USA by Rail

plus Canada's main routes

the Bradt Travel Guide

D0097080

John Pitt

edition
8

www.bradtguides.com

Bradt Travel Guides Ltd, UK
The Globe Pequot Press Inc, USA

CANADA

NOTE
FOR CANADA'S MAIN RAIL
ROUTES, SEE PAGE 305.

Hike amidst lofty peaks in
the Glacier National Park
page 11

Marvel at the alpine splendour
of the Rocky Mountains
page 71

Drink in the views over Lake Michig
from the top of Chicago's Willis To
page

Wander through restored ghost
towns in the Mojave Desert
page 130

Board a wooden tram to see
the sights of San Francisco
page 60

Meander along the floor of
the Grand Canyon, a mile-deep
channel cleaving the earth
page 130

PACIFIC OCEAN

MEXICO

VANCOUVER
Richmond
Surrey
Bellingham
Mt Vernon
Edmonds
Everett
SEATTLE
Tacoma
Wenatchee
Olympia-Lacey
Ellensburg
Ephrata
Centralia
Moses Lake
Kelso-Longview
Bingen-
White Salmon
Vancouver
Wishram
PORTLAND
Salem
Hood
River
The Dalles
Albany
Eugene
Cottage Grove
Madras
Redmond
Roseburg
Bend
Grants Pass
Chemult
Medford
Burns
Ashland
Klamath Falls
Arcata
Dunsmuir
Redding
Chico
Willits
Marysville
Truckee
Colfax
Sparks
Reno
OAKLAND
Carson City
EMERYVILLE
SACRAMENTO
SAN
Stockton
FRANCISCO
Yosemite
San José
Merced
Madera
Monterey
Salinas
Fresno
Hanford
Corcoran
Wasco
San Luis Obispo
Bakersfield
Santa Barbara
Barstow
LOS ANGELES
Anaheim
Palm Springs
Indio
SAN DIEGO

Sandpoint
Libby
Whitefish
Browning
West
Glacier
Glacier
Park
Shelby
Havre
Spokane
Cut Bank
Pullman
Moscow
Lewiston
Pasco
Hermiston
Pendleton
Grangeville
La
Grande
McCall
Baker
City
Vale
Ontario
Nampa
Boise
Twin Falls
Winnemucca
Elko
Ogden
SALT LAKE CITY
Provo
Helper
Helena
Green
River
Grand
Junction
St. George
LAS VEGAS
Laughlin
Kingman
Grand Canyon
Needles
Williams
Flagstaff
Winslow
Gallup
Camp Verde
PHOENIX
Yuma
Maricopa
TUCSON
Benson
Lordsburg
Deming

Stanley
Rugby
Glasgow
Malta
Minot
Wolf Point
Williston

Laramie
Cheyenne
Fort Collins
Longmont
Loveland
Fort Morgan
McCook
Granby
Boulder
Glenwood
Winter
DENVER
Springs
Park
Colorado Springs
Pueblo
Lamar
Garden
City
Do
Cit
La Junta
Trinidad
Raton
Lamy
Las Vegas
ALBUQUERQUE
Belen
Socorro
Truth or Consequences
Hatch
Las Cruces
EL PASO
FORT
Alpine
Sanderson
Del Rio
ANT

KEY
Railway ———
Amtrak Thruway Motorcoach -------

Get soaked on a trip to the Niagara Falls
page 274

Immerse yourself in high culture at the Met Museum, people-watch in Central Park or chow down on matzo balls at a downtown diner — all in New York
page 181

Delve into Montreal's Gallic-tinged nightlife
page 242

mple Portuguese, Malaysian or Korean cuisine in multicultural Toronto
page 275

Join the revellers in New Orleans' pulsating Carnival
page 138

Snorkel or dive in the deep green waters off the Florida Keys
page 216

Lake Superior
Lake Michigan
Lake Huron
L. Ontario
L. Erie

ATLANTIC OCEAN

Gulf of Mexico

Bradt

Quebec
MONTREAL
St Lambert
Rouses Point
St Albans
Ottawa
Burlington-Essex Junction
Plattsburgh
White River Junction
Rutland
Schenectady
Albany-Rensselaer
BOSTON
Springfield
Providence
Hartford
New Haven
NEW YORK

Haughton
Marquette
Escanaba
St Ignace
Mackinaw City
Duluth
Hinckley
Hudson
Menomonie
Chippewa Falls
Wausau
Traverse City
TORONTO
Aldershot
Niagara Falls
Rochester
Syracuse
ST PAUL
MINNEAPOLIS
Eau Claire
Shawano
Green Bay
St Catherines
Grimsby
BUFFALO
Red Wing
Winona
Wisconsin Dells
London
Madison
MILWAUKEE
Grand Rapids
Pontiac
DETROIT
Jamestown
Rockford
Kalamazoo
Windsor
Battle Creek
CHICAGO
CLEVELAND
Altoona
PHILADELPHIA
Trenton
Joliet
Hammond/Whiting
Toledo
Harrisburg
Atlantic City
Galesburg
Dwight
Pontiac
PITTSBURGH
Cumberland
BALTIMORE
Wilmington
Creston Osceola Ottumwa
Bloomington-Normal
Lorton
WASHINGTON, DC
Fort Madison
Lincoln
INDIANAPOLIS
CINCINNATI
Charleston
Charlottesville
Richmond
La Plata
Springfield
Williamsburg
Virginia Beach
Quincy
Carlinville
Louisville
Huntington
Clifton Forge
Norfolk
Independence
Jefferson City
Alton
Washington
Lynchburg
Newport News
 rence
Sedalia
Centralia
Danville
Petersburg
Lees Summit
Hermann
St LOUIS
Carbondale
Burlington
Greensboro
Durham
Cary
Rocky Mount
Warrensburg
Kirkwood
Winston-Salem
High Point
Raleigh
Wilson
Poplar Bluff
Fulton
Salisbury
Kannapolis
Selma
Newbern-Dyersburg
Charlotte
Southern Pines
Walnut Ridge
Gastonia
Fayetteville
Spartanburg
Hamlet
Dillon
Greenville
Camden
Florence
MEMPHIS
Toccoa
Clemson
Kingstree
Gainesville
Columbia
OMA CITY
Denmark
LITTLE ROCK
Charleston
Malvern
Marks
Birmingham
Anniston
ATLANTA
Yemassee
Arkadelphia
Greenwood
Opelika
Savannah
Marshall
Texarkana
Tuscaloosa
Jesup
Longview
Bossier City
Yazoo City
Montgomery
ineola
Shreveport
Meridian
Nacogdoches
Jackson
Chipley
Madison
Lake City
JACKSONVILLE
gor
Hazlehurst
Laurel
Hattiesburg
Palatka
Brookhaven
Atmore
Crestview
Tallahassee
Waldo
Daytona Beach
McComb
Picayune
Pensacola
Ocala
DeLand
Hammond
Slidell
Biloxi
MOBILE
Wildwood
Winter Park
Lake Charles
Baton Rouge
Gulfport
Pascagoula
Dade City
ORLANDO
Lafayette
Bay St Louis
Lakeland
Kissimmee
USTON
Beaumont
NEW ORLEANS
TAMPA
Winter Haven
New Iberia
Sebring
Schriever
Pinellas Park-Clearwater-St Petersburg
Okeechobee
West Palm Beach
Bradenton
Delray Beach
Sarasota
Deerfield Beach
Port Charlotte
Fort Lauderdale
Fort Myers
Hollywood
MIAMI
Key West

USA
by Rail
Don't
miss…

Grand Canyon
A mile-deep channel gouged
out of the earth, this surreal
landscape is the ultimate
American sight
(RC/DT) page 130

Niagara Falls
This dramatic natural wonder
straddles the USA and Canada
(EI/DT) page 274

San Francisco
With 43 hills, travelling on an iconic tram is a must for visitors to this laid-back city
(SE/DT) page 60

Rocky Mountains
Fantastic views abound in this range running through Colorado, Wyoming, Montana and Idaho
(MZ/DT) page 71

New York City
The Brooklyn Bridge affords a magnificent view of lower Manhattan
(AM/DT) page 179

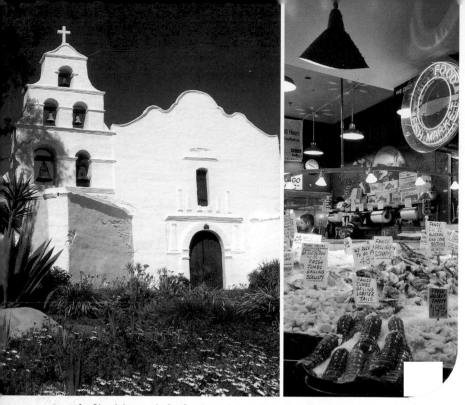

above left San Diego is home to the first Franciscan mission in California, and contains many other restored early buildings (JB/DT) page 98

above right Dating from 1907, Pike Place Market in Seattle is a labyrinth of shops, restaurants, galleries and stalls (S/DT) page 51

below From the brooding presence of El Capitan to ranks of giant sequoias and shimmering alpine lakes, Yosemite National Park packs in an almost indecent number of breathtaking sights (MZ/DT) page 93 *top* San Francisco's Chinatown, the largest outside Asia, is a city-within-a-city with numerous temples, restaurants and traditional shops (J/DT) page 60

centre Once the producer of many crops, today California's sunny Napa Valley is particularly renowned for its wine industry (SS) page 59

right With its stylish buildings and coffee culture, Portland rivals Seattle for the accolade of 'America's most liveable city' (SS) page 54 *above*   The desolate landscapes of Monument Valley have starred in many westerns (RA/DT) page 84

below   The Las Vegas Strip is the ultimate paean to hedonism, with adrenaline-fuelled casinos, never-ending buffets and relentless neon lights (PQ/DT) page 124

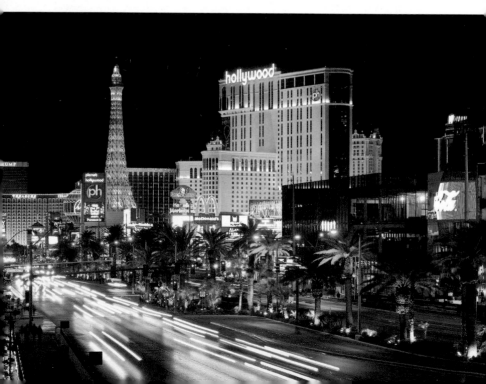

AUTHOR

John Pitt studied economics and philosophy at East Anglia University before working at the Ministry of Defence and in local government. Since 1990, he has travelled extensively in North America, including over 75,000 miles by train, and has written on travel for Thomas Cook as well as for magazines and newspapers such as the *Sunday Times*, the *Daily Telegraph* and the *Daily Mail*.

AUTHOR'S STORY

Anything can happen on a train, and when Amtrak's *Pennsylvanian* paused early one evening at Lancaster a young Amish couple came on board. The man looked like Gary Cooper and had a neat beard, a wide-brimmed hat and a long, black coat. His wife wore traditional dark clothes, black boots and a bonnet, and carried their baby asleep in a black shawl. Suddenly we were in the middle of a scene from the film, *Witness*. All afternoon we had travelled among the flat fields and white farmhouses of Pennsylvania Dutch country, where the churches have wooden bell towers and cars are a rarity. Now and then a horse-drawn buggy would trot surreally along a dusty road or wait beside the tracks for the train to pass. By the time we reached Lancaster it seemed quite natural to have an Amish family join us and share their picnic.

Chance encounters are part of what makes an American train journey such a rewarding experience even when, as a writer, I'm trying to make notes for a book. One day it might be a group of schoolgirls heading for Niagara Falls, the next it's Australian backpackers in Arizona. US trains are friendly places so you are sure to run into someone interesting before very long, and you can learn a great deal by sitting next to a Kansas City mortician or a drag artist on her way to entertain the troops in San Diego. Between the small towns and big cities you can also appreciate the country's sheer size and variety, and understand what this land was like before McDonald's and Coca-Cola. As Homer Simpson said, 'Nothing beats flying across the country on a train.'

PUBLISHER'S FOREWORD   *Hilary Bradt*

A trip across America by train is surely one of *the* great romantic journeys: it is evocative of old movies, it has the scent of adventure, and it promises broad and beautiful landscapes. More practically, it also ensures that you're minimising your carbon footprint. Moving into its eighth edition, John Pitt's book has long established itself as the essential resource for those tourists who recognise that travelling is as much a part of the experience as arriving.

Eighth edition February 2012   First published 1992

Bradt Travel Guides Ltd, IDC House, The Vale, Chalfont St Peter, Bucks SL9 9RZ, England
www.bradtguides.com
Published in the USA by The Globe Pequot Press Inc,
PO Box 480, Guilford, Connecticut 06437-0480

Text copyright © 2012 John Pitt
Maps copyright © 2012 Bradt Travel Guides Ltd
Photographs copyright © 2012 Individual photographers (see below)
Project manager: Maisie Fitzpatrick

ISBN-13: 978 1 84162 389 4
British Library Cataloguing in Publication Data
A catalogue record for this book is available from the British Library

Photographs Alamy: Jeff Greenberg (JG/A); Amtrak (AM); Dreamstime: Ronald Adcock (RA/DT), Asterixvs (A/DT), Jay Beiler (JB/DT), Natalia Bratslavsky (NB/DT), Richard Charpentier (RC/DT), Songquan Deng (SD/DT), Elephantopia (E/DT), Serban Enache (SE/DT), Eric Inghels (EI/DT), Alexey Malashkevich (AM/DT), Dan Peretz (DP/DT), William Perry (WP/DT), Photoquest (PQ/DT), Dean Riley (DR/DT), Silvestrovairina (S/DT), Dragi Stankovic (DS/DT), Minyun Zhou (MZ/DT); SuperStock (SS); Wikipedia: Douglas Rahden (DR/WP)
Front cover The *California Zephyr*, West route (AM)
Title page Lifeguard hut, Miami (DS/DT), *The Empire Builder* (AM), Clock at Grand Central Terminal, New York (DP/DT)
Part openers Page 47: The *Coast Starlight* (AM); page 275: The *Rocky Mountaineer* (AM)
Back cover Chinatown, San Francisco (J/DT); The *Empire Builder* (AM)

Maps David McCutcheon
Colour map Relief map bases by Nick Rowland FRGS

Typeset from the author's disk by Wakewing, High Wycombe
Production managed by Jellyfish Print Solutions; printed in India

Acknowledgements

The author would like to thank the following for their generous help in the preparation of this book. Craig White, Barbara Bach, Ann Owens, Christine Suchy, Kathleen Gordon and Terry Rowley at Amtrak; Lyne Perreault and Guy Faulkner at VIA Rail; Kate Selley and Diana Cima at Rocky Mountaineer; Tamra L Hoppes at GrandLuxe Rail Journeys; Breanne Feigel at Canadian Pacific; Jim Williams at the USA Hostel Handbook; Kathryn Potter at the American Hotel & Lodging Association; Tim Thompson at the Alaska Railroad; Mark S Bassett at the Nevada Northern Railway Museum; Rebecca Laurie at the Colorado Historical Society; William W Sherrick at the New Hope & Ivyland Railroad; Paul Hammond at the California State Railroad Museum; Craig Lacey at the Heber Valley Railroad; Jerry Thull at the Grand Canyon Railway; Pam Butler at the Durango & Silverton Railroad; Joanne Hirasaki at Roaring Camp Railroads; Rebecca McGlynn at the Ontario Northland Railway; Craig S O'Connell and other Friends of Amtrak; Stephen Grande; Albert M Tannler in Pittsburgh; Wanie Biggs in San Francisco; Raymond Parker in New Orleans; Ann Terry in Washington, DC; Nelson Sanchez and Tom Bynum in New York; Heidi Gardner at Trailfinders; Anna Crew at BUNAC; Christopher Muller at RailServe.com; Rita Plahetka; Marjorie and Wayne Preston in Florida; Natasha Smith; Vangie S Palacios; Lynne Williams; Brian and Alison Henley; Michael B Gehl; George William; Eileen Rose.

UPDATES AND FEEDBACK REQUEST

Railways, hotels and tourist attractions sometimes make changes. If you notice any of these or have other comments about your trip please email information@usa-by-rail.com or contact Bradt on ☏ 01753 893444 or e info@bradtguides.com. Alternatively you can add a review of the book to www.bradtguides.com or Amazon. Periodically our authors post travel updates and reader feedback on the website. Check www.bradtguides.com/guidebook-updates for any news. Current prices for Amtrak and VIA Rail passes can be found on the website www.usa-by-rail.com.

Contents

LIST OF MAPS

Introduction

All aboard!

Ever since they came on the scene, American trains have had a strong hold on the popular imagination, inspiring countless stories, songs, scandals, films and legends. Their rugged charm sets them apart from more mundane means of transport and their ecological soundness is again in fashion. Trains pollute less, rarely suffer from weather delays and won't give you jet lag. You can choose your companions, read a book, let your thoughts unfurl, take a snooze, sleep horizontally and generally enjoy most of the comforts of home. One reason for travelling by train is especially compelling: it's much more fun.

American passenger trains go to most big cities as well as to Disney World, Niagara Falls and the Grand Canyon. Pampered by helpful attendants, you can travel from coast to coast, explore the Rocky Mountains and ride directly alongside two oceans. You cross many rivers, lakes and deserts, often seeing places which cannot be visited any other way. Less expensive than flying, more comfortable than the bus, trains keep you relaxed and in touch with an ever-changing landscape as the world becomes a moving picture, framed.

Amtrak coaches have generous reclining seats, air conditioning, bright observation domes and snug bunks. This may not be the fastest way to travel but the civilised pace is perfect for sightseeing. If the scenery palls you can always go for a stroll, enjoy a meal, make friends in the bar or watch a movie. At night a gentle rocking and the steady, muffled rhythm of the wheels are sure to lull you to sleep.

Not many people would mourn buses if they became obsolete, and few entertain fond thoughts about airports, but children still count freight cars and wave as the train goes by. Instead of leaving you exhausted and surly, trains create a sense of adventure and romance. No wonder many still find the sound of a locomotive whistle at midnight a sure sign that it's time to move on. As the bell clangs and the conductor calls out 'All aboo-aard!', you soon discover why North American rail travel remains such a beguiling experience.

THE UNITED STATES

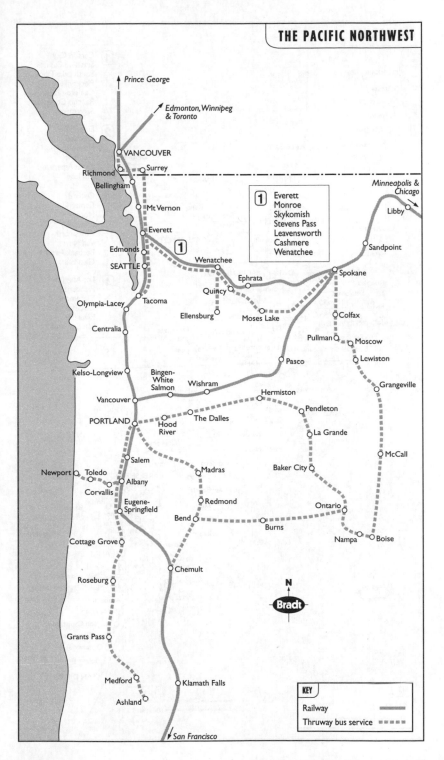

THE PACIFIC NORTHWEST

Prince George

Edmonton, Winnipeg & Toronto

VANCOUVER

Surrey

Richmond

Bellingham

Mt Vernon

Everett

Edmonds

SEATTLE

Olympia-Lacey

Tacoma

Centralia

Kelso-Longview

Bingen-White Salmon

Vancouver

PORTLAND

Hood River

The Dalles

Salem

Newport

Toledo

Albany

Corvallis

Eugene-Springfield

Cottage Grove

Roseburg

Grants Pass

Medford

Ashland

Chemult

Madras

Redmond

Bend

Klamath Falls

San Francisco

Wenatchee

Ephrata

Quincy

Ellensburg

Moses Lake

Wishram

Hermiston

Pendleton

La Grande

Baker City

Burns

Ontario

Nampa

Boise

McCall

Grangeville

Lewiston

Moscow

Pullman

Colfax

Spokane

Pasco

Sandpoint

Libby

Minneapolis & Chicago

Minneapolis & Chicago

1
Everett
Monroe
Skykomish
Stevens Pass
Leavensworth
Cashmere
Wenatchee

N

Bradt

KEY

Railway	———
Thruway bus service	•••••••

CALIFORNIA

↑ Seattle

○ McKinleyville
○ Arcata
○ Eureka
○ Fortuna
○ Rio Dell
○ Garberville
○ Leggett
○ Laytonville

○ Willits

○ Ukiah

Cloverdale ○

Healdsburg ○

Santa Rosa ○
Rohnert Park ○
Petaluma ○
Richmond ○
OAKLAND/EMERYVILLE ○
SAN FRANCISCO ○

○ Redding

○ Red Bluff

○ Chico

Oroville ○   Nevada   Truckee
Grass   City
Marysville ○   Valley ○   Reno ○   Sparks
Lake of the Pines Jct ○   Soda Springs
Rocklin ○   Colfax
Roseville ○   Auburn ○   CARSON CITY

①

South Lake Tahoe

Davis ○   ○ SACRAMENTO
Vallejo-
Marine
World ○   Suisun-Fairfield ○
Napa ○   Antioch-Pittsburg ○
Berkeley ○   Martinez ○   Stockton ○
②   Tracy ○
East Dublin-Pleasanton ○   Livermore ○   Riverbank ○   Yosemite
Turlock-   National Park
San José ○   Denair ○   Merced ○   Mariposa ○
Santa Cruz ○   Gilroy ○   Madera ○
Watsonville ○   Salinas ○
Seaside ○   Soledad ○   ○ Fresno
Monterey/Carmel ○   King City ○
Lemoore ○   ○ Hanford
Kettleman City ○
Paso Robles ○   ○ Corcoran

Denver →

LAS VEGAS

○ Atascadero
○ San Luis Obispo   ○ Wasco
○ Grover Beach   BAKERSFIELD
Tehachapi ○
Santa Maria ○   Mojave ○
Guadalupe ○   Lompoc ○   Rosamond ○   Boron ○   Barstow
Solvang ○   Lancaster ○
Lompoc/Surf ○   Palmdale ○
Fillmore ○   Santa Clarita ○
Goleta (UCSB) ○   Van Nuys ○   LOS ANGELES
SANTA BARBARA   Carpinteria ○   Santa Paula ○   ④
Ventura ○   Oxnard ○   San Bernardino ○
③   Palm Springs ○
San Pedro ○   Commerce ○   Palm Desert ○
Long Beach ○   Fullerton ○
Anaheim ○   ○ Indio
Santa Ana ○
San Juan Capistrano ○   San
San Clemente ○   Antonio →
Oceanside ○
Solana Beach ○
○ SAN DIEGO

Albuquerque →

N
Bradt

①	Carson City Stateline Casinos South Lake Tahoe Placerville Cameron Park Rancho Cordova Sacramento
②	Emeryville Oakland Hayward Fremont Great America San Jose
③	Oxnard Camarillo Moorpark Simi Valley Chatsworth Van Nuys Burbank Airport Glendale
④	Los Angeles Pasadena Claremont Ontario Riverside San Bernardino

KEY
Railway ——————
Thruway bus service - - - - - - -

0 ——— 100km
0 ——— 100 miles

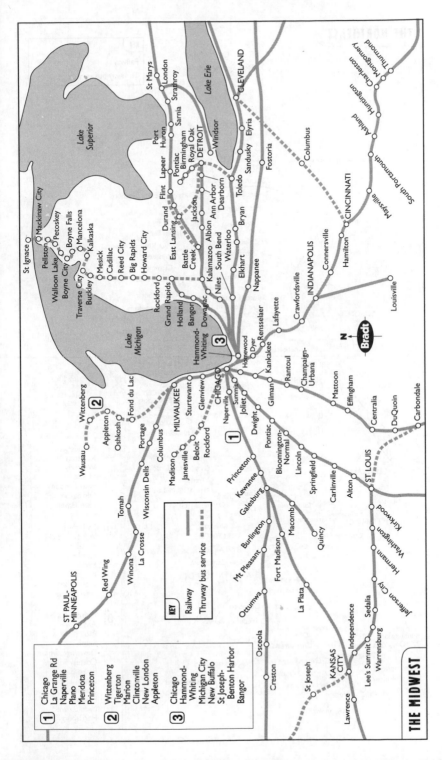

THE MIDWEST

KEY

Railway

Thruway bus service

1
Chicago
La Grange Rd
Naperville
Plano
Merdota
Princeton

2
Wittenberg
Tigerton
Marion
Clintonville
New London
Appleton

3
Chicago
Hammond-
Whiting
Michigan City
New Buffalo
St Joseph-
Benton Harbor
Bangor

N
Bradt

ix

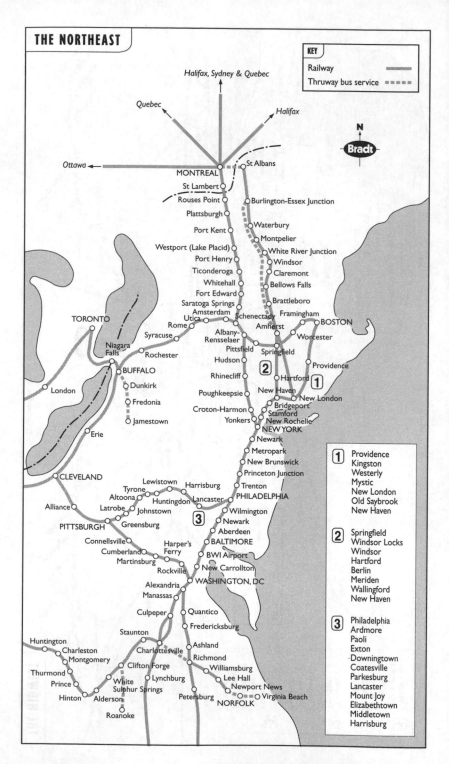

THE NORTHEAST

KEY
Railway
Thruway bus service

N
Bradt

Halifax, Sydney & Quebec
Quebec
Halifax
Ottawa
MONTREAL
St Albans
St Lambert
Rouses Point
Burlington-Essex Junction
Plattsburgh
Waterbury
Port Kent
Montpelier
Westport (Lake Placid)
White River Junction
Port Henry
Windsor
Ticonderoga
Claremont
Whitehall
Bellows Falls
Fort Edward
Brattleboro
Saratoga Springs
Amsterdam
Framingham
TORONTO
Utica
Schenectady
BOSTON
Rome
Amherst
Syracuse
Albany-Rensselaer
Worcester
Niagara Falls
Pittsfield
Springfield
BUFFALO
Rochester
Hudson
Providence
Dunkirk
Rhinecliff
2
London
Fredonia
Poughkeepsie
Hartford
1
Jamestown
Croton-Harmon
New Haven
New London
Bridgeport
Erie
Yonkers
Stamford
New Rochelle
CLEVELAND
NEW YORK
Newark
Metropark
Lewistown
Harrisburg
New Brunswick
Tyrone
Princeton Junction
Altoona
Huntingdon
Lancaster
Trenton
Alliance
Latrobe
Johnstown
PHILADELPHIA
PITTSBURGH
Greensburg
3
Wilmington
Connellsville
Newark
Harper's Ferry
Aberdeen
Cumberland
BALTIMORE
Martinsburg
BWI Airport
Rockville
New Carrollton
Alexandria
WASHINGTON, DC
Manassas
Culpeper
Quantico
Fredericksburg
Staunton
Huntington
Ashland
Charleston
Charlottesville
Richmond
Montgomery
Clifton Forge
Williamsburg
Thurmond
Lynchburg
Lee Hall
Prince
White Sulphur Springs
Newport News
Hinton
Alderson
Petersburg
Virginia Beach
Roanoke
NORFOLK

1
Providence
Kingston
Westerly
Mystic
New London
Old Saybrook
New Haven

2
Springfield
Windsor Locks
Windsor
Hartford
Berlin
Meriden
Wallingford
New Haven

3
Philadelphia
Ardmore
Paoli
Exton
Downingtown
Coatesville
Parkesburg
Lancaster
Mount Joy
Elizabethtown
Middletown
Harrisburg

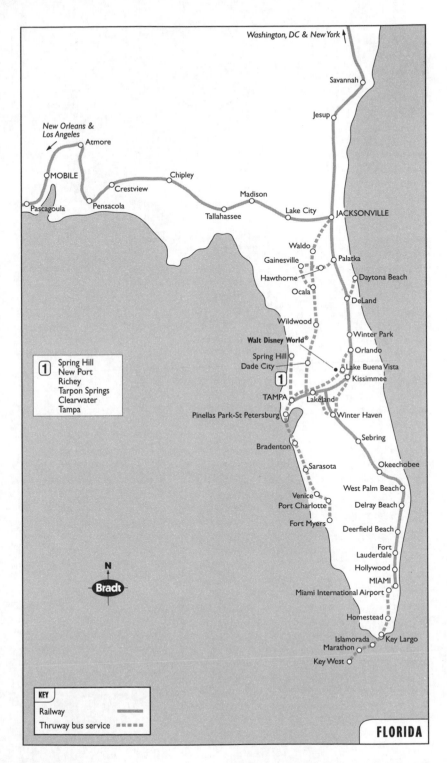

Washington, DC & New York

Savannah

Jesup

New Orleans &
Los Angeles

Atmore

MOBILE

Chipley

Crestview

Pascagoula

Pensacola

Madison

Tallahassee

Lake City

JACKSONVILLE

Waldo

Gainesville

Palatka

Hawthorne

Daytona Beach

Ocala

DeLand

Wildwood

Winter Park

Walt Disney World®

Orlando

Spring Hill

Lake Buena Vista

Dade City

Kissimmee

1   Spring Hill
    New Port
    Richey
    Tarpon Springs
    Clearwater
    Tampa

TAMPA

Lakeland

Pinellas Park-St Petersburg

1

Winter Haven

Sebring

Bradenton

Okeechobee

Sarasota

West Palm Beach

Venice

Delray Beach

Port Charlotte

Fort Myers

Deerfield Beach

Fort
Lauderdale

N

Hollywood

Bradt

MIAMI

Miami International Airport

Homestead

Islamorada

Key Largo

Marathon

Key West

KEY

Railway ⎯⎯⎯

Thruway bus service ------

FLORIDA

Part One

GENERAL INFORMATION

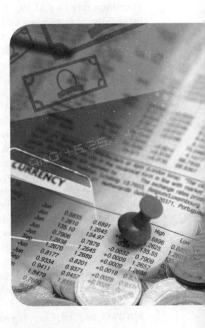

Location North America, bordering both the north Atlantic Ocean and the north Pacific Ocean

Neighbouring countries Canada and Mexico

Size/area 9,631,418km^2

Climate Mostly temperate, but tropical in Hawaii and Florida, arctic in Alaska, semi-arid in the great plains west of the Mississippi River, and arid in the Great Basin of the southwest. Low winter temperatures in the northwest are ameliorated occasionally in January and February by warm chinook winds from the eastern slopes of the Rocky Mountains.

Status Federal republic

Population 313,232,044 (July 2011)

Capital Washington, DC

Other main cities New York, Los Angeles, Chicago, Houston, Philadelphia, Phoenix, San Diego, Dallas, San Antonio, Detroit

Economy The largest economy in the world, with a per-capita GDP of $46,400. Agriculture 1%; industry 22%; services 77% (2009).

GDP $14.14 trillion (2009)

Languages English is spoken by approximately 82% of the population; Spanish is regarded as the second national language.

Religion Protestant 51%, Roman Catholic 24%, Mormon 2%, Jewish 2%, Muslim 1%, other 10%, none 10%

Currency US dollar; $1 = 100 cents

Exchange rate £1 = $1.59, €1 = $1.37 (November 2011)

International telephone code +1

Time There are four different time zones in the continental USA: Eastern Standard Time, Central Standard Time, Mountain Standard Time and Pacific Standard Time. Two further time zones apply in Alaska and Hawaii.

Electrical voltage 120V/60Hz standard plugs have two parallel flat pins ('American' type) or have two pins with an earth connector.

Weights and measures The USA is one of the few countries not to have adopted the International System of Units as its official system of weights and measures. Although the metric system has been lawful in the USA since 1866, it has been slow in displacing the adaptation of the British Imperial System known as the US Customary System (miles, gallons, etc).

Flag The Stars and Stripes has 13 horizontal stripes of red alternating with white. A blue rectangle in the upper hoist-side corner has 50 small, white, five-pointed stars arranged in nine offset horizontal rows of six stars alternating with rows of five stars. The 50 stars represent the 50 states; the 13 stripes represent the 13 original colonies.

National anthem 'Star Spangled Banner'

National flower American rose

National bird/animal Bald eagle

National sports Baseball, basketball, American football, ice hockey

RAILWAYS In 2008, Class I railroads operated on a total of 94,082 miles of the 139,887-mile United States network, with 151,000 employees, 24,000 locomotives and 416,000 freight cars. Over 1.9 billion tons of freight were carried.

From Horsepower to Amtrak

THE IRON HORSE

The development of the United States in the 19th and early 20th centuries largely coincided with the epic story of its railroads. Trains contributed hugely to prosperity and provided a sense of national identity, coming to symbolise the country's strength, optimism and pioneering spirit. For over 170 years Americans have been proud to call themselves 'locomotive people'.

It may be symbolic that one of the country's first railroads had as its purpose the hauling of granite for the Bunker Hill Monument, which was being built to commemorate a defining episode in America's War of Independence. Gridley Bryant's Granite Railway used horsepower to operate over three miles of track at Quincy, Massachusetts, in 1826. America's first steam-powered locomotive was the English-built *Stourbridge Lion*, inaugurated in August 1829 on the Delaware & Hudson Canal Company's line at Honesdale, Pennsylvania. But the story really began on 19 February 1827, when a group of Baltimore residents decided to build the country's first public railroad between their city and the Ohio River. Charles Carroll, by then the only surviving signatory of the Declaration of Independence, laid the cornerstone on 4 July 1828, and two years later the experimental engine *Tom Thumb*, weighing less than a ton, reached 18mph on 13 miles of Baltimore & Ohio track.

America's first (and the world's second) regular steam train service went into operation on Christmas Day 1830 on the South Carolina Canal & Railroad, when the *Best Friend of Charleston* took a passenger train out of Charleston on a line built to transport cotton from central Georgia. Completed three years later, the Charleston & Hamburg was for a time the world's longest railway (135 miles/217km).

Other lines soon followed, most notably the New York Central from Albany to Buffalo and the Philadelphia & Columbia (the first to be government-sponsored). Like most early lines, they served local needs and few people imagined the railway's full potential. Canal owners and road transport companies opposed them, partly on safety grounds, and doctors warned of the dangers inherent in such reckless speeds. Indeed, accidents did often happen. Few rights of way were fenced off and early railroad cars were little more than stagecoaches with flanged wheels, whose grip on the track was sometimes uncertain.

Despite these problems, total trackage increased to 3,000 miles by the early 1840s and to 9,000 miles (4,800–14,500km) by 1850 (when it was three times the length of the canal system). By the late 1850s, America had built half the world's railroad mileage in existence, and French traveller Guillaume Poussin wrote that 'the locomotive appears to be the personification of the American'.

Early locomotives such as *Tom Thumb* and the *Best Friend of Charleston* had upright boilers but these were soon replaced by engines using horizontal, English-style boilers which allowed greater capacity. Mid-century engines were most usually handsome American-type (4-4-0) wood burners, brightly painted and extravagantly decorated with polished brass. Other elegant innovations included a bell, whistle, headlight and pilot (or cowcatcher, invented by Charles Babbage and perfected by engineer Isaac Dripps). Bulbous chimneys reduced emissions and sparks, a cab gave weather protection to the crew and a sandbox was added to improve traction, allegedly after a plague of locusts on a line in Pennsylvania. Typical examples from this period can be seen in the 1903 silent film *The Great Train Robbery* and in D W Griffith's 1916 epic *Intolerance*.

The first ticket offices were at stagecoach stops or in hotels, but characteristic railroad depots soon developed, usually as one-storey buildings located parallel to the tracks. Large cantilevered canopies protected passengers and freight from inclement weather. Clock towers were often added at a later date as stations became more elaborate and companies adopted distinctive styles of architecture to make their railroads easily identifiable.

The New York Central brought together ten small railroads in the northeast whose lines ran roughly parallel with the Erie Canal, later extending them to St Louis. The Erie Railroad went from the Hudson River north of New York to Lake Erie and Chicago, enabling New York City to enjoy fresh milk every day and consume more strawberries than anywhere else in the world. Chicago by this time had 11 railways and saw 70 trains a day, making it the busiest rail centre in the world.

From 1856, the Illinois Central linked Chicago to Cairo, at the junction of the Mississippi and Ohio rivers, with federal land grants assisting the line's construction through 700 miles (1,130km) of thinly populated country. The far west's first railway, the Sacramento Valley, opened in the same year between Sacramento and the gold mines at Folsom.

Southern railways made slower progress, but by the 1860s, 1,000 miles (1,600km) of track existed in each of Georgia, Tennessee and Virginia, and a network of lines served all states west of the Mississippi. This proved vital to both sides during the Civil War, when railroads and trains became major targets. In 1862, General Bragg's army of 30,000 men travelled nearly 800 miles (1,300km) to the key rail centre of Chattanooga from Mississippi by Confederate railway. The following year, 23,000 Union troops and their equipment journeyed 1,200 miles (1,900km) from Virginia to relieve Chattanooga. Their expedition took 12 days and required 30 trains with a total of 600 coaches. More than 35,000 lives were lost in bitter fighting before the battle ended. Later in the war, General Sherman's army of 100,000 men in Georgia needed 16 trains a day to keep it supplied. Without railways the North might never have broken Confederate resistance. Northern lines were better developed than those in the South and military traffic was given priority, but the Confederate government failed to take over responsibility for railroads in its territory. By the end of the Civil War, half the South's railroads were out of action while those in the North were more dominant than ever.

THE GOLDEN AGE

Even before the Civil War, railroads had come to represent unity for a country divided by geography and culture. In 1862, at a crucial time for the Union, President Lincoln signed the Pacific Railway Act making possible America's first transcontinental route. Abraham Lincoln had earlier played a part in railroad history in 1856, when as a young man he represented the Rock Island & Chicago Railroad, which had built the first bridge across the Mississippi River between Rock Island, Illinois, and Davenport, Iowa. Riverboat operators previously had a monopoly on the large-scale movement of passengers and goods and tried to block the bridge's construction (it was nicknamed 'Hell Gate of the Mississippi' in St Louis). Fifteen days after the bridge's gala opening, a steamboat, the *Effie Afton*, struck one of its piers and a stove on the boat overturned, setting fire to the bridge and causing extensive damage. The owners of the steamboat sued the railroad company but Lincoln brilliantly demonstrated that the accident occurred because the steamboat's starboard paddle wheel failed. He also stressed the vital importance of allowing railroads to span the Mississippi, saying that east-to-west travel was 'growing larger and larger, building up new countries with a rapidity never before seen in the history of the world'.

The Central Pacific Railroad set out to build a line eastwards from Sacramento, California, while the Union Pacific Railroad would go west from the Missouri River. Each company received generous federal loans and was given ownership of huge tracts of land – ten sections (each one mile square) for every completed mile. Despite experiencing the worst winter on record, with temperatures down to –40°C, track was laid at a phenomenal rate, using mostly Irish or ex-army labour on the Union Pacific and Chinese immigrants, paid between one and three dollars a day, on the Central Pacific. The thousands of workers from Kwantung Province imported by the CP became known as 'Celestials' after their 'Celestial Kingdom' homeland. They were often lowered down sheer cliff faces in baskets attached to ropes to drill into rock, pack in explosives and light a fuse before making a rapid return up the rope. Many 'basket men' failed to make it to safety before the explosion took place. A total of 19 tunnels (15 of them on the Central Pacific) were blasted out of solid rock with black powder at the rate of 14 inches a day. Nitroglycerine was tried in 1867, but had to be abandoned when it was found to be dangerously unstable.

At ten spikes to the rail and 400 rails to the mile, it required approximately 21 million strokes of the hammer to complete the line. In 1867 alone, 235 miles of track were finished and Charles Crocker's Central Pacific team won a $10,000 bet from Thomas Durant of the Union Pacific after workers each lifted more than 100 tons of steel to lay ten miles in a single day (still a record). At one time the Union Pacific employed 10,000 labourers and an equal number of working animals. Hunters slaughtered vast quantities of buffalo to keep the workers supplied with meat and ramshackle tent towns sprang up along the way. These 'Hell on Wheels' settlements became notorious for land speculators, gambling, drinking and prostitution. Most collapsed as soon as the railroad moved on but some remained to become permanent towns.

Over 1,774 miles (2,860km) of track had been constructed by the time the two lines met ahead of schedule at Promontory Point, north of Utah's Great Salt Lake. Half a million people, including newspapermen, dignitaries and railway employees (though Chinese labourers were specifically excluded), gathered on 10 May 1869 to watch the Golden Spike ceremony complete one of the greatest engineering feats of the century. The ceremony was rather disorganised, due partly to the size of the crowd. Leland Stanford of the Central Pacific had brought four ceremonial spikes, the famed 'Golden Spike' being presented by David Hewes, a San Francisco construction magnate. It was inscribed with the names of Central Pacific directors as well as the words 'The Last Spike' and 'May God continue the Unity of our Country as this Railroad unites the two great oceans of the world'.

A second gold spike was presented by the San Francisco *News Letter*, a silver spike by Nevada and a spike made from iron, silver and gold by Arizona. All four were dropped into a pre-bored laurel wood tie during the ceremony and at 12.47 the actual last spike – an ordinary iron one – was driven into a regular tie. The spike had been wired to send the sound of the strikes over the telegraph to the nation but Leland Stanford and the Union Pacific's Thomas Durant frequently missed their aim as they took turns to drive it home. A single word, 'done', was telegraphed to the nation anyway, resulting in widespread celebrations. Meanwhile, construction supervisors actually drove in the final spike.

The Central Pacific's *Jupiter* and the Union Pacific's *No 119* were present at the ceremony and replicas of both appear in the final scenes of John Ford's excellent 1924 pictorial history *The Iron Horse*. Cecil B DeMille told the story less convincingly in *Union Pacific*. The original 'Golden Spike' is now on display behind glass at Stanford University in Palo Alto, California. The temporary town of Promontory remained as a 'Hell on Wheels' settlement for a few weeks but never became a permanent city.

The first engines to cross the continent were the Central Pacific's *Success* and *Excelsior*, built by Rogers and delivered by rail. The first trains to carry passengers and cargo along the route ran on 11 May 1869, with emigrants travelling west and a consignment of Japanese teas going east. The *Jupiter* was scrapped for iron in 1901 and the Union Pacific's *No 119* went the same way two years later. The Lucin Cutoff took most traffic away from Promontory in 1904 and the last tie of laurel was destroyed in the 1906 San Francisco earthquake. The old rails over the 123-mile (197km) Promontory Summit line were salvaged in 1942 for the war effort in ceremonies marking the 'Undriving of the Golden Spike', when collectors picked over the area for ties and materials.

A re-enactment of the last spike ceremony took place in 1948, using miniature locomotives provided by the Southern Pacific, and in 1951 a monument to the event was erected at Ogden's Union Station. Congress established a seven-acre (2.8ha) piece of land as the Golden Spike National Historic Site and the National Golden Spike Society was formed to promote it. The site was enlarged to 2,176 acres (880ha) in 1965, and is now administered by the National Park Service. To mark the centennial of the transcontinental railroad, the Golden Spike Monument was moved 150ft (46m) northwest and the National Park Service began the reconstruction of two railroad and telegraph lines, together with switches and siding connections.

The engines used in the 1969 ceremonies were modified to resemble the originals and from then until 1980 the annual re-enactment used vintage locomotives on loan from Nevada. In 1980, with water from Liberty Island in New York Harbour and Fort Point in San Francisco Bay, two replica locomotives, built by Chadwell O'Connor Engineering of Costa Mesa, California, were introduced. Costing $1.5 million, these were the first steam engines to be manufactured in the United States for a quarter of a century, and today they operate from May until August and from Christmas to New Year's Day. Visitors can also walk and drive along the old grades and see exhibitions relating to the railroad's construction.

Elsewhere, the Southern Pacific linked southern California to New Orleans in 1883 and two years later the Atchison, Topeka & Santa Fe line ran from Kansas City to Los Angeles along the Southern Pacific route. Cross-country travel now took five days instead of a month. When the Santa Fe first reached Los Angeles only 10,000 people lived in southern California, but more soon arrived as competition brought fares from New York down to as little as $1. Many farmers in the south returned from the Civil War to find themselves homeless and impoverished and so took the only jobs they could find – building railroads. Being farmers, they were often referred to as 'hoe boys' or 'hobos'. Unable to settle, many later went on to wander the country, riding on the same rails they had built.

The Iron Horse began to open up the west and create rapid development in cities along the way, creating the foundations on which modern western states such as

Washington, Idaho, Montana and Wyoming were constructed. The Union Pacific advertised five million acres of farmland in Kansas and Colorado to prospective German immigrants. Colonisation agents were employed to recruit people in the east or from abroad, especially 'hard-working, thrifty' people from England, Scandinavia and the Netherlands, urging them to settle where the air was clean and the land dirt cheap. Some immigrants travelled west free, sharing a wagon with their personal belongings, livestock and machinery. Educational trains up to ten coaches long were sent out to teach farmers how to grow more and better crops – the Poultry Train featured a famous talking rooster. In a remarkably short time the railways transformed America's heartland into one of the most productive food-growing areas in the world.

Tourists also began to arrive as brochures promoted hunting and fishing trips as well as the scenery, abundant produce ('The King of Fruits – 150 recipes for Apple Dishes'), and settlement opportunities in the 'Golden West', 'where money grows on trees'. The Atchison, Topeka & Santa Fe Railway, commonly called the Santa Fe, cleverly publicised its route along the Santa Fe Trail by naming its trains the *Chief* and *Superchief*. Their exotic interiors were decorated with rare woods such as Macassar ebony and African rosewood and the company used the slogan 'see Indian country by train' on its calendars and posters. Native Americans were recruited to present a romanticised picture of the west and artists were commissioned to paint both landscape and people. Detours were made, allowing urban Americans to see the outback for the first time and feel a sense of adventure as they overcame their fear of the west. The first brochures were published to tell passengers what they would be seeing *en route*. Koch and Oakley's *Railway and Navigation Guide*, published in the 1890s, advised: 'Keep your temper and don't get left at the water tank where you have alighted to enjoy the mountain scenery.'

Other railways tried different means to attract passengers, selling or giving away such items as ashtrays, letter openers, match safes, spoons and scissors. Almost anything which could be stamped with a name or slogan was tried, including paperweights in the shape of locomotives or, in one instance, an Idaho baking potato. Such promotional items are now greatly sought after by rail fans, as are early books, posters, timetables, railroad songs and train recordings. Some people collect hardware such as destination signs, lanterns, silverware, locks, keys, telegraph instruments and hand brakes, or even bricks from demolished stations.

The Northern Pacific Railroad opened up the northwest in the 1880s and acquired more land than has been owned by any other single company in the United States. In 1883, the company's charismatic president, Henry Villard, spent nearly a quarter of a million dollars to celebrate the railway's completion. He invited financiers, newspaper reporters and dignitaries from Europe, as well as hundreds of American politicians, bankers, railroad officials, investors and journalists. Five trainloads of guests, including former president Ulysses S Grant, converged on Gold Creek, west of Helena, where a sign read 'Lake Superior 1,198 miles, Puget Sound 847 miles'. Sitting Bull spoke in Sioux through a translator in a speech that began: 'I hate all white people. You are thieves and liars.' The interpreter hastily improvised flowery compliments in English and the speech was greeted with rapturous applause, much to Sitting Bull's amusement.

James J Hill built a similar transcontinental route, the Great Northern, between St Paul, Minnesota, and Seattle. Born in Rockwood, Ontario, the clever, determined and obsessive Hill arrived in St Paul by steamboat in 1856 and started working for the Mississippi River Steamboat Company, fixing freight and passenger rates. After the Civil War he joined the St Paul & Pacific Railroad, which he later bought. He also advised on the construction of the Canadian Pacific but resigned when he saw that it would become a competitor to his own transcontinental line, which he built without government funds or loans: 'Most men who have really lived have had their great adventure. The railway is mine.'

Construction of the Great Northern reached Great Falls in 1887, the fast rate of laying track being ensured by excellent planning and the use of 8,000 men and 3,300 teams of horses. Immigrants were carried west for $10 provided they agreed to settle along the route and farmers were offered free imported cattle. More than six million acres of Montana were settled in two years and the line reached Puget Sound in 1893. The success of his railroad meant that Hill was able to take over the Northern Pacific in 1896.

Unlike the Northern Pacific, most railroad construction west of the Mississippi received federal land grants, eventually totalling 131 million acres. Rail companies charged reduced rates for government traffic in return. As well as the four great transcontinental routes, many smaller lines were built throughout the west and by 1890, a network of 164,000 miles (264,000km) covered virtually the whole country. Few Americans then lived more than 25 miles (40km) from the track. Large, often grandiose, new stations opened at South Street, Boston (1890), St Louis (1894), Washington, DC (1907) and New York (Pennsylvania 1910, Grand Central 1913).

Standard-gauge track and Standard Time (adopted in 1883) helped integration. Railroad timekeeping became so good that farmers set their clocks according to passing trains. Safety innovations included air brakes and automatic coupling. Trains became longer, faster and more efficient as coal-burning engines replaced less powerful wood burners. 'American' types gave way to heavier Atlantics (4-4-2) and Pacifics (4-6-2). Refrigerated wagons were introduced to ship beef from Chicago and oranges from Florida as the railways brought increasing control over nature.

Compressed gas and electricity superseded candlelight in passenger carriages and hot-water heating replaced wood-burning stoves after the Civil War, with corridors and steam heat arriving by the turn of the century. The paint on these new, 85ft-long (25m) coaches was varnished to make it shiny, and the word 'varnish' is still slang for a First Class passenger car. Express services for passengers and special freight were introduced as the economy grew at an ever greater pace.

Sleeping and dining cars, rarely seen before the Civil War, afterwards became much more common. George Pullman's $20,000 *Pioneer* sleeper boasted thick carpets, chandeliers, polished walnut, crimson plush upholstery and marble wash-stands. Pullman, originally a cabinet maker by trade, instructed his craftsmen to build 'palaces on wheels' in which the wealthy would wish to travel. The owner of the Penn Railroad was one of the first to buy a lavishly equipped private coach complete with drawing room, dining room and private galley. Delmonico dining cars, introduced in 1868, meant passengers no longer had to snatch hurried meals at scheduled stops along the way. Parlour cars, forerunners of present-day lounge and club cars, also went into service at about this time. The rich could buy their own lavish private vehicle or hire an entire 'hotel train', complete with barber shop and dance floor.

Railroads became America's first big business, dominating economic life for three-quarters of a century, but the golden age had its less appealing aspects. Train routes made obsolete the Pony Express, the overland stagecoach, and much of the Mississippi riverboat trade. They devastated wildlife, brought the bison to near-extinction, and helped destroy a way of life for many Native Americans. Unionisation brought better pay, at least for train crews, but a dispute on the Baltimore & Ohio in 1877 spread to other companies and resulted in riots. Following wage cuts, a strike at the Pullman factory in 1894 led to sympathy action throughout the Midwest. Rail traffic in America came to a halt as the dispute turned violent. People were threatened, property burned and at least 34 people died when the government sent in 12,000 troops to break up the strike. Union leader Eugene Debs was jailed.

Fraud, corruption and coercion became commonplace. The huge profits attracted a profusion of crooks and bribery sometimes appeared the only way to get business done. Owners often bought up newspapers, politicians, and even the law. Jay Gould, 'Commodore' Cornelius Vanderbilt ('the public interest be damned') and the Central Pacific's 'scrupulously dishonest' Collis Huntington were famous for their ruthlessness. 'Jubilee Jim' Fisk defrauded Erie Railroad stockholders of $64 million. Competition increased in some places but the railways too often exploited their monopoly and public opinion turned against them. The Interstate Commerce Commission was set up in 1887 to control their excesses and the financier Pierpoint Morgan, whose business fortune was said to total more than the combined value of all other property in the 22 states west of the Mississippi, was surprised and hurt when forced to break up his railroad empire.

In 1868, with the first transcontinental line near completion, the great American writer, politician and political economist Henry George predicted that trains would alter California for ever: 'It will not merely open a new route across the continent; it will be the means of converting a wilderness into a populous empire in less time than many of the cathedrals and palaces of Europe were built.' He foresaw that it would lead to great wealth concentrated in the hands of a relatively small number of people. The Central Pacific and Union Pacific were the two largest corporations in the country and the 'Big Four' grew immensely rich from their investment.

Nevertheless, the country had reason to be grateful for the railroads. They brought prosperity, opened up the west, carried the mail and helped turn the United States into a major world power. Ralph Waldo Emerson wrote that, 'the old universe was thrown on to the ash-heap and a new one created'. Railroads changed perceptions of time and space, measuring distance not by miles but by hours and minutes. They made many people rich and gave even penniless hobos a means of transport they could afford. Trains became an indelible part of national culture, inspiring countless stories and featuring in folk songs, blues, jazz, country and gospel music, from 1859's 'North Western Railway Polka' to Johnny Cash's 'Rock Island Line' and 'Wreck of The Old 97'. 'Midnight Special' was one of many songs in which a train symbolised the American desire for escape. 'Bound For Glory', 'Heavenbound Train' and 'Downbound Train' made the railway journey a metaphor for life. On 'The Black Diamond Express To Hell', Sin was the engineer, Pleasure the headlight and the conductor was the Devil. 'Big Rock Candy Mountain' was originally a hobo song, later sanitised for children, and it was down by the railroad track that Johnny B Goode learnt to play guitar so well.

The first American narrative film, *The Great Train Robbery*, was directed in 1903 by Edwin S Porter. Its action-packed plot was inspired by a real-life robbery that took place in August 1900, when four members of the 'Hole in the Wall' gang led by George Leroy Parker (Butch Cassidy) held up the No 3 train on Union Pacific Railroad tracks near Table Rock, Wyoming. They made the conductor uncouple the passenger cars from the rest of the train, blew up the mail car safe and escaped with $5,000 in cash. Instead of the ten-minutes-long film being made in Wyoming, it was shot at Thomas Edison's New York studio and on part of the Lackawanna Railroad. *The Great Train Robbery* starred the world's first cinematic cowboy hero, Gilbert M 'Bronco Billy' Anderson, along with Billy Whiskers, Marie Murray and George Barnes.

Trains have featured in countless movies in the century since, including classics such as *Double Indemnity, Butch Cassidy and the Sundance Kid,* Alfred Hitchcock's *Strangers on a Train,* and 2004's IMAX 3D animation, *The Polar Express.*

THE 20TH CENTURY

By 1900, there were 1,000 railroad companies and 193,000 miles of track. More than a million people worked on the railroads – one out of every 23 Americans – and the USA probably had the best trains in the world. The New York Central's *Twentieth Century Limited* – 'a gentlemen's club on rails' – was inaugurated on the Water Level route in 1902, becoming the fastest and most luxurious way to travel between New York and Chicago. The *Twentieth Century* was the pride of the fleet and a national institution, its name synonymous with prestige and comfort. This train gave the world the expression 'red-carpet treatment', as at New York and Chicago stations a 260ft-long carpet bearing the New York Central's logo would be rolled out for passengers. Every other transcontinental route also had its prestige train intended to impress. Such rolling palaces on wheels included the Great Northern's *Oriental Limited* and later its *Empire Builder.* Northern Pacific's *North Coast Limited* boasted a clothes-pressing service, a barber, shower rooms and a buffet serving 'fine cigars and beverages'. The Union Pacific had its *City of Portland* and the Milwaukee Road's *Olympian* featured a Parlour car with a powerful moveable floodlight with which to view the scenery by night. The Florida East Coast Railway's *Florida Special* had a pre-dinner string quartet and swimsuited models to entertain passengers. Another luxury train, the *Overland Limited,* provided passengers with fresh flowers and Persian carpets and served champagne for breakfast.

By the late 1920s, most city-to-city travel was by rail, with more than 15,000 passenger trains running every day over 254,000 miles (405,000km) of track. The peak was reached in 1929, when 20,000 passenger trains operated every day – one for every 600 Americans. The 1932 film *Union Depot* gives a vivid picture of the atmosphere inside a busy station of the time. Traders gathered at stations to sell their wares and card sharps often made a living out of cheating naive passengers, resulting in notices warning people not to play cards with strangers – still good advice.

In the beginning, the Pullman Company would hire only African-American men for the job of porter, which was eventually to have significant cultural and political consequences when A Philip Rudolph used the power of the labour union to demand substantial social changes for African-Americans. The Brotherhood of Sleeping Car Porters, which he founded, became the first African-American union to gain a contract with a major US corporation. Rudolph later went on to become an important figure in the 1960s civil rights movement.

The 20th century brought other dramatic changes. In a sign of things to come, 1916 saw more than three million automobiles registered in the USA. Over-expansion by the railroads led to financial problems, though these were temporarily disguised when World War I made heavy demands for the movement of freight and people. President Wilson set up the Railroad Administration to put the whole network under government control. With this extra workload the unions became more powerful, demanding an eight-hour day and the end of piecework. Over 100,000 women were recruited, mostly in clerical positions, though nearly all would lose their jobs when railways became private again after the war.

Many of the women recruited during World War II were given more responsible jobs and some remained for another 40 years. A few women had worked on the railways ever since the mid 19th century, sometimes making a living as professional gamblers. Former slave women sold food to passengers on the Chesapeake & Ohio line and attractive females were always in demand to christen a new engine or stretch of track.

Engines continued to become more efficient as 'compounding' (using steam more than once) and 'articulation', together with huge Mallet-type locomotives, allowed prodigious numbers of freight cars to be moved in a single train. Larger fireboxes and 'superheating' also improved productivity. Steam railroads served almost every large community by 1920, and were augmented by many local electric and street railways providing passenger services and encouraging cities to expand.

As the 20th century progressed, diesel replaced steam as the chief source of power. Steam engine numbers reached a peak of 72,000 in the 1920s, but no more were put into service after 1953. The last regular service operating under steam was on the Norfolk & Western in April 1960. The first successful diesel service had been the streamlined *Pioneer Zephyr*, which in 1935 averaged 77.5mph (125km/h) on its inaugural run from Denver to Chicago. Streamliner designers boasted that they took their engines from trucks and their styling from automobiles. These trains were undeniably luxurious but rarely attracted enough passengers to pay their way.

Railroads were badly hit by the Great Depression. Passenger traffic in 1932 was less than two-thirds of the total in 1929. Freight tonnage and railroad employment almost halved. Increasing numbers of hobos rode boxcars and flats to search for work. A million Americans are thought to have 'caught out' (jumped) trains during the 1930s, although it was a dangerous pursuit and thousands died from being crushed between carriages or falling from moving trains. Around a quarter of a million teenagers hopped freight trains at the height of the Depression, joining the adult drifters who wandered from town to town. In makeshift hobo camps called 'jungles', these teenaged transients would often encounter prostitution (both hetero and homosexual), gambling and violence. The number of adolescents on freight trains became an epidemic that inspired the 1933 Hollywood film, *Wild Boys of the Road*, which aimed to show the dangers of such a life. For some, the movie had the opposite effect, encouraging them to catch the next freight out of their home town.

Even today, 'riding the rods' offers the chance to travel free and hobo encampments can sometimes be seen alongside the track. 'First Class' hobo travel means a boxcar offering protection from the elements and great panoramic views through the open doors. A wise hobo stays near the front of the car so that he is not thrown out of the door if the train suddenly stops. He tries never to walk between the rails, cross under couplers or carriages, 'catch out on the fly' (jump on a moving train) or join anyone else in a boxcar. Other hobo slang includes: accommodation car – the caboose of a train; angelina – a young inexperienced hobo; banjo – a small portable frying pan; bindle stick – belongings wrapped in cloth and tied around a stick; bone polisher – a mean dog; cannonball – a fast train; catch the westbound – to die; cow crate – a railroad stock car; crums – lice; doggin' it – travelling by bus; road kid – a young hobo learning the ways of the road; rum dum – a drunkard; soup bowl – a place to get soup, bread and drinks; yegg – a travelling professional thief.

Being a hobo remains hazardous and many were horrifically murdered during the 1990s in a series of killings for which there have been few arrests. Hobos such as Danville Dan, Steamtrain Maury and Guitar Whitey continued to ride the rails in the 1960s and 1970s, sharing food, cigarettes and alcohol as they roamed 200,000 miles of track across the land. Evading the 'bulls' (railroad security guards), they became part of an underworld culture that would later attract students, accountants and other 'weekend riders' looking for thrills. Writer James Michener described this as 'the last red-blooded American adventure'.

As the century progressed, mass car ownership, improved highways and air travel took away rail traffic, reducing revenues. America was the world's first nation to transfer its affection from trains to the automobile. Almost 98% of inter-city passengers travelled by rail in 1916, and in 1920 the US rail network carried a record 1.2 billion passengers. By 1975 numbers were down to 6% and falling. Freight traffic also declined, although less rapidly.

Despite improved efficiency and lower wages, railways increasingly ran into massive deficit. By the end of the Depression half were bankrupt and many of those which remained were only rescued, temporarily, by World War II. Military and civilian traffic in 1944 totalled an amazing 97 billion miles (155 billion kilometres), stretching resources to breaking point. Retired railway workers and old wooden railroad cars were brought back to help the war effort. After the war the locomotive fleet was mostly worn out and there was a dramatic fall in business. More streamlined trains were introduced, along with domed observation cars, high-level seating and economy sleepers. The Santa Fe slogan was 'If you want to feel like a star, travel like a star' and for a while the railways continued to carry more traffic than all other means of transport put together. The Interstate Commerce Commission insisted that they operate passenger services but by 1970 only 500 inter-city trains were left.

By 1962, freight traffic was lower than at any time since the Depression. Tracks started turning to rust as railways merged or were forced into bankruptcy. The greatest collapse was that of the Penn Central (formed only two years earlier) in 1970. Ironically, the last time many lines made a profit was when hauling concrete to build the new interstate highways. To stay in business, the Union Pacific halved its workforce and increased productivity by 55% in less than ten years. Federal government, under pressure to save America's trains, passed the 1970 Rail Passenger Service Act, and a year later the Railroad Passenger Corporation set up Amtrak (short for American Trackage) to take over most long-distance passenger routes. The Southern Railway, the Denver & Rio Grande Western, the Reading, the Georgia, the Chicago, South Shore & South Bend, and the Chicago, Rock Island & Pacific were the only lines to stay independent, but most gave up their passenger services soon afterwards. The Chicago, Rock Island & Pacific line, which last saw trains more than 20 years ago, has been leased by the Union Pacific Railroad to the Missouri Central Railroad, which hopes to restore freight and possibly passenger trains.

The dire state of the freight industry in the early 1970s also forced the government to set up Conrail (the Consolidated Rail Corporation) to take over six bankrupt railroads in the northeast. An estimated $13 billion in subsidy was spent before the company was privatised in 1987. Like other private rail companies, Conrail shed labour, cut costs and sought new business. Services and revenues gradually improved, helped by a change in the government regulations which had put railroads at a disadvantage to truckers. Freight could now be transferred more easily between trains, trucks and ships. Containers gave faster delivery times and rates were cut by two-thirds. More powerful and efficient locomotives were introduced, train crew size reduced and unprofitable routes abandoned or sold, leaving the remaining lines more profitable. For the first time in decades, business found it could save on transport costs by using rail instead of road. Consequently, since the mid 1980s, haulage has increased by a third and revenues have reached more than $31 billion.

This remarkable recovery has led to a series of mergers, resulting in further cost savings as fewer freight cars need to be shunted into sidings or change trains before reaching their destination. From 31 rail companies in 1980 there are now eight, four of which control 90% of the traffic. The Burlington Northern and Santa Fe joined forces in 1995, and in 1996 the Union Pacific and Southern Pacific merged to create the largest and most powerful transport organisation in the world. Conrail was valued at $10 billion in 1997 when its operations were competed for by the CSX and Norfolk Southern, both based in Virginia. Further mergers seem likely, antitrust rules permitting, bringing shorter routes and more cost savings. In 2009, investment guru Warren Buffett paid $44 billion for the Burlington Northern Santa Fe, which owns 390 railroad lines in the United States. Each Burlington Northern train takes 280 trucks off the highways. Explaining his biggest ever deal, Buffett said that: 'Our country's future prosperity depends on its having an efficient and well-maintained rail system.'

Today's railroads employ 192,000 people to maintain and operate almost 200,000 miles of track, with 26,000 locomotives pulling 1.6 million freight and passenger cars. More rational line usage by freight companies should result in fewer delays for Amtrak passengers and the corporation's future seems much more assured. New equipment and other improvements continue to be introduced and Amtrak has received more than $15 billion from the government since 1971. Amtrak's management personnel numbers have been cut by over a third in recent years and the workforce as a whole by several thousand, making it one of the world's most efficient rail operators.

Even in the age of cyberspace, trains still have their uses. President Bill Clinton took a four-day train journey through West Virginia, Kentucky, Ohio, Indiana and Michigan on his way to the 1996 Democratic convention in Chicago, travelling aboard the *21st Century Express* on the kind of whistle-stop campaign not seen since the days of Harry Truman. Clinton went from the blue-collar mining and steel towns of Appalachia to Lake Michigan. At stops *en route* he could wave to cheering crowds from the train's podium as he drummed up interest in his campaign and made a series of proposals designed to appeal to America's heartland. The bullet-proof royal-blue car with gold curtains and dark wooden panelling had formerly been used by Franklin Roosevelt. Other sections of the 16-car train contained Secret Service personnel, satellite communications equipment and enough gadgetry to start a small war.

Before President-elect Barack Obama took office he made a point of using the same privately owned Georgia 300 rail car on his inaugural weekend to travel from Philadelphia to Washington's Union Station, primarily because Abraham Lincoln also came by train along this route in 1861. Lincoln travelled for 12 days all the way to Washington from the state capital of Springfield, Illinois, where Obama announced his presidential bid in 2007. President Obama has always championed the railroads and voted to support state investment. When he was a senator, Vice President Joe Biden returned home to Wilmington from Washington by train almost every night for three decades to be with his sons after his first wife and daughter were killed in a car crash.

President Obama's decision to make this symbolic journey was at first resisted by officials on security grounds as the ten-car 'Obama Express' stopped in Wilmington (where Joe Biden and his family boarded) and Baltimore (where 40,000 people turned out for a rally) and made several 'slow rolls' through places where large crowds of onlookers had gathered on a bitingly cold day. The coach was fitted with internet facilities for the trip, on which the new president was accompanied by his family, journalists and a number of hand-picked 'everyday Americans'.

When terrorists attacked and destroyed New York City's World Trade Center on 11 September 2001, Amtrak trains had continued to operate throughout the crisis, bringing crucial emergency supplies and personnel to the scene. Trains also played a vital role in the recovery efforts after the devastation caused by Hurricane Katrina in 2005. The New Orleans terminal was spared major damage – at one point it was used as a temporary jail – and Amtrak was able to start moving residents from the city when a special 12-car train arrived from Baton Rouge able to carry 600 passengers. Food and water were loaded onto the train before it left for New Orleans. By the Monday after the hurricane, Amtrak was able to operate four runs a day and would later provide the first commercial transportation out of the city with the departures of the *City of New Orleans* to Memphis and Chicago and the *Crescent* to Atlanta and New York.

As well as providing such essential services, environment-friendly trains relieve traffic congestion and conserve energy. They use fuel efficiently, are not greedy for land and encourage economic growth. They are also the most enjoyable way to see America, which has some of the world's finest long-distance routes, and by using them as often as possible you help ensure their survival and prosperity.

2

American Trains Today

AMTRAK TRAINS TODAY

The system Amtrak inherited in 1971 was dilapidated after being starved of investment for many years. Rolling stock was falling apart, roadbeds crumbling, stations dangerous and staff, not surprisingly, felt demoralised. The corporation initially served just 340 cities, with 21 routes operating over 20,000 miles (32,000km) of track. Most employees still worked for the rail companies Amtrak had taken over and continuing losses seemed inevitable. Things improved surprisingly quickly, though, as extra trains were scheduled and modern equipment purchased. In 1971, Amtrak announced a schedule of 184 trains, serving 314 destinations, and services began on 1 May 1971, when *Clocker No 235* departed New York Penn Station at 00.05 bound for Philadelphia. Train reservations and tickets were still laboriously written by hand until Amtrak introduced an automatic system with computerised ticketing, well before airlines caught on to the same development. In efforts towards greater efficiency Amtrak has also introduced a mobile satellite communications and tracking system to link trains and support facilities.

Since the beginning, most even-numbered trains have travelled north and east and odd-numbered trains travel south and west. Exceptions include *Pacific Surfliners*, which use the opposite numbering system inherited from their former operator, the Santa Fe Railway, and some Empire Corridor trains.

Amtrak's slogan – 'the tracks are back' – was emblazoned on everything from lapel badges to bumper stickers. Stations were spruced up and made secure, running times significantly improved and staff again had reason to be cheerful. In Amtrak's first year passengers travelled over three billion miles, rediscovering historic trains like the *California Zephyr* and *Sunset Limited*. Many trains operate like first-class mobile hotels, with room service, overnight shoeshines and mints left on your pillow by the sleeping-car attendant.

Conrail took over six bankrupt railroads in the northeast in 1976 and allowed Amtrak to acquire its first tracks, and the corporation today owns 730 route miles (about 3% of the total nationwide). This primarily consists of the electrified Boston–New York–Washington route and some routes in Michigan. In other parts of the country, Amtrak trains use tracks owned by freight railroads. Amtrak owns 17 tunnels consisting of 29.7 miles of track and 1,186 bridges consisting of 42.5 miles of track. In co-operation with contract railroads and local government, 30 new stations have been built and 35 others renovated.

Heavy maintenance facilities are located in Wilmington and Bear (Delaware) and Beech Grove (Indiana), and there are other maintenance facilities in Boston, Chicago, Hialeah (Florida), Los Angeles, New Orleans, New York City, Niagara Falls, Oakland, Rensselaer (New York), Seattle and Washington, DC.

Employee numbers have risen from 1,200 in 1972 to approximately 19,000 today. Amtrak has 1,519 railroad cars plus 80 *Auto Train* vehicle carriers and 101 baggage cars, and operates 469 locomotives. On weekdays, Amtrak operates up to 300 trains per day, excluding commuter trains, and trains run every minute of the year. In 2009, Amtrak earned $2.35 billion in revenue and incurred $3.51 billion in expenses, covering 67% of its operating costs. Excluding depreciation, a non-cash cost, Amtrak covered 80% of its operating costs. No country in the world operates a passenger rail system without some form of public support for capital costs and/ or operating expenses.

Amtrak has ordered 130 new single-level rail cars in a five-year, $298.1 million contract awarded to the CAF assembly plant in Elmira, New York, with the first one scheduled for completion in 2012. The cars will be similar to the Viewliner model and will include 25 sleeping cars, 25 diners, 55 baggage cars and 25 baggage/ dormitory cars. This is the first step in Amtrak's plan to replace its entire fleet of passenger cars and locomotives over the next 30 years. The company has also ordered 70 new electric locomotives from Siemens for $466 million. Designed for use in the northeast, the first of these is due to join the fleet in 2013.

Amtrak's Northeast Corridor is the busiest railway in North America, carrying almost ten million passengers a year. More than 2,600 trains operate over some portion of the Washington–Boston route each day. More than a quarter of a million riders every weekday generate more than 4.4 million daily passenger miles. The busiest Amtrak stations are in New York, Washington, DC, Philadelphia, Chicago, Los Angeles, Boston, Sacramento, Baltimore and San Diego.

If Amtrak was an airline it would be the country's eighth largest. It serves more than 28 million passengers a year and clocks up a total of five billion passenger miles (a passenger mile is one person transported one mile) on 21,000 miles of routes. Trains travel to most cities in 46 states and the District of Columbia. The states not served are Alaska, Hawaii, South Dakota and Wyoming, although Wyoming does have Amtrak Thruway buses. There are plans also to serve such places as Las Vegas, Abilene, Louisville, Boise and Nashville, and for a luxury transcontinental route (60 hours from coast to coast). Other possibilities include more Midwestern trains out of Chicago, an *Aztec Eagle* train from San Antonio to Monterey in Mexico, and the reintroduction of the *Pioneer* route between Chicago and Seattle.

More people each month are turning to trains as a convenient and enjoyable alternative to congested highways and crowded airports. Of the 510 communities currently served by Amtrak, 130 have no air service, 113 are without inter-city buses and 35 have neither air nor bus services. Altogether, 65 million people a year in the USA travel by train and without them there would be 167,000 more cars on the road.

Amtrak is the country's largest provider of contract-commuter services for state and regional authorities, and an average of nearly 925,000 people every weekday depend on commuter rail services that use Amtrak-owned infrastructure, dispatching, shared operations, or ride commuter trains operated by Amtrak under contracts with local or regional agencies. Commuter services are provided for Caltrain (California), Coasters (California), Maryland Area Regional Commuter (MARC), Metrolink (California), Shoreline East (Connecticut) and Virginia Railway Express (VRE).

Amtrak also provides maintenance services for the Sounder Commuter Rail system in the Seattle area.

David Gunn became President of Amtrak on 15 May 2002, electing to ride to work on the Washington Metro rather than a fancy *Crown Victoria* car provided by his railroad. After giving up a trio of these cars he sent the Amtrak police officer assigned to them back to regular patrol duty. Gunn had earned a formidable reputation, having previously successfully run both of the largest transit systems in the United States and Canada, serving as President of the New York City Transit Agency from 1984 to 1990 and as Chief General Manager of the Toronto Transit Commission from 1995 to 1999. He also headed transit systems in Philadelphia and Washington, DC. He came out of retirement to take on the job as a challenge to turn Amtrak around and stated his determination to maintain and improve the national system.

An early economic-stimulus bill placed before Congress by President Obama included a commitment of $8 billion to construct high-speed rail systems – the most dramatic national pledge to rail since the Pacific Railway Act under President Lincoln. This was intended to be the first stage in a six-year, $53 billion high-speed rail investment plan to modernise the national system with inter-city rail hubs. One prime corridor candidate for upgrading is the Chicago-centred Midwest network including St Louis, Cleveland, St Paul–Minneapolis and Detroit. Other candidates include the Pacific Northwest (Seattle–Portland–Eugene), South Central (San Antonio–Dallas–Tulsa), Florida (Miami–Orlando–Tampa), Northern New England/New York (Boston–Springfield–Albany–Buffalo) and Southeast-Gulf Coast (Raleigh–Charlotte–Atlanta–New Orleans–Houston). Major improvements are needed on the existing Northeast Corridor (Washington–Boston), where Acela trains still run at about half the speed of France's TGV service.

David Gunn was fired by the board of directors in November 2005, despite his success in reducing layers of management overhead, eliminating the controversial express business and improving labour relations. Amtrak had been targeted by the Bush Administration for closure or sell-off since its election in 2000, and more than previous Amtrak presidents Gunn was willing to oppose the political and budget positions of the President of the United States. His view was that no form of mass passenger transportation in the United States is self-sufficient as the economy is currently structured, with highways, airports and air traffic control all receiving large government support. The current Amtrak president is Joseph H Boardman, formerly Administrator of the United States Federal Railroad Administration. In 2010, he announced a 30-year plan to invest $117 billion in deploying high-speed rail in the Northeast Corridor. The system would narrow the commuting time between Washington and New York City from 162 minutes to 96 minutes and the commuting time between New York City and Boston from 215 minutes to 84 minutes.

The National Association of Railroad Passengers (NARP) is the largest national advocacy organisation for train and rail transit passengers (*www.narprail.org*). NARP aims to expand the quality and quantity of passenger rail in the United States and has around 20,000 members, whose benefits include excellent newsletters, discounts on most Amtrak fares and the Grand Canyon Railway, and an 'I'd Rather Be on the Train' bumper sticker. Newsletters about current Amtrak activities can also be found on the websites of Friends of Amtrak (*www.trainweb.org/crocon/amtrak.html*) and the National Corridors Initiative (*www.nationalcorridors.org*).

AMTRAK FACILITIES AND SERVICES

TICKETS Coach Class is the standard Amtrak ticket. Business Class (available mainly on Acela/Northeast Corridor routes) are First Class services which offer extra facilities (see *Equipment* later in this chapter, page 22). Sleeping-car accommodation is also First Class. Since most long-distance trains require advance reservations you normally have to reserve and purchase separate tickets if you wish to break your journey *en route*. Business Class, available on some trains in the northeast, Midwest and on Empire services, provides coaches with more room around the seats and extra facilities such as changing rooms and telephones.

Fares naturally depend on the distance travelled and standard of service provided, though special offers, seasonal rates and excursion deals often provide big reductions. Ticket prices are often 50% or 75% less than the equivalent air fare, especially if you travel off-peak. This may be influenced by the season, day of the week or time of day, depending on the route. Check Amtrak's website (*www. amtrak.com*) or your travel agent for news of the current special deals. Sleeping-car accommodation is always charged for in addition to the journey fare.

Accompanied children aged two–15 pay half fare (limited to two half fares per adult) and those aged under two travel free if they share an adult's seat. There are further reductions for group travel, a group being 20 people or more. You can buy one-way standard-rate tickets on board but a penalty will be added if the ticket office was open at the time of your departure. For information on discounts for children, students, senior citizens and group travel, see page 28. Where space is available you can upgrade accommodation on board, including sleepers and Business Class, and sometimes obtain a discount on the usual rate. Ask the conductor or chief of on-board services. Tickets can be delivered by mail if paid for by credit card but Amtrak accepts no responsibility for lost, stolen or destroyed tickets.

Quik-Trak self-service machines with touch-screen menus are now in use at most major stations. These accept credit and debit cards and enable you to purchase Coach Class tickets to any city listed on the machine. You can also pick up tickets for previously made reservations by entering your reservation number.

All ticket information can be found on Amtrak's award-winning website.

RESERVATIONS Coach seating on unreserved trains is not guaranteed and is allocated on a first-come, first-served basis. Coach Class and all First Class and sleeping-car accommodation on all-reserved trains should be booked well in advance, particularly during summer when some routes may be very busy. If travelling overnight through particularly scenic areas try to make your departure date just before a full moon.

Reservations can be obtained up to 11 months ahead via Amtrak's website, through any Amtrak station ticket office (try to avoid busy times) or at designated travel agents, including those abroad. Many travel agents in North America are connected into the Amtrak computer booking system. Alternatively, you can call 'Julie', Amtrak's state-of-the-art voice-recognition system (☏ *1 800 USA RAIL or* ☏ *1 800 872 7245; for group reservations,* ☏ *800 USA 1GRP*). You will be given a reservation number and hold date by which time you must collect your tickets. Tickets can be paid for when you make your reservations and picked up at any time ⸱ prior to travel, but reservations will be cancelled if collection is not made by then. Telephone lines are open 24 hours a day, 365 days a year, but you may receive a faster service by calling early in the morning or late at night.

A service charge is made for prepaid tickets. If you need to upgrade and find no sleeper is available try calling again at a later date, if possible early in the morning, as there are sometimes compartments and coach seats available as a result of cancellations or 'no-shows'.

AMTRAK VACATIONS Plan a rail vacation the easy way by calling Amtrak Vacations (☏ *1 800 268 7252*). This allows you to make all your arrangements for train tickets, hotel reservations, car rental and sightseeing. You can also book Air Rail tickets for travel with United Airlines and United Express, allowing you to fly one way and take the train the other.

MULTI-RIDE TICKETING OPTIONS Many Amtrak short-distance trains offer multi-ride ticket options, including a ten-ride ticket valid for 45 days. A calendar-month ticket (similar to a monthly pass) is valid for one calendar month.

Multi-ride tickets cannot be booked on Amtrak's online booking system or bought on board trains, but are available at Quik-Trak self-serve ticket machines and at staffed Amtrak stations. Note that restrictions may vary by route and destination.

You can also call ☏ 800 USA RAIL, speak to an Amtrak reservations agent and have a multi-ride ticket mailed to you at home or at work. A call is needed every time you want a new ticket mailed and you should allow at least ten days before your first intended travel date.

SECURITY Amtrak's security measures require customers to provide acceptable photo identification when purchasing/obtaining tickets – whether in stations or on board trains – or checking baggage. Acceptable forms of identification include a valid driver's licence, passport or government-agency ID.

USA RAIL PASS Amtrak rail passes enable you to visit any destination in Amtrak's system throughout the United States. They are available in three travel durations and travel segments: 15 days/eight segments, 30 days/12 segments and 45 days/18 segments. A travel segment is specified as any time you get on and then get off a vehicle (train, bus, ferry or other allowable leg) regardless of distance travelled. Each segment booked counts towards the total number of segments permitted for the pass. Travel must begin within 180 days of the date that your pass is purchased.

A USA Rail Pass entitles you to travel in regular Coach Class seats and is valid on all Amtrak trains except the *Auto Train*, *Acela Express* and the Canadian portion of trains operated jointly by Amtrak and VIA Rail. Travel is restricted to four one-way trips between two cities, and to all cities in between, over the same route.

On some trains, you can upgrade to Business Class or sleeping-car accommodations for the appropriate surcharge. Children aged two to 15 years travel for half-price when accompanied by a full fare-paying adult, and two children are permitted per adult fare. One child under two years old may ride free with each fare-paying adult.

You can purchase a USA Rail Pass at any time on Amtrak's website using a credit card or by contacting an international sales representative (see *Appendix 3*, page 337). Passes cannot be bought on board trains. The following prices currently apply:

15 days (eight segments)	$389.00 (adult)	$194.50 (child aged two–15)
30 days (12 segments)	$579.00 (adult)	$289.50 (child aged two–15)
45 days (18 segments)	$749.00 (adult)	$374.50 (child aged two–15)

The pass is not a ticket, so you must make reservations and pick up your ticket(s) before boarding any train. Seats available for USA Rail Pass passengers are limited so you should make reservations as far in advance as possible and not wait until the day of departure, since there is then a greater chance that seats may not be available on your desired train. If your plans are not flexible, non-USA Rail Pass seats may be available at an additional cost. For more information, call ☏ 1 800 USA RAIL (☏ *1 800 872 7245*).

For travellers outside the United States, reservations can be made by sending your name, desired travel date(s), USA Rail Pass confirmation number and the train(s) on which you want to travel to e inat5@sales.amtrak.com prior to arriving in the United States, or call ❧ (001) 215 856 7953 during regular business hours (08.30–17.30 Monday–Friday EST). If you are already in the United States, call ❧ 1 800 USA RAIL (❧ *1 800 872 7245*) and speak to a reservations agent. You can pick up your pass and tickets at any staffed Amtrak ticket office in many Amtrak stations by showing your USA Rail Pass or pass confirmation number. Travel on Amtrak requires full identification so bring a valid passport or US-issued identification card, such as a driver's licence or picture ID card.

Refunds are only allowed before travel begins. The pass as well as all tickets issued with it must be turned into an Amtrak ticket agent no later than the day before the date of the first use written on the pass. A cancellation fee may apply, which might be substantial if sleeping-car accommodations are cancelled less than 24 hours in advance.

CALIFORNIA The California Rail Pass allows up to seven days of travel in California over a consecutive 21-day period for $159 (adults) and $80 (children two–15). Eligible trains are the *Capitols, San Joaquin* and *Pacific Surfliner* corridor trains, most connecting Thruway services, and the *Coast Starlight* between Los Angeles and Dunsmuir, California. The California Rail Pass is not valid on long-distance trains, such as the *Sunset Limited*, the *Southwest Chief*, the *California Zephyr* and the *Texas Eagle*. On the *Coast Starlight*, travel to or from points outside California requires a separate fare, calculated between Dunsmuir and the out-of-state origin or destination. A pass holder is entitled to regular Coach Class travel, which may be upgraded to Business Class or sleeping-car accommodations by paying an extra charge.

California Rail Passes are not available for purchase online so you need to call a travel agent or Amtrak at ❧ 1 800 USA RAIL (❧ *1 800 872 7245*). In addition to holding the pass, you must make reservations on all trains and obtain hard-copy tickets for all travel prior to boarding. The pass is not valid without a corresponding ticket. You should also carry identification as this may be requested.

Travel during any part of a calendar day counts as using that day and travel is limited to not more than four one-way journeys on a given route segment. The California Rail Pass is not transferable and must be used within one year of purchase. Refunds are only available if it has not been used, and if the pass and all tickets issued against it are returned to Amtrak. A penalty may apply to sleeping-car accommodations not cancelled at least seven days before departure. The pass cannot be combined with other offers, discounts or promotions unless specifically allowed under the terms of these offers.

PAYMENT You can pay for Amtrak tickets and dining-car meals with cash or by credit or debit card, or by travellers' cheques designated in US dollars. Personal cheques must be drawn on a US bank and be for a minimum of $25. Two pieces of identification are required, including one with your photograph or signature. Amtrak will not accept personal cheques in California, except from customers aged 62 or over.

REFUNDS If you change your plans you should apply for a refund as soon as possible to avoid penalties. In most cases a fee will be charged. No change fees are charged as long as you buy another Amtrak ticket of equal or greater value or take a credit towards future travel. The only time a fee would apply is if you ask for money back, when there is a service charge equal to 10% of the ticket's value, up to a maximum of $100. The same service charge applies to refunds for on-board accommodations as long as the reservation is cancelled at least one hour before departure. For sleeping-car accommodations cancelled less than 24 hours before the train's departure, the cost of the on-board accommodation can still be credited towards future travel within one year. Partly used special fare and excursion tickets may have limited refunds.

Reimbursement can be received from ticket offices, online or by mail from Amtrak Customer Refunds (*30th St Station, 2995 Market St, Philadelphia, PA 19104-2898*). Send your ticket via certified mail. Travel agency-sold tickets must usually be refunded through the agent, although Amtrak will make refunds on the spot if this is due to service disruption or downgrading.

TIMETABLES Amtrak ticket offices and travel agents can provide free timetables for individual routes, the northeast and for the National network. Up-to-date timetables can also be found on the Amtrak website (*www.amtrak.com*). Times shown are local, taking into account any zone changes *en route*. You should confirm your departure time the day before travelling, especially if the tickets were bought several weeks in advance. In the autumn, on the day clocks go back, trains may be deferred for an hour in order to arrive 'on time'. On the day clocks go forward in spring, a new timetable comes into effect and trains attempt to make up time lost before reaching subsequent stations. Arizona and parts of Indiana do not observe daylight saving time.

Generally speaking, Amtrak's timekeeping performance in recent years has compared favourably with that of airlines, although circumstances beyond the corporation's control can lead to delays. Freight trains sometimes have to take precedence and Amtrak trains crossing into Canada may be held up by customs and immigration inspections. Connections of less than 60 minutes are not guaranteed (90 minutes between arriving long-distance trains and local trains in the Northeast Corridor) so you should allow at least an hour between trains. Even a guaranteed connection may sometimes be missed. If this happens, alternative transport on Amtrak or another carrier will usually be provided and, in exceptional circumstances, overnight accommodation arranged.

If you have limited time to change trains ask the conductor on the train where you should go to get your next one when you reach the depot. This will save you having to hunt for signs or wait in a queue for information. Note that some cities have more than one station. Trains may not pause for as long as the timetable indicates at scheduled stops, so listen to the announcements or ask an attendant before deciding to stretch your legs on the platform. Stay within sight and hearing of the train and be prepared to reboard at a moment's notice or you may be left behind. Anyone intending to meet a train can check times of arrival and departure by calling ☎ 1 800 USA RAIL (☎ *1 800 872 7245*) and listening to the automated information.

THRUWAY BUSES Amtrak's Thruway bus service provides co-ordinated train/bus connections with through fares and ticketing. Where a Thruway bus is necessary to complete your journey the cost is included in the rail fare.

Timetables show some of the connecting services provided by other carriers to destinations not served by Amtrak or Thruway buses. Reservations and tickets for these services can be obtained from Amtrak but you should note that they may leave from another terminal.

AIRPORT CONNECTIONS Several Amtrak stations (including BWI Thurgood Marshall and Newark Liberty International) are adjacent to airports with connecting services provided by the airport. Others, especially in larger cities, have a range of transfer options available between the station and airport.

BOARDING You should arrive at least half an hour before departure time (or two hours for the *Auto Train*). It is important that you go to the right coach, so tell the gate attendant your destination and he will direct you. Red Caps (porters) are there to assist with luggage if required. Choose a window seat for a better view of the scenery, a little more privacy and a corner to lean against when sleeping. An aisle seat will give you more freedom to move without disturbing other passengers. Try not to sit too near the front as the view there may be more restricted.

METROPOLITAN LOUNGE Chicago and Portland, Oregon, have Metropolitan waiting rooms located away from the crowds. They provide a staffed reception desk, comfortable chairs, television, telephones, fax machines, computer links, a conference area, rest rooms, newspapers, luggage stores and a superior class of muzak. They also offer complimentary coffee, soft drinks and doughnuts. Metropolitan lounges are available (on arrival or departure) to sleeping-car-service passengers.

CLUBACELA First Class ClubAcela lounges are located in Boston South Station, New York Penn Station, Philadelphia 30th Street Station and Washington Union Station. They are available to passengers travelling with First Class or long-distance tickets.

Facilities include complimentary soft drinks, juice, pastries and snacks; comfortable and quiet seating; reservations and ticketing assistance; newspapers and periodicals; free local telephone calls; credit-card long-distance telephones with data ports for computer usage; complimentary use of photocopy and fax machines; internet access; conference rooms equipped with speaker phones and VCRs available for rental; information on local dining and entertainment options; train information; advance boarding (where available); and Quik-Trak ticketing machines (where available).

FIRST CLASS LOUNGE Unattended, separate sleeping-car passenger and Amtrak Guest Rewards Select Plus member waiting rooms are available in St Paul–Minneapolis, St Louis, New Orleans, Raleigh and Miami.

EQUIPMENT

Superliner Manufactured by the Pullman-Standard Company for Amtrak between 1979 and 1981, these spacious, twin-decked coaches operate on all long-distance routes west of the Mississippi as well as on some in the east. Designed to be 'the finest trains anywhere in the world', they have air-cushioned suspension and were built with extra sound-absorbing materials. Each Superliner car measures 85ft (26m) long and 16ft (5m) high, weighs 75 US tons (68 tonnes) and has large windows with excellent views, especially from the upper level. The reclining seats, about equivalent to flying First Class, provide leg and foot rests, folding trays and personal reading lights.

A new generation of Superliner II cars, built by the Bombardier company, has been introduced on the *Auto Train* and several western routes. These have bigger windows and larger compartments than the first range of Superliners.

Dining cars cater for up to 72 people and are on the upper level above the kitchen. Sightseer lounge cars and most kinds of sleeping accommodation are also usually available. Rest rooms (toilets) are mostly on the lower level, with at least one accessible to disabled passengers. Facilities include toilet, washbasin, mirror, infant changing table, soap, tissues and a 120V AC electric point. Luggage may be left at the lower level on entry or stored in overhead racks.

Amfleet Designed for short and medium journeys and operating mostly in the east, Amfleet coaches were built by the Budd Company of Philadelphia. They offer reclining seats, fold-down trays, overhead luggage racks and personal reading lights. Amfleet II coaches, intended for longer journeys, provide leg rests and more space. At least one rest room caters for disabled passengers. Dinette and lounge cars serve light meals which you can take to a table or back to your seat.

Business Class Business Class cars have a double seat on one side of the aisle and a single on the other, with complimentary at-your-seat food and drinks service, including wine, as well as free newspapers and hot towels. Custom Class includes a newspaper and complimentary coffee, plus tea or juice in a café car shared only with Business Class passengers.

California Fleet Bi-level coaches feature large picture windows and headphone connections for recorded music. There are telephone and fax facilities as well as electrical outlets for laptop computers and handheld games. These coaches operate on the *San Joaquins* route and elsewhere in southern California. They were purchased by the state and are operated by Amtrak in partnership with the California Department of Transportation.

Pacific Surfliner With aerodynamic styling and ultra-efficient engineering, these latest bi-level trains are operated in partnership with Caltrans in southern California. Each five-car train has 422 seats and includes one Business Class car with personal audio and visual systems. Coach Class cars have wide reclining seats, panoramic windows, electrical outlets for laptop computers, Railfone and a digital information display showing station arrivals. Surfliner trains are designed to be easily accessible, especially for mobility-impaired passengers.

Acela Pronounced 'Ah-cell-ah', the name combines the words 'excellence' and 'acceleration'. *Acela Express* trains have replaced most Metroliner services in the Northeast Corridor, using new equipment and making fewer stops. The sleek trains, built by Bombardier and Alstom in Vermont, New York and Quebec, use tilt technology to achieve speeds of up to 150mph and cut the time between New York City and Washington, DC, to 2¾ hours. *Acela Regional* trains serve more destinations.

Besides a faster trip with fewer stops, the *Acela Express* provides a superior on-board experience, with reserved First Class and Business Class seating and upmarket amenities such as an electrical outlet at your seat, adjustable lighting and a tray table large enough for a laptop. Meetings can be held at one of 32 conference tables and there is a bistro-like café car with an extensive menu.

Regional *Regional* services offer coach-car accommodations with reclining seats, fold-down trays and overhead reading lights. Business Class passengers have more leg room and receive complimentary non-alcoholic beverages in the café car.

Cascades Service Sporting distinctive, 7ft-tall tail fins, Amtrak's sleek Cascades trains were built in Spain by Talgo and in Seattle by General Motors. They incorporate tilt technology and consist of 12 cars, each half the length of a normal Amtrak car, including a bistro and a dining car. They were bought in partnership with the Washington State Department of Transportation (*PO Box 47407, Olympia, WA 98504-7407;* ✆ *1 800 872 7245 or* ✆ *360 705 7901 (in Olympia); www. amtrakcascades.com*) to operate along the Northwest Corridor. For safety reasons they are currently limited to 79mph but improvements to the track will eventually allow them to reach speeds of up to 110mph.

The comfortable coaches are painted in bold colours, officially known as Double Latte and Evergreen, and feature plush seats and Railfone as well as video and stereo services. Business Class includes wider seats, more leg room, television screens and laptop computer outlets, plus complimentary snacks, drinks and newspapers.

For more information, see contact details above.

SLEEPING Reclining seats, dimmed lights and a free pillow from the attendant complement a gentle rocking and the hypnotic rumble of the wheels: obtaining a comfortable night's sleep is easy even when travelling Coach Class given a certain amount of practice. You also save money on hotels. For the best results you should choose a seat in the middle of the car away from the noise of sliding doors, and take a coat or blanket to ward off sometimes over-enthusiastic air conditioning. Souvenir blankets are sold on most long-distance trains. The pillows provided by Amtrak are fairly small so you may wish to take a larger one of your own. Alternatively, you could take a pillow case and ask the attendant for two pillows to put inside.

All sleeping-car accommodation is designated First Class. Compartments are ingenious but small, and become no bigger as your journey progresses, so it helps if you enjoy camping. You do get extra privacy and there is a strange pleasure to be had from hurtling through the night in your personal travelling capsule. Try to obtain a compartment in the centre of the coach away from the vibration of the wheels. You can either make up your own bed or let the attendant do it for you, and he may even leave a goodnight sweet on your pillow. Towels, soap and bed linen are provided. Remember that sleeping-car walls are usually thin so keep the noise down at night.

Complimentary tea, coffee or fruit juice (plus a newspaper) are served 06.30–09.30 to passengers in sleeping-car accommodation and your fare includes all meals in the dining car. Sleeping-car passengers are entitled to make use of Amtrak's Metropolitan lounge waiting rooms both before and after their journey.

Superliner bedrooms All Superliner bedrooms have adjustable climate controls, individual reading lights, a fold-down table, garment rack and an electrical outlet.

Roomette Ten roomettes on the upper level and four on the lower level each accommodate two adults. Two reclining seats face each other or slide together to form the lower berth, and a second berth folds out from the wall. Features include a picture window, narrow closet (wardrobe) and an aisle window with curtains. Rooms are compact so it pays to leave most of your luggage in the lower storage area and take only a small bag into your bedroom. Rest rooms are provided on the lower or upper level. Room dimensions: 3ft 7in by 6ft 6in.

Bedroom Five bedrooms are located on the upper level, each sleeping two adults in berths which fold down. Daytime seating consists of a large sofa and an armchair. Adjoining rooms can sometimes be combined into a suite for up to four people. Features include a closet and an aisle window with curtains. There is space for two medium-sized suitcases. Rest-room facilities include a shower, washbasin and toilet. Room dimensions: 6ft 6in by 7ft 6in.

Family bedroom One family bedroom on the lower level sleeps two adults and two children, with daytime seating consisting of two chairs and a long sofa. Only a few family rooms are available on each trip so book well in advance if possible. Upper and lower berths are for adults, with two short berths for children. Family bedrooms extend the full width of the car, giving windows on each side. The windows are smaller, though, which makes watching the scenery less easy. Being on the lower level puts you closer to the wheels so you may find travelling slightly noisier, although this should not affect sleeping. There is space for up to three suitcases and a rest room is provided on the lower level. Room dimensions: 5ft 3in by 9ft 6in.

Accessible bedroom Each sleeping car has a bedroom on the lower level intended for up to two people, including one passenger with special mobility requirements. Features include an attendant call button. Two berths fold down for sleeping and for daytime use there are two reclining seats. There is space for two suitcases. The accommodation includes meals and drinks served in your room by the car attendant. Rest-room facilities (which are curtained off) include a toilet, washbasin and hand grips. Room dimensions: 6ft 6in by 9ft 6in.

Viewliners These Amtrak-designed cars were the first single-level sleepers to be manufactured in the US for 40 years. Introduced on routes in the east and Midwest they have replaced the Heritage sleepers which pre-dated Amtrak. Viewliners are larger and give a smoother ride. Their modular design means that each bedroom is a separate structure, making them quieter, and there are more windows so that upper-berth passengers can have a view. All Viewliner bedrooms have adjustable climate controls, an electrical outlet, reading lights, built-in audio and a video screen for movies. A shower room is also available. Room dimensions: 6ft 8in by 7ft 1in.

Standard bedroom Designed for one or two people. Two reclining seats convert into a bed at night and an upper berth drops down from the ceiling. There is a picture window and another window above for extra light. Rest-room facilities include a toilet, mirror and washbasin, and a shower is located nearby. If you are in a Viewliner by yourself, sleep in the top bunk, leaving more room to store your belongings below and have access to the toilet. Room dimensions: 3ft 7in by 6ft 6in.

Deluxe bedroom Extra space is provided for two people, with an armchair and a sofa. The sofa converts into a wide berth below an upper berth. Rest-room facilities include a private shower, toilet, mirror and washbasin. Two deluxe bedrooms can be combined into a suite for four people. Room dimensions: 6ft 6in by 7ft 3in.

Accessible bedroom This is a deluxe bedroom equipped for passengers with special mobility requirements, with all facilities accessible by wheelchair. There is a reclining seat and upper and lower berths. Meals and drinks can be served to those with disabilities. Rest-room facilities include a private shower, toilet, mirror and washbasin. Room dimensions: 6ft 6in by 7ft 3in.

DINING Most long-distance trains have a complete dining-car service, providing breakfast (06.30–10.30), lunch (11.30–14.30) and dinner (16.30–21.00). A meal service is generally available for passengers boarding 30 minutes before the end of each meal period.

Regional specialities such as barbecued spare ribs or fresh salmon are sometimes added to the standard steak, chicken and lasagne menu, and there are special meals for vegetarians and children. Dessert is usually a choice of fruit pie (à la mode if you wish), cake or cheesecake. Breakfast is likely to consist of fresh fruit, cereal, bagels and muffins with cream cheese, jelly and butter. For kosher, low sodium or low cholesterol food you should let Amtrak know your requirements at least 72 hours before travelling. Call ☎ 1 800 USA RAIL and ask for the Special Services desk.

Advance dinner reservations are normally taken by the chief of on-board services or dining-car attendant moving through the train. This minimises waiting time, since on arrival you can be seated straight away by the steward. The tables usually seat four so you may find yourself eating with strangers, which can be an entertaining and revealing experience. Amtrak uses china dishes and linen tablecloths on the *Capitol Limited*, *Coast Starlight* and *Southwest Chief*, and has plans to extend these civilised touches to other trains. *Auto Train* passengers receive a full dining-car service but buffet-style dining cars operate on most Florida routes.

Lunch is usually better value than dinner for those keeping to a tight budget. Entrées range from about $8 to $14, and anything alcoholic tends to be expensive. Many people bring their own supplies of food and drink on board, but this is not encouraged and may be impractical for longer journeys. You can buy snacks such as sandwiches, pizza, soup, salad, drinks and sweets to take back to your seat or consume in the dinette or café car, which usually opens from 06.00 to midnight. Business Class provides a meal service to your seat.

LOUNGE AND DOME CARS Superliners have a Sightseer lounge car, giving views through huge windows that extend part way over the roof. Here you can mingle with fellow passengers, watch a movie (most likely a comedy or light drama) on the television monitor in the evening, get a drink at the bar, buy a sandwich or coffee, and watch the changing landscape pass by outside. Movies and sometimes cartoons or travelogues are also occasionally shown during the afternoon. You can also buy souvenir blankets, playing cards and postcards. Seating is on a first-come, first-served basis but it is good manners not to monopolise a seat all day.

Hospitality hour in the lounge is an excellent opportunity to sample exotic drinks, snack on hors d'oeuvres and break the ice by meeting new people. The relaxed atmosphere on board seems to encourage Americans in particular to tell their life stories to a complete stranger. This special kind of friendliness is encouraged by the thought that, unless you make a considerable effort, you are unlikely ever to see them again.

Amfleet lounge and dome cars offer similar services to Superliners, with more 'land cruise' experience and wide-angle viewing on eastern and Midwestern routes.

QUIET CAR Many Northeast and West Coast Corridor trains, as well as the *Hiawatha* service, have a quiet car where passengers are asked not to use mobile phones, pagers or the sound feature of laptop computers, and to speak only in subdued tones. Seating is on a first-come, first-served basis and cannot be reserved specifically.

BAGGAGE Trains can accommodate up to two items of carry-on luggage (maximum weight 50lb/22.7kg each) per passenger, but Amtrak encourages you to use its checked baggage service whenever possible. Carry-on bags with shoulder straps are easier to handle. All bags must be visibly tagged with the name and address of the passenger. There is storage space in overhead racks and at the end of the car. When occupying sleeping accommodation you can bring on board as much as will safely fit into your bedroom, although sometimes this will not be much. Additional bags can be left in the storage area outside your room.

Amtrak usually accepts no liability for loss or damage to carry-on luggage but you should report any problems to the attendant as soon as possible. Although it's usually safe to leave things behind on your seat when you visit the diner or lounge car, you should take expensive cameras or other items of value with you just in case.

Where a check-in service is provided, you are allowed to check up to three items of baggage weighing no more than 50lb (22.7kg) each or 150lb (68kg) altogether. You pay a surcharge if this is exceeded but items slightly over the limit are usually permitted. Well-secured boxes or cartons weighing less than 50lb will also be accepted. If you require special assistance with your bags you should let Amtrak know when making reservations. Many stations provide free luggage trolleys. Others have handcarts for which a small charge is made, partly refunded when you return the cart to a vending machine.

Bags should be labelled with your name and address and checked in at least half an hour before departure. Checked baggage may be sent by a different route and get to your destination before you do. It will be held for up to two days without charge following your arrival. Amtrak's liability for checked baggage is limited to $500 per passenger, but you can purchase additional insurance up to $2,500. Claims for loss or damage must be submitted within 30 days. For more details ask for a copy of *Checked Baggage Service*, available at most stations or by mail.

An increasing number of trains now offer bicycle and ski racks. Space for bikes remains limited, though, so you should make reservations well ahead of your journey.

RED CAPS Assistance with baggage is provided free of charge by uniformed Red Cap porters at most large stations. Items handled by Red Caps are not checked baggage and are your responsibility once loaded onto the train. Make sure you obtain a claim check for each bag in case anything is mislaid. Amtrak recommends you accept help only from a Red Cap.

SAFETY Try to arrive early in order to avoid rushing for your train. Don't leave luggage in the aisle or in the vestibules between cars. Always wear shoes when moving about the train and use handrails when boarding or climbing stairs. Only touch connecting doors on the 'press' plate to open them.

SMOKING Smoking is prohibited on all Amtrak trains apart from the *Auto Train* as well as on Thruway buses and in stations. Some long-distance trains provide semi-official smoking stops announced by the train crew at certain stations along the way. If you smoke on a non-smoking train you may, without a warning, be asked to get off at the next stop.

TIPPING You do not have to tip Amtrak personnel, although most people reward bar staff, waiters and sleeping-car attendants, especially after a long trip. Some of the older, more wily attendants can judge how many dollar bills you have in your roll just by looking at it. The IRS taxes Amtrak officials based on what they expect the crew to receive in tips, so $1 at breakfast is usual and a few dollars at dinner. Red Caps should be tipped $1 per bag, or more where extra help has been provided. Train-operating personnel such as conductors are never tipped.

ALCOHOL Except in sleeping cars you are not officially supposed to consume your own supplies of alcoholic drinks.

PERSONAL ELECTRONIC DEVICES Earphones or headphones must be used when listening to radios, personal stereos or portable televisions. Keep the volume down to prevent 'leakage'.

LAPTOP COMPUTERS Electrical outlets for use with computers are available in Metropolitan lounges. Some trains also provide electrical sockets for use with laptops but train power current is not always stable so a surge protector should be used.

PETS Only certified guide or service animals accompanying passengers with disabilities are permitted on board. Documentation is required.

CHILDREN Even more than adults, children love to travel by train, especially since this is often a rare treat. When travelling with children you should take a good supply of books, games and other amusements, such as quiet toys. Children must always be supervised by an adult while in the lounge car and should never be left unattended. Most trains have rest rooms with infant changing facilities. Chicago's Union Station and the *Auto Train* have special play rooms and a private area for nursing mothers.

Children aged under eight are not allowed to travel unaccompanied. Children aged between eight and 14 can do so during daylight hours, provided there are no transfers and both boarding and detraining stations are staffed. Prior written permission is required from the person in charge at the boarding station. The full adult fare will be charged. Call ✆ 1 800 USA RAIL for more information.

SENIOR CITIZENS Those aged over 62 get a 15% discount off most coach fares. Some blackout dates apply and discounts are not available on Metroliners, the *Auto Train* or sleepers. For information on discounts for accommodation and other matters of interest contact the National Council of Senior Citizens (*8403 Colesville Rd, Suite 1200, Silver Spring, MD 20910-3314;* ✆ *1 301 578 8800*).

STUDENTS Those with a Student Advantage card can get 15% off most Amtrak fares as well as reductions for hotels, car hire and theatres. Call ✆ 1 800 96 AMTRAK if you are a university or secondary-school student, or visit www.studentadvantage.com.

GROUP AND CONVENTION TRAVEL Generous extra discounts are available if you can rustle up a group of people to travel together between the same origin and destination. Amtrak offers discounts for groups of at least 20 people, and can even handle groups of 100 or more, depending on the train and time of year travel is taking place. You can choose from a 20% discount or one free escort ticket for each 20 paying passengers. Amtrak's 15% senior citizen and half-fare children's discounts may be applied to eligible members of the group. These discounts are not valid on all trains and further restrictions may apply.

To make reservations you can use the online group travel form on Amtrak's website, call ✆ 1 800 USA 1GRP (✆ *1 800 872 1477*) or email e groupsales@amtrak.com.

PASSENGERS WITH DISABILITIES Except for the *Auto Train* and Metroliners, disabled passengers are entitled to 25% off regular one-way coach fares. Amtrak also offers a discounted companion fare for people travelling with a passenger with a disability. Disabled children pay half the disabled adult fare and guide dogs accompanying blind or deaf passengers travel free.

Wheelchair lifts are available at most stations. Passengers can receive special assistance at a station or on board provided 72 hours' notice is given. Most trains have special rest rooms and sleeping accommodation, and meals can usually be served at your seat by the attendant. Call ✆ 1 800 USA RAIL for details and ask for a copy of *Access Amtrak*, a guide to services for the elderly or disabled. Explain your needs when making reservations and remember to bring any medication you require.

Amtrak Thruway and other bus connections are not accessible by wheelchair, although folding chairs can be stored. Disabled passengers must occupy a standard seat and be able to board the bus unassisted.

Hearing-impaired people can obtain information or make reservations by teletypewriter (✆ *1 800 523 6590*). The service operates nationwide 24 hours a day, seven days a week. Many states supply access details in their brochures and a wide range of materials for people with disabilities, including information sheets, are available from the Society for the Advancement of Travel for the Handicapped (SATH) (*347 Fifth Av, Suite 610, New York, NY 10016;* ✆ *1 212 447 7284; www. sath.org*).

RAILFONE An on-board telephone service is available on Metroliners and most other trains between Boston and Washington, DC, as well as on some trains in California and the Midwest. You can make a call to anywhere in the world from a private booth, charging directly by credit card.

ENTERTAINMENT Movies, travelogues and card games are sometimes featured in the lounge car, as are games of trivia and scavenger hunts where you win a modest prize by giving the correct answers to a quiz or coming up with a specific object. Desperately competitive types should carry their birth certificate, a $2 bill and a photograph of their pet. Games of bingo are sometimes organised in the dining car.

On some routes an official guide will board the train to describe the history and wildlife of the landscape through which you are travelling.

PHOTOGRAPHY Seeing the country by train provides passengers with almost too many photo opportunities. For best results a medium-speed film (ASA 64 or above) is recommended for shooting scenery through the windows. If your camera's shutter speed is adjustable (and light conditions permit) set it at either 1/125sec or 1/250sec. Taking photographs from a moving train can result in blurred images, so to cope with this you should boost the shutter rate. If you have a digital camera with an auto-advance option, use this to take photographs continuously and try to use fast film, ideally 400 ISO. Most digital still cameras can also capture short video clips, though a video camera will produce better results. Keeping the lens close to the window will help eliminate glare and reflections, or you can use a polarising filter. For interior shots using flash you can avoid reflections by not pointing directly at the windows.

ON-BOARD SERVICE The conductor is in charge of the train's crew and responsible for collecting tickets, identifying stops and ensuring the safety of the train. The chief of on-board services supervises the attendants on overnight long-distance trains.

Each coach attendant looks after a particular car and is a good person to make your friend. He or she will help with boarding, detraining, arranging seats, answering questions, bringing pillows and generally making your journey more agreeable. You are assigned a seat when you board and should not change it without consulting the attendant.

The sleeping-car attendant will help with your luggage, make up rooms for day or night use and bring your orders from the lounge car. In the morning he/she will provide complimentary tea, coffee or fruit juice and deliver a copy of the latest local newspaper to your room.

Service crew members such as car attendants, waiters and chefs ride the train all the way (except on the *Sunset Limited*) and have their own sleeping accommodation. Train personnel, such as conductors and engine crew, change every six or eight hours on long-distance routes.

CROSSING BORDERS For US and Canadian citizens, a passport is strongly recommended and may be required for all crossings of the US–Canadian border. Citizens of other countries must have a passport. Citizens of many countries must also have a visa, a US Employment Authorisation Card (a temporary work permit), or a Canadian Form IMM 1000 (for naturalised Canadian citizens or permanent residents). Passengers under 18 years old who are not accompanied by an adult must bring a letter from a parent or guardian giving them permission to enter Canada. Except for citizens of the US and Canada, a valid visa is required for return to the United States after visiting Mexico, even after a one-day trip (see also *Chapter 3, Red tape*, page 33).

If in doubt check with your US embassy or contact the Immigration and Naturalisation Service in Washington, DC (see *Chapter 3*, page 34 and *Appendix 2*, page 335). Passengers without proper documentation are prohibited from entering the US or Canada and will be detrained before reaching the US–Canadian border.

CHARTER SERVICES An entire train, or an exclusive Amtrak coach attached to a regular scheduled service, can be hired for group travel. Handsomely furnished, privately owned cars are also available, offering the chance to experience a different type of train travel. The *Overland Trail* uses a 1949 lounge car restored to its former glory, making monthly trips between Los Angeles and San Diego. The 39-seat passenger car, complete with barber shop and shower, was built in 1949 by the Pullman-Standard Car Manufacturing Company for the Southern Pacific Railroad. It was specifically ordered for the *San Francisco Overland*, a train jointly operated by the Southern Pacific, Union Pacific and the Chicago & North Western railroads between Chicago and Oakland. The 2981 car travelled millions of miles during its railroad career until in 1966 the beautiful lounge was stripped and converted into a dance floor. Purchased by Amtrak in 1971, it finished its 'revenue' railroad career assigned to Amtrak's Reno *Fun Train*, serving as a bar/dance car running between Oakland in California and Reno, Nevada. For more information contact Overland Trail (*2054 S Halladay St, Santa Ana, CA 92707;* ❧ *1 800 539 7245 or* ❧ *1 714 546 6923;* e *overlandtrail@cs.com; www.overlandtrail.com*).

For other private railcars available for charter, contact the American Association of Private Railroad Car Owners Inc (*630 Constitution Av NE, Washington, DC 20002;* ❧ *1 202 547 5696*).

COMPLAINTS AND SUGGESTIONS If you have any comments, compliments or suggestions regarding Amtrak services you can write to the Amtrak Customer Satisfaction Center (*Washington Union Station, 60 Massachusetts Av NE, Washington, DC 20002-4285*) enclosing your ticket receipt. Alternatively, contact the website (*www.amtrak.com*).

In July 2000, on the same day it unveiled its new logo, Amtrak introduced a guarantee of commitment to passenger satisfaction by promising to compensate for unsatisfactory experiences. If you did not receive a safe, comfortable and enjoyable trip you would be entitled to a certificate good for future Amtrak travel at equal cost. To encourage employees to 'take personal initiative and do what is necessary to solve guest problems' they were offered a bonus equal to the average Amtrak ticket price (about $50) for every month that 99.9% of customers are satisfied.

NON-AMTRAK SERVICES

Many cities have their own **suburban and commuter services**, either operating independently or in association with Amtrak, and these sometimes provide a more frequent or cheaper alternative for shorter journeys. The best metropolitan services operate out of Chicago, Houston, Denver and Seattle. Details can be obtained at the local Amtrak station or information bureau. City-operated services often use locally the same routes served by Amtrak's longer-distance trains, but the stops and timings may be different.

The **Alaska Railroad** (*Alaska Passenger Service, 411 W 1st Av, Anchorage, AK 99501;* ❧ *1 907 265 2494 or* ❧ *800 544 0552; www.alaskarailroad.com*) operates to Denali, Seward and Fairbanks, using three large-windowed Vistadome cars, and is one of the few railroads in the USA to carry both freight and passengers. Trains travel through 350 miles of national park land with pristine mountain scenery and wildlife that includes moose, caribou, grizzly bear and beaver. You pass close to Bartlett Glacier (named in 1907 after Frank Bartlett, the Alaska Central Railroad's civil engineer at the time) and cross the continental divide at its lowest rail pass point (2,363ft) in the Rocky Mountains. You also cross the Mears Memorial Bridge, a 700ft steel structure which is one of the world's longest single-span bridges and which marked the completion of the Alaska Railroad in 1923.

Services operate daily from May to September, otherwise only at weekends. A Gold Star service is offered daily between Anchorage and Fairbanks. Two custom-made coaches currently operate – one southbound and the other on the northbound *Denali Star*. These unique rail cars feature a viewing platform on the second level. A Whittier trip follows the shore of Turnagain Arm, where you may be lucky enough to see beluga whales.

3

Practical Information

WHEN TO VISIT

Most people choose summer, when days are warmer and longer and most of the attractions will be open, but this can create problems. Hotels are more expensive, restaurants more crowded and train reservations harder to come by. Large numbers of people, many as foreign as yourself, crowd around the very things you have come to see, and sometimes it can be too hot for comfort. Usually the weather is fine, though, and it can be exciting to travel when half the country seems on the move.

Train reservations, flights and accommodation are more readily available in winter, often at reduced prices. You see fewer tourists and more of the real America, with only an hour's wait for the Washington Monument elevator. The sun still often shines, at least in the south, and the skiing season is open. Landscapes, especially the Rocky Mountains, can look even more spectacular when sprinkled with snow.

For many people, spring and autumn (known as 'fall' to Americans) are probably the best times to visit. During spring, flowers bloom in the mountains and the countryside is at its greenest. New England's forests always put on a dazzling show for autumn 'peepers'.

CLIMATE The United States is a huge country with a diverse geography so the climate varies accordingly. Temperatures in some places can go well above 100°F (38°C) or as cold as –40°F (–40°C). Some places see dramatic differences between seasons; others scarcely change at all.

The north experiences European-type summers, but other regions, especially the southwest, become considerably hotter. The south and Midwest are often humid. In winter the northwest continues to follow a European pattern, while the northeast and Midwest become much colder. Florida, southern California and the southwest stay mostly warm throughout the year.

Although spring and autumn are good times to visit, these seasons can be quite short. In the Midwest, summer and winter sometimes swap places within a few days. Autumn is the hurricane season along the Gulf of Mexico and tornadoes can occur in central regions during the spring.

RED TAPE

Travellers to the US should have a full passport valid for at least six months after the intended date of return, although the US has an agreement with most countries, including the UK, automatically to extend the validity of a passport for six months past its expiration date. A British passport therefore needs to be valid only for the duration of your stay. Passport information (for the UK) is available on the website www.open.gov.uk.

Children should have their own passport or be included in that of a parent or guardian. Canadians and permanent legal residents of the USA do not require a visa, nor do citizens of the UK, Australia, New Zealand, Argentina, Uruguay, Singapore, Brunei, Japan and most countries in western Europe, provided you intend to stay for no more than 90 days. You must have an unexpired passport that is machine-readable, identified by the presence of two typeface lines printed at the bottom of the biographical page that can be read by machine. These lines electronically provide some of the information contained on the upper part of the biographic page. If you are in doubt as to whether or not your passport is machine-readable, you should check with the passport-issuing authority of your country. Families require individual passports for each traveller in order to travel visa-free, regardless of the fact that they may hold machine-readable passports. Travellers not in possession of machine-readable passports will require either B-1 (business) or B-2 (tourist) visas.

Passports issued on or after 26 October 2005 must include a 'biometric identifier'. If your passport is issued prior to this date, provided it is an individual machine-readable passport, you may continue to use the passport to travel visa-free even though it does not have the biometric identifier. If your passport was issued after 26 October 2006, you must have an e-passport containing an integrated computer chip to travel to the US on the Visa Waiver Program (VWP).

To travel visa-free you also require a return or onward ticket and a completed form I-94W, obtainable from airline and shipping companies *en route*. UK travellers to Canada planning to cross the land border into the USA no longer require a visa.

British passports must state that the holder is a British citizen. If the passport states 'British subject' the holder must apply for a visa, and visa-free travel does not apply if you intend to work, study or stay in the US for more than 90 days. You may then require either a B-1 visa (for business) or a B-2 visa (tourist). Application forms are available from travel agents, airlines, US embassies and consulates. Applications must be made by post or through a travel agent or courier two weeks (preferably a month) before your departure date.

Indefinite visas are no longer provided (the maximum is now ten years) but those in existence remain valid for ten years from the date they were issued. A visa is still valid in an expired passport if you also have a current passport. Make sure that when your expired passport was cancelled it was not clipped by the authority in such a way as to damage the visa and thereby make it invalid. If you are travelling visa-free and your passport is valid for less than 90 days you will only be admitted until the date your passport expires. If you hold a visa of any classification you are not required to hold a return ticket and may enter the US on a one-way ticket.

If in doubt, contact your US embassy for the latest requirements (in the UK call the premium-rate number ❧ 0905 544 4546). Visa information is also available on the website www.travel.state.gov/visa/index.html.

Where appropriate you should obtain in advance an International Student Identification Card, an American Youth Hostel card and an international driver's licence.

IMMIGRATION Before passing through immigration control you are given a form to complete, asking where you will be staying and the date you intend to leave. This is attached to your passport and must be shown on your departure. If you lose the certificate or wish to extend your stay you should contact the nearest Citizenship and Immigration Services (USCIS) office. For more details contact US Citizenship and Immigration Services (*20 Massachusetts Av NW, Washington, DC 20529;* ❧ *1 800 375 5283; http://uscis.gov*).

Immigration officers may ask for some evidence that you can support yourself during your visit, usually reckoned on the basis of a minimum $150 per week. Take plenty of travellers' cheques and perhaps a copy of your latest bank statement or evidence of current employment. Resist any temptation to test the officers' sense of humour.

On arrival in the US, visitors are photographed with a digital camera and inkless prints are taken of your right and left index fingers with a scanner, to be checked against those of suspected terrorists and criminals. Assuming you are not one of these people, your details will be stored separately and you will be free to enter the US. This procedure applies to residents of all countries, including those in the Visa Waiver Program (VWP). People will also be asked to 'check out' when they leave the country, enabling the authorities to know whether someone is still in the US or staying longer than permitted.

Travellers to the United States under the Visa Waiver Program must now provide details online 72 hours prior to travel on an automated electronic travel system known as an Esta. Once obtained, an Esta is valid for a period of two years, or for the validity of the traveller's passport (whichever is shorter). To register, visit the official website at https://esta.cbp.dhs.gov or contact your country's US embassy (*http://london.usembassy.gov* for London). An Esta is free but a charge is made to cover administration costs. Beware of fraudulent unauthorised websites which charge you for information about Estas and for submitting Esta applications to the Department of Homeland Security (DHS) on your behalf.

All persons, including US citizens, entering the United States from the Americas, Canada, Mexico, the Caribbean and Bermuda are now required to have a passport or other accepted document that establishes the bearer's identity and citizenship. For more information, visit www.travel.state.gov or www.dhs.gov.

It's a good idea to keep copies of all your travel documents in your email account so that, if necessary, they can be accessed *en route*. If your passport is lost or stolen, for example, your embassy in the US should be able to issue a temporary one from a scanned copy.

CUSTOMS As well as personal belongings you can bring in 200 cigarettes and 100 cigars. If aged over 21 you can also import one litre of wine, beer or spirits for your own use or as a gift. Food, illegal drugs, firearms and endangered species products such as ivory are forbidden. If carrying prescribed drugs, only take the quantity a person in your condition would normally require, and keep them in their original containers. You are allowed to take in or bring out any amount of currency but if it comes to more than $10,000, including travellers' cheques, you should report it to customs. The penalty for not doing so could be severe.

For more information, contact the customs office of your US embassy or the Director, Passenger Programs, US Customs Service (*1331 Pennsylvania Av NW, Washington, DC 20004-1710;* ↘ *1 202 347 7039; www.customs.ustreas.gov*).

Write to PO Box 7407, Washington, DC 20044 for a copy of *Know Before You Go*.

GETTING THERE AND AWAY

Competition has reduced the cost of flights, particularly over the north Atlantic, but fares vary tremendously according to date and season. Low season generally runs from November to March, excluding Christmas. Midweek flights tend to be cheaper and it usually pays to fly into a gateway airport such as Boston, Los Angeles or New York (John F Kennedy and Newark), though places such as Cincinnati, served by Delta (📞 *1 404 715 2600; www.delta.com*) and Charlotte, served by British Airways (📞 *800 247 9297 or* 📞 *0844 493 0787 (in the UK)*) are worth considering.

The main airlines flying from Europe include American (*www.aa.com*), British Airways (*www.ba.com*), United Airlines (*www.united.com*) and Virgin Atlantic (*www.virgin-atlantic.com*). Air India, El Al and Kuwait Airlines may be cheaper to book through agents such as Trailfinders in the UK (📞 *020 7937 5400*).

Charter flights are not necessarily less expensive but may offer a greater choice of departure airports, especially to Florida. British operators include Monarch (📞 *0871 225 3555*) and Thomson (📞 *0871 231 4787*). For the latest deals check the internet, national press or teletext for flight-only advertisements.

HEALTH

REGULATIONS No inoculations are required for visitors from Europe. Visitors from elsewhere should check with their US embassy.

MEDICAL INSURANCE The USA has no free health service available to overseas visitors. A hospital room alone can cost $300 per night so horror stories about people being financially ruined by illness or accident are not apocryphal. Make sure you take out sufficient insurance cover for your entire stay, including provision to be flown home for treatment if necessary ($5 million is recommended). Airlines and travel agents usually try to sell you their own policies but check the small print and compare prices. If you plan a long stay it may be cheaper to buy annual cover.

TREATMENT Hospital clinics will often provide simple treatments and some have a 24-hour emergency room. Most towns have a late-opening pharmacy. If you need regular medication you should be sure to take sufficient to last for your visit. For prescribed drugs you should obtain a letter from your doctor explaining why you need them. If you wear glasses, carry an extra pair.

SAFETY

WOMEN TRAVELLERS The United States is a relatively safe place and most crime victims are young single men, not female tourists. Nevertheless, women travellers are wise to take special care to avoid sexual harassment, physical assault or theft. Sleeping in train or bus stations is generally not accepted. Getting off a train late at night to look for lodging is not a good idea, so try to arrange your accommodations in advance. If you have to wait for a train alone, especially at night, find a group to stand near to or go to a café until it's time for the train to arrive. Avoid sitting or walking in empty areas, no matter what time of day. Be aware of the people around you and do not stand alone listening to your MP3 player. Budget considerations should not be allowed to prevent you from being safe, so consider upgrading to a better hotel or take a taxi if you need to get out of a bad area of town. Dress appropriately, preferably like a local, and avoid ostentatious jewellery. You may wish to stay clear of bars and other places with a predominantly male clientele. If you feel uncomfortable – leave.

CRIME Most people survive a visit to the United States without being mugged, assaulted or robbed, but sensible precautions should always be taken. Don't keep all your valuables in one place; then if some are stolen you still have an emergency fund. Keep to downtown or well-lit areas at night and avoid going to secluded places alone. Your hotel desk clerk will advise on safety for the part of town in which you are staying.

Try to be inconspicuous. Don't flash money around in public but carry a small amount to surrender if threatened. Carry your camera in a bag, use the hotel safe for valuables and always lock your hotel door. Watch over your belongings and be wary of pickpockets or bag snatchers in crowded places such as train and bus stations. Don't ask strangers to keep an eye on your things. At stations, only trust your bags to a uniformed member of staff. Report any theft to the police and ask for a reference number to show to your insurance company.

When driving, don't stop if flagged down by anyone other than the police, and keep all windows and doors locked. If you get lost, drive to a well-lit area before asking directions. When leaving your car, lock any bags and packages in the boot and park in a busy place. Never hitchhike or pick up hitchhikers.

Many cities have residential areas which are effectively segregated by race so ask advice before venturing where your presence might be too distinctive. All policemen and some security guards carry guns. Do not run away if challenged.

DRUGS The authorities take a dim view of illegal drug use even in California, where possession of small amounts of cannabis may be overlooked. Apart from the dangers inherent in dealing with shifty characters on street corners you are more than likely to be ripped off. If caught with drugs the best you can hope for is to be put on the next flight home, and you will find it less easy to get into America another time. If you do run into trouble you should contact your nearest consulate, which will recommend a lawyer.

SEX The dangers of casual sex are well known. AIDS is a serious problem in the USA, where upwards of 1.2 million people are thought to be HIV positive. In many cities a majority of prostitutes carry the virus and Nevada is the only state where prostitution is legal. Enjoy the bars and nightlife but save your affections for those you can trust.

Some states, particularly in the south and Midwest, have laws restricting certain types of sexual behaviour that may be permitted where you come from. In most places the age of consent is 16, although it may be up to 18. Statutory rape (consensual sex with a minor) is treated legally in the same way as any other rape.

INSURANCE Make sure your policy protects against cancellation or delays, loss of baggage or passport, and claims for negligence. LIS (personal liability insurance) will protect you if you are sued by third parties in the event of an accident. PAI (personal accident insurance) provides a one-off payment in the case of death or serious injury (see *Health*, page 36, for information on medical insurance). PEC (personal effects coverage) will pay for lost or stolen items, including those stolen from a car. If you plan to indulge in adventurous sports such as skiing or white-water rafting you may have to pay an extra premium. For motor insurance, see *Getting around*, page 39.

Take copies of all your insurance policies with you and make a separate note of their numbers and any emergency phone numbers.

WHAT TO TAKE

Pack as lightly as possible, especially the bags you carry on board. You may find it useful to take a pair of binoculars, a good book, a deck of cards, maps (preferably showing rail lines), a light blanket, a pillow or large pillow case, earplugs or an eyeshade if you are a light sleeper, bathing and grooming items, a pocket torch, sunglasses, a cheap digital watch with an alarm, a small first-aid kit, bottled mineral or spring water (which will probably taste better than that provided at the drinking fountain), fresh fruit, nuts and other snacks. Wear comfortable clothes, especially shoes. There are no places on board to get cash, except by cashing a travellers' cheque, so take enough money to last the journey. A neck wallet or money belt will allow you to keep money hidden safely beneath your clothes.

MONEY

The American dollar (or buck) is worth 100 cents. Coins are one cent (penny), five cents (nickel), ten cents (dime), 25 cents (quarter), 50 cents (half dollar) and one dollar. Dollar and half-dollar coins seem almost as scarce as two-dollar bills (now no longer printed). The most common denomination banknotes, all confusingly similar in size and colour, are for one, five, ten, 20 and 50 dollars. You need plenty of coins for telephones, buses, vending machines and tips so carry enough cash on arrival to last for two or three days. US dollars are widely accepted in Canada.

US-dollar travellers' cheques are the safest and most convenient currency, with American Express and Thomas Cook the most widely recognised varieties. You can use them as cash in hotels, restaurants and shops (take your passport for identification). Signs saying 'no checks' generally refer to personal cheques. Lost or stolen cheques can be replaced by contacting the issuing company by phone (✆ 1 800 528 4800 (American Express)). Keep a note of your cheque numbers separately from the cheques themselves. Prepaid travel cards (or 'Money Cards') are becoming a popular electronic alternative to travellers' cheques. They can be pre-loaded with a set amount of money before you travel then used anywhere that Visa is accepted. As long as transactions are in the currency loaded onto the card, there is usually no transaction charge. There is a low-rate charge for cash withdrawals, in addition to ATM provider charges.

Charge and credit cards such as American Express, Visa and MasterCard are accepted throughout the USA. Handy when paying a deposit for hotels, car hire or tickets by phone, they can also be used to obtain cash at banks and bureaux de change. Always make a note of the card number and keep it separately. In case of loss or theft you should notify the police and call the card company's emergency number immediately. It pays to take two credit cards with you because hotels and car-hire companies often 'block' an amount for themselves as a deposit and do not release it for some time after you have paid the bill. A second card helps in emergencies or if your first card balance gets too low. You could also ask your card company for a higher limit before you travel.

Banks generally open at 09.00 on weekdays, closing at 15.00 on Monday–Thursday, or 17.00 on Friday. Not all of them will change foreign currency or travellers' cheques and, even if they do, the commission may be high. In an emergency you can have money transferred from your bank account at home to an associated US bank, or to an office of Thomas Cook. International money orders take about a week to arrive by airmail. If you become desperate, consulates will reluctantly help you to obtain money from home.

PRICES Unless you are rich or feeling extravagant you should reserve the uptown streets for window shopping, looking for bargains where tourists are less in evidence. Books and records are particularly good value and are often found at a discount. DVDs, video tapes and computer games may not be compatible with your equipment at home but music cassettes and CDs should be fine. Clothing is also a good buy and

New York's garment district has many bargain stores. American clothing and shoe sizes are different from British or European sizes, so try things on before you buy.

Car hire, gas (petrol) and cigarettes are often only a third the price of their European equivalents. You can save even more on petrol by using a self-service station and paying with cash. US gallons (3.8 litres) are five-sixths the volume of imperial gallons (4.5 litres).

Local buses and subways provide excellent value, especially with a travel pass. Tourist bureaux should have the details. Taxis, on the other hand, can be expensive, although occasionally there is no safe or reliable alternative.

In most states a sales tax ranging from 3% to 9% is added to retail prices except on some foods and other goods, and these taxes may also apply to hotel rooms, airline tickets and car rental. Municipalities often impose their own taxes, too, so prices shown are usually less than you actually have to pay.

TIPPING You may think that tipping is a class-conscious anachronism inappropriate for a country where everyone has been proclaimed equal. This is not a good line to adopt with the average cab driver. He expects 10% or 15%, as do bartenders and hairdressers, and in restaurants 20% is more usual. Follow the practice of other customers or you may notice an abrupt change in the standard of service. Tipping is not necessary in self-service cafés or fast-food restaurants.

Most hotels don't include a service charge so a tip is expected. Hotel, airport and railway porters receive $1 per bag. Of course, you don't have to tip anyone who is rude or unhelpful. Amtrak service is free but attendants should be rewarded for exceptional assistance (see also page 27).

GETTING AROUND

BY CAR Trains and buses may not take you everywhere you wish to go so you may need to hire a car. You are allowed to drive for up to a year in the USA provided you hold a valid licence in a country (such as the UK) which has ratified the Geneva Road Traffic Convention. An international driving licence is not essential but will be more readily accepted by a traffic cop than the home country version. The speed limit is mostly 25mph (40km/h) in towns and 65mph (110km/h) on highways, freeways, interstates and major roads outside towns. Limits are strictly enforced. Always carry your licence when driving – it is a legal requirement.

Rental companies have a minimum age restriction (usually 21) and sometimes a maximum. Check the limits when booking and take your passport as proof. National firms have offices in most cities and can be reached on the following toll-free numbers or websites – **Hertz** (❧ 800 654 3131; www.hertz.com); **Avis** (❧ 1 800 230 4898; www.avis.com); **Budget** (❧ 1 800 527 0700; www.budget.com); **Dollar** (❧ 1 800 800 3665; www.dollar.com); **Thrifty** (❧ 1 800 847 4389; www.thrifty.com). For cheap transport, companies with names like Rent-A-Wreck (❧ 1 877 877 0700; www.rent-a-wreck.com) hire out battered but roadworthy cars past their prime.

Local companies may be less expensive but national ones allow you to rent a car in one place and leave it in another, though this may be expensive. Prices depend on location, size of vehicle and rental period. Economy cars are smallest, followed by compact and standard (the normal American size). Virtually all have automatic gears. The cheapest rates are obtained if you book well ahead, especially online.

Make sure you obtain third party insurance of at least $0.5 million, and ask for a collision damage waiver (CDW) or loss damage waiver (LDW) that includes protection against vandalism and theft. Avoid 'fuel purchase plans' where you have

3

to prepay for a full tank of petrol or pay for what you have used when you return the car with a part-filled tank. The hire company will charge an exorbitant amount (by US standards) for the refill fuel.

If you plan to drive extensively you may find it more economical to take out car insurance before leaving home. American policies don't always include third party protection and in some states insurance is voluntary – two good reasons for having full medical cover (see page 36). Members of affiliated organisations can obtain free assistance and route maps from the American Automobile Association (*1000 AAA Dr, Heathrow, FL 32746;* ☏ *1 800 222 4357; www.aaa.com*).

Cars for the disabled Some rental companies provide hand-controlled cars (call their toll-free numbers to check). For further information contact the Society for Accessible Travel & Hospitality (SATH) (*347 Fifth Av, Suite 605, New York, NY 10016;* ☏ *1 212 447 7284; www.sath.org*).

🏠 ACCOMMODATION

All big cities have international-style hotels such as Hiltons and Hyatts where you can expect first-class service. Prices vary with the season but a double room is likely to cost upwards of $100 per night. Single rooms cost almost as much as doubles or triples so it pays to travel in company. Hotels may offer American plan (meals included) or European (without meals). Rates are lower if you book for a week or more and some chains offer discounts with prepaid vouchers.

Smaller hotels are more individual and charge $25–75 per night for a single room. The local tourist bureau will help you choose a place in a safe area convenient for sightseeing. Bed and breakfast is becoming easier to find, especially in rural areas. Standards are high and prices start at around $35. Check with the tourist bureau or contact one of the agencies or directories for details. Those covering the whole country include:

BedandBreakfast.com 700 Brazos St, Suite B-700, Austin, TX 78701; ☏ 1 512 322 2710 or ☏ 1 800 462 2632; www.bedandbreakfast.com
Bed & Breakfast Inns ONLINE 909 N Sepulveda Bd, 11th Fl, El Segundo, CA 90245;

☏ 800 215 7365 or ☏ 1 310 280 4363; e info@bbonline.com; www.bbonline.com
BnBFinder 55 Broad St, Suite 3F, New York, NY 10004; ☏ 1 888 469 6663; e info@bnbfinder.com; www.bnbfinder.com

Motels can cost as little as $25 a night but vary greatly in quality and service. Ask to see the room before accepting. The best motels will have a restaurant, a shop and possibly a swimming pool. Major chains include Holiday Inn, Travelodge, Marriott, Ramada and Best Western. Econo Lodge (☏ *1 877 424 6423; www.econolodge.com*)

ACCOMMODATION CODING			
Based on the price of a double room:			
Exclusive	$$$$$	US$200+	£100+
Upmarket	$$$$	US$150–200	£75–100
Mid range	$$$	US$100–150	£50–75
Budget	$$	US$50–100	£25–50
Shoestring	$	<US$50	<£25

and Super 8 (☎ *1 800 800 8000; www.super8.com*) are among the most economical places to stay. Unfortunately, motels tend to be a long way from downtown, making them less convenient for rail travellers.

An alternative, particularly for young people, is the **YMCAs** (2,600 altogether) found in most large cities in the USA. Many have swimming pools, cafés, a library and sports facilities. Single and double rooms are usually available to men and women. For information contact YMCA of the USA (*101 N Wacker Dr, Chicago, IL 60606;* ☎ *800 872 9622;* e *info@ymcaworldservice.org; www.ymca.net*).

America also has more than 300 YWCA centres, for women only. Contact YWCA USA (*2025 M St, NW Suite 550, Washington, DC 20036;* ☎ *1 202 467 0801; www.ywca.org*).

Hundreds of **youth hostels** provide some of the best value and friendliest accommodation, often located in a historic building. Some have family rooms. *The Hostel Handbook* for the USA and Canada, written by Jim Williams, gives details of almost 600 hostels. The listings include all hostels affiliated with Hostelling International and all the independent hostels. You can view online listings and purchase the book from their website. Contact The Hostel Handbook (*730 Saint Nicholas Av, New York, NY 10031;* ☎ *1 212 926 7030;* e *editor@hostelhandbook.com; www.hostelhandbook.com*).

Most hostels close during the day and operate a midnight curfew. Cooking facilities are provided but alcohol and drugs are forbidden. For about $15 a night you get a bed in a dormitory (segregated by sex) but must supply your own sleeping bag. Although no age restrictions apply you are more likely to enjoy your stay if you remain young at least in spirit. International Youth Hostel membership can be taken out before travelling or guest membership purchased on arrival.

For more information contact Hostelling International-USA (*8401 Colesville Rd, Suite 600, Silver Spring, MD 20910;* ☎ *1 301 495 1240;* e *hostels@hiusa.org; www.hiusa.org*).

For Canada contact Hostelling International-Canada (*205 Catherine St, Ottawa, ON K2P 1C3;* ☎ *1 613 237 7884 or* ☎ *1 800 663 5777 (for reservations);* e *info@ hihostels.ca; www.hihostels.ca*).

Camping sites, public and private, can be found in most parts of the country. Unrestricted camping is still possible in wilderness areas (with a permit from the nearest park rangers' office) and some youth hostels permit camping. Reservations are recommended for state sites and those in national parks. For information contact the Director, National Park Service (*1849 C St NW, Washington, DC 20240;* ☎ *1 202 208 3818; www.nps.gov*).

Kampgrounds of America is a private organisation with 75,000 campsites throughout North America. Contact KOA (*PO Box 30558, Billings, MT 59114;* ☎ *1 406 248 7444; www.koakampgrounds.com*).

If staying in one place for a few weeks it might be worth checking the price of **apartments and rooms**. Usually you need to rent for at least a month. Ask around and check in local newspapers under 'furnished rooms'. For college rooms available for let during summer you should enquire at the university housing office or local visitors bureau.

✖ EATING AND DRINKING

FOOD Americans dine out more than most people so finding somewhere to eat is rarely a problem. New York City alone boasts 15,000 places, from unpretentious cafés and hamburger bars to some of the finest restaurants in the world. Fast food staples such as hot dogs, burgers, pizzas, Kentucky Fried Chicken and McDonald's are sure to make you feel at home, although American versions are likely to be superior.

You may be lucky enough to find one of the few remaining 1940s-style diners. An authentic place should have chrome fittings, a jukebox, ornate mirrors, counter seats and booths. Like coffee shops, diners are great for sampling the traditional American breakfast of eggs (cooked your way), crispy bacon, pancakes (with maple syrup), sausage, buttered toast and hash browns (fried grated potato). All washed down with coffee, tea (for the adventurous) or the ubiquitous Pepsi and Coca-Cola. Some places serve breakfast 24 hours a day.

Desserts are a major temptation, from homemade apple pie to chocolate fudge. No country has fancier doughnuts or better Danish pastries, not to mention chocolate-covered, peanut-filled pretzel nugget ice cream. Other ice-cream varieties you may meet include garlic, lobster and many more.

America's diverse population produces a formidable range of cuisines. Some of the world's best Chinese food can be found in the Chinatowns of cities such as San Francisco and Los Angeles. You can sample black-eyed peas and grits in the south, steaks in Texas, and lobster, crabs or clam chowder in New England. Chicago invented the deep-pan pizza and in New Orleans eating is a way of life.

Some restaurants offer all you can eat for a fixed charge or have two for the price of one deals. Lunch is usually better value than dinner, but look for early-bird specials where evening meals are discounted until 17.00–18.00. Mexican food is tasty and cheap and salad bars, delis and supermarkets provide the basis for an inexpensive picnic. Sandwich bars sell any filling or bread you can think of, including the famous bagels with cream cheese.

DRINK The water is safe to drink and Americans prefer it iced. If a glass is not delivered with your meal you only have to ask. Any soft drink is a soda. Pepsi and Coke come in small, medium (meaning large) and large (meaning gigantic) sizes. Sprite and 7-Up may be familiar but root beer is definitely an acquired taste.

Bars range from the seedy to the glamorous and from cheerful to film-noir gloomy. The clientele may consist of businessmen, sports fans, gays, singles, television addicts or any other all-American type. Look for cut-price drinks during happy hour, which sometimes stretches much further than 60 minutes. Arrive looking respectable between 17.00 and 19.00 and you can often fill up on free hors d'oeuvres as you sample a margarita or mint julep.

Drinks served 'on the rocks' have ice added while those 'straight up' do not. If you fail to specify you will usually get the ice. Measures are generous and spirits often 90° proof (45% vol) so don't underestimate your consumption. Draught, canned and bottled beer will most likely be served well chilled, with brands such as Budweiser familiar to many non-Americans. Canadian or Mexican brands can also often be found. Various low-alcohol and alcohol-free 'Lite' beers are widely available. Groups can save money by ordering draught beer in a (usually half-gallon/2-litre) jug or pitcher. American wines, especially those from California, can be excellent.

Some states, including Utah, have laws restricting the sale of alcohol in various ways or in certain areas. The minimum legal age for the purchase of alcohol is 21, so if you look young enough you may be asked for identification. It is an offence in most cities to consume alcohol in a public place.

PUBLIC HOLIDAYS

Banks, post offices, businesses, museums and government agencies are likely to be closed on the following dates:

USA

New Year's Day	1 January
Martin Luther King's Birthday	Third Monday in January
Lincoln's Birthday	First Monday in February
Presidents' Day	Third Monday in February
Memorial Day	Last Monday in May
Independence Day	4 July
Labor Day	First Monday in September
Columbus Day	Second Monday in October
Election Day	4 November
Veterans Day	11 November
Thanksgiving	Fourth Thursday in November (the day after Thanksgiving is also effectively, if not officially, a holiday)
Christmas Day	25 December

Some states celebrate George Washington's Birthday (12 February) instead of Presidents' Day or make 12 October Columbus Day.

CANADA Public holidays in Canada include the following:

New Year's Day	1 January
Good Friday	
Easter Sunday	
Easter Monday	
Victoria Day	Next to last Monday in May
Canada Day	1 July
Labor Day	First Monday in September
Thanksgiving	Second Monday in October
Christmas Day	25 December
Boxing Day	26 December

Travelling on holidays, even when possible, is sure to be crowded. However, if it is unavoidable, remember to book tickets and accommodation well ahead.

SIGHTSEEING

CityPasses (☎ 1 888 330 5008; e info@citypass.com; www.citypass.com) are available for visitors to New York, Boston, Philadelphia, Chicago, Seattle, Hollywood and San Francisco. The San Francisco programme includes unlimited rides aboard cable cars and all other Muni transportation. Each booklet contains actual tickets, not vouchers, to six of the most popular attractions and cultural institutions (except Hollywood, which includes eight), together with information about the best times to visit. Tickets are valid for nine days once the booklet has been presented to the first attraction.

Passes can be purchased at any CityPass attraction as well as many US travel agencies, visitor centres and at the website.

STUDENT CARD

Students can claim discounts ranging from air fares to accommodation to sightseeing. An International Student Identity Card (ISIC) gives generous deductions for VIA Rail train travel in Canada and for hotel chains such as Travelodge and Howard Johnson throughout North America. Discounts are available on airlines and for airport shuttle services in New York, Boston, San Francisco and Washington, DC, as well as at Busch Gardens, Sea World, Elvis Presley's Graceland, and the Rock and Roll Hall of Fame and Museum in Cleveland. There is a 24-hour emergency assistance service which card holders can call toll-free from anywhere in the world.

Cards can be bought at www.istc.org and STA Travel (see *Appendix 1*, page 331) or on the ISTC website. To be eligible you must be a full-time student. Ask for a directory when buying your card or look for current discounts on the International Student Travel Confederation website www.istc.org.

TIME ZONES

Mainland USA has four time zones. Seattle (Pacific Standard Time) is an hour behind Denver (Mountain Standard Time), two hours behind Chicago (Central Standard Time) and three hours behind New York (Eastern Standard Time). Amtrak schedules take account of this and show local times for arrival and departure.

Canada and most of the USA, apart from Arizona and some of Indiana, observe Summer Time (Daylight Saving Time). Clocks are set ahead an hour at 02.00 on the last Sunday in April. Standard Time returns when clocks go back an hour on the last Sunday in October.

MEDIA AND COMMUNICATIONS

TELEPHONES The US telephone system is famous for its efficiency and economy. Public phones are found in train and bus stations as well as in stores, hotels, restaurants and bars. You don't have to be a customer to use one. Read the instructions before making your call and have lots of change handy, or pay with a credit card by calling ❧ 1 800 CALL ATT. Local calls usually cost 25 cents. Press '1' before the area code when calling from out of town, and for operator assistance press '0'.

If you need to find a local number and have no directory, call ❧ 1 555 1212. For long-distance information call ❧ 1 (area code) 555 1212. Directory enquiries are free from pay phones. The international dialling code for the USA and Canada is 1. No international code is required for calls from the US to Canada and vice versa. Simply use the area code in the usual way.

Calls prefixed 800 or 1 800 are toll-free and any toll-free number can be obtained by calling ❧ 1 800 555 1212. Toll-free numbers can be dialled from outside the US but in that case they are charged at the same rate as any other international call. Use only the 800 part of the prefix, not the whole 1 800.

Calling home is cheaper from a public telephone than from a hotel, which may add a surcharge. It is easiest to call collect (reverse charges) and the international operator can be contacted on ❧ 1 800 874 4000. The international prefix for calls from the USA is 011, which must be followed by the relevant country code (eg: 44 for the UK). Use a private telephone and dial direct between 23.00 and 08.00 for the lowest call rates.

In most places the emergency number for police, fire or ambulance is ✆911. No coin is required. If in difficulty call the operator on 0 or 01.

INTERNET Email can be sent or received immediately by those with access to the internet and there is no need to lug around a notebook computer or modem. Instead, look for cybercafés, web terminals, libraries or arrange to meet friends with internet connections along the way. You may also gain brief access to the web in computer/internet company showrooms (ask the salesperson nicely) or at universities and colleges. If this is not possible they may be able to recommend somewhere suitable.

With an email account through an internet service provider, or if you sign up for a free POP mail account, you can access your mailbox while travelling. You will need to know your email server name as well as your username and password. Write these down and test the system before leaving home. Your server name will most likely be the information after the '@' mark in your email address and your username is usually the information before the mark.

If you want to keep the messages in your mailbox to read again when you get home, leave them on the server. Otherwise, make sure you select the 'Delete' option. Free email providers include Gmail (*www.google.com*), Hotmail (*www.hotmail.com*) and Mail2Web (*www.mail2web.com*). Do not leave your email account unused for more than two or three months or it may be closed.

POSTAL SERVICE The US mail service is less wonderful than America's telephones, so when sending postcards home you should allow at least a week for delivery. Either put them in the appropriate box or hand them over the counter at a post office, where you will find information on mailing rates. Post offices open 09.00–17.00 on weekdays and 09.00–12.00 on Saturdays. Large cities often have one branch that opens 24 hours a day. You can also buy stamps (at 25% extra cost) from shops or vending machines.

Street-corner mailboxes are dark blue and may be mistaken by the unwary for litter bins. Allow between two and four days for letters to be delivered within the US, or a day more without the Zip (area) code. The correct code can be obtained from the telephone directory, at a post office, or by calling ✆ 1 800 ASK USPS (✆ *1 800 275 8777*). This toll-free number also has details of mailing costs, post office hours and other information.

Packets or parcels weighing 16oz (0.5kg) or more must be presented to a postal clerk or mailing agent. This is an anti-terrorist policy designed to eliminate the risk of terrorism on aircraft.

Mail can be delivered c/o General Delivery at any main US post office, which will keep it for up to a month. To collect your letters you will need a passport or other identification.

NEWSPAPERS America has more daily newspapers than any other country in the world. There is no national press apart from the *Wall Street Journal* and *USA Today*, but the *Los Angeles Times* and *New York Times* are widely distributed outside their own cities. Local papers are inexpensive (some only 25 cents), heavy (especially at weekends) and great value for the funny pages alone. You can buy them from station shops and street-corner vending machines. A local paper gives you insight into a town's character and provides up-to-date information about clubs, hotels, shops and theatres. Look for restaurant and cinema advertisements offering special deals.

Foreign newspapers are hard to find even in big cities, although public libraries should be able to track down a week-old copy of something reassuring.

WORKING

Working illegally can result in stiff penalties, including being deported and banned from re-entering the USA for up to five years. To work legally you must obtain a special visa (J-1 or H-2) prior to departure. Forms are available from US employer sponsors. For more information contact the Federal Consumer Center (*Lista, Pueblo, CO 81009;* ✆ *1 888 878 3256; www.pueblo.gsa.gov*).

If you get on well with children and are aged 18 or over you can apply to work at one of America's 12,000 summer camps. Most are in the northeast but some can be found as far west as California and Oregon. Work starts in June and lasts for about nine weeks. You can also be employed as a family companion – providing child care and doing light household duties. You receive a return flight, the necessary work permit, pocket money, board and lodging, plus two months' free time for independent travel. Contact **Camp America** (*37A Queens Gate, London SW7 5HR;* ✆ *020 7581 7373;* e *enquiries@campamerica.co.uk; www.campamerica.co.uk*).

BUNAC (the British Universities North America Club) (*16 Bowling Green Lane, London EC1R 0QH;* ✆ *020 7251 3472;* e *enquiries@bunac.org.uk; www.bunac. org/uk. In the USA: PO Box 430, Southbury, CT 06488;* ✆ *1 203 264 0901;* e *info@ bunacusa.org; www.bunac.org/usa*) has summer camp and other work programmes in the US and Canada. Jobs last for up to 12 months in Canada (US programmes run during the summer, typically from June to September) and are for students only. Early application is strongly advised. Support is provided from a New York office and there are good travel deals, loan plans and free job directories. **Real Gap Experience** (*1 Meadow Rd, 1st Fl, Tunbridge Wells TN1 2YG;* ✆ *01892 516 164;* e *info@realgap.co.uk; www.realgap.co.uk*) has several programmes for visitors hoping to work in North America. The H-2B Seasonal Work Visa programme offers this visa to any UK resident aged 18–38 who is looking for the opportunity to work in the States. The visa is available for the summer and winter seasons yearly and offers jobs ranging from ski instructors to hotel and restaurant positions. For full jobs listings visit www.realgap.co.uk/paid-work-abroad. The J-1 Career Training Visa is available to UK residents with a degree and one year of experience in their degree field, or those without a degree but five years of experience in the same field. They are available in Accounting, Advertising, Architecture, Business Administration, Computer Science, Engineering, Finance, Hospitality and Tourism, Information Media and Communications, Management, Marketing and Sales, Public Law and Public Relations. The Student Summer J-1 Visa is specifically designed for university students on their summer break. Work for up to four months and travel for a month afterwards. This visa allows students to take a job that Real Gap Experience has on offer or to find a job on their own. Real Gap also has volunteer jobs in America, conserving the environment in the national parks of the west, at a wildlife rehab centre in America's south or as a real-life cowboy on a ranch in Wyoming.

Part Two

TRAINS AND ROUTES IN THE UNITED STATES

Each of the following sections gives details of a different long-distance Amtrak train. Scheduled stops are shown in ALL CAPITALS, followed by figures in parentheses giving the time to the next stop. Other towns and places of interest *en route* are shown in lower case and are also followed by figures in parentheses but trains do not actually stop in these places, eg: Kent (20/32). This shows that when you are travelling in the direction described in the text you will pass through Kent 20 minutes after departing from the previous scheduled stopping station, SEATTLE. Going on from Kent it will be 32 minutes to the next stop at TACOMA (see page 52 for this example). Routes can therefore be read in either direction, changing left for right and arrival for departure as appropriate. However, you should note that the timetable means that some places can only be seen by day when you are travelling in one direction.

ACCOMMODATION Accommodation has been selected wherever possible for easy access from the rail station or from the downtown area. Consideration is also given to safety and value for money, hotels being listed in descending order of price per room.

TELEPHONE CODES Where a telephone code is separately listed in the information given for a town or city, unless otherwise noted it applies to all visitor attractions, places to stay, etc, included within that town's entry, whether these are actually situated within the city limits or some distance away.

THE MAPS The strip maps that illustrate the routes are inevitably schematic. They are not to scale and curves have been straightened, although the north indicators will show you roughly which direction you are travelling in. Please refer to the area maps on pages VIII–XIII for a more accurate impression of the routes.

4

The *Coast Starlight*
Seattle–Los Angeles

General route information

One of Amtrak's most popular and scenic routes, this is a particular favourite with young people. Not surprisingly, a party atmosphere often develops, starting in the lounge car and spreading throughout the train. On the 35-hour, 1,377-mile journey you can see snow-covered mountains, deep forest valleys and long stretches of Pacific shoreline. When travelling south, choose a seat on the right of the train for the best views.

Between San Francisco and Los Angeles the *Coast Starlight* follows tracks formerly used by the Southern Pacific Railroad's *Coast Daylight*, and one of that train's last steam engines was brought out of retirement to haul the American Bicentennial Freedom Train.

Rangers from the Klondike Gold Rush National Historical Park provide a narrative commentary between Seattle and Portland on select trains from Thursday through Monday, Memorial Day to Labor Day. Rangers from the Juan Bautista de

ESSENTIAL INFORMATION

FREQUENCY Daily. The **southbound** service leaves Seattle mid morning to arrive in Portland by early afternoon, Emeryville (for San Francisco) early next morning, Santa Barbara by early evening and Los Angeles mid evening. Travelling **north**, trains leave Los Angeles mid morning to reach Santa Barbara just after midday and Emeryville by mid evening. You arrive in Portland the following afternoon and Seattle by mid evening.

DURATION 35 hours

RESERVATIONS All reserved. Book well ahead during summer and at weekends. Passengers for San Francisco have bus transport from Emeryville included.

EQUIPMENT Superliner coaches

SLEEPING Superliner bedrooms

FOOD Complete meals, snacks, sandwiches and drinks. The dining car offers freshly prepared meals served on real china and table linens. At-seat meal service is available to Coach Class passengers.

LOUNGE CAR Movies, games, hospitality hour. The Arcade Room entertains children of all ages with arcade-style video games (parental supervision required). The Pacific Parlour car (for First Class passengers) has a library, large-screen movies, wine tastings, fresh flowers and candlelit evenings. Parlour cars are refurbished Santa Fe Heritage coaches with polished wood panelling.

BAGGAGE Check-in service at most stations

SEATTLE
Olympia
Lacey / Tacoma
Centralia
N
Bradt
Kelso-
Longview
Vancouver
PORTLAND
Salem
Albany
Eugene-
Springfield
Chemult
Klamath
Falls
Dunsmuir
Redding
Chico
Davis
Sacramento
Martinez
Emeryville
OAKLAND
SAN FRANCISCO
San José
Salinas
Paso Robles
San Luis
Obispo
Santa
Barbara Oxnard
Simi Valley Van Nuys
LOS ANGELES

Anza National Historic Trail between Santa Barbara and San Luis Obispo or Oakland also provide a commentary on certain days throughout the year.

As on some other routes, First Class passengers on the *Coast Starlight* may be presented with a gift, such as a glass mug or an umbrella decorated with the train's logo, as well as a 'personal amenities' kit that includes shampoo, soaps and lotions, and can receive complimentary on-board internet access via Amtrak Connect.

Joining the train

SEATTLE Surrounded by mountains, Lake Washington and Puget Sound, the Emerald City was named after Chief Sealth of the Damish and Suquamish tribes. Seattle sees only 56 days of sun a year but has less rainfall than New York or Atlanta, so the city is not quite so wet as outsiders may imagine. Water provides an important leisure resource, however, and countless marinas provide enough space for two boats to every three people.

Seattle was the birthplace of Jimi Hendrix (buried in Greenwood Cemetery in the suburb of Renton), Starbucks coffee, grunge rock and the Microsoft company. Lately one of America's most fashionable cities, famous for its coffee houses, Seattle has been the setting for movies such as *The Fabulous Baker Boys*, *Sleepless in Seattle* and *Singles*, as well as television's *Frasier*. A month-long film festival is held each spring and the Folklife music festival takes place around Memorial Day.

Seattle basics

Telephone code 206

Station *(Ticket office* ⊕ *06.15–20.00. Waiting room* ⊕ *06.00–22.30)* Handsome King St Station at 303 S Jackson, with its distinctive 240ft clock tower modelled after Venice's campanile, was built by the Great Northern Railway in 1905. In 2008, this impressive landmark building was purchased from the Burlington Northern Santa Fe Railway by the City of Seattle as a $26.5 million project to restore the building's historic character & grandeur. Lockers, vending machines, newspapers, handcarts, Red Caps, ATM banking, taxi stand.

Connections Amtrak trains operate daily into Canada, & Thruway buses connect incoming & outgoing *Coast Starlight* trains with Vancouver, BC, in about 4hrs.

Local transport Metro buses (553 3000) are free in the downtown area. Seattle has some of the worst traffic problems in the USA so it pays to use public transport. The fastest monorail in the country (905 2600) operates a startling 2min service between the downtown Westlake shopping mall & the Seattle Center.

Taxis Yellow 622 6500; Farwest 622 1717

Car rental Budget, 19030 28th Av S; 800 527 0700

🚌 **Greyhound** Eighth Av & Stewart; ☎ 628 5526

✈ **Seattle-Tacoma Airport** Located 14 miles south & accessible by Gray Line Downtown Airporter (☎ 626 6088) & Metro bus #174. **Tours** Gray Line (☎ 624 5077) has coach & boat excursions. Guided sea kayak tours with Alki Kayak (☎ 953 0237).

ℹ **Visitors bureau** Seventh & Pike; ☎ 461 5840; e visinfo@visitseattle.org; www. visitseattle.org; ☉ w/days, summer daily

🏠 **Accommodation** Contact Pacific Bed & Breakfast, 2040 Westlake Av N, #307, Seattle, WA 98109; ☎ 439 7677 or Seattle Hill Hse, 1113 E John St, Seattle, WA 98102; ☎ 323 4455.

YMCA, 909 Fourth Av; ☎ 382 5003. Incorporates the Traveller's Aid office. Over 200 rooms for men or women, **$**. YWCA, 1118 Fifth Av; ☎ 461 4888. Women over 18 only, **$**. Green Tortoise Hostel, 105 Pike; ☎ 340 1222; www. greentortoise.net, **$**.

Hotels include the Fairmont Olympic at 411 University; ☎ 621 1700, **$$$$**; Sorrento, 900 Madison; ☎ 622 6400, **$$$$**; Sixth Av Inn, 2000 Sixth Av; ☎ 441 8300, **$$$**; Day's Inn Town Center, 2205 Seventh Av; ☎ 448 3434, **$$**; Inn at Queen Anne, 505 First Av N; ☎ 282 7357, **$$$**; Moore Hotel, 1926 Second Av; ☎ 448 4851, **$$**.

Recommended in Seattle

Seattle Center 305 Harrison; ☎ 684 7200 or ☎ 684 7100; www.seattlecenter.com. This legacy of the 1962 World's Fair, a min or so from downtown by monorail, has over 70 acres (28ha) of parkland & entertainments, dominated by the 605ft (198m) Space Needle (☎ 905 2100; www.spaceneedle.com). Take an elevator to the observation deck for lofty views of the city, Puget Sound & Mount Rainier.

The Waterfront Where gold arrived during the 1897 Klondike rush, ex-Australian streetcars now run along waterfront tracks. Ferries to Canada & Alaska go from Pier 48, & to Bremerton & Bainbridge Island from Pier 52, giving wealthy island commuters inspiring views of snow-capped mountains & an occasional whale.

Ye Olde Curiosity Shop Pier 54, sells souvenirs & has a museum of bizarre relics (☎ 682 5844). Pier 55 has Argosy Cruises (☎ 623 1445) & excursions from Pier 56 go to Tillicum Village on Blake Island (☎ 933 8600).

Seattle Aquarium Pier 59, has coral reef & underwater dome (☎ 386 4300; www. seattleaquarium.org).

Pike Place Market Between downtown & the Waterfront at First & Pike; www.pikeplacemarket. org; ☉ daily; free. This 1907 market is a warren of shops, restaurants, galleries & stalls selling every kind of fish, fruit & vegetable. Great for street entertainment, people-watching & dodging the flying salmon.

Pioneer Square Covering 12 blocks from Second Av to the Waterfront. The square is where

Seattle began in the 1850s with the setting up of a sawmill & where logs were skimmed along Skid Road. During the gold rush this became a dangerous place & in the Depression it was a refuge for down-and-outs (the original 'Skid Row'). Art galleries, restaurants & shops now occupy restored buildings & daily Underground Tours (☎ 682 4646) explore the basements of Old Seattle.

Klondike Gold Rush National Historic Park 117 S Main; ☎ 553 7220; ☉ daily; free. Depicting the excitement & hardship, with old mining photographs & clothes. Chaplin's *The Gold Rush* is shown on w/end afternoons.

Museum of Flight 9404 E Marginal Way S; ☎ 764 5720; www.museumofflight.org; ☉ daily; admission charge. Chronicles the history of flying from the Wright Brothers up to the space age.

Northwest Railway Museum 38625 SE King in Snoqualmie; ☎ 425 888 3030; www. trainmuseum.org; ☉ daily; admission charge. One of the largest displays in the country, with steam locomotives, passenger & freight cars, & specialised railway equipment that built & maintained the right of way. Built in 1890, Snoqualmie Depot has been fully restored & there are train rides through the upper Snoqualmie Valley.

Seattle Art Museum Downtown 1300 First Av; ☎ 344 5275; www.seattleartmuseum.org; ☉ daily; admission charge. The largest art museum in the region, with Native American paintings, African masks, old masters & contemporary works.

Pacific Science Center 200 Second Av N; ↘
443 2001; www.pacsci.org; ⊕ daily; admission

charge. Explore the tropical butterfly house & see robotic dinosaurs. IMAX films in 3D.

All aboard!

The *Coast Starlight* leaves King Street Station with Smith Tower, once one of the city's tallest buildings, on your right. You pass the Kingdome sports stadium, also on the right, and for the next few miles travel through industrial scenes where factories are owned by the likes of Westinghouse, Nabisco and Ford.

Boeing Field (7/45) Seattle's largest manufacturing company is on your right. The airport is used for testing and sometimes by private planes. Boeing's original factory, a red-brick building seen across the runway, is now the Museum of Flight.

The *Coast Starlight* continues through residential areas, with the Green River on your right.

Kent (20/32) Look left for an interesting old train station and Longacres racetrack.

After the train crosses the Green River, half an hour from Seattle, the urban landscape begins to give way to small farms and dairies. The train crosses the White River and makes a long right turn towards the east, crossing the Puyallup River.

Puyallup (40/12) This town, like the river, was named after a Native American tribe. A pioneer named Ezra Meeker who had crossed the plains with an ox team in 1882 to set up home here returned to New York in 1906, marking the Oregon Trail with many monuments.

You go through downtown and attractive western suburbs then cross Clark's Creek, travelling southwest through tall pine forest. Look for the bright, dandelion-like flowers of gosmore, or 'cat's ear'.

TACOMA (52/42) Note the eccentric domed Transit Center Building. Tacoma was chosen as the terminus of the North Pacific Railroad in 1873 and was transformed from rustic frontier outpost into a bustling commercial city with the finest hotel on the North Pacific shore. It became known as 'the city of destiny', where much of the state's lumber reached the sawmills. The old Milwaukee, St Paul & Pacific Railroad freighthouse, located a few blocks south of Amtrak's station, has found a new life as Tacoma's public market. Timber is still an important industry here, along with shipbuilding. The **visitors bureau** is at 1516 Pacific (↘ *800 272 2662; www.traveltacoma.com*).

Tacoma overlooks Commencement Bay in the east and the Tacoma Narrows highway bridge to the west. **Point Defiance Park, Zoo and Aquarium** is famous for its sharks and giant Pacific octopuses (↘ *253 591 5337; www.pdza. org; admission charge*). The **State History Museum** can be found at 1911 Pacific Avenue (↘ *888 238 4373; www.wshs.org; admission charge*).

The *Coast Starlight* leaves Tacoma alongside the city waterway. Old City Hall, with its elaborate clock tower, can be seen perched beside the North Pacific Railroad building on cliffs to your left.

A few minutes later the train goes through a tunnel and turns due south, emerging on the shoreline of Puget Sound with the Olympic Mountains beyond. This idyllic coast has dozens of coves and piers, with pleasure boats coming and going. Look also for herons and bald eagles gliding above the rivers, which have names such as Nisqually, Nooksack and Skookumchuck.

Stellacoom (26/16) A ferry terminal serves Anderson and McNeal islands, visible across Henderson Bay to your right. Brilliant yellow broom grows beside the track.

OLYMPIA–LACEY (42/20) Olympia is Washington's state capital, with a Capitol dome that claims to be the largest domed masonry building in the country. Amtrak's station is at 6600 Yelm Highway SE. The 900,000-acre (360,000ha) Olympic National Park is accessible along US Highway 101.

Soon after pulling out of Olympia, the *Coast Starlight* crosses the Skookumchuck River.

CENTRALIA (20/45) This food-processing and logging town was founded in 1875 by a former slave from Virginia called George Washington. Early settlers built the blockhouse in Fort Borst Park as a defence against marauding Indians. Amtrak's picturesque brick station (*ticket office* ☺ *09.00–16.30*) is at 210 Railroad Avenue. As the train departs you glimpse the Mount St Helens volcano across fields to your left. A massive eruption in 1980 killed 57 people, together with thousands of birds, animals and fish. Traces of grey ash can still be seen, although grass and a few trees now grow on 'pumice plain'.

The train continues south through Chehalis then crosses the Newaukum River.

Winlock (18/27) 'The egg capital of the world', where the planet's largest egg nestles in a monument to your right. Winlock's mighty chicken industry is celebrated with an annual festival.

Castle Rock (35/10) You cross the Toutle River, with the Cowlitz River on your right. Mud was pushed this far from the St Helens explosion 40 miles away. The volcano is now a 110,000-acre (45,000ha) park where you can take a flight over the summit and buy souvenirs sculpted from the debris.

KELSO–LONGVIEW (45/40) 'The smelt capital of the world', where vast numbers of these small fish swim up the Cowlitz River each year to spawn, Kelso also has a major lumber industry and deep-water port. The **Cowlitz County Historical Museum** (*405 Allen;* ☏ *360 577 3119; www.co.cowlitz.wa.us/museum*) features a settler's log cabin built in 1884, Native American artefacts and other exhibits of local historical interest.

On a clear day, three of America's most impressive mountains can be seen as you leave. Mount St Helens (8,400ft/2,560m) and Mount Adams (12,307ft/3,750m) are to your left, and Mount Rainier (14,410ft/4,390m) to your right. Between May and October, Gray Line tour buses operate from Seattle to Rainier National Park.

Columbia River (8/32) To your right, the train joins the river which used to represent the border between the United States and Canada. The *Coast Starlight* route follows the Columbia River as far as Vancouver in Washington State, with Oregon on the opposite shore. Look for gigantic rafts of logs being transported downstream.

Trojan Power Plant (12/28) This nuclear energy plant stands on the Oregon side of the river.

Kalama (15/25) Look right for a giant totem pole. The landscape begins to turn into marsh as you approach Lake Vancouver, meeting its shoreline on the right.

VANCOUVER (40/25) Not to be confused with Vancouver, Canada. The Hudson's Bay Company built Fort Vancouver as a trading post in 1824, making this the oldest non-Indian settlement in the northwest USA. Amtrak's station (*ticket office* ☺ *08.30–20.30. Waiting room* ☺ *08.15–21.00; information* ☏ *360 694 7307*) is at 1301 West 11th. The *Coast Starlight* leaves Vancouver and soon afterwards crosses the Columbia into Oregon by way of Hayden Island. You then cross the Willamette River near Portland before crawling among freight yards, industrial plants and ocean-going ships being loaded. Look for the *River Queen*, an old steamboat now converted into a restaurant.

PORTLAND (25/65) Spread along the Columbia River between the Cascade Mountains and the Pacific, Oregon's only metropolis is a seaport famous for its many gardens, fountains and parks, and for having one of the country's largest bookstores, which covers an entire city block. The eco-friendly 'City of the Roses' considers itself a rival to Seattle for the accolade of 'America's most liveable city'.

Portland basics

☏ **Telephone code** 503

⚊ **Station** (*Ticket office & waiting room* ☺ *07.15–21.15; information* ☏ *273 4864*) Union Station is at 800 NW Sixth Av. Built in 1896 on what had been a lake in an old part of town, the large echoing building boasts chandeliers, ceiling fans, evocative pictures & an antique weighing machine. Metropolitan lounge, vending machines, newspapers, handcarts, Red Caps, café/shop, restaurant, left-luggage room, taxi stand.

Connections Thruway buses go to Pendleton & Boise, Idaho.

🚐 **Local transport** Portland is well served by TriMet buses (☏ *238 7433*) & the MAX light railway. Both are free downtown.

🚕 **Taxis** Green Cab ☏ *234 1414*; Broadway; ☏ *227 1234*

🚕 **Car rental** Enterprise, 452 SW Pine; ☏ *275 5359*

🚐 **Greyhound** 550 NW Sixth Av, close to Union Station; ☏ *243 2357*

✈ **Portland International Airport** Located 8 miles (13km) northeast by Raz Tranz bus (☏ *684 3322*), TriMet bus #12, or MAX Red Line service train every 15mins.

Tours Gray Line ☏ *285 9845*; Rose-Smith ☏ *201 1921*. Columbia & Willamette River cruises

from Cascade (☏ *223 3928*). Whale-watching with Marine Discovery (☏ *800 903 2628; www. marinediscovery.com*).

ℹ **Visitors bureau** 701 SW Sixth Av; ☏ *275 8335*; e info@travelportland.com; www. travelportland.com; ☺ winter Mon–Sat, summer daily.

🏠 **Accommodation** Contact Portland International Guesthouse, 2185 NW Flanders St; ☏ *224 0500* or ☏ *877 228 0500*; e info@ pdxguesthouse.com; www.pdxguesthouse.com, or White House B&B, 1914 NE 22nd Av; ☏ *800 272 7131* or ☏ *287 7131*; e web@portlandswhitehouse.com; www.portlandswhitehouse.com.

YMCA, 9500 SW Barbur Bd; ☏ *223 9622*; www. ymca-portland.org. YWCA, 1111 SW Tenth; ☏ *294 7400*. Women only, **$**. AYH Youth Hostel, 3031 SE Hawthorne Bd; ☏ *236 3380*, **$**.

For hotel reservations in Portland, ☏ *1 877 678 5263*. Hotels include the Benson at 309 SW Broadway; ☏ *228 2000*, **$$$$$**; Clyde, 1022 SW Stark; ☏ *224 8000*, **$$$**; Lucia, 400 SW Broadway; ☏ *225 1717*, **$$$$**; Hotel deLuxe, 729 SW 15th Av; ☏ *219 2094*, **$$$$**; Days Inn City Center, 1414 W Sixth Av; ☏ *221 1611*, **$$$$**; Mark Spencer, 409 SW 11th Av; ☏ *224 3293*; www.markspencer.com, **$$**.

Recommended in Portland

Rose Festival ☏ *227 2681*; e info@rosefestival. org; www.rosefestival.org. A week of mostly

free parades, concerts, sporting events & bands honours the city's favourite flower in early Jun.

Washington Park 4001 Canyon Rd; ☎823 3636. Douglas firs, a Japanese garden & statues can be found here, along with 400 varieties of rose.
Oregon Zoo 4001 SW Canyon Rd; ☎226 1561; oregonzoo.org; ⊕ daily; admission charge. Only 2 miles from downtown by TriMet bus #63 or the Westside MAX. Beavers, otters & nocturnal cats live in natural settings. Steam & diesel trains operate around the zoo & through the forested hills to Washington Park.
Portland Art Museum 1219 SW Park Av; ☎226 2811; www.portlandartmuseum.org; ⊕ daily; admission charge. One of the 25 largest museums in the country, featuring works by Renoir & Monet as well as Native American art & English silver.
Pioneer Courthouse Fifth Av & Morrison; ☎326 5830; ⊕ daily; free. The oldest public building in the northwest dates from the 1860s.

You can climb a stairway up to the cupola & get a view of downtown & Pioneer Courthouse Sq.
Classical Chinese Garden 127 NW Third Av & Everett; ☎228 8131; www. portlandchinesegarden.org. Located in the middle of Portland, this is the largest urban Suzhou-style garden outside China. Rugged rocks & serpentine walkways are reflected in the lake.
Oregon History Center 1200 SW Park Av; ☎222 1741; www.ohs.org; ⊕ Tue–Sun; admission charge. State history comes to life in this spectacular building with interactive exhibits.
Oregon Museum of Science & Industry 1945 SE Water Av; ☎797 4000 or ☎1 800 992 8499; www.omsi.edu; ⊕ daily; admission charge. Hands-on fun, with live demonstrations, a planetarium & laser shows. Visit the USS *Blueback* submarine, see the Omnimax cinema & check out the latest touring exhibitions.

All aboard!

Departing Portland, the *Coast Starlight* quits the Burlington Northern Santa Fe (BNSF) route followed so far and switches to the Union Pacific (UP). You cross the Willamette River on a steel bridge then pass through Milwaukie, Gladstone and Chackamas suburbs. As the train heads into the flat Willamette Valley, the Cascades and Mount Hood (11,235ft/3,425m) can be seen to your left. The Coast Range is on the right.

Oregon City (30/35) The original capital of Oregon Territory, this was the end of the Oregon Trail. More than 200,000 people travelled the 2,000-mile trail when 'Oregon fever' swept the country over 150 years ago. The first Protestant church and first Masonic lodge west of the Rockies were built here. An interpretive center at 1726 Washington (☎ 503 657 9336) has films, exhibits and a multi-media show which explain the famous pioneer route.

Waterfalls appear on your right, with lumber factories and giant logs next to the river. In springtime, look for fields of daffodils and tulips near the city of Canby.

Aurora (45/20) Reached after the train crosses the Pudding River, Aurora was founded by Germans in the 19th century as America's first commune.

Woodburn (50/15) A nostalgic Southern Pacific steam engine stands on the left. As the train continues, you travel among fields of strawberries, raspberries, blackberries and loganberries.

SALEM (65/28) Oregon's capital is one of the oldest cities in the state, with many historic buidlings. Willamette University, the oldest in the west, can be seen to your right as the train arrives. Also look right for the white marble Capitol topped by a gold-plated statue of a man with an axe (the *Spirit of Oregon*). The beautiful 1919 station building has been fully restored, with hanging light globes in the lobby recast according to the original designs.

The *Coast Starlight* pulls out of Salem past the city airport to your left. Between the towns of Turner and Marion, 15 minutes later, look for a llama farm on your right. Formerly kept for their wool, the llamas are now used as pack animals on expeditions into the mountains.

Jefferson (20/8) You cross the Santiam River.

ALBANY (28/40) Founded in 1845, Albany was connected by railroad in 1870 after citizens paid the O & C company $50,000 to be included in the line. This agriculture and lumber town now supplies almost all the grass seed sold in America. It also hosts the world championship timber carnival, with everything from tree climbing to axe throwing. Amtrak's station is at 110 West Tenth.

The **visitors bureau** is at 250 Broadaldbin SW (☎ *1 800 526 2256;* e *info@ albanyvisitors.com; www.albanyvisitors.com*).

The *Coast Starlight* leaves Albany and crosses the Calapooia River, entering a region known as 'the plains of Lebanon'.

Tangent (15/25) The town was named after the long, straight stretch of track here. The buttes seen on the left, created by prehistoric volcanoes, contain fossils and mammoth bones. To your left are some of the fields producing grass seed. Between here and Eugene look out for farms growing mint, another local speciality.

Harrisburg (25/15) The snow-covered Three Sisters Mountains appear in the left distance before the train crosses the Willamette River. Southern Pacific rail yards and Lane County jail are seen to your right as you near Eugene and travel through Junction City.

EUGENE–SPRINGFIELD (40/165) Home to the Nike Corporation, 'The lumber capital of the USA' is the westernmost city served by Amtrak. Look for huge stacks of timber being sprayed with water to reduce the fire risk. Named after a settler called Eugene Franklin Skinner, who built the first cabin here in 1846, Eugene is now the second-largest city in Oregon and the 'running capital of the universe' (home town of Mary Decker Slaney). This region is famous for its mild climate and for fishing and boating on the McKenzie River. The ticket office of Amtrak's renovated green and white station at 433 Willamette opens from 04.30 to 21.00 and 23.00 to 00.45.

The 1908 station and 1955 mail shed addition have become a safe and convenient multi-modal transportation facility, accommodating Amtrak passengers, motorists, bus users, cyclists and pedestrians, and local Amtrak staff. The $4.5 million project (including approximately $3.5 million in federal funds) was designed so that the station would meet the aesthetic and functional needs of a modern transit facility while preserving the building's historic features.

The *Coast Starlight* leaves past the University of Oregon campus on the right before crossing the tree-lined Willamette River into Springfield, the sister city to Eugene.

Tracks curve right as the train climbs slowly for 70 miles into the Cascade Mountains, winding through 22 tunnels and several snow sheds towards the source of the Willamette. Snow sheds are wooden or concrete structures built over the track to protect it from avalanches and accumulating snow. Spectacular waterfalls, wild flowers, rhododendrons and dense vegetation feature in the alpine scenery of Willamette National Forest on both sides.

Lookout Point Reservoir (30/135) The dam and reservoir are on your left, with Diamond Peak (8,750ft/2,670m) to the south. The Three Sisters Mountains appear in the left distance.

Westfir (60/105) Spanning the Willamette River to your right is one of the many covered bridges in this region.

Oakridge (65/100) The train starts climbing 'the hill' to Cascade Summit, an ascent of 3,600ft in 44 miles (1,100m in 70km). You cross Salmon Creek then follow Salt Creek on the right.

Salt Creek Canyon (80/60) Views of the tracks above and below dramatically demonstrate the steepness of your climb. There is another 2,700ft (800m) to go from the health resort of McCredie Springs to the summit along 30 more miles (48km) of track. The tops of tall trees appear beside the train windows and dense, dark evergreens cover the mountains to your right. In autumn, the occasional maple makes a spectacular splash of crimson or yellow.

Willamette Pass (120/45) Source of the Willamette River, with the slopes of Willamette Path ski resort visible ahead.

Cascade Summit (140/25) The line is 4,800ft (1,460m) above sea level here. Maiden Peak (7,811ft/2,380m) overlooks the deep-blue water of Odell Lake to your left. The purple and green Cascade Mountains are all around, giving breathtaking views as the train gently descends among Douglas firs, waterfalls and wild flowers towards the Oregon–California border. Look for quail creeping in the grass banks between tunnels.

CHEMULT (165/70) Diamond Peak (8,750ft/2,670m) can be seen on your right. Buses connect Chemult with Bend, a resort 60 miles (96km) to the northeast.

After Chemult you pass Mount Thielsen and Mount Scott (both over 9,000ft/2,750m) to your right. Diamond Lake is also on the right a few minutes later as you enter the Winema National Forest. Logging operations appear on both sides as you continue towards Klamath Marsh. Half an hour from Chemult the train joins the Williamson River on the right, following it intermittently through a canyon for the next 15 miles (24km) after crossing at Kirk.

Chiloquin (55/15) America's largest museum of logging is in nearby Collier State Park. The train continues down Calimus Hill to Modoc Point.

Upper Klamath Lake (60/10) One of the country's largest freshwater lakes, where in summer you may see white pelicans. You follow the eastern shore of the lake for 18 miles, with Mount McLaughlin (9,495ft/2,894m) to your right. Mount McLaughlin has been known by a number of different names over the years, including Snowy Butte and Mount Pitt (after the Pit River).

KLAMATH FALLS (70/160) Sawmills appear on your left near the station. Geothermal springs once used by Klamath Indians for cooking are now harnessed to heat homes, and the Klamath County Museum explains this underground activity along with pioneer history. Amtrak's station is at 1600 Oak.

The *Coast Starlight* departs with the Klamath River to your right then travels via two short tunnels and crosses the state line, 20 miles (32km) south, into

California. You may catch a first glimpse of the Cascades' highest peak, Mount Shasta (14,160ft/4,453m), snow clad and ethereal by moonlight as the train speeds through the small Butte Valley communities of Dorris and Mount Hebron.

Grass Lake (80/80)

This is the highest point on the route and from here the *Coast Starlight* descends around the base of Mount Shasta, cutting through solidified lava flows. Black Butte is seen on the left before you travel down via the alpine town of Mount Shasta City into the Sacramento River Canyon. The train follows this winding canyon for 32 miles (51km) and passes a spectacular waterfall.

DUNSMUIR (160/100)

A base for the Southern Pacific railway, Dunsmuir is also an all-year recreation centre. The train departs and continues its slow descent from the high tableland. The grey granite spires of Castle Crags appear to the right.

REDDING (100/70)

Located at the north end of the Sacramento Valley, close to Lake Shasta and Lassen National Park. Shasta Dam, three times the height of Niagara Falls, backs up the Sacramento, McLoud and Pit rivers. Amtrak's station is at 1620 Yuba.

Look left as the train continues to see the Sierra Nevada, and right for views of the Coast Range.

CHICO (70/110)

Home of one of California State University's campuses, Chico was originally settled by gold miners. Fortunes were later made by those who came to farm, since most things seem able to grow here, including rice, peaches and olives. General John Bidwell established the town and his mansion now forms part of a state park. Nearby is Oroville Dam, the largest earth-filled dam in America.

Marysville (40/70)

Another former gold prospectors' town and centre for agriculture, with Yuba City adjacent to the west. Marysville is an important railroad town, with classification yards and locomotive workshops.

Roseville (90/20)

The train turns southwest here, crossing the American River just before Sacramento.

SACRAMENTO (110/20)

California's capital since 1854, to the scorn of some who live in glitzier cities further south. The 1849 gold rush started nearby at Sutter's Mill (gold was actually first found in 1848) and the Pony Express ended its inaugural run here in 1860. A rail link over the Sierra Nevada soon afterwards brought the first trains.

Many 19th-century houses have been preserved and a reconstructed **Fort Sutter** stands on the east side of town. The 1869 **State Capitol** features ornate plaster and splendid oak staircases. Sacramento is the hub of a food-producing area specialising in almonds, peaches and pears, and the **visitors bureau** is at 1608 I (✆ *800 292 2334; www.discovergold.org*).

Amtrak operates from the historic renovated station at 401 I. Close by is the **California State Railroad Museum**, seen to your left (*125 I;* ✆ *916 445 7387 or* ✆ *916 445 6645 (for recorded information); www.csrmf.org;* ☉ *daily; admission charge*). The Transcontinental and Sacramento Valley railroads began in Old Sacramento and this massive museum on an 11-acre (4.5ha) site displays 21 restored locomotives, railroad cars and 46 exhibits, including a 1929 St Hyacinthe Pullman sleeper. The Central Pacific depot at First and J is a reconstruction of Sacramento's 1876 depot and shows bustling train travel in the late 19th century. Steam trains travel on holidays and at weekends (April–September) on the **Sacramento Southern Railroad** for a six-mile round trip through the Feather River Canyon (☎ *916 445 7387*). More nostalgia is on hand at the hardware store where the Central Pacific and Southern Pacific were planned by the Big Four, the men behind the building of the first transcontinental railway line – Leland Stanford, Charles Crocker, Mark Hopkins and Collis Huntington. Together with single-minded and clear-eyed designer Theodore Judah, these financiers and merchants had the idea for a transcontinental route which would make it easier to trade with the east coast and would encourage more trade with Asia. The store museum recreates the boardroom and has much archive material. The Southern Pacific Railroad eventually came to own a fifth of California's land.

The Capitol's gilded dome can be seen to your left as the train leaves, crossing the Sacramento River with a drawbridge on the left. As you travel through the flat landscape of the Sacramento Valley look for fields which are sometimes flooded to grow rice. The Coastal Range is to your right and the attractive Sierra foothills away to your left as you cross the Yolo Bypass on a long low trestle.

DAVIS (20/40) Part of the University of California is based here and Davis has enlightened policies promoting recycling and energy conservation. Bicycle pathways exist throughout the city to discourage car use. Amtrak's Spanish adobe-style station on the right is a historic landmark that dates from 1913 and carries a Southern Pacific logo.

As the *Coast Starlight* leaves past the university campus look right to see some of the research animals, including llamas and pygmy goats. You also pass fields of sunflowers.

Suisun-Fairfield (25/15) Note the pretty pink and cream station building on your left, a scheduled stop for the *California Zephyr*. The white pillars of Solano County Courthouse are to your right at the end of Union Avenue. Large military transport aircraft can be seen at the Travis Air Force base on your left.

The train races on over flat agricultural land past a ridge on the right, beyond which is the Napa Valley. As you cross Suisun Marsh at up to 79mph (130km/h), look for ducks, herons and cattle. Boeing's experimental wind farm generates electricity on your right.

Mothball Fleet (30/10) To your left, near the shoreline of Suisun Bay, floats a large fleet of transport ships kept neatly lined up in 'mothballs'. Many date from World War II but some saw action in Vietnam and the Gulf War of 1991. Also to your left are docks packed with imported Japanese cars. In the left distance is Mount Diablo (3,849ft/1,170m). The beacon on top of the mountain was extinguished after Pearl Harbor but is lit once a year by war veterans.

You cross the impressive Benicia-Martinez Bridge spanning the Carquinez Strait. Before the double-track steel bridge opened in 1930, trains had to be ferried across the water in sections. Benicia, on your right, was the state capital from 1853 to 1854. Look for oil tankers in the harbour as you near Martinez.

MARTINEZ (40/40) Named after a Spanish governor, Martinez was the birthplace of baseball star Joe DiMaggio and the Martinez, forerunner of the Martini. It was also the home of John Muir, an early environmentalist and father of the modern conservation movement. Amtrak's station at 401 Ferry is the connecting point for services along the San Joaquin Valley. The city's museum occupies an old house to the left of the station building.

Amtrak Thruway shuttle buses make a 20-minute journey from Martinez to **Six Flags Marine World** (*1001 Fairgrounds Dr, Vallejo;* ☏ *707 643 ORCA (6722); www. sixflags.com*). Marine World is home to thousands of animals, including tigers, sharks, dolphins, walruses, killer whales and a herd of elephants. Among the thrill rides is *Medusa* – the tallest, fastest and longest rollercoaster in northern California.

The *Coast Starlight* continues along the rocky shore of Pablo Bay and Carquinez Strait to the right, with gulls, yachts and fishing boats. You go through Crockett and pass the California & Hawaii Sugar factory and several large oil refineries. Mare Island Shipyard and California's Maritime Academy are on the far side of the strait. To the right also are the Marin County Hills and Mount Tamalpais (2,604ft/791m).

Richmond (25/15)
Over 100,000 people worked at Richmond's Kaiser Shipyards during World War II. The town is now a San Francisco suburb, its modern station on the right linked to the Bay Area Rapid Transit system. Look for BART trains lined up on the left.

San Francisco's skyline appears across the bay to your right as you leave and speed through Berkeley. The Golden Gate Bridge is to the north and Oakland Bay Bridge (eight miles/13km long, including approaches and toll plaza) to the south.

Golden Gate Racetrack (5/35)
Look for the racecourse on your right, next to an aquatic park.

EMERYVILLE (40/5)
Home of the Pixar Animation Studios as well as many biotech and software companies. Passengers for San Francisco disembark at Amtrak's station at 5885 Horton for transfer by shuttle bus into San Francisco's downtown area, connecting via the Oakland Bay Bridge with the Ferry Building at 425 Mission, Pier 39 on Fisherman's Wharf, the San Francisco Shopping Center at 835 Market and the Caltrain Station at Fourth and King.

SAN FRANCISCO
Free shuttle buses connect the Emeryville train station with downtown San Francisco in about 30 minutes.

The 'City by the bay' is famous for its Golden Gate Bridge, fog in the morning, vertiginous streets, elegant houses and Alcatraz. Home of Dashiell Hammett and Sam Spade, San Francisco was the birthplace of beatniks, hippies and the topless bar. Finance, industry and a large gay community coexist in the cosmopolitan atmosphere. With 'Silicon Valley' to the south, the city has lately become home to some of the world's most successful dot.com companies, creating hundreds of 25-year-old millionaires. Spaniards arrived here in 1776 but the city prospered only after it became a part of the United States. When gold was discovered in 1848, ships and wagon trains, then the railroads, began bringing thousands of settlers across the Sierra Nevada. San Francisco's Chinatown was founded (like the one in Vancouver, Canada) by immigrants who worked on the transcontinental railroad. Neither the 1906 earthquake nor the tremors of 1989 have dissuaded a million people from making the city their home.

San Francisco basics

☏**Telephone code** 415
Station (*Ticket office* ⊕ *06.00–22.20.*
Waiting room ⊕ *06.00–22.50*) Amtrak's
handsomely refurbished Ferry Building terminal

at 101 The Embarcadero is close to downtown.
Ferries cross at hourly intervals between here &
Oakland's Jack London Sq, calling at Alameda &
passing under the Bay Bridge.

Connections Caltrain services operate to San José & Gilroy (☎ 800 660 4287). Thruway buses go to Santa Cruz. Futuristic BART trains leave from Market St & are a fast & inexpensive way to explore Oakland, Berkeley, Fremont & Concord (☎ 510 465 2278). Alameda-Contra Costa Transit District buses serve the East Bay area (☎ 510 891 4700).

🚌 **Local transport** San Francisco can best be seen on foot or by cable car. Or you can use buses & the Muni Metro, a light railway running partly underground. For information on buses, cable cars & Muni trains, ☎ 673 6864.

🚕 **Taxis** Luxor ☎ 282 4141; Yellow ☎ 333 3333

🚗 **Car rental** Hertz, 433 Mason; ☎ 771 2200

🚌 **Greyhound** Transbay Terminal, 425 Mission; ☎ 495 1569

✈ **San Francisco International Airport (SFO)** 14 miles (22km) south on US Highway 101. American Airporter buses connect to a downtown terminal at Taylor & Ellis (☎ 202 0733), or you can take a BART train or SamTrans bus #397 (☎ 800 660 4287).

Tours Super Sightseeing, Pier 9; ☎ 777 2288. Bay cruises from the Blue & Gold Fleet at Pier 39 (☎ 705 8200). Air tours from Commodore Seaplane (☎ 332 4843).

ℹ **Visitors bureau** Hallidie Plaza, Market & Powell; ☎ 391 2000 or ☎ 391 2001 (for the latest events); e visitor-info@sfcvb.org; www.onlyinsanfrancisco.com; ⊕ daily

🏠 **Accommodation** Contact Bed & Breakfast San Francisco; ☎ 415 899 0060; e reservations@bbsf.com; www.bbsf.com, or Red Victorian Bed & Breakfast, 1665 Haight; ☎ 864 1978; www.redvic.net. Everything from expensive, classic hotels to downbeat rooming houses can be found, with budget accommodation in Japantown & Oakland.

Central (IYHF) Hostel, 312 Mason, 1 block from Union Sq; ☎ 788 5604. Free continental breakfast & Wi-Fi. Max 4 beds per dorm room, private rooms with bathroom available, **$**.

International (IYHF) Hostel, Bldg 240, Fort Mason; ☎ 771 7277. Overlooks the Golden Gate Bridge. Mostly dormitory rooms, **$**. City Center Hostel, 685 Ellis; ☎ 474 5721. Newly renovated, 75-room hostel offers both private rooms & 4- or 5-bed dorms, all with private bathrooms, **$**.

For the latest accommodation offers contact the visitors bureau hotel reservation service, ☎ 1 888 782 9673 (☎ 1 888 STAY N SF). Hotels include the Crescent, 417 Stockton; ☎ 400 0500, **$$**; Essex, 684 Ellis; ☎ 474 4664, **$$**; Sheehan, 620 Sutter; ☎ 775 6500, **$$**; Amsterdam, 749 Taylor; ☎ 673 3277, **$$**; Grant Plaza, 465 Grant Av; ☎ 434 3883, **$**; Ansonia, 711 Post; ☎ 673 2670, **$$**.

Recommended in San Francisco

Golden Gate Bridge Linking the city with Marin County to the north is one of the world's best-known & most impressive landmarks. At 2 miles (3.2km) long – 7 miles (11km) including approaches – it incorporates 80,000 miles (128,000km) of cable & is painted orange rather than gold. Magical views of San Francisco from the Marin County side.

Golden Gate Park Between Fulton & Lincoln Way is one of the world's largest manmade parks, where many museums & the odd buffalo can be found among 1,000 acres (400ha) of lakes, redwoods & eucalyptus. Information from the office at Fell & Stanyan (☎ 831 2700).

Maritime Museum At the foot of Polk St; ☎ 561 6622; www.maritime.org; ⊕ daily; museum free, pier admission charge. Photographs, models & relics showing west coast seafaring life from sail to steam are located in a building shaped like a 1930s liner. Excellent ranger-guided tours of the historic ships moored at nearby Hyde St Pier.

Cable Car Barn & Museum 1201 Mason; ☎ 474 1887; www.cablecarmuseum.com; ⊕ daily; museum free. Cable cars travel 9 miles (14.5km) of track at up to 9mph & are America's only historic landmarks with wheels. Observe this unique system in operation & see old cable cars (including the first, built in 1873), along with other exhibits & films.

Fisherman's Wharf On the waterfront between Taylor & the Embarcadero, the wharf has gift shops, salt air, cruise boats & hordes of tourists. Open-air stalls sell freshly cooked seafood while sea lions bark for fish & gulls glide above the water. **Downmarket** pleasures include a wax museum, the Guinness World of Records & Ripley's 'Believe It Or Not!'.

The Cannery 2801 Leavenworth; ☎ 771 3112; www.thecannery.com. Built in 1894 as a fruit-canning factory, the Cannery has been converted into a mall with dozens of shops, a comedy club, restaurants & art galleries. Jack's Cannery Bar boasts more beers on tap than almost anywhere in the country. There are stalls & cafés among century-old olive trees in the courtyard & street performers entertain on summer w/ends.

Coit Tower Located on top of Telegraph Hill, just east of North Beach; ☎362 0808; ⊕ daily; admission charge. The wealthy eccentric Lillie Hitchcock Coit left San Francisco $125,000 to build this memorial to volunteer firemen. Completed in 1933, the tower has great views & impressive murals depicting California during the 1930s.

Ansel Adams Center for Photography 250 Fourth; ☎495 7000; ⊕ Sun–Tue; admission charge. The museum features 5 galleries with exhibitions of contemporary & historical photography. One is dedicated solely to the work of Ansel Adams.

Wells Fargo Museum 420 Montgomery; ☎396 2619; ⊕ Mon–Fri; free. A history museum for one of California's largest banks, located on the site where Wells Fargo first opened for business in 1852. Among the hundreds of relics are a Concord Coach used by Wells Fargo in the 1860s, an impressive display of gold dust & ore, pistols, photographs, early posters & mining equipment.

Alcatraz ☎800 410 8233 (for ferry information & tickets); www.alcatraz.us; admission charge.

A million visitors every year come on boats from Pier 41 to the isle of pelicans, former residence of Al Capone, 'Machine Gun' Kelly & the 'Birdman'. The prison's first 53 inmates, including Capone, were brought on a 1,000-mile journey in a train equipped with barred windows & reinforced doors. Each man was clamped in leg irons & chained to his seat. The rock closed as a federal penitentiary in 1963 but still has the power to freeze your spirit. Make reservations early (at least 1 week ahead during summer) & dress warmly for the excellent tours led by national park rangers.

Golden Gate Railroad Museum Formerly located on the naval base at Hunter's Point, now temporarily at Niles Canyon; ☎822 8728; e info@ggrm.org; www.ggrm.org; admission free. The museum started in 1975 when pharmacist Michael Mangini acquired an old steam engine he saw in the San Mateo Fairgrounds parking lot & began restoring & repairing the vintage ex-SP #2472 Pacific-type locomotive. In May 1991, #2472 steamed under its own power for the first time to make its debut at that year's Railfair & since then the GGRM has continued collecting artefacts & rolling stock & securing the machinery & parts needed to establish the museum as a 'hands-on' facility for the public. It also operates charters & excursions using #2472 as motive power.

All aboard!

Buses leave from the Ferry Building and cross the Oakland Bay Bridge, with great views to your left of the city, Alcatraz and the Golden Gate Bridge. To your right are Oakland and the tall Gothic tower of the University of California at Berkeley. The *Coast Starlight* continues south from Emeryville to Oakland.

OAKLAND (5/70) Known as 'the place where the trains stopped', Oakland lacks San Francisco's glamour but does have inexpensive accommodation less readily found on the other side of the bay. A pedestrian bridge takes you across from Amtrak's new glass and steel station to Jack London Square, named after Oakland's former resident and author of *The Call of the Wild*. Other notable citizens have included Gertrude Stein, Jessica Mitford and the Black Panthers. The **visitors bureau** is at 463 11th (☎ *510 839 9000; www.oaklandcvb.com*).

The **Oakland Museum** (*1000 Oak;* ☎ *510 238 2200; www.museumca.org; admission charge*) features Californian art and a simulated journey from sea level to the Sierra Nevada. Nearby are the Victorian houses of Old Oakland and the **Pardee Museum** (*www.pardeehome.org; admission charge*), built in 1868–69 by Enoch Pardee, a gold rush immigrant, & once the home of the 'earthquake governor', George Pardee. **Lake Merritt**, a unique fresh & salt-water lake close to the city centre, has a wildlife refuge and boating.

The train leaves and gathers speed through industrial suburbs with the Bay Bridge still visible to your right.

Jack London Square (5/65) Oakland's main tourist attraction on your right features the Jack London Museum, the USS *Potomac*, Franklin Roosevelt's yacht and dozens of waterfront restaurants. Also on your right is the former Alameda naval base.

Oakland Coliseum (20/50) This massive circular construction on your right is home to the Oakland A's baseball team. The BART train line is to your left.

Alameda Stadium (25/45) The Alameda County stadium can be seen on your right before you continue across mudflats via Drawbridge, an officially certified 'ghost town' which was formerly the home of railroad workers, bootleggers and duck hunters.

Moffett Field (50/20) Beyond the lower end of San Francisco Bay are the giant hangars of this naval air station.

Marriott's Great America Park (60/10) Look right for rollercoasters and other amusement rides as the mudflats are left behind.

Santa Clara (65/5) The enclosed sports stadium of Santa Clara University can be seen to your right in this computer industry centre of 'Silicon Valley'. Just south of town you travel among extensive Southern Pacific rail yards and pass a historic brick roundhouse.

SAN JOSE (70/70) California's oldest city and first capital was founded in 1777 as Pueblo de San José de Guadalupe. Larger than San Francisco in area and population, San Jose has fruit and wine industries as well as many companies specialising in aerospace and computer technology. The **Mission of Santa Clara de Assisi** is a reminder of earlier days. Amtrak's recently restored station is at 65 Cahill and Caltrain commuter services operate between here and San Francisco.

The *Coast Starlight* travels on through the Santa Clara Valley, one of the richest farming regions in America. To your left are Mount Hamilton (4,430ft/1,350m) and the Diablo Mountains, with the beautiful Santa Cruz Range to your right.

Gilroy (30/40) 'The garlic capital of the world', where tons of garlic-laden food are cooked and eaten by devotees at the town's August festival. You can see and sometimes smell these plants growing near the tracks. Marilyn Monroe was once crowned as Gilroy's 'garlic queen'. To your right are St Mary's Church (with its gold bell) and the City Hall clock tower.

Pajaro Gap (40/30) You cross the Santa Cruz Mountains, via Chittenden Pass and the San Andreas Fault on a bridge near Logan, into the Pajaro Valley – 'the valley of the birds'. Look for herons, divers and buzzards, as well as more of the Santa Cruz Range to your right. Exotic eucalyptus trees flourish beside the tracks.

Watsonville (45/25) First settled during the 18th-century gold rush, Watsonville has many attractive Victorian houses. This area specialises in growing apples, lettuces and strawberries. Spanish explorer Don Gaspar de Portola was the first European to discover the nearby redwoods.

Castroville (60/10) 'The artichoke capital of the world', where tall, bushy plants grow in fields of black earth to your right. In 1949, an unknown Marilyn Monroe was named the town's first 'artichoke queen'.

SALINAS (70/110) The centre of America's salad bowl, where huge crops of lettuce, sugar beet and other vegetables fatten beneath a benevolent sun. Salinas was the birthplace of John Steinbeck, who described his home town in *East of Eden*. His beautiful Victorian house at 132 Central Avenue is now a restaurant and museum, and the public library owns a collection of his manuscripts. Amtrak's station is at 11 Station Place, from where Thruway buses serve Monterey (immortalised by Steinbeck in *Cannery Row*) and Carmel.

Big Sur, where Jack Kerouac, Henry Miller and Orson Welles lived, is 15 miles (24km) to the west.

You leave Salinas past an incongruous Firestone factory standing in fields to your right then travel 100 miles along the Salinas River Valley. San Benito Mountain (5,258ft/1,600m) is the highest peak of the Diablo Range to your left. The rugged Santa Lucia Mountains are on your right.

Soledad (20/90) Built as a mission town in 1791 – the name is Spanish for 'solitude' – Soledad was the setting for John Steinbeck's novel, *Of Mice and Men*. The large, modern prison to your left once held the Black Panther leader, Eldridge Cleaver.

The *Coast Starlight* continues along the Salinas Valley with the river to your right and Pinnacles National Monument on the left. Just before Rocky Point tunnel (1,305ft/400m long), look left for an airfield where light planes used for crop spraying are based.

King City (45/65) 'The most metropolitan cow town in the west', where many crates of agricultural produce await transportation on your right. John Steinbeck's father was the town's first railroad agent.

San Lucas (65/45) A statue of Christ protects the cemetery seen to your right.

Camp Roberts (85/25) The camp is the headquarters of California's National Guard.

San Miguel (95/15) On your right is the 18th-century Mission San Miguel Arcángel, its two-storey adobe structure enclosing the best-preserved interior of all California's missions. *Coast Starlight* tracks from Oakland to Los Angeles closely follow the Spanish mission path, El Camino Real ('the Royal Road'), founded between 1769 and 1823 by Franciscan father Junipero Serra. The 21 missions and four chapels along the Camino Real from San Diego to Sonoma were each a day's journey apart.

PASO ROBLES (110/60) A new station has been built at 800 Pine beside the old, burned-down Southern Pacific depot.

Atascadero (15/45) The golf course on your right is bounded by the Santa Lucia foothills. Atascadero's red-brick City Hall houses a history museum.

Cuesta Pass (40/20) A quintessential railroad experience begins as the train climbs into the Santa Margarita Mountains, negotiating five tunnels and giving magnificent views of the Santa Lucias. Los Osos Valley is below and Highway 101 opposite. Look for rocky outcrops, adventurous sheep, pine trees, eucalyptus and scrub oak. Splendid white oaks can be seen in the valley below.

The descent from Cuesta Grade represents a fall of more than 1,000ft in 11 miles (300m in 18km), with the old wooden trestle over Stenner Creek visible ahead.

Horseshoe Curve (55/5) The *Coast Starlight* winds down to San Luis Obispo, taking two spectacular sweeping curves that bring the entire train into view. On your right is the California Men's Colony, a state penitentiary from which Timothy Leary once made his escape. As the train crosses Stenner Creek, look left for California's Polytechnic State University.

SAN LUIS OBISPO (60/125) This oasis of palm trees, sunshine and Spanish architecture began in 1772 as the Mission San Luis Obispo de Tolosa. Many of the buildings on Marsh Street were built for rail workers' families when it was an important railroad town. **San Luis Obispo County Historical Museum** (*696 Monterey;* ✆ *805 543 0638; http://historycenterslo.org;* ☺ *Wed–Mon; free*) explores the history of the county. The **visitors bureau** is at 811 El Capitan Way (✆ *800 634 1414; www.sanluisobispocounty.com*).

Amtrak's station is at 1011 Railroad Avenue, from where buses leave for the amazing **Hearst Castle** (*750 Hearst Castle Rd, in nearby San Simeon;* ✆ *1 800 444 4445; www.hearst-castle.org;* ☺ *daily*). California's main tourist attraction after Disneyland was the home of William Randolph Hearst, the real-life entrepreneur and newspaper tycoon who became Orson Welles's inspiration for *Citizen Kane*. The 'Mediterranean Revival' mansion boasts 130 telephones and is crammed with baths, swimming pools, marble statues, armour, Persian rugs and flamboyant furniture from around the world. Former guests have included Charlie Chaplin, George Bernard Shaw, Buster Keaton, Cary Grant and Winston Churchill.

As the train leaves San Luis Obispo note the historic locomotive turntable on your right.

Grover City (15/110) Obsolete rail coaches to the right now house a restaurant. The *Coast Starlight* continues south, crossing the Santa Maria River.

Pismo Beach (20/105) Eucalyptus trees and dunes to your right conceal the resort of Pismo Beach, famous for its clams.

The train climbs Callendar Hill then travels through Guadalupe and the Santa Maria Valley before emerging from the Schuman Canyon.

Vandenberg Air Force Base (50/75) For half an hour the train proceeds through the Strategic Air Command western missile test range, home of B-52 planes and firing site for Minuteman missile tests. Minuteman Beach is to your right. Further south, at Purisma Point, several satellite launch pads can be seen on the right and Vandenberg airfield to your left. The base is military territory so no photography is allowed.

Pacific Ocean (51/74) More peaceful scenes appear on your right as the train travels for over 100 miles through heather moorland with splendid views out across the Pacific Ocean.

Surf (60/65) You cross the Santa Ynez River with more launch pads on your right and oil rigs out to sea.

Space Shuttle (65/60) The big white buildings on your left were used during the Space Shuttle development programme and are now abandoned.

Point Arguello (70/55) This has been the site of many wrecks and an automatic lighthouse on the cliffs warns passing ships of the danger. Look out for dolphins and migrating grey whales in spring and autumn. The train's tracks run over a trestle above Jalama Beach Park at the southern end of Vandenberg Air Force Base.

Point Conception (80/45) Note the historic lighthouse still in use on the bluff as you continue south along the cliff tops. Ocean views here are shared only with grazing cattle since this area is inaccessible to the public except by train. The Santa Ynez Mountains begin in the left distance and extend south beyond Santa Barbara.

Gaviota (95/30) The name is Spanish for 'seagull'. You cross on high trestles above Gaviota Pass and Tajiguas Creek.

Refugio State Beach (100/25) Picnic tables dot the beach to your right. Oil rigs and production platforms then come into view as the train accompanies the Santa Barbara Channel, discovered in 1542 by the Portuguese explorer Juan Cabrillo. He was buried on San Miguel Island, seen out to your right, after he died there the following year.

The *Coast Starlight* temporarily leaves the coast and goes inland towards Santa Barbara, passing on the right the bell tower of the University of California at Santa Barbara.

Santa Barbara Mission (123/2) The 'Queen of the Missions' on your left was founded in 1786 and has been in use ever since. The only mission with twin towers, its fountain is fed by an aqueduct.

SANTA BARBARA (125/45) Originally the home of Chumash Indians, this resort and retirement area is located invitingly between a palm-lined beach and the Santa Ynez foothills. Santa Barbara was discovered by Sebastian Vizcaino on St Barbara's Day in 1602 and it was here in 1782 that Spain built its last New World fortress, the Presidio Real. Spanish influence continues in the white adobe and red-tiled architecture, much of which had to be reconstructed after a 1925 earthquake.

The **visitors bureau** is located at 1601 Anacapa (✎ *805 966 9222 or* ✎ *800 676 1266; www.santabarbaraca.com*).

Amtrak's station is at 209 State, an unsafe area at night. To the left of the station is the Moreton Bay fig tree, planted in 1877 and the largest of its kind in America. Branches spread more than 160ft (50m) to provide welcome shade. The **Museum of Art** (*1130 State;* ✎ *805 963 4364; www.sbma.net*) has American and Impressionist works as well as art from Asia and a children's gallery.

The **South Coast Railroad Museum** is seven miles (11km) west (*300 N Carneros Rd, Goleta;* ✎ *805 964 3540; www.goletadepot.org;* ⊕ *Wed–Sun; donation*). Amtrak's *Pacific Surfliner* trains travelling north of Los Angeles serve Goleta station. A 1901 Southern Pacific wood-frame depot has been relocated in Lake Los Carneros Park and restored to house model trains, rare photographs and miniature train rides.

The *Coast Starlight* leaves Santa Barbara among some of the city's finest residential areas.

Andree Clark Bird Refuge (4/41) The wildlife sanctuary next to a freshwater lagoon on your right is home to herons, egrets, cormorants and many migrating birds.

Miramar (5/40) The old station house to your left has been converted into a restaurant.

Summerland Beach (6/39) Nude bathers are sometimes seen frolicking to your right. Bates Beach, a similar venue to watch for or recoil from, is passed 15 minutes further on. From here to Ventura the train, like Highway 101, travels along the shoreline.

Look for surfers at Carpintera Beach and Emma Woods Beach, where on a clear day you can see out to the Channel Islands. At Mussel Shoals a causeway leads to the island on which oil production began in 1964. More oil platforms appear in the channel before you cross the Ventura River and again head inland.

Ventura (30/15) The county fairgrounds are to your right and the 1809 San Buenaventura Mission to your left. The mission's unique wooden bells are preserved in a museum.

A Spanish expedition of 1542 was the first to discover Ventura, now a scheduled stop for some *Pacific Surfliner* trains. Nearby is the Ojai Farm Hostel (℡ 805 646 0311) with free pickup from Amtrak's station.

The *Coast Starlight* continues south, crossing the Santa Clara River on a long low trestle.

OXNARD (45/20) Founded in 1897 by the four Oxnard brothers, who made their fortune out of raising sugar beet. Now a centre for citrus and other fruit production, Oxnard is the home of California's strawberry festival.

The train travels east into the beautiful Simi Valley with the Simi Hills to your right. The Santa Susanna Mountains are to your left.

Camarillo (10/10) A mission-type church stands on the hill to your left.

SIMI VALLEY (20/30) Ronald Reagan's Presidential Library is located in this predominantly white suburb of Los Angeles. In 1992, a local jury acquitted four white policemen of using excessive force to arrest a black motorist, Rodney King, and the verdict led to riots in cities across America.

After Simi Valley the *Coast Starlight* tackles the imposing Santa Susanna Mountains, where tunnels and passes take you through a stark landscape of rocks and cacti. This was a film location for the *Lone Ranger* television series, James Cagney's *White Heat* and Alfred Hitchcock's *North by Northwest*.

Chatsworth (20/10) On the border of Los Angeles County, this is the San Fernando Valley – land of the swimming pool. Millions of Angelinos live the suburban life in an area the size of Chicago.

VAN NUYS (30/30) The modern glass-and-concrete station is a stop for Amtrak's *Pacific Surfliner* trains. Look for factories belonging to General Motors and Schlitz as the scenery becomes industrial. Van Nuys Airport appears to your right before the train passes beneath the San Diego freeway.

Hollywood-Burbank Airport (5/25) The airport is a test area for the Lockheed factory seen beyond runways to your left.

Burbank (10/20) The city of Burbank is to the left. Disney, Warners and Columbia film studios, as well as NBC Television, have facilities among the Santa Monica Hills on your right. This is where the helicopter scenes for television's *MASH* were shot.

Glendale (15/15) The ornamental Spanish-style 1920s station has starred in many movies and has recently been renovated.

Soon after Glendale you see Forest Lawn Memorial Park next to Griffith Park on your left. Made famous as Whispering Glades in Evelyn Waugh's novel *The Loved One*, Forest Lawn is the burial place of Clark Gable, Carole Lombard, Jean Harlow and Errol Flynn. Tasteful highlights include a stained-glass version of Leonardo's *Last Supper*. The *Coast Starlight* travels on deeper into the city of Los Angeles.

Los Angeles River (23/7) The concrete channel to your right is another favourite film location, notably for *Point Blank*, *Chinatown* and *Repo Man*. The channel stays dry most of the year but at times of flooding becomes a river. The train crosses the channel then passes beneath the Golden State and Pasadena freeways before winding slowly towards Union Station.

Dodger Stadium (25/5) Perched on a bluff to your right is the home of epic baseball. Also look right for Elysian Park and the impressive Los Angeles skyline. Los Angeles County jail is on your left.

LOS ANGELES Palm trees, beaches, blondes, surfing, freeways, smog and David Hockney swimming pools: Los Angeles is a sprawling place with an atmosphere all its own. Founded by the Spanish in the 18th century as El Pueblo de Nuestra Señora de la Reina de Los Angeles (the City of Our Lady, Queen of the Angels) its name grew shorter as the town became bigger. Completion of the transcontinental railroad in 1869, together with oil, Hollywood and a near-perfect climate, brought millions of settlers in search of the good life.

America's second-largest city now spreads ten million people over an area as big as Rhode Island and true Angelinos would never live anywhere else. The sun really does shine 90% of the year, although smog can be a problem in summer.

Los Angeles basics

⬦**Telephone code** 213

⬦**Station** (*Ticket office & waiting room* ⏲ *24hrs; information* ⬦*624 0171*) Los Angeles Union Station at 800 N Alameda is one of the world's prettiest railway stations, built in Spanish Mission & Art-Deco styles with gardens shaded by palm trees. It was constructed in the 1930s on part of the original Chinatown & has starred in many movies, including *Bugsy*. Vending machines, ATM banking, newspapers, handcarts, Red Caps, restaurant, left-luggage room, shop, taxi stand.

Connections Thruway buses go to Santa Barbara, Long Beach & Bakersfield & there are plans for a daily train service between Los Angeles & Las Vegas, Nevada, using Talgo equipment. This would restore part of the route once used by Amtrak's *Desert Wind* train.

🚌**Local transport** Los Angeles used to boast the largest electric railway in the world, its *Pacific Red* streetcars often appearing in early silent films. As in other cities, the oil, tyre & car companies bought up the railway in order to close it down. Metro Rail's Blue Line (⬦*626 4455*) from Long Beach to Los Angeles opened in 1990 & the system has expanded to 5 rail lines & 79 miles of track, carrying more than a billion passengers in 20 years.

MTA buses take in most city attractions, with free maps from the customer service centre (*5301 Wilshire Bd;* ⬦*1 800 COMMUTE* (⬦*266 6883*)). MTA bus #1 leaves from the corner of Broadway &

Arcadia for Hollywood. DASH shuttle buses (☏ *808 2273*) operate Mon–Sat, connecting Union Station with Chinatown & the downtown area. For Metrolink commuter trains serving southern California, ☏1 800 371 5465 or ☏213 347 2800 from outside the area.

🚗 **Taxis** LA Taxi ☏627 7000; United ☏483 7604

🚗 **Car rental** Budget (at the terminal) ☏617 2977; Beverly Hills Rent-A-Car, 9732 Little Santa Monica Bd; ☏800 479 5996. LA is the ultimate city of the automobile, with 6,500 miles (10,000km) of road & freeway & 24 million vehicle trips on an average day. Renting a car is no problem but finding your way around is more tricky. If you have the time & inclination, the Automobile Club will supply maps & advice.

🚌 **Greyhound** 1716 E Seventh; ☏629 8401. Also at 1715 Cahuenga Bd, Hollywood; ☏466 6381.

✈ **LAX Airport** 16 miles (26km) southwest of downtown by the Super Shuttle (☏ *310 782 6600*). Alternatively you can get there via MTA bus # 439.

Tours Gray Line goes to Hollywood, Beverly Hills & the film studios (☏ *800 828 6699*). Other companies include Starline (☏ *800 959 3131*) & Hollywood Fantasy (☏ *323 469 8184*). The Los Angeles Conservancy (*304 S Broadway;* ☏*623 2489*) offers walking tours & Dearly Departed Tours (☏ *800 979 3370*) provides morbid & sometimes irreverent tours to places where famous people have died or been involved in various scandals. These include the Highland Gardens/Landmark Hotel (Janis Joplin), the Knickerbocker Hotel (D W Griffith) & the Hollywood sign (where a failed English actress, Peg Entwistle, was the first person to commit suicide).

ℹ **Visitors bureau** 685 S Figueroa; ☏689 8822; www.discoverlosangeles.com

🏠 **Accommodation** Los Angeles has 12 million visitors a year so there are plenty of rooms to choose from. Consult the local press for w/end rates & special offers. For B&B contact Baywood Inn Bed & Breakfast, 1370 Second St, Baywood Park, CA 93402-1112; ☏805 528 8888; e frontdesk@baywoodinn.com; www.baywoodinn.com.

International (IYHF) Hostel, 3601 S Gaffey; ☏310 831 8109. Take MTA bus #246. **$**. Banana Bungalow-Hollywood, 5920 Hollywood Bd; ☏877 977 5077. Take the Metro Redline to Hollywood & Vine. Dormitory rooms, **$**. Hollywood International Hostel, 6820 Hollywood Bd; ☏323 463 0797. Dormitory rooms, **$**. Santa Monica AYH Hostel, 1436 Second; ☏310 393 9913. Take MTA bus #33. Dormitory rooms, **$**, dbl, **$$**.

Hotels include the Palomar, 10740 Wilshire Bd; ☏310 475 8711, **$$$$**; Metro Plaza, 711 N Main; ☏680 0200, **$$$$**; Figueroa, 939 S Figueroa; ☏627 8971, **$$**; Park Plaza, 607 S Park View; ☏381 6300, **$$**; Milner, 813 S Flower; ☏627 6981, **$$**; Orchid, 819 S Flower; ☏623 9904, **$**; Stillwell, 838 S Grand Av; ☏627 1151, **$**.

Recommended in Los Angeles

El Pueblo de Los Angeles State Park
Opposite Amtrak's station. Los Angeles began here in 1781 & the city's oldest house, the Avila Adobe, which dates from 1818 is at 10 E Olvera. This street also features Mexican restaurants & cheerfully tacky souvenir shops. Look also for the Masonic Hall (1858), Old Plaza Church (1822), Old Plaza Firehouse (1884) & Sepulveda House (1884). Free film & walking tours from the **visitor centre** (*622 Main;* ☏*628 1274; www.lasangelitas.org*).

Natural History Museum 900 Exposition Bd; ☏763 3466; www.nhm.org; ⊕ daily; admission charge. 2 world-famous habitat halls show African & North American mammals in their natural environments, & the museum is home to Megamouth, the world's rarest shark. The Lando Hall of California History has fascinating exhibits showing the southwest from the 1500s through to downtown Los Angeles in 1940.

Mann's Chinese Theater 6925 Hollywood Bd; ☏323 464 8111. Match your favourite actor's cement prints in front of this outlandish pagoda. Nearby, almost 2,500 bronze stars in the **Walk of Fame** celebrate the great & not so great of Tinseltown.

LA County Museum of Art 5905 Wilshire Bd; ☏323 857 6000; www.lacma.org; ⊕ Thu–Tue; admission charge. LACMA is one of the finest art museums in the country, with more than 100,000

works spanning the history of art from ancient times to the present & major special exhibitions. **J Paul Getty Center** 1200 Getty Center Dr; ☎310 440 7300; www.getty.edu; ⊕ Tue–Sun; free. With panoramic views of Los Angeles & the Pacific Ocean, the museum has 54 galleries to display one of the richest collections in the world, including medieval manuscripts & 65,000 photographs, as well as paintings by Cézanne, Goya, Leonardo, Michelangelo, Monet, Titian, Turner & Van Gogh. Metro Rapid Line 761 stops at the main gate on Sepulveda Bd. The Roman-inspired Getty Villa at 17985 Pacific Coast Highway in Malibu has Greek, Roman & Etruscan antiquities arranged by themes. Take Metro bus #534.

La Brea Tar Pits 5801 Wilshire Bd; ☎323 934 7243; ⊕ daily; admission charge. Bubbling black deposits contain hundreds of fossilised mammals, seen at the Page Museum & observation pit. The fossils are up to 40,000 years old & include camels, mammoths & mastodons.

Griffith Park 4730 Crystal Springs Dr; ☎323 913 4688; ⊕ daily, admission charge to the zoo & some other attractions. This 4,107-acre (1,650ha) city park is the largest in the country & incorporates a planetarium, bird sanctuary, miniature railway, carousel & zoo (☎602 273 1341). Take bus #96.

Universal Studios 1000 Universal City Plaza, Universal City; ☎1 800 UNIVERSAL; www.universalstudios.com; ⊕ daily; admission charge. The 2nd-biggest tourist attraction in southern California has spectacular rides such as Jurassic Park, King Kong in 3D & the Simpsons Ride, with character voices performed by stars of the TV show. You can enter the world of Shrek & experience the chilling, machine-controlled future with the Terminator.

Travel Town 5200 Zoo Dr, in the northwest corner of Griffith Park; ☎323 662 5874; www.traveltown.org; ⊕ daily; free. The museum has 14 steam locomotives, including one of the oldest in the United States, built for the original Western Pacific Railroad in 1864 & used by the Central Pacific during construction of the Transcontinental Railroad. There are also many passenger cars, freight wagons & cabooses (brake cars). Trains ride for 1 mile along a 16in-gauge (42cm) track, crossing several bridges & an 80ft (27m) tunnel.

Forest Lawn Memorial Park 1712 S Glendale Av, Glendale, near Griffith Park; ☎323 254 3131 or ☎1 800 204 3131; www.forestlawn.com; ⊕ daily; free. This is the last resting place of Buster Keaton, Stan Laurel, Clara Bow, W C Fields, Alan Ladd & Charles Laughton.

Lomita Railroad Museum Just south of Los Angeles at 2137 W 250th, Lomita; ☎310 326 6255; www.lomita-rr.org; ⊕ Thu–Sun; admission charge. Includes live steam engines, memorabilia & a replica of the Boston & Maine's Greenwood station at Wakefield, MA. On display is a Southern Pacific Railroad Mogul steam locomotive & tender, a 1910 Union Pacific caboose & a 1913 Southern Pacific wood boxcar.

5

The *California Zephyr*
Chicago–Emeryville (for San Francisco)

General route information

The original *California Zephyr* streamliner was inaugurated in 1949 on this route, operated collectively by the Chicago, Burlington & Quincy Railroad, Denver & Rio Grande Western Railroad and Western Pacific Railroad. Sold as a 'cruise train' to compete on spectacular scenery rather than speed, it had Vista-Dome cars, 'Zephyrette' hostesses and coast-to-coast sleeping cars in conjunction with the Pennsylvania Railroad. One of the world's great trains, Amtrak's revived *California Zephyr* travels for two days and nights over farmland, prairie, deserts, rivers and mountains. Western pioneers came this way, as did gold prospectors, the Pony Express and the first long-distance telegraph line. The *Zephyr* follows America's earliest transcontinental rail route for much of its 2,438-mile (3,922km) journey, and many people take this train just to explore the Rocky Mountains.

Joining the train

CHICAGO The proclaimed capital of America's third coast is one of the country's largest and most ethnically diverse cities. Writers such as Saul Bellow, Nelson Algren

ESSENTIAL INFORMATION

FREQUENCY Daily. The **westbound** service leaves Chicago early in the afternoon to arrive in Omaha late in the evening and Denver by early next morning. You reach Salt Lake City by midnight on the second evening, Reno the following morning and Emeryville (for San Francisco) mid afternoon. Travelling **east**, you leave San Francisco early in the morning to arrive in Reno by late afternoon and Salt Lake City during the night. You reach Denver by early evening and Omaha early on the second day, arriving in Chicago mid afternoon.
DURATION 51 hours 20 minutes
RESERVATIONS All reserved
EQUIPMENT Superliner coaches. Sightseer lounge car.
SLEEPING Superliner bedrooms
FOOD Complete meals, snacks, sandwiches, drinks
LOUNGE CAR Movies, games. A California State Railway Museum history guide provides a commentary between Reno and Sacramento. In spring and summer, National Park Service rangers provide a narrative between Grand Junction and Denver.
BAGGAGE Check-in service at major cities

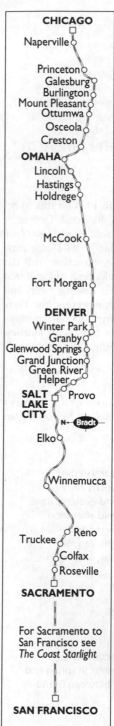

CHICAGO
Naperville

Princeton
Galesburg
Burlington
Mount Pleasant
Ottumwa
Osceola
Creston
OMAHA
Lincoln
Hastings
Holdrege

McCook

Fort Morgan

DENVER
Winter Park
Granby
Glenwood Springs
Grand Junction
Green River
Helper
SALT
LAKE   Provo
CITY
        N—Bradt
Elko

Winnemucca

        Reno
Truckee
        Colfax
        Roseville

SACRAMENTO

For Sacramento to
San Francisco see
The Coast Starlight

SAN FRANCISCO

and Sara Paretsky have lived in 'the city of big shoulders', as have Al Capone (gangster) and Mother Cabrini (first American saint). Harrison Ford and Raymond Chandler, whose father was a railway engineer, were born here, and Ernest Hemingway grew up in the middle-class suburb of Oak Park. Muddy Waters, Howlin' Wolf and John Lee Hooker made blues history on the South Side.

Chicago began in 1833, but stayed a village until railways connected it to the east coast in 1852. Destroyed by fire in 1871 soon after the rail link with San Francisco was completed, the city rebuilt itself as a centre for industry, finance and the arts. The Junction Railway's stockyards were where cowboys brought their cattle, and although these have long closed down, Chicago retains a hard-headed commercial spirit. More mainstream and less pretentious than New York or Los Angeles, the city has become the fashionable home of television's *ER* and *Oprah*.

The first 11-storey skyscrapers were erected here, leading to the Chicago School of Architecture and subsequently Frank Lloyd Wright and Mies van der Rohe. You can see three of the world's ten tallest buildings and superb architecture in every modern style, as well as outdoor sculpture, an elevated railway and the brooding Chicago River. Chicago boasts 29 miles (46km) of beaches but it can be bitingly cold in winter, when ice sometimes floats on Lake Michigan.

Chicago basics

☏ **Telephone code** 312 downtown; 773 for the rest of the city

🚂 **Station** (*Ticket office* ⏲ *06.00–21.00. The Great Hall waiting room* ⏲ *05.30–midnight*) Chicago has long been a port for ships arriving on Lake Michigan via the St Lawrence Seaway. It has also been called the railroad hub of the world, with Union Station at 225 S Canal the centre of America's rail network. The cathedral-like Great Hall features huge marble columns, statues, sweeping staircases, balconies, original wooden benches & a soaring arched ceiling. This magnificent waiting room has appeared in many films, including Brian de Palma's *The Untouchables*. *The Narrow Margin*, set mostly on board the Central Pacific's *Golden West Limited*, has intriguing shots of how the station looked in 1951.

Amtrak operates from a more modern part of the building, with a fountain into which you can throw pennies for luck. A separate waiting room is reserved for Amtrak passengers (*Metropolitan lounge* ⏲ *08.30–20.00*). Lockers, vending machines, ATM banking, newspapers, handcarts, Red Caps, restaurants, shops, taxi stand.

Connections No Thruway bus connections.

🚌 **Local transport** Metra (☏ *322 6777*) runs commuter trains out of Union Station & City Transit Authority, the nation's 2nd-largest public transportation system, has buses covering the whole city, with a stop outside the Adams St exit. CTA buses & a subway augment the El railway (☏ *836 7000; www.transitchicago.com*). Pace buses (☏ *847 364 7223;*

www.pacebus.com) operate to the suburbs. Free maps from the tourist bureau & the Metra information window at Union Station.

Chicago also has an underground Pedway system of pedestrian walkways that makes navigation easy even in bad weather. From the Illinois Center at Michigan Av & the Michigan Av Bridge a network of walkways lead to stores in the Loop area & to major train stations, with an entrance elevator in Loop buildings & subway stations. Maps of the Pedway are available in hotels & at the Illinois Center.

🚕 **Taxis**   Flash ☎ 773 561 4444; Checker ☎ 243 2537

🚗 **Car rental**   Hertz, at Union Station; ☎ 928 0538

🚌 **Greyhound**   630 W Harrison; ☎ 408 5800. Also located at Union Station.

✈ **O'Hare Airport**   One of the world's busiest, O'Hare is 20 miles northwest by coach or El train. Continental Airport Express buses (☎ 888 284 3826) run every few mins between downtown & the airport. CTA trains are just as frequent & much cheaper ($1.50).

Tours   Gray Line ☎ 251 3107; Chicago Tours ☎ 888 881 3284. Untouchable Tours visits infamous gangster scenes (☎ 881 1195). For views of the city from Lake Michigan call Mercury (☎ 332 1353) or Chicago From the Lake (☎ 527 1977).

From May to Sep the Loop Train offers free 40min tours of downtown attractions. Tours are conducted each Sat afternoon by guides from the Chicago Architecture Foundation (☎ 922 3432) & tickets can be obtained at the Chicago Cultural Center on the morning of the tour.

ℹ **Visitors bureau**   The Cultural Center is located in what was once Chicago's first central library building at 77 E Randolph; ☎ 877 244 2246; www.explorechicago.org; ⊕ daily. The **Visitor Center**, also open daily, is located at 163 E Michigan Av in the pumping station adjacent to the water tower, sole survivors of Chicago's great fire.

🏠 **Accommodation**   Contact Chicago Bed & Breakfast, PO Box 14088, Chicago, IL 60614; ☎ 951 0085; www.chicago-bed-breakfast.com.

Getaway Hostel, 616 W Arlington Pl; ☎ 773 929 5380. Private & dormitory rooms, **$**. International Hostel, 6318 N Winthrop Av; ☎ 773 262 1011. Family rooms available. Take bus #151. Members & non-members, **$**. Some hotels offer w/end & summer packages. Call the Hotel Association (☎ 346 3135). For discount hotel rates call Hot Rooms (☎ 1 800 468 3500 or ☎ 773 468 7666; e hotrooms@hotrooms.com; www.hotrooms.com).

Hotels include the Drake, 140 E Walton Pl; ☎ 787 2200, **$$$**; Blackstone, 636 S Michigan Av; ☎ 447 0955, **$$$**; River Hotel, 75 E Wacker Dr; ☎ 777 0990, **$$$**; Allegro, 171 W Randolph; ☎ 236 0123, **$$**; Cass, 640 N Wabash Av; ☎ 787 4030, **$$**; Travelodge, 65 E Harrison; ☎ 427 8000, **$$**.

Recommended in Chicago

Willis Tower   233 S Wacker & Jackson, near the station; ☎ 875 9447; www.willistower.com; ⊕ daily; admission charge. Formerly the Sears Tower. Edward Sears, a former railway clerk, co-founded Sears, Roebuck, the world's largest mail order company. Railways proved ideal for distributing the catalogue & its goods, including entire houses. This building, completed in 1973, was the world's tallest for 25 years, reaching 110 storeys & 1,454ft/443m (1,729ft/527m including added antennae). Ear-popping elevators shoot you to the 103rd-floor Skydeck (*www.theskydeck.com*) for views of the city, Lake Michigan & 4 states. Go before sunset & watch the city come alight.

John Hancock Observatory   875 N Michigan Av; ☎ 751 3680; www.hancockobservatory.com; ⊕ daily; admission charge. Even at 327ft lower than the Willis Tower, the John Hancock Center observation deck gives wonderful views of Lake Michigan & the city. The 94th-floor observatory is more than 1,000ft (300m) above Chicago & features an outside Skywalk, a virtual-reality tour of more than 80 city sites, 3D 'talking' telescopes & a Chicago history wall.

John Shedd Aquarium   1200 Lake Shore Dr; ☎ 939 2438; www.sheddaquarium.org; ⊕ daily; admission charge, free on community discount days. When the aquarium began in 1927, live specimens were transported here aboard a specially built fish car, the Nautilus, later replaced by the Nautilus II (now on display in the Railway Museum at Monticello, Illinois). Today's splendid building holds thousands of fish as well as the largest indoor collection of marine mammals in the world, including beluga whales, seals, sea otters & dolphins. Don't miss the penguins & the amazing alligator snapping turtle.

Art Institute   111 S Michigan Av; ☎443 3600; www.artic.edu; ☺ daily; admission charge, Thu evening free. One of the world's top galleries features Impressionist, American & Renaissance works alongside major exhibitions. Crowded at w/ends.

Museum of Science & Industry   57th & Lake Shore Dr; ☎773 684 1414; www.msichicago.org; ☺ daily; admission charge. Includes a German U-Boat, a British Spitfire, the Apollo 8 spacecraft & many automobiles, plus Omnimax film shows. Among the railroad engines is the New York Central's *No 999*, which in 1893 was the first locomotive to exceed 100mph (160km/h). A Santa Fe miniature railroad operates model trains over 1,000ft (300m) of track.

Navy Pier   600 E Grand Av; ☎595 PIER or ☎800 595 PIER (outside Chicago); www.navypier.com. A city landmark with 50 acres (20ha)of parks, gardens, shops, restaurants & attractions, including a Ferris wheel, carousel & children's museum. The 3,000ft pier was one of several planned for the city but the only one actually to be constructed (in 1916).

Robie House   5757 S Woodlawn; ☎708 848 1976; www.wrightplus.org; ☺ Thu–Mon; admission charge. Designed by Frank Lloyd Wright, this spectacular building features 174 art-glass windows & doors. Daily tours & special events. The house is managed by the Frank Lloyd Wright Foundation.

Pullman Community   11111 Forestville Av; ☎773 785 8901. America's earliest railway sleeping cars were made here by the businessman & inventor George Mortimer Pullman's Palace Company. They were the first to have electric

lights & folding berths. Pullman's company town was designed in 1885 by an English architect, Solon Beman, as a model community for 12,000 workers. Some were expert carriage makers who had arrived from Germany. Most of the town was built around the factory between 1880 & 1884, & included a church, school & library but no saloon. Workers lived in houses which reflected their level of skills.

Pullman is a designated landmark district & most of the original buildings in the town are still standing. The Hotel Florence, built in 1881, is the community's showpiece but hundreds of homes are undergoing restoration. Pullman is located about 14 miles south of downtown but can easily be reached by Metra train on the Illinois Central Gulf Railroad.

The Historic Pullman Foundation Visitor Center is at 11141 S Cottage Grove Av (☎*773 785 8901 for group tours of 20 or more people; www. pullmanil.org*), 14 miles south of downtown Chicago. Take CTA bus #111 or Metra train. Guided walking tours leave from the Visitor Center on the first Sun of the month between May & Oct.

A Philip Randolph/Pullman Porter Museum   10406 S Maryland; ☎773 928 3935; www.aphiliprandolphmuseum.com; ☺ Thu–Sat; admission charge. Located in the Pullman District, this museum gallery is named after Asa Philip Randolph, chief organiser of the Brotherhood of the Sleeping Car Porters (BSCP) & once regarded by some people in government as 'one of the most dangerous Negroes in America'. Wonderful photographs & memorabilia show the struggle between corporate power & disenfranchised workers in 1937, when Randolph chartered the first African-American labour union.

All aboard!

The *California Zephyr* departs Chicago on BNSF Railway Company tracks with the city skyline diminishing to your right. You should pass the eastbound *Zephyr* a few minutes out of Union Station. The westbound train continues at a modest pace through industrial scenes followed by many miles of suburbs such as Hinsdale, Westmont and Downer's Grove.

NAPERVILLE (30/60) Chicago's main western suburb has attractive restored buildings and a four-mile-long river walk. Commuter trains provide connections to La Grange, Cicero and Aurora.

Aurora (10/50) A stone roundhouse and other early railway buildings can be seen to your right. Double-decked commuter trains wait on your left. Aurora has been a transport junction since stagecoach days and in 1908 was the first American city to have electric street lights. The Chicago, Burlington & Quincy Railroad was formed here in 1849. Not just a place but a state of mind, Aurora was the setting for the excellent *Wayne's World*.

Look right as the train leaves to see the Caterpillar Tractor company's water tower and factory. You then cross the Fox River before travelling among corn fields and the small communities of Plano, Sandwich, Somonauk and Mendota.

PRINCETON (60/60) 'The pig capital of the world' began as a New Englander settlement in 1833. It was the home of John Bryant, a founder of the Republican Party, and the anti-slavery Underground Railroad had a 'station' here. Richard Widmark grew up in Princeton and first began acting at Lake Forest College. An old caboose from the Burlington Railway can be seen to your left just before the train station.

Wyanet (15/45) Look for some of the large local population of pigs and cattle.

Kewanee (30/30) Located next to the Spoon River, this was another early New Englander settlement. The town's name is a Native American word for 'prairie chicken'.

Galva (40/20) Swedish dissidents set up the utopian community of Bishop's Hill among these wooden houses in the 19th century.

GALESBURG (60/50) Former home town of George Washington Ferris, creator of the original Ferris wheel, and Olmsted Ferris, who invented popcorn. The Marx brothers are said to have received their nicknames here during a poker game in 1914. The **National Railroad Hall of Fame** is at 200 East Main (℡ *309 345 4634; www.nrrhof.org*) and Galesburg hosts the Railroad Days festival each June. To your right is the copper spire of Knox College. Galesburg was another station on the secret Underground Railroad for escaped slaves. A 1930s Hudson engine with its coach and caboose stands to the right of Amtrak's attractive canopied station. Thruway buses connect with *Texas Eagle* trains stopping at Springfield.

Monmouth (20/30) Wyatt Earp was born here and the railway brought a large block of granite to Monmouth to build a monument in his honour. You travel on through a region of cattle farms and corn fields. Nearing the Mississippi River you start to see woodland, marshes and wildfowl.

Mississippi River (45/5) The train crosses on a 2,000ft-long (600m) steel bridge, giving wonderful views of the river and its forested banks. A graceful highway bridge reflects in the water to your right. The Mississippi is the world's third-longest river, stretching 2,350 miles (3,780km) to the Gulf of Mexico and draining a third of the United States. Before the railway bridge opened in 1868, passengers crossed here by ferry. During winter they sometimes went over the ice on foot. Crossing the river takes you from Illinois into Iowa.

BURLINGTON (50/30) The nearby Shoquoquon Hills were one of the few places in this area where flint could be found, so Native Americans came to regard them as neutral territory. Strategically placed next to the river, Burlington became a natural railroad centre and capital of both Wisconsin and Iowa. Look for the steam locomotive to the left of Amtrak's station at 300 S Main. This location played an important part in the history of rail technology when George Westinghouse developed the air brake on adjacent Burlington Hill from 1863 onwards.

The *California Zephyr* passes slowly through an older part of town, with warehouses and an ammunition factory on the left, before travelling among wide fields of maize and oats.

Danville (15/15) Trees surround a town once used by stagecoaches and the Pony Express.

MOUNT PLEASANT (30/40) The Old Settlers & Threshers Reunion celebrates America's frontier heritage each September in this typical Midwestern town. Vintage steam locomotives pull wooden coaches and cabooses on the **Midwest Central Railroad** (✆ *319 385 2912; www.mcrr.org*). The red building to your right is Iowa's Wesleyan College, dating from 1842. America's first toll roads with plank surfaces were laid between here and Burlington.

Soon after leaving Mount Pleasant the train crosses the Skunk River. Note the dilapidated Rock Island Line building on your right as you approach Ottumwa. Celebrated by Leadbelly and other balladeers, the Rock Island Line had a colourful history, beginning in 1852 when the first train out of Chicago sported a rainbow-painted locomotive and six bright-yellow coaches. Jesse James and his gang carried out their first hold-up on a Rock Island train, derailing its locomotive and killing the engineer. The railroad faced bankruptcy several times but somehow managed to struggle on over its weather-beaten tracks until the 1970s.

OTTUMWA (40/70) Named after a Native American tribe when this was a trading post on banks above the Des Moines River, Ottumwa subsequently became a business centre and 'home town' to *MASH*'s Radar O'Reilly.

You leave Ottumwa and cross the Des Moines River on its way to join the Mississippi.

OSCEOLA (70/30) Settlers in the 19th century discovered the first 'Delicious' apple tree 30 miles (48km) to the north of here at Winterset, where John Wayne was born and christened Marion Morrison. Osceola was named after a Seminole warrior chief whose wooden statue stands on your left beyond the station. Des Moines is 50 miles (80km) to the north.

As the train travels east look for some of the covered wooden bridges made famous by Robert Waller's book *The Bridges of Madison County*, and by the subsequent film starring Clint Eastwood. The story takes place in Winterset and this small town has been invaded by romantics attempting to trace the steps of the star-crossed lovers.

CRESTON (30/105) This railroad town set on a ridge between the Des Moines and Missouri valleys is the *Zephyr*'s highest point east of the Missouri River. The beautiful, restored yellow-brick rail depot to your right is a national landmark that now houses the Chamber of Commerce, a museum and Creston City Hall. Farmers' co-operatives' silos, also on your right, provide the town's best viewing platform.

The train continues among cornfields, neat towns, woods, quiet rivers, cattle and horse farms. Sometimes you may catch sight of a roving coyote.

Stanton (40/65) Look right for the famous water tower shaped like a coffee pot, complete with handle. Also to your right is the town's courthouse building.

Council Bluffs (75/30) This pioneer trading post became the eastern end of the Union Pacific Railroad leading to California. A former Rock Island depot at 1512 Main houses the **Railswest Railroad Museum** and model railroad (℡ *712 323 5182; www.thehistoricalsociety.org/Depot.htm*).

The **Union Pacific Railroad Museum** is at 200 Pearl Street (℡ *712 329 8307; www.uprr.com;* ☺ *Tue–Sat; free*). Artefacts, photographs and documents trace the development of the railroad and the American West. The collection dates from the mid 1800s, and features original editions of reports from survey teams that searched for the best land route for the construction of the nation's first transcontinental railroad.

Missouri River (80/25) From its source in the Montana Mountains (where the Gallatin, Jefferson and Madison rivers converge), the Missouri River comes through here to join the Mississippi at St Louis. Crossing 'Big Muddy' takes you from Iowa into Nebraska.

Offutt Air Force Base (90/15) The airfield and Strategic Air Command Museum are seen to your left before you approach Omaha through extensive freight yards.

OMAHA (105/60) This was the birthplace of Fred Astaire, Marlon Brando, Montgomery Clift, Malcolm X and Henry Fonda, and is the home of businessman Warren Buffett, the 'Sage of Omaha'. Mormons wintered here in 1846 on their way to Utah and Omaha played an important part in the great days of westward migration, being a stop on the first transcontinental railroad. The Union Stockyards have been in business since 1884 and the city deals mostly in grain and cattle raised on the prairies.

Omaha basics

℡ **Telephone code** 402

🚂 **Station** *(Ticket office & waiting room* ☺ *midnight–06.30 & 21.30–23.59; information* ℡ *342 1501)* Amtrak's modest brick station is a mile from downtown at 1003 S Ninth. Vending machines, handcarts, taxi stand. Next to the Amtrak station is a massive old Burlington Northern building.

Connections Thruway buses connect with Kansas City & St Joseph.

🚌 **Local transport** MAT bus information & maps are available at the Park Fair Mall, 16th & Douglas (℡ *341 0800; www.metroareatransit. com*).

🚕 **Taxis** Happy Cab ℡ 333 8294; Checker ℡ 339 0110

🚗 **Car rental** Midwest, 14116 W Center Rd; ℡ 333 3434

🚌 **Greyhound** 1601 Jackson; ℡ 341 1906

✈ **Eppley Airport** Can be reached by MAT bus #16 from Tenth St.

Tours The *River City Star*, 151 Freedom Park Rd; ℡ 342 7827; www.rivercitystar.com. The riverboat offers a wide range of day & night cruises along the Missouri River.

ℹ **Visitors bureau** 1001 Farnam; ℡ 444 4660; e info@visitomaha.com; www.visitomaha.com; ☺ Mon–Fri. For the events hotline, ℡ 444 6800.

🏠 **Accommodation** For B&B contact the Cornerstone Mansion, 140 N 39th; ℡ 558 7600.

Hotels include the Doubletree, 1616 Dodge; ℡ 346 7600, **$$$$**; Quality Inn, 2808 S 72nd; ℡ 397 7137, **$$$**; Crowne Plaza, 655 N 108th Av; ℡ 496 0850 or ℡ 800 227 6963, **$$$**; Hampton Inn, 3301 S 72nd; ℡ 391 8129, **$$**; Super 8, 7111 Spring; ℡ 390 0700, **$**; Candlewood Suites, 360 S 108th Av; ℡ 877 859 5095, **$**.

Durham Western Heritage Museum 801 S Tenth; ☎ 444 5071; www.durhammuseum. org; ⊕ Tue–Sun; admission charge. The Union Pacific collection, formerly housed in the UP headquarters building at 12th & Dodge, is now located here. The museum describes the railroad's long & sometimes controversial history, & includes an auditor's office, Abraham Lincoln's funeral car with its original furnishings, & the surveying instruments of General Grenville M Dodge, who was the Union Pacific's chief engineer & responsible for constructing some of America's most vital early routes. There is also a research facility & library. The photograph collection contains an estimated 590,000 images, some of which can be viewed in the UPRR Photo Gallery (*www.uprr.com/aboutup/photos*). The famous picture of the Golden Spike ceremony shows General Dodge shaking hands with Samuel S Montague of the Central Pacific.

Old Market Farnam to Jackson sts, Tenth to 13th; ☎ 341 7151 or ☎ 346 4445; www. omahaoldmarket.com. Bookstores, art galleries, antique shops, pubs & more than 30 restaurants populate this historic neighbourhood.

Murdock Historical Society & Museum 9014 310th; ☎ 867 3331; www.murdockmuseum.org; ⊕ Sun; free. The settlement of Murdock began in 1890 when it was a water stop on the Rock Island Railroad. Many German settlers moved to this area & the Historical Society Museum tells their story.

Joslyn Art Museum 2200 Dodge; ☎ 342 3300; www.joslyn.org; ⊕ Tue–Sun; admission charge. Nebraska's only fine arts museum opened in 1931. The encyclopaedic collection features works from antiquity to the present with a special emphasis on 19th- & 20th-century art from Europe & America. Designed as a cultural centre for the community, the museum was built as a gift to Omaha from Sarah Joslyn in memory of her husband George, a prominent Omaha businessman & community leader.

Greenwood Depot Museum 340 N Broad, in Greenwood; ☎ 789 3175. Cass County's only preserved depot is almost 130 years old & contains history of the town & surrounding area.

Malcolm X Birthsite 3448 Pinkney; ☎ 455 5253; ⊕ daily; free. Visit the house where the 1960s civil rights activist Malcom X was born on 19 May 1925.

Henry Doorly Zoo 3701 S Tenth; ☎ 733 8401; www.omahazoo.com; ⊕ daily; admission charge. Gorillas, orang-utans & white tigers live beside the Missouri River in Omaha's greatest tourist attraction, which has the largest indoor rainforest in the world. The aquarium features sharks & king penguins. Union Pacific has funded a new engine house from where steam trains chug through the grounds on a 30in-gauge line originally laid with help from the Union Pacific in 1968.

Boys Town Located 10 miles west of the city at 137th & W Dodge Rd; ☎ 1 800 625 1400; www. boystown.org; ⊕ daily; free. Boys Town was founded in 1917 as a home for underprivileged youngsters by Father Flanagan, played in the *Boys Town* film by Spencer Tracy. Boys Town is now a National Historic Landmark with attractions that include Father Flanagan's House, a working farm & 2 Gothic chapels.

Strategic Air & Space Museum 28210 W Park Hwy in Ashland; ☎ 944 3100; www. strategicairandspace.com; ⊕ daily; admission charge. The museum includes a flight simulator & has many aircraft & missiles to show the entire development of military aviation.

All aboard!

The *Zephyr* leaves past high-rises to the right and rolls on across Nebraska, crossing the Platte River midway between Omaha and Lincoln. The course of this river was followed west by Mormons, and later by the Pony Express and settlers on the Oregon Trail.

LINCOLN (60/90) Nebraska University appears to your left as the train approaches the station with the state fairgrounds to your right. Amtrak occupies the north end of an old Burlington & Northern building, using a renovated waiting room called the Great Hall. Lincoln's 400ft-high (120m) State Capitol, known as the 'tower of the plains', can be seen on your left and is the only unicameral (single house) state legislature in the country. The statue on its gold dome represents a man scattering seed. Lincoln's **visitors bureau** is at Seventh and P (☏ *402 434 5348; www.lincoln. org/visiting*).

HASTINGS (90/50) The town is a centre for trade and manufacturing, especially of farm machinery and Kool-Aid, invented here in 1927. Grand Island, 30 miles (48km) north, is home to the **Stuhr Museum of the Prairie Pioneer** (*3133 W Hwy 34;* ☏ *308 385 5316; www.stuhrmuseum.org;* ⊕ *daily; admission charge*). The cottage where Henry Fonda was born is one of 60 authentic buildings in Railroad Town, which recreates a prairie community of the late 19th century. The railyard includes an 1890 depot, turntable, steam locomotives and rolling stock.

The countryside becomes progressively drier as the *California Zephyr* pulls out of Hastings and travels west, moving gradually from farmland into predominantly cattle country.

Kenesaw (15/35) You cross the Oregon Trail once used by wagon trains.

HOLDREGE (50/70) Named after George Holdrege, a former manager of the Chicago, Burlington & Quincy Railroad.

MCCOOK (70/115) This was a division point on the railroad before becoming an oil town.

Nebraska–Colorado state line (70/45) As you change from Central to Mountain Time, watches go back an hour (forward when travelling east). The *California Zephyr* leaves Nebraska and travels towards Denver over the high plains of eastern Colorado, which used to be buffalo territory.

FORT MORGAN (115/80) The fort dates from 1864, since when the town has grown rich on oil and cattle. Fort Morgan is the burial place of science fiction writer Philip K Dick and was the boyhood home of Big Band musician Glenn Miller.

Pike's Peak (60/20) This 14,110ft (4,300m) mountain is just visible on the far left horizon. It was on top of Pike's Peak in 1893 that Katherine Lee Bates was inspired to write the words to 'America the Beautiful'. The Rockies are 80 miles (130km) away to your right.

Commerce City (65/15) Denver's chief industrial suburb boasts America's busiest sheep market and largest sugar beet factories. Look for extensive cattle yards beside the track.

Riverside Cemetery (70/10) The pioneer graveyard to your right dates from 1876. As the train passes beneath Interstate 70, look for Denver's skyline on your left. The front of the train comes into view on the right, turning north before reversing into the station.

DENVER (80/120) 'The mile-high city' was a gold rush town founded in 1858, when flakes of gold were discovered at nearby Cherry Creek. Many narrow-gauge railroads were built to serve the camps and in 1876 a route was opened via the steep black rock walls of Clear Creek Canyon to the town of Central City. It was here that George Pullman was working as a miner when he thought of the idea for his sleeping car.

The Union Pacific bypassed Denver on its transcontinental route but citizens built their own railroad to meet it at Cheyenne, Wyoming. This line and the Kansas City railroad helped transform Denver from a frontier town (where Bat Masterson patrolled the saloons) into one of the fastest-growing cities in the United States, with a population of over two million (not counting the Carringtons). Skyscrapers glitter in the brilliant light and older parts of the city have been restored.

Denver invented the cheeseburger and brews more beer than anywhere else in the world, yet still claims to have America's thinnest residents. The dry climate and high altitude make this city unique, so treat its pure sunlight with respect and allow a few days to become acclimatised before undertaking anything too strenuous. Many ski resorts are close by and equipment can easily be hired.

Denver basics

☎Telephone code 303

⚐ Station (*Ticket office & waiting room* ⊕ *05.00–21.30; information* ☎ *534 2812*) When Union Station at 1701 Wynkoop opened in 1881 it was the biggest train station in the west & the largest building in Colorado. Built in Italian Romanesque style with neoclassical additions, it received 80 trains a day & served a million passengers a year. Lockers, ATM banking, Red Caps, newspapers, handcarts, snack bar, shop, taxi stand.

Connections Thruway buses connect with Boulder, Cheyenne & Laramie, as well as Colorado Springs & Pueblo.

🚌 Local transport RTD light rail trains & buses (☎ *299 6000; www.rtd-denver.com*) serve downtown & the suburbs, with maps & schedules from the station. A free MallRide shuttle service runs along 16th St, between RTD's Civic Center Station & Union Station.

🚕 Taxis Yellow ☎ 777 7777; Freedom ☎ 292 8900

🚗 Car rental Avis, 1900 Broadway; ☎ 839 1280

🚌 Greyhound 1055 19th; ☎ 293 6555

✈ Denver International Airport The airport cost $4.3 billion, covers an area twice the size of Manhattan & has its own underground railway. The RTD 'SkyRide' has frequent bus services from the airport to dozens of locations downtown.

Tours Gray Line city & mountain excursions leave from the Cherry Creek Shopping Center at 3000 E First Av (☎ *289 2841*). The Denver Rail Heritage Society operates riverfront rides on summer w/ends (☎ *458 6255*). Walking tours can be taken with Denver History (☎ *720 234 7929; www.denverhistorytours.com*).

ℹ Visitors bureau 1600 California; ☎ 892 1505; www.denver.org; ⊕ Mon–Sat; closed Sun & holidays. For a free guide to Denver, ☎ 800 233 6837 or visit the website.

🏠 Accommodation Adagio Bed & Breakfast, 1430 Race; ☎ 370 6911; www.adagiobb.com.

International Youth Hostel, 630 E 16th Av; ☎ 832 9996. Dormitory rooms, **$**.

Hotels include the Brown Palace, 321 17th; ☎ 800 321 2599, **$$$$**; Fairfield Inn, 1680 S Colorado Bd; ☎ 691 2223, **$$$**; Residence Inn, 2777 Zuni; ☎ 458 5318, **$$$$$**; Broadway Plaza, 1111 Broadway; ☎ 893 0303, **$$**; Comfort Inn, 401 17th; ☎ 296 0400, **$$**; Standish, 1530 California; ☎ 534 3231, **$**.

Recommended in Denver

Larimer Square This historic part of the city, once the haunt of outlaws, has Victorian houses, courtyards, gaslights, craft shops, restaurants & nightclubs.

US Mint 320 W Colfax; ☎ 405 4761; www. usmint.gov; ⊕ Mon–Fri; free tours (reservations are required & can be booked through the website) but no free samples! The mint, located in an Italian Renaissance-style building, is the largest single producer of coins in the world, producing 10 billion a year. It also boasts more gold bullion (an estimated $100 billion worth) than anywhere outside Fort Knox. Souvenir coins are on sale.

Denver Art Museum 13th & Acoma; 📞720 865 5000; www.denverartmuseum.org; ☺ Tue–Sun; admission charge. The spectacular 28-sided museum building houses over 40,000 works, including the world's finest Native American art collection. The New-World gallery has 5,000 pre-Columbian & Spanish colonial works, & there are pictures by Georgia O'Keeffe, Degas, Matisse, Monet, Picasso & Renoir. The spirit of the American West is captured by artists such as Frederic Remington & Norman Rockwell.

State Capitol 200 E Colfax; 📞866 2604; ☺ Mon–Fri; free tours. Murals, unique Colorado onyx & a dome covered with gold leaf, plus balcony views towards the Rockies & north to the Wyoming border. The 15th step on the west side is exactly 1 mile above sea level.

Black American West Museum & Heritage Center 3091 California, opposite Amtrak's station; 📞720 242 7428; www. blackamericanwestmuseum.com; ☺ Tue–Sat; admission charge. A third of working cowboys in the Old West were African-Americans, often freed slaves who travelled west after the Civil War. This museum uses photographs, personal belongings, clothing & oral histories to tell the story of black pioneers, buffalo soldiers, African-American cowboys & businessmen who helped settle the west.

Coors Brewery 13th & Ford St in Golden; 📞866 812 2337; www.coors.com; ☺ Mon–Sat. The Coors Brewery has been in business since 1873 & this is the largest single brewing site in the world. Over 10 million people have taken the free tour, which takes you through the entire brewing process & lets you sample the products in the hospitality lounge.

Colorado Railroad Museum 17155 W 44th Av in Golden, 12 miles west of Denver; 📞279 4591; www.coloradorailroadmuseum.org; ☺ daily; admission charge. The replica 1880s-style masonry depot has 50,000 rare photographs & artefacts. The sprawling grounds contain more than 50 narrow- & standard-gauge locomotives, cars & other rolling stock, including some of the oldest in the state. A large model railroad recreates local lines such as those at Cripple Creek, Telluride & Tennessee Pass. Over 2,000 miles of tracks once probed the local mountain canyons, & there are short steam train rides at w/ends.

Forney Transportation Museum 4303 Brighton Bd; 📞297 1113; www.forneymuseum. com; ☺ Mon–Sat; admission charge. The museum features locomotives, including a 1941 Union Pacific 'Big Boy', as well as horse-drawn vehicles & antique cars such as Amelia Earhart's *Kissel Kar* & a Mercedes belonging to Hitler's US ambassador.

All aboard!

The *California Zephyr* departs on Union Pacific tracks, having arrived on the BNSF line from Chicago. Look back to your right for terrific views of Denver.

Arvada (20/100) You pass through another major suburb with the Front Range of the Rockies ahead. Mount Evans (14,264ft/4,350m) is on your left and Long's Peak (14,255ft/4,345m) on your right. The road up to Mount Evans is the highest paved road in North America.

Rocky (40/80) The train takes an S-shaped curve to gain height among the foothills. Winds can reach 100mph (160km/h) here so the track is protected at Big 10 Curve by railroad cars anchored with sand. The *Zephyr* climbs a 2% gradient and enters the first of 29 tunnels, with Coal Creek Canyon on your left.

Plainview (50/70) Look for spectacular sightings of the barren Colorado plains 1,500ft (450m) below and the whole city of Denver back to your right. Rocky Flats nuclear weapons factory can be seen in the foreground. To your right are Colorado University and the city of Boulder. The train rumbles on into the Rockies through South Boulder Canyon.

Gross Reservoir (60/60) A 340ft-high (100m) dam provides Denver with 14 billion gallons (62 billion litres) of water. Look out for deer and elk as you enter the Roosevelt National Forest with the continental divide ahead.

Moffat Tunnel (105/15) The tunnel is over six miles (10km) long and is the highest point (9,239ft/2,820m) on Amtrak's network. Before the tunnel opened in 1928, reducing the distance between Denver and Salt Lake City by 65 miles (100km), trains took five hours to cross the continental divide around James Peak (13,260ft/4,040m). Now the journey takes only ten minutes before you emerge from darkness into dazzling light.

Winter Park Ski Resort (115/5) Ski slopes appear close by on your left.

WINTER PARK (120/20) One of many mountain parks in a densely wooded region which is famous for pine trees, tourists and ranching. The train station is actually in Fraser – called 'the icebox of America' because temperatures sometimes get as low as –50°F (–46°C). Look on a ridge to your right to see the Devil's Thumb rock formation.

Tabernash (5/15) Named after a Native American chief. Before the Moffat Tunnel opened, helper (pusher) locomotives would be added here to enable trains to climb over Rollins Pass.

Fraser Canyon (10/5) The *Zephyr* accompanies the clear, trout-laden Fraser River, where President Eisenhower often came to fish.

GRANBY (20/180) This area of meadow lands is known as Middle Park. Trail Ridge Road (the world's highest car road) runs through Rocky Mountain National Park to your right. Evidence has been found locally of people who pre-date all known Native American tribes.

After Granby the train joins the Colorado River near its source and accompanies it for more than 200 miles (320km), making this one of the longest stretches of river followed by a train route anywhere in the world.

Hot Sulphur Springs (15/165) Thermal springs heat the indoor swimming pool to your right.

Byers Canyon (16/164) Spiky rock formations tower above the track and Highway 40 can be seen on your left. Watch for herds of deer and the occasional buffalo as the train picks up speed through prime cattle country.

Kremmling (35/145) The town is on your right and Mount Powell (13,534ft/4,125m) to your left.

Gore Canyon (40/85) Sheer rock walls reach 1,500ft (450m) and make the canyon accessible only by train. The Gore Range to your left touches 13,000ft (4,000m). Coming out of the canyon you travel through meadows and ranch land. Just before Bond you see the old State Bridge to your left.

Bond (100/80) A historic railroad town where the Rio Grande branch line to Steamboat Springs can be seen above on the right. The cut-off line between Bond and Dotsero was built by the Denver & Salt Lake Railroad.

Red Canyon (110/65) Spaniards called this place Colorado (meaning red) after seeing the vivid colours of these strange rock formations.

Dotsero (140/40) An 1885 survey of the Colorado River marked this point '.0' or 'dot-zero' on its maps and it represents the midpoint of the *California Zephyr*'s journey. The Eagle River joins the Colorado on your left.

Glenwood Canyon (155/10) Brightly coloured rocks, cliffs, aspen trees and evergreens proliferate as you follow the river. Interstate 70, one of the longest highways ever built, is on the far shore.

GLENWOOD SPRINGS (180/100) A centre for fishing, hiking and white-water rafters who come to brave the rapids. The ski resorts of Snowmass and Aspen, where you might bump into Jack Nicholson or Martina Navratilova, can be reached by bus. On your right is one of the world's largest outdoor swimming pools, heated all year round by Yampa Hot Springs. Beyond the pool is Theodore Roosevelt's favourite, Colorado Hotel. John Henry 'Doc' Holliday, the gambler, gunfighter and part-time dentist, lived and was buried here when he died at the age of 35. Sheriff Pat Garrett was also buried nearby. Amtrak's attractive stone and red-tile station to your left has unusual square Chinese-style towers.

As the train leaves along a typical Rocky Mountain valley, look for rafters riding on the Roaring Fork River joining the Colorado to your left.

New Castle (30/70) Named after Newcastle, England. Massive oil shale deposits have been discovered in this area and some are visible in the cliffs to your right. Also to your right is Mount Baxter (11,188ft/3,410m). In 1896, 54 workers died in a local coal mine explosion and a second disaster in 1931 killed 37 more. The mine continues to burn.

Grand Valley (70/30) The aptly named Parachute Mountains can be seen to your right.

De Beque-Palisade (80/20) The beautiful and majestic Grand Mesa on your left is the world's largest flat-top mountain (over 10,000ft/3,000m). This region produces great quantities of fruit, especially peaches and apricots. As you approach Grand Junction among fruit fields, vineyards and orchards, look for a goat farm on your right.

GRAND JUNCTION (100/85) Where the Gunnison and Colorado rivers meet the Denver and Rio Grande railroads. Amtrak's station is on the left at 339 S First. Grand Junction is a centre for agriculture and the coal industry, as well as a base for visitors travelling to Mesa Verde National Park, Grand Mesa Forest and Colorado National Monument. The last's red cliffs are visible to your left as you leave.

Ruby Canyon (20/65) Another splendid photo opportunity as the train winds through beautifully coloured rocks carved by the Colorado River out of the Uncompahgre Plateau. Bald and golden eagles ride currents of air along the canyon walls and above the river. Several sets of *moki* steps on your right show where Anastosia Indians used to climb, and a sign marks the Colorado–Utah border. Moki steps are small depressions carved into the rock by early inhabitants to make climbing easier.

At Westwater the Colorado goes south and enters a quite different landscape, travelling 150 miles (240km) through sandy desert. Watch for antelope as you cross the dried riverbeds of this arid region, which used to be below sea level. The massive eroding mesas to your right are the intricately carved Book Cliffs, made from sandstone and shale. La Sal Mountains can be seen in the left distance.

Thompson (60/25) The white and green station on the left is a flag stop, so trains halt only on request. Look beyond the station for the Sweet Grills Café featured in the film *Thelma and Louise*.

Rich in uranium, this part of Utah has dramatic and sometimes desolate scenery. Nearby are Arches National Monument, Dead Horse Point, Canyonlands National Park and Monument Valley (star of many John Ford westerns, including *Stagecoach*).

GREEN RIVER (85/70) Look for fields of cantaloupes and watermelons before you cross the Green River and enter the town of the same name. Green River Bible Church is to your right. An altitude of 4,075ft (1,240m) makes this the lowest point on the line between Denver and Salt Lake City. To your left are Mount Marvine (11,600ft/3,540m) and Thousand Lake Mountain (11,306ft/3,450m).

HELPER (70/120) Named after the extra locomotives once attached here to westbound freight trains to enable them to climb the mountains. The **Western Mining and Railroad Museum** (*294 S Main;* ✎ *435 472 3009; wmrrm.org; free admission, donation requested*) is housed in the Old Helper Hotel building and tells the history of the railroad, mining and the lifestyles of the multi-ethnic immigrants who came to the area between 1880 and about 1936 to work on the railroad and in the coal mines. Burlington Northern freight wagons stand on your right and Helper remains a busy centre for shipping coal, of which this region has enough to supply America for hundreds of years.

You leave past a western downtown district to your left, where a large brick building on the hillside belongs to the Utah Railway. As the train heads into the Wasatch Mountains by way of Soldier Summit it is joined on the left by the Price River. The conglomeration of machinery to your right, ten minutes from Helper, is a coal-processing plant.

Castle Gate (15/105) So called because the rock walls resemble a castle. Also high up on the right is Balancing Rock, topped by a flying flag. The train robber Butch Cassidy lived in this area and is said to have held up the Pleasant Valley Coal Company here for $7,000 in gold in 1897.

Soldier Summit (60/60) The 7,440ft (2,270m) peak's name commemorates Southern Army soldiers who were caught in a sudden snowstorm and buried here in 1861. Look for the abandoned mine to your right. The train descends sharply from this summit of the snow-capped Wasatch Mountains by a series of horseshoe curves into the Spanish Fork River Canyon. You may catch sight of deer and elk as you travel between the rusty red and white canyon walls.

Thistle (100/20) Heavy rains caused a mudslide in 1983 which deluged the village of Thistle along with the river and parts of the Rio Grande tracks. The route had to be closed for three months while a 3,000ft (910m) tunnel was constructed beneath Billy's Mountain. Old tracks can be seen below to your left and remnants of the village are visible just before the tunnel.

Look for llamas and horses in fields to your right as the train approaches Springville.

Springville (115/5) The colonial building on the right was once a school.

PROVO (120/55) Founded by Mormons in 1849, Utah's third-biggest city is the headquarters of Brigham Young University (America's largest private college) as well as the Osmond family. Provo's nondescript industrial buildings and car-wrecking yards are set among beautiful mountain ranges, with the Uinta and Manti La Sal national forests close by.

The *Zephyr* crosses the Provo River with US Steel's Geneva Works to the right. Mount Timpanogos (11,750ft/3,575m) is also to the right and Mount Nebo on your left.

Utah Lake (15/40) The lake is to your left with the Tintic Mountains in the distance.

Riverton (25/30) Kennecott copper mine, once the largest in the world, is among the hills to your left. Nearing Salt Lake City, look right for the Salt Lake Temple and domed State Capitol.

SALT LAKE CITY (55/250) Founded in 1847 by Brigham Young and other pioneers seeking to practise their beliefs in freedom, Mormon influence still dominates this pretty valley between the Wasatch Mountains and the Oquirrh Range. The Golden Spike ceremony which completed the first transcontinental rail route took place 40 miles (60km) north of here at Promontory Summit.

Salt Lake City is an attractive place with clean air, wide streets and downtown crossing signals that chirrup endearingly. Nearby ski resorts include Alta (America's second oldest) and Sundance (proprietor Robert Redford). Five national parks with dramatic rock scenery are within a single day's drive.

Salt Lake City basics

Telephone code 801
Station (*Ticket office & waiting room* ☺ *midnight–05.30 & 22.00–23.59; information* ☏*531 0188*) The station used by Amtrak is at 340 S 600 W. Lockers, vending machines, handcarts, restaurant, taxi stand.
Connections Thruway buses go to Ogden, Utah, & Boise, Idaho, as well as south to Las Vegas, Nevada.
Local transport Utah Transit Authority buses (☏*743 3882; www.rideuta.com*) visit most tourist attractions. UTA also provides an extensive bus & light rail (TRAX) service to the ski resorts & Provo as well as throughout the valley.
Taxis City ☏363 5500; Yellow ☏521 2100
Car rental Advantage, 460 S Redwood Rd; ☏973 4499
Greyhound 300 S 600 W; ☏355 9579

Salt Lake City International Airport 5 miles west of the city by UTA bus #50.
Tours Gray Line ☏433 6510. City Tours ☏534 1001. For a free 15min guided tour on the open-air trolley (☺ *Mon–Sat*) giving an overview of the Mormon sites, ☏240 6279.
Visitors bureau 90 S West Temple; ☏0800 541 4955; www.visitsaltlake.com; ☺ daily; free guide
Accommodation For B&B contact Alpine Cottage/saltair, 164 S 900 E, Salt Lake City, UT 84102-410; ☏533 8184.
Avenues (AYH) Youth Hostel, 107 F; ☏359 3855; e Info@saltlakehostel.com; www. saltlakehostel.com. Take UTA bus #3 from Amtrak's station. Members & non-members, **$**. Ute Hostel, 21 E Kelsey Av; ☏595 1645. Free transport to & from the airport & train station. Some private rooms. Dormitory rooms, **$**.

Hotels include the Brigham Street Inn, 1135 E South Temple; ☏364 4461, **$$**; Crystal Inn-Downtown, 230 W 500 S; ☏328 4466, **$$**; Little America Hotel, 500 S Main; ☏596 5700, **$$**; Days Inn Central, 315 W 3300 S; ☏486 8780, **$$**; Salt City Inn, 1025 N 900 W; ☏328 8520, **$$**; Carlton, 140 E South Temple; ☏800 633 3500, **$**.

Recommended in Salt Lake City

Temple Square 50 W South Temple; ☏240 2534; www.visittemplesquare.com. The heart of the Church of Jesus Christ of Latter-Day Saints is a 6-spired temple which can only be entered by Mormon Church members. Film shows & tours take place elsewhere. The Mormon Tabernacle Choir (☏240 4150) broadcasts a TV & radio programme each Sun morning (*free*) & there are daily recitals on the temple's 11,623-pipe organ, complete with light effects. Free concerts take place in summer on Tue & Fri evenings in Brigham Young Historic Park (☏240 3323).

Buildings of interest within walking distance including the Lion House at 63 E South Temple, an elegant mansion named after the stone lion sculpted for the front porch, & the 1847 Deuel Pioneer Log Home, one of the first log houses built in the Salt Lake Valley. Brigham Young's Beehive House at 67 E South Temple (☏240 2671) provides free tours & traditional candy.

The Church Office Building 50 E North Temple; ☏240 2190; ☉ Mon–Fri; free. The tallest structure in Salt Lake City is this world headquarters of the Church of Jesus Christ of Latter-Day Saints. An observation deck on the 26th floor gives spectacular views of the valley & surrounding mountains.

Family History Library 35 N West Temple; ☏240 2584; ☉ Mon–Sat; free tours. Trace your family line among over 2 million rolls of microfilm, 742,000 microfiche and 300,000 books in the largest library of its kind in the world.

Family Search Center Joseph Smith Memorial Bldg, 15 E South Temple; ☏240 4085; www.familysearch.org; ☉ Mon–Sat; free. Another likely place to check out your ancestors, with a vast collection of compiled genealogical data on 475 computers & the aid of helpful staff.

The Capitol At the north end of State St; ☏538 1800; ☉ Mon–Sat. This impressive state house was constructed from marble & granite beneath a copper dome.

Pioneer Memorial Museum 300 N Main; ☏538 1050; ☉ daily; free. Pioneer artefacts including clothes & vehicles are looked after by ladies every bit as formidable as those in the photographs.

Trolley Square 602 E 500 S; ☏521 9877; ☉ Mon–Sat; free. Originally a fairground, this city block was the site of the Utah Light & Railway Company's trolley system carbarn complex. Now a registered historic place, it has been carefully converted into a shopping & entertainment centre. Walking tour highlights include the original 97ft-high water tower & a stained-glass dome from the First Methodist Church in Long Beach, California.

Gardner Mill 1100 W 7800 S; ☏566 8903; www.gardnervillage.com; ☉ Mon–Sat; free. Scottish immigrant Archibald Gardner was one of the original settlers with Brigham Young & he set up mills here in the 19th century. His main mill is now a restaurant & many historic buildings have been moved here to recreate a village, complete with a stream winding among connecting pathways & covered bridges.

Hansen Planetarium 110 S 400 ☏456 7827; www.hansenplanetarium.net; ☉ daily; admission charge. Built in 1904, this planetarium is the place to watch Utah skies. Star shows, laser/music concerts & science exhibits, including the International Space Station (ISS) project.

Great Salt Lake State Marina PO Box 16658, Salt Lake City, Utah 84116; ☏250 1898; www.stateparks.utah.gov/parks/salt-lake. Located about 16 miles west on Interstate 80, the lake was once part of Lake Bonneville & the water's high salt content makes swimming here a buoyant experience. The park is open all year round for picnics, boating & wildlife-watching.

All aboard!

The *California Zephyr* makes a long service stop before leaving on Union Pacific tracks, touching the edge of the Great Salt Lake before crossing Bonneville Salt

Flats. The run between here and Elko is Amtrak's longest without a scheduled halt. As you pass from Mountain to Pacific Time, watches should go back an hour (forward when travelling east).

ELKO (250/120) Legend has it that Elko was named by Charles Crocker, a superintendent of the Central Pacific Railroad who liked elk. The name Elko is also a Native American word for 'white woman'. The town was founded as a railhead for the White Pine mines in 1869 and was a stop for wagon trains on the Humboldt River Overland Trail. It is now a base for the region's many sheep and cattle ranches. Each spring the town holds the world chariot race championships.

As the train travels west, look for the Ruby Mountains to your left and the Independence Range on your right.

WINNEMUCCA (120/175) The *Zephyr* makes a service stop in this town that changed its name from French Ford to that of a Paiute Indian chief. In 1900, Butch Cassidy's gang robbed the town's First National Bank, brimming with cash for local gold and silver mines. Formerly a trading post where wagons crossed the Humboldt River, Winnemucca is now a distribution point for agriculture and livestock.

The *California Zephyr* changes to Southern Pacific tracks before following the Humboldt River.

Lovelock (80/95) The Trinity Range is to your right and the Humboldt Mountains to your left. You cross the Humboldt Sink, a muddy region located in the middle of a desert.

Fernley (140/35) The Truckee River joins on the right and the train begins to trace it back to the High Sierras as far as Truckee.

MUSTANG RANCH (145/30) The red-tiled building to your left is Nevada's best-known little whorehouse.

Sparks (165/10) Note the old wooden station with its canopy, tower and peeling cream paint. Sparks has long been a railroad town and is a major distribution centre since the introduction of Nevada's tax-free warehousing scheme. Southern Pacific freight wagons stand on the left and the Nugget Casino on the right. Pyramid Lake's bird sanctuary, famous for pelicans, is 30 miles to the north.

As you leave Sparks and approach Reno look left to see MGM's massive Grand Sierra Casino.

RENO (175/55) 'The biggest little city in the world' tries hard to be Las Vegas but still retains its charm. What started as a Mormon settlement became more riotous once silver was discovered. Gambling was legalised in 1931, after which Reno began accumulating the neon-clad casinos which draw fun-seekers to Virginia Street, located on either side of Amtrak's Spanish-style station. If you plan to gamble, or just want to know what goes on behind the mirrors, you can take a behind-the-scenes tour. The station was built in 1926 by the Southern Pacific Railroad and was also used by the Virginia & Truckee Railroad. It was enlarged in 2007, and trains now dip down through downtown in what is locally called 'The Trench'. The **visitors bureau** is at 4001 S Virginia (☏ *775 827 7713 or* ☏ *800 FOR RENO (800 367 7366); www.visitrenotahoe.com)*.

The Harrah's Hotel's collection of antique cars is now housed in the **National Automobile Museum** (*10 S Lake;* \ *775 333 9300; www.automuseum.org*), and the **Liberty Belle Saloon** features old slot machines. Lake Tahoe, North America's largest alpine lake, is 35 miles (56km) southwest.

The *Zephyr* departs with the dome of St Thomas Aquinas Church a calming presence on your left. You travel through ranch country into Tahoe National Forest then cross the Sierra Nevada Range, which climbs to over 7,000ft (2,100m). Gold prospectors were the first white men to follow this route, which later became a heroic challenge to pioneer railroad constructors.

The train accompanies the fast-running Truckee River most of the way to the town of Truckee. On weekends (daily during summer) a guide from the California Railroad Museum joins the train across the Sierras to describe the line's history and places of interest.

Verdi (15/40) A hydro-electric generator on the far side of the Truckee River is powered by water brought along wooden flumes from the mountains. The first train robbery took place here on 4 November 1870, less than 18 months after the railroad arrived. The same *Atlantic Express* was robbed again less than 24 hours later in Independence, Nevada, and some of the loot is said to still be buried locally.

Nevada–California state line (20/35) Look right for the border mark. Wooden flumes on the cliffs to your left are relics of the mining industry.

Floriston (30/25) A splendid yellow mansion stands on the left.

Boca (40/15) The small dam to your right is all that remains of a town drowned beneath the reservoir. Boca formerly earned a living by supplying ice packed in sawdust to San Francisco. It once registered California's lowest-ever temperature (–45°F/–42°C) and became known as 'the coldest place in the nation'.

TRUCKEE (55/125) Named after Paiute Winnemucca's father, Chief Trukizo, and located on the banks of the Truckee River, the town had 14 lumber mills by the time the railroad arrived. Truckee managed to burn down six times between 1871 and 1882, but Chaplin filmed some of the remaining wooden buildings on Main Street for *The Gold Rush*.

Truckee is a gateway to Lake Tahoe and the ski resorts of Squaw Valley and Sugar Bowl. Pullman railway cars used to run from Oakland to Lake Tahoe but the branch line, abandoned in the 1940s, is now a cycle track. Amtrak's long, low station is on the right. For **tourist information**, the Truckee Visitors Center is at 10065 Donner Pass Road (\ *530 587 8808*).

After leaving town the train starts to ascend the Donner Pass in a sequence of horseshoe curves, providing fine views of the Truckee River basin below. All the trees are less than 100 years old because the original forest was demolished to feed wood-burning locomotives.

Donner Lake (15/110) Blizzards in 1846 trapped 87 Illinois settlers who had been travelling to California. By the time a relief party arrived here on 19 February 1847, nearly half the settlers, including five women and 14 children, had frozen to death or died from starvation. Others were reduced to cannibalism or had gone mad in the greatest single natural disaster of America's westward expansion. The place became known as Donner Pass after the Donner family, who were among the settlers. A museum on Donner Pass Road depicts their ordeal and describes the building of the Central Pacific Railroad.

Mount Judah (25/100) Nearing Judah's summit the slopes of Sugar Bowl ski resort can be seen on both sides of the track, joined by an overhead trestle. The train then enters a tunnel through the mountain named after the Central Pacific's designer, Theodore Judah.

Norden (35/90) Snowfall averages 34ft (10m) a year so building and maintaining this track is a remarkable achievement. The *City of San Francisco* was once snowbound here for four days but today's trains are often able to run when the nearby highway becomes impassable.

There used to be 37 miles (60km) of snow sheds between Truckee and Sacramento, leading some to describe the route as 'like railroading in a barn'. Sheds were usually made from wood and often caught fire during the days of steam power. Special fire trains had to be kept in readiness and only four miles (6.5km) of sheds now remain. On a mountain to your left is the small box which was once a fire lookout point.

Soda Springs (40/85) Lake Van Norden and the Soda Springs ski resort are to your left. On the other side of the valley to your right is Castle Peak, shaped like a fortress. Beside it is Black Butte Mountain (8,030ft/2,450m).

Emigrant Gap (65/60) Lake Spalding's irregular outline appears to your right as the train crosses Interstate 80. Trees sometimes grow almost horizontally in the alpine scenery. Pioneers used to lower wagons by rope into the beautiful Bear Valley on your right after travelling through Emigrant Gap.

Blue Canyon (70/55) Named after the blue haze produced by sawmills, this was a gold rush town and a servicing stop for steam trains.

American River Canyon (90/35) Astonishing views appear to your left as the train inches along evergreen-covered cliffs 1,800ft (550m) above the north fork of the American River. The remains of gold mine workings can be seen opposite in a valley that stretches all the way to Sacramento.

Alta (100/25) A red fire station stands on the right. Among the hills are flumes originally constructed by gold miners and which are now used to carry water to the farms below.

Gold Run (105/20) Note the old post office building to your left. Until it became illegal in 1884, hydraulic gold mining washed away huge sections of the hillside. The *California Zephyr*'s tracks run alongside the old mine site.

Cape Horn (118/7) This is the steepest slope on the *Zephyr*'s entire journey. Chinese labourers constructing the route were lowered on ropes to hack out a rocky ledge for the track. Lewis Metzler Clement was hired by Theodore Judah as one of the Central Pacific's chief assistant engineers and was primarily responsible for designing and building the section of the line between Truckee and Colfax, including Cape Horn, all the tunnels and the snow sheds. Although not present at the Golden Spike ceremony he is shown in the famous Thomas Hill painting standing behind Judah (who was by then dead) and Charles Crocker. Clement later worked on constructing the cable-car system in San Francisco.

Colfax can be seen ahead to your left as the train curves left over a highway.

COLFAX (125/60) Look left for a flea market and an ancient Southern Pacific railroad car housing a bank. During the gold rush, goods were brought to Colfax by mule for transfer into the mountains. The town became the Central Pacific's 'end of track' in 1865. Pears, grapes and prunes are now grown around the former 'mother lode' town.

As the *Zephyr* eases down the western side of the Sierra Nevada (the snowy mountains) look for drifts of wild lupins and red and yellow poppies.

Auburn (25/35) When gold was discovered at Coloma, just south of here, Auburn supplied the camps and administered claims. Among several preserved buildings is the 1893 fire house on your right, which boasted the first volunteer fire department west of Boston. Outlaws were publicly hanged in the grounds of the gold-domed Placer County Courthouse on your left.

As you leave, the town cemetery can be seen on a hill to your right before the train descends through less mountainous terrain and enters the fields, ranches and orchards of the Sacramento Valley.

Rocklin (45/15) Local granite was used as ballast (for laying railroad tracks) but only one quarry remains open.

ROSEVILLE (60/25) The *California Zephyr* picks its way carefully among the complexities of the Southern Pacific's rail yards. Note the large locomotive-maintenance shop next to a wooden station building to your left.

McClellan Air Force Base (10/15) The airfield and depots can be seen on your right. Closed in 2001, this former logistics and maintenance facility is now a civil–military airfield and business park. Approaching Sacramento, both sides of the track are engulfed by the Blue Diamond Company – the largest almond-processing plant in the world. Most of California's yearly crop of one million pounds (450 tonnes) find their way here and groves of almond trees can often be seen.

SACRAMENTO (25/20) For Sacramento and the rest of the *California Zephyr* route to San Francisco, see *Chapter 4, The* Coast Starlight (pages 49–70). The *Zephyr* makes a scheduled stop at Suisun-Fairfield.

The *San Joaquin*
San Francisco–Bakersfield
(via Emeryville/Oakland)

General route information

With fig trees, vineyards, date palms, orchards and oil wells, the San Joaquin Valley is definitive California: a heady blend of warmth and almond blossom. *San Joaquin* trains travel more than 300 miles (480km) between Emeryville/Oakland and Bakersfield, giving access to several national parks and some of the richest farm country in America.

Joining the train

SAN FRANCISCO For San Francisco, Emeryville/Oakland and the route to Martinez, see *Chapter 4, The* Coast Starlight (pages 49–70). *San Joaquin* trains initially travel north from Oakland towards Martinez, stopping *en route* at Richmond (described in the *Coast Starlight* chapter).

All aboard!

MARTINEZ (25/22) As the train leaves Martinez it parts company with the *California Zephyr* and *Coast Starlight* tracks, which continue over the bridge to

ESSENTIAL INFORMATION

FREQUENCY Four trains operate daily in each direction. Departure times are early morning, mid morning, early afternoon and late afternoon.
DURATION Six hours 15 minutes
CONNECTIONS Connecting buses link Emeryville with San Francisco, and Bakersfield with Los Angeles and Santa Barbara. An extensive Amtrak Thruway bus system operates in the Bay Area and throughout the Sacramento Valley. Trains and buses are funded by Amtrak and Caltrans (the California Department of Transportation) and are a good way to explore some of the less well-known parts of the state. Schedules are available from Amtrak agents or by post from Timetable, c/o Caltrans, Rail Program, PO Box 942874, Sacramento, CA 94274-0001. Information about Amtrak services in California can also be found on the website www.amtrakcalifornia.com.
RESERVATIONS All reserved
EQUIPMENT Bi-level California coaches. Railfone.
FOOD Complete meals, snacks, sandwiches, drinks
BAGGAGE Check-in service on all trains. Bicycle racks.

Antioch-Pittsburg
Martinez
Richmond — Stockton
Emeryville
Modesto
□ OAKLAND
SAN FRANCISCO

Turlock-Denair

Merced

Madera

N
Bradt

Fresno

Hanford

Corcoran

Wasco

BAKERSFIELD □

your left. Storage tanks and a Shell oil refinery appear on the right.

Mothball Fleet (12/10)
Across the bay to your left lies a fleet of transport ships kept in 'mothballs'. Many date from as long ago as World War II but some saw action in Vietnam and as recently as the Gulf War in 1991.

Between here and Antioch-Pittsburg, *San Joaquin* trains change from Southern Pacific tracks to those of the Santa Fe Railroad.

ANTIOCH-PITTSBURG (22/35)
You begin to escape the Bay Area's influence as the Sacramento and San Joaquin rivers converge to your left. Look for the deep-water channel linking Stockton, 80 miles (128km) from the sea, with San Francisco.

STOCKTON (35/25)
The Magnolia District has 19th-century houses and this inland port and distribution centre was the location for John Huston's *Fat City*. Amtrak's station is at 735 S San Joaquin, from where Thruway buses go north to Sacramento. Additional train and Thruway connecting bus services are available in Stockton at the Robert J Cabral Station (SKT), 949 E Channel Street. The Stockton **visitors bureau** is located in the Historic Waterfront Warehouse at 445 W Weber Avenue (✆ 209 547 2770; *www.visitstockton.org*).

After leaving town the train travels through a landscape where hundreds of vineyards supply local wineries. You cross the Stanislaus River.

MODESTO (25/15)
Served by ferries during the 1880s gold rush, further development came to neighbouring Riverbank with the arrival of the Santa Fe Railway.

Hetch Hetchy Aqueduct (3/12)
The train crosses the concrete-lined aqueduct which supplies the Bay Area with water from the Sierra Nevada. A few minutes later you cross the Tuolumne River.

TURLOCK-DENAIR (15/22)
The station is at Santa Fe Avenue in Denair, although adjacent Turlock is much larger. The Diablo Mountains can be seen in the right distance.

As the *San Joaquin* crosses the Merced River, look for the numerous almond trees growing on both sides – an especially wonderful sight when they blossom in late winter.

Atwater (15/7)
Note the preserved World War II planes at the air base to your left. As you approach Merced the town's 1875 courthouse can be seen on your right.

MERCED (22/30) Built in Renaissance style and restored, the **Courthouse Museum** at 21st and N streets (✆ 209 723 2401; www.mercedmuseum.org) dominates the main square with a figure of Justice perched on its cupola. Amtrak's station is at 324 W 24th, from where Thruway buses will take you east to one of America's finest experiences, **Yosemite National Park**. Highlights include El Capitan (a granite dome twice as tall as the Rock of Gibraltar) and Yosemite Falls (2,425ft/740m). Late spring and early summer are the best times to visit. A visitor centre opens daily in the park or you can contact PO Box 577, Yosemite National Park, CA 95389 (✆ *209 372 0200; www.nps.gov/yose*).

The train pulls out of Merced past a Goodyear factory on the right.

Planada (5/25) Kadota fig trees grow raggedly on your left as you continue through some of America's most productive land. Other local specialities to look for include pistachio nuts, rice, tomatoes, peaches and grapes. Back to your left before the train crosses the Fresno River you can see the Sierra Nevada's Cathedral Mountains (13,000ft/4,000m).

MADERA (30/25) A busy farming town, located in the geographical centre of California and famous for its wines and olives.

San Joaquin River (10/15) A golf course is on your right as you cross the river.

Fresno State College (20/5) The campus is seen to your right before the train enters Fresno, passing a water tower and the Santa Fe Railway offices.

FRESNO (25/30) 'The raisin capital of the world', where Sunmaid's packing facility covers 73 acres (30ha). Grapes grown south of here are mostly turned into raisins while those produced further north become wine. The Meux Mansion, located a block from the station, is an ornate Victorian house originally built for a doctor.

Fresno's station at 2650 Tulare is Amtrak's busiest stop between Emeryville and Bakersfield. It is also the nearest station to **Sequoia** and **Kings Canyon national parks** in southern Nevada. These are quieter than Yosemite but still have fantastic mountains, caves, meadows and sequoia trees (the largest living things in the world). For **information** contact 47050 Generals Highway, Three Rivers, CA 93271-9700 (✆ *559 565 3341; www.nps.gov/seki*).

The *San Joaquin* leaves Fresno with the water tower of Sunmaid's old plant on your right. You continue among sun-baked vineyards and cross the Kings River.

HANFORD (30/20) Named after James Hanford, a Southern Pacific paymaster who sometimes paid his company's employees in gold. Hundreds of Chinese came to work on constructing the railroad and left behind the Taoist temple in China Alley. You can also visit Hanford's neoclassical courthouse and the Courthouse Square jail, which resembles the Bastille in Paris. Amtrak's station is at 200 Santa Fe Avenue, from where Thruway buses connect to San Luis Obispo and Visalia, the central valley's first settlement.

The train travels on, making good time through the flat landscape of orchards, vineyards and alfalfa fields. Irrigation means prolific crops can be grown over an area the size of the Netherlands.

CORCORAN (20/25) Note the grain elevators and cotton gin to your right beyond Amtrak's unstaffed station at the corner of Whitley and Otis Avenue. Corcoran is the home of a California state prison built on what was once Tulare Lake, home of the Tachi Indians.

Allensworth Park (10/15) The park on the right is in the middle of the Tulare Lake region.

WASCO (25/22) This is another predominantly agricultural town, famous for growing roses. Amtrak's stop is at 700 G and Highway 43.

Shafter (2/20) Look for more grapes and almond trees before the *San Joaquin* passes through Kern County oilfield, where pumps can be seen working on both sides of the track. The area's largest refinery is to your left as you near Bakersfield. A few minutes from town, the train crosses a canal then enters the Santa Fe yards with an old roundhouse to your right.

BAKERSFIELD Home of country music's Merle Haggard and Glen Campbell, Bakersfield rapidly expanded when oil was discovered at the turn of the century. **Kern County Museum and Pioneer Village** (*3801 Chester Av;* ✆ *661 852 5000; www.kcmuseum.org*) has more than 50 buildings dating from 1865 to World War II.

The station is at 601 Truxtun Avenue, from where Amtrak buses link with many places in the Los Angeles area, as well as with trains from Los Angeles to San Diego.

7

The *Pacific Surfliner*
Los Angeles–San Diego

General route information

Pacific Surfliner (formerly *San Diegan*) trains travel one of Amtrak's busiest routes, serving two major cities and a growing population. For part of the journey the *Pacific Surfliner* hugs the Pacific shoreline and other pleasures include Disneyland, San Juan Capistrano and the Tijuana Trolley.

Joining the train

LOS ANGELES For Los Angeles city information, see *Chapter 4, The* Coast Starlight (pages 49–70).

All aboard!

As the *Pacific Surfliner* leaves Los Angeles look for City Hall's white tower dominating the skyline to your left. Between here and Fullerton the train passes through the residential and industrial suburbs of Los Angeles County.

Los Angeles River (5/27) The train accompanies a concrete channel to your left. Designed for flood control and usually dry, the channel has been a location for dozens of movie chases.

ESSENTIAL INFORMATION

FREQUENCY Departures are approximately every two hours in both directions from early morning until late evening (a total of 12 daily round trips, with many trains continuing to Santa Barbara, Sacramento or San Luis Obispo). The journey between Los Angeles and San Diego takes just under three hours (half an hour less on the *Pacific Surfliner Express*).
DURATION Three hours
CONNECTIONS Amtrak Thruway buses and some local trains, as well as the *Coast Starlight*, connect Los Angeles with Santa Barbara along the San Fernando Valley
RESERVATIONS Unreserved except for Pacific Business Class
EQUIPMENT Bi-level Surfliner coaches. Business Class. Railfone.
FOOD Snacks, sandwiches, drinks
BAGGAGE Check-in service on most trains. Bicycle and surfboard racks.

LOS ANGELES

Fullerton

Anaheim

Santa Ana

Irvine

San Juan
Capistrano

Oceanside

Solana
Beach

SAN DIEGO

Redondo Junction (10/22) Amtrak Superliners for the *Coast Starlight*, *Sunset Limited* and *Southwest Chief* are set up in the yards and roundhouse to your right.

Commerce (15/17) This was formerly a stop for two trains a day in each direction.

Santa Fe Springs (22/10) Oil wells, tanks and derricks gradually accumulate on both sides.

FULLERTON (32/9) An attractive restored Santa Fe station with pink stucco and red tiles stands on your left next to the grand Union Pacific depot, which was moved to this site and is now a restaurant. The Donald Duck citrus juice plant also features on your left. Fullerton is a suburban stop as well as the station for two of the state's most popular venues.

Recommended near Fullerton

Disneyland 1313 Harbor Bd, Anaheim; ☎714 781 4565 (for recorded information); http://disneyland.disney.go.com; ☉ daily; admission charge. Opened in 1955, the original fun park has been added to ever since. California's largest tourist attraction features Tomorrowland, the Indiana Jones Adventure, Splash Mountain (the world's longest flume ride) & a twice-nightly Fantasmic! light show. Disneyland's Victorian-style railroad train circles the park every few mins.

Knott's Berry Farm 8039 Beach Bd, Buena Park; ☎714 220 5200; www.knotts.com; ☉ daily. This recreated ghost town comes with shops, restaurants & a hundred rides, including Montezooma's Revenge (0–55mph (88km/h) in 5 seconds) & the Corkscrew (first upside-down rollercoaster). Steam engines & equipment formerly owned by the Denver & Rio Grande Western & Rio Grande Southern operate over a 36in-gauge track. Train rides included in the admission charge.

All aboard!

As the *Pacific Surfliner* pulls out of Fullerton you can just make out Disneyland's replica Matterhorn to your right. Approaching Anaheim, look right also for the enormous sports stadium located beyond the station.

ANAHEIM (9/9) One of the country's fastest-growing cities, this was the birthplace of Leo Fender, pioneer of the electric guitar. Founded by German settlers and former gold miners from San Francisco, Anaheim's name combines the nearby Santa Ana River with *heim* (German for 'home'). The Rams (football) and Angels (baseball) perform in the stadium next to an ultra-modern railway station at 2150 E Katella Avenue.

The train leaves for another brief run to Santa Ana through Orange County, famous for Valencia oranges.

Orange (4/5) Seen away to your right with an old station building on the left.

SANTA ANA (9/10) This was the birthplace of Michelle Pfeiffer. The restored downtown area and more recent developments feature traditional Spanish architecture. Amtrak's station is at 1000 E Santa Ana Boulevard.

As the train leaves, look right for the two giant hangars which accommodated World War II air balloons and now house US Marine helicopters. The Santa Ana Mountains are to your left.

US Marine Corps (8/2) The air base is on the left.

IRVINE (10/10) You continue south from here through a land of orange groves interspersed with the occasional small town.

SAN JUAN CAPISTRANO (10/30) Amtrak's station at 26701 Verdugo features a restaurant and live jazz performances. The 1776 mission where Juanero Indians converted to Christianity was damaged by an earthquake but part of the adobe building still stands in neatly kept grounds to your left. The famous San Juan Capistrano swallows leave in October, returning (fairly) punctually on 19 March each year.

Soon after leaving town, the train joins the Pacific Ocean on your right, staying in touch with its shoreline until Del Mar. Enviable houses cling to cliffs on your left.

San Clemente (10/20) Two trains a day stop in San Clemente, where Richard Nixon lived at Casa Pacifica for some of his time as president. The beach is one of the prettiest in California.

San Onofre Nuclear Plant (16/14) Look right for this ominous presence next to the beach, where the extra-warm water attracts heedless surfers.

Camp Pendleton (25/5) One of many naval facilities to be found in this part of the state. Yachts and pleasure boats bob in the busy marina to the right.

OCEANSIDE (30/17) Amtrak and Greyhound share the transit centre at 235 S Tremont. Mission San Luis Rey is on nearby Mission Avenue. Oceanside is the home of the Legoland Museum, featuring a castle, miniature Lego cities and a safari adventure complete with Lego animals.

Carlsbad (5/12) Look out for a military boys' school to your right before the train passes a gigantic power plant, also to the right.

Del Mar Racetrack (15/2) The racetrack is immediately to your left.

SOLANA BEACH (17/30) The nearby town of Del Mar is famed for its conservatism and exclusive beach apartments. A hundred annual events take place at the Del Mar fairgrounds, where Thoroughbred Club meetings are a regular meeting place for Hollywood names.

The *Pacific Surfliner* shifts away from the ocean at this point and travels inland through rugged country towards its final destination. Look out for the celebrated Torrey Pines on both sides as you descend through Soledad and Rose Canyons.

University of San Diego (20/10) The campus is to your left.

Lindbergh Airport (25/5) Runways and buildings appear on the right.

SAN DIEGO The state's oldest city has smog-free sunshine, Spanish architecture and an easy-going atmosphere. Portuguese explorer Juan Cabrillo discovered this bay in 1542, but settlement began much later when a garrison and California's first Spanish mission were built. San Diego became part of the United States in 1847, after which the Santa Fe Railway brought rapid expansion to a city which continues to grow. It is now the seventh-biggest city in the country and has the world's largest military complex (125,000 acres).

San Diego basics

☎ Telephone code 619
▄▄ Station (*Ticket office ⊕ 05.15–22.00. Waiting room ⊕ midnight–01.15 & 04.45–23.59; information ☎ 239 9021*) Amtrak's station at 1050 Kettner Bd is a beautiful, spacious building close to the waterfront in an older part of downtown. Built in a mixture of Spanish Mission & Colonial Revival styles the depot was originally constructed by the Atchison, Topeka & Santa Fe Railway for passengers arriving at the 1915 Panama–California Exposition, replacing the California Southern Railway's 1887 Victorian depot. From 1916 to 1951, the depot also served the San Diego & Arizona Railway (later SD & AE) as the Union Depot.

Luggage store, ATM, Red Caps, taxi stand. The station is the home of the research library of the San Diego Railroad Museum & the Santa Fe Historical Society library.

Connections No Thruway bus.
🚌 Local transport The city is easy to negotiate on foot or by bicycle. San Diego Transit buses (☎ 238 0100) operate a comprehensive service. Passes can be used on all SDT routes as well as the San Diego Trolley (downtown & from the station to San Ysidro on the Mexican border) & the Bay Ferry from Broadway Pier to Coronado. Coaster runs commuter rail services to Oceanside (☎ 800 262 7837).

🚕 Taxis Yellow ☎ 858 760; San Diego Cab ☎ 226 8294
🚗 Car rental Avis, 3180 N Harbor Dr; ☎ 688 5000
🚐 Greyhound 120 W Broadway; ☎ 239 6737
✈ Lindbergh Airport 3 miles (5km) north of downtown by SDT bus #992.
Tours Harbour cruises from Hornblower (☎ 686 8700) & trips to Santa Catalina Island with California Cruisin' (☎ 296 8000).
ℹ Visitors bureau 2215 India St; ☎ 232 3101; e sdinfo@sandiego.org; www.sandiego.org; ⊕ daily
🏠 Accommodation The Cottage, for B&B, is at 3829 Albatross; ☎ 299 1564. San Diego Bed & Breakfast Guild; ☎ 800 619 7666; www. bandbguildsandiego.org.

The San Diego Hostel, about 10mins' walk from Amtrak's station, is at 726 Fifth Av; ☎ 232 3100. Dormitory, **$**, sgl, **$$**. AYH Hostel, 3790 Udall, Point Loma; ☎ 223 4778. Take bus #35. Members & non-members, **$**. The nearest campsite is Campland On The Bay, 2211 Pacific Beach Dr; ☎ 858 581 4200. Take bus #30.

Hotels include the Churchill, 827 C; ☎ 234 5186, **$$**; Sofia, 150 W Broadway; ☎ 234 9200, **$$$$**; Days Hotel, 543 Hotel Circle S; ☎ 297 8800, **$$$**; Bristol, 1055 First Av; ☎ 232 6141, **$$$$**; Comfort Inn, 660 G; ☎ 238 4100, **$$**; Baltic Inn, 521 Sixth Av; ☎ 237 0687, **$**.

Recommended in San Diego

Balboa Park 2125 Park Bd. The park information centre is at 1549 El Prado (☎ 239 0512; www.balboapark.org). The park has over 1,000 acres (400ha) of gardens, trees & lawns, as well as the world's largest outdoor pipe organ.

The California–Pacific Exposition succeeded the Panama–California Exposition here in 1935, & Spanish-style buildings house 14 excellent art galleries, museums & theatres. A pass gives access to all the museums, most of which are free on the 1st Tue in the month; a free tram service operates around the park.

San Diego History Center 1649 El Prado in Balboa Park; ☎232 6203; www.sandiegohistory. org; ⊕ Tue–Sun; admission charge. Changing exhibits & lectures are used imaginatively to interpret San Diego's regional history.

Aerospace Museum 2001 Pan American Plaza in Balboa Park; ☎234 8291; www. aerospacemuseum.org; ⊕ daily; admission charge. Aviation history from the Wright Brothers to the space age is brought to life with over 65 aircraft, including a replica of the *Spirit of St Louis* monoplane in which Charles Lindbergh made his first flight in 1927 from a San Diego airfield. The first transcontinental flight, from New York to San Diego, took place in 1923.

Museum of Contemporary Art 1001 Kettner Bd; ☎234 1001; www.mcasd.org; admission charge. The museum has 2 distinct, complementary locations & includes collections, exhibitions & programmes that focus on present-day art & artists. Another part of the museum is located next to the ocean at 700 Prospect in La Jolla (☎858 454 3541 – for 24hr recorded information).

Model Railroad Museum 1649 El Prado, on the lower level of the Casa De Balboa in Balboa Park; ☎696 0199; www.sdmodelrailroadm.com; ⊕ daily; admission charge, but children under 15 enter free. The largest of its kind in the world, with 4 gigantic layouts.

San Diego Zoo 2920 Zoo Dr, Balboa Park, north of the museums; ☎231 1515; www.sandiegozoo. org; ⊕ daily; admission charge. Koalas, tigers, giant pandas, rhinos & gorillas are among the 4,000 creatures (over 800 species) living in the world's best zoo. Children's area, tours & an aerial tramway.

Old Town Historic Park 4002 Wallace (information centre); ☎220 5422. Restored buildings, galleries & restaurants occupy the site of the first (1769) Spanish settlement. Highlights include the **Machado y Silvas Adobe**, San Diego's first schoolhouse & the

Casa de Estudillo, built in 1827 by a presidio commander who would watch bull & bear fights from its cupola.

Whaley House Built in 1856 on a former gallows site, this was the first 2-storey brick building in southern California & has been officially designated as a haunted house by the US Department of Commerce. Free walking tours leave daily from the information centre. For Old-Town trolley tours, ☎298 8687.

Gaslamp Quarter 614 Fifth Av; ☎233 5227; www.gaslamp.org. Many of the buildings in this area from Broadway to the waterfront were erected in the late 19th century & have been returned to their former glory, serving now as shops, restaurants & nightclubs. You can take a walking tour narrated by the former Gaslamp Quarter saloon owner & gunslinger, Wyatt Earp. Call the Gaslamp Quarter Foundation (☎233 4692) for information & reservations.

La Jolla This affluent northern suburb is famous for its beaches, scuba diving & chic residents. Raymond Chandler used La Jolla as the setting, renamed Poodle Springs, for his last novel *Playback*. Chandler's former home can be seen at 6005 Camino de la Costa. La Jolla's racetrack also features in the film of Jim Thompson's *The Grifters*, along with several shots of San Diegan trains.

San Diego Railroad Museum Located at the Campo Depot, State Highway 94 & Forrest Gate Rd in Campo, 50 miles (80km) to the east; mail address: 1050 Kettner Bd, #5, San Diego, CA 92101-3339; ☎478 9937 (w/ends) or ☎465 7776 (w/days); www.sdrm.org; admission charge. Over 80 pieces of railroad equipment, including steam & diesel locomotives of the Southern Pacific & California Western railroads, passenger cars, freight cars & cabooses can be seen at the restored depots at La Mesa & Campo.

Steam train excursions using vintage equipment over parts of the San Diego & Arizona Railway take place on w/ends, & diesel-powered trains travel to Tecate in Mexico.

Tijuana Not classic Mexico, and less wild than it used to be, but 'the world's most visited city' is an easy trip from San Diego. The trolley and bus #932 will take you the 17 miles to the border, although beggars and the concrete walkway make crossing on foot a bleak experience. San Ysidro is the world's busiest international border crossing, with 60 million people a year passing through.

Tijuana offers cheap drinks, accommodation, food, shopping and bullfights. US dollars are welcome as you shop for blankets, leather goods, jewellery and tequila. For more information visit the website www.tijuana.com.

Note: except for citizens of the US and Canada, a valid visa is required for return to the United States, even after a one-day visit.

8

The *Empire Builder*
Chicago–Seattle

General route information

The *Empire Builder* crosses the Mississippi River and travels more than 2,200 miles (3,500km) past wheat fields, cattle ranges, forests, mountains and glacial lakes. America's northern plains were mostly wilderness until the freewheeling tycoon James J Hill built his Great Northern Railway between St Paul, Minnesota, and Seattle. Amtrak's *Empire Builder* takes its name from the train called after him, which ran on this route during the heyday of rail travel.

Joining the train

CHICAGO For Chicago city information, see *Chapter 5*, *The* California Zephyr (pages 71–90). The *Empire Builder* leaves on the complex tracks of the Chicago, Milwaukee, St Paul & Pacific Railroad (also known as the Soo Line or Milwaukee Road), following what was a plank road in the days of horse-drawn wagons.

ESSENTIAL INFORMATION

FREQUENCY Daily. The **westbound** service leaves Chicago mid afternoon to arrive in Milwaukee by late afternoon and St Paul–Minneapolis late in the evening. You reach Havre on the second afternoon, West Glacier by mid evening and Spokane during the night, arriving in Seattle or Portland by mid morning. Travelling **east**, trains leave Seattle or Portland late in the afternoon to reach Spokane at midnight and West Glacier early next morning. You reach Havre by early afternoon and St Paul–Minneapolis early the following morning, arriving in Milwaukee early afternoon and Chicago by late afternoon.
DURATION 46 hours
RESERVATIONS All reserved
EQUIPMENT Superliner coaches
SLEEPING Superliner bedrooms
FOOD Complete meals, snacks, sandwiches, drinks
LOUNGE CAR Movies, games, hospitality hour. During spring and summer months, National Park Service guides from the Klondike Gold Rush National Historic Park provide a narrative commentary between Seattle and Shelby. Rangers from the Fort Union Trading Post are similarly on board between Williston and Shelby, and Rangers from Knife River Indian Villages between Minot and Malta or Shelby (Memorial Day through Labor Day).
BAGGAGE Check-in service at most stations

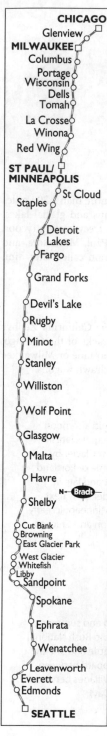

CHICAGO
Glenview
MILWAUKEE
Columbus
Portage
Wisconsin
Dells
Tomah
La Crosse
Winona
Red Wing
ST PAUL/
MINNEAPOLIS
St Cloud
Staples
Detroit
Lakes
Fargo
Grand Forks
Devil's Lake
Rugby
Minot
Stanley
Williston
Wolf Point
Glasgow
Malta
Havre
N— Bradt
Shelby
Cut Bank
Browning
East Glacier Park
West Glacier
Whitefish
Libby
Sandpoint
Spokane
Ephrata
Wenatchee
Leavenworth
Everett
Edmonds
SEATTLE

Some of the fastest-ever trains, capable of well over 100mph (160km/h), ran between Chicago and Milwaukee in the 1930s when this route was known as 'the world's greatest steam railroad speedway'.

All aboard!

On your right as the train pulls out of Chicago is the Chicago River, with the Merchandise Mart Building and the cylindrical towers of Marina City. Also to your right are a Rock-Ola jukebox factory and the tapered Hancock Building. The Willis Tower is to your left. You continue among the older buildings and spired churches of Chicago's northside.

Niles (4/20) The Niles version of Pisa's leaning tower appears on your left.

GLENVIEW (24/60) The train pauses at this busy suburban station before changing from Metra tracks to those of Canadian Pacific (CP) to continue north through residential areas, farms and industrial plants owned by the likes of Fiat. Look for the patriotic water tower to your left.

Glenview Naval Station (2/58) This air base is visible on the left.

Gurnee (15/45) Look right for the Six Flags' Great America Amusement Park.

Wadsworth (20/40) The Des Plaines River comes into view on your left, and a few minutes later the *Empire Builder* crosses the Illinois–Wisconsin state line into 'America's dairyland'.

Franksville (40/20) 'The kraut capital of the world' was named after the Frank Pure Food Company, seen on the left.

Mitchell Field (50/10) The international airport can be seen to your right. As the train nears Milwaukee and crosses the Monomonee River, look left for two of the city's finest churches. **St Josaphat's**, with its distinctive dome, was North America's first Polish basilica, built in 1901 by immigrants using material salvaged from the post office building in Chicago. Next to it are the gold spires of **St Stanislaus Cathedral**.

Also on your left as the train snakes into the station are the octagonal dials and square tower of the **Allen Bradley clock**, an enduring local landmark.

MILWAUKEE (60/70) 'The Genuine American City' is Wisconsin's largest and is famous for *Happy Days*, Miller beer and Harley-Davidsons. Milwaukee stands on a Lake Michigan bay which Potawatomi Native Americans called 'Millioki' or 'the gathering place by the waters'. In the 19th century, many thousands of immigrants came from Italy, Ireland, Poland, Scandinavia and especially Germany. One of them was the future Israeli premier, Golda Meir. Milwaukee's different ethnic groups give the city a lively cultural atmosphere and its annual Summerfest on the lakefront is the largest music festival in the world.

Milwaukee basics

Telephone code 414

Station (*Ticket office* ☺ *05.30–21.00. Waiting room* ☺ *05.30–22.00*) Union Station is at 433 W St Paul Av, not a safe area by night. Lockers, newspapers, Red Caps, restaurant, taxi stand.
Connections No Thruway bus.

Local transport Many attractions are within walking distance of the Milwaukee River & a skywalk system means you can get around easily without going outdoors. Milwaukee County Transport at 1942 N 17th (*344 6711*) operates a near-24hr bus service.

Taxis Yellow *271 1800*; American United *220 5000*

Car rental Avis, 916 E State *272 0892*; Budget, 603 N Fourth St; *276 1634*

Greyhound 433 W St Paul Ste 150; *272 2156*

General Mitchell Airport 6 miles (10km) from downtown by bus #80

Tours MCT has summer excursions to historic sights & the lakeshore. Walking tours are

available from Historic Milwaukee (*277 7795*). Boat trips are offered by Milwaukee Boat Line (*294 9450*).

Visitors bureau 400 W Wisconsin Av; *273 7222* or *800 554 1448*; e visitor@milwaukee. org; www.milwaukee.org; ☺ Mon–Fri

Accommodation Contact Little Red House Bed & Breakfast, 9212 Jackson Park Bd, Wauwatosa, WI 53226; *479 0646*; e mjwey@ earthlink.net.

Hostelling International Summer Hostel, 1530 W Wisconsin Av; *961 2525* or *800 554 1448*.

Hotels include the Wyndham, 139 E Kilbourn Av; *276 8686*, **$$$$$**; Astor, 924 E Juneau Av; *271 4220*, **$$$**; Radisson, 2303 N Mayfair Rd; *257 3400*, **$$$**; Courtyard Milwaukee Downtown, 300 W Michigan; *291 4122*, **$$**; Residence Inn Milwaukee Downtown, 648 N Plankinton Av; *224 7890*, **$$$**; Metro, 411 E Mason; *272 1937*, **$$$$$**; Pfister, 424 E Wisconsin Av; *273 8222*, **$$$$**.

Recommended in Milwaukee

Milwaukee Art Museum 700 N Art Museum Dr; *224 3200*; www.mam.org; ☺ Tue–Sun; admission charge. Almost 25,000 works of art from ancient to contemporary are housed in the city's 'masterpiece on the lakefront', designed by Eero Saarinen. A $63 million expansion with its wing-like design gave the city skyline a new profile when it opened in 2001.
Milwaukee Public Museum 800 W Wells; *278 2702*; www.mpm.edu; ☺ Wed–Mon; admission charge. A recreation of Old Milwaukee, a tropical rainforest & the first known total habitat diorama are included among 6 million objects & specimens in one of the largest museums in the United States.
Mitchell Park Conservatory 524 S Layton Bd; *649 9800*; ☺ daily; admission charge. 3 giant

glass domes, each 85ft high & 140ft wide (26m by 43m), house collections of plants in desert, tropical & temperate environments. Brightly coloured birds & iguanas live among the exotic rainforest flowers of the tropical dome.
Milwaukee County Zoo 10001 W Blue Mound Rd; *256 5412* or *771 5500*; www. milwaukeezoo.org; ☺ daily; admission charge. Around 2,500 creatures, including endangered trumpeter swans & black rhino, live among 200 wooded acres (81ha). There are 300 species of mammals, birds, reptiles, fish & invertebrates plus a children's zoo, guided tours & a miniature train safari ride (mid-Apr–mid-Oct). Take bus #10.
Pabst Mansion 2000 W Wisconsin Av; *931 0808*; www.pabstmansion.com; ☺ daily;

admission charge. Built by the sea captain, beer baron & philanthropist Frederick Pabst in 1892, the mansion boasts 37 rooms, 14 fireplaces & 12 baths as well as stained glass, carved woodwork & ornamental iron. The mansion was the home of Roman Catholic archbishops for 67 years & is now being restored to its original splendour. Guided tours.

Old World Wisconsin Off Hwy 67 at nearby Eagle; ☎262 594 6301; www.oldworldwisconsin. org; ☉ daily; admission charge. This open-air museum captures the lifestyles, ideas & challenges of 19th- & early 20th-century rural immigrants.

Historic Cedarburg Located 20mins north of Milwaukee at Washington Av & Spring in Cedarburg; ☎800 237 2874; www.cedarburg. org. First settled by Irish immigrants in the 1840s, Cedarburg prospered with the coming of the railroad in 1870 & German families who built dams & mills along the fast-running Cedar Creek. Over 100 main-street businesses, many of them antique shops, occupy registered historic buildings surrounded by attractive limestone houses. Special events & festivals take place all year round.

All aboard!

As the *Empire Builder* departs Milwaukee, look for the Mitchell Park Conservatory's three graceful domes. The County Stadium is to your left and the Miller Brewery, which made Milwaukee famous, on your right. The train travels through city suburbs for 20 minutes towards America's heartland of lakes and farms.

Pewaukee Lake (30/40) The shoreline and town are visible to your left before you cross the Rock River three times. Lake Oconomowoc also comes into view on the left, with Pine and Okauchee lakes to your right. Look for wheat fields, silos, cattle and horse-drawn farm wagons.

Watertown (50/20) The steeple of St Bernard's Church pokes above trees on your right just before the campus of Marantha College. The train then crosses the Crawfish River.

COLUMBUS (70/30) Zion Evangelical Lutheran Church is to the left of Ludington Street Station. The steeple bell, presented by Germany's emperor, was cast from pieces of French cannon captured during the Franco–Prussian War. Beside the church stands the 1892 City Hall.

Wyocena (25/5) Santa's rocket stays grounded in a salvage yard to your right. Wyocena Lake is famous for angling and commercial fishing.

PORTAGE (30/20) The town was founded as a stopover between the Fox and Wisconsin rivers to serve traders and settlers. They had to portage (carry) goods across this strip of land when going from Lake Michigan to the Mississippi. Milwaukee Road freight cars gather on the left of Amtrak's station at 400 W Oneida. Madison is 25 miles (40km) to the south.

Wisconsin River (15/5) The river on your left cuts through many miles of finely streaked rock. A Baptist Indian church and cemetery can be seen high up to your right.

WISCONSIN DELLS (20/45) Situated in a sandstone canyon created by the winding Wisconsin River, natural beauty and an amusement park combine to make this one of the state's chief attractions. Rafting and boat trips are popular pastimes along the river.

Amtrak's station is at 100 LaCrosse Street, and the **Park Lane Model Railroad Museum** (✆ 608 254 8050) in nearby Reedsburg features 2,000 model trains of various vintages.

The *Empire Builder* continues northwest and crosses the Wisconsin River.

Mauston (20/25) The spire of St Patrick's Church is to your right. Lake Decorah, also to your right, was formed by a dam built across the Lemonweir River.

Camp Douglas (30/15) The flow of the Wisconsin River over centuries has produced the splendid red sandstone rock formations seen in Mill Bluff State Park to your left.

TOMAH (45/40) Tomah's chamber of commerce occupies a Milwaukee Road Pullman car on the left, its sign supported by characters from the comic strip *Gasoline Alley*. The strip's creator, Frank King, grew up in Tomah. Wisconsin's annual dairyland tractor pull brings competitors to the city from the whole Midwest.

Tomah Lake is to your left as the *Empire Builder* leaves town and suddenly enters a landscape of steep hills.

Tunnel City (5/35) The train runs along a single track through the 1,350ft (410m) tunnel.

Sparta (15/25) Look right for the airport. You join the La Crosse River on your right and follow it for the next 25 miles (40km) until it joins the Mississippi.

Bangor (25/15) An imposing village hall appears on your right before the train crosses the river.

LA CROSSE (40/40) Situated at the junction of the Mississippi, Black and La Crosse rivers, the town was named after a term French trappers gave to a game they saw being played by Native Americans. Amtrak's station is at 601 St Andrew.

After leaving La Crosse, the *Empire Builder* crosses the Mississippi River for the first time, going from Wisconsin into Minnesota. Islands in midstream divide the Mississippi into three channels. Once across the river you enter one of the route's most attractive stretches, accompanying the Mississippi into hardwood forest. The train bowls along for 40 miles (64km) past farmland and riverboat towns, with the river at times becoming as wide as a lake.

Number 7 Dam (5/35) The dam and lock system on your right is one of several built in attempts to tame the river.

Number 6 Dam (20/20) Another dam appears on the right.

WINONA (40/60) The city's name is a Sioux word for 'first-born daughter'. Sugar Loaf Mountain, rising 500ft (150m) to your left, was a ceremonial meeting place for the Sioux. Chief Wa-Pa-Sha's outline could be seen there before quarrying altered the mountain's shape. Winona has grown from its early sawmill days to become a centre for shipping and manufacturing.

Look out for the large grain elevators standing on your right as the train leaves the station.

Number 5 Dam (10/50) Another dam built in the federally financed series.

Weaver (15/45) This is 'the white bass capital of the world', with many fishing camps located in the area. The *Empire Builder* crosses the Zumbro River.

Wabasha (30/30) At the 1856 Anderson House (the oldest hotel in the state) services include free shoeshines, hot bricks to warm your bed and pet cats to keep you company.

Lake Pepin (35/25) Where the Chippewa River joins the Mississippi. Lake Pepin is home to eagles and claims to be the place where water skiing was invented. Watch out for the romantic riverboat steamer.

Frontenac (50/10) This small town dates back to a French fort built in 1723. Mount Frontenac ski resort is to your left. As the train nears Red Wing look left for the 1891 Minnesota State Training School, resembling a German castle.

RED WING (60/65) The name came from a Dakota chief whose emblem was a swan's wing dyed scarlet. Red Wing today is famous for shoes and pottery. In 1905, the Milwaukee Road built a station which the city acquired from the Milwaukee's successor, the Soo Line, and Amtrak leases a waiting room restored to its original condition. The St James Hotel is to your left.

Cannon River (5/60) Look right to see the Prairie Island nuclear power station before you cross the Vermillion River.

Hastings (20/45) A domed 1871 courthouse stands on your left, with another lock and dam system to your right. The *Empire Builder* continues north, again crossing the Mississippi River.

St Paul Airport (45/20) The airport appears across the river to your left, with the city skyline on palisades to the right.

Harriet Island (50/15) During summer, picturesque riverboats go from the island on your right to Fort Snelling. As you approach St Paul, look right for the cathedral and left for a castle-like Schmidt Brewery.

ST PAUL–MINNEAPOLIS (65/80) The 'Twin Cities' began as frontier towns on the banks of the Mississippi, settled by immigrants from Scandinavia, Germany and Great Britain. Two million people now live in the metropolitan area.

Minneapolis, home of Prince, is brasher and noisier. The state capital, St Paul, was the birthplace of F Scott Fitzgerald. Some of the world's most powerful computers are built in St Paul, and there are hundreds of lakes and parks.

Twin City basics

Telephone codes 612 in Minneapolis; 651 in St Paul
Station (*Ticket office* ☉ *06.30–23.30. Waiting room* ☉ *06.00–23.59*) Amtrak's modern Midway Station at 730 Transfer Rd, St Paul, serves both cities. Lockers, vending machines, handcarts, taxi stand. Take bus #7 to the downtown areas. Amtrak expects to move to St Paul's 1923 Union Depot at 214 E Fourth St when refurbishment of this impressive neoclassical building is completed in 2012.

Connections Amtrak Thruway buses connect with Duluth, birthplace of Robert Allen Zimmerman (better known as Bob Dylan).
🚌 **Local transport** Minneapolis & St Paul have glass-covered skyways which make it easy to get about on foot, even in winter. MTC bus maps & timetables are available from 560 Sixth Av N (✆ 373 3333).

Metro Transit also operates 12 miles of light rail, connecting 3 of the Twin Cities' most popular destinations – downtown Minneapolis, St Paul–Minneapolis international airport & Mall of America in Bloomington.
🚕 **Taxis** (St Paul) Diamond ✆ 642 1188; Yellow ✆ 222 4433
🚕 **Taxis** (Minneapolis) Town ✆ 331 8294; Yellow ✆ 824 4000
🚗 **Car rental** Thrifty, 1313 Nicollet Av; ✆ 333 2050 (Minneapolis) & Enterprise, 395 E 7th; ✆ 225 9766 (St Paul)
🚌 **Greyhound** (St Paul) 166 W University Av; ✆ 222 0507
🚌 **Greyhound** (Minneapolis) 950 Hawthorn Av; ✆ 371 3325
✈ **Twin Cities International Airport** 8 miles (13km) from downtown by Airport Express (✆ 827 7777) & MTC bus #54.
Tours Metro Connections, 1219 Marquette Av, Minneapolis (✆ 333 8687 or ✆ 800 747 8687).

Gray Line, 21160 Holyoke Av N, Lakeville (✆ 952 469 5020). Mississippi stern-wheel riverboats leave from Harriet Island (✆ 651 227 1100).
ℹ **Visitors bureau** 250 Marquette Av S; ✆ 612 767 8000; www.minneapolis.org. Also at 75 W Fifth in St Paul; ✆ 292 3225; e info@visitsaintpaul.com; www.visitsaintpaul.com; ☺ daily.
🏠 **Accommodation** For B&B contact Elmwood Hse Bed & Breakfast, 1 E Elmwood Pl, Minneapolis, MN 55419; ✆ 822 4558; e innkeeper@elmwoodhouse.us; www.elmwoodhouse.us. Or contact Chatsworth Bed & Breakfast, 984 Ashland Av, S Paul, MN 55104; ✆ 227 4288. The University of Minnesota housing office often has inexpensive rooms; ✆ 624 2994. Minneapolis International Hostel is at 2400 Stevens Av S; ✆ 874 0407; e reservations@minneapolishostel.com; www.minneapolishostel.com.

Minneapolis hotels include the Whitney, 150 Portland Av; ✆ 375 1234, **$$**; Crowne Plaza Northstar, 618 Second Av S; ✆ 338 2288, **$$$$**; DoubleTree, 1101 La Salle Av; ✆ 332 6800, **$$$**. St Paul hotels include the St Paul, 350 Market; ✆ 292 9292, **$$$$$**; Crowne Plaza Riverfront, 11 E Kellogg Bd; ✆ 292 1900, **$$$$**; Super 8 Inn, 1739 Old Hudson Rd; ✆ 771 5566, **$$**.

Recommended in the Twin Cities

Minneapolis Institute of Arts 2400 Third Av S; ✆ 888 642 2787; www.artsmia.org; ☺ Tue–Sun; free. Among 100,000 exhibits spanning 5,000 years are Rembrandts, Chinese jade, Roman sculptures & an Egyptian mummy. Tours, films & lectures.
American Swedish Institute 2600 Park Av, Minneapolis; ✆ 871 4907; www.americanswedishinst.org; ☺ Tue–Sun; admission charge. This chateauesque mansion, built in 1908 for the newspaper publisher Swan J Turnblad, has wooden panels & carvings, Swedish art, glassware, furniture & a reference library. The Svenskarnas Dag, one of the largest festivals in the United States, takes place each Jun in Minnehaha Park.
Landmark Center 75 W Fifth; ✆ 292 3225; www.landmarkcenter.org; ☺ daily; free. St Paul's 1902 Federal Court building has been restored to

its Romanesque splendour, with guided tours of the chambers & courtrooms.
James Hill House 240 Summit Av, St Paul; ✆ 297 2555; www.mnhs.org/places/sites/jjhh; ☺ Wed–Sat; admission charge. Canadian-born James Jerome Hill owned the St Paul-Pacific Railroad & was closely involved with the building of the Canadian Pacific. He gained control of the Great Northern Railroad (later to become the Burlington Northern) after a stock exchange battle, & no expense was spared when he constructed this mansion in 1891. The house is one of many fine residences on Summit Av, where F Scott Fitzgerald lived.

The James J Hill Library owns a vast & complete collection of Hill's business & private papers, including thousands of letters. As well as financing & constructing railroads, he ran experimental farms, helping to increase livestock & crop yields for those who came to settle along the line. In 1915, the Panama–Pacific Exposition in San Francisco named him 'Minnesota's greatest living citizen'.

Hill retired in 1907, handing over the Great Northern to his son, Louis W Hill, but he continued to go into the office to supervise business until his death in 1916. Every train & steamship on the Great Northern came to a stop for 5mins in his honour on the day of his funeral.

Twin City Model Railroad Museum 1021 Bandana Bd E, St Paul; ✆ 647 9628; www.tcmrm. org; ☉ Tue–Sun; admission charge. 3,000ft^2 (280m^2) of O-gauge railroad are located in former Northern Pacific maintenance shops. On display outside are locomotives from the Grand Trunk Western & Northern Pacific railways, as well as passenger & boxcars.

Minnesota Transportation Museum 193 Pennsylvania Av E, St Paul; ✆ 402 7497 or ✆ 228 0263; www.mtmuseum.org. The museum operates the Jackson St Roundhouse in St Paul, the Como Harriet Streetcar line in Minneapolis & the Steamboat *Minnehaha*.

The museum also operates the Osceola & St Croix Valley Railway, PO Box 176, Osceola, WI 54020 (✆ 715 755 3570; www.mtmuseum.org). The railway is located east of the St Croix River, about a 1hr drive from the Twin Cities, & has steam & diesel train rides.

Lake Superior Railroad Museum Lovingly restored steam engines & coaches (including the *Gallery Car* exhibit with its works of art rescued from the ashes of a fire that destroyed the old Union Depot in Ashland, WI) are housed in an old railway depot at 506 W Michigan in Duluth (✆ 218 727 8025; www.lsrm.org). There are also daily train rides on the **North Shore Scenic Railroad** (✆ 218 722 1273; www. northshorescenicrailroad.org).

All aboard!

After a service stop, the *Empire Builder* leaves St Paul on Burlington Northern Santa Fe (BNSF) tracks for the rest of its journey to Seattle/Portland. Minneapolis can be seen in the left distance, dominated by the 57-storey IDS Tower.

ST CLOUD (80/60) Located on the shores of the Mississippi, St Cloud ships granite from local mines. To your right is the largest granite wall in the world, surrounding the St Cloud Reformatory completed by the inmates in 1889.

STAPLES (60/60) This former railroad town became run-down but has lately attracted new industries.

DETROIT LAKES (60/55) The 400 lakes nearby are a popular venue for fishing and other outdoor pursuits. Amtrak's station is at 116 Pioneer.

Red River (53/2) You cross the river and go from Minnesota into North Dakota, the Sioux State.

FARGO (55/60) Named after William Fargo of the Wells Fargo Express Company, North Dakota's largest city is at the heart of the Red River Valley. In the late 19th century, this was the main hub of the North Pacific Railroad. Amtrak's station at 420 Fourth Street N also serves Moorhead in Minnesota. **Bonanzaville USA** (✆ 701 282 2822; www.bonanzaville.com), in West Fargo, relives pioneer days with a village reconstructed from original buildings, including two rail depots.

GRAND FORKS (60/80) Located where the Red Lake River meets the Red River, Grand Forks is the home of North Dakota University. Buses connect downtown with Amtrak's station at 5555 DeMers Avenue and Thruway buses go north to Winnipeg in Canada.

DEVIL'S LAKE (80/60) Catchily nicknamed 'the goose- and duck-hunting capital of America', the town stands next to North Dakota's largest lake. Sioux and Chippewa Indians called this the Evil Spirit Lake, telling of water monsters, thunderbirds and overturned canoes.

The *Empire Builder* continues its way across the vast yellow and gold expanses of the northern plains, above which can often be seen eagles and huge flocks of wild geese.

RUGBY (60/65) The geographical centre of North America boasts a stone monument and museum to support its claim. The Canadian border is less than 50 miles (80km) from Amtrak's red-brick station on your left.

Look for crops of sunflowers and fields of ploughed black earth as the train travels on over the plains. Near Minot look left for the converted green railroad car used as part of a plant nursery. Also to your left are several picturesque railway buildings and a large letter 'M'.

MINOT (65/50) Located on the Souris River, this service stop was called the 'magic city' when it seemed to grow overnight after the Great Northern Railroad arrived. Minot remains an important divisional point with extensive marshalling yards, and the city prospers thanks to oil and the military. Amtrak's utilitarian station is on your left.

The landscape opens out dramatically as large, flat fields of wheat stretch to the horizon on all sides.

STANLEY (50/65) This small town's economy is based mainly on grain and livestock production. Mountrail County Courthouse can be seen to the right of the single-storey station with its fading green sign.

WILLISTON (65/80) Oil discoveries at the western edge of Lake Sakakawea during the 1950s turned Williston into a boom town. Several wells with patiently nodding pumps can be seen along the train's route. Look also for the steam locomotive to your right just before the station.

The *Empire Builder* joins the Missouri River on the left and follows it along the Missouri Breaks for the next 60 miles (96km). Garrison Dam on the Missouri greatly increased this region's farming activity and rows of tall grain elevators stand next to many small stations along the way.

Fort Buford (15/65) Where Chief Sitting Bull surrendered after the Battle of the Little Bighorn in Montana (1876). The army officers' quarters, a cemetery and other relics can be seen at the fort.

Fort Union (20/60) On your left is one of the 19th century's liveliest fur-trading posts. Wild West excitement returns each June with the Fort Union Rendezvous.

North Dakota–Montana state line (22/58) You officially enter big sky country and change from Central to Mountain Time. Watches go back an hour (forward when travelling east).

For most of the next 700 miles (1,100km) the train rolls across the grassland plains of northern Montana, where cattle are more frequent than people and sheep more frequent than cattle. Watch out also for woodchuck, wolverine and herds of antelope.

Culbertson (50/30) Just west of town the *Empire Builder* crosses Big Muddy Creek into Fort Peck Indian Reservation, where Sitting Bull lived after surrendering. The train then crosses the Poplar River.

WOLF POINT (80/45) This small town is set among hundreds of thousands of acres of Montana's high plains. Note the wolf silhouette on the welcome sign, recalling frontier days when this was a wolf-trappers' trading post. Each July, Wolf Point hosts the Wild Horse Stampede – 'the granddaddy of Montana rodeos'.

Fort Peck Dam (30/15) Built in 1940, the earth-filled dam is 250ft (75m) tall and forms a 383-square-mile (990km^2) lake. As the train leaves Fort Peck Reservation and approaches Glasgow, look right for a large letter 'G' on the hillside.

GLASGOW (45/55) The neat station stands to your left and a church to your right. Fossils and dinosaur bones discovered nearby are displayed at the Fort Peck Museum.

The train accompanies the Milk River west to Havre (pronounced 'Have-er') and somewhere between here and Malta, assuming both trains are on time, you should pass the eastbound *Empire Builder*.

Tampico (15/40) The small town is visible to your right.

Sleeping Buffalo Hot Springs (35/20) A large bell hangs on the Saco Methodist church to your right. The town of Saco got its start because of the need of a place for a Great Northern Railroad water tank. The railroad agents could not decide on a name, so they spun a globe and a finger landed on Saco, Maine. The *Empire Builder* passes Nelson Reservoir and part of Lake Bowdoin, also to your right. The wildlife refuge on the left is a resort for waterbirds.

MALTA (55/70) The town's name is also said to have been determined by a spin of the globe by a Great Northern official, whose finger came to rest on the island of Malta in the Mediterranean. Local cattle empires inspired the western artist Charles Russell and ranching is still big business.

The *Empire Builder* makes a fast run from Malta to Havre, passing many more grain elevators alongside the track.

Wagner (10/60) The Wild Bunch dynamited the Adams Express car on Great Northern's *Oriental Limited* here in 1901 and stole $68,000. Gang members Butch Cassidy and the Sundance Kid took no part in the robbery as both had already set sail for Buenos Aires to escape the law.

You travel beside the northern edge of Fort Belknap Indian Reservation, with the Bear Paw Mountains ahead to your left. In 1877, Chief Joseph of the Nez Perce Indians surrendered to the US Army after a 1,700-mile (2,700km) retreat with the words: 'From where the sun now stands I will fight no more forever.' On your left beyond the highway are the Little Rocky Mountains.

HAVRE (70/95) This is an Amtrak service stop so you should have plenty of time to detrain and inspect the S-2 locomotive standing on a pedestal to the left of the station. It was one of the last 14 steam engines acquired from the Baldwin works for main-line service by the Great Northern in 1930. They were the most powerful steam locomotives built until then. Some continued in freight service after the previous *Empire Builder* was streamlined and switched to diesel power in 1947.

Native Americans used to hunt buffalo by driving them over nearby cliffs, and a museum at the site shows some of the animals' skeleton remains. Havre has expanded greatly since the discovery of natural gas in this area.

Fort Benton, located 70 miles south of Havre, has a larger-than-life bronze statue of Old Shep, a sheepdog who appeared at the town's Great Northern railway station one day in 1936 as the casket of his dead master was being loaded on a train to be sent back east to relatives. The dog watched the train depart and for the next 5½ years he maintained a vigil at the station, scanning passengers alighting from the four trains that arrived each day as he waited for his master to return. Tragedy struck in 1942, when the old and deaf Shep failed to hear the 10.17 and slipped on an icy rail trying to get away, disappearing under the engine. He was buried on a lonely bluff looking down on the depot and the Great Northern Railroad put up an obelisk, with a painted wooden cut-out of Shep next to it and white stones spelling out 'SHEP'. Lights illuminated the display at night, and it can still be seen today.

Milk River (5/90) The river departs to the north, entering Canada before finding its source in Montana's Glacier National Park.

SHELBY (95/30) Named after Peter Shelby, General Manager of the Montana Central Railroad, this characteristic prairie town is located at the heart of Montana's oil region. Look for freight wagons and grain elevators standing beside the track. A railway branch line goes north from the station on your right through the Crowsnest Pass to Lethbridge in Alberta.

Shelby was the unlikely venue in 1923 for a heavyweight boxing championship fight between Jack Dempsey and Tom Gibbons. Chaos ensued when the match was cancelled before being reconvened in front of 7,000 fans and 17,000 gatecrashers, many of whom arrived by chartered train. Dempsey won but received no prize money after his manager vanished with $300,000. Several banks failed and the city never hosted another fight.

CUT BANK (30/32) Winter temperatures in this small, oil-producing town are among the nation's coldest. Sweetgrass Hills and the Canadian border are only 25 miles (40km) away to your right.

The *Empire Builder* departs on tracks supported by a trestle across Cut Bank Creek and you get your first views ahead of the Rocky Mountains. This horizon becomes increasingly impressive as you near Glacier National Park, but if you wish to be sure of seeing this section of the route by daylight you should travel during summer or take an eastbound train.

Lewis and Clark Monument (20/12) An obelisk on your left commemorates Lewis and Clark's search for a pass through the mountains when they made the first overland journey across North America during 1804–06.

BROWNING (32/20) The train stops here when East Glacier Park Station is closed during winter. Browning is at the heart of the Blackfeet Indian Reservation and a good place to shop for Native American goods. The **Museum of the Plains Indian** (✆ *406 338 2230*) features the art and history of many Northern Plains tribal peoples including the Blackfeet, Crow, Northern Cheyenne, Sioux, Assiniboine, Arapaho, Shoshone, Nez Perce, Flathead, Chippewa and Cree.

The train continues towards the Rockies, approaching East Glacier Park Station on a high trestle over Two Medicine River.

EAST GLACIER PARK (20/60) The station opens in summer to provide a gateway into one of America's most stunning national parks, which opened in 1910 and features 200 lakes, 10,000ft (3,000m) mountains and 50 living glaciers. For **information** on boating, hiking and skiing, ☏ 406 888 7800.

Timber was brought from Oregon and Washington by the Great Northern to build Glacier Park Lodge, seen to your right beside the 1913 station. When the station closes out of season, access to the park may still be possible via Browning or Essex. Having enjoyed relatively easy conditions so far the *Empire Builder* now has to tackle the jagged barrier ahead.

Marias Pass (15/45) The continental divide at this point is lower (5,216ft/1,590m) than anywhere else between Canada and New Mexico. Native Americans may have crossed Mystery Pass but Meriwether Lewis and William Clark were unable to chart an accurate route. It was John Stevens, working as a surveyor for the Great Northern, who finally discovered a passage in 1889. Almost freezing to death in temperatures of –40°F (–40°C), he fully earned the statue dedicated to him on your right.

Also on the right is a fence constructed to keep out grizzly bears. The monument to your left honours President Theodore Roosevelt, after whom the adjacent highway was named.

As the train descends the western side of the pass the scenery becomes even more breathtaking, with waterfalls and deep gorges cutting through the rugged mountains.

Flathead River (45/15) Joining from your left, the river is crossed on another trestle.

ESSEX (60/35) A flag stop, so trains only halt at this village if requested. The Izaak Walton Inn to your right was named after the English writer and angler.

WEST GLACIER (35/35) Entrance to the western part of **Glacier National Park**, where yearly snowfall can reach over 200 inches (500cm). The *Empire Builder* again crosses the Flathead River.

Columbia Falls (20/15) Look for the preserved steam engine on your left and an Anaconda aluminium plant to your right.

WHITEFISH (35/110) A German-style station on the left complements the alpine scenery. Whitefish is located in a valley of the Flathead National Forest close to the resorts of Whitefish Lake and Big Mountain. Flathead Lake, the greatest expanse of water west of the Mississippi, is 25 miles (40km) to the south.

Flathead Tunnel (40/70) You travel seven miles (11km) through one of the longest tunnels in the world.

LIBBY (110/55) The town is in the middle of **Kootenai National Forest**, popular with hunters and fishermen. Libby's sawmills and log-processing plants are sometimes open to visitors.

Between here and Sandpoint the train goes from Montana into Idaho, changing from Mountain to Pacific Time. Watches go back an hour (forward when travelling east).

SANDPOINT (55/80) Sandpoint stands next to Lake Pend Oreille and close to the Schweitzer ski area.

Travelling on through the night, the *Empire Builder* leaves Idaho for Washington, the Evergreen State.

SPOKANE (80/120) 'The monarch of the inland empire' stands next to the Spokane River and is surrounded by farmland. An important railroad junction, this is where the Great Northern route meets the Spokane, Portland & Seattle line. The old Great Northern clock tower remains a prominent downtown landmark and Amtrak's station is at W 221 First.

Bing Crosby attended Spokane's Gonzaga University and the library owns photographs, memorabilia and a bronze statue. The **Northwest Museum of Arts and Culture** (*2316 W First Av*; ☎ *509 456 3931; www.northwestmuseum.org*) has 68,000 objects including fine art, historic regional paintings and a huge collection of American Plateau Indian culture. The **Grand Coulee Dam**, one of the largest concrete structures in the world, is 80 miles (128km) east. Famously sung about by Woody Guthrie, the dam was begun in 1933 as part of President Roosevelt's New Deal.

The *Empire Builder* divides into two trains at Spokane; in this chapter we continue to Seattle. For the route to Portland, see the next chapter (pages 000–000).

EPHRATA (120/65) The town is set among fertile land irrigated by water from the Columbia River project.

Rock Island Dam (35/30) The dam to your left holds back the Columbia River, which the *Empire Builder* crosses five minutes later.

WENATCHEE (65/25) The city was named after a Salish Indian word that means 'river which comes from canyons' or 'robe of the rainbow'. Wenatchee is one of the apple capitals of the world and orchards in the Cascades foothills have perfect weather conditions for producing a seventh of the country's crop. The **Wenatchee Valley Museum and Cultural Center** (*127 Mission*; ☎ *509 664 3340*) shows the rich history of north central Washington and has spirited demonstrations of apple sorting.

The train pulls out past warehouses and lumber yards then accompanies the Wenatchee River to your left. To enjoy the best scenery for the next hour or so you should stay on this side of the train. This region is one of the last refuges for the spotted owl, a consequent source of conflict between conservationists and loggers.

Cashmere (15/10) Look for more apple warehouses. Turkish delight-type sweets called aplets (made from apples) and cotlets (from apricots) are local specialities.

The train crosses the Wenatchee River several times as it approaches the Cascade Mountains.

LEAVENWORTH (25/150) Bavarian-style buildings appear among the orchards as the *Empire Builder* starts a long, steep climb, entering the first of many tunnels before again crossing the river.

Merritt (35/115) The train slows further as it gains height among streams, mountains and marshland.

Icicle Canyon (40/110) The best views are now to your right. Keep a look out for goats, elk, deer and perhaps beaver.

Cascade Tunnel (50/100) Completed in 1929, the tunnel is another of the world's longest, at 7.79 miles (12.53km). It helped replace 43 miles (69km) of stiff grades with an easier 34-mile (54km) route. Stevens Pass is 500ft (150m) higher at 4,061ft (1,225m). The tunnel lasts 15 minutes before the train emerges to begin a 65-mile (105km) descent to Everett, giving delightful views of the Cascades and Puget Sound.

The *Empire Builder* crosses the Skyomish River, which it follows to Everett. A waterfall appears on the left but the best scenery remains to your right. This is *Twin Peaks* country, with wooden houses, cloud-topped mountains, pine forests, fast-running streams and huge logging trucks. The modest towns look as if they belong in a Norman Rockwell painting.

You cross the Skyomish River on another dramatic high trestle, with the Mount Baker-Snoqualmie National Forest ranger station to your right.

Skyomish (75/75) A logging town which has an interesting historic Burlington Northern station.

Sunset Falls (90/60) The falls are to your left before you again cross the river. Look also for Indian Falls, Table Rock and Index Mountain.

Grotto (92/58) A small village stands among the mountains to your right. The train crosses the river twice more, leaving the Cascades for less demanding terrain.

Monroe (125/25) Note the old station building away from the tracks to your right.

EVERETT (150/25) As a natural inland port, Everett was a focal point for the fishing and lumber industries even before the railroad came. Boeing's 747/767 assembly plant is contained here in what may be the world's largest building. Trailways Northwest buses connect with Vancouver, British Columbia.

South of the city you join Puget Sound on your right for the next 15 miles (24km), with the Olympic Mountains in the distance. Islands in the sound include Bainbridge and Whidbey, linked to the mainland by ferry.

EDMONDS (25/30) 'The gem of the Puget Sound', Edmonds is mostly residential and its Old Milltown shopping arcade was developed inside an old Ford garage. The *Empire Builder* stops at 211 Railroad Avenue, near the dock where ferries leave for Kingston and the Olympic Peninsula.

Shilshole Bay (15/15) Innumerable boats are moored in the marina to your right. Bainbridge Island, where Michael Douglas lived in the movie *Disclosure*, is across the water. You cross Salmon Bay inlet then travel briefly inland past Chittenden Locks to your left, part of a waterway system linking the bay with Lake Washington. On your right is a statue of the Norwegian explorer Leif Ericsson.

The train returns to the shoreline by way of a US Navy reservation, then travels along Seattle's waterfront. Pier 70 to your right is America's largest restored wooden building. The former warehouse has 40 shops and restaurants and is connected to downtown by a trolley running on tracks beside the train. Seattle's Space Needle comes into view on your left before the *Empire Builder* passes through a mile-long (1.6km) tunnel to complete its journey at King Street Station.

SEATTLE For Seattle city information, see *Chapter 4, The* Coast Starlight (pages 49–70).

9

The *Empire Builder*
Spokane–Portland

Joining the train

SPOKANE (80/150) For Spokane, the route from Chicago and onward to Seattle, see the previous chapter (pages 10–14).

All aboard! *Duration: seven hours 15 minutes*

Through-coaches for this branch of the *Empire Builder* service to Portland continue via Pasco.

PASCO (150/115) This is the furthest seagoing vessels can voyage up the Columbia River. The Columbia and Snake rivers meet in this territory, which was claimed by the British until it became part of the United States in 1846. Before a railroad bridge was built across the Columbia in 1883, connecting Pasco with railroad tracks leading over the Cascade Range to Puget Sound, steel barges were used to transport Northern Pacific railroad cars across the water. The barges were operated by the Pacific Steamship Company, which gave the town its name. An alternative explanation is that Virgil Bogue, a construction engineer for the Northern Pacific, named the town after Cerro de Pasco, a city in the Peruvian Andes where he had helped build a railroad. The station at Clark and Tacoma also serves Kennewick and Richland.

North McNary (30/85) Named after Charles McNary, who was a US senator for Oregon from 1917 to 1944.

Columbia River (75/40) The state of Oregon can be seen on the opposite side as you travel the water-level route through the Columbia River Gorge – a land of stone cliffs, lakes, streams, meadows and woods.

Roosevelt (80/35) Barges shipping grain are a common sight on the river between here and Vancouver.

John Day Dam (100/15) The dam is 5,900ft (1,800m) long and was completed in 1968 at a cost of $487 million. Masses of pylons take away enough electricity to supply Portland three times over. The locks carry eight million tons of shipping a year and incorporate one of the highest (113ft/35m) single lifts in the world.

Maryhill (105/10) Just past an emu and ostrich farm to your left, look right for a glimpse of the Maryhill Castle Art Museum. Also on the hill to your right is a concrete replica of Stonehenge, built to honour troops who died in World War I.

For Chicago to
Spokane, see the main
Empire Builder section

CHICAGO

SPOKANE

Pasco

N← **Brad**

Wishram

Bingen-
White Salmon

VANCOUVER

For Vancouver to
Portland, see
The Coast Starlight

PORTLAND

WISHRAM (115/30) Named after a Native American settlement known to Lewis and Clark, Wishram is the site of a legendary 'beanery' – one of the cheap restaurants built and operated by the railway for its workers.

On the far side of the Columbia are the Union Pacific tracks used until 1997 by Amtrak's *Pioneer* train from Seattle and Salt Lake City. A bridge ahead takes the Burlington Northern line south to Klamath Falls.

Avery (2/28) The pyramid of Mount Hood can be seen to the south as you continue through the Columbia Gorge.

Dalles Dam (10/20) Dalles is French for 'trough' and describes the narrow channel formed by the river. The 8,700ft (2,650m) zigzag-shaped dam provides irrigation and power, and created Horsethief Lake. The town of Dalles is on the opposite shore.

Mount Hood (15/15) Look left for another view of Oregon's tallest mountain, 11,235ft (3,425m) and permanently snow-capped.

Lyle (25/5) The train crosses the Klickitat River, with the Native American burial ground of Memaloose Island to your left.

BINGEN-WHITE SALMON (30/80) Jointly named after the White Salmon River and a German town called Bingen. The city of Hood River can be seen on the far shore.

For the next 55 miles (88km) the landscape changes from near-desert to rainforest as the *Empire Builder* travels through the Columbia Gorge, carved into ancient rocks by the river. Lewis and Clark were the first white people to venture this far and settlers on the Oregon Trail would often refuse to risk crossing the powerful river.

Cooks (15/65) Wind Mountain (2,500ft/760m) is to your right. One of this region's few remaining log flumes transports lumber to a sawmill beside the river.

Stevenson (30/50) Amtrak's *Pioneer* formerly stopped at Cascade Locks across the water.

Bridge of the Gods (33/47) The bridge ahead to your left replaced a stone bridge which Native Americans say their god destroyed when he was angered by his sons arguing over a maiden. The sons became Mount Hood and Mount Adams and the maiden was transformed into Mount St Helens.

Sheridan's Point (35/45) Philip Sheridan, a cavalry officer and later a Civil War general, defended settlers from Indian marauders here in 1855 when he was a young officer. He notoriously remarked that the only good Indians he ever saw were dead ones. The final spike was driven nearby in 1908 to complete the Spokane, Portland & Seattle route between Pasco and Vancouver.

Bonneville Dam (36/44) This was the Columbia's first great dam, worked on by Woody Guthrie. The half-mile (0.8km) feat of engineering created Lake Bonneville. Look for the fish ladder which allows migrating salmon to swim upstream.

Beacon Rock (40/40) The 840ft (255m) Beacon Rock is claimed to be the second-largest free-standing monolith in the northern hemisphere, just behind the Rock of Gibraltar. El Capitan is twice as tall but the term 'monolith' usually defines a 'single rock'. Named by Lewis and Clark, it was an unmistakable guide for travellers.

Multnomah Falls (42/38) The second-highest waterfall in the country cascades 620ft (190m) on the Oregon side. Look also for rafts of logs, paper mills and sawmills.

Cape Horn (48/32) The train leaves the Columbia Gorge by way of a 2,369ft (720m) tunnel through the western Cascades. Just before Vancouver you can glimpse a smart Spokane, Portland & Seattle railroad car to your left.

VANCOUVER (80/22) For Vancouver and the rest of the *Empire Builder* route to Portland, see *Chapter 4, The* Coast Starlight (pages 49–70).

10

The *Southwest Chief*
Chicago–Los Angeles

General route information

Amtrak's fastest trip from Chicago to the Pacific is along part of the Santa Fe Trail first used by Native Americans and Spanish conquistadores, then by mule caravans, wagon trains, stagecoaches and gold prospectors. The train travels 2,265 miles (3,645km) through eight states, passing wheat fields, ranches, missions, pueblos, mountains and deserts. Sometimes the canyons you go through are only a few feet wider than the train. Close by this route are Santa Fe, Taos and the Grand Canyon.

The *Southwest Chief* follows a Santa Fe Railway line which the *Super Chief* first took in 1937, cutting 15 hours from the time of its predecessor, the *Chief*. The *Chief* in turn had succeeded two other luxury trains, the *Southwest Limited* and the *Santa Fe De Luxe*. Even as late as the 1970s, Frank Sinatra was inclined to hire a luxury private car to travel with his friends between San Bernadino and Chicago.

Joining the train

CHICAGO For Chicago city information and the route as far as Galesburg, see *Chapter 5, The* California Zephyr *(pages 71–90)*. In addition to the stops made

ESSENTIAL INFORMATION

FREQUENCY Daily. The **westbound** service leaves Chicago mid afternoon to arrive in Kansas City late in the evening and Dodge City early next morning. You reach Albuquerque late in the afternoon, Flagstaff (for the Grand Canyon) by mid evening and Los Angeles early on the third day. Travelling **east**, trains leave Los Angeles early in the evening to reach Flagstaff early next morning, Albuquerque by early afternoon and Dodge City about midnight. You arrive in Kansas City early on the third day and Chicago by mid afternoon.
DURATION 40+ hours
RESERVATIONS All reserved
EQUIPMENT Superliner coaches
SLEEPING Superliner bedrooms
FOOD Complete meals, snacks, sandwiches, drinks
LOUNGE CAR Movies, travelogues, hospitality hour. National Park Service guides are on board between Albuquerque and La Junta, Colorado, as follows: From Bent's Old Fort (La Junta), from the Pecos National Historic Park (Pecos, New Mexico) and from Petroglyph National Monument (Albuquerque).
BAGGAGE Check-in service at most stations

by the *California Zephyr*, the *Southwest Chief* serves the renovated station in Mendota – the first long-distance train to stop there in 26 years. The train travels all the way to Los Angeles on tracks of the BNSF Railway Company (BNSF).

GALESBURG (42/45) Settled by Presbyterians from Oneida, New York, Galesburg was the scene of a Lincoln–Douglas debate in 1858. It was also the home of George Washington Ferris (creator of the first Ferris wheel) and Olmsted Ferris (inventor of popcorn). Amtrak's station is at 225 S Seminary Street.

Mississippi River (35/10) North America's greatest waterway appears to your right. A few minutes later the train crosses the river from Illinois into Iowa by means of the longest (3,347ft/1,020m) double-track, double-decked bridge in the world. The structure pivots to allow larger boats to pass beneath.

Approaching Fort Madison, note the Santa Fe steam engine on your left. The old Santa Fe station is a museum.

FORT MADISON (45/65) The train's only stop on its brief passage through Iowa is this industrial city. US soldiers set fire to the original fort in 1813 to divert attacking Indians while settlers escaped through a tunnel to the Mississippi. This event is commemorated by One Chimney Monument to your right.

Fort Madison is Amtrak's closest stop to Keokuk, five miles south along the river.

Nauvoo (10/55) The old Mormon town seen across the Des Moines River is being restored as a monument. Soon after Nauvoo you cross the Des Moines River from Iowa into Missouri.

LA PLATA (65/130) A small farming town in a region famous for deer, pheasant and turkey hunting. La Plata Lake is on your left and Kirksville, home of Northeast Missouri University, ten miles (16km) to the north.

Marceline (35/95) Childhood home of Walt Disney, who invented Mickey Mouse while riding on the *Southwest Chief*. Walt Disney Park to your right features a steam locomotive from the Santa Fe Railway.

Mendon (45/85) Waterfowl migrate to Canada from Swan Lake Game Reserve, seen on your right. Hunters account for several hundred thousand birds each year.

Bosworth (50/80) You cross the Grand River, bordered by pecan trees.

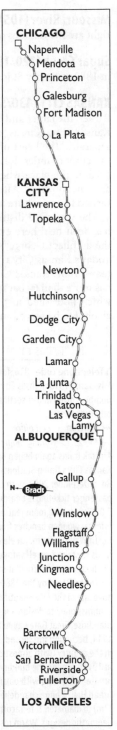

CHICAGO
Naperville
Mendota
Princeton
Galesburg
Fort Madison
La Plata

KANSAS CITY
Lawrence
Topeka

Newton
Hutchinson
Dodge City
Garden City
Lamar
La Junta
Trinidad
Raton
Las Vegas
Lamy
ALBUQUERQUE

Gallup

N Bradt

Winslow
Flagstaff
Williams
Junction
Kingman
Needles

Barstow
Victorville
San Bernardino
Riverside
Fullerton

LOS ANGELES

10

Missouri River (105/25) The train crosses on a 135ft-high (40m) bridge. To your right are the remains of Fort Osage, built in 1808.

Sugar Creek (120/10) The town was a haunt of the outlaw Jesse James, who died in 1882 at nearby St Joseph.

KANSAS CITY (130/50) Birthplace of Harry S Truman, Jean Harlow and Charlie Parker, the larger and better-known Kansas City is in Missouri rather than Kansas. Kansas City, Kansas, is immediately across the Missouri River but is politically separate. 'The heart of America' was named after Kanza Indians who traded with the city's founder, John Calvin McCoy. A settlement on a bend in the river later became the place where wagon trains were equipped for the Santa Fe, California and Oregon trails. After the Civil War, with the coming of the railroad, Kansas City turned to agriculture and transport for a living.

The stockyard district reflects Cowtown history and the Royal Livestock Show has been held here every year since 1899. Around the turn of the 20th century, the architect George Kessler set out to create 'one of the loveliest cities on earth'. Today's Kansas City rivals Paris for boulevards and claims to have more fountains than Rome. Kansas City has been 'the home of the barbecue' since the 1920s and has more than 60 barbecue restaurants. The city is also famous for its jazz tradition, which flourished in the 1930s prohibition era when the authorities still allowed alcohol to be served in this 'wide-open town'.

Kansas City basics

❧**Telephone code** 816, for Kansas City, Missouri; 913 for Kansas City, Kansas. All numbers given in this section are 816 code unless otherwise noted.

ᜊ **Station** (*Ticket office ⏰ 05.45–14.15 & 14.45–23.15. Waiting room ⏰ 06.00–23.59*) Amtrak trains again began operating out of Kansas City's Union Station at 30 W Pershing Rd in December 2002, with a new $4.6 million passenger ticketing & boarding facility. The 2,000ft² waiting room features 5 of the splendid original wooden benches from the station's North Waiting Room. An elevated walkway leads to stairs & an elevator provides access to the boarding platform. Kansas City outgrew its old Union Depot by the 1880s & Jarvis Hunt, an advocate of the City Beautiful movement, was commissioned to design a new building. His grandiose 'Great Gateway to the West' opened in 1914, becoming the second-largest train station in the country (with almost 80,000 trains visiting in 1917). Among the building's features were an ornate 95ft ceiling with oak leaf clusters in the Grand Hall, 3 huge chandeliers, a clock over 6ft (2m) in diameter, & terracotta floors in elegant geometric designs. Warm rose-brown-marble decorated, separate male & female lounges, & the North Waiting Room was longer than a football field.

The station also housed fine restaurants, the city's largest barbershop, a post office, a drug store, a small jail, a Harvey House coffee shop & an emergency hospital. The complex was lit, heated & cooled by its own power plant, & 3 sub-levels smoothed traffic between passengers, baggage transportation & local citizens using the station's services.

Union Station became notorious in 1933 for the Kansas City Massacre in which 5 people died in an attempt to free the notorious underworld figure Frank 'Gentleman' Nash from Federal custody. Charles Arthur 'Pretty Boy' Floyd became Public Enemy Number One, with a $23,000 dead-or-alive reward on his head. After fleeing Kansas City, Floyd made his way to Ohio, where he died there after being shot by FBI agents in 1934. His body left East Liverpool in a baggage car & 20,000 people attended his funeral. To some people of his home state, Oklahoma, he was a folk hero – the 'Robin Hood of the Cookson Hills' – & was written into legend through Woody Guthrie's ballad.

During World War II, half of all military personnel passed through Kansas City on troop trains but rail travel declined in the 1950s. The North Waiting Room was closed, the grand structure began to deteriorate & Amtrak temporarily relocated to a small boarding office nearby. Local preservationists, with help from Kansas & Missouri taxpayers, raised the necessary funds & Union Station reopened in 1999 after a $118 million renovation. Now an entertainment centre, it has a hands-on Science City for children, theatres, a 5-storey cinema, restaurants, shops & offices. For information about programming & events, ☎ 460 2020; www.unionstation.org.

Connections Thruway buses go to Tulsa & Oklahoma City.

Local transport Kansas City covers 300 square miles (770km²), so most people get around by car. Metro buses (☎ 221 0660) operate downtown.

Taxis Yellow ☎ 471 5000; Checker ☎ 444 4444

Car rental Thrifty, 2001 Baltimore; ☎ 842 8550

Greyhound 1101 N Troost; ☎ 221 2835

Kansas City International Airport 20 miles (32km) northwest by KCI Shuttle Bus (☎ 243 5000) or Metro bus #246.

Tours Self-guided walking tours from the Historic Kansas City Foundation, 20 W Ninth (☎ 931 8448; www.historickansascity.org) & Plaza Merchants Association, 4745 Central (☎ 753 0100).

Visitors bureau Union Station & at 11th & 1100 Main; ☎ 221 5242 or ☎ 800 767 7700; e info@visitkc.com; www.visitkc.com; ⊕ Mon–Fri

Accommodation Contact Bed & Breakfast in Kansas City; ☎ 913 888 3636. Downtown hotel rates can be expensive but look for w/end deals.

Hotels include the Raphael, 325 Ward Parkway; ☎ 756 3800, **$$$$**; Westin Crown Center, 1 Pershing Rd; ☎ 474 4400, **$$$$**; Best Western, 501 Southwest Bd; ☎ 913 677 3060, **$$**; Travelodge, 1600 Parvin Rd; ☎ 453 5210, **$$$**; Intercontinental, 401 Ward Parkway; ☎ 756 1500, **$$$**; Drury Inn-KC Stadium, 3830 Blue Ridge Cut-off; ☎ 923 3000, **$$**.

Recommended in Kansas City

The parks Among the city's 300 parks is America's 2nd largest, Swope Park, with its Starlight Theatre, the Kansas City Zoo & 2 golf courses. Others include Loose Park (famous for its roses) & Shawnee Mission Park.

Crown Center 2405 Grand Av, opposite the station; ☎ 274 8444; www.crowncenter.com; ⊕ daily; free concerts in summer. This complex of shops, offices & hotels incorporates an indoor waterfall & the headquarters of Hallmark Cards.

Country Club Plaza 2 miles south of Crown Center at 4745 Central; ☎ 753 0100; www. countryclubplaza.com. This was America's first (1922) shopping precinct & has pretty Spanish-style architecture, fountains & sculpture. The Plaza Art Fair takes place each Sep.

Kansas City Museum 3218 Gladstone Bd; ☎ 460 2020; www.unionstation.org/kcmuseum; ⊕ Tue–Sun; donation. Housed in the mansion of lumber tycoon R A Long, the museum includes a replica trading post.

Science City Union Station, 30 W Pershing Rd; ☎ 460 2020; www.sciencecity.com. This beautiful, restored 1914 train station features an interactive science museum, restaurants, shops & theatres. Take a behind-the-scenes tour with characters from the station's past.

American Jazz Museum 18th & Vine; ☎ 474 8463; www.americanjazzmuseum.com; ⊕ Tue–Sun; admission charge. The story of jazz & performers such as Louis Armstrong, Charlie 'Bird' Parker, Duke Ellington & Ella Fitzgerald is celebrated in one of the country's most interactive museums. This ultra-modern building is shared by a visitor centre, a theatre & the **Negro Leagues Baseball Museum** 1616 E 18th; ☎ 221 1920; www.nlbm.com; admission charge. The museum opened in 1991 & is located in the historic Lincoln Building.

1859 Jail Museum 217 N Main, Independence; ☎ 252 1892; www.jchs.org/jail/museum; ⊕ daily; admission charge. Frank James was a resident within the massive, limestone walls of the jail during Wild West days. As well as the 2-storey County Jail, with its barred windows & double iron doors, the museum features a schoolhouse & marshal's office.

All aboard!

The *Southwest Chief* departs Kansas City, Missouri, and crosses the state line into Kansas City, Kansas.

LAWRENCE (50/32) This was a 'station' on the Underground Railroad founded by abolitionists before the Civil War. In 1863, Quantrill's pro-Confederate guerrillas attacked the peaceful town, killing 150 of its citizens. Kansas University began here in 1866.

The 1906 Santa Fe depot at Baldwin, 12 miles (19km) south, has vintage equipment, memorabilia and diesel-powered trips from May to October on the historic **Midland Railway** (✆ *913 721 1211; www.midland-ry.org*).

TOPEKA (32/130) The capital of Kansas is home to the Menninger Foundation, a world leader in the treatment of mental illness, and the clinic owns an important collection of Sigmund Freud's papers.

Emporia (65/65) Home of Emporia State University and the *Emporia Gazette*. The newspaper's editor, William White, gave the city its Peter Pan Park.

NEWTON (130/35) One of America's largest Mennonite settlements, Newton was founded in 1872 by immigrants from Russia. Seed they brought for winter wheat helped Kansas become 'the world's breadbasket'. Amtrak's station also serves Wichita, 20 miles (32km) further south.

HUTCHINSON (35/95) The largest wheat market anywhere in the world, boasting 50 massive grain elevators. Nearby is one of the world's biggest salt mines.

Between here and Dodge City the train travels through oil country, with nodding pumps seen on both sides of the track.

Kinsley (65/30) A sign to your right states that Kinsley is exactly 1,561 miles (2,510km) from both San Francisco and New York.

DODGE CITY (95/42) This former trading post and army fort began to prosper when the Santa Fe Railway arrived in 1872. Dodge soon became the cowboy capital of the world, shipping longhorn steers brought on cattle drives from Texas and the south. Lawlessness took hold of 'the wickedest little city in America' until Bat Masterson, Wyatt Earp and Doc Holliday restored order. The hangman's tree still survives and many gunfighters and outlaws who died were buried on Boot Hill to your left. The railyards still ship great quantities of cattle and wheat. Front Street, to your right, looks much as it always did, although calmer these days.

The **tourist bureau** is at 400 W Wyatt Earp Boulevard (✆ *620 225 8186; www. visitdodgecity.org*). Amtrak's Santa Fe Station, a national historic landmark, is at Central and Wyatt Earp. Two sundials on your right signify a change of time zone which actually takes place further west.

Cimarron (15/27) Where the Santa Fe Trail crosses the Arkansas River, seen to your left.

GARDEN CITY (42/75) Apparently named by a passing hobo who admired the garden of its founder's wife, the city claims to have the world's largest swimming pool and most capacious grain elevator. Nearby are the world's biggest buffalo herd and a massive natural gas field.

Holcomb (5/70) The murders described in Truman Capote's *In Cold Blood* took place here. This part of the Sunflower State has many fields filled with these impressive plants, grown for their oil and as cattle feed.

Coolidge (50/25) The train leaves Kansas and enters Colorado, changing from Central to Mountain Time, so watches go back an hour (forward when travelling east).

The *Southwest Chief* crosses the Arkansas River, which it then follows west to La Junta. The valley is famous for vegetables and fruit, especially cantaloupe melons.

LAMAR (75/45) As the train nears the station in 'the goose hunting capital of America', look left to see the Madonna of the Trails statue erected by the Daughters of the Revolution.

John Martin Dam (10/35) The dam forms a reservoir frequented by herons and cranes.

Las Animas (25/20) Named after the Río de las Animas Perdidas (the river of lost souls) where a wagon train of settlers camped and disappeared overnight, presumably having been attacked by Native Americans.

Bent's Old Fort (35/10) The settlement seen among the trees to your right was built in the 1840s to protect fur traders and service wagon trains on the Santa Fe Trail. Kit Carson worked at the adobe fort, which has been restored.

LA JUNTA (45/75) The Santa Fe Trail meets the Cimarron cut-off here and La Junta is the Santa Fe Railway's divisional headquarters. Outlaws such as Belle Star inscribed their names on nearby rocks. On a clear day you can see Pike's Peak on your right even though it stands 100 miles north.

After La Junta the *Southwest Chief* leaves the valley and swings south to make a fast run across the Commanche National Grassland.

Sunflower Valley (50/25) Farms in this region produce enormous crops of wheat, corn and sugar beet. As the train approaches Trinidad, look right for the snow-covered Sangre de Cristo Range and the twin Spanish Peaks of the Colorado Rockies. Native Americans called these mountains 'the breasts of mother earth'.

TRINIDAD (75/65) The name (meaning 'trinity') appears to your left on the hill known as Simpson's Rest, after the pioneer who was buried there. Fisher's Peak (10,000ft/3,038m) is also to your left.

Trinidad became known for the battle fought between Spanish and US settlers on Christmas Day in 1867, and the town's **history museum** (☏ *719 846 7217*) reveals the struggles of early settlement life. Amtrak's station is at 110 Pine Street.

Purgatoire River (5/60) The *Southwest Chief* crosses the river and begins the steep climb to Raton Pass.

Morley (20/45) Look for an old coal mine and the ruins of a Spanish mission on the hill to your right.

Wootton Ranch (35/30) On your right is the ranch owned by Dick Wootton, a noted frontier scout and Indian fighter, paid for by the Raton Pass toll road he established. The road became obsolete when the railway was built. The original Santa Fe Trail can be seen to your right and Interstate 25, which the train accompanies most of the way to Albuquerque, is off to your left.

Raton Pass (40/25) Highest point (7,588ft/2,310m) on the *Southwest Chief's* journey, the ascent to this pass is the steepest on the route. Entering a half-mile-long (0.8km) tunnel, you go from Colorado into New Mexico.

RATON (65/105) Thruway buses connect with Colorado Springs and Denver's Union Station. A railroad and mining town nestled in the foothills of the Sangre de Cristo Mountains, Raton is Amtrak's nearest stop to the Philmont Ranch, a 137,441-acre (55,600ha) estate owned by the Boy Scouts of America.

Clifton House Ruins (5/100) The house to your left, built in 1867 and known as the Red River Hotel, was a resting place on the Santa Fe Trail.

Maxwell (20/85) The 1.75 million-acre Maxwell wildlife refuge belonged to Lucien Maxwell – hunter, trapper and a friend of Kit Carson.

Springer (35/70) After following the Canadian River, the train crosses the Cimarron River with Baldy Peak (12,441ft/3,795m) on the far right. Keep a look out for antelope.

Wagon Mound (60/45) The butte to your left, shaped like a wagon and horses, was one of many landmarks on the Santa Fe Trail.

Shoemaker Canyon (80/25) The train crosses then follows the Mora River. Pines and cottonwoods flourish in what was once a trade route for Plains and Texas Indians.

Watrous (85/20) To your left are the ruins of Fort Union, founded in 1851 as one of the largest forts in the southwest. Ahead to your right are the higher Sangre de Cristo Mountains, called 'the blood of Christ' by Spanish settlers because of the hardships suffered crossing them.

LAS VEGAS (105/100) Not to be confused with any other Las Vegas. Look right just before the station to see La Castenada Hotel, a former Harvey House. The first of Englishman Fred Harvey's dining rooms opened at Topeka, Kansas, in the spring of 1876 on the Atchison, Topeka & Santa Fe line. Orders taken on the train were ready to be served as soon as passengers arrived. Theodore Roosevelt joined his Rough Riders at La Castenada for a reunion in 1899 following their exploits in Cuba during the Spanish–American War of the previous year.

Native Americans knew this region for thousands of years before Coronado discovered it in 1541. White settlers began to arrive in the 1830s, and the town grew faster when the railroad came in 1879. Prosperity also attracted outlaws such as Jesse James and Billy the Kid.

As the train pulls out, look for an old railway roundhouse to your right. The letter 'H' on the hill to your left signifies New Mexico Highlands University.

Bernal (20/80) The ruins of a Las Vegas–Santa Fe stagecoach relay station can be seen off to your right. Martinez Canyon is to your left.

Starvation Peak (30/70) A band of 30 early 19th-century Spanish settlers are said to have climbed the small, flat-topped mesa ahead to your left. They defended themselves from Navajo Indians by throwing rocks but were eventually starved to death.

S-Curve (35/65) The *Southwest Chief* descends a zigzag sequence of curves. Both ends of the train come into view as you travel through a wild landscape of dry riverbeds and pink earth.

Pecos River (45/55) The 1775 Mission of San Miguel is to your left.

Rowe (65/35) Pecos Indians lived here in New Mexico's largest pueblo. After conversion to Christianity by the Spanish in 1617, they built the adobe mission seen in ruins across the valley to your right. Known as the **Pecos National Monument**, it rests on land donated by the actress Greer Garson. The pink pillars on the right mark the entrance to her Forked Lightning ranch.

The *Southwest Chief* travels on past Glorieta Mesa to your left, with Santa Fe National Forest on your right.

Glorieta (80/20) One of the Civil War's most westerly battles took place here in 1862, when a Texan supply train was destroyed by Union forces. A Baptist retreat centre can be seen to the right.

Between Glorieta and Lamy the train descends Glorieta Pass – a 1,000ft drop over ten miles (300m in 16km). The route twists through dry, red-rock canyons and hills thick with juniper, tamarisk, scrub oak and ponderosa pine.

Apache Canyon (95/5) A narrow granite gorge cuts into one of the oldest parts of the Rocky Mountains, where the rock face is sometimes only inches from the train as it snakes through the canyon.

LAMY (100/65) Named after Jean Baptiste Lamy, a 19th-century missionary. The ruins of his school can be seen to your left as the train arrives. To your right is the Legal Tender saloon. Lamy Shuttle buses connect with the train and you can book through-tickets (✆ *505 982 8829*). Amtrak's adobe-style station is at 152 Old Lamy Trail.

Connections from Lamy

Santa Fe The southwest's oldest city, founded in 1610, and the country's highest (7,000ft/2,100m) state capital. Crooked streets follow the contours of the earth and the flat-roofed buildings come in every shade of adobe. Formerly the royal city of the conquistadores, known as La Villa Real de Santa Fe de San Francisco de Asis, Santa Fe still has fine Spanish architecture, along with opera, art galleries, restaurants and probably too many tourists.

Handmade silver jewellery is sold by Native Americans on the pavement outside the Palace of the Governors and you can visit San Miguel Mission, the oldest house in the United States. The Loretto Chapel's Miraculous Staircase was built by a mysterious man who arrived from nowhere and left without payment after completing his task. Santa Fe's **visitor centre** is at 201 W Marcy (✆ *505 955 6200 or* ✆ *800 777 2489; www.santafe.org*).

The **Santa Fe Southern Railway** is at 410 S Guadalupe (✆ *1 888 989 8600; www. sfsr.com*). You can ride in vintage passenger cars along a working freight line through high desert scenery on a four-hour round trip from the historic depot in Santa Fe to Lamy. Construction difficulties prevented the Santa Fe Railway's tracks reaching Santa Fe itself until 1880, when this line and the beautiful adobe-style station were built by the Atchison, Topeka & Santa Fe Railway. Trains operate on Saturday (year round) and Friday (from April to October).

Taos Some 75 miles (120km) further north, Taos has an adobe pueblo culture going back at least 900 years, and it was here that D H Lawrence and his wife Frieda came in the 1920s to seek mystical enlightenment. His ashes are buried in a shrine on their former ranch, which has spectacular views across the desert to distant mountains. For **visitor information** about Taos, ☎ 575 751 8800; www.taoschamber.com.

All aboard!

As the *Southwest Chief* leaves Lamy and travels through tracts of barren countryside you begin to lose sight of the Sangre de Cristo Mountains back to your right.

Los Cerrillos (15/50) The Ortiz Mountains are in the left distance. This area is rich in minerals, including silver and turquoise, and was the site of the earliest (1830s) US gold mine. The film *Young Guns*, telling the story of Billy the Kid and the Lincoln County War, was made on location in Los Cerrillos. Amtrak scenes for the first *Superman* film were also shot here on one of the network's fastest sections of track.

Santo Domingo (30/35) The settlement on your right dates from 1598. Look for the beehive-shaped *hornos* – ovens used for baking bread.

San Felipe (35/30) This pueblo was established more than 500 years ago. A Catholic church and a Native American *kiva* (religious council chamber) can be seen to your right.

Sandia Crest (55/10) The mountain over on your left in the **Cibola National Forest** is 10,678ft (3,250m) high. These 'watermelon mountains' go bright red at sunset, when trees on the slopes resemble seeds.

As the train nears Albuquerque, look right to see the tower and gold globe of the Federal Office building.

ALBUQUERQUE (65/140) A centre for business, government and the military, Albuquerque is sought after for its dry, invigorating climate. Named after a Portuguese duke, the city was ruled by Spain and Mexico before being won for the United States in 1846. The railroad arrived in 1880, after which Albuquerque became the site of the main locomotive works of the Santa Fe Railway. Today's population of 400,000 represents a quarter of the total figure for the entire state of New Mexico.

Albuquerque basics

☎ **Telephone code** 505

ᴍᴍ **Station** Amtrak uses the Alvarado Transportation Center at 320 First St SW (*Ticket office* ⊕ *09.45–17.00. Waiting room* ⊕ *24hrs*). Tiwa Indians sell pretty silver & turquoise jewellery on the platform. Free baggage store, vending machines, handcarts, taxi stand.

Connections Thruway buses travel to Truth or Consequences & El Paso.

🚌 **Local transport** Albuquerque's free D-RIDE downtown service includes the Rail Runner Express as a way for rail passengers to travel to some of the area's most popular destinations after arriving at the Alvarado Transportation Center. Services run every 7mins on w/days ☎ *243 7433*). Travel part of legendary Route 66 by taking a bus down Central Av, Albuquerque's 'main street'.

🚕 **Taxis** Yellow ☎ 247 8888; Albuquerque ☎ 883 4888

🚗 **Car rental** In a city 20 miles long by 25 miles wide (32km by 40km), a car can be essential. Hertz, 3400 University SE; ☎ 842 4235.

🚌 **Greyhound** 320 First St, next to the Amtrak station; ☎ 243 4435

✈ **Albuquerque International Sunport Airport** 5 miles (8km) from downtown by ABQ bus #50 or the Sunport Shuttle (☎ *883 4966*)

Tours Albuquerque Tours has tours of the city as well as Taos & Santa Fe (☎ *888 307 4147*). Walking tours of the Old Town start from the Albuquerque Museum of Art and History (☎ *243 7255*).

ℹ **Visitors bureau** 20 First Plaza; ☎ 800 284 2282; e info@itsatrip.org; www.abqcvb.org; ⏰ Mon–Fri

🏠 **Accommodation** Contact Adobe & Roses Bed & Breakfast, 1011 Ortega NW, Albuquerque, NM 87114; ☎ 898 0654; or the Mauger Estate, 701 Roma; ☎ 242 8755.

KOA's nearest campsite is at 12400 Skyline NE; ☎ 296 2729. Route 66 Hostel, 1012 Central Av SW; ☎ 247 1813, **$**. The hostel is within walking distance of the train station, & there are free pickups from Albuquerque & El Paso.

Hotels include the Hotel Albuquerque, Old Town, 800 Rio Grande; ☎ 843 6300, **$$$**; Hotel Parq Central, 806 Central Av SE; ☎ 242 0040, **$$$**; Hotel Blue, 717 Central NW; ☎ 924 2400, **$$**; Andaluz, 125 Second; ☎ 242 9090, **$$$**; MCM Eleganté, 2020 Menaul; ☎ 884 2511, **$$$**; Rodeway Inn, 2108 Menaul; ☎ 884 2480, **$$**; Rio Grande Inn, 1015 Rio Grande Bd NW; ☎ 843 9500, **$$**.

Recommended in Albuquerque

Old Town Off Central Av & Rio Grande Bd; ☎ 248 1087. Colourful activity around the plaza with artists, craft shops, good food & adobe architecture. The most impressive building is the 1706 San Felipe de Neri Church.

Albuquerque Museum of Art and History 2000 Mountain Rd, in Old Town; ☎ 243 7255; www.cabq.gov/museum; ⏰ Tue–Sun; admission charge, free Sun morning & 1st Wed in every month. Shows the history of Albuquerque & the Middle Rio Grande Valley from the founding early Spanish settlements to the present. The art collection concentrates on works by regional artists, contemporary & historical.

Indian Pueblo Cultural Center 2401 12th; ☎ 843 7270; www.indianpueblo.org; ⏰ daily; admission charge. Traditional food, crafts, fetishes, carvings & dancing. The shop has a wide range of posters, music & books relating to Native American culture. Take bus #36.

Sandia Peak East of Albuquerque off Interstate 25. As well as mountains & desert you can see the impressive lights of night-time Albuquerque & Santa Fe. Look too for wildlife such as mule deer, black bear, racoons, bobcats & various types of squirrels. Birds include golden eagles, hawks, jays, ravens & canyon wrens.

The Sandia Peak Tram (☎ *856 7325; www. sandiapeak.com*) travels up the longest (14,657ft) tramway in the world, rising 4,000ft (1,200m) in 15mins. Sandia Crest (10,680ft/3,255m) is 300ft (90m) higher & can be reached by road from the east. The tramway closes for 2 weeks each spring & autumn for maintenance.

National Atomic Museum 601 Eubank Bd SE; ☎ 245 2137; www.atomicmuseum.com; ⏰ daily; admission charge. Documentary film & exhibitions reveal how atomic bombs were developed for use at Hiroshima & Nagasaki. Much of the early atom research was carried out at Los Alamos, 60 miles (96km) to the north. The museum incorporates robotics & nuclear medicine exhibits as well as information about atomic timekeeping, micro worlds, nuclear arms control & renewable energy.

New Mexico Museum of Natural History and Science 1801 Mountain Rd; ☎ 841 2800; www. nmnaturalhistory.org; ⏰ daily except Christmas & non-holiday Mon in Jan & Sep; admission charge. Meet New Mexico's giant dinosaurs, walk through a volcano or explore the solar system. Footprint fossils date back to animals that lived in New Mexico 280 million years ago – 60 million years before dinosaurs. See Dynamax movies on a huge 5-storey screen.

All aboard!

The *Southwest Chief* departs this service stop past the University of New Mexico's sports stadium on the left. Rio Grande Park and Zoo are to your right.

As the train starts to leave the Rio Grande Valley behind and enters New Mexico's desert country, a guide from the Inter-Tribal Indian Ceremonial Association describes some of the route's highlights. The Ladron Mountains are to your right and the Manzano Range on the far left horizon. As you cross the Rio Grande, look for lavender-coloured tamarisk trees (salt cedars).

Isleta Indian Reservation (15/125)
St Augustine Church to your left dates from 1613 and is still in use. Away to your right is an extinct volcano, Mount Taylor (11,301ft/3,445m).

The train crosses the Puerco River, a tributary of the Rio Grande, and begins a 3,000ft (900m) climb to the continental divide.

Kneeling Nuns (48/92)
The distinctive rock formation on your right resembles two nuns praying at an altar.

Route 66 (50/90)
Crossing the track on a wooden bridge is the road which ran for 2,000 miles (3,200km) between Chicago and Los Angeles. The last official Route 66 marker was taken down in 1977, but the highway lives on in Bobby Troup's song and Jack Kerouac's *On the Road*.

Mesita Pueblo (55/85)
The pueblo to your left is one of several seen as you cross the Laguna Indian Reservation. Gypsum cliffs on the right reveal local uranium workings. The *Southwest Chief* joins the San José River on the left before crossing it several times ahead.

Laguna Pueblo (60/80)
This is the youngest and largest of the pueblos on this route.

Paraje Pueblo (63/77)
Look for the mission building to your left.

Acomita (65/75)
An adobe church stands on the left. Just to the south of here, 850 years ago, Acoma Indians built a pueblo on top of a 365ft (110m) mesa.

McCarty's Pueblo (68/72)
The stone-built pueblo is part of an Acoma Indian Reservation to your left, where a 200-year-old church dominates the bluff.

Anzac (75/65)
Mount Taylor produced the black lava beds to your left, much favoured by warmth-loving rattlesnakes.

From here to Gallup the *Southwest Chief* travels among the Red Cliffs, some of which are 7,000ft (2,100m) high. The desert sun can produce spectacular changes of colour. Native Americans say that the hills became red after a wounded stag shed blood while escaping from hunters.

Grants (90/50)
This railroad town became 'the carrot capital of the USA' and a centre for uranium mining. An Anaconda uranium smelter can be seen to your right.

Bluewater (100/40)
Mount Taylor is on the right.

Continental divide (110/30) The train crosses at Campbell's Pass.

Fort Wingate Depot (124/16) Army ammunition bunkers are securely hidden in the hillside to your right.

Pyramid Rock (130/10) Behind this landmark on your right is the spire of Church Rock, where a jilted Indian maiden is said to have jumped to her death.

Red Rock State Park (132/8) Each August, 50 tribes gather on the right for ceremonial dancing and games.

GALLUP (140/90) 'The Indian capital of the world', where half the population are Native Americans, is a good place to buy silver jewellery, baskets, pottery, rugs and blankets. The tribes include Acoma, Zuni, Hopi, Navajo and Apache.

Amtrak's station at 210 E Highway 66 gives access to the Four Corners region comprising the Painted Desert, Petrified Forest, Mesa Verde National Park and South Colorado Mountains.

New Mexico–Arizona state line (10/80) Arizona does not observe Daylight Saving Time, so watches go back an hour (forward when travelling east) only from November to April.

The train continues through a stark desert country of mystical beauty, the wide plains interrupted by mesas and buttes. Sharp winds have carved the red and yellow sandstone into wonderful spires and caves. Part of the Painted Desert and Petrified Forest can be seen to your left.

Holbrook (70/20) The train makes a street crossing at Holbrook, trading place for Hopi, Navajo and Apache. To your right is the Blevins House where in 1887, Perry Owens, Sheriff of Apache County, shot a horse thief and three other men. The flamboyant Owens later became a US deputy marshal and businessman in Seligman.

The *Southwest Chief* accompanies the Little Colorado River for the next few minutes. The giant electricity-generating plant you see on your right consumes four million tons of coal a year.

WINSLOW (90/60) About 20,000 years ago, a meteor hit the earth 23 miles (37km) west of here, causing a crater 600ft deep and 4,000ft wide (180m by 1,200m). 'Meteor city' is another trading post for Hopi and Navajo. Amtrak's pink stucco station at E Second Street is a fine example of Spanish-style architecture.

Canyon Diablo (30/30) The train crosses on a 544ft-high (165m) bridge, with a trading post and store ruins to your right, then continues through further canyons and high desert country. In the days of steam power, tank cars of water had to be hauled into this arid region to feed the locomotives.

You continue through Padre Canyon. Approaching Flagstaff, look right among the San Francisco Peaks for Mount Agassiz (12,340ft/3,760m) and the highest mountain in Arizona, Humphrey's Peak (12,670ft/3,860m).

FLAGSTAFF (60/35) Situated almost 7,000ft (2,100m) above sea level, the town was named after local settlers who celebrated America's 100th birthday by making a flagstaff out of a pine tree stripped of branches. Amtrak's picturesque station is at 1 E Route 66, where Thruway buses connect with Phoenix and the Grand Canyon.

Open Road/Gray Line Tours (📞602 997 6474 or 📞800 766 7117; www.openroadtours. com) offers a Colorado River Float Trip, a Grand Canyon Railroad excursion that includes a 23-mile (37km) east rim tour, travel through the Painted Desert and a stop at the Cameron Trading Post on the Navajo Indian Reservation. You can also take a 30-minute helicopter ride (optional) as an inclusion to the Grand Canyon tour. Additional services include shuttles between Phoenix Sky Harbor Airport and Flagstaff Amtrak Station.

The Colorado River, which from the rim of the **Grand Canyon** looks little more than a thin green thread of water, created this natural wonder revealing two billion years of geological history. The canyon is about 190 air miles (306km) long and ranges between 600 yards (549m) and 18 miles (29km) wide, averaging ten miles (16km). This 1,900-square-mile (4,921km²) phenomenon is actually 600 interlinked smaller canyons and much of the rain which falls here has evaporated in the heat before it reaches the bottom.

The best way to appreciate the Grand Canyon is to walk one of its trails, that on the south rim being easiest. You can also go down into the canyon itself, but temperatures often reach 100°F (38°C) in summer and fall below freezing in winter, so take sensible precautions.

Five million people visit the canyon each year. Mule-back rides need to be booked well in advance and flights are available from Grand Canyon Airlines (📞 866 235 9422; www.grandcanyonairlines.com). For tours and lodge accommodation contact the Reservations Department, Grand Canyon National Park (PO Box 129, AZ 86023; 📞928 638 7888; www.nps.gov/grca).

The *Southwest Chief* leaves Flagstaff to travel among some of the Coconino Forest's many ponderosa pines. Lowell Observatory, from where the planet Pluto was discovered, stands on a hill to your right.

WILLIAMS JUNCTION (35/120) The **Grand Canyon Railway** operates steam trains from the 1908 depot at nearby Bill Williams Avenue to the edge of the canyon on a line built by the Atchison, Topeka & Santa Fe Railway (see *Chapter 29, US Steam Today*, page 289). Free shuttle buses operate between Williams Grand Canyon Railway station and Amtrak's Williams Junction station (reservations required).

Seligman (45/75) This mining and cattle-trading town was founded by the railroad in 1882 at the junction of the Santa Fe line and a route south to Prescott.

KINGMAN (120/64) Another historic railroad town.

Arizona–California state line (50/14) As the train crosses the Colorado River near Lake Havasu you change from Mountain to Pacific Time. Since Arizona does not observe Daylight Saving Time, watches go back an hour (forward when travelling east) only from November to April.

NEEDLES (64/160) California's easternmost city was named after neighbouring rock pinnacles and this part of the Mojave Desert often registers the country's hottest temperatures. Connecting Thruway buses link Needles with Las Vegas and Lake Havasu City.

BARSTOW (160/35) Capital of the Mojave, Barstow began as a station on the Santa Fe Trail before becoming a BNSF railroad town. To your right, set among cypress trees, is one of the few surviving Harvey House buildings, Casa del

Desierto (house of the desert). This elegant restored building is now home to Amtrak's station, the Chamber of Commerce, the **Mother Road Route 66 Museum** (*www.route66museum.org*) and the **Western America Railroad Museum** (*www.barstowrailmuseum.org*).

Fred Harvey built 47 restaurants and hotels in the 19th century to service the railways and help civilise the west. Hundreds of people would leave the train, enjoy 'the best food and lodging anywhere', and be back on board inside an hour. Waitresses, chosen for their youth and attractiveness, wore immaculate black dresses and lived in dormitories guarded by matrons. They had to forgo half their salary if they married in the first year of employment but 5,000 still found western husbands. Judy Garland made the waitresses immortal in *The Harvey Girls*. Barstow is now a tourist centre, with military bases and NASA's Goldstone satellite station close by.

Leaving the station, the train manoeuvres through a complex of Santa Fe marshalling yards before setting out towards the San Bernardino Mountains.

Edwards Air Force Base (15/20) Beyond the Kramer Mountains to your right is the landing site for NASA's space shuttle. Craig Breedlove chose this six-mile runway in 1996 to test his *Spirit of America* vehicle for an attempt at the land speed record and sound barrier. The late Francis Vincent Zappa, who was born in Baltimore, Maryland, moved with his parents to the nearby desert town of Lancaster because of his childhood asthma.

Oro Grande (25/10) Wrightwood Mountain is to your left, along with several cement mines and processing plants.

VICTORVILLE (35/65) You cross the Mojave River, which runs 20ft (6m) below ground and forms dangerous quicksand. Another cement plant appears on the right.

The *Southwest Chief* starts a long climb among spectacular rocks and Joshua trees to Cajon Pass. The Union Pacific and Southern Pacific railroads also use this route to approach Los Angeles from the east. At their highest point the tracks reach more than 3,800ft (1,160m) as they travel the border between the San Bernardino and San Gabriel mountains. The San Andreas Fault is seen as a raised blue line along the hills.

Stunning rock formations feature on both sides as the train begins a slow, twisting 2,743ft (835m) descent towards San Bernardino. Desert scenes give way to a greener country of jacarandas, palm trees and bougainvillaea.

SAN BERNARDINO (65/20) Note the handsome grounds and Spanish Mission-style station to your right, with its four domed towers. Other Spanish buildings blend with modern architecture and the heritage of Mormon settlers who came here from Salt Lake City 100 years ago. A citrus fruit industry has existed since the first navel orange crop was grown locally in 1873, and the McDonald brothers opened their first hamburger stand in San Bernardino during the 1930s. The **visitors bureau** is at 1955 Hunts Lane, Suite 102, San Bernardino, CA 92408 (✆ 1 800 867 8366; *www.san-bernardino.org*).

To your left as the train leaves is southern California's highest peak, Mount San Gorgonio (11,502ft/3,500m).

RIVERSIDE (20/50) The March Air Force Base is in Riverside, now part of the inexorable Los Angeles expansion.

Santa Ana Mountains (25/25) You travel through a canyon formed by the Santa Ana River on your left. Prado Dam was built at the head of the canyon to control flooding.

Yorba Linda (30/20) Birthplace of Richard Nixon, where the modest house constructed by his Quaker father stands next to the $21 million presidential library. Despite Watergate, Orange County still celebrates Richard Nixon Day.

FULLERTON (50/35) A restored Santa Fe station with pink stucco and red tiles can be seen on the right, next to a grand Union Pacific depot which was moved to this site and converted into a restaurant. A Donald Duck citrus juice plant is also on the right. Fullerton is a suburban stop as well as being the station for **Disneyland**, the **Movieland Wax Museum** and **Knott's Berry Farm**. For details of these attractions, see the Fullerton entry in *Chapter 7, The Pacific Surfliner* (page 96).

From here to Los Angeles the train passes through residential and industrial suburbs of Los Angeles County.

Santa Fe Springs (10/25) Oil wells, tanks and derricks abound on both sides.

Redondo Junction (25/10) Amtrak superliners are set up for the *Coast Starlight*, *Sunset Limited* and *Southwest Chief* in the yards and roundhouse to your left.

Los Angeles River (30/5) The train accompanies a concrete channel on your right. Designed for flood control and normally dry, the channel has been a location for dozens of movie chases. As the *Southwest Chief* nears Los Angeles, look for City Hall's white tower dominating the skyline to your right.

LOS ANGELES For Los Angeles city information, see *Chapter 4, The Coast Starlight* (pages 68–70).

The *Sunset Limited*
Orlando–Los Angeles

General route information

The *Sunset Limited* is the only way to travel from coast to coast on a single train and it takes almost three days to make the 2,764-mile (4,472km) journey. After going north from Orlando to Jacksonville the train heads west into two sunsets. You visit the swamps of bayou country, flirt with the Mexican border and cross Texas range lands before seeing mountains, deserts and the orange groves of California.

The original *Sunset Limited* began in 1895 as a Southern Pacific all-Pullman service, complete with silver finger-bowls, operating between San Francisco and New Orleans. Passengers could continue to New York by steamship.

ESSENTIAL INFORMATION

FREQUENCY Three trains a week in each direction. Please note that at the time of writing the service between Orlando and New Orleans remains suspended because of the effects of Hurricane Katrina. Future service has yet to be determined.

The **westbound** service leaves Orlando early on Tuesday, Thursday and Sunday afternoons to reach Jacksonville by early evening (when the service between Orlando and New Orleans is operational). You leave New Orleans around midday on Wednesday, Friday and Monday to reach Houston by mid evening and San Antonio during the night. You reach El Paso by late afternoon, Tucson late evening and Los Angeles early on Friday, Sunday or Wednesday morning.

Travelling **east**, trains leave Los Angeles late on Sunday, Wednesday and Friday afternoons, reaching Tucson after midnight and El Paso early next morning. You arrive in San Antonio late evening, Houston early morning and New Orleans late afternoon. The rest of the route to Orlando is currently suspended.

DURATION 68 hours (48 hours between New Orleans and Los Angeles)
RESERVATIONS All reserved
EQUIPMENT Superliner coaches
SLEEPING Superliner bedrooms
FOOD Complete meals, snacks, sandwiches, drinks
LOUNGE CAR Movies, games, hospitality hour. National Park Service guides from the Amistad National Recreation Area travel between New Orleans and Houston to provide a narrative along this part of the route.
BAGGAGE Check-in service at main stations

Joining the train

ORLANDO For Orlando city information and the route to Jacksonville, see *Chapter 17, The* Silver Star (pages 202–16).

JACKSONVILLE (60/50) The *Sunset Limited* begins its long journey west by crossing the cattle ranches and farms of northern Florida – a land of twisted cypress trees, oaks, swamps and lakes, with birds such as herons, egrets and flamingoes.

LAKE CITY (50/50) Suwannee State Park can be seen on both sides of the track. Lake City used to be known as Alligator, after a Seminole Indian chief, and is located on the banks of the graceful Suwannee River. A museum honours Stephen Foster, the composer of 'Swannee River' and 'Camptown Races'. The only significant Civil War battle fought in Florida took place at nearby Olustee.

As the train travels among more cypress trees and cattle ranches, look for the attractive lake to your right just before Madison.

MADISON (50/65) In the 19th century, this was one of the world's great centres for processing cotton. The *Sunset Limited* pauses at a modest platform building on the right, beyond which can be seen an impressive example of mechanical engineering.

You continue through farms and woodland where alligators lurk beneath gnarled trees. Approaching Tallahassee, the train passes through Chaires then crosses US Highway 27. Look to your right for the old Capitol Building and the clean, white high-rises of downtown.

TALLAHASSEE (65/120) You pass a redundant platform to your right before the train stops at Tallahassee's station. This former freight depot is one of the oldest station buildings in Florida. Florida A & M University can be seen on the hill to your right.

Tallahassee was named by Apalachee Indians from their words for town (*talwa*) and old (*ahasee*). It became Florida's capital as a compromise between the previous capitals of St Augustine and Pensacola. The 'canopy roads' at the centre of the town are cool, lush tunnels formed beneath oak trees dripping with Spanish moss.

The city is home to **Wakulla Springs**, one of the deepest natural springs in the world, where several *Tarzan* movies and *The Creature from the Black Lagoon* were made. Wildlife areas include **Falling Waters State Park** with its forests, lakes, mysterious caverns and waterfalls, and the **Apalachicola National Forest** where you may see bald eagles or even black bears. For more information about

Tallahassee and the surrounding region contact the **visitors bureau** at 106 E Jefferson (✆ *850 606 2305; www.visittallahassee.com*).

As the *Sunset Limited* pulls out, look in the right distance for the stadium of Florida State University. The train continues through a landscape scarcely populated except for an occasional small house or village. Between here and Chipley you change from Eastern to Central Time, so watches go back an hour (forward when travelling east).

CHIPLEY (120/70) Named after Colonel William Chipley, responsible for building the Louisville & Nashville Railroad between Tallahassee and Pensacola in 1883. Chipley is Amtrak's nearest stop to the resort of Panama City.

The white building with a red roof to your left is Washington County's Agricultural Center. As the train continues west through the 17th-century resort of De Funiak Springs, look for azaleas, magnolia trees and Victorian houses.

CRESTVIEW (70/60) The town is situated on the Old Spanish Trail, a historic trade route between Jacksonville in Florida and El Paso, Texas. This is Amtrak's nearest stop to Fort Walton Beach and Destin on the Gulf of Mexico. Crestview's Eglin Air Force Base is one of the largest (724 square miles/1,875km^2) in the world.

The *Sunset Limited* travels on across Florida's panhandle. Approaching Pensacola, look left for glimpses of Escambia Bay.

PENSACOLA (60/65) The city's name derives from the local Pansfalaya tribe. To your left, beyond the site of an old railway station, is the Grand Pensacola Hotel. This area was occupied by Spanish conquistador Don Tristan de Luna in 1559, but his settlement was later abandoned. Fort San Carlos was built in 1698 as the region went through Spanish, French and British ownership before being ceded to the US in 1821. A US Navy base was established in 1825.

Pensacola also has splendid white beaches, historic houses and the **National Museum of Naval Aviation** at 1750 Radford Boulevard (✆ *850 452 3604; www. navalaviationmuseum.org*). Apache leader Geronimo and some of his followers were held for several years at Fort Pickens after being brought here by train. Fort Pickens, Fort McRee and Fort Barrancas now form part of the **Gulf Islands National Seashore Park**, which stretches for 150 miles (240km) to Gulfport. This is one of the world's best fishing areas and the Barrier Islands are home to rare brown pelicans. It was the dredging of channels around the islands which inspired John Grisham's novel *The Pelican Brief*.

The train continues among fields growing watermelons, strawberries, sweet potatoes and corn. The Gulf Breeze region between Pensacola and Biloxi is famous for UFO sightings, perhaps because there are so many local military bases.

Florida–Alabama state line (25/40) Look for scrub oaks, cypresses and pine trees, often half smothered by kudzu vines.

ATMORE (65/80) Originally called Williams Station, the town was a small supply stop on the Mobile & Great Northern Railroad. In 1880, the Louisville & Nashville Railroad took over and extended the line to Mobile. The town was renamed after Charles Pawson Atmore, chief ticket agent on the Louisville & Nashville.

To your right as you leave is Atmore's fire station, beside which is parked an old US Air Force plane. Between here and Mobile the train crosses the Alabama and Tombigbee rivers.

MOBILE (80/35) Founded by the French in 1704, Mobile has become a modern industrial city. Look for the new convention centre building next to Amtrak's station. On your left is Mobile Bay, one of the largest ports in the world, where a great Civil War naval battle took place. The battleship USS *Alabama* is preserved as a memorial to those who fought in World War II.

As you leave, look left for Mobile's international speedway track. You can also see Fort Condé, which was once the French headquarters in Louisiana Territory.

Alabama–Mississippi state line (25/10) The *Sunset Limited* crosses into the Magnolia State.

PASCAGOULA (35/24) Industrial scenes dominate as you cross the Singing River, which can sometimes be heard making strange humming sounds. Legend says that a group of Pascagoula Indians committed suicide by walking into its waters singing because they feared being massacred by the Biloxi tribe.

Industrial buildings appear on both sides and the Ingles Shipyard is to your left. The train departs and crosses the Pascagoula River Swamp, rich in birds and animals. In the left distance you can see trees on the island of Petit Bois.

Ocean Springs (20/4) A white gazebo to your left marks where Ocean Springs was briefly the capital of Louisiana. The healing springs which made this area famous were known to Native Americans, who often came to drink from the water of the Great Spirit.

As you near Biloxi look left for Biloxi Bay, with Deer Island in the distance. The big white building to your left houses Mississippi's largest aquarium.

BILOXI (24/15) Note the interesting old train station on the left. Pierre Le Moyne d'Iberville claimed Biloxi Bay for the French in 1699 and a settlement at Fort Maurepas became the original capital of Louisiana Territory. Biloxi has existed under six flags, including that of the West Florida Republic. Some of the town's famous shrimp boats and canning factories can be seen to your left.

Also to your left as you leave are the extensive Keesler Air Force Base and Barq's root beer plant. The train then passes Beauvoir, where Confederate president Jefferson Davis spent the last 12 years of his life.

GULFPORT (15/28) Founded in 1887 by William F Hardy as the terminal for his Gulf & Ship Island Railroad, this is Mississippi's largest port and the home of the **Marine Life Oceanarium**. Gulfport became a seaside resort during the 1920s, when the rail line was purchased by the Illinois Central. The town's beaches and sailing waters are protected by islands, including Ship Island, which form the western end of the **Gulf Islands National Seashore Park**.

Pass Christian (18/10) One of the world's longest manmade beaches was built from Pass Christian to Biloxi after World War II. 'The Pass' also has the oldest yacht club in the south.

Approaching Bay St Louis, the train crosses St Louis Bay. US Highway 90 is to your right and the Gulf of Mexico to your left.

BAY ST LOUIS (28/70) This became a tourist resort after the New Orleans, Mobile & Chattanooga Railroad arrived in 1869. Look for some of the city's fine trees, including oaks, magnolias, azaleas and bald cypresses. Wonderful views can be had of the bay and Mississippi Sound from this coast's only bluff, shared by pelicans and blue herons.

The *Sunset Limited* continues through swamp country – the haunt of alligators and wild boar.

Mississippi–Louisiana state line (25/45)
You cross into the Pelican State and ahead to your right is Lake Catherine. Lake Pontchartrain lies beyond.

A few minutes before New Orleans the city skyline appears to your left, together with Lake Borgne and a NASA space facility. Also to your left is the Rosedale Cemetery with its above-the-ground tombs. The New Orleans population was formerly plagued by yellow fever and high infant mortality, with more than 8,000 people dying in 1853 alone. Many turned to voodoo for comfort or decided to live it up, believing they might not be around tomorrow.

NEW ORLEANS (70/70)
The 'Big Easy' features jazz, blues, Mardi Gras, voodoo and creole cooking, and more churches per person than anywhere else in the country. Immortalised by Tennessee Williams and William Faulkner, New Orleans was founded by the French in 1718, taken over by the Spanish, then bought by the US for $15 million in 1803. Settlers from France, Spain, Britain, Germany and the Caribbean have given it a uniquely cosmopolitan atmosphere.

Relaxed charm and a ragged beauty make New Orleans the perfect place for letting *les bon temps* roll. Apart from Las Vegas, this is one of the few places in America without a closing-time law. Louis Armstrong and Fats Domino were born here and blues, soul and Cajun music are played in hundreds of music clubs. **Jazz venues** include Mahogany Hall at 309 Bourbon Street and Preservation Hall at 726 St Peter.

The effect of Hurricane Katrina on New Orleans in August 2005 was catastrophic because of the failure of the levees that should have protected the city. Over 200,000 properties were damaged or destroyed by the floodwaters and more than 1,500 people died. Reconstruction and recovery work still has a long way to go in some areas, especially the Ninth Ward that was worst affected. Despite this, the most celebrated and historic parts of the city, including the French Quarter, Garden District and St Charles Avenue, not only remain intact but are also thriving.

New Orleans basics

Telephone code 504

Station (*Ticket office* ⊕ *05.45–22.00. Waiting room* ⊕ *05.00–22.00*) Amtrak shares with Greyhound the modern Union Passenger Terminal at 1001 Loyola Av. Metropolitan lounge. Lockers, vending machines, handcarts, restaurant, shop, taxi stand.

Connections Thruway buses go to Baton Rouge.

Local transport The RTA (248 3900; www.norta.com) operates buses & streetcars, including those along the Riverfront & St Charles Av.

Taxis Sunset Cab 282 0002; United 522 9771

Car rental Budget, 1317 Canal; 565 5600

Greyhound 1001 Loyola Av; 525 6075

Airport Jefferson Transit Airport Downtown Express (818 1077) & Airport Shuttle (866 596 2699) buses go to Louis Armstrong International Airport at Kenner, 15 miles (24km) west of downtown

Tours City & plantation tours, as well as excellent Hurricane Katrina tours from Gray Line (569 1401) & Dixie (522 9422). Steamboat river cruises on the *Creole Queen* (529 4567) & the *Natchez* (569 1401). Free walking tours leave from Jean Lafitte Historical Park, 419 Decatur St (589 2636).

Visitors bureau 2020 St Charles Av; 800 672 6124; www.neworleanscvb.com; ⊕ daily

Accommodation A wide range of hotels is available, from ultra modern to historic. Call the Tourist Commission (℡ *566 5011*) or contact New Orleans & French Quarter Accommodations (℡ *524 9918*). Marquette House AYH Hostel, 2249 Carondelet; ℡ 523 3014; www.neworleansinternationalhostel.com. Members & non-members, **$**. India House Hostel, 124 S Lopez; ℡ 821 1904; www.indiahousehostel.com, **$**.

Hotels include the Roosevelt, 123 Baronne; ℡ 648 1200, **$$$$**; Bourbon Orleans, 717 Orleans; ℡ 523 2222, **$$$**; Cornstalk, 915 Royal; ℡ 523 1515, **$$$**; French Quarter Landmark, 920 N Rampart; ℡ 524 3333, **$$$**; Studio 6, 12330 I-10 at Bullard Av; ℡ 240 9778, **$$**; LaSalle, 1113 Canal; ℡ 523 5831, **$**.

Recommended in New Orleans

French Quarter (*www.frenchquarter.com*) The Vieux Carré (Old Square) centres on Jackson Sq, where the first settlers arrived in 1718. The finely decorated wrought iron on the houses was made in Birmingham, England. You can soak up the atmosphere best at the French Market & along Bourbon St.

Jackson Square Originally the Place d'Armes, where soldiers marched & public executions took place. Later it became a park & was renamed after General Andrew Jackson, whose statue stands opposite the cathedral. See artists, street musicians & entertainers free & have your future told by tarot cards.

Pontalba Apartments Constructed on 2 sides of Jackson Sq over 100 years ago for the Baroness Micaela Pontalba, these buildings have handsome balconies & ironwork, eg: the 1850 House at 523 St Ann (℡ *568 6968;* ⊕ *Tue–Sun; admission charge*).

Louisiana State Museum 751 Chartres St; ℡ 568 6972; http://lsm.crt.state.la.us; admission charge. The museum oversees a complex of 5 national landmarks reflecting Louisiana's history & culture. The properties, all located in the French Quarter, are the Cabildo, Presbytère, 1850 House, Old US Mint & Madame John's Legacy. 2hr walking tours through the Vieux Carré start at the 1850 House Museum Store on Jackson Sq at 523 St Ann.

Old US Mint 400 Esplanade Av; ℡ 1 800 568 6968; http://lsm.crt.state.la.us/mintex.htm; ⊕ Tue–Sun; admission charge. This 1835 building is the only one to have served as both a Confederate & a US mint. It now houses carnival exhibits & the **New Orleans Jazz Collection**, including Louis Armstrong's first trumpet, as well as a history of coins.

The Cabildo 701 Chartres; ℡ 568 6968; http://lsm.crt.state.la.us/cabex.htm; ⊕ Tue–Sun; admission charge. This was the site of the Louisiana Purchase Transfer & was built between 1795 and 1799 as the seat of the Spanish city council in New Orleans. The building has also served as the Louisiana Supreme Court & became part of the Louisiana State Museum in 1911. Reopened in 1994 after being damaged by fire, the Cabildo focuses on Louisiana's early history.

Mardi Gras The greatest free show on earth takes place during the month before Lent, with parades, bands & every kind of revelry. Book your accommodation in good time. **Mardi Gras World** (*1380 Port of New Orleans Pl;* ℡ *361 7821; www.mardigrasworld.com*) has a collection that includes thousands of carnival props & giant figures.

Confederate Civil War Museum 929 Camp; ℡ 523 4522; www.confederatemuseum.com; ⊕ Wed–Sat; admission charge. The 2nd-largest collection of Confederate memorabilia in the world, & the oldest continually operating museum in Louisiana, housed in Memorial Hall. The collection includes uniforms, guns, swords, photographs, paintings & 125 battle flags.

Texas-Pacific Depot 739 Third St, Gretna, just across the river. This landmark was built in 1905 to replace a pre-Civil War wood structure & was the starting point of all Texas-Pacific rails going north & west of the Mississippi. After passengers boarded in New Orleans, the cars were ferried across the river & assembled into a train in front of Gretna Station. It became redundant once a rail bridge was opened in 1935 but has been restored.

The Ogden Museum of Southern Art University of New Orleans, 925 Camp; ℡ 539 9600; www.ogdenmuseum.org; ⊕ Wed–Mon; admission charge. The largest & most comprehensive collection of southern art in the world tells the story of the south through its art, music & education. Among many artists represented in the museum's collection are Benny Andrews, William Dunlap, Ida Kohlmeyer, Will Henry Stevens, Kendall Shaw & George Ohr. 'Ogden After Hours' on Thu evenings features live performances of southern music in an intimate setting.

All aboard!

As the *Sunset Limited* departs after a lengthy service stop, look right for the Superdome sports. The buildings on your left belong to *The Times-Picayune* and Xavier University.

Huey P Long Bridge (20/50) Seen ahead to your left, the bridge was named after a state governor and US senator prominent in Louisiana and national politics during the 1930s. Before the 4.4-mile (7.1km) bridge opened in 1935, trains had to cross the river on barges. The *Sunset Limited* inches carefully over the Mississippi with views of the Avondale Shipyard and other industrial plants to your right. The New Orleans skyline becomes visible as the river curves away to your left, showing how the Crescent City earned its name.

The train slowly descends from the bridge and enters a bayou country of swamps, forests, mansions and Spanish moss. 'Bayou' comes from a Choctaw word meaning 'sluggish stretch of water'. The French-born pirate and smuggler Jean Lafitte hid in this region during the early 19th century. In summer, Jean Lafitte National Park Service guides join the train between here and Lafayette.

Harahan (30/40) The cemetery to your right has graves above the ground to accommodate the swampy conditions.

Mississippi River (40/30) Look for grain-loading facilities next to the river as you travel beside the levees.

Highway 90 (45/25) To your left is the highway which the train will accompany for 1,100 miles to El Paso. You pass an oil refinery on the right then lose sight of the Mississippi to the north.

Des Allemands (50/20) The name is French for 'of the Germans'. The bayou is on your right, and to your left are the first of many sugarcane fields. The land is so wet that much of this line had to be constructed on pilings.

Bayou LaFourche (65/5) You cross the bayou at the town of the same name.

Bayou Blue (67/3) The train crosses just before Schriever.

SCHRIEVER (70/80) An industrial town which serves as a base for offshore oil drilling. In 2010, an explosion on the Deepwater Horizon oil rig in the Gulf of Mexico killed 11 men working on the platform. The huge oil spill that followed caused extensive damage to marine and wildlife habitats as well as to the Gulf's fishing and tourism industries.

The *Sunset Limited* crosses Chacahoula Swamp, its graceful cypress trees decorated with Spanish moss.

Bayou Boeuf (15/65) To your left is more evidence of the oil industry as the McDermott plant assembles giant rigs. The pontoon helicopters service platforms in the Gulf of Mexico. A few minutes after leaving Bayou Boeuf you cross Bayou Chene.

Morgan City (25/55) Named after Charles Morgan, who built this section of the line when it belonged to the Louisiana & Texas Railroad. The intercoastal waterway

11

to your left stretches from Brownsville, Texas, to New York, giving inland industries access to the Gulf.

Atchafalaya River (26/54) Over 200ft (60m) deep, the river has busy embankments on both sides.

Garden City (40/40) Look for a plantation house and estate to your right.

Jeanerette (65/15) A church and another above-the-ground cemetery can be seen on the right. As the train approaches New Iberia, several mansions and the towers of St Peter's Church appear to your right.

NEW IBERIA (80/22) Commercial activity coexists with French and Spanish heritage among the town's ante-bellum homes. Edward McIllhenny, founder of the Tabasco Sauce Company, created Avery Island as a sanctuary for egrets, herons and ibises.

Between here and Lafayette you travel through typical southern Louisiana countryside, with more mansions and sugarcane fields in evidence after you cross the Vermillion River.

LAFAYETTE (22/80) Henry Longfellow called these bayous, forests and flowers 'the Eden of Louisiana'. The French-speaking locals arrived when the British took over Nova Scotia, then called Acadia, from France during the colonial wars of the 18th century, and Cajuns are their descendants.

Lafayette is 'the capital of Acadiana' and home to many oil companies, as well as the University of Southwestern Louisiana. Amtrak's stop is at 100 Lee Avenue. This brick-built station, originally constructed by the Texas & New Orleans Railroad in 1911, was badly damaged by fire in 2001, but has been restored as part of the city's modern transportation facility.

Rayne (15/65) 'The frog capital of the world' holds jumping contests at its annual frog festival.

Mermenteau River (40/40) You cross the river connecting Lake Charles with the intercoastal waterway. Between here and the lake, look for rice paddies and the flooded cages of crayfish farms.

LAKE CHARLES (80/80) A small, attractive brick-built station with a gabled roof stands next to the old station. Although barely 16ft (5m) above sea level, the deep-water port at Lake Charles ships vast quantities of oil, chemicals and cement.

Calcasieu River (5/75) As the *Sunset Limited* crosses the river note the duelling pistol design on the highway bridge to your left, a reminder that pirates once operated here.

Orange (40/40) You cross the Sabine River and enter the Lone Star State of Texas. The landscape remains Louisiana-like for a while, with cypresses, rice fields and the odd alligator. Between Orange and El Paso the train travels for 941 miles (1,500km) across Texas.

BEAUMONT (80/100) The town produces many professional footballers and was the home of Mildred 'Babe' Didrikson-Zaharias. When 18 years old, this remarkable athlete won six events in three hours during trials for the 1932 Los Angeles Olympics, subsequently setting two world records in the Games. In the 1940s and 1950s, she was the world's top woman golfer, winning 17 tournaments in a row.

Nearby, the Lucas Gusher began delivering 75,000 barrels of oil a day in 1901 at Spindletop Field. Port Arthur, birthplace of Janis Joplin, is five miles southeast. Look for irrigated rice fields to your right about half an hour after the train leaves Beaumont.

Trinity River (50/50) You cross as the train approaches the small town of Liberty.

San Jacinto River (70/30) You cross the river (on its way to Galveston Bay) and see in the far left distance the 570ft (170m) San Jacinto Monument.

Approaching Houston, the train passes Santa Fe rail yards to the left, busy with long lines of freight wagons. As the city skyline comes into view note the Allied Bank spires and the chisel-shaped towers of the Pennzoil Building.

HOUSTON (100/250) The largest city in Texas covers more than 500 square miles (1,300km²) and is a brash, bustling place where both international banker and redneck can feel at home. Houston was founded in 1836 by New York property developers who called their creation 'Baghdad on the bayou'. The boom in oil subsequently brought prosperity and many tall buildings.

A 50-mile (80km) ship canal links 'Bayou City' to Galveston on the coast. The oil business has its ups and downs but Houston remains hot in more ways than one, sharing the same latitude as the Sahara. For most of the year the weather is subtropical, but air conditioning prevails.

Houston basics

☏ Telephone code 713
⋙ Station *(Ticket office & waiting room* ⏱ *13.30–23.00 Mon, 04.00–23.00 Tue/Wed/Fri, 04.00–13.30 Thu/Sun, closed Sat; information* ☏ *224 1577)* Amtrak's insignificant station is at 902 Washington Av, near downtown but not in a safe area. It was built by the Southern Pacific Railroad in 1959 to replace a much more attractive one, from which the benches in the present waiting room were salvaged. Lockers, vending machines, handcarts, taxi stand.
Connections Thruway buses connect to Galveston & with Amtrak's station in Dallas.
🚌 Local transport Metro buses (☏ *635 4000; www.ridemetro.org)* operate throughout the city & to outlying places. METRORail is a fast, convenient way to travel to downtown, midtown & the Museum District.
🚕 Taxis Yellow ☏ 236 1111; Liberty ☏ 695 6700
🚗 Car rental Budget, 6021 E Sam Houston Parkway; ☏ 281 454 4479
🚐 Greyhound 2121 S Main; ☏ 759 6565

✈ George Bush Intercontinental Airport 25 miles (40km) north by Airport Express (☏ *523 8888)*. Airport Direct buses run between the airport & the downtown Airport Direct Passenger Plaza (☏ *635 4000)*. Hobby Airport (formerly Howard R Hughes Airport & used for domestic flights) is 8 miles (13km) southeast.
Tours Discover Houston Tours at 912 Prairie St (☏ *222 9255; www.discoverhoustontours.com)* has w/day walking tours featuring Texas history & Art Deco architecture
ℹ Visitors bureau The main visitor centre is at City Hall, 901 Bagby, with a satellite kiosk at Katy Mills Mall; ☏ 437 5200; e houtour@ghcvb.org; www.visithoustontexas.com; ⏱ daily.
🏠 Accommodation Contact Angel Arbor Bed & Breakfast, 848 Heights Bd; ☏ 868 4654.
The International Hostel is at 5302 Crawford St; ☏ 523 1009; www.houstonhostel.com. Members & non-members, **$**.
Hotels include the Westin Galleria, 5060 W Alabama; ☏ 960 8100, **$$$$**; Icon, 220 Main;

224 4266, **$$$$**; Doubletree, 2001 Post Oak Bd; ☎961 9300, **$$$$**; La Quinta Inn, 1625 W Loop S; ☎355 3440, **$$$**; Sheraton Brookhollow, 3000 N Loop W; ☎688 0100, **$$$$**; Econo Lodge, 6630 Hoover St US 290 & Bingle Rd; ☎956 2828, **$$**.

Recommended in Houston

Port of Houston 7300 Clinton Dr; ☎670 2400; www.portofhouston.com. The Houston Ship Channel has been a catalyst for growth ever since the first journey of a steamship up Buffalo Bayou in 1837. You can watch the non-stop activity in America's 2nd-largest & rather polluted port from a platform on Kirby Drive. Boat trips are available as well as free tours of the MV *Sam Houston*, for which you require reservations.

Reliant Park 8400 Kirby Dr; ☎832 667 1842; www.reliantpark.com; stadium tours Mon–Thu; admission charge. Formerly known as the Astrodome, this facility includes the Reliant Stadium, home to the Houston Texans & the Houston Livestock Show & Rodeo. Called the 8th wonder of the world when it opened in 1965, the original 'Dome' was the world's first large (45,000 seats) indoor venue for a major league field sport.

Gulf Coast Railroad Museum 7390 Mesa Dr; ☎631 6612; www.houstonrrmuseum.org; ☉ Apr–Nov Sat; admission charge. Historic engines, passenger coaches & freight cars are on display with a visitor centre housed in a former Santa Fe baggage car. The collection also includes lanterns, coffin carts & a huge neon sign that once stood atop Houston's now-demolished Grand Central Station.

Sam Houston Park 1100 Bagby & Lamar; ☎655 1912; www.heritagesociety.org/park.html; ☉ daily; museum free, admission charge to tour the historic buildings. A green space in the midst of downtown, with historic buildings such as the 1847 Kellum-Noble House (the oldest brick house in Houston) & an 1891 Lutheran Church. The Texas History Museum features items from the 16th century to the present.

Space Center Houston 20 miles (32km) south at 1601 Nasa Parkway off I-45 in Clear Lake; ☎281 224 2100; www.spacecenter.org; ☉ daily; admission charge. Better known as the headquarters of the manned space programme, the Center has rockets, lunar vehicles, moon samples & training simulators. Film shows & tours daily. Take bus #246.

San Jacinto Battleground 20 miles (32km) southeast on TX 225; ☎281 479 2421; www.sanjacinto-museum.org; museum ☉ daily; free, admission charge to film shows. Sam Houston defeated General Antonio Lopez de Santa Anna here in 1836 to create an independent Texas. Great views from the world's tallest (570ft/170m) monument tower (elevator admission charge). You can also take a tour of the World War I/II battleship USS *Texas*, commissioned in 1914.

All aboard!

After Houston the *Sunset Limited* embarks on its longest run without a scheduled stop. The landscape changes as you begin to leave the Gulf Coast's green humidity for drier conditions. Cacti replace live oaks and Spanish moss, and there are fields of soya beans and cotton. Look also for some of this region's many birds, including flocks of delicate white egrets.

Sugarland (50/200) A large Imperial Sugar processing plant appears to your right just before you cross the Brazos River.

Richmond and Rosenberg (60/190) These towns were infamous in prohibition days for their brazen gambling and fast women. A brick courthouse stands on the right. Soon after Richmond, look right for rice elevators storing some of the local crop.

Colorado River (110/140) The train crosses the Texas Colorado River – no relation of its larger namesake.

Columbus (111/139) The dome and clock of a historic courthouse can be seen to your left. Approaching the station, look left also for the ancient live oak which was once the town's hanging tree.

Weimar (125/125) The old train depot on your left is now a library.

Randolph Air Force Base (220/30) Look for runways on your left and a Mission-style tower to your right.

SAN ANTONIO (250/185) This modern, relaxed city is the place where 20 million tourists (including other Texans) come to unwind. Only 160 miles (250km) from the border, it has sometimes been called the northernmost town in Mexico.

Named by explorer Domingo Teran when he arrived on St Anthony's Day in 1691, San Antonio has lived under six flags. Influences are evident in the Spanish missions, Mexican ambience, fiestas and cattle stockyards – not forgetting the Alamo. April's fiesta is a Mexican Mardi Gras featuring a river parade, rodeos and a 'night in Old San Antonio'.

San Antonio basics

☏Telephone code 210
▰ Station (*Ticket office & waiting room* ⊕ *midnight–07.15 & 21.00–23.59*) The modern station is at 350 Hoefgen. Amtrak previously used the adjacent Southern Pacific Station, also known as the Sunset Station, built in 1902 in elegant Spanish style with a vaulted ceiling, colourful stained glass & an imposing black marble staircase. The Sunset Station is now an entertainment complex with nightclubs, an outdoor dance hall & scores of shops.
Connections Thruway buses connect with Laredo.
▰ Local transport VIA buses (☏ *362 2020; www.viainfo.net*) serve the metropolitan area. VIA trolleys serve 4 routes downtown & are an inexpensive way to explore all the major attractions. Transfers between the streetcars are free.
▰ Taxis Yellow ☏ 222 2222; National ☏ 434 4444
▰ Car rental Budget, 4437 Fredericksburg Rd; ☏ 737 8979
▰ Greyhound 500 N St Mary's; ☏ 270 5824

✈ San Antonio International Airport 8 miles (13km) north by bus #2
Tours Alamo (☏ *228 9776*) & San Antonio City (☏ *212 5395*) tour the Alamo & missions. The trolley makes a 45min circuit of downtown. San Antonio River Tours (☏ *244 5700*) offers 2½-mile trips by boat along the River Walk.
🛈 Visitors bureau 317 Alamo Plaza; ☏ 800 447 3372; e sacvb@SanAntonioVisit.com; www.SanAntonioVisit.com; ⊕ daily
🏠 Accommodation Contact Joske House Bed & Breakfast, 241 King William; ☏ 271 0706. International Hostel, 621 Pierce; ☏ 223 9426. Members & non-members, **$**. Take bus #20.

Hotels include Riverwalk Inn, 329 Old Guilbeau; ☏ 212 8300, **$$$**; Menger, 204 Alamo Pl; ☏ 223 4361, **$$$$**; Rodeway Inn Downtown, 900 N Main; ☏ 223 2951, **$$**; Seven Oaks, 1400 Austin Hwy; ☏ 824 5371, **$$**; Economy Inn, 2434 S W Loop; ☏ 673 7490, **$$**; O'Brien Historic Hotel, 116 Navarro; ☏ 527 1111, **$$$**; Rose Park Inn & Suites, 312 South W W White Rd; ☏ 359 6767, **$$**.

Recommended in San Antonio

Paseo Del Rio 110 Broadway; ☏ 227 4262; www.thesanantonioriverwalk.com. A 2-mile (3.2km) downtown walk through parkland beside canals & the meandering river, with music, bars, floating restaurants, boat rides & a cosmopolitan parade of people. At twilight, fireflies & lanterns glow while cicadas hum among the pecan trees & palms. In 2009, a $72 million extension opened to reach the **San Antonio Museum of Art** at 200 W Jones Av;

11

978 8100; www.samuseum.org; ⊕ Tues-Sun; admission charge. SAMA houses the largest collection of ancient Egyptian, Greek, Roman and Asian art in the southern United States. It also has a fine collection of Latin American art, from pre-Columbian times to the present, and a wide range of contemporary works.

The Alamo 300 Alamo Plaza; ☎225 1391; www.thealamo.org; ⊕ daily; donation. Mission San Antonio de Valero (The Alamo) is one of the city's oldest buildings & the most-visited attraction in Texas. In 1836, 189 defenders (including Davy Crockett & Jim Bowie) died fighting General Santa Anna's overwhelming forces after a 13-day siege which came to symbolise the Texan battle for independence.

The cool, rectangular chapel is set among subtropical gardens surrounded by high stone walls. Museum & guided tours organised by the doughty Daughters of the Republic of Texas, who rescued the mission from dereliction in 1905 & have looked after it ever since.

King William District These imposing Victorian houses on the southern edge of downtown were built for German merchants. The Steves Homestead, built in 1876, is at 509 King William (☎227 9160; ⊕ daily; admission charge). The Guenther House at 205 E Guenther (☎227 1061; ⊕ daily; free) was built for the founder of Pioneer Flour Mills.

Spanish Governor's Palace 105 Plaza De Armas; ☎224 0601; ⊕ daily; admission charge. 'The most beautiful building in San Antonio' once housed officials of the Spanish province of Texas. It was completed in 1749 & features period furnishings, a cobblestone patio & a fountain.

Botanical Gardens 555 Funston Pl; ☎207 3250; www.sabot.org; ⊕ daily; admission charge. A miniature representation of the Texas landscape, from Hill Country wild flowers to formal rose gardens. Includes an exhibition hall, tropical house, desert house, palm house, fern room & orangery.

Tower of the Americas 600 HemisFair Park; ☎207 8615; www.toweroftheamericas.com; ⊕ daily; admission charge. This 750ft (228m) tower, built for the HemisFair in 1968, symbolises progress made by Western civilisations. Glass-walled elevators take you over 500ft (152m) to the restaurant & observation level for panoramic views of the city & surrounding area.

Texas Transportation Museum 11731 Wetmore Rd, McAllister Park; ☎490 3554; www.txtransportationmuseum.org; ⊕ Thu–Sun; admission charge. Featuring locomotives, rolling stock, a Southern Pacific station & a model railroad. Short steam train rides operate on the Longhorn & Western railroad.

The Missions Apart from the Alamo, 4 others can be seen on the Mission Trail starting at S Alamo & Market (*all missions* ⊕ *daily; free*). The **visitor centre** (☎932 1001; www.nps.gov/saan) is next to Mission San José & has a free film showing early life at the mission.

Mission Concepción, 807 Mission Rd; ☎534 1540. The oldest unrestored mission, dating from 1731, still has original frescoes.

Mission San José, 6701 San José Dr; ☎932 1001. Largest & most impressive, with a church, granary & aqueduct. Mariachi mass on Sun. The 'Queen of the Missions' also has impressive carvings & the famous Rose Window.

Mission San Juan, 9101 Graf; ☎534 0749. Quiet, with a pretty bell tower & guided nature trail, the mission was established in 1731 after relocation from east Texas.

Mission San Francisco de la Espada, 10040 Espada; ☎627 2064. The dam & aqueduct built in the 1730s between this remote mission & Mission San José are still in working order.

All aboard!

The *Sunset Limited*, accompanied by through-cars of the *Texas Eagle*, continues from San Antonio into prairie country. Cactus plants, sage and yuccas thrive in these arid conditions as the train descends from the Anacacho Mountains to the Rio Grande Valley. Native Americans used the spiked leaves of yucca plants to make shoes and baskets.

Laughlin Air Force Base (175/10) The base can be seen away to your left across the flatlands.

DEL RIO (185/160) The Queen City of the Rio Grande, otherwise known as 'the wool and mohair capital of the world', Del Rio is famous for sheep, goats and the Val Verde winery (the oldest in Texas). Immediately to the south is the Mexican town of Ciudad Acuna, visible on bluffs across the river.

The train is joined on the left by the Rio Grande, the 'big river' separating the United States from Mexico.

Amistad Reservoir (15/145) *Amistad* is Spanish for 'friendship', and the reservoir was a joint project between the US and Mexican governments. About 30 miles long and 20 miles wide (48km by 32km), it dams the Rio Grande near its junction with the Devil River.

As the *Sunset Limited* climbs 3,500ft (1,000m) over the next 200 miles (320km), watch for prickly pear cacti, more yuccas and the woolly grandpa's beard. Between April and June, prickly pears produce bright magenta flowers. Persimmons, mesquite and greasewood (the creosote bush) also grow here.

Pecos River (50/110) The train crosses a dramatic river canyon on the state's highest railroad bridge (321ft/98m tall and 1,390ft/420m long).

Eagle Rock Canyon (70/90) In 1883, the last spike was driven nearby to complete the nation's second transcontinental railway. Look for strange rock formations jutting from the canyon wall.

Langtry (71/89) Where 'Judge' Roy Bean ran the 'Jersey Lilly' saloon and dispensed his version of justice west of the Pecos. It was claimed that his reverence for the actress Lily Langtry caused him to change the town's name from Vinegaroon. In fact, the town was named after George Langtry, foreman of the immigrant Chinese crew working here to build the Southern Pacific Railroad.

Dryden (140/20) Look for parts of a wall that was built to keep out Pancho Villa's raiders.

SANDERSON (160/100) Roy Bean owned another saloon here when the town had a wild reputation, and outlaws and rustlers mingled with cattle ranchers and sheep men. The last train robbery in Texas took place in 1912, when two masked men boarded the Southern Pacific's train #9 and forced it to stop midway between Dryden and Sanderson. They were Ole Hobek and Ben Kilpatrick, the latter sometimes being known as The Tall Texan when he rode with Butch Cassidy's 'Hole in the Wall' gang. Both men died during the robbery and were displayed in Sanderson before being buried in the town's Cedar Grove cemetery.

Amtrak's station at 201 W Downey is a flag stop. The train leaves with the ruined brick walls of Sanderson's Wool Commission to your right. Wool remains an important industry, but sheep and goat ranching become impractical further west because of predators such as coyotes, pumas, bobcats and eagles. An Apache cave and cooking mound can be seen away to your right.

Haymond (60/40) The former cow camp is now a ghost town, with its cemetery and deserted buildings on your right.

Warwick Flat (65/35) A crossing place on the Comanche War Trail, which ran for 1,000 miles (1,600km) from upper Texas to Chihuahua. As the train travels among the Glass and Del Norte Mountains look for deer, pronghorn antelope, jackrabbits and javalina (wild pigs). Mount Ord (6,814ft/2,075m) is to your left and Altveda Mountain (6,860ft/2,090m) on your right.

Approaching Alpine, you see the town's rodeo grounds to your right. The letters 'SR' engraved on a hill signify Sul Ross University.

ALPINE (100/220) Capital of Texas's largest county, Brewster, with Mitre Peak (6,100ft/1,860m) on your right. The Spanish-style station at 102 W Holland is used by tourists visiting **Big Bend National Park**.

The *Sunset Limited* continues through colourful canyon lands to Paisano Pass, the highest point (5,074ft/1,550m) on this journey. Chinati Peak (7,730ft/2,350m) is ahead to your left.

Marfa Ghost Lights (20/200) For many years mysterious lights have appeared among the Chinati Mountains and across the desert to your left. The lights were even seen by pioneers on wagon trains during the 1840s.

Marfa (25/195) The town was founded in the early 1880s as a railroad water stop and named after Marfa Strogoff, a character in Jules Verne's novel, *Michael Strogoff*. The domed, stone building to your right is a Presidio County courthouse dating from 1886 and the adobe walls of a World War II POW camp can be seen to your left. Also on your left, a few minutes west of Marfa, is the wooden windmill that was used as a location in the James Dean film, *Giant*.

Valentine (60/160) Bear Mountain (7,247ft/2,208m) and Mount Livermore (8,332ft/2,540m) are to your right. As the train descends further from the high plains, fields begin to appear and Van Horn is ahead in the right distance.

Quitman Mountains (90/130) You change from Central to Mountain Time, so watches go back an hour (forward when travelling east). For the first time in 24 hours the train parts company with Highway 90, which continues further north.

Hot Wells (100/120) A ruined adobe school appears on the right and the Eagle Mountains to your left.

Sierra Blanca (120/100) Look for the last adobe courthouse still functioning in Texas. The Sierra Blanca Peak (6,970ft/2,070m), located among mountains to your right, looks lighter because it contains soapstone.

Fort Hancock (150/70) The fort's remains are to your right. Beyond them can be seen the Finlay Mountains.

As the train approaches Fabens, look right for cheerful decorations displayed on the graves in a Mexican cemetery.

Fabens (180/40) A splendid Mission-style church stands on the left next to a cotton gin.

Ysleta (190/30) Texas's longest-surviving ethnic group, the Tigua Indians, live in Ysleta, which has the second-oldest (1682) church in the country.

The train travels through industrial scenes towards El Paso, with oil and copper refineries on both sides. The shell-shaped building to your left is the civic auditorium.

EL PASO (220/85) Encircled by the mile-high (1,600m) Franklin Mountains, this laid-back city was named after a pass (El Paso del Río del Norte) formed by the Rio Grande. Nearby are **Carlsbad Canyon National Park**, Las Cruces and Cloudcroft ski resort. El Paso's population expanded rapidly with the arrival of the Southern Pacific, Texas & Pacific and the Atchison, Topeka & Santa Fe railroads in 1881.

The first Margarita cocktail was mixed here in 1945 and many films have been shot in El Paso, including *No Country for Old Men*. Amtrak's renovated station at 700 San Francisco dates from 1904/05 and was designed by Daniel Burnham, the architect for Washington's Union Station. The **tourist bureau** is at 1 Civic Center Place (℡ *915 534 0601 or* ℡ *1 800 351 6024; www.elpasocvb.com*).

El Paso maintains close links with Ciudad Juarez in Chihuahua, Mexico, seen above palisades to your left as the train departs. To your right are the campus and stadium of the University of Texas. On top of the Sierra de Cristo Rey ahead to your left is a 33ft (10m) statue of the crucifixion known as the *Christ of the Rockies*. Pilgrims climb four miles to the 4,576ft (1,390m) summit to celebrate the Feast of Cristo Rey at this meeting place of Texas, Mexico and New Mexico.

Rio Grande (5/80) A cement plant appears to your right and a mineral refinery to your left before the train crosses the river and enters New Mexico.

Sunland Park (7/78) The race track is on your right.

US–Mexican border (10/75) A white post 30ft (10m) to the left of the tracks indicates the border line. The mountains on both sides are the Portillos. It was just to the north of here that the infamous Lincoln County cattle wars were fought in 1881, resulting in the shooting of Billy the Kid by Pat Garrett at Mesilla.

In 1916, this barren land witnessed the passage of Pancho Villa's marauders on their way to attack the town of Columbus and provoke a brief US–Mexico conflict.

Florida Mountains (75/10) Florida Peak is prominent close by to your left. A hole in the ridge at 7,300ft (2,200m) is known as the Window Peak. On your right the Cooke's Peak Range rises to 8,408ft (2,560m). The train crosses the Mimbres River near Deming, with the clock tower of Luna County Courthouse to your left.

DEMING (85/50) The city was named after Mary Ann Deming Crocker, wife of Charles Crocker, one of the Big Four of the railroad industry. A silver spike was driven here in 1881, to commemorate the meeting of the Southern Pacific and the Atchison, Topeka & Santa Fe railroads, completing the second transcontinental railroad in the United States.

Deming is the venue each August of the world's only duck races. Over 70,000 irrigated acres (28,000ha) nearby produce wine, peanuts, pecans, beans, cotton and grain sorghum. A mild climate among the Cooke's and Florida mountains makes this a popular retirement town. Similar secluded resorts can be found further north near Silver City, where Billy the Kid grew up. Amtrak's station in Deming is at 400 E Railroad Avenue, close to Rock Hound State Park.

Continental divide (25/25) The lowest elevation (4,587ft/1,400m) for any rail crossing of America's divide, where water falling to the west flows into the Pacific and to the east into the Atlantic.

LORDSBURG (50/110) Lordsburg began as a railroad town in a hollow between the Burro and Pyramid mountains. The US Government bought this land from Mexico in 1854 to enable the rail line to be built to California.

On your right soon after Lordsburg you pass a dry lake where mirages transform the sand into sheets of water.

Steins (20/90) The final battle between Apache chief Cochise and the US Army took place here.

New Mexico–Arizona state line (25/85) Arizona does not observe Daylight Saving Time, so watches go back an hour (forward when travelling east) only between April and October.

Cochise's Face (35/75) On a ridge of the tawny Chiricahua Mountains rising 9,795ft (2,985m) to your left is the commanding outline of Cochise, gazing at the sky. The Peloncillo Mountains away to your right are rich in gold, silver and copper.

Dos Cabezas (60/50) Look in the Sulphur Hills to your left for this 'two heads' rock formation, named after Cochise and the Indian agent Thomas Jeffords.

Wilcox (65/45) From this altitude of 4,167ft (1,270m) the *Sunset Limited* will descend 3,000ft (900m).

Wilcox Playa (70/40) A dry lake creates convincing mirages, even reflecting the mountains to your left.

Dragoon (95/15) During wars with the US Army between 1861 and 1872, Cochise and the Chiricahuas occupied the Dragoon Mountains to your left. The train crosses the San Pedro River.

BENSON (110/55) Formerly a stop on the Butterfield stagecoach run from St Louis to San Francisco, a 2,800-mile (4,500km) journey which took 55 days. When the railway came in 1880, Benson developed as a shipping point for mines around Tombstone, 25 miles (40km) to the south.

The *Sunset Limited* leaves past the Rincon Mountains on the right and travels through a series of canyons down the Pantano Wash. The buildings away to your right, 15 minutes from Benson, were a television film set for *Little House on the Prairie*.

East and westbound trains proceed on different lines for part of the way between Benson and Tucson, allowing the eastbound *Sunset Limited* an easier climb. Tracks are sometimes half a mile (0.8km) apart.

Durant Castle (25/30) Look for this large house situated high up on your right.

Vail (27/28) You travel the higher of two overlapping bridges – eastbound trains use the one below – and catch sight of the train ahead as you continue down into the rose-coloured Texas Canyon.

Santa Rita Shrine (37/18) A pink Catholic church is surrounded by desert to your right.

Davis Monthan Air Force Base (47/8) Thousands of planes stand mothballed in the aircraft 'boneyard' to your right, preserved by dry desert air. Beside the track is the **Pima Air Museum** featuring World War II bombers (*6000 E Valencia Rd;* ☎ *520 574 0462; www.pimaair.org*).

As the train nears Tucson it enters the rail yards of the Santa Fe Pacific (formerly the Southern Pacific).

University of Arizona (50/5) Look for the stadium and campus to your right. Low down on the southern horizon is the Santa Rita Range.

TUCSON (55/60) The city began in 1776 as a supply station for the Mission San Xavier del Bac, located on the banks of the Santa Cruz River. Today it is a centre for farming, government and high-tech industry. It was capital of Arizona from 1867 to 1877, and Spanish, Mexican and Confederate flags have flown here at various times.

Tucson is 60 miles (96km) from the Mexican border and surrounded by mountains – the Santa Ritas to the south, Santa Catalinas to the north, Rincons in the east and Tucsons to the west. Being 1,000ft (300m) higher than Phoenix, temperatures are slightly cooler.

Tucson basics

☎ **Telephone code** 520

⊷ **Station** (*Ticket office & waiting room* ⊕ *midnight–03.00 Mon, 18.00–23.59 Tue, midnight–01.30 & 19.30–23.59 Wed/Fri/ Sun, midnight–03.00 & 18.00–23.59 Thu/Sat; information* ☎ *623 4442*) The Mission-style station is at 400 E Toole.

Connections Thruway buses connect with Phoenix.

🚍 **Local transport** Sun Tran (☎ *792 9222; www.suntran.com*) operates buses & a modern downtown streetcar system is planned.

🚕 **Taxis** Yellow ☎ 624 6611; John's Taxicab ☎ 409 3215

🚗 **Car rental** Budget, 4570 N Oracle Rd; ☎ 544 6118

🚌 **Greyhound** 471 W Congress; ☎ 792 3475

✈ **Tucson International Airport** 6 miles (10km) south by bus #16

Tours Gray Line; ☎ 622 8811. Lost Souls Tours (☎ *795 1117*) meet at the Amtrak train station behind Hotel Congress & visit haunted downtown Tucson.

ℹ **Visitors bureau** 100 S Church Av; ☎ 624 1817; e info@mtcvb.com; www.visittucson.org; ⊕ daily

🏠 **Accommodation** Contact Cactus Quail Bed & Breakfast, 14000 N Dust Devil Dr, Tucson, AZ 85739; ☎ 825 6767. Congress Hostel, 311 E Congress; ☎ 622 8848. Members & non-members, **$**.

Hotels include the Doubletree Reid Park, 445 S Alvernon Way; ☎ 881 4200, **$$$$$**; Arizona, 181 W Broadway Bd; ☎ 624 8711, **$$$**; Windmill Inn-St Philip's, 4250 N Campbell Av; ☎ 577 0007, **$$$**; Motel 6, 1031 E Benson Highway; ☎ 628 1264, **$$**; Tucson City Center, 475 N Granada Av; ☎ 622 3000, **$$**; Country Inn & Suites, 705 N Freeway; ☎ 867 6200, **$$**.

Recommended in Tucson

Presidio Historic Park Located 45 miles south of Tucson at 1 Burruel; ☎ 398 2252. Tucson became a walled city (or presidio) when the Spanish built a barrier against Native Americans. Many historic places are within walking distance of the station, including the Pima County courthouse which preserves a small part of the wall. It also has a mosaic-tiled dome & a courtyard fountain. El

Tiradito (the wishing shrine) makes dreams come true for believers who light a candle. The park is some way from Tucson, Amtrak's nearest stop, but well worth a visit.

Arizona State Museum 1013 E University Bd; ☎ 621 6302; www.statemuseum.arizona.edu; ⊕ daily; admission charge. The oldest & largest anthropological museum in the southwest features the history of the American southwest & northern Mexico. Combines prehistoric, historic & contemporary items with high-tech displays.

Arizona History Museum 949 E Second St ☏ 628 5774; www.arizonahistoricalsociety.org; ☺ Mon–Sat; admission charge. Southern Arizona history from the Spanish colonial to the territorial eras. The exhibits include Geronimo's rifle & 18th-century Spanish silver sculptures. Other Arizona Historical Society museums include the **Sosa-Carrillo-Frémont House** (☏ 622 0956; ☺ daily; free). One of Tucson's oldest adobe houses has been restored using period furniture of the 1880s. Walking tours on Sat.

Saguaro National Monument 3693 S Old Spanish Trail; ☏ 733 5158; www.nps.gov/sagu; ☺ daily; admission charge. Located in 2 sections, east & west of the city. The eastern section has older & taller stands of the giant saguaro cactus, which can live for 200 years & grows in only 2 states. White saguaro blossom, the state flower, appears in May & Jun.

Mission San Xavier del Bac 9 miles (15km) southwest of Tucson at 1950 W San Xavier Rd; ☏ 294 2624; www.sanxaviermission.org; ☺ daily; donation. Father Eusebio Kino arrived in 1692 & built a church 2 miles (3km) to the north. This mission, the most elaborate & beautiful in America, was completed 100 years later. Sometimes called 'The White Dove of the Desert', the mission is located on the Tohono O'dham Indian Reservation, where you can also sample Indian fry bread.

Pima Air and Space Museum 6000 E Valencia Rd; ☏ 574 0462; www.pimaair.org; ☺ daily; admission charge. 5 hangars contain more than 300 military, civilian & commercial aircraft, including President John F Kennedy's Air Force One & a replica of the Wright brothers' *Flyer*. Experience simulated space flights & a full motion simulator. Walking & tram tours.

Tombstone 65 miles (105km) southeast on Route 80. The **Old Courthouse State Historic Park** is at 219 Toughnut (☏ 457 3311; www.azstateparks.com/Parks/TOCO/index.html). 'The town too tough to die' began as a mining settlement & was the scene of the 1881 OK Corral shoot-out between Wyatt Earp, 'Doc' Holliday & the Clantons. Tombstone is quieter now but looks little different from when it was 'the next best thing to hell on earth'. Big Nose Kate's saloon, the church, Boot Hill cemetery & the Epitaph Building are intact, & the OK Corral appears much as it did on the day of the gunfight. The **Tourist Association** is at PO Box 995, Tombstone, AZ 85638-0995 (☏ 888 457 3929).

PHOENIX The *Sunset Limited* does not currently stop in Phoenix but buses connect the city with Tucson and Amtrak's Maricopa Station in about two hours.

Arizona's capital sprawls over 393 square miles (1,020km²), surrounded by impressive mountains. The original settlement was made on the ruined villages of Anasazi and Mogollon Indians, who lived here from before the time of Christ until the 15th century and used irrigation to tame the desert. The Anasazi grew maize, made fine-art pottery and constructed sophisticated architecture but their civilisation was mysteriously destroyed. Settlers prophesied that a city would rise again like the legendary phoenix bird. Roosevelt Dam, 75 miles (112km) to the north, harnessed the Salt River in 1911 and helped fulfil the prophecy.

Phoenix boasts the highest water fountain in the world at 560ft (171m). The city has 300 days of sunshine a year and only seven inches (17cm) of rain, with summer temperatures sometimes up to 120°F (49°C).

Phoenix basics

☏**Telephone code** 602

🚂 **Station** The magnificent Mission Revival-style Union Station on Harrison St at Fourth Av was built by the Santa Fe & the Arizona Eastern (Southern Pacific) railroads in 1923. A milestone in the city's development, Union Station brought tourism on a grand scale. At its peak after World War II, Union Station was served by 18 trains a day, including Southern Pacific's *Sunset Limited* between Los Angeles & New Orleans, & the *Golden State Limited* on the Los Angeles–Chicago route. The *Golden State* made its last run in 1968,

& Amtrak re-routed the *Sunset Limited* away from Phoenix in 1996. Since then, the *Olympic Torch* train has stopped here twice & GrandLuxe tourist trains have occasionally used Union Station.

Connections Greyhound buses link Tucson with Phoenix & a taxi service operates from Maricopa (✆ *520 568 4404*). Thruway buses operate between Amtrak's Flagstaff Station & Phoenix.

🚐 **Local transport** Valley Metro (✆ *253 5000; www.valleymetro.org*) operates buses as well as a new light rail service.

🚕 **Taxis** Yellow ✆ 252 5252; Aguilas ✆ 455 6249
🚕 **Car rental** Enterprise, 1638 S 7th; ✆ 257 4177
🚐 **Greyhound** 2115 E Buckeye Rd; ✆ 389 4200
✈ **Sky Harbor International Airport** 4 miles (6.5km) southeast. Valley Metro connects to the airport at the light rail station at 44th & Washington sts using the PHX Airport Shuttle. A free PHX Sky Train will replace the Airport Shuttle when construction is completed in late 2012.

Tours Gray Line; ✆ 226 8060. The Capitol walking tour includes the Capitol Museum & Confederate Monument. Desert excursions from Arrowhead Tours (✆ *942 3361*).

i **Visitors bureau** 125 N Second; ✆ 254 6500; e visitors@visitphoenix.com; www.visitphoenix. com; ☺ Mon–Fri

🏠 **Accommodation** For B&B contact Maricopa Manor, 15 W Pasadena Av, Phoenix, AZ 85013; ✆ 274 6302 or ✆ 1 800 292 6403.

Metcalf House Youth Hostel, 1026 N Ninth; ✆ 254 9803. Dormitory rooms, **$**. YMCA, 350 N First Av; ✆ 257 5134, **$**.

Hotels often have low-rate specials during summer, if you can take the heat. They include the Lexington, 1100 N Central Av; ✆ 252 2100, **$$$**; Ramada Inn, 401 N First; ✆ 258 3411, **$$$**; Crescent, 2620 Dunlop Av; ✆ 943 8200, **$$$**; San Carlos, 202 N Central Av; ✆ 253 4121, **$$**; Hyatt Regency, 122 N Second; ✆ 252 1234, **$$$$$**.

Recommended in Phoenix

Heritage Square 115 N Sixth St; ✆ 262 6412; ☺ Mon–Sun; admission charge. Restored 19th-century houses give an idea how Old Phoenix looked, eg: the 1895 Rosson House.
Encanto Park 15th Av & Encanto; ☺ daily. An oasis in the middle of the city, featuring a lake, nature trails & a swimming pool.
Desert Botanical Garden 1201 N Galvin Parkway in Papago Park; ✆ 480 941 1225; www. dbg.org; ☺ daily; admission charge. The garden is an important conservation institution with 169 rare, threatened or endangered plant species from the world's deserts, especially the southwestern US & northern Mexico. Over 1,350 varieties of cactus are among the 50,000 plants located in 145 acres, 5 miles east of downtown. Take bus #3.
Phoenix Art Museum 1625 N Central Av; ✆ 257 1222; www.phxart.org; ☺ Wed–Sun; admission charge. The largest visual arts museum between Denver & Los Angeles features 14,000 exhibits, including art from Asia, the Americas & Europe to 1900, along with contemporary works.
Heard Museum 2301 N Central Av; ✆ 252 8848; www.heard.org; ☺ daily; admission charge, free tours. One of the best places to experience the cultures & art of Native Americans of the southwest. 10 galleries & outdoor courtyards

feature traditional & contemporary Native American art.
Phoenix Zoo 455 N Galvin Parkway, near the Botanical Garden; ✆ 273 1341; www.phoenixzoo. org; ☺ daily; admission charge. Approximately 1,200 animals & birds live in replicated natural habitats here, including rare Arabian oryx; there are also 2½ miles of walking trails.
Arizona Railway Museum 330 E Ryan Rd in Chandler, 20 miles (32km) southeast; ✆ 480 814 8645; www.azrymuseum.org; ☺ Sat/Sun from Labor Day to Memorial Day; donation. Located in a building resembling a train depot, the museum tells the history of southwestern railways.
Verde Canyon Railroad North of Phoenix at 300 N Broadway in Clarkdale; ✆ 800 582 7245; www.verdecanyonrr.com; ☺ Wed–Sun, plus Mon in peak season; admission charge. A 20-mile (32km) round trip takes you to the ghost-town depot at Perkinsville over a line built in 1911 for the United Verde Copper Company. You travel through North Verde River Canyon & the Sycamore Wilderness area, which can only be visited by train. You cross the SOB Canyon on a 175ft-high (50m) trestle, then go through a 680ft (200m) tunnel blasted with 20,000lb (9,000kg) of dynamite.

11

Parts of *How The West Was Won* were filmed among the canyon's Sinagua ruins & abandoned gold mines. You can see cacti, wild flowers, bald eagles, javalinas, blue herons & deer, & sometimes beavers, mountain lions & black bears. The line was formerly operated by the Santa Fe, Prescott & Phoenix Railroad, which hauled freight until 1988.

All aboard!

To your right as the *Sunset Limited* pulls out of Tucson are the Santa Catalina Mountains, including Mount Lemmon (9,157ft/2,790m). The train begins a journey of more than four hours to Yuma, although a stop is planned for Maricopa.

Pima Air Park (30/30) The base on your left refurbishes jets for sale around the world. The Little Owl Head Mountains are to your left and the Tortolita Range directly ahead. In this fertile country you see fields of cotton, pecans, cabbage and broccoli.

Picacho Pass (40/20) Picacho Peak (3,382ft/1,030m) is to your left and the Picacho Range to your right.

Look for stands of candelabra-like saguaro cactus on both sides of the track for the next few miles as desert predominates. A saguaro can grow to 50ft (15m) and store 2,000 gallons (9,100 litres) of water. Look also for the portly barrel cactus, prickly pears, tangling chollas and the spindly ocotillo shrub. The last acquired its name (Spanish for 'little torch') because of the bright-red flowers it sprouts after winter rain.

MARICOPA (60/180) Amtrak's new station on N John Wayne Parkway in Maricopa serves Phoenix, 25 miles to the north, as well as the surrounding area. The elegant old round tail observation car on display was originally brought from Los Angeles Union Station to serve as a ticket office and waiting room.

Nearby Superstition Mountains were sacred to the Apache thunder god and a search for Apache gold has been going on here ever since. Hundreds of miners and their guards were massacred in the 1860s after being sent to look for the treasure by a Mexican cattle rancher. The Lost Dutchman mine, believed to be located somewhere in the canyons to your right, was never found again after its German prospector was shot trying to return to his find. An Apache girl reputedly had her tongue cut out for showing him the gold.

As the *Sunset Limited* continues across the Sonoran Desert, home of the gila monster lizard, look for distant rocks eroded into natural sculptures. The flat rectangular ones are known as mesas. Others have been carved into recognisable figures, such as a praying monk and a weeping Apache.

YUMA (180/135) A resort set in farmland which is irrigated from the Colorado River. The former Yuma Prison is now a state park.

Colorado River (20/115) Crossing the river takes you from Arizona into California. Since Arizona does not observe Daylight Saving Time, watches go back an hour (forward when travelling east) only from October to April.

Indio (110/25) 'The date capital of the world' hosts a date festival each February.

PALM SPRINGS (135/75) Half of Palm Springs is owned by the Cahuilla tribe, who were given a vast area of desert by the US Government in return for the right to build a railroad. The Cahuillas thought they already owned the land, which subsequently became some of the world's most exclusive real estate and made them America's richest Native Americans.

Colton (65/10) The train crosses the Santa Ana River, with the San Gabriel Mountains to your right. Look for giant, electricity-generating turbines seen from both sides of the train.

ONTARIO (75/10) Part of Southern California's Inland Empire region, located 37 miles inland of the Pacific Ocean. The international airport is on your left.

POMONA (10/45) Named after the Roman goddess of fruit, although residential development has mostly replaced orchards and vineyards. Singer Tom Waits was born in the back of a taxi just outside the hospital here in 1949. Los Angeles County Fair, held in September, attracts more people than any other similar event in the country. Amtrak uses the Southern Pacific station at 100 W Commercial.

The train leaves with St Joseph's Church to your left and St Paul's Mission-style church on the right, next to the California Polytechnic.

San Gabriel River (15/30) You cross this often dried-out riverbed.

El Monte Airport (17/28) The airport to your right was named after nearby Mount Wilson (5,700ft/1,730m).

The train crosses the concrete-lined Rio Hondo then enters a short tunnel to Temple City, dramatically emerging along the centre strip of the San Bernadino Freeway.

California State University (33/12) The campus is to your right as you part company with the freeway.

LA County Hospital (37/8) Look right for the hospital's tall buildings. On your left is the concrete channel of the Los Angeles River, with Dodger Stadium visible ahead on a hill. The *Sunset Limited* crosses the river then passes the post office building's twin domes and the tower of City Hall on the right. LA's county jail is to your left just before the station.

LOS ANGELES For Los Angeles city information, see *Chapter 4, The* Coast Starlight (pages 68–70).

11

12

The *Texas Eagle*
Chicago–San Antonio (for Los Angeles)

General route information

From Lake Michigan to the Alamo, the *Texas Eagle* makes a 1,306-mile (2,100km) journey down the centre of America, travelling through Lincoln land then crossing the Mississippi before continuing through the Ozarks to Arkansas and Texas. Pine forest and lakes north of Dallas give way to cattle country as you approach San Antonio, where through-coaches to Los Angeles join the *Sunset Limited*. The *Texas Eagle* has one of the highest passenger growth rates of all the Amtrak routes.

Joining the train

CHICAGO For Chicago city information, see *Chapter 5, The California Zephyr* (pages 71–4). The *Texas Eagle* operates between Chicago and Joliet over the Canadian National Railway, travelling initially through industrial suburbs.

ESSENTIAL INFORMATION

FREQUENCY Daily. The **southbound** *Texas Eagle* leaves Chicago mid afternoon to reach St Louis by mid evening and Little Rock early next morning. You arrive in Dallas early in the afternoon and San Antonio by late evening. On some days (see below) coaches continue to Los Angeles by joining the *Sunset Limited* (see page 133). Travelling **north**, trains leave San Antonio early in the morning to reach Dallas by late afternoon and Little Rock late evening. You arrive in St Louis early next morning and Chicago by mid afternoon. A through service west of San Antonio operates tri-weekly, departing Chicago, Poplar Bluff and intermediate stations on Sunday, Tuesday and Thursday. Eastbound trains departing Los Angeles on Sunday, Wednesday and Friday arrive in Dallas on Tuesday, Friday and Sunday, and stations between Walnut Ridge and Chicago on Wednesday, Saturday and Monday.
DURATION 32 hours 25 minutes (Chicago–San Antonio); 65 hours 20 minutes (Chicago–Los Angeles)
RESERVATIONS All reserved
EQUIPMENT Superliner coaches
SLEEPING Superliner bedrooms
FOOD Complete meals, snacks, sandwiches, drinks
LOUNGE CAR Movies, games, hospitality hour. A guide from the San Antonio Missions National Historical Park provides a narrative on select weekends from Memorial Day through Labor Day.
BAGGAGE Check-in service available at main cities

All aboard!

Look back for fine views of the city as you cross the Chicago River, which provided French explorers with a passage from Lake Michigan almost as far as the Mississippi River. A few minutes out of Union Station the *Texas Eagle* crosses the Chicago Sanitary Ship Canal, a waterway which reverses the Chicago River's flow. The canal forms part of an inland system which runs 30 miles (48km) from Chicago to Lockport, linking the Great Lakes with the Mississippi.

Bridgeport (15/30) First settled by Irish immigrants who built the Illinois & Michigan (I & M) Canal, Bridgeport was the home of Chicago's influential former mayor, Richard J Daley.

Willow Springs (30/15) Look left for deer hiding in a wooded enclave.

Lambert (32/13) The train crosses the Calumet Sag Channel joining Lake Michigan with the Sanitary Ship Canal. You then continue to Joliet through the urban parkland of the I & M National Corridor.

Lockport (38/7) Restored buildings can be seen to your right as the *Texas Eagle* accompanies a towpath.

Illinois State Prison (41/4) Joliet's notorious correctional centre is to your right.

JOLIET (45/52) Named after the 17th-century French-Canadian explorer Louis Jolliet, this manufacturing town has busy rail and water connections, including four riverboat casinos. Amtrak's station is at 50 E Jefferson.

From Joliet to Fort Worth, the *Texas Eagle* operates on tracks of the Union Pacific Railroad. You continue with the Des Plaines River and conservation area to your right, next to the I & M Canal. To your left are a limestone quarry and a US Army arsenal where munitions are stored underground.

Kankakee River (15/37) The train crosses this tributary of the Illinois River.

Braidwood (20/32) The tall towers on your left are part of a Con-Edison nuclear energy plant.

Dwight (35/17) In 1860, the then Prince of Wales visited Dwight's small, white pioneer Gothic church. The station to your right dates from 1892. Beyond it is a brick building

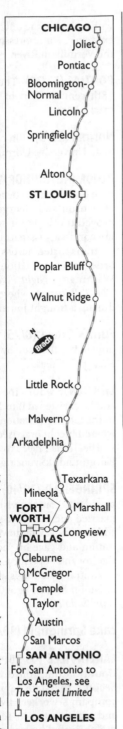

The Texas Eagle   Chicago–San Antonio

12

CHICAGO
Joliet
Pontiac
Bloomington-Normal
Lincoln
Springfield

Alton
ST LOUIS

Poplar Bluff
Walnut Ridge

Little Rock
Malvern
Arkadelphia
Texarkana
Mineola
FORT WORTH   Marshall
DALLAS   Longview
Cleburne
McGregor
Temple
Taylor
Austin
San Marcos
SAN ANTONIO
For San Antonio to Los Angeles, see *The Sunset Limited*

LOS ANGELES

with a clock – the only one of three banks designed by Frank Lloyd Wright still in existence. An impressive windmill can be seen to the left before the train crosses the Vermillion River.

PONTIAC (52/30) The town was named after a Native American chief of the 18th century. Part of the original Route 66 was constructed right next to the tracks here.

Normal (25/5) Illinois Normal School was a teachers' college which became the State University. Dormitories and other campus buildings appear to your right.

BLOOMINGTON-NORMAL (30/33) Abraham Lincoln delivered his final speech here on his way to becoming president in 1860. This was the birthplace of Adlai Stevenson and George Pullman also lived here. Pullman's luxury Pioneer car proved too wide for some railroads until Mrs Lincoln used one following her husband's assassination in 1865. Alterations were made so that his body could be transported across country to Springfield. The journey took two weeks in order to let the nation pay its respects along the route. A reconstruction of the Washington *Night Flyer* train of 1861 can be seen in a Dick Powell film called *The Tall Target*, where Lincoln is saved from assassination by 'John Kennedy' during a fraught journey.

Funk's Grove (8/25) Illinois's only tract of virgin timber, mostly maple, was donated to the state by Eugene Funk of Funk Seeds. Just before Lincoln you cross Kickapoo Creek.

LINCOLN (33/30) The only town named after Lincoln before he became president, and he christened it in 1853 using melon juice. A 'slice of watermelon' statue stands to the left of the station. Also to your left is the domed Logan County Courthouse where Lincoln practised law.

The *Texas Eagle* crosses the Sangamon River near Springfield, with the Illinois Fairgrounds to your right.

SPRINGFIELD (30/40) Lincoln spent 25 years in Springfield before becoming president. You can visit the only house he ever owned, the place where he was married and the grave in which he and his family are buried. He made his farewell address on leaving town in 1861 at a rail depot a short distance from the present station and gave his 'house divided' speech at the Old State Capitol. The present Capitol and Supreme Court can be seen to your right.

Amtrak's station is at Washington and Third and the **Illinois Visitor Center** is at Union Station at 500 E Madison (☎ *217 557 4588; www.visit-springfieldillinois. com;* ☺ *daily*).

Lake Springfield (10/30) The *Texas Eagle* crosses the western tip of the lake.

CARLINVILLE (40/30) Carlinville is a flag stop only. The spired Macoupin County Courthouse on your left dates from when Carlinville hoped to become the state capital. When Standard Oil operated local coal mines the company's workers lived in Sears, Roebuck houses which were prefabricated and transported in sections by train. The mines are closed but some of the prefabricated houses remain.

Macoupin Creek (5/25) The *Texas Eagle* crosses at Beaver Dam State Park.

ALTON (30/40) Birthplace in 1926 of the legendary jazz musician, Miles Davis. This Mississippi River port's newspaper editor, Elijah Lovejoy, was lynched in 1838 by a mob opposing his anti-slavery views. The town later became a supply point for the Union Army.

Unseen to your right as you cross the Wood River is Lewis and Clark State Park, where the Missouri and Mississippi rivers meet. Lewis and Clark's expedition wintered here before beginning their explorations west.

Cahokia Diversion Canal (10/30) Levees on both sides try to prevent flooding when the Mississippi rises. During the summer of 1993, the worst floods in history brought chaos to this region, covering 16,000 square miles (41,000km²) of crops in eight states and killing at least 40 people.

The Native American city of Cahokia stretched across 2,200 acres here and was inhabited from around AD700 to 1400. The inhabitants, known as Mississippians, had a culture based on cosmology and built sacred ritual mounds as large as Egypt's Great Pyramid. It is thought that deforestation caused devastating floods which ruined crops and made the population flee their 'Native American Jerusalem'.

Lenox (11/29) The train travels next to tracks which run between St Louis and Detroit and were used by the celebrated *Wabash Cannonball* train.

Granite City (14/26) Steel and other heavy industries accumulate as you approach St Louis.

Mississippi River (22/18) You cross high above the river on the Merchants Railroad bridge, leaving Illinois for Missouri. Look for barges on the river and the St Louis skyline to your left.

Eads Bridge (30/10) The train passes beneath the city's oldest bridge, which had the longest steel spans anywhere when it was completed in 1874.

Gateway Arch (35/5) The landmark to your right is America's tallest (630ft/192m) monument, with a cathedral at its base. Old riverboats can be seen moored on your left.

Busch Memorial Stadium (38/2) The former site of the St Louis Cardinals' baseball ground, demolished in 2005, is to your right.

ST LOUIS (40/240) This gateway to the west was founded by Pierre Laclede in 1764 on high ground where the Mississippi River joins the Missouri. Named after King Louis IX of France, St Louis was acquired by President Jefferson as part of the 1803 Louisiana Purchase. The original fur-trading post became a place for wagon trains to gather before heading west, so the massive 630ft stainless-steel Gateway Arch designed by Eero Saarinen makes an appropriate symbol.

Scott Joplin invented ragtime when he lived here and W C Handy's 'St Louis Blues', the most recorded song of all time, also helped put the city on the music map. Jazz musicians came by riverboat and train from New Orleans to join blues artists from the Mississippi Delta to create new musical styles. Their influence can still be heard in the many live music clubs and bars. Other famous St Louisans include singer/guitarist Chuck Berry, dancer Josephine Baker, actor Vincent Price and Beat Generation writer William S Burroughs.

St Louis basics

❯Telephone code 314

⇌ Station (*Ticket office* ⊕ *03.30–23.30. Waiting room* ⊕ *24hrs; information* ❧*331 3300*) Amtrak's modern station at 551 S 16th replaces the famous old Union Station. Lockers, vending machines, taxi stand.
Connections No Thruway bus.
🚌 Local transport Metro (❧*231 2345; www. metrostlouis.org*) operates buses, including the Levee Line between Union Station & the river. The MetroLink light rail system extends 38 miles from Lambert-St Louis International Airport to Shiloh-Scott (Air Force Base), Illinois College, stopping along the line at major retail, business, recreational & cultural centres, as well as the Convention Center. Passengers can travel from Union Station to Laclede's Landing & all points in between (❧*982 1400 or* ❧*877 982 1410;* ⊕ *Mon–Fri*). The Metro also now has a 2nd line that goes to the St Louis Galleria & to Shrewsbury.
🚕 Taxis County Cab and Yellow Cab ❧993 8294
🚕 Car rental Enterprise, 9305 National Bridge Rd; ❧800 227 9449
🚌 Greyhound 1450 N 13th; ❧231 4485

✈ Lambert-St Louis International Airport 14 miles (22km) northwest by MetroLink train or Metro bus
Tours Gray Line/Vandalia; ❧800 542 4287. During summer you can take the downtown St Louis Tram tour. Open-air cars pause at the major attractions & a pass permits unlimited stops. 2 replica 19th-century steamboats, the *Tom Sawyer* & *Becky Thatcher*, offer 1hr narrated trips on the river (❧*621 4040*).
ℹ Visitors bureau Kiener Plaza & 701 Convention Plaza; ❧421 1023 or ❧800 916 0092; e visinfo@explorestlouis.com; www. explorestlouis.com; ⊕ daily
🏠 Accommodation Contact Lehmann House Bed & Breakfast, 10 Benton Pl, St Louis, MO 63104; ❧422 1483. Huckleberry Finn AYH Hostel, 1904 S 12th; ❧241 0076; www.huckfinnhostel. com. Take bus #59. Members, **$**.
   Hotels include the Fleur-de-Lys Mansion, 3500 Russell Bd; ❧773 3500, **$$$$**; Westin St Louis, 811 Spruce; ❧621 2000, **$$$$$**; Adam's Mark, 315 Chestnut; ❧241 7400, **$$$$**; Drury Inn Union Station, 201 S 20th, adjacent to Union Station; ❧231 3900, **$$$**; Pear Tree Inn Union Station, 2211 Market; ❧241 3200, **$$$**; Napoleon's Retreat, 1815 Lafayette Av; ❧772 6979, **$$$**.

Recommended in St Louis

City Museum 701 N 15th; ❧231 2489; www.citymuseum.org; ⊕ daily; admission charge. Located in a factory built in 1909 for the International Shoe Company, the museum features history, science & architecture. Among the highlights are a working glass studio, a giant fish tank & Art City – where artists can be seen at work.
National Museum of Transportation 3015 Barrett Station Rd; ❧615 8668; www. museumoftransport.org; ⊕ daily; admission charge. America's greatest collection of railway engines & equipment, including 70 locomotives, plus streetcars, buses & aircraft.
Union Station 18th & Market; ❧421 6655. Opened in 1894, this splendid Romanesque-style

building with its great clock tower was once the world's largest & busiest train station. Now a National Historic Landmark, the station has been restored & transformed into a shopping mall & entertainment venue with paddle boats, a Ferris wheel & a carousel. The Grand Hall features a superb barrel-vaulted gilt ceiling, stained glass over the entrance, scale models of trains, & statues. The station's past & present can be discovered on self-guided walking tours. Actor Kurt Russell filmed part of *Escape from New York* in Union Station.
Museum of Westward Expansion Located beneath the Gateway Arch at 11 N Fourth St; ❧655 1700; ⊕ daily; museum free, admission charge to the observation deck. The museum

depicts wagon trains & pioneer life, with clothing, tools, weapons, household goods & personal items. The Saarinen Arch's observation deck (twice the height of the Statue of Liberty) gives unbeatable views of the city.

Laclede's Landing On the riverfront, between the Eads & Martin Luther King bridges; ☎241 5875; www.lacledeslanding.com. This historic district stands next to the site of Pierre Laclede's original encampment. Dozens of shops & restaurants line 19th-century cobblestone streets decorated with cast-iron lamps.

Cupples House 221 N Grand Bd; ☎977 6630; www.slu.edu/x27031.xml; ⊕ Tue–Sat; admission charge. This restored Romanesque mansion dates from 1888 & has 42 rooms, 22

fireplaces, wooden floors, gargoyles & elegant stone carvings, as well as an art gallery.

Missouri History Museum In the Jefferson Memorial Bldg, Forest Park; ☎746 4599; www.mohistory.org; ⊕ daily; free. Missouri Historical Society displays include Charles Lindbergh's flight suit & items from the 1904 World's Fair.

Scott Joplin State House 2658 Delmar Bd; ☎340 5790; ⊕ daily; admission charge. Dating from just after the Civil War, this was the home of the composer Scott Joplin in the early 1900s.

Anheuser-Busch Brewery 1127 Pestalozzi; ☎577 2626; www.budweisertours.com; ⊕ daily; free. Tour the world's largest brewery, admire the Clydesdale horses & sample a free beer. Take bus #40.

All aboard!

The *Texas Eagle* departs on the Missouri Pacific section of the Union Pacific Railroad for a run of almost four hours through Mark Twain country to Poplar Bluff.

Mississippi River (30/210) The shipyard to your left constructs boats for use on the river.

Jefferson Barracks (35/205) Chief Blackhawk of the Sac Indians was imprisoned at this 18th-century military post.

Pevely (70/170) The *Texas Eagle* parts company with the Mississippi River.

Big River (120/120) You cross to the north of Ironton in an area that has some of the world's largest lead and iron ore mines.

POPLAR BLUFF (240/50) Winner of the 'all American city' award, Poplar Bluff is a manufacturing centre located among farmland. Nearby are the Ozark Mountains and Wappapello Lake. The historic station with its impressive steps was built in 1910 by the St Louis, Iron Mountain & Southern Railway. It was renamed the Union Pacific Depot in 1983, and later added to the National Register of Historic Places. The **Mo-Ark Regional Railroad Museum** (*303 Moran St;* ☎ *573 785 4539; http://moarkrail. org; ⊕ w/end afternoons*) has photographs of early railroading days, an early steam engine and dining car display, and a large model train layout. For many years, train crews would stay in the hotels and boarding houses that once lined the city's streets.

Missouri–Arkansas state line (20/30) You cross into the smallest state west of the Mississippi.

WALNUT RIDGE (50/106) The restored 1920s Italianate–Mediterranean-style train station, originally belonging to the Missouri Pacific Railroad, is also used by the local Chamber of Commerce and tourist centre and serves the nearby cities of Jonesboro, Paragould and Pocahontas. Close by are Lake Charles State Park and one of Arkansas's first settlements, Old Davidsonville.

Newport (26/80) Newport prospered after the Cairo & Fulton Railroad arrived. At neighbouring Jacksonport, Confederate troops massed beside the White River during the Civil War.

Arkansas River (105/1) You cross the river dividing North Little Rock from Little Rock then see the Capitol dome and city skyline to your left.

LITTLE ROCK (106/45) French explorers called this 'La Petite Roche' but Arkansas's biggest city has been the state capital since 1821. Until Governor Bill Clinton ran for president, Little Rock was best known for its strict 1950s segregationism.

The present Capitol is a smaller version of the one in Washington, DC. An older, Greek-style **state house** at 300 W Markham features Arkansas history and a display in honour of President Clinton, whose Presidential Center opened in 2004. Little Rock is dominated by the TCBY tower (named after The Country's Best Yogurt) and hosts the annual autumn state fair. Amtrak's depot is at Union Station Square and the **visitors bureau** at 615 E Capitol Avenue (✆ *501 370 3232; www.littlerock.com*).

The *Texas Eagle* leaves with the Capitol again to your left. The train eases through suburbs before entering hillier country covered with forests of pine and hardwood.

Benton (30/15) Most of America's aluminium comes from the local bauxite mines. You cross the Saline River soon after leaving Benton.

MALVERN (45/21) The original town of Rockport, located on the Ouachita River, transferred here and changed its name to Malvern Station. Known as 'The brick capital of the world', Malvern has three Acme brick plants and hosts an annual 'Brickfest'. Amtrak's stop at 200 E First also serves **Hot Springs National Park**, established in 1832 and formerly served by a narrow-gauge railroad called the Diamond Jo that replaced the previous stagecoach connection. Hot Springs **visitors bureau** is at 134 Convention Boulevard (✆ *1 800 SPA CITY or* ✆ *501 321 2835; www. hotsprings.org*).

Ouachita River (20/1) You cross the river, with Arkadelphia to your right.

ARKADELPHIA (21/80) The former steamboat landing stage is famed for its colleges and aluminium plants. A few minutes before reaching Prescott, the *Texas Eagle* crosses the Little Missouri River.

Prescott (25/55) Note the red-roofed station on your right. To the west is the 'Trail of Tears' travelled by Cherokee Indians. Forced by the US Army to move to Oklahoma reservations, a quarter of the Cherokee nation died from inadequate food and clothing in the winter of 1838.

Hope (40/40) Look right for an old brick-kiln chimney. 'The watermelon capital of the world' claims the all-time record (265lb/120kg) and was the birthplace of Bill Clinton. Richard Ford, author of *Independence Day*, lived here while working on the Louisiana-Pacific Railroad.

Between Hope and the Red River you can see boisdarc trees, often with enormous green seed pods. Their exceptionally hard wood was used for horse-drawn farm implements.

Red River Valley (55/25) You cross the river on its way south, eventually to join the Mississippi. The valley's red earth washes into the water and gives the river its name. Soya beans and grain grow on land which once raised cotton.

Homan (65/15) Pecan trees on both sides of the track prove this really is the south.

Texarkana Airport (70/10) Runways and buildings appear to your left.

TEXARKANA (80/75) When the train stops, its front end is in Texas while the rear remains in Arkansas. Texarkana's unique position calls for two mayors and two police departments, and the post office is the only federal building to straddle a state line. Texarkana was the birthplace of one-time presidential candidate Henry Ross Perot, whose medals are displayed at the local Boy Scout Center. Amtrak's station is at 100 E Front.

The *Texas Eagle* departs, travelling south along the Texas border.

Sulphur River (20/55) Look left for a paper mill as you cross.

Atlanta (30/45) Prehistoric Native American settlements have been found nearby.

Jefferson (50/25) One of the state's earliest steamboat ports, where an old cemetery can be seen on the right. Nearby Caddo Lake has a water garden of bayous, cypress trees, Spanish moss, lotuses and water lilies.

MARSHALL (75/25) Marshall was an important centre for the Texas & Pacific Railway Company (the T&P) from the 1870s. Lady Bird Johnson and George Foreman, entrepreneur and former heavyweight boxing champion respectively, were born here. When Texas seceded from the Union in 1861, this became one of its largest cities, making ammunition and saddles for the Confederate army. After the fall of Vicksburg, Marshall became the Missouri governor capital. Shreveport, Louisiana, is 25 miles (40km) to the west. The fine Texas & Pacific depot museum and station have lately been renovated (*www.marshalldepot.org*).

LONGVIEW (25/45) A railroad surveyor changed the town's name from Earpville in 1870 after admiring the view from a farmer's front porch. Rail service arrived two years later, when Longview became the head of the former Southern Pacific line. In 1930, the city's fortunes were transformed dramatically with the discovery of the East Texas Oilfield, the largest in the United States outside Alaska. Amtrak Thruway buses connect the lovingly restored T & P station with Houston, Nacogdoches, Galveston and Shreveport.

Gladwater (20/25) Located in the middle of east Texas oil country, where the industry has expanded since the first major discovery of 1931. Production fields can be seen on both sides of the track and a Texaco refinery is to your left.

MINEOLA (45/95) The train's route follows the Sabine River for the next 50 miles (80km) through country famous for beef cattle and Quarter Horses.

Big Sandy (10/85) Garner Ted Armstrong's Ambassador College is bounded by white-fenced fields on your right.

Grand Saline (20/75) Named after the 700ft-deep (210m) salt mine seen to your left.

Mesquite (45/50) A large building to your left houses the Mesquite Rodeo. Thorny mesquite scrub trees are a common sight throughout the southwest.

As the Dallas skyline appears to your right, look for the Texas fairground's Ferris wheel in the distance.

DALLAS (95/65) The train halts opposite the Hyatt Hotel, mesmerised by its reflection in the glass façade familiar from television's *Dallas*. 'The city that should never have been' had few natural resources and no proper transport links until the railroad arrived. Founded as a log-cabin trading post in 1841, it became a utopian colony of artists and scientists.

Today's Dallas specialises in banking, oil and transport. The city has more shops, Cadillacs and divorces than anywhere else, as well as the world's largest computer centre. Neighbouring Fort Worth is more relaxed.

Dallas basics

✎ Telephone code 214
⚌ Station (*Ticket office* ⊕ *08.00–17.30. Waiting room* ⊕ *05.00–23.59; information* ✎ *653 1101*) Union Station at 400 S Houston is a splendid renovated building decorated with white marble. Lockers, vending machines, newspapers, handcarts, restaurant, shops, information centre, taxi stand. A walkway leads to the Hyatt Regency Hotel & Reunion Tower.
Connections No Thruway buses.
🚐 Local transport Dallas is primarily designed for cars but DART commuter rail, light rail & bus services (✎ *979 1111*) operate downtown & to the suburbs. The McKinney Av heritage streetcar operates daily, connecting to the Cityplace Station on the DART rail system (✎ *855 0006*).
🚕 Taxis Yellow ✎ *426 6262*; Ranger Cab ✎ *421 9999*
🚗 Car rental Hertz, 1200 Ross Av; ✎ *979 9494*
🚐 Greyhound 205 S Lamar; ✎ *849 6831*
✈ Dallas/Fort Worth Airport Larger than Manhattan, the airport is 16 miles (25km) west,

with bus connections to both downtown areas. Take the Super Shuttle from 729 E Dallas Rd (✎ *817 329 2000*). The Trinity Railway Express (or TRE) commuter rail line serves Union Station & Dallas/Fort Worth Airport Station (✎ *817 215 8600*).
Tours All In One ✎ *698 0332*; Gray Line (✎ *800 256 4723*) has tours around Dallas, Fort Worth & to the Southfork Ranch.
ℹ Visitors bureau Old Red Courthouse, 100 South Houston; ✎ *571 1300*; www.dallascvb.com; ⊕ daily
🏠 Accommodation Corinthian Bed & Breakfast, 4125 Junius St; ✎ *818 0400*.

Hotels include the Hyatt Regency, 300 Reunion Bd; ✎ *651 1234*, **$$$$**; Stoneleigh, 2927 Maple Av; ✎ *871 7111*, **$$$**; Radisson, 6060 N Central Expressway; ✎ *750 6060*, **$$$**; Crowne Plaza, 1015 Elm; ✎ *742 5678*, **$$$**; Knights Inn Market Center, 1550 Empire Central; ✎ *638 5151*, **$$**; Lumen, 6101 Hillcrest Av; ✎ *219 2400*, **$$$$$**.

Recommended in Dallas

Reunion Tower 300 Reunion Bd; ✎ *712 7145*; www.reuniontower.com; ⊕ daily; admission charge. The best views of Dallas are from the restaurant & observation deck of this 50-storey building next to Union Station. Spectacular light displays from the high geodesic dome after dark.

Old City Park 1717 Gano; ✎ *421 5141*; ⊕ Tue–Sun; admission charge. Historic buildings relocated from the surrounding area include a blacksmith's shop, general store, railway depot, church & pre-Civil War mansion.

Fair Park 2 miles east of downtown on First & Grand Av; ☎670 8400; www.fairpark.org. Art Deco Texas centennial buildings date from 1936. The park has been the site of the annual Texas state fair since 1887 & has symphony concerts, opera, rollercoaster rides & 8 museums.

Museum of the American Railroad Located in State Fair Park; ☎428 0101; www. dallasrailwaymuseum.com; ⊕ Wed–Sun (daily during Oct's state fair); admission charge. Features locomotives, passenger cars, freight wagons & Dallas's oldest train station. The museum plans to move the Fair Park collection to a new site in Frisco (see website for details).

Museum of Nature & Science Also in Fair Park, at 3535 Grand Av; ☎428 5555; www. natureandscience.org; ⊕ daily; admission charge. Formed in 2006 by merging the Dallas Museum of Natural History, the Science Place & the Dallas Children's Museum, the new museum occupies 3 landmark structures in Fair Park. Its Nature Building houses more than 200,000 items & authentic environments have been recreated, with the first mounted Texas dinosaur & a chance to handle some of the exhibits.

Southfork Ranch About 30mins' drive north of Dallas at 3700 Hogge Dr, Parker; ☎972 442 7800; www.southfork.com; ⊕ daily; admission charge. Tour the ranch where TV's *Dallas* was filmed & see the gun that was used to shoot J R Ewing. Lucy's flamboyant wedding dress is among the other memorabilia. Guided tours.

World Aquarium 1801 N Griffin; ☎720 2224; www.dwazoo.com; ⊕ daily; admission charge. Wander safely through a jungle filled with rare plants, monkeys, toucans, crocodiles, jaguars & piranhas. The aquarium features a 22,000-gallon walk-through tunnel with views of giant catfish, cichlids, huge turtles, stingrays & sea dragons.

Dallas Zoo 650 South R L Thornton Frwy; ☎670 5656; www.dallaszoo.com; ⊕ daily; admission charge. View more than 1,400 animals from a monorail train as you travel through the wilds of Africa.

The Sixth Floor Museum at Dealey Plaza 411 Elm; ☎747 6660; www.jfk.org; ⊕ daily; admission charge. The old Texas schoolbook depository now contains a museum which recreates the southeast window area as it looked on 22 November 1963 when President John F Kennedy was assassinated. The museum uses films, photographs, radio broadcasts & reconstructions to tell the story. Dramatic views of Dealey Plaza & tours.

All aboard!

You leave Dallas with Dealey Plaza to your right. President Kennedy was shot here and the familiar scene still provokes a shiver. The train goes over the overpass that JFK's motorcade sped under after he was shot.

The *Texas Eagle* crosses the Trinity River with the massive white Texas Stadium to your right.

Grand Prairie (25/40) Dallas naval air station and the Ling-Tempco-Vought aircraft factory are on your left.

Arlington (35/30) Part of the University of Texas can be seen to your right, with Six Flags Over Texas amusement park in the distance.

Handley (45/20) Look left for the manmade Arlington Lake. Lee Harvey Oswald, John F Kennedy's alleged assassin, was buried in Rose Hill Cemetery to your right.

FORT WORTH (65/40) The sister city of Dallas became a shipping point for cattle when citizens financed a 26-mile (42km) link to the Texas & Pacific Railroad in 1876. After this line opened, cattle no longer had to be driven north to Kansas. Fort Worth has acquired other industries since but an old Cowtown flavour still persists. Amtrak's modest station is at 101 Jones and the **visitors bureau** is at 508 Main, Sundance Square (☎ *817 698 3300; www.fortworth.com*).

The **Grapevine Vintage Railroad** (✆ *800 457 6338; www.grapevinetexasusa. com*) operates steam trains with vintage 1920s coaches from Thursday to Saturday, starting from the Fort Worth stockyards. Formerly known as the *Tarantula Train*, it travels over a 21-mile route to Grapevine on tracks of the St Louis Southwestern Railway (sometimes called the 'Cotton Belt'), going through the centre of town with excellent views of the skyline as you cross the Trinity River on massive trestles and follow part of the Chisholm Trail. The station at 140 E Exchange Avenue is the largest train station in the southwest.

The *Texas Eagle* goes south from Fort Worth on a Burlington Northern/Santa Fe Railroad line towards the small towns and villages of Texas hill country. This area has an exciting history of Comanche raids and cattle drives.

CLEBURNE (40/60) The town was named after Confederate General Pat Cleburne in 1867, having previously been known as Camp Henderson. Cleburne deals in agricultural crops and livestock, especially longhorn cattle.

Balcones Fault (15/45) Limestone hills suddenly rise out of the prairie as the train follows this fault line to San Antonio.

Brazos River (17/43) After crossing the Noland River you cross the Brazos, which runs to your left into Lake Whitney (15,000 acres/6,000ha of water created by a dam).

Meridian (28/32) Watch for Angora goats being raised for their mohair. Look also for fields of cotton, still a commonplace sight in the south.

Bosque River (30/30) You cross the river then accompany it for the next 30 miles (48km).

Clifton (40/20) Founded by Swedish and Norwegian settlers. To your right is one of the region's many limestone quarries.

Middle Bosque River (55/5) The *Texas Eagle* crosses the river shortly before Crawford.

MCGREGOR (60/32) Amtrak's stop for McGregor's bigger neighbour Waco, 20 miles (32km) to the east. David Koresh and his henchmen allegedly shot dozens of Branch Davidian cult members in 1993 during a siege by federal agents at nearby Mount Carmel. Many members died as fire swept through their ranch. Former president George W Bush's Prairie Chapel Ranch is six miles north at Crawford.

In 1896, Missouri, Kansas & Texas Railroad agent William G Crush decided to take two obsolete 35-ton locomotives, paint one green and one red, and put them on a track facing each other a few miles apart on a wide stretch of Texas prairie near Waco. The crews fired up the engines, each pulling seven boxcars, set them moving then jumped off as the trains raced towards each other, picking up speed to 45mph until they met in a spectacular crash. The trains were completely destroyed as the boiler of one locomotive exploded into a cloud of steam, sending iron and debris into the crowd. The publicity stunt was a great success, attracting more than 40,000 paying spectators, but the debris killed two people and seriously injured others. Crush was fired from his job, though he was rehired by 'the Katy' the following day. Scott Joplin immortalised the disaster with a march, *The Great Crush Collision*.

Moody (10/22) A small town which boasts a very large (2,200ft/670m) television antenna.

TEMPLE (32/55) The Gulf, Colorado & Santa Fe Railroad connects with the Missouri, Kansas & Texas here, making this a key junction. Close by are Fort Hood and Killeen.

The town was named after a Santa Fe surveyor in 1880 and the 'Prairie-Beaux Arts' depot was completed in 1911, featuring the Santa Fe trademark (a cross in a circle) formed in brick. In 1989, Santa Fe vacated the depot and by the early 1990s, it was completely abandoned. The city of Temple bought the building and approved $2.4 million for its restoration, which was completed in the year 2000. The **Santa Fe Depot Railroad and Heritage Museum** (*315 West Av B;* ✆ *254 298 5171; www.rrhm.org;* ⊕ *Mon–Sat; admission charge*) has vintage furniture and equipment, including a working telegraph machine. Temple also has the Santa Fe Depot from the McClennan County town of Moody and there are plans to move this to the site of the new museum.

The *Texas Eagle* continues on the Union Pacific line through ranch land and tree-covered hills.

Little River (25/30) You cross the river near the town of the same name.

San Gabriel River (40/15) As you cross look right for pecan trees growing on the river's banks.

TAYLOR (55/42) Founded in 1876 pending the arrival of the International & Great Northern Railroad, this rail town was named Taylor Station then Taylorsville after Edward Moses Taylor, a railroad official. In 1882, the Missouri, Kansas & Texas Railroad was extended to Taylorsville and was joined with the Missouri Pacific to link east and west. The town officially became Taylor in 1892 and still ships much of the prairie's ranch and farm produce. This was the birthplace of cartoonist and voice actor Frederick Bean 'Tex' Avery, creator of such animated greats as Daffy Duck and Bugs Bunny.

Round Rock (22/20) A residential town for many who commute to Austin.

Camp Mabry (35/7) The US Army base can be seen to your right.

AUSTIN (42/40) Capital of Texas and a former capital of the Texas Republic, Austin was founded in 1839 on hills beside the Colorado River. Richard Linklater's 1991 film *Slacker* was set in Texas University at Austin and the city has become an important film-making centre. The official 'live music capital of the world' is home to thousands of musicians and has more music venues per capita than anywhere else in the country. Austin is also home to the Lyndon Johnson Library and the Harry Ransom Center, where among nine million manuscripts are three versions of *Lady Chatterley's Lover*.

This being Texas, the Capitol Building is 7ft taller than the one in Washington, DC. Amtrak's station is at 250 N Lamar Boulevard, and the **tourist bureau** is at 301 Congress Avenue (✆ *800 926 2282; www.austintexas.org*).

Colorado River (2/38) Look back to your left as you cross for views of Austin's skyline, dominated by the Capitol's ornate pink dome.

Aquarina Springs (37/3) The clear springs to your right are the source of the San Marcos River, which you cross as you enter San Marcos.

SAN MARCOS (40/85) Home of Southwest Texas State University, alma mater of Lyndon Johnson, the town hosts an annual cooking contest for chilli aficionados. The train crosses the Guadalupe River.

New Braunfels (20/65) This town was founded in 1845 by a German prince called Carl von Solms-Braunfels.

San Antonio International (50/35) The airport can be seen to your right.

Olmos Park (52/33) The train travels through the middle of a golf course with Trinity University away to your left.

As San Antonio comes into view on the left, look for the InterFirst Building, the 750ft (225m) Tower of the Americas and the green-roofed Tower Life Building (San Antonio's oldest skyscraper).

King William District (75/10) Victorian houses appear to your left beyond the Pioneer flour mill.

Lone Star Brewery (78/7) The brewery museum is seen on your right just before you cross the San Antonio River.

SAN ANTONIO For San Antonio city information and through-travel to Los Angeles, see *Chapter 11, The* Sunset Limited (pages 133–53). For passengers between Chicago and Los Angeles, the train lays over in San Antonio overnight for between seven and 9½ hours to accommodate train-coupling operations. You are welcome to remain on board during this layover or enjoy the sites of the city. Access to train cars may be limited and temporary power outages will occur, including loss of air conditioning.

The *City of New Orleans*
Chicago–New Orleans

General route information

The *City of New Orleans* train divides the United States neatly into two as it travels more than 900 miles (1,450km) from the Great Lakes to the Gulf of Mexico. Between Chicago and New Orleans are prairies, farms, plantations and the Mississippi Basin where Civil War history was made. You also visit Memphis, birthplace of the blues and rock and roll.

A previous overnight train on this route was the Illinois Central's premier 'All-Pullman' *Panama Limited*, so called because hundreds of construction workers came this way to build the Panama Canal. Amtrak changed the name after Arlo Guthrie's recording of Steve Goodman's song became popular in the 1970s.

Joining the train

CHICAGO For Chicago city information, see *Chapter 5*, *The* California Zephyr (pages 71–4).

All aboard!

The *City of New Orleans* leaves Union Station then reverses for a few minutes before continuing forward with the city's skyline to your left. This train travels on Canadian National (CN) tracks for its entire jorney. After crossing the Chicago River, look left for Soldier Field and a view of Lake Michigan.

ESSENTIAL INFORMATION

FREQUENCY Daily. The **southbound** service leaves Chicago mid evening to reach Memphis early next morning and New Orleans by mid afternoon. Travelling **north**, the train leaves New Orleans mid afternoon to reach Memphis by late evening and Chicago by early morning.
DURATION 19 hours
RESERVATIONS All reserved
EQUIPMENT Superliner coaches
SLEEPING Superliner bedrooms
FOOD Complete meals, snacks, sandwiches, drinks
LOUNGE CAR Movies, games, hospitality hour. A National Park Service guide provides commentary along the route during summer.
BAGGAGE Check-in service available at main stations

CHICAGO
Homewood
Kankakee

Champaign-Urbana

Mattoon
Effingham

Centralia

Carbondale

N
Bradt

Fulton

Newbern-
Dyersburg

MEMPHIS

Greenwood

Yazoo City

Jackson

Hazlehurst
Brookhaven
McComb

Hammond

NEW ORLEANS

Chicago State University (20/25) Campus buildings appear on your right just before you cross the Calumet River.

HOMEWOOD (45/30) A leafy suburb served by the Metra/IC commuter rail line, with its neat red-tiled station building seen to your right.

You continue through several more attractive suburbs interspersed with stretches of farmland.

KANKAKEE (30/65) The town stands next to the Kankakee River. Chicago's best-known architect, Frank Lloyd Wright, once lived here and many of the houses feature elaborate stonework, domes and spires.

You travel on through an increasingly rural landscape. Look for farmhouses and gently rolling fields of mostly cotton and soya beans.

Gilman (20/45) An agriculture and railroad town which used to be a scheduled stop for *City of New Orleans* trains travelling north.

Rantoul (45/20) Originally known as Neipswah, an Illiniwek Indian word for 'where the minks are'. This used to be a scheduled stop for *City of New Orleans* trains.

Chanute Field (47/18) The large former US Air Force training base is now an aviation museum.

CHAMPAIGN-URBANA (65/35) Champaign is a commercial and manufacturing centre and the inspiration for an obscure Bob Dylan song, 'Champaign, Illinois', written with the rockabilly great Carl Perkins. Less industrial Urbana has been home to the University of Illinois since 1867. Amtrak is based in the handsome Illinois Terminal Building at 45 E University Avenue.

MATTOON (35/22) Another manufacturing town set among Illinois farm country. Lincoln Log Cabin State Park is close by and Eastern Illinois University 12 miles (19km) east at Charleston.

The train continues among more fields, trees, farmhouses and barns.

EFFINGHAM (22/45) Grain elevators and industrial scenes dominate both sides of the track.

Little Wabash River (8/37) You cross this tributary of the Ohio.

CENTRALIA (45/50) Amtrak's modest modern station at 110 S Oak is a flag stop. Founded by the Illinois Central

Gulf Railroad in 1854, Centralia's busy yards are among this region's most impressive.

CARBONDALE (50/105) Home of Southern Illinois University, Carbondale is in the Shawnee Hills region. The town acquired its name as the centre of a coal-mining area. Amtrak's station is at 401 S Illinois, near the traditionally styled Illinois Central Railroad (ICG) depot, built in 1903 and now restored. Thruway buses connect for passengers coming to join the train from Kansas City via St Louis. Nearby Crab Orchard wildlife refuge is a sanctuary for wintering birds such as Canada geese.

Cairo (60/45) 'Little Egypt' stands where the Mississippi and Ohio rivers meet at the borders of three states – Illinois, Missouri and Kentucky. General Grant occupied this commanding position during the Civil War. Before that the Illinois Central line ended in Cairo and passengers had to continue their journey to New Orleans by Mississippi steamboat. One of the river pilots then was Samuel Clemens, later to become known as Mark Twain. He said that the south began in Cairo (pronounced 'Kay-ro'), and included the town in *The Adventures of Huckleberry Finn*.

Illinois–Kentucky state line (62/43) You cross the border southeast of Cairo by crossing the Ohio River.

FULTON (105/50) The city stands directly beside Fulton, Tennessee. Huge South and Central American banana cargoes used to be distributed by refrigerated rail car from this 'banana crossroads of the USA'.

Kentucky–Tennessee state line (2/48) The *City of New Orleans* crosses into the Volunteer State just south of Fulton.

NEWBERN-DYERSBURG (50/90) Named after William Dyer, a colonel in the War of 1812, Dyersburg processes cotton and other farm produce. It was once one of Tennessee's largest ports.

After travelling most of the way from Chicago in darkness, the train nears Memphis around dawn. As you travel beside the Mississippi River look right for the shiny 32-storey Great American Pyramid which connects to Mud Island.

On your left is Confederate Park and beyond that the old Cotton Row market. Immediately before the station, look left to see the Beale Street District.

MEMPHIS (90/120) The train trundles through a nondescript part of the city before making a service stop at Amtrak's beautifully restored Central Station, built in 1914. Set on bluffs overlooking the Mississippi, Memphis was named by Andrew Jackson in 1819 after the capital of ancient Egypt. It soon became a port and the largest city in Tennessee, with the world's biggest mule-trading market.

Memphis's railroads and a strategic position on the river made it an ideal supply base during the Civil War. The Memphis to Charleston railroad was taken over by Union forces after victories at Fort Pillow and Shiloh. In 1862, eight Confederate steamers were sunk here within an hour on the Mississippi River.

The city remains a major port but hardwoods, soya and other agricultural products have replaced cotton as the chief cargo. Birthplace of Tennessee Williams and the Piggly Wiggly supermarket, Memphis was officially named by *American Heritage* magazine as a 'Great American Place', only the second US destination to be given this award. The first award went to Saratoga Springs and subsequent ones have been given to Tucson, Arizona, and Hampton Roads, Virginia. The **visitors bureau** is at 47 Union Avenue (✆ *901 543 5300; www.memphistravel.com*).

A free shuttle bus service runs every hour between Graceland, the Sun Studios and Beale Street. **Tours** can be had from Blues City (✆ *901 522 9229; www. bluescitytours.com*) and riverboat cruises on the *Memphis Queen* (✆ *901 527 2628; www.memphisriverboats.net*). The room and balcony where Martin Luther King was killed at the Lorraine Motel in 1968 are kept as a memorial.

Blues and Dixieland jazz feature in the handsomely restored Victorian **Beale Street** buildings (✆ *901 526 0115; www.bealestreet.com*) of W C Handy's home town, which was also the birthplace of Stax Records. Elvis Presley, Roy Orbison, Johnny Cash, the Everly Brothers, Dolly Parton and many others made their earliest recordings at Sam Phillips's **Sun Records studio** (*706 Union Av;* ✆ *901 521 0664; www.sunstudio.com*), a brownstone building preserved in its original state.

Graceland (*3734 Elvis Presley Bd;* ✆ *901 332 3322 or* ✆ *1 800 238 2000; www. elvis.com/graceland*), where 'The King' died in August 1977, is ten miles to the south. This is the country's second most-visited residence (after the White House). Go early and avoid a grilling wait in summer humidity for a tour of the mansion's surprisingly modest rooms, admire Elvis's 1955 pink Cadillac and put flowers beside his bronze gravestone.

The **Peabody Hotel** (*149 Union Av;* ✆ *901 529 4000; www.peabodymemphis.com*), where the Tom Cruise film *The Firm* was made, has been restored to its original ornate splendour. Live ducks fed on strawberries and lettuce leaves are paraded from their rooftop home each day to splash in the lobby's marble fountain.

The train pulls out of Memphis among freight and storage facilities then travels through wooded, undulating country. Between here and New Orleans you mostly accompany the route of Interstate 55.

After 25 minutes, the Mississippi River appears again to your right beyond a line of trees as the train enters delta country – a flat land of cotton fields, woods and small towns with dirt roads and Baptist churches. It was here that early blues singers such as Charley Patton and Robert Johnson played and made their first recordings. Others later took the train and their music north to Chicago.

You pass through Marks, a likely future stop for this train, and North Money. Extensive cotton fields can be seen on both sides. As you approach Greenwood, look left to see a lake and church among the trees.

GREENWOOD (120/55) The *City of New Orleans* holds up traffic as it pauses across the town's main street. Amtrak's neat brick station is to your right, with the town beyond.

You leave past a decaying railway building to your left then pass modern houses before seeing more cotton fields, processing plants and mansions. The train moves deeper into the south, passing small towns with white clapboard churches. There are houses with verandas, dusty roads, abandoned shacks and muddy, meandering rivers lined with trees. Woods and green fields start to predominate as you near Yazoo City.

YAZOO CITY (55/60) Note the impressive church to your left and an abandoned station building to your right.

The train departs through attractive forest and crosses several narrow, almost dry streams. You see cypress trees, sleepy towns and sun-bleached barns. Look also for log stacks being sprayed with water to keep them cool.

One of America's most famous train wrecks occurred just east of here on a rainy night in April 1900. The *Cannonball Express*, speeding to make up time between

Memphis and Canton, ploughed into the back of a stationary freight train at Vaughan. The train's headstrong engineer, John Luther 'Casey' Jones, died on board *No 382* but his skill saved others' lives. A friend of his wrote the well-known song and sold it for a case of gin. Vaughan's depot has a museum in Casey Jones's honour.

JACKSON (60/28) Named after Andrew Jackson, Mississippi's capital and largest city began as a trading post beside the Pearl River and had to survive being burned down during the Civil War. You can tour the gold-domed Capitol and Greek-style Governor's Mansion. Amtrak's renovated station is at 300 W Capitol and the **visitors bureau** is at 111 E Capitol (☎ *601 960 1891; www.visitjackson.com*).

As you depart, look left for the old 1840 Capitol (now a history museum) and the Arts Center Planetarium.

Crystal Springs (24/4) 'The tomato capital of the world' is famed for its bumper crops. This is also a well-known turkey-hunting area.

HAZLEHURST (28/19) Birthplace in 1911 or 1912 of Robert Johnson, the most influential blues artist of all time. The city was named after George Hazlehurst, chief engineer and surveyor for the New Orleans, Jackson & Great Northern Railroad. Lumber and other freight wagons gather to your left with the station and town to your right.

You leave among pine forests, massive lumber yards and processing plants. As well as timber, this region produces pine oil and turpentine.

Wesson (13/6) The preserved Old Wesson Hotel on your left once had a casino where passengers could while away their time and money between trains.

BROOKHAVEN (19/22) A recruiting town during the Civil War, Brookhaven deals in oil, timber and farm produce. The red-brick and tile station seen among magnolias to your right is Amtrak's nearest stop to **Natchez**, home of 'King Cotton'. Natchez is considered the prettiest town on the Mississippi, with many of its ante-bellum homes furnished in authentic style. Visitors are escorted around by brisk society matrons during the Natchez Pilgrimage (four weeks in March/April, three weeks in October).

You leave Brookhaven among the town's older residential suburbs, with the Bogue Chitto River to your left.

MCCOMB (22/50) The station also houses the **McComb Railroad Museum** (☎ *601 684 2291; www.mcrrmuseum.com*), which has more than 1,400 catalogued items. Outside can be seen a 200-ton steam locomotive, one of the two largest steam engines in the Illinois Central Railroad fleet, as well as the only aluminum refrigerator car ever built and a 1966 cupola-style caboose. The town was named after Colonel Henry McComb, who took charge of rebuilding the New Orleans, Jackson & Great Northern Railroad after the Civil War. McComb's camellias and azaleas are especially fine during spring. Illinois Central freight yards appear to your left as the train travels past lines of wagons loaded with logs.

Magnolia (10/40) Named after the state's official flower, the giant magnolia. Look right for colonial mansions hiding among the trees.

Tangipahoa River (12/38) You cross the river, which continues to your left.

Mississippi–Louisiana state line (20/30) The border is crossed just south of the small town of Osyka. You travel among beautiful ranches and pine trees, with modest houses fronted by porches and rocking chairs.

Kentwood (27/23) Look left soon after Kentwood for the Camp Moore Cemetery and Museum. The camp was a training ground for Confederate troops during the Civil War.

Amite (36/14) New Orleans-type ironwork decorates some of the houses. This area, known as the Florida Parishes, belonged to Florida until 1810. Strawberry plantations appear on both sides until the train approaches Hammond through thick forest.

Independence (45/5) On your right are Southeastern Louisiana College and an above-the-ground cemetery, or 'city of the dead'.

HAMMOND (50/60) 'The strawberry capital of the world', from where vast quantities of fruit used to be sent aboard the *Crimson Flower* train to Chicago and New York. The red-brick station with its pointed octagonal tower was built in Queen Anne Revival style by the Illinois Central Railroad in 1912.

You depart past warehouses, a flea market and freight cars loaded with wood chippings. Note the rusting Illinois Central caboose to your left just before Ponchatoula.

Ponchatoula (6/54) A *Louisiana Express* locomotive stands on the left at a picturesque station building. You pass three large greenhouses and, a few minutes later, enter Cajun country. In this eerily beautiful land of forests, swamps and water hyacinths, egrets fly among the evergreen live-oaks and cypress trees are draped with Spanish moss. During earlier days, trains sometimes had to stop for the engineer to remove an occasional alligator sunning itself on the rails.

Interstate 55 (7/53) The highway to your right strides across the wet wilderness on two arched bridges supported by concrete pillars. Look right for water lilies among the reeds, rushes and trees. You may spot alligators and such exotic birds as pelicans, black herons and egrets.

The *City of New Orleans* curves left around oceanic Lake Pontchartrain, the state's largest expanse of water, as the train travels for 49,884ft, or 9¾ miles, on the longest continuous railway curve in the world.

Pass-Manchac (10/50) You cross the waterway linking Lake Pontchartrain with Lake Maurepas to your right.

Moisant Field (33/27) New Orleans's international airport appears on the left beyond factories and warehouses.

Xavier University (51/9) Look right for campus buildings as you approach New Orleans with the skyline ahead to your left featuring the massive Superdome. The train continues to crawl towards the city before making a safety stop and reversing into the station.

NEW ORLEANS Thruway buses connect with Baton Rouge. For New Orleans city information, see *Chapter 11, The* Sunset Limited (pages 137–8).

14

The Northeast Corridor
Boston–Washington

General route information

This is the fastest and busiest route and the only one where Amtrak owns both track and stations. Since 1986, Amtrak has been the dominant carrier, moving more passengers between New York and Washington than any airline. It would require 10,000 packed DC-9s to carry the same number of passengers each year between these cities. *Acela Express* trains capable of 150mph (240km/h) have been introduced on Amtrak's 'main street' and services are frequent and fast. *En route* you encounter cities, rural scenery and splendid seascapes.

Some trains go all the way between Boston and Washington while others operate over just part of the line. Pennsylvania Railroad services used to rejoice in names such as *Constitution, Judiciary, Potomac* and *President* but Amtrak's trains are now more prosaically given mere numbers. Trains may not stop at every station indicated, so check when buying your ticket.

More economical *Acela Regional* trains have reduced the time between Boston and New York by as much as 90 minutes, with a corresponding 40% increase in passengers. *Acela Regional* trains now make the journey in four hours and the *Acela Express* cuts this by another hour. *Acela Express* trains operate hourly between New York, Washington, DC, and intermediate cities, as well as round trips between New York and Boston. *Acela Regional* trains serve more stations.

Acela Regional coaches have been refurbished with improved seats and overhead lights and have a more modern colour scheme. They also give a much smoother ride. The motive power is mostly provided by Bombardier/Alstom 8,000-horsepower locomotives capable of up to 125mph (200km/h).

Acela Express trains consist of one First Class and four Business Class cars, with a total seating of 304 passengers. First and Business Class are more comfortable than *Acela Regional* coaches, with lumbar support, moveable armrests and headrests,

---

ESSENTIAL INFORMATION

FREQUENCY Over 40 trains daily, running almost 24 hours a day out of New York. Metroliners operate hourly between New York and Washington, taking three hours for the journey.

DURATION Seven hours (Acela); eight hours (Regional)

RESERVATIONS Most trains are reserved

EQUIPMENT Amfleet and Acela coaches. Through-trains from Boston to Washington have Club cars. Railfone.

FOOD Most trains provide snacks, sandwiches and drinks

BAGGAGE No check-in service

BOSTON
□
Back Bay
Station
Route 128

Providence
Kingston
Westerly
Mystic
New London
Old Saybrook
New Haven

Bridgeport
Westport
Stamford
New Rochelle
NEW YORK CITY
□
Newark

Metropark
Princeton Junction
Trenton

N
Bradt

□
PHILADELPHIA

Wilmington
Aberdeen

Baltimore

BWI Airport

New Carrollton
□
WASHINGTON

laptop computer outlets, conference tables, extra telephones, deluxe rest rooms and personal controls for lights and audio.

Acela Express trains reach up to 150mph (240km/h) on their 231-mile sprint between Boston and New York, and travel at 135mph (216km/h) from New York to Washington, taking 6½ hours for the whole 457-mile Boston–Washington run on 'America's Super Railroad'.

Many Northeast Corridor trains have a quiet car, where passengers are asked not to use mobile phones, pagers, or the sound feature of laptop computers, and to speak only in subdued tones. This provides a quiet atmosphere for those who want to work or rest without distractions. There is no additional charge, but seating is first come, first served and cannot be reserved specifically. Announcements are made in stations and on the trains as to the location of the quiet car.

Joining the train

BOSTON English Puritans arrived in the 17th century, and the Revolution began here when British troops fired on colonists during the 'Boston Massacre' of 1770. New England's largest city became the hub of the solar system, where 'the Lowells spoke only to Cabots and the Cabots spoke only to God'.

Today's Boston is one of America's most sophisticated and attractive cities. Modern buildings, green spaces and the Cheers bar mingle successfully with older parts of the city.

Boston basics

☎Telephone code 617

⚌ Station (*Ticket office ⏰ 04.45–22.00. Waiting room ⏰ 24hrs; information ☎ 345 7442*) Amtrak's restored South Station at Atlantic Av & Summer was Boston's first Beaux Arts building. When completed in 1899, this station was the busiest railway terminal in the world. ClubAcela lounge. Lockers, newspapers, Red Caps, restaurants, shops, ATM banking, taxi stand.

Connections Amtrak *Downeaster* trains to New Hampshire & Maine arrive & depart from Boston's North Station at 135 Causeway St (*North Station ticket office ⏰ 06.00–21.00 Mon–Fri, 08.00–20.30 Sat/Sun. Waiting room ⏰ midnight–01.00 & 06.00–23.59*).

All other Amtrak services in Boston depart from South Station & Back Bay Station. Passengers transferring between the *Downeaster* & other Amtrak services must arrange their own transfer between stations in Boston. Passengers travelling with significant luggage or young children should transfer by taxi to their continuing Amtrak train at South Station. Other passengers should connect to their continuing Amtrak train at Back Bay Station using the Orange Line subway.

🚌 Local transport MBTA (*10 Park Plaza; ☎ 222 3200*) operates commuter trains from South Station to points south & west, & to points north & northwest from North Station.

You can see the city best on foot, with help from an MBTA system that includes bus, trolley & subway (the 'T'). A subway stop is located in the station & a 'T passport' offers unlimited travel on buses & the subway as well as discounts at various attractions.

🚕 **Taxis** Red Cab ☎ 734 5000

🚗 **Car rental** Thrifty ☎ 1 800 367 2277; Budget ☎ 1 800 527 0700

🚌 **Greyhound** 700 Atlantic Av, South Station; ☎ 526 1801

✈ **Logan Airport** East Boston, easy to reach by bus, car, taxi, the MBTA's Blue Line subway & Silver Line SL1 buses, as well as the Logan Express bus service.

Tours Gray Line ☎ 720 6342. National park rangers lead Black Heritage Trail walking tours, beginning at the Robert Gould Shaw & 54th Regiment Memorial on the corner of Park & Beacon (☎ 617 742 5415). Harbour & island trips from Bay State Cruises (☎ 877 783 3779).

ℹ **Visitors bureau** 2 Copley Pl; ☎ 536 4100 or ☎ 888 733 2678; www.bostonusa.com. There is an information booth on Boston Common

at Tremont & Park (🕑 *daily*), & the National Historical Park Service is at 15 State (☎ *242 5642; www.nps.gov/bost*).

🏠 **Accommodation** Contact the B & B Agency of Boston, 47 Commercial Wharf, Boston, MA 02109; ☎ 0800 248 9262; www.boston-bnbagency.com; or Host Homes of Boston, PO Box 117, Boston, MA 02468; ☎ 800 600 1308; www.hosthomesofboston.com.

International (IYHF) Hostel, 12 Hemenway; ☎ 536 9455; www.bostonhostel.org. Members & non-members, **$**. Irish Embassy Hostel, 232 Friend; ☎ 973 4841. Free barbecue. *Beds from $15*. Berkeley Hostel, 40 Berkeley; ☎ 375 2524; www.ywcaboston.org. Members & non-members, **$$**.

For discount rates contact Citywide Reservation Services, 839 Beacon St Inc; ☎ 859 8880. Hotels include the Park Plaza, Park Sq; ☎ 426 2000, **$$$$$**; Lenox, 61 Exeter; ☎ 536 5300, **$$$$$**; Eliot, 370 Commonwealth Av; ☎ 267 1607, **$$$$$**; Copley Sq, 47 Huntington Av; ☎ 536 9000, **$$$$$**; Ramada, 800 Morrissey Bd; ☎ 287 9100, **$$$**; Courtyard, 275 Tremont; ☎ 426 1400, **$$$$$**.

Recommended in Boston

Museum of Fine Arts 465 Huntington Av; ☎ 267 9300; www.mfa.org; 🕑 daily; admission charge. Includes art from Egypt, Asia & Europe, with more than 40 works by Monet, as well as portraits of eminent Americans such as George Washington. The new Art of the Americas wing features works from ancient American gold to paintings to period rooms.

Museum of Science Science Park; ☎ 723 2500; www.mos.org; 🕑 daily; admission charge. The museum has a planetarium with laser displays & a theatre showing films on a giant screen.

Freedom Trail ☎ 357 8300; www.thefreedomtrail.org; most places on the Trail 🕑 daily; free. Most of Boston's historic buildings can be explored by following the Freedom Trail, marked somewhat erratically in red on the pavements. Information & a free map are available from the booth on Boston Common. Highlights include the Old State House, the Old South Meeting House, Paul Revere's House & the USS Constitution from the War of 1812.

Bunker Hill Monument A 221ft (67m) obelisk memorial erected between 1827 & 1843 to

commemorate the battle fought nearby during the War of Independence. The granite was brought from Quincy, MA, to the site on the Granite Railway, built specially for that purpose. There are 294 steps to the top for excellent views of the city & harbour.

Museum of Afro-American History 46 Joy; ☎ 725 0022; www.afroammuseum.org; 🕑 Tue–Sun; free. Located in what was once the first publicly funded school for African-Americans, the museum has many exhibits showing their contribution to the city's history.

John F Kennedy Library and Museum Near the University of Massachusetts in Dorchester; ☎ 514 1600; www.jfklibrary.org; 🕑 daily; admission charge. Photographs, films & memorabilia trace the Kennedy family history. You can listen to JFK's speeches & review the Nixon–Kennedy debates in an impressive building designed by I M Pei.

Isabella Stewart Gardner Museum 280 The Fenway; ☎ 566 1401; www.gardnermuseum.org; 🕑 Tue–Sun; admission charge. Built in 1903 around a courtyard in the style of a 15th-century

14

Italian palace, the museum's art collection includes Renoirs & many Renaissance works. **Harvard University Art Museums** 32 Quincy in Cambridge; ☎ 495 9400; www.artmuseums. harvard.edu; ⊕ daily; admission charge (1 admission covers all museums); Sat free before noon. The Sackler has Roman, Egyptian & Islamic antiquities. The adjacent Fogg Museum features European, Asian & American art, & the Busch-Reisinger Museum specialises in art from Germany.

All aboard!

The Capitol, seen high above the city as the train departs, is topped by a marble dome and a statue of 'the independent man'. For the best coastal views choose a seat on the left of the train when travelling south.

BACK BAY STATION (5/10) A subterranean station serves Copley Square and the downtown hotels. This is also a stop for commuter trains, which pause only to receive passengers (or discharge them if travelling north).

You leave and continue for several minutes below ground, occasionally surfacing amid concrete car parks for glimpses of Boston's skyline back to your right.

ROUTE 128 (10/28) A south suburban halt where trains pause only to receive passengers (or discharge them if travelling north). Route 128 is one of Amtrak's main weapons in its battle with the airline shuttle services, being closer to New York and more convenient than Logan Airport for most people in southern and western Boston. The new station is a bright and spacious building with a glass-fronted waiting room facing the tracks and new platforms.

You pass freight and warehouse facilities on your right, then travel through suburbs and woodland before entering the flat landscape of eastern Massachusetts.

Attleboro (20/8) The **Attleboro Arts Museum** is at 86 Park Street (☎ *508 222 2644; www.attleboroartsmuseum.org*). Look left as you depart to see an imposing white church and steeple.

Approaching Providence you cross the border into Rhode Island. The city's green-domed Capitol and skyscrapers are ahead with freight yards to the right.

PROVIDENCE (28/22) The capital of America's smallest state has many interesting 18th- and 19th-century buildings. The 1786 John Brown House at Benefit and Power is furnished in period style. The Roger Williams Memorial is located on the site of the original 1636 settlement. Other highlights include the Capitol and the Athenaeum Library where Edgar Allan Poe courted Sarah Whitman (his inspiration for Annabel Lee). The **visitors bureau** is at 1 Sabin (☎ *401 751 1177 or ☎ 1 800 233 1636; www.pwcvb.com*).

Amtrak trains stop at 100 Gaspee, a new building next to the Capitol. Note the impressive postmodern apartment block to your left as the train pulls out.

East Greenwich (12/10) The old seaport's 1773 General Varnum House and garden are preserved in their original condition. Narragansett Bay and its colourful yachts come into view to your left before the train departs temporarily inland through wooded countryside.

KINGSTON (22/10) Some of the buildings in this quiet town date from when it was an 18th-century trading centre for plantation owners. The George Fayerweather House was built by the blacksmith son of a slave. Look for the lumber company mural to the right of a picturesque grey station flanked by evergreens. Located in West Kingston, this is Amtrak's nearest stop to Newport, famous for its naval base, mansions and jazz festival. Other sights in this former colonial seaport include the Friends Meeting House (1699) and the Old Colony House (1739).

You continue west among woods, streams and marshes.

WESTERLY (10/10) An 18th-century town situated on the border between Rhode Island and Connecticut. Ancient industrial buildings stand on the opposite side of the track from the solid brick and red-tile station. Between here and New Haven the train accompanies an attractive shoreline to your left.

Stonington (5/5) This well-preserved coastal town boasts Connecticut's first lighthouse (now a museum). You can tour vineyards in summer and take boat trips to the Isle au Haut.

As you depart past a marina and dry dock, look right for a Christmas tree plantation and several old railroad cars converted into unusual homes.

MYSTIC (10/10) Built in 1905, the wooden station on your right has been restored to its pink and yellow glory. The town is on the banks of the Mystic River and owes its existence to the sea and shipbuilding. Vessels constructed here include one of America's first ironclad warships, the *Galena*, and the clipper *Andrew Jackson*, which sailed to San Francisco round Cape Horn in a record 89 days. **Mystic Seaport Museum** (✆ *860 572 5388; www.mysticseaport.org*) owns one of the largest outdoor displays in the country, with a 19th-century whaling ship, the *Charles Morgan*, moored in a recreated New England village. This was the last wooden whaler ever built (in 1841) and you can tour its cramped conditions and ghoulish vats.

You pass another marina then continue along an embankment where water and pleasure craft can be seen on both sides. The pretty shoreline ahead features many inlets, trees and herons.

NEW LONDON (10/20) Trains cross the River Thames (rhymes with 'shames') on a steel bridge before entering a large Romanesque station designed by Henry Hobson Richardson. Over 100 years old, this brick and granite building was one of Amtrak's first major restoration projects. Thruway buses connect with the Foxwoods Casino. The Cross Sound ferry is based adjacent to Amtrak's station and travels to Orient Point on Long Island.

New London was among North America's earliest settlements and grew rich on whaling. The **Lyman Allyn Museum** (*625 Williams;* ✆ *860 443 2545; www. lymanallyn.org*) is dedicated to a whaling captain and seagoing tradition continues at the US Coastguard Academy. The training vessel *Eagle* can usually be seen either moored to your left or in full sail on the river. New London's shipyards launched the world's first nuclear submarine, *Nautilus*.

From here to Old Saybrook trains run mostly alongside the beach, with the waters of Niantic Bay just a few feet from the track. Look for sunbathers, fishing boats and enviable homes.

Connecticut River (14/6) You cross the river on a drawbridge then continue among marshes.

OLD SAYBROOK (20/30) The blue and white station dates from 1873. Long Island Sound and some of its small islands can be seen to your left as the train speeds along this coastal stretch. Approaching New Haven you see a power plant and docks to your left before the train crawls through rail yards into the station.

NEW HAVEN (30/25) The first planned city in the USA, this is where the first sulphur matches and Colt revolvers were made. Other firsts claimed are the hamburger, pizza and frisbee, named after apple-pie plates from the Frisbie Baking company. Founded in 1638 as Quinnipiac and renamed two years later, New Haven became one of the strictest Puritan towns. Dr Benjamin Spock was brought up here, where his father was a lawyer with the New Haven Railroad. The **visitors bureau** is at 127 Washington Avenue (✆ *203 777 8550; www.visitnewhaven.com*).

Amtrak's restored Union Station is at 50 Union Avenue. Look right for Amtrak trains from Springfield and Hartford joining the main Northeast Corridor line as Metro-North trains wait on your left.

New Haven surrounds a green with three historic churches and you can take a cruise on the sound from Long Wharf dock. Nearby are Fort Nathan Hale, the Pardee-Morris House and **Yale University**, named after its early benefactor, Elihu Yale. Bill and Hillary Clinton first met here at Law School. Free guided tours of Yale include the 1752 Connecticut Hall, the Harkness Tower (221ft/66m tall) and the Center for British Art. A Gutenberg Bible is one of 400,000 books in the Beinecke Library.

You leave among rail yards, houses and factories to continue through southern Connecticut.

Milford (5/20) Milford is the scene of an annual oyster festival. As you travel southwest you cross the Housatonic and Pequonnock rivers.

BRIDGEPORT (25/24) Connecticut's largest city contains 1,300 acres (525ha) of parkland and the state's largest zoo. City Hall was named after a socialist mayor, Jasper McLevy (in office 1933–57). Amtrak is at 525 Water.

To your right as you leave is the **Barnum Museum** (✆ *203 331 1104; www. barnum-museum.org*), containing an Egyptian mummy and the clothes worn by General Tom Thumb. Showman Phineas Taylor Barnum (also a Bridgeport mayor) was buried in Mountain Grove Cemetery, where Tom Thumb's grave is marked by a supposedly life-size 2ft (60cm) statue. Ocean-going ships can be seen in the harbour to your left.

WESTPORT (10/14) A handful of New Yorkers commute further north but this is as far as most will travel. Houses here and along the coast to Stamford are among this area's most expensive and fashionable. Nearby Sherwood Island is popular for swimming and boating on Long Island Sound.

As the train nears Stamford, look ahead to your right for the most modern part of the city.

STAMFORD (24/18) Research City claims to have more international corporations than anywhere except New York or Chicago. Smart new office blocks and malls have transformed the downtown skyline.

Amtrak shares the glass and concrete Transportation Center on Washington Boulevard with Metro-North trains, seen to your left, and a walkway links the platforms.

Greenwich (6/12) First settled by the Dutch, Greenwich is the home of many film and television stars and is possibly the richest town in Connecticut. Places of interest include the Bush-Holley House (of colonial 'saltbox' design) and the US Tobacco Museum.

From here the train loses touch with Long Island Sound and travels through an increasingly urban and bleak landscape towards New York City.

NEW ROCHELLE (18/30) Amtrak trains part company with Metro services, which operate out of New York's Grand Central Station.

Pelham Bay (4/26) Massive Co-op City apartment blocks appear to your right as you cross the bridge. Calvary Hospital is to your left.

The train crosses the Hutchinson River then slows down as it passes through a deprived South Bronx before entering Hell Gate Viaduct. The Hell Gate Bridge, 320ft (96m) above the East River, was the world's largest steel-arch bridge when it was completed in 1917, and served as a model for the bridge across Sydney Harbour in Australia. The Hell Gate Route (or New York Connecting Railroad) was built to link the New York, New Haven & Hartford line with the Pennsylvania Railroad.

Manhattan State Hospital (10/20) Look right for this sombre 1930s building and your first views of Manhattan. The train crosses Randalls and Wards islands before going through Astoria. Rail yards and commuter trains extend on both sides as you enter a tunnel on Long Island, burrowing beneath the East River and Manhattan to reach Pennsylvania Station.

NEW YORK CITY (30/15) *Manhattan, Wall Street, 42nd Street, West Side Story* and *Breakfast at Tiffany's* – everyone has visited New York in the movies. The birthplace of Bogart and Bacall is a world leader in fashion, finance and the arts, inspiring admen and bankers as much as painters, writers and musicians.

New Amsterdam began in 1625, and the following year Peter Minuit bought Manhattan Island from the Indians for $24. Today its population is three million, plus 11 million commuters.

Nowhere else has such energy and style, although homelessness and urban decay seem as much a part of the fabric as Fifth Avenue and the St Patrick's Day parade. Not everyone loves New York, but no-one forgets the experience.

| 4

New York City basics

☎Telephone codes 212 for Manhattan; 718 for Queens, Brooklyn, the Bronx & Staten Island. All numbers given in this section have Manhattan codes unless otherwise stated.

☛ Station (*Ticket office ⊕ 05.10–21.50. Waiting room ⊕ 24hrs; information ☎630 6400. ClubAcela lounge ⊕ 05.15–02.00 Mon–Fri, 07.00–02.00 Sat/Sun & is particularly swish – a welcome respite from the busy waiting room outside*) Amtrak uses **Pennsylvania Station** at Seventh Av & 32nd, beneath Madison Square Garden. It has been made cleaner & safer lately but remains a poor substitute for the building it replaced in the 1960s, built by McKim, Mead & White. Thomas Wolfe described the original Penn Station as 'vast enough to hold

the sound of time' & it can be seen in the 1942 film *The Palm Beach Story.*

Baggage room, newspapers, restaurants, snack bars, shops, ATM banking, taxi stand, subway.

Connections The Long Island Railroad (☎718 217 5477) & New Jersey Transit (☎973 275 5555) also operate from Penn Station.

The magnificent, atmospheric Grand Central Terminal at 89 E 42nd & Park Av is where John Barrymore won Carole Lombard after their cross-country train journey in the 1934 film *Twentieth Century*. Completed in 1913 by Cornelius Vanderbilt, the largest train station in the world replaced a smaller 1898 station which had proved to be unable to cope with increased traffic. In 1902, an explosion in the open rail yards had killed 15 people with fumes, smoke & steam. It was decided therefore to electrify the trains & construct a roof over the entire complex, excavating 48ft (14m) into Manhattan Island to create 3 separate levels. 8 underground tracks carried 700 trains per day while above ground a new New York grew, including all the buildings on Park Av. The $180 million station had been financed by selling air space above.

A 'city within a city', Grand Central originally had tennis courts, an art gallery, a bakery, a betting parlour & a hospital. Restored in magnificent style & rededicated in 1998, the station has 5 brass chandeliers (each with 100 lights), Tennessee marble floors, frescoes, grand balustraded staircases & triumphant arched windows where people walk in a wall of glass. Look for the Vanderbilt family's oak leaves emblem incorporated into the vaulted ceiling of the main concourse. The Oyster Bar, located in the bowels of the station, continues to serve shellfish stew, pan roasts & oysters across splendid marble counters & a new steakhouse occupies the north balcony. A murmur from the 'whispering gallery' outside the Oyster Bar's entrance can be heard clearly in the far corners of the cavernous hall.

By 1946, more than 65 million passengers a year were using Grand Central & rush hour can still be frantic. Metro-North (℡ 532 4900) operates over 500 commuter trains daily to the suburbs of New Jersey & Connecticut. Sadly, Amtrak stopped using Grand Central in April 1991. Despite attempts to deal the building a similar fate to the old Penn Station, campaigners such as Jackie Kennedy kept this spectacular building safe. The Municipal Art Society (℡ 935 3960) gives free tours each Wed afternoon.

Local transport Manhattan's logical grid of streets & avenues makes it easy to find your way around, although driving or finding a place to park can be a nightmare. The **visitors bureau** has maps & schedules for public transport & more details are available from the NYC Transit Authority (347 Madison Av, NY 10017-3739). A MetroCard provides a week's unlimited travel on the subway & buses throughout the city for only $17. For all bus & subway information, ℡ 718 330 1234. John Tauranac produces excellent subway guides & maps.

Taxis A taxi stand is located on 31st St between Seventh & Eighth avs. Otherwise look for a yellow cab with a lighted sign & hail it by raising your arm. In case of complaints or lost property contact the Taxi Commission (℡ 692 8294).

Car rental National, 252 W 40th; ℡ 1 800 227 8368

Greyhound Port Authority Terminal, 625 Eighth Av; ℡ 971 6300

Airports Call Air-Ride (℡ 800 247 7433) for recorded information about transport to all 3 New York airports.

The largest is John F Kennedy in Queens, which can be reached by taxi, bus or limousine. New York Airport Express bus services operate between JFK, the Port Authority & Grand Central Station, with transfers to Penn Station from Grand Central (℡ 718 875 8200; www. nyairportservice.com). Journey time from JFK to Grand Central is about 1hr.

AirTrain JFK is an 8.1-mile light rail system that connects JFK to the New York City area's mass transit system. A trip from JFK to Jamaica or Howard Beach subway will average about 12mins, plus 60–75mins for the subway journey to midtown Manhattan.

LaGuardia Airport in Queens is served by several MTA bus lines, including the M60, linking LaGuardia to the New York City Subway & Long Island Railroad. A proposed extension of the subway system would allow a 'one seat' ride to LaGuardia from Manhattan.

Newark Airport is 14 miles (22km) southwest & was briefly, in the 1930s, the world's busiest airport. Express Shuttle buses (℡ 315 3006) connect to midtown Manhattan & Olympia buses (℡ 964 6233) run from Newark to Grand Central. AirTrain Newark Links (℡ 888 397 4636) is a light rail service to the Newark Liberty International Airport Train Station.

Tours Gray Line; ℡ 445 0848. Harlem Heritage walking tours (℡ 280 7888) are conducted by people who live & work in Harlem, giving an insider's view of the community. 3hr boat cruises around Manhattan from Circle Line at Pier 83, W 42nd at the Hudson River (℡ 563 3200). Helicopter flights from Liberty (℡ 967 2099). The Staten Island ferry (℡ 718 815 2628) chugs around the harbour & Statue of Liberty, making 50 crossings each way on w/days between the

Whitehall ferry terminal in Lower Manhattan & St George ferry terminal on the island. The 5-mile journey takes 25mins & is free to foot passengers.

The Jazz Trail takes place about once a month around Queens, visiting the former houses of musicians such as Louis Armstrong, Dizzy Gillespie, Lena Horne & James Brown. Take the subway from Times Sq or the Long Island Railroad from Penn Station to Flushing Town Hall (137–35, Northern Bd; ✆718 463 7700).

ℹ **Visitors bureau** 810 Seventh Av, between 52nd & 53rd; ✆484 1200; www.nycgo.com; ⏲ 08.30–18.00 Mon–Fri, 09.00–17.00 Sat/Sun

⌂ **Accommodation** Contact Bed & Breakfast Network of New York at 130 Barrow St, New York, NY 10014-2866; ✆645 8134. B&B Lodges, 1598 Lexington Av; ✆917 345 7914; www.bblodges. com. Located in the Upper East Side close to Central Park & the #6 subway on 103rd – 10mins to central Manhattan. 12 comfortable apts & suites with private kitchens & bathrooms, from **$$$**.

HI-New York Hostel, 891 Amsterdam Av; ✆932 2300. The world's largest hostel, with 672 beds. Family rooms available. Members & non-members, **$**. Vanderbilt YMCA, 224 E 47th; ✆912 2500. A classic-style building on the fashionable East Side. TV, AC, swimming pool, gym & restaurant (with room service). For men & women, **$$**. West Side YMCA, 5 W 63rd; ✆875 4100. Located off Central Park West in a European-style building close to Upper West Side attractions. TV, AC, swimming pool, fitness facilities, restaurant, **$$**.

Hotel room prices are often very high apart from some w/end rates. Hotels include the Algonquin, 59 W 44th; ✆840 6800, **$$$$$**; Sofitel, 45 W 44th; ✆354 8844; www.sofitel. com. An upmarket hotel with marble bathrooms & elegant Art-Deco style, **$$$$$**. Hotel 41 at Times Sq, 206 W 41st; ✆703 8600; www. hotel41nyc.com. Close to theatres & central Manhattan sights, **$$$$$**. Wyman Hse, 36 Riverside Dr; ✆799 8281; www.wymanhouse. com. Tastefully restored townhouse with 6 spacious suites overlooking Riverside Park & the Hudson River. 3 nights' min, **$$$$$**. Hilton New York, 1335 Av of the Americas; ✆586 7000; www. newyorktowers.hilton.com. Close to Central Park & MOMA. Almost 2,000 rooms & 3 ballrooms, including the biggest in New York, **$$$$**. Hotel 414, 414 W 46th; ✆399 0006; www.414hotel. com. Pretty courtyard for guests. Great value, with continental b/fast included, **$$$**.

Recommended in New York City

Statue of Liberty On Liberty Island, reached by Circle Line ferry from Battery Park; ✆363 3200; www.nps.gov/stli. 'Liberty enlightening the world' was designed by Frederic Bartholdi & paid for by the French. The statue reopened in 2004 after being closed for security reasons. Visitors can now view inside the structure through a glass ceiling & have access to the observation deck for panoramic views of New York City & the harbour. There is a choice of 2 tours: the Statue of Liberty Observatory Tour & the Statue of Liberty Promenade Tour. Both include a guided tour through the Statue of Liberty Museum which includes the Lady's original torch. To climb the staircase within the statue to the crown you should purchase a special ticket from Statue Cruises, which can be reserved up to a year in advance. Only 240 people a day are permitted to ascend the strenuous 354 steps. Reservations for all visits can be made with Statue Cruises (✆877 523 9849; www.statuecruises.com).

Immigration Museum On nearby Ellis Island; ✆363 3200; www.nps.gov/elis; ⏲ daily; free. The museum now occupies the building which 12 million immigrants passed through between 1892 & 1954.

The Frick Collection 1 East 70th; ✆288 0700; www.frick.org; ⏲ Tue–Sun; admission charge. The collection, housed in an elegant mansion built by Henry Clay Frick, one of America's most successful steel & railroad tycoons, includes masterpieces of Western painting, sculpture & decorative art, displayed in a serene & intimate setting. Among the 16 galleries are the Fragonard Room & the Living Hall, with works by Holbein, Titian, El Greco & Bellini.

Empire State Building 350 Fifth Av; ✆736 3100; www.esbnyc.com; ⏲ daily; admission charge. The people's favourite skyscraper was the world's tallest building when completed in 1931 & kept the record for 40 years. The 86th- & 102nd-floor observation decks still give great

14

views of New York but arrive early to miss the crush.

St Patrick's Cathedral Fifth Av & 50th; ☎753 2261; www.saintpatrickscathedral.org; ☉ daily; free. The Gothic towers of New York's Roman Catholic cathedral contrast with the adjacent Rockefeller Center's Art Deco.

Central Park Bounded by 59th & 110th sts, & by Fifth Av & Central Park West; www.centralparknyc.org; ☉ daily. Watch New York at play, listen to concerts & enjoy free Shakespeare performances. The park has America's oldest carousel, a zoo & Strawberry Fields, dedicated to John Lennon. Free maps & details of latest events from the **Mid-Park Visitor Center** at 65th (☎794 6564; ☉ Tue–Sun; for guided walks, ☎360 2726).

Metropolitan Museum of Art 1000 Fifth Av at E 82nd; ☎535 7710; www.metmuseum.org; ☉ 09.30–17.30 Tue–Thu & Sun, 09.30–21.00 Fri–Sat; admission charge. More than 4 million people each year visit this vast Victorian Gothic building to see the largest art collection in the USA. More like a dozen museums in one, with great works by Picasso, Rembrandt, Vermeer & French Impressionists, Egyptian art, a Chinese Ming-period courtyard, the Frank Lloyd Wright room & a terrific sculpture garden on the roof. For concerts & lecture tours, ☎570 3949. The Met is always busy so go early, although some galleries do not open until late on Sun morning.

Museum of Modern Art 11 W 53rd, between Fifth & Sixth avs; ☎708 9400; www.moma.org; ☉ Wed–Mon; admission charge. One of the world's finest collections includes Monet's Water Lily room & works by Picasso, Matisse, Miró & Jackson Pollock.

United Nations First Av & 46th, overlooking the East River; ☎963 8687; www.un.org; ☉ daily; admission charge for tours, free tickets to observe meetings. Take a guided tour of the Secretariat Bldg, General Assembly Hall & Hammarskjold Library.

Stock Exchange 20 Broad; ☎656 5165; www.nyse.com. Formed in 1792 when a group of brokers met at the junction of Wall & William sts, where kerbside brokers sold railroad stocks in the 1860s. The Stock Exchange is currently closed to visitors but the **Wall Street Experience** (☎917 868 7009; www.thewallstreetexperience.com) has revealing tours designed & guided by insiders. Tours start opposite the Exchange at 15 Broad St.

NY Transit Museum Located in an authentic 1930s subway station at the corner of Boerum Pl & Schermerhorn St in downtown Brooklyn; ☎718 694 1600; www.mta.info/museum; ☉ Tue–Sun; admission charge. The first New York subway opened in 1904 & 2.4 billion people a year now now ride the subways, buses & railroads. The museum has many subway cars, including early wooden ones, as well as photos & interactive exhibits showing how the city's subways & railroads were built. The museum also has a gallery annex with exhibitions at Grand Central Station.

All aboard!

The train pulls out of Pennsylvania Station by way of a 2.5-mile (4km) tunnel beneath the Hudson River, surfacing three minutes later in New Jersey. The Hudson tunnels were the first structural links across the river between New Jersey and New York City. Train services began when Penn Station opened in 1910.

The city's outline on the far left features the Empire State Building and the Giants Stadium is beyond a New Jersey Turnpike bridge to your right.

Hackensack River (10/5) You cross with an impressive bridge to your left and lose sight of New York. The train follows then crosses the Passaic River before going through a New Jersey Transit depot at Harrison.

NEWARK (15/14) New Jersey's largest city is one of the country's great manufacturing centres. It was the birthplace of the novelist Stephen Crane, author of *The Red Badge of Courage*. The Thomas Edison Historic Site in the suburb of West Orange preserves Edison's laboratory, his early gramophone and the first movie camera. Edison was once a newsboy on the Grand Trunk Railway.

Amtrak's echoing Art Deco Pennsylvania Station in Newark is at Raymond Plaza W and has a beautifully restored waiting room. The train leaves past PATH trains, warehouses and brick-built factories, picking up speed as it travels through commuter stops such as Lincoln.

Elizabeth (6/8) The former New Jersey capital, an influential town during the American Revolution, is bound to Newark by continuous suburbs and was named one of 'America's greenest cities' by *Popular Science* magazine. Look right for a General Motors factory.

Rahway (10/4) Interesting old brownstone buildings appear on both sides.

METROPARK (14/15) Amtrak's station is at 100 Middlesex-Essex Turnpike. You cross the Garden State Parkway and continue among industrial plants owned by some of America's biggest companies. The scene is occasionally brightened by a stretch of farmland and near New Brunswick you cross the Rariton River.

New Brunswick (7/8) A scheduled stop for some Amtrak trains, New Brunswick has frequent New Jersey Transit services to Newark and Trenton. Look right for Rutgers University (founded in 1776) and the headquarters of Johnson & Johnson.
The train continues through semi-rural scenes until factories, chemical plants and warehouses take over again on the approach to Trenton.

PRINCETON JUNCTION (10/5) The university's ivy-clad campus to your right features Albert Einstein's house. Other inhabitants have included future presidents Woodrow Wilson and Aaron Burr. The art museum features pictures by Cézanne, Van Gogh and Picasso, and panels in University Chapel are carved from Sherwood Forest wood. For **visitor information,** ✆ 609 258 6115. A few Amtrak trains stop at Princeton Junction and New Jersey Transit trains go to Princeton from Penn Station in New York City.

TRENTON (15/32) Home of New Jersey's State Museum and the 1792 Capitol Building. Amtrak's rather lived-in station with open platforms is at 72 S Clinton Avenue.
Look right for the Capitol's gold dome as you leave among older parts of the city. The train slows down to cross the Delaware River near where Washington crossed in 1776 to attack a garrison of British-financed mercenaries. The bridge to your right proclaims that 'Trenton makes, the world takes'. Crossing the river transports you from New Jersey into Pennsylvania.

Holmesburg Junction (20/12) Holmesburg Prison is to your right and the Tacony-Palmyra Bridge arches across the Delaware River, seen beyond trees to your left.

Schuylkill River (30/2) You pass two spired churches then cross the river and enter Philadelphia through Fairmount Park. The zoo is on your left.
An old signalbox mural announces 'the city of brotherly love' as the train crawls among freight yards and half-derelict buildings, with Philadelphia's skyline in the left distance. Nearing the station, look left for Boathouse Row and the Parthenon-style Museum of Art with its famous *Rocky* steps.

PHILADELPHIA (32/22) 'On the whole I'd rather be in Philadelphia' was W C Fields's malign epitaph on his birthplace when he thought he was dying. The city

14

has also been the home of Benjamin Franklin, Sammy Davis Jr, Dizzy Gillespie and Live Aid. Elfreth's Alley, occupied since 1772, is America's oldest street.

William Penn founded Philadelphia on a peninsula between the Schuylkill and Delaware rivers in 1682, and it became America's capital from Independence until 1800. By then it was the world's second-largest English-speaking city. Apart from historic buildings and museums, Philly is known for its cheesesteaks, pretzels and alarming crime rate.

Philadelphia basics

Telephone code 215

Station (*Ticket office* ⊕ *05.15–21.35 Mon–Fri, 06.10–21.35 Sat/Sun. Waiting room* ⊕ *24hrs; information* ⬙*824 1600. ClubAcela lounge* ⊕ *06.00–21.00*) Stately 30th St Station at 30th & Market is one of Amtrak's busiest terminals, restored at great expense. Electronic train information, newspapers, Red Caps, restaurants, shops, ATM banking, taxi stand.

Connections SEPTA trains operate to the suburbs & Philadelphia Airport (⬙*580 7800*). PATCO high-speed trains to New Jersey leave from Eighth & Market (⬙*922 4600*). For New Jersey Transit trains to Atlantic City & southern New Jersey, ⬙*800 772 2287.*

Amtrak ticket holders can travel free by commuter train between 30th St & the downtown Penn Center Station at 1617 John F Kennedy Bd (*ticket office* ⊕ *09.10–14.00 & 15.00–17.30 Mon–Fri*).

Local transport The historic district is best explored on foot, using maps from the tourist bureau, & SEPTA operates buses, trolleys & the subway (⬙*580 7800*).

Taxis Yellow ⬙*333 3333*; Quaker City ⬙*728 8000*

Car rental Avis ⬙*386 6426*; Budget ⬙*764 5980*. Both located in 30th St Station.

Greyhound 1001 Filbert; ⬙*931 4075*

Airport The airport is 8 miles (13km) southwest by Boston Coach (⬙*800 672 7676*) & Airport Express trains to either the University City Station on Convention Av or to 30th St Station (call SEPTA for times).

Tours Gray Line; ⬙*568 6111*. Philadelphia on Foot; ⬙*800 340 9869*. Philadelphia Trolly & The Big Bus Company Tours (⬙*389 8687*) take in most sights. Water cruises on the *Spirit of Philadelphia* (⬙*923 1419*) & the riverboat *Liberty Belle* (⬙*629 1131*).

Visitors bureau 1700 Market; ⬙*636 3300*; www.philadelphiausa.travel; ⊕ 09.00–17.00 daily

Accommodation Contact Philadelphia Bed & Breakfast, City Center, 1804 Pine, Philadelphia, PA 19103; ⬙*735 1137*.

HI Hostel, Chamounix Mansion, a historic building in Fairmount Park; ⬙*878 3676*. Some family rooms. Members & non-members, **$**. YWCA, 225 S 15th St; ⬙*790 9006*, **$**.

Hotels include the Four Seasons, 1 Logan Sq; ⬙*963 1500*, **$$$$**; Holiday Inn Midtown, 1305 Walnut; ⬙*735 9300*, **$$$**; Best Western, 501 N 22nd; ⬙*568 8300*, **$$$**; Alexander Inn, 12th & Spruce; ⬙*923 3535*, **$$$**; Chestnut Hill, 8229 Germantown Av; ⬙*242 5905*, **$$$**; Comfort Inn Downtown, 100 N Christopher Columbus Bd; ⬙*627 7900*, **$$$**.

Recommended in Philadelphia

Museum of Art 26th & Benjamin Franklin Parkway; ⬙*763 8100*; www.philamuseum. org; ⊕ Tue–Sun; admission charge (donation on Sun). 300,000 works, including Van Gogh (*Sunflowers*), Picasso, Renoir, Rubens & Cézanne (*Bathers*), plus American crafts, a Japanese tea house & an Indian temple. Guided tours.

Fairmount Park Covering 4,500 acres (1,800ha) from downtown to the city's northwest

boundary, the park features forests, waterways, sports fields & museums. Highlights include Boathouse Row (19th-century buildings used by rowing clubs), Strawberry Mansion & Memorial Hall (dating from the 1876 centennial).

Christ Church Beyond Franklin Court to Market. The pews in this church have been occupied by such luminaries as George Washington & Benjamin Franklin. Services are held on Sun

City Hall Broad & Market; ☎686 2840; ⊕ Mon–Fri. Completed in 1900 & topped by a 37ft (11m) bronze statue of William Penn, this 548ft (166m) tower is one of the world's tallest and largest all-masonry, load-bearing structures without a steel or iron frame. Free tours & observation deck.

Franklin Institute Science Museum 222 N 20th St; ☎448 1200; www.fi.edu; ⊕ daily; admission charge. Includes a science centre, planetarium & theatre. The museum has many hands-on & walk-through exhibits, & the garden features high-tech displays & a maze.

Independence Park The national park visitor centre is at Sixth & Market; ☎800 537 7676; www.independencevisitorcenter.com; ⊕ daily. This historic square mile draws 5 million tourists every year & buildings (*most* ⊕ *daily; free*), include the following:

Independence Hall Chestnut St. Opened in 1732, this is where the Declaration of Independence (1776) & Constitution (1787) were adopted. You can tour the Assembly Room & Old City Hall, where the US Supreme Court held sessions from 1791 to 1800.

Liberty Bell Pavilion Market St. Cast in England in 1751, the State House Bell hung in Independence Hall for 200 years before moving to its new glass-walled home.

Old City Hall On Chestnut at Fifth. This was the home of the US Supreme Court between 1791 & 1800. See the prisoner's dock & jury box as well as restored furniture.

Rodin Museum 22nd & Benjamin Franklin Parkway; ☎568 6026; ⊕ Tue–Sun; donation; free tours. The largest collection of Rodin drawings & sculptures (including *The Thinker*) outside Paris.

All aboard!

The train departs Philadelphia past the National Publishing Company Building to your left and the ivy-league university's Franklin Field to your right, next to the Convention Hall. You continue among residential suburbs and smokestack industry, with the tall cranes of the Pennsylvania Shipbuilding yard on your left.

Commodore Barry Bridge (11/11) The imposing steel structure to your left spans the Delaware River between Chester, Pennsylvania, and New Jersey. Look for ships being loaded below.

Pennsylvania–Delaware state line (15/7) The Delaware River is to your left as you enter the Small Wonder State at Marcus Hook. A Phoenix Steel factory stands to your right, with chemical plants and Sun Oil refineries on both sides. Chimneys burn off waste in dramatic bursts of flame.

Brandywine Creek (18/4) You cross the creek, flowing into the Christina River to your left. The Christina eventually joins the Delaware.

From here to Wilmington the train progresses through Fort Christina Park, site of the first (1638) Swedish settlement. The **Holy Trinity** (**Old Swede's**) **Church** and graveyard on your right date from 1698 and are still in use. As you travel among more factories look right near Wilmington for the station's decorative clock tower.

WILMINGTON (22/25) 'The chemical capital of the world', where Eleuthère du Pont founded a gunpowder mill in 1802. The site is now occupied by the **Hagley Museum and Library** (☏ *302 658 2400; www.hagley.org*), which collects and interprets the history of American enterprise. Wilmington's 1871 opera house boasts a splendid cast-iron façade. Look left for the cutter *Mohawk*, retained as a memorial to the Battle of the Atlantic in World War II. Amtrak's large, refurbished Victorian-style station at 100 S French Street, formerly known as Pennsylvania

Station, was designed in 1907 by Frank Furness. The 12th-busiest station in the country, it boasts terracotta window arches, marble steps and a clay-tiled roof. Train travel is close to the heart of US Vice President Joe Biden, who famously commuted between his home in Wilmington to Washington on Amtrak during his 36-year Senate career, taking over 7,000 round trips. He was also the driving force behind Wilmington Station's $37.7 million renovation project, and in 2011, he cut a ribbon to dedicate the renamed Joseph R Biden Jnr Railroad Station. Two years earlier, he announced that Amtrak would receive $1.3 billion in federal stimulus money to expand passenger rail capacity, calling the system 'an absolute national treasure and necessity'.

The train leaves past freight yards and a Berger Brothers factory before travelling beneath a highway bridge with a twin-spired church to your right.

Newark (8/17) A scheduled stop for some trains but not to be confused with Newark, New Jersey. The University of Delaware appears to your right. To your left is a vast Chrysler plant which originally manufactured tanks.

Delaware–Maryland state line (14/11) You cross into Maryland, exotically sculpted by Chesapeake Bay and the Potomac River. At the town of Hancock the state is only five miles wide. Stone markers (one white, one black) in a field to your right indicate the state boundary, which is also the Mason–Dixon Line. This divided, and some say still divides, north and south.

Elkton (15/10) Wedding chapels here witnessed thousands of quickie marriages during the 1930s. You pass a quarry to your right before continuing through a colonial countryside of streams, woods and traditional buildings.

Northeast River (16/9) The tree-lined river to your left flows towards Chesapeake Bay.

Perryville (20/5) The train slows down to cross the Susquehanna River. Look left for a marina and Chesapeake Bay, with sailboats and the supports of a former bridge. Three more bridges span the river upstream to your right.

Havre de Grace (23/2) This neat town on the south shore of the bay was burned by the British during the War of 1812.

ABERDEEN (25/22) Home of Aberdeen Proving Grounds and the US Army Ordnance Museum, this is a stop for a few Amtrak trains.

The train gathers speed as it travels southwest and crosses the mile-wide (1.6km) Bush River, with attractive houses and boat jetties ranged along the banks. **Susquehanna Wildlife Refuge** can be seen to your left as green fields, forests and grain silos appear.

Edgewood (9/13) William Paca, one of the signatories to the Declaration of Independence, was born near this prosperous small town. You cross the Gunpowder River, also a mile (1.6km) wide, and pass the Maryland National Guard headquarters on your left.

Industrial scenes return as the train nears Baltimore and travels beneath Interstate 40. Look for an old brownstone district to your right and Baltimore's downtown skyline ahead to your left before the train curves left into a tunnel.

BALTIMORE (22/12) Birthplace of the American railroad and one of the country's busiest ports, Baltimore has been the home of Billie Holliday, F Scott Fitzgerald, Babe Ruth, *Homicide – Life on the Street* and *The Wire*. The great writer and satirist H L Mencken – the 'Sage of Baltimore' – was born here in 1880 and lived most of his life at 1524 Hollins Street. During the 1830s, Edgar Allan Poe lived in poverty at 203 N Amity. When he died in 1849, he was buried in the grounds of Westminster Church. Lexington Market, the world's largest continuously running market, has been in operation in Baltimore since 1782.

Amtrak's renovated Beaux Arts-style station, opened in 1911, stands on your left at 1500 N Charles. There are plans to build a 77-room hotel on the top three floors – a first for any Amtrak station. MTA light rail connections are available to the harbour and elsewhere (✆ 410 539 5000) and you can experience panoramic views of the revived city and its harbour from the World Trade Center. The **visitor center** is at 401 Light (✆ 877 225 8466; *www.baltimore.org*; ⊕ 09.00–18.00 daily).

The **Baltimore & Ohio Railroad Museum** (*901 W Pratt;* ✆ *410 752 2490; www.borail. org;* ⊕ *daily; admission charge*) is the oldest, most comprehensive American railroad collection in the world. A huge restoration project took place after a record-breaking 2003 snowstorm devastated the museum's national landmark 1884 Roundhouse. The 'birthplace of American railroading' displays engines (including the original *Stourbridge Lion*), rolling stock, replicas and model trains, as well as the nation's earliest passenger and freight station. The train continues through a tunnel to another district of traditional brownstones. Look for the pretty Renaissance-style church to your left and a Calvert whiskey distillery to your right before the train speeds up through a more wooded landscape. The water tower at Piney Orchard is balanced on stilts.

BALTIMORE/WASHINGTON INTERNATIONAL AIRPORT (12/10)
Concrete platforms and an overhead walkway are set among attractive trees. This international airport is one of several serving Washington, DC, but is not a stop for all trains.

NEW CARROLLTON (10/10)
A key transport junction in Washington's northern suburbs, where the station and yards of Metro Rail can be seen beside Amtrak's depot.

After New Carrollton you enter the District of Columbia across the narrow Anacostia River and see the 555ft (170m) **Washington Monument** to your right. Also on your right, beyond Amtrak's maintenance facility, are the dome and tower of the **Shrine of the Immaculate Conception**. The train creeps among extensive rail yards before finally entering Union Station.

WASHINGTON
'Southern efficiency and northern charm' was President Kennedy's mischievous description of Washington, an elegant neoclassical city designed by Pierre Charles L'Enfant on what had been a swamp. The architecture, boulevards and green spaces provide a fine setting for Washington's main business – government.

Events include the cherry blossom festival in April and an Independence Day parade in July. Tourist areas are clean and impressive but the nation's capital has a darker side. Drugs and other crime make parts of the city unsafe, so stay on the beaten track. Summer can be oppressively humid.

Washington basics

✆ **Telephone code** 202
▬ **Station** (*Ticket office* ⊕ *04.30–22.00 Mon–Fri, 05.00–22.00 Sat/Sun. Waiting room*

⊕ *24hrs for Amtrak ticket holders; information* ✆ *484 7540. ClubAcela lounge* ⊕ *04.45–22.00)* Union Station is at 50 Massachusetts Av (✆ *906*

| 4

3000 or ☎ *1 800 527 2554; www.unionstationdc. com*). The station, built with white granite from Vermont, is as grand as Washington's other public buildings & is one of Amtrak's showpieces. The most-visited destination in the city, with over 32 million visitors a year, is also downtown's most impressive shopping centre. Ancient Rome's Baths of Diocletian inspired Daniel Burnham's waiting room design, the 96ft (29m) ceiling decorated with 70lb (32kg) of gold leaf. The main concourse, with its marble floor & glazed terracotta columns, is long enough (750ft/225m) to hold the Washington Monument horizontally.

The station was completed in 1908 at a cost of more than $25 million, with the cost to construct the station building alone being $4 million. It originally included a bakery, butcher's shop, bowling alley, YMCA, hotel, ice house, liquor store, Turkish baths, nursery, police station & mortuary. The dining room could handle 1,000 people at one sitting & there were separate men's & women's waiting rooms, each with heavy mahogany benches & built-in steam heaters. Union Station employed 5,000 people & became known as the 'crossroads of America'. It was made a National Historic Landmark in 1964 but, as the railroads declined, the building fell into decay. It was reopened in 1988 after America's largest-ever restoration project, which took 2 years & cost $160 million. Major exhibitions & cultural events are hosted here & private events such as the Presidential Inaugural Ball & citywide galas are celebrated in the grand halls.

Dozens of shops & restaurants, 9 movie theatres, a post office, lockers, vending machines, ATM banking, newspapers, handcarts, Red Caps, taxi stand, subway. Amtrak also has ticket offices at 1721 K Street & in the Capitol Bldg.

Connections No Thruway bus.

🚌 **Local transport** Washington is best appreciated on foot, most places of interest being within walking distance of the station, although the length of the mall can be deceptive. Metrobus operates throughout the city as well as into Maryland & northern Virginia, and the expanding Metrorail subway (☎ *637 7000; www. wmata.com*) has a stop at the station & services as far as northern Virginia & Maryland. MARC commuter trains (☎ *866 743 3682*) & the Virginia

Railway Express (☎ *703 497 7777 or* ☎ *1 800 RIDE VRE or 1 800 743 3873*) operate on w/days from Union Station.

🚕 **Taxis** Diamond ☎ 387 4011; Yellow ☎ 544 1212

🚗 **Car rental** National ☎ 842 7454; Budget ☎ 289 5374. Both located in Union Station.

🚌 **Greyhound** 1005 First NE; ☎ 289 5160. Greyhound plans to move to a new depot, possibly at Union Station.

✈ **Airports** Dulles International Airport, 25 miles (40km) west, is the main international flight centre. Washington National is in Arlington, Virginia, 4 miles (6.5km) from downtown by subway. Baltimore/Washington International (BWI) is 45 miles (72km) northeast by bus, Amtrak & MARC trains. For Washington Flyer buses to all airports, ☎ 888 WASHFLY (☎ *888 927 4359*).

Tours The Old Town Trolley (☎ *832 9800*) visits the main attractions, including Arlington Cemetery & Union Station. Unlimited stops are permitted *en route*. Gray Line coach tours (☎ *289 1995*) operate from the station.

ℹ **Visitors bureau** 901 Seventh NW; ☎ 789 7000; www.washington.org; ◷ 09.00–16.30 Mon–Fri, 09.00–16.00 Sat. Also at Union Station.

🏠 **Accommodation** Contact the Dupont at The Circle, 1604 19th St NW, Washington, DC 20009; ☎ 332 5251; or Bed & Breakfast Accommodations, PO Box 12011, Washington, DC 20005; ☎ 328 3510.

AYH Hostel, 1009 11th NW; ☎ 737 2333; www. hiwashingtondc.org. Dormitory rooms, free tours & movies, **$**. The city's oldest continuously operating hotel, the Hotel Harrington, is at 436 11th & E (☎ *628 8140 or* ☎ *800 424 8532*). Handily located for the museums & monuments, it has AC, a restaurant & cable TV with HBO. Large family rooms are also available, **$$$**.

Washington DC Hotels (☎ *800 847 4832; www. washingtondchotels.com*) has special rates & package deals among the 40,000 hotel rooms. Hotels include the Madera, 1310 New Hampshire Av; ☎ 296 7600, **$$$**; Liaison Capitol Hill, 415 New Jersey Av; ☎ 638 1616, **$$$**; Four Points by Sheraton, 1201 K St NW; ☎ 289 7600, **$$$$$**; Phoenix Park, 520 N Capitol NW; ☎ 638 6900, **$$$$$**; Comfort Inn Downtown, 1201 13th NW; ☎ 877 321 9066, **$$**; Allen Lee, 2224 F; ☎ 331 1224, **$$**.

The Capitol At the east end of the mall; ☎225 6827; ⊕ Mon–Sat; free tours. The nation's most important building was completed in 1800, when the Senate & House of Representatives met in joint session on 22 November. The familiar white dome is a later addition. In addition to its use by Congress, the Capitol is a museum of American art & history.

Supreme Court First & E Capitol; ☎479 3000. Housed in a white marble building, the court sits for 2 weeks each month from Oct to Jun (you are invited to watch). At other times, members of staff give free lectures on w/days.

White House 1600 Pennsylvania Av; ☎456 7041; www.nps.gov/whho. This official residence has been occupied by every US president since George Washington. Tours (for US citizens) can be arranged by contacting your Member of Congress & reservations must be confirmed at least 1 month prior to the visit. For more information, ☎456 7041. Visits to the White House by non-US citizens must be made through their embassies in Washington, DC.

Washington Monument On the Mall at 15th & Constitution Av; ☎426 6841; www.nps.gov/wamo. The tallest (555ft/170m) structure in the city & the highest free-standing masonry edifice in the world. A line in the marble a quarter of the way up shows where building work stopped during the Civil War. Finally completed in 1888, the monument provides stunning views from narrow slits in the observation deck. Expect a long wait for the elevator to the top.

Lincoln Memorial At the west end of the mall; ☎426 6841; www.nps.gov/linc; ⊕ daily; free. A classical Greek temple overlooks a reflecting pool. The walls around Abraham Lincoln's 19ft (5.8m) statue are inscribed with the words of his Gettysburg Address. Appropriately, this is where Martin Luther King made his 'I have a dream' speech.

National Archives Seventh & Constitution Av; ☎357 5000; www.archives.gov; ⊕ Mon–Sat; free. A classical-style building which contains over 3 billion items, including the Declaration of Independence, the Constitution & the Bill of Rights.

Smithsonian Institution The Castle visitor centre is at 1000 Jefferson Dr; ☎633 1000; www. si.edu/visit; ⊕ daily; free. This complex of 14 museums & galleries, mostly located between Sixth & 14th, include the following:

National Postal Museum 2 Massachusetts Av, next to Union Station; ☎633 5555; www. postalmuseum.si.edu; free admission. The story of the US Mail service is entertainingly demonstrated with motor vehicles, aircraft, a stagecoach & a reproduction railroad mail car (the last one was retired in 1977). You can print & mail a free personalised postcard.

Air and Space Museum Independence Av & Sixth; www.nasm.si.edu; free admission. The most-visited museum in the world features the Wright Brothers' *Flyer*, Lindbergh's *Spirit of St Louis*, the *Apollo 11* command module & a piece of moon rock billions of years old. Film shows, planetarium & tours.

Museum of American History 14th & Constitution Av; www.americanhistory.si.edu; free admission. Includes the original *DeWitt Clinton* locomotive & *John Bull*, America's oldest working steam locomotive. Built in England, the parts for the engine were purchased by New Jersey entrepreneur & engineer Robert Stevens in 1931 & shipped to the United States. Isaac Dripps, a skilled mechanic from Belfast, was hired to assemble the locomotive, which was later used on Stevens's successful Camden & Amboy Railroad in New Jersey. The engine got its famous cowcatcher, whose real function was not to deflect livestock but to add a new pair of wheels up front for better traction, thanks to the invention of Isaac Dripps. The rugged *John Bull* was in service for 35 years & was acquired by the Smithsonian in 1885. Look also for a gold crescent moon on the cylinder of a 1926 Pacific engine from the Southern Railway's *Crescent Limited*. Passengers on the *Crescent Limited* could pay extra for valet or ladies' maid services & its Pullman cars were trimmed with real gold leaf. The museum also has Henry Ford's Model T, Edison's phonograph, Washington's false teeth, Muhammad Ali's gloves, & the flag which inspired the national anthem.

Museum of Natural History Tenth & Constitution Av; www.mnh.si.edu; free admission. The 45.5-carat Hope Diamond (biggest blue diamond in the world) & the Fenkovi African elephant (the largest ever recorded) are among 60 million exhibits.

14

The Northeast Corridor
New Haven–Springfield (for Boston)

Joining the train

Several Northeast Corridor trains branch north at New Haven to travel inland through some of Connecticut's most appealing countryside.

All aboard! *Duration: one hour 15 minutes*

NEW HAVEN (30/17) For New Haven city information and the main Northeast Corridor route, see the preceding chapter (pages 173–89).

WALLINGFORD (17/7) Look for a spired church to your right.

MERIDEN (7/10) Located between Mount Beseck and the Hanging Hills. **Meriden's Heritage Museum** recreates life in the 1700s and you can see Long Island Sound from the tower of **Castle Craig**, accessible through Hubbard Park. Amtrak's station is at 60 State.

Beaver Pond (4/6) The pond is to your left and Silver Lake to your right.

BERLIN (10/10) Berlin was famous in the 18th century for manufacturing tinware. Amtrak's station also serves nearby New Britain.

HARTFORD (10/8) Birthplace of Katharine Hepburn. Founded in 1633, the former landing post known as Sucking became Connecticut's capital in 1875. Look for the Capitol's gold-plated dome high up to your right as the train arrives. The white-domed **Old State House**, designed by Charles Bulfinch, is now a museum. Hartford's Library and Supreme Court are opposite the Capitol Building and contain the table where Abraham Lincoln signed the emancipation document. Amtrak's small station is at Union Place and the **tourist bureau** is at 31 Pratt (❄ 800 446 7811; *www.enjoyhartford.com*; ☺ 10.00–17.00 daily).

When Hartford's English colonists displaced the Dutch, the latter called them *jankes* (thieves), so inventing the word 'Yankee'. Around 50 companies now make this the 'insurance capital of the world' and the Travelers Insurance skyscraper on the site of the Charter Oak is one of America's tallest buildings at 527ft (160m). The homes of Mark Twain (*Tom Sawyer*) and Harriet Beecher Stowe (*Uncle Tom's Cabin*) are preserved at Nook Farm.

Connecticut River (5/3) The river is to your right. Between here and Old Saybrook it runs through one of America's prettiest valleys.

WINDSOR (8/5) The town was originally settled in 1663 among colonial tobacco farms. You continue north across the Farmington River.

WINDSOR LOCKS (5/20) The 19th-century canal to your right supplies water for Dexter and Sons, a paper products manufacturer. Windsor Locks' **Bradley Air Museum** owns more than 50 aircraft, including a 1909 Bleriot. The train crosses the Connecticut River.

Enfield (10/10) A future president of New Jersey College, Jonathan Edwards, preached here in colonial days.

Connecticut–Massachusetts state line (15/5) You leave the Constitution State for the Bay State.

SPRINGFIELD A 17th-century trading post on the banks of the Quinnitukqut (Native American for 'long tidal') River has become an industrial city and host to the Eastern States Exposition. Springfield's **Armory** contains a huge military collection and the **Basketball Hall of Fame** honours the sport's inventor, James Naismith. Free sights downtown include the **Natural History Museum** and the **Connecticut Valley Historical Museum**. The **visitors bureau** is at 1441 Main (✆ 413 787 1548) and Amtrak's station at 66 Lyman.

Some trains continue from Springfield to Boston. For this part of the route, see *Chapter 23, The* Lake Shore Limited (pages 249–58).

BOSTON ▫

For Springfield to Boston, see
The Lake Shore Limited

Brad

Springfield ◊

Windsor Locks ◊

Windsor ◊

Hartford ◊

Berlin ◊

Meriden ◊

Wallingford ◊

NEW HAVEN ▫

The Northeast Corridor   New Haven–Springfield

15

16

The *Crescent*
New York–New Orleans

General route information

Southern hospitality envelops staff and passengers as Amtrak's friendliest train travels the Northeast Corridor route then passes through Civil War country to Atlanta, Birmingham and the south. You pass through 12 states and the District of Columbia.

The *Crescent* began in 1891 as the Washington & Southwestern *Vestibule Limited*, an overnight train between Washington and Atlanta. Operated by the Richmond & Danville Railroad, the predecessor of the Norfolk Southern (whose line the present train uses south of Washington), the *Vestibule Limited* offered luxurious staterooms, a library and an observation car. It became a through-train from New York City to New Orleans in 1906, and was later renamed the *Crescent City Limited*. The Southern Railway continued this service until Amtrak took over in 1979.

Joining the train

NEW YORK For New York City information and the route to Washington, see *Chapter 14, The Northeast Corridor* (pages 173–89).

Chapter 14, The Northeast Corridor (pages 173–89).

ESSENTIAL INFORMATION

FREQUENCY Daily. The **southbound** train leaves New York early in the afternoon, reaching Washington by early evening and Greensboro just after midnight. You arrive in Atlanta early next morning, Birmingham by late morning and New Orleans mid evening. Travelling **north**, trains leave New Orleans early in the morning to reach Birmingham by early afternoon, Atlanta mid evening and Greensboro during the night. You arrive in Washington early on the second day and New York by early afternoon.
DURATION 30 hours
RESERVATIONS All reserved
EQUIPMENT Amfleet coaches
SLEEPING Viewliner bedrooms
FOOD Complete meals, snacks, sandwiches, drinks
LOUNGE CAR A National Park Service guide accompanies the train to provide passengers with a commentary along part of the route. An interpretive guide from the Martin Luther King Jr National Historic Site provides a narrative between Atlanta and New Orleans from Memorial Day to mid-August.
BAGGAGE Check-in service at most stations

WASHINGTON The *Crescent* departs by way of a tunnel, emerging with the Capitol Building to your right. Also to your right are the Bureau of Engraving, the Washington Monument and the Jefferson Memorial. To your right as you cross the Potomac River is the 14th Street road bridge.

The Pentagon (5/10) The nerve centre of America's military network, with 23,000 personnel occupying the world's largest office building (3.7 million ft^2 or 340,000m^2). Nearby Arlington Cemetery was the last resting place for General Pershing, Admiral Byrd and the boxer Joe Louis. President John F Kennedy's grave is marked by an eternal flame.

You pass the National Airport to your left then a huge Crystal City hotel and office development to your right, built on former railroad property. As the train approaches Alexandria, look left for long lines of Metro trains.

ALEXANDRIA (15/30) The massive grey stone building to your right is the George Washington Memorial Masonic Temple. Amtrak's attractive station at 110 Callahan Drive is one of many on this line which have been renovated.

Alexandria, 'the cradle of history', began in the 1740s as a port on the Potomac River. A million visitors each year now come to see the hundreds of restored buildings, a cobblestone waterfront and the nation's second-oldest apothecary shop. Gadsby's Tavern in Market Square was the traditional focus for business and social gatherings. Tours of **Old Town Alexandria** start at the Ramsay House (*221 King;* ℡ *703 838 4200*). The *Spirit of Mount Vernon* travels along the Potomac River to George Washington's colonial estate, where you can visit his grand farmhouse, smokehouses and slave quarters.

After Alexandria, the *Crescent* changes from CSX tracks and travels on to New Orleans with the Norfolk Southern (NS).

MANASSAS (30/30) The town was fiercely fought over during the Civil War, when two battles around a strategic rail junction in 1861 cost 24,000 lives and earned Thomas 'Stonewall' Jackson his nickname. The present brick station on your right at 9431 W dates from 1915 and has original wood panelling in the waiting room. Bristow Air Park is to your left.

The *Crescent* passes a cemetery and grain elevators on the right before travelling among forests and farms.

Remington (20/10) Look right for a farmers' market before you cross the Rappahannock River. Factories and warehouses accumulate on the right as you approach Culpeper.

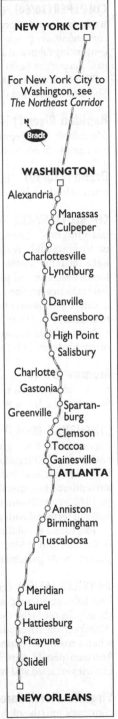

CULPEPER (30/60) The Union Army had a headquarters here during the Civil War and the **Museum of Culpeper History** (*803 S Main;* ☎ *540 829 1749; www.culpepermuseum. com; admission charge*) features the charming Burgandine House, a fully restored 18th-century log cabin and a working Native American village. The attractive downtown area of Culpeper can be seen beyond the red-brick station to your right.

The *Crescent* continues southwest, accompanying the Blue Ridge Mountains and Shenandoah National Park to your right.

Rapidan River (15/45) More Civil War battles were fought at nearby Cedar Mountain, Port Republic and the Wilderness. You travel through lush farmland adorned with dogwoods and apple trees.

Orange (30/30) The James Madison law office appears to your left just before the town. Also look left for Montpelier Station and President Madison's estate.

CHARLOTTESVILLE (60/65) Named after King George III's wife, Charlotte, the last Queen of America, this is where Thomas Jefferson founded the University of Virginia and created his Monticello home on a nearby hill. Other residents have included Meriwether Lewis, William Faulkner, Sissy Spacek and Presidents James Madison and James Monroe, whose **Ash Lawn Estate** is open to the public. Amtrak's new station is next to Union Station at 810 W Main, where Thruway buses connect with Warrenton and Dulles International Airport. The **visitors bureau** is at 610 E Main (☎ *434 293 6789; www.visitcharlottesville.org*).

To your right as you leave town is the University of Virginia Medical Center, then other academic buildings and the distinctive rotunda.

Monroe (55/10) Sweet Briar College is across the highway to your right as the train continues past rolling green fields with hedgerows, cattle, barns and streams. You cross the James River on a high trestle then enter Rivermont Tunnel.

LYNCHBURG (65/65) Named after John Lynch, who founded a ferry service here after the town grew rich on tobacco. Lynchburg has many Victorian houses and is one of Virginia's chief industrial and education centres. Amtrak's station is at Kemper and Park Avenue. Appomattox Courthouse, where Robert E Lee surrendered to General Grant, is 21 miles (33km) east. Kemper Street Station, built in 1912 by the Southern Railway, has been handsomely restored as a modern bus and rail terminal with antique charm.

The *Crescent* continues through mellow Piedmont countryside and the forests of the Blue Ridge Mountains, which extend from Pennsylvania down to Georgia as part of the Appalachian Range.

DANVILLE (65/60) Located beside the Dan River, Danville boasts 'the world's best tobacco market' and the largest textile mill in the world. The town became (briefly, in 1865) the Confederate capital, and was later the birthplace of Lady Astor. A marker on Riverside Drive commemorates the 'wreck of the old 97' in 1903, when a mail train crashed at 90mph on the grade between Lynchburg and Danville. Thirteen people were killed, including engineer Joseph Broady. Three crates of canaries escaped and were found flying surreally in the wreck's smoky aftermath.

Virginia–North Carolina state line (5/55) The train crosses the border as it continues into the night.

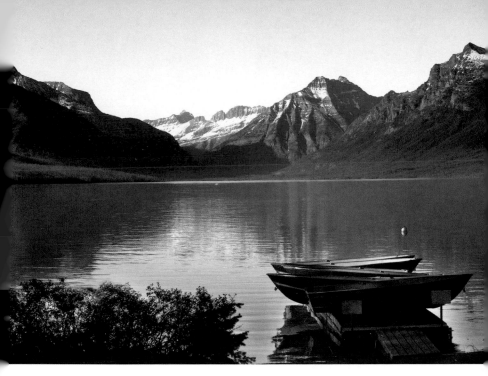

above   Glacier National Park boasts 430 glaciers, numerous alpine lakes and glorious mountain passes (WP/DT) page 111

below   Despite its desolation, Death Valley is visited every year by nearly a million visitors, who flock to see its salt flats, valleys, canyons and dunes (SS) page 86 *top left* The residents of San Antonio unwind on the Paseo del Rio, a riverside walk offering music bars, floating restaurants and people-watching galore (A/DT) page 143

top right Albuquerque has a distinctly Mexican feel with its brightly painted houses (NB/DT) page 126

above The *California Zephyr* glides through one of Colorado's picturesque canyons (AM) page 71

left Every year at Carnival New Orleans springs to life with a bombastic display of dancing, parades and music (SS) page 138 *above* The nightclubs and beaches of Miami's South Beach art deco district are a byword for glamour (E/DT) page 214

below Barely connected to the USA, there's one road in and one road out of Key West (JG/A) page 216

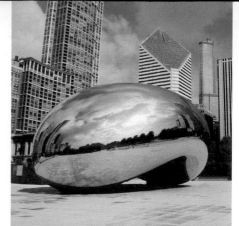

right   The bean-like sculpture *Cloud Gate* forms the centerpiece of Millennium Park, one of Chicago's main draws (DR/DT) page 71

below left   Occupied since 1772, Elfreth's Alley in Philadelphia is the USA's oldest street (SS) page 184

beow right   The shores of Lake Michigan, the only one of the Great Lakes to lie fully within the USA, are popular with Midwesterners and seasonal visitors alike for their scenic beauty (SS) page 154

bottom   Washington DC is far more than a mere administrative hub: countless museums, restaurants and galleries lie in the shadow of the Capitol dome (SD/DT) page 187

above   Old-style eateries can be found all over
         New York City (SS) page 179

right   Central Park is the place to marvel at
         NYC's inline skaters, catch a free open-air
         theatre performance or take a whirl on
         America's oldest carousel (SS) page 182

below   Built at the height of the Great Depression,
         the Rockefeller Center is a vast art deco
         complex that includes Radio City Music
         Hall, an array of public artwork and
         several outdoor plazas (SS) page 182

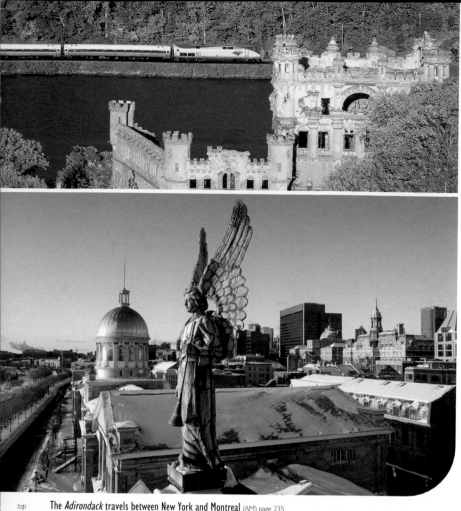

top   The *Adirondack* travels between New York and Montreal (AM) page 235

above   Montreal and the rest of Quebec Province typically receive more snow than Moscow in winter (SS) page 242

below   The aurora borealis may be seen from much of Canada's frozen expanses, as here near Whitehorse, Yukon (SS) page 325 *above* **A male grizzly bear near Prince Rupert, British Columbia** (SS) page 316

right **Vancouver's Stanley Park is home to a large collection of monuments, including totem poles, statues and plaques** (SS) page 315

below **The *Rocky Mountaineer* offers a magnificent view of Mount Robson, the highest peak in the Canadian Rockies** (SS) page 320

The *Alberni Pacific*, an ex-logging locomotive, winds its way through forests up to the McLean Hill National Historic Site (SS) page 328

GREENSBORO (60/25) Famous for an annual golf tournament and a Revolutionary War battle where British general Cornwallis defeated General Greene at Guilford Courthouse.

HIGH POINT (25/40) So named because it represents the highest point on the route between Charlotte and Goldsboro. The 'home furnishings capital of the world' has many furniture manufacturers and the 'world's largest chest of drawers' – a 38ft-tall office building designed to look like a Goddard-Townsend block front chest.

SALISBURY (40/50) Daniel Boone grew up in this colonial town set among pretty hills and lakes. Amtrak's station is at Depot and Liberty.

A short distance to the north, at 411 S Salisbury Avenue in Spencer, is the **North Carolina Transport Museum** (❨ *704 636 2889; www.nctrans.org; ☉ daily; free*). Located on the site of what was once the Southern Railway Company's largest steam locomotive repair facility, the museum features an authentic train depot, antique automobiles and a 37-bay Roundhouse that includes 25 locomotives, dozens of rail cars and other exhibit areas with memorabilia from Native American times to the present. The museum also offers seasonal train rides.

CHARLOTTE (50/25) Another city named after George III's wife, Charlotte became the first place in America where gold was found. Railroads converged on what is now the largest city in the Carolinas. An important financial centre, this is also America's main producer of cotton cloth. Each May the **World 600 Auto Races** take place at the Motor Speedway.

Charlotte was the birthplace, in a log cabin, of President James Polk, and you can take a self-guided tour of the Old City from the **visitor center** at 330 S Tryon (❨ *800 231 4636; www.visitcharlotte.com; free guided walking tours most Fris*). Highlights include a settlers' cemetery and the blushing pink splendour of Overcarsh House. Latta Plantation Park has costumed guides and a 19th-century merchant's house.

GASTONIA (25/55) The *Crescent* makes a slight detour west to take in this industrial town, near where a Revolutionary War battle was fought at Kings Mountain.

North Carolina–South Carolina state line (5/50) You cross between the two Carolinas and enter the Palmetto State, travelling through countryside famous for peaches.

SPARTANBURG (55/40) A manufacturing town which was named after the Spartan regiment of the South Carolina militia.

GREENVILLE (40/35) Another major textile town, where inexpensive clothes can be bought at many factory outlets. Bob Jones University became established here in 1827, and Greenville was the birthplace of Joanne Woodward and Jesse Jackson. The small modern station is part of a large building containing offices of the Norfolk Southern Railroad.

CLEMSON (35/35) A university town which until 1943 was called Calhoun, after the 19th-century politician John Calhoun.

South Carolina–Georgia state line (20/15) As the *Crescent* travels deeper into the south through wooded countryside, look for examples of the fast-growing *kudzu*

vines. These were imported from Japan to combat soil erosion but have become a menace throughout the south, spreading over the ground to smother all in their path.

TOCCOA (35/40) Home of Toccoa Falls (186ft/56m) and a college of the same name. Note the traditional station building to your right and an impressive spired church on your left.

The *Crescent* departs past warehouses and freight trains to travel among tree-covered hills, lumber yards, orchards and occasional fields. Near Gainesville, factories and freight trains gather on both sides.

GAINESVILLE (40/55) The town is on the eastern edge of Lake Sidney Lanier, Georgia's largest lake. The Lake Lanier Islands are a popular recreation area with beaches, campsites, fishing and boating. Amtrak's charming brick station at 116 Industrial Boulevard also serves Athens, home of the University of Georgia (America's oldest state college).

The train pauses across a barriered road junction before continuing among more factories, lumber yards and freight wagons. Look right for a flea market after you pass beneath a highway bridge.

As the day becomes lighter you begin to travel through less mountainous scenery, with cattle, horses and dark ploughed fields.

Norcross (35/20) Industry returns as MARTA commuter trains assemble. Look for the old green Pullman car sidelined to your left.

Oglethorpe University (40/15) The campus is to your right. As you near Atlanta, the city's imposing skyscrapers can be seen ahead to your left.

ATLANTA (55/130) Birthplace of Spike Lee and venue for the 1996 Olympic Games, Atlanta is America's fastest-growing city. The unofficial capital of the south has the most affluent black middle class in the country and one of America's highest crime rates. Magnolias still bloom along the older streets and spring fills Atlanta's parks with flowering azaleas and dogwoods.

The city began in 1837 as a railroad town called Terminus but was renamed after the Western Atlantic Railroad. By the time of the Civil War, more rail lines converged here than anywhere else in the south, and the city became a prime target for General Sherman's Union forces. The war's destruction failed to halt growth for long and many large corporations are now resident, including Coca-Cola and CNN. The glass building to the left of the station belongs to AT&T.

Atlanta basics

✆Telephone code 404

⚏ Station (*Ticket office & waiting room* ⊕ *07.00–21.30; information* ✆ *881 3061*) Amtrak's renovated Brookwood (Peachtree) station is at 1688 Peachtree, 3 miles (5km) north of downtown (take bus #23). Built by the Southern Railway in 1918 as a small suburban halt, the station is barely adequate today even though slightly expanded. Lockers, vending machines, handcarts.

Connections No Thruway buses.

🚌 Local transport MARTA operates buses & subway trains (✆ *848 5000; www.itsmarta.com*)

🚕 Taxis Ambassador ✆ *724 0220;* Checker ✆ *351 1111*

🚗 Car rental Avis, 143 Courtland; ✆ *659 4814*

🚌 Greyhound 232 Forsyth; ✆ *584 1728*

✈ Hartsfield Airport The world's busiest airport, both in terms of passengers & number of flights, is 10 miles (16km) south by MARTA train (☎ *848 5000*) & Airport Express bus (☎ *800 842 2770*)

Tours American Coach/Gray Line; ☎ 800 593 1818. Walking tours from the Preservation Center, 327 St Paul Av (☎ *688 3353; www. preserveatlanta.com*).

ℹ️ **Visitors bureau** 233 Peachtree; ☎ 521 6600; www.atlanta.net; ⊕ 08.30–17.30 Mon–Sat

🏠 **Accommodation** Contact Bed & Breakfast Atlanta; ☎ 875 0525 or ☎ 800 967 3224; www. bedandbreakfastatlanta.com.

International Hostel, 223 Ponce De Leon Av; ☎ 875 9449, **$**.

Hotels include the Holiday Inn, 101 International Bd; ☎ 524 5555, **$$$**; Marriott Buckhead, 3405 Lenox Rd; ☎ 261 9250, **$$$**; Quality Inn, 89 Luckie; ☎ 524 7991, **$$$**; Howard Johnson, 5375 Peachtree Industrial Bd, Norcross; ☎ 678 736 6610, **$$$**; Motel 6, 311 Courtland; ☎ 659 4545, **$$**; Midtown Manor, 811 Piedmont Av; ☎ 872 5846, **$$**.

Recommended in Atlanta

State Capitol 206 Washington; ☎ 656 2846; www.sos.ga.gov/archives/state_capitol; ⊕ Mon–Fri; free tours. Topped by a dome of gold leaf mined in north Georgia, the 1889 building houses state offices, Confederate flags & the **Georgia History Museum.**

Stone Mountain Park and Village 16 miles east of Atlanta on US 78; ☎ 770 498 5690; www. stonemountainpark.com; ⊕ daily; admission charge. This 3,200-acre (1,296ha) park attracts 6 million visitors a year, giving it the 3rd-largest attendance in the United States (after the Disney parks). The site includes the world's largest granite outcrop, where you can see carved figures of Jefferson Davis, Robert E Lee & Stonewall Jackson on horseback.

Antebellum Plantation & Farmyard Featuring 19 restored historic buildings from around the state of Georgia, built between 1783 & 1875. This is the largest collection of period furniture & decorations in the south, reflecting the diverse lifestyles of 18th- & 19th-century Georgia residents.

Stone Mountain Scenic Railroad The railroad takes visitors on a 5-mile excursion around the mountain's base aboard a full-size locomotive. Opened in 1962, the railroad features diesel engines, built in 1950 & 1956, pulling newly renovated 1940s open-air train cars. The train departs from a scale replica of the Main Train Depot from late 19th-century downtown Atlanta.

Governor's Mansion 391 W Paces Ferry Rd; ☎ 261 1776; ⊕ Tue–Thu; free. Built in Greek Revival style, the mansion has a fine collection of federal period furnishings.

Martin Luther King Center & Historic District The King Center at 449 Auburn Av

(☎ *526 8900; www.thekingcenter.org;* ⊕ *daily; free*) was established in 1968 by Coretta Scott King & has a library, films & museum. Atlanta was a focal point for the 1960s civil rights movement. You can visit Dr King's birthplace & see the Ebenezer Baptist Church (⊕ *daily; donation*) where he preached.

Jimmy Carter Library 441 Freedom Parkway; ☎ 865 7100; www.jimmycarterlibrary.org; ⊕ daily; admission charge. The Jimmy Carter Library is the only presidential library in the southeastern United States. Documents & memorabilia, including some of the nation's historic treasures, are on exhibit.

Southeastern Railway Museum 3595 Buford Hwy in Duluth, 20 miles (32km) northeast of Atlanta; ☎ 770 476 2013; www.srmduluth.org; ⊕ Wed–Sat; admission charge. Among the rolling stock are vintage steam engines, wooden cars & Pullmans such as the 1911 car Superb used by President Harding. Train rides in restored coaches. In 2008, the former Southern Railway System depot previously used in downtown Duluth was relocated to the museum & is being restored.

Southern Museum of Civil War and Locomotive History 2829 Cherokee, Kennesaw; ☎ 427 2117; www.southernmuseum. org; ⊕ daily; admission charge. 25 miles north of Atlanta, Kennesaw is the only town in America where it is illegal for citizens not to own a gun. The museum features *The General*, an 1855 Rogers steam engine that was stolen at Big Shanty by northern soldiers in 1862 along with 2 cars of a Western & Atlantic passenger train. *The General* was captured halfway to Chattanooga after being pursued at 60mph by southern troops aboard the locomotive *Texas*. The 'great locomotive chase' inspired the classic 1926 film, *The General*, starring Buster Keaton, who was born close to the sounds of a rail junction & had a lifelong obsession with trains.

Chattanooga Located 110 miles (176km) northwest of Atlanta; www.choochoo.com. Chattanooga is dominated by Lookout Mountain, the top of which can be reached on the world's steepest passenger railway line. The 1909 Southern Railway terminal has been renovated, its magnificent 85ft (24m) dome becoming the lobby of a hotel where you can spend the night in restored Victorian passenger cars & eat in an original dining car (☏ 423 266 5000). The station also holds the largest HO-gauge model railway in the world.

The original 'Chattanooga Choo-Choo' was a passenger train which first operated from Cincinnati in 1880. Almost all trains going south passed through Chattanooga then, & this one later encouraged Glenn Miller to make a million-selling record. A vintage wood-burner locomotive resembling *The General* used on that first run is displayed at the terminal. The state has plans to reopen a regular train route between Chattanooga & Atlanta.

All aboard!

The *Crescent* leaves Atlanta through western industrial suburbs. Extensive freight yards sprawl to your right and the Chattahoochee Brick Company is to your left. The train crosses Interstate 75 and the Chattahoochee River before re-entering a landscape of tree-covered hills and ridges.

Douglasville (35/95) One of many quiet towns encountered on this section of the route. An imposing Commercial Bank and the Young Refining Corporation Building are to your right.

Villa Rica (50/80) Look right for the Golden Hosiery Mills factory set among pine trees and dogwoods.

Bremen (65/65) The Hubbard Slacks Company is seen to your right before the *Crescent* moves slowly out of Bremen. You pass a church on your left then start climbing a series of S-shaped curves into the hills.

Tallapoosa (75/55) Note one of Georgia's finest golf courses on your left as you approach town. The American Thread Company is to your right. The *Crescent*'s tracks run on an island along the centre of Main Street and an ancient steam engine can be seen on display.

The train picks up speed as it crosses the attractive Tall River then climbs further into forested hills. Look for logs being loaded aboard railway wagons on your left before you cross the Tallapoosa River.

Georgia–Alabama state line (90/40) You pass from Eastern to Central Time, so watches go back an hour (forward when travelling east). The landscape becomes ever more densely wooded as you enter Talladega National Forest at the southern end of the Appalachian Mountains.

Heflin (105/25) This was once a gold rush town. In the left distance is Alabama's highest mountain, Mount Cheaha (2,407ft/735m).

ANNISTON (130/90) One of the state's main manufacturing centres, with an old brick station building on the right. Also on the right is the Lee Brass Foundry, one of the largest in the world.

Anniston Depot (10/80) World War II Sherman tanks guard silos at the US Army's largest military depot, stretching away to your right.

Lincoln (15/75) Look for a modest blue railroad building on your right.

Pell City (30/60) A Chrysler factory appears to your right before the train enters Chula Vista Mountain Tunnel, the only tunnel on this line.

Gahaba River (65/25) You cross by means of two high bridges. The river continues on your left as undulating, forest-covered hills give way to industrial scenes near Birmingham.

Irondale (70/20) Freight wagons assemble on the right. Look right also for the Sloss furnace, dating from 1890. The Dr Pepper Company appears to your left.

RED MOUNTAIN (85/5) A 55ft (17m) statue on the mountain to your left represents Vulcan, the Roman god of fire and forge. Made for the 1904 St Louis World's Fair, this is the largest (60 tons/54,000kg) cast-iron statue ever constructed. A stairway inside leads to an observation deck at the top.

BIRMINGHAM (90/60) Alabama's biggest city has been the home of Willie Mays, Nat King Cole and Hank Williams Jr. Amtrak's stop at 1819 Morris Avenue stands opposite a cluster of dismal factories with tall brick chimneys. To your left is the University of Alabama Medical School.

Founded in 1871 at the crossing of two railroad lines, Birmingham rapidly became the south's leading industrial centre, based on iron and steel production. Named after its English equivalent, the city also has parks and gardens filled with roses and dogwood trees. The **visitors bureau** is at 2200 Ninth Avenue N (℡205 458 8000; www.birminghamal.org).

The *Crescent* departs among rail yards, with Vulcan still dominating the skyline to your left.

Bessemer (22/38) To your right are the Royster Guano Company and a former Pullman-Standard factory. Assuming both trains are on time, you should soon be passing the northbound *Crescent*.

TUSCALOOSA (60/90) The University of Alabama, home of the 'Crimson Tide' football team, is to your right as you approach the beautiful brick and stucco station. Named after a Choctaw chief, Tuscaloosa used to be Alabama's capital.

The train skirts a golf course to your left then travels southwest through swamp country. Sleepy towns, sunburned houses and characterful general stores appear between the forest plantations and logging sites.

Mound State Monument (15/75) Prehistoric mounds to your right were used by Native Americans for ceremonial purposes, although the temple on the highest one is more recent.

Black Warrior River (35/55) The *Crescent* slows down to clank across a steel drawbridge into further swamp country. Another track runs along the raised bed to your left.

Tombigbee River (45/45) Note the white cliffs as you cross this part of the Tenn-Tom project which links the Tennessee, Ohio and Upper Mississippi rivers with the Gulf of Mexico.

Livingston (70/20) Named after Edward Livingston, who negotiated the Louisiana Territory purchase in 1803.

York (75/15) Look for picturesque stores to your right and a sawmill to your left.

Alabama–Mississippi state line (80/10) The train continues south among cotton fields and magnolias.

MERIDIAN (90/60) Birthplace of delta country blues artist Jimmie Rodgers, the 'singing brakeman' whose memory lives on at a museum and the town's music festival. Rodgers worked on the railroad and wrote many songs about his experiences. 'Waiting for A Train' told the story of a hobo who jumped freights to look for work during the 1930s Depression.

Meridian is an important rail junction, where tracks radiate in six directions. In the shunting yards beyond the remodelled station you can see rolling stock from many lines, including the Southern Railway, the Delaware & Hudson and the Illinois Central Gulf. The splendid station was built in traditional style and is remarkably large, considering it sees only two Amtrak trains a day (one in each direction).

As the *Crescent* leaves, look for a faded Gulf Mobile Sohio Railroad building falling apart to your left.

Key Field (8/52) Light aircraft are housed in the hangars to your right and other planes belong to the Mississippi National Guard. You cross Chunky Creek and pass a natural gas facility to your left.

LAUREL (60/30) This is a crew-change point for the *Crescent*. Laurel is a trading centre for farmers, with a fire station on the left and disused tracks that run into the trees. Amtrak has a waiting room at the north end of the large brick station building, originally built in 1913 by the New Orleans & Northeastern Railroad.

The *Crescent* crosses the Leaf River just before Hattiesburg Station, where an old baggage car can be seen confined between two steam locomotives.

HATTIESBURG (30/60) Home of Southern Mississippi University and the Magnolia Classic golf tournament, Hattiesburg was founded on the railroad and lumber industries. The impressive restored station at 308 Newman was built in 1910 for the New Orleans & Northeastern Railroad. To the right of its wide platform and large wooden canopy stands a futuristic coal-fired electricity-generating plant.

You leave past a square-towered church on your left.

Poplarville (40/20) Birthplace of Theodore Bilbo, a US senator and segregationist who was Governor of Mississippi in the 1920s–40s.

PICAYUNE (60/15) This is the *Crescent's* final stop in the state of Mississippi. Picayune was founded in 1904 by Eliza Jane Poitevent Nicholson, poet and publisher of the New Orleans Times-Picayune newspaper, named after a Spanish coin used throughout colonial America. The town received little damage from Hurricane Katrina so has become a permanent home for many who relocated from the Mississippi Gulf Coast and New Orleans. Amtrak's modern station was built in the style of a classic early 20th-century passenger station, including a port cochère (covered carriageway) and waiting room. Note the old open wooden pavilion to provide shelter for waiting passengers.

Pearl River (5/10) Crossing the river takes you into the flat, subtropical landscape of southern Louisiana.

SLIDELL (15/55) Slidell was founded around 1882 during construction of a major new railroad from New Orleans to Meridian, Mississippi, connecting there with Cincinnati, Ohio and eventually with New York City. The New Orleans & Northeastern Railroad established a building camp at the first high ground north of Lake Pontchartrain which eventually grew into the city. In 2005, Slidell suffered extensive damage from the effects of Hurricane Katrina, experiencing a massive storm surge from Lake Pontchartrain. It remains a residential suburb for many who commute into New Orleans. Main Street is to your left beyond the station.

Lake Pontchartrain (10/45) Taking the *Crescent* is worthwhile just to experience this spectacular six-mile (10km) crossing of Lake Pontchartrain's eastern tip. The train runs along a causeway immediately above the lake's surface, giving sensational views across 630 square miles (1,630km²) of water. The scene is especially wonderful at sunset (or sunrise if travelling east). Look for fishing shanties on stilts and a road bridge to your left.

Soon after leaving Lake Pontchartrain, you glimpse the New Orleans skyline ahead to your left. Look also for Tulane University and the Greenwood Cemetery with above-the-ground graves. On arrival in New Orleans the *Crescent* pauses before reversing into the station.

NEW ORLEANS For New Orleans city information, see *Chapter 11, The* Sunset Limited (pages 137–8).

17

The *Silver Star*
New York–Miami

General route information

Another train with a party atmosphere, the *Silver Star* travels between the great northeastern cities and Florida's subtropical resorts, passing through historic Virginia, tracts of pine forest and Old Savannah. Beyond Lake Okeechobee you visit many of the beach communities leading to Miami, the furthest south that you can travel by train in the US.

Joining the train

NEW YORK For New York City and the *Silver Star* route to Washington, see *Chapter 14, The Northeast Corridor* (pages 173–89). For the route from Washington to Alexandria, see *Chapter 16, The* Crescent (pages 192–201).

All aboard!

ALEXANDRIA (15/90) Soon after leaving Alexandria the *Silver Star* crosses the first of several inlets leading to the Potomac River.

Lorton (14/76) Amtrak's new northern *Auto Train* depot is to your right. The *Silver Star* crosses the Occoquan River and Neabsco Creek.

ESSENTIAL INFORMATION

FREQUENCY Daily. The **southbound** service leaves New York mid morning to reach Washington mid afternoon, Richmond late afternoon and Raleigh by mid evening. You arrive in Savannah and Jacksonville early next morning, Orlando by mid morning and Miami early evening. Travelling **north**, trains leave Miami early mid morning to reach Orlando early evening, Jacksonville late evening and Savannah during the night. You arrive in Richmond around midday, Washington mid afternoon and New York by early evening.

DURATION 28+ hours

RESERVATIONS All reserved

EQUIPMENT Amfleet coaches. Movies are shown in coaches, with headphones available for purchase.

SLEEPING Viewliner bedrooms

FOOD Complete meals, snacks, sandwiches, drinks

BAGGAGE Check-in service at most stations

Possum Point (20/70) A huge Virginia Power electricity-generating plant appears to your left.

Quantico Base (30/60) Amtrak's *Carolinian* train makes a stop inside this 60,000-acre (24,000ha) US Marine Corps base, where the museum features World War II tanks and aircraft. Look left for the airfield and assault course.

You continue with the Potomac away to your left and travel south among forests and rivers.

Falmouth (36/54) Soon after this small residential and manufacturing town you cross the muddy Rappahannock River, across which George Washington famously threw a silver dollar. A highway bridge is to your right.

Fredericksburg (40/50) Another stop for the *Carolinian*. Washington lived in Fredericksburg as a boy and Mary Washington's garden at 1200 Charles still has the box hedges she planted. George's brother, Charles, owned the Rising Sun Tavern. The **visitors bureau** is at 706 Caroline (✆ *540 373 1776; www.simplyfredericksburg.com/tourism*) and Amtrak's station at Caroline and Lafayette Boulevard. Nearby Fredericksburg and Spotsylvania Military Park explains events at four Civil War battlefields.

The train leaves with Fredericksburg's airport and runways to your left.

Meade Pyramid (45/45) This memorial to the Civil War general George G Meade can be seen to your left.

Jackson Shrine (55/35) Stonewall Jackson died in the modest white house to your left at Guinea. You cross the Mattaponi and Pamunkey rivers as the train travels through pleasant countryside. Logging operations and marshes are often close to the sides of the track.

Ashland (80/10) As the train runs carefully beside the town's main street look left for picturesque Randolph-Macon College. Dating from 1830, it was originally for women only.

RICHMOND (90/30) State capital since 1779, Richmond was the Confederate capital for much of the Civil War. The old tobacco town has recently revived after a period of decline, and the Cultural Link trolley runs from the Science Museum at 2500 W Broad to take in 35 historic landmarks. Richmond's **tourist bureau** is at 401 N Third (✆ *804 783 7450; www.visit.richmond.com*).

The **Museum of the Confederacy** owns the world's largest collection of Civil War memorabilia, including General Lee's sword and Stonewall Jackson's forage cap

NEW YORK CITY

For New York City and the Silver Star route to Washington, see *The Northeast Corridor*

WASHINGTON

For the route from Washington to Alexandria, see *The Crescent*

Alexandria
Richmond
Petersburg

Rocky Mount

Raleigh
Cary
Hamlet — Southern Pines
Camden
Columbia

Denmark

SAVANNAH

N
Bradt

JACKSONVILLE

Palatka

Deland

Winter Park
TAMPA — ORLANDO
Lake- — Kissimmee
land
Winter — Sebring
Haven
Okeechobee
West Palm Beach
Delray Beach
Deerfield Beach
Fort Lauderdale
Hollywood
MIAMI

(*1201 E Clay;* \ *855 649 1861; www.moc.org; admission charge*). There are free tours of the Capitol, which Thomas Jefferson helped design, and of the Philip Morris plant (the largest cigarette factory in the world). Amtrak's impressive modern station on your right is some way from downtown but is open 24 hours a day.

The train curves right through massive yards bustling with goods traffic. As you near the James River, the University of Richmond can be seen to your left.

James River (14/16)
You cross the rock-strewn waterway with an Interstate 95 highway bridge to your right. As you approach Petersburg, houses begin to replace the trees.

Centralia (20/10)
Centralia is the headquarters of the main US Army clothing supply depot.

Chester (24/6)
Several battles were fought here during the Civil War. Look for the remains of an 1863 campsite to your left.

PETERSBURG (30/80)
The *Silver Star* stops at the single-storey South Street Station on your right at Ettrick. The Civil War ended 75 miles (128km) west of here when Grant accepted Lee's surrender at Appomattox Courthouse. The actor Joseph Cotton was born in Petersburg.

Virginia University appears high up to your left as the train departs Ettrick. You cross another muddy river, the Appomattox, into Petersburg proper. Just to the south is Fort Hell, a large Civil War fort.

The train continues through Carson and Stoney Creek then crosses the Nottoway River.

Meherrin River (30/50)
After you cross the river near Emporia look for fields producing prolific crops of peanuts.

Virginia–North Carolina state line (35/45)
The Georgia Pacific Plywood factory straddles the border to your right. The train enters the Tar Heel State, so named after a promise Jefferson Davis made to tar the heels of soldiers to make them stand their ground.

Roanoke River (45/35)
You cross the river on its way from the Blue Ridge Mountains to the Atlantic. This area around Weldon was the setting for the Sally Field film *Norma Rae*.

Enfield (65/15)
Peanut storage warehouses appear on both sides before the train travels through a region of swamps renowned for their oversized crocodiles. North Carolina Wesleyan College can be seen to your right at Battleboro. Approaching Rocky Mount, you cross over the Tar River.

ROCKY MOUNT (80/80)
North Carolina grows the largest tobacco crop in America and much of it comes here to be marketed, along with cotton and other produce. In the old days most of the tobacco was transported from here by rail. Amtrak's station is at 101 Hammond.

Wilson (20/60)
Wilson is a scheduled stop for *Palmetto* and *Carolinian* trains. Local manufacturing companies include Levi Strauss (jeans) and Ralston Purina

(pet food). An annual tobacco auction brings people from all over the country, and warehouses and curing facilities feature on both sides of the track.

Selma (45/35) A modest town serving adjacent farm communities, this is another stop for the *Palmetto* and *Carolinian*. Several houses have pictures of locomotives painted on their sides.

The *Silver Star* travels on past oil storage tanks then crosses the Neuse River before going through Wilson Mills. Look for more tobacco plants and peanut fields. Fox hunters can sometimes be seen during spring and autumn.

RALEIGH (80/14) The 'city of oaks' was named after its founder, Sir Walter Raleigh, and proclaimed North Carolina's unalterable seat of government. Raleigh's statue takes pride of place near the Capitol, completed in 1840 and restored for the US bicentennial. Beautifully preserved Victorian houses stand on streets lined with oak trees, magnolias and dogwoods. Raleigh has many educational establishments and high-tech industries, and *Money* magazine voted it the best place to live in America.

The **North Carolina Museum** depicts life from the first settlements through Revolutionary days to the Civil War (*2110 Blue Ridge Rd;* ☎ *919 839 6262; www. ncartmuseum.org; admission free*). Amtrak's porticoed station at 320 W Cabarrus was built by the Southern Railway in 1950. For information on the Victorian neighbourhoods contact the **visitor centre** at 500 Fayetteville (☎ *919 834 5900; www.visitraleigh.com*).

North Carolina Central Prison (5/9) The jail's forbidding walls are to your left.

North Carolina State University (7/7) Seen to your right before the train

continues among lakes, streams and hills thick with pine trees.

CARY (14/61) Located in the heart of the Research Triangle region, this is the fifth-fastest-growing city in the US, with the most PhDs per capita of any city larger than 75,000 people. Begun in 1750 as a settlement called Bradford's Ordinary, the coming of the North Carolina Railroad (NCRR) 100 years later placed it on a major transportation route. Amtrak's current station was built in 1996 after Cary's historic station had been demolished in the 1970s.

You continue through the small communities of Merry Oaks and Moncure. On the approach to Southern Pines look left for the corrals where racehorses are prepared.

SOUTHERN PINES (61/30) The train holds up traffic among manicured bushes at a road junction. The large building beyond the station is an arts centre.

HAMLET (30/70) A proud sign proclaims this 'the all-American city'. This was the birthplace of jazz saxophonist John Coltrane, and is located at a major junction of two CSX rail lines. Log trains are set up in rail yards to the right of canopied Main Street Station, which is a registered historic building. Dating from 1900, it was originally called the Seaboard Air Line Passenger Depot. Between 2001 and 2004, its Queen Anne-style station house was moved across a set of tracks for safety reasons, and converted into a museum by the North Carolina Department of Transportation. The station was jacked up, rotated 90° and moved 210ft to its new foundation. Hamlet's **National Railroad Museum and Hall of Fame** is at 120 E Spring Street (☎ *910 582 238*).

After Hamlet, industry gives way again to forests, fields and white-spired churches.

Carolinas state line (7/63) You move from North into South Carolina then cross the Pee Dee River north of Cherub and enter the Sand Hills.

Bethune (50/20) Located just south of the Lynches River, Bethune is one of the country's chief egg producers.

CAMDEN (70/30) Home of three racetracks and the Colonial Cup steeplechase, Camden is among South Carolina's oldest cities, often fought over during the Revolution. A stage of Alexander Graham Bell's first transcontinental telephone call was completed here in 1915.

COLUMBIA (30/55) The state capital since 1786, when government moved to the banks of the Congaree River from Charleston. The Hampton-Preston Mansion shows how Confederate general and statesman Wade Hampton lived in the 19th century. The **visitors bureau** is at 1101 Lincoln (✆ *803 545 0002*). Nearby are Fort Jackson and the state fairgrounds. Look for the stationary red caboose at Amtrak's station.

The **South Carolina Railroad Museum** is 25 miles (40km) to the north at Rockton (✆ *803 635 9893; www.scrm.org*). Locomotives and rolling stock include a Seaboard office car and a hospital/command car. The museum's railroad, known today as the Rockton, Rion & Western, began life in 1883 as the Rock City Railway. Some of America's last steam trains ran between Rockton and Greenbrier, and on the first and third Saturdays from June to October you can take a ride along the restored line.

DENMARK (55/80) A railroad town which is situated in the middle of swampland.

South Carolina–Georgia state line (55/25) You enter what was once Great Britain's 13th colony.

SAVANNAH (80/130) General James Oglethorpe and a group of English colonists founded Savannah on a bluff next to the river in 1733. Tobacco and cotton wealth soon resulted in great warehouses, mansions and a booming cotton exchange. America's first planned city was designed by Oglethorpe, who laid out a grid of streets and filled the squares with mountain laurel, oaks, azaleas and dogwoods. In *Treasure Island*, Robert Louis Stevenson refers to Savannah as a place of beauty and style. It was here, despite the rarity of snow, that James L Pierpoint composed *Jingle Bells*.

The cotton market and prosperity suffered after the Civil War, but 1,000 buildings have been restored. Savannah has lately become better known by appearing as the setting for movies such as *Midnight in the Garden of Good and Evil* and *Forrest Gump*. Bus and carriage tours are available from the **Historic Savannah Foundation** at 321 E York (✆ *912 233 7787; www.myhsf.org*). The **visitor centre** is in a former Central of Georgia railway station at 301 Martin Luther King Boulevard (✆ *912 944 0455; www.savannahvisit.com*).

The **history museum** next to the visitor centre occupies a railway shed on the site of the Siege of Savannah in 1779 (*303 Martin Luther King Jr Blvd;* ✆ *912 651 6825; www.chsgeorgia.org; admission charge*). There are presentations of the siege as well as displays of historic train engines and dining cars. Amtrak's station, built in 1962 by the Atlantic Coast Line Railroad, is four miles (6.5km) from downtown at 2611 Seaboard Coastline Drive.

The *Silver Star* departs through freight yards and travels among swampland, trees, farms and villages. Watch out for egrets and anglers along the banks of the many streams.

Hunter Airfield (5/125) A US Army establishment is seen to your left just before you cross the Ogeechee River.

Richmond Hill (10/120) The car magnate Henry Ford once owned a plantation here.

Altamaha River (45/85) You cross a river which flows into the intracoastal waterway.

JESUP (50/80) The town formed at the intersection of two railroads, the Macon & Brunswick Railroad and the Savannah, Florida & Western Railroad, and named after Morris K Jesup, who financed the line which is now part of the Seaboard Coast Railroad. Others argue that the town's name originated from General Thomas S Jesup, a hero from the American Indian War. This is a scheduled stop for *Silver Meteor* trains. Nearby are Brunswick and St Simons Island. Look for the Jesup Shrimp Inc Building to your right and a very old freight wagon to your left as you pass through town.

After Jesup, the train travels inland through eastern Georgia among more logging operations.

Big Satilla Creek (70/60) You cross the creek and a few minutes later cross the Satilla River.

Folkston (85/45) About 60 trains a day pass through Folkston, drawing many rail fans to the town's specially built viewing platform. West and south of here is the 650-square-mile Okefenokee Swamp and wildlife refuge, where the beguiling scenery and animal life can best be seen from a canoe or by walking the canal trails. Campsites are raised on platforms to outwit alligators.

Georgia–Florida state line (95/35) The *Silver Star* crosses high above the St Mary's River into the Sunshine State, which grows by around 1,000 people a day.

JACKSONVILLE (130/60) An industrial centre that is the largest US city by area, reaching from the St John's River to the Atlantic. The most attractive part of the city is down by the river, with its boardwalk and park. The **Cummer Art Gallery** is in a former lumber baron's mansion and **Jessie Ball du Pont Park** features the 800-year-old Treaty Oak tree under which settlers and Native Americans concluded a truce. The **visitors bureau** is at 208 N Laura (✆ *800 733 2668 or* ✆ *904 421 9156; www. visitjacksonville.com*).

Sunset Limited trains travel west from Amtrak's station at 3570 Clifford Lane to New Orleans and Los Angeles, as well as south to Orlando. The *Silver Star* crawls out of Jacksonville among rail yards, crossovers, warehouses and loading facilities. The St John's River to your left is one of the few which flow 'up' from south to north.

You continue past Doctor's Inlet and Black Creek, then travel through a constantly changing countryside of hardwood forests, lakes and rivers. Palm trees start to appear among the hills.

Ortega River (16/44) You cross with the St John's River still to your left and a marina to your right. Beyond the river you can see the extent of Jacksonville.

US Naval Air Station (20/40) The base is across the highway to your left, alongside an armed forces' reserve centre.

St John's River (35/25) The river appears again among trees to your left as the train goes through a land of woods, Spanish moss, small lakes and alligators. More than 300 species of birds live in this area, including bald eagles, black rails, bridled terns and yellow-breasted chats. Just before Palatka you cross a tributary of the St John's River.

PALATKA (60/52) The name is a Native American word for 'forbidding place'. Exotic palm trees grace the station to your left as the *Silver Star* stops twice to accommodate the train's length. Thruway buses connect with Ocala and Gainesville. Palatka is Amtrak's closest station to St Augustine, the oldest European settlement in the United States.

The train leaves past azalea bushes and holds up traffic at a road crossing – something which happens often on this part of the route. As you cross the St John's River, dairy farms and orchards begin to appear.

Pierson (35/17) 'The fern capital of the world' grows most of America's crop, much of it exported around the world.

DeLeon Springs (46/6) The town was named after Juan Ponce de Leon, a Spanish explorer who discovered Florida in 1512 while on a quest for the fountain of perpetual youth.

DELAND (52/40) Founded by Henry Deland in 1876 and the home of Stetson University (named after the hat maker). A ferry goes from 2309 Riverride Road to Hontoon Island, famous for Timucuan Indian settlements. The station is at 2491 Old New York Avenue, was originally built in 1918, and restored by Amtrak in 1988. Look out for the famous station cat. Thruway buses go to Daytona Beach, 25 miles (40km) east, where the 500 auto races are held each January and February and draw countless fans to the international speedway.

St John's River (12/28) The *Silver Star* crosses on a steel bridge.

Sanford (20/20) After the South Florida Railroad arrived in 1884, joining Sanford to Jacksonville, this became a steamboat port and shipping point for the produce of central Florida. Amtrak's station is at 800 Persimmon Avenue. The *Auto Train* terminates at 600 Persimmon Avenue, where sidings for dealing with cars can be seen to your left.

You travel on among factories and housing estates with a large cement plant to your left. Urban scenes persist most of the way to Winter Park.

WINTER PARK (40/15) The train trundles through the streets of one of Winter Park's quiet, leafy neighbourhoods. The park itself is to your left. Rollins College, the oldest in the state, has a Spanish-style campus and the Cornell Fine Arts Centre. You continue through more suburbs to Orlando.

Florida Hospital (5/10) The imposing structure stands on both sides of the track and is connected by an overhead walkway.

Church Street Station (11/4) The old train station on your left has become part of an entertainment complex, complete with 19th-century steam engine and street parties. Other delights include the Cheyenne Saloon and can-can-dancing waitresses at Rosie O'Grady's Bar. Tours feature the history of the original rail depot (✆ 407 422 2434). Look for the high-rise buildings of Orlando ahead.

ORLANDO (15/20) Tourism has turned a modest agricultural town set among lakes and citrus groves into a 400-square-mile city of a million people. Millions more visitors arrive throughout the year. Don't stray too far from the searchlights of the major attractions or you are almost certain to become lost.

Try to get to the theme parks early – at least half an hour before opening time – when the weather is cooler and fewer people are around. Queues for rides are usually shorter when a parade is on. Take snacks and plastic bottles to fill at the water fountains. Make sure you have a good breakfast before you go to give you energy, and alternate days at the parks with trips to the beach or you may find things too exhausting.

Orlando's daytime temperatures often reach 90°F (32°C) and even the coldest months rarely get below 50°F (10°C). As elsewhere in Florida, humidity can be high.

Orlando basics

✆ **Telephone code** 407

Station (*Ticket office & waiting room* ⏱ *07.30–20.15; information* ✆ *423 4882*) Amtrak's cheerful whitewashed station is at 1400 Sligh Bd. The splendid Mission-style building, lately refurbished, has beautiful columns supporting the platform canopy. Baggage store, vending machines, newspapers, handcarts, Red Caps, taxi stand.

Connection Shuttle buses link to all the Disney resorts & the fare is half that of a taxi.

🚌 **Local transport** Most hotels are some distance from downtown, & the big attractions further still, but there is plenty of scheduled transport. The main companies are Phoenix (✆ *574 7662*) & Gray Line (✆ *522 5911*). LYNX buses operate in Orlando & to the airport (✆ *841 2279*).

Red Line I•RIDE Trolleys (✆ *866 243 7483; www.iridetrolley.com*) travel to International Dr every 20mins & serve the south International Drive Resort area. Green Line trolleys begin & end on International Dr, arriving every 30mins, but primarily travel along Universal Bd.

🚕 **Taxis** Mears Transportation ✆ *422 2222*; Ace Metro ✆ *855 1111*

🚗 **Car rental** Avis ✆ *851 4656*

🚌 **Greyhound** 555 N John Young Parkway; ✆ 292 3424

✈ **Orlando International Airport** 12 miles (19km) south of downtown by LYNX bus #11 & the Mears Shuttle (✆ *423 5566*).

Tours Orlando Tours ✆ *800 303 5107*; Gray Line ✆ *522 5911*

ℹ **Visitors bureau** 8723 International Dr, Suite 101, Orlando, FL 32819; ✆ 363 5872; www. orlandoinfo.com; ⏱ 08.30–18.30 daily

🏠 **Accommodation** Orlando has hundreds of hotels, especially around International Dr (known locally as 'I-Drive'). Rooms on Disney property tend to be more expensive but offer discounts off-season (Sep–Dec). Book well in advance at the Disney Central Reservations Office, Box 10100, Lake Buena Vista, FL 32830-1000 (✆ *934 7639*).

Hotels in Orlando include the Peabody, 9801 International Dr; ✆ 352 4000, **$$$$$**; Renaissance, 6677 Sea Harbour Dr; ✆ 351 5555, **$$$$**; Heritage Inn, 9861 International Dr; ✆ 352 0008, **$$**; Radisson, 8444 International Dr; ✆ 345 0505, **$$**; Ramada, 8342 Jamaican Court; ✆ 363 1944, **$$**.

Recommended in Orlando

Disney World For information, advance tickets & a free guide, contact Box 10100, Lake

Buena Vista, FL 32830; ✆ 939 1289; http:// disneyworld.disney.go.com. This 27,400-acre

17

(11,000ha) complex opened in 1971 & is the world's most popular tourist attraction. Over 30 million visitors come each year & more than 750 million passengers have ridden the world's largest monorail system. Other highlights include the Magic Kingdom (rollercoasters, Mickey Mouse & horrendous queues), the Epcot Center (cutting-edge technology), Disney's Hollywood Studios (animation techniques, classic films & the Star Tours simulator) & 2 water parks: Blizzard Beach & Typhoon Lagoon. Admission is by day ticket or by 'passport' for several days.

The Animal Kingdom is a fantasy zoo with an African savanna safari park conjured out of featureless farmland. Florida oaks have been pruned to resemble acacias & 40,000 other trees planted. Among the 1,700 animals are elephant, black rhino, cheetah & mhorr gazelle, which are extinct in the wild.

Sea World 7007 Sea World Dr, 20 miles (32km) southwest of Orlando; ☎888 800 5447; www. seaworld.com; ☺ daily; admission charge. Features killer whales, stingrays, sea lions, penguins & some of Florida's few remaining manatees. You can hand-feed dolphins & enjoy close encounters with sharks from the safety of a glass tunnel. Take Greyhound or city bus #50.

Universal Studios 1000 Universal Studios Plaza; ☎363 8000; www.universalorlando.com; ☺ daily; admission charge. The largest movie studio & theme park in the world has more than 40 rides, shows & film sets.

The adjacent Islands of Adventure site lets you travel back to Jurassic Park & the Lost Continent. For VIP tours lasting 4hrs, ☎363 8295. Admission to the Islands of Adventure includes entrance to The Wizarding World of Harry Potter with its twin, high-speed rollercoasters.

Lake Eola Park Rosalind & Central; ☎246 2827; ☺ daily; free. A favourite picnic & walking place in central Orlando, with swan-shaped paddle boats for hire on the lake.

Wekiwa Springs State Park 1800 Wekiwa Circle, Apopka, 20mins northwest of downtown; ☎884 2008; www.floridastateparks.org/wekiwasprings; ☺ daily; free. A beautiful park with fishing, camping, swimming & canoeing on the Wekiva River or Rock Springs Run.

Trainland of Orlando 8990 International Dr; ☎363 9002; ☺ daily; admission charge. Includes the world's largest model train layout & live steam passenger rides.

Kennedy Space Center Located at Cape Kennedy (or Cape Canaveral), a 1hr drive to the east; ☎321 449 4444; www.kennedyspacecenter.com; ☺ daily; admission charge. Bus tours take in the museum, rocket garden & shuttle launch site. Includes an IMAX film show, the Astronaut Hall of Fame & a 373ft (124m) *Saturn V* rocket saved by cancellation of the *Apollo* project.

All aboard!

After suburban Orlando, the *Silver Star* heads west among orange groves, lakes, trees and rivers. Florida has plans for a bullet train which would travel the 250 miles between Orlando and Miami in 90 minutes.

KISSIMMEE (20/60) Amtrak's nearest station to Disney World, but Orlando provides more hotels and better local transport connections. Kissimmee was originally built on reclaimed swampland late in the 19th century, and this region is served by a network of rivers, canals and lakes. The oldest cattle auction in Florida takes place in Kissimmee each Wednesday. Amtrak's station is at 416 Pleasant and the **visitors bureau** at 1925 E Irlo Bronson Memorial Highway (☎ *407 742 8200; www.visitkissimmee.com*).

Thruway buses connect with Waldo, Gainesville, Ocala, Wildwood and Dade City. The college town of Gainesville was a major rail junction until the workshops moved away in 1929, and a vintage Seaboard caboose can be seen next to the old railroad station in Waldo. Ocala is one of the state's many centres for training and breeding thoroughbred horses and is close to one of Florida's oldest tourist attractions, **Silver Springs**, with its glass-bottom-boat rides and white alligators

(352 236 2121; *www.silversprings.com*). Nearby is the 366,000-acre (148,000ha) **Ocala Forest Wilderness**. Dade City was formerly Amtrak's stop for the winter resort of Zephyrhills.

As the train pulls out of Kissimmee note the **Monument of the States** among the downtown buildings to your left. This 70ft-high (21m) structure is made out of rocks from every state in the Union.

A few minutes later the *Silver Star* passes Lake Tohopekaliga before continuing among orange groves. Look for bald eagles and wading birds such as white ibis, blue herons and egrets.

Auburndale (20/40) The large citrus juice plants belong to Minute Maid and the Adams Company.

LAKELAND (60/35) *Silver Star* trains stop at Lakeland twice, before and after Tampa. Southbound trains disembark only before Tampa and board only afterwards, while northbound trains reverse this order. The train stops at the attractive 1998 station that replaced a larger Atlantic Coast Line Railroad station west of town. Lakeland Civic Center is to your right and a power plant to your left.

TAMPA (35/35) The name 'Tampa' is a Seminole word for 'sticks of fire'. Settlement began when Fort Brooke was established in 1824, but most of Florida's early tourist development concentrated on the east coast. Henry Plant's railway reached Tampa late in the 19th century, when he built the 'world's most elegant' Tampa Bay Hotel. During the Spanish–American War this became a headquarters for Theodore Roosevelt. Florida's state fair takes place in Tampa each February.

St Petersburg, adjacent to the south, is quieter and more residential. From the resorts along this coast you can see a variety of wildlife including cormorants, pelicans, dolphins and, if you are really lucky, a rare and charming manatee.

Tampa basics

Telephone code 813

Station (*Ticket office & waiting room* ⊕ 08.15–18.15; *information* 221 7600) Amtrak has an Italian-style station at 601 Nebraska Av & Twiggs. Lockers, vending machines, handcarts, taxi stand.

Connections Thruway buses connect with Pinellas-St Petersburg, Orlando, Sarasota, Fort Myers & Clearwater Beach.

Local transport HART buses operate in the Tampa region (254 4278) & the Pinellas Suncoast Transit Authority (PSTA) (727 530 9911) in St Petersburg.

Taxis Yellow 253 0121; Independent 727 327 3444

Car rental Budget, 7223 West Hillsborough Av; 885 8836

Greyhound 610 E Polk; 229 2174

Tampa International Airport 6 miles (10km) from downtown; you can get there by limousine or HART bus. Contact the Super Shuttle (727 572 1111) for transport to St Petersburg's Clearwater Airport.

Tours Swiss Chalet; 985 3601. For dolphin-watching cruises contact Dolphin Landings (727 367 4488).

Visitors bureau 615 Channelside Dr; 223 2752 or 800 44 TAMPA or 1 800 448 2672; www.visittampabay.com; ⊕ 09.30–17.30 Mon–Sat, 11.00–17.00 Sun. Other information centres are located at the Channelside entertainment complex in downtown Tampa (223 2752) & at 13805 58th St N in Clearwater (727 464 7200).

Accommodation Gram's Place, 3109 N Ola Av, is a combination of bed & breakfast & hostel, inspired by the music of Gram Parsons; 221 0596.

Tampa hotels include the Sheraton Tampa Riverwalk, 200 N Ashley Dr; 223 2222, **$$$$**; Best Western Bay Harbor, 7700 Courtney

Campbell Parkway; ☎281 8900, **$$$$**; Hyatt Regency, 2 Tampa City Center; ☎225 1234, **$$$$**; Wyndham Tampa, 700 N Westshore Bd; ☎289 8200, **$$$**; Red Roof Inn, 10121 Horace Av; ☎681 8484, **$$**; Holiday Inn Busch Gardens, 2701 E Fowler Av; ☎936 8200, **$$$**.

Recommended in Tampa

Busch Gardens 3000 E Busch Bd; ☎888 800 5447; www.buschgardens.com; ☺ daily; admission charge. Take bus #5 to Florida's chief tourist attraction after Disney World. The gardens have more than 3,000 birds & animals, with a monorail to transport you among the lions & rhinos.

Ybor City 1600 E Eighth Av; ☎241 8838; www.ybor.org. Tampa's Cuban city-within-a-city features Spanish-style buildings, restaurants & shops. Many of Tampa's first residents were Cuban refugees from the Spanish–American War who brought with them their cigar-making skills. You can see cigars being hand rolled at the Cigar Factory, 1901 13th (☺ *daily; free*). The **Ybor City Museum** is at 1818 E Ninth Av (☎*247 6323; www.ybormuseum.org;* ☺ *daily; admission charge*).

Henry B Plant Museum 401 West Kennedy Bd; ☎254 1891; www.plantmuseum.com; ☺ Tue–Sun; donation. Housed in the 1891 Tampa Bay Hotel, a National Historic Landmark built by the railroad magnate, Henry Bradley Plant. This quintessential Victorian hotel was constructed in flamboyant Turkish & Moorish style with minarets, domes, cupolas, horseshoe arches & long verandas. Filled with opulent European furniture & art, the museum tells the story of the hotel & of Florida's tourist industry.

Tampa Bay History Center 801 Old Water St; ☎228 0097; www.tampabayhistorycenter. org; ☺ daily; admission charge. This history & heritage museum preserves & teaches the history of the Tampa Bay area with exhibits showing the geographical, historical & cultural influences shaping the region from 12,000 years ago to the present.

Tampa Museum of Art 120 W Gasparilla Plaza; ☎274 8130; www.tampamuseum.com; ☺ daily; admission charge. The new museum has a range of 20th-century art as well as a famous collection of Greek & Roman antiquities. Lectures, walking tours & children's activities.

Salvador Dalí Museum 1000 Third S, St Petersburg; ☎727 823 3767; www.salvadordalimuseum.org; ☺ daily; admission charge. The museum claims to have the world's most comprehensive collection of the eccentric Spanish Surrealist's work.

All aboard!

You return across central Florida and approach Lakeland again past a huge Publix warehouse.

LAKELAND (35/20) Home of Florida Southern College, where many of the buildings were designed by Frank Lloyd Wright. This is the centre of a vast citrus fruit region and Lakeland has the state's main trading exchange and juice extraction plants. The world's largest phosphate mine is nearby.

WINTER HAVEN (20/45) A Bordo Citrus plant stands opposite the station.

West Lake Wales (8/37) Beyond a disused station to your left is a 255ft-high (78m) stone and marble carillon called the **Bok Tower**. The tallest structure in Florida, this neo-Gothic and Art Deco structure was named after E W Bok, the influential editor of *Ladies' Home Journal* around the turn of the century. The Singing Tower's 60 bronze bells weigh up to 12 tons each.

Frostproof (25/20) White beehives can be seen among the orange trees. The town failed to live up to its name in the winter of 1983, when the local crop was severely damaged.

SEBRING (45/30) Farming, packing and distribution were established here in the early 1900s. The famous international motor racing track is to your left.

Lake Istokpoga (7/23) The lake is visible among trees to your right before you cross the Kissimmee River, on course between Lake Kissimmee and Lake Okeechobee (the largest lake in the southern United States). On the far side is the swamp wilderness of **Everglades National Park**, where alligators lurk among floating islands of sawgrass and reed.

OKEECHOBEE (30/50) The name is a Hitchiti Indian word for 'big water'. A few minutes later you pass the dykes restraining Lake Okeechobee on your right.

The *Silver Star* travels for the next 59 miles (95km) through cattle country at up to 79mph (127km/h) on the longest straight stretch of track east of the Mississippi. It takes an eight-car passenger train approximately 1.13 miles (1.8km) to stop when travelling at this speed. Look for a Florida Steel factory to your right.

Indiantown (25/25) The town was named after Seminole Indians. The train rattles across a bridge over the St Lucie Canal connecting Lake Okeechobee with the Atlantic.

United (33/17) The airfield is owned by Pratt and Whitney.

WEST PALM BEACH (50/20) This is the start of Florida's Gold Coast, with its mansions, condominiums, posh shops and polo fields. Three bridges link West Palm Beach with the island community of Palm Beach. Clear Lake is to your right. Amtrak's beautiful Spanish-style station on your left at 201 S Tamarind Avenue opened in 1925 as a Seaboard Air Line Railroad depot and also served the Florida East Coast Railway. The Seaboard Air Line (motto 'Through the heart of the South') was the main rival to the Atlantic Coast Line for luxury services between New York and Florida and its *Cherry Blossom Special* was the first air-conditioned train on this route.

The **Flagler Museum** in Palm Beach honours Henry Morrison Flagler, founder of the Florida East Coast Railway. When his line, some of which was built by slaves from the Bahamas, reached the island of Palm Beach he set about creating the most exclusive resort in the country by constructing the Breakers Hotel, where string orchestras and opera singers such as Dame Nellie Melba were imported to entertain his rich friends. The present Renaissance-style hotel is a 'palace by the sea' built on the original site of Flagler's hotel in the 1920s. It boasts 567 rooms, 140 acres of gardens and two golf courses.

The opulent Flagler Museum is located in his stately Whitehall mansion at Cocoanut Row and Whitehall Way (✆ *561 655 2833; www.flagler.org*) and features an Italian Renaissance library, Louis XIV music room, Elizabethan breakfast room, Swiss billiard room and a dining room imported from Warwick Castle in England. In Palm Beach you can also find the Estée Lauder mansion, the Kennedy compound and a former home of John and Yoko Lennon.

You leave West Palm Beach past the airport to your right. Plans to expand the runways were blocked when a population of rare gopher tortoises was discovered. The train continues among houses and waterways, interrupted by the occasional industrial scene.

DELRAY BEACH (20/10) An attractive, low-key resort which began as a settlement for artists. Delray Beach is the home of Florida's tennis championships and the

Morikami Museum of Japanese Art (*4000 Morikami Park Rd*; ☏ *561 495 0233; www.morikami.org; admission charge*).

Boca Raton (4/6) Another airport appears to your left. Boca Raton's dusty pink buildings were created by the architect Addison Mizner in a mixture of European styles and have an authentic 1920s atmosphere. Set among palm trees, shady cloisters and herb gardens, this is one of the few places on the coast where beaches and dunes remain in their natural state.

DEERFIELD BEACH (10/15) Palm trees line both sides of the track as you approach the station. The **South Florida Railway Museum** (*1300 W Hillsboro Beach Bd in Deerfield*; ☏ *954 698 6620; www.sfrm.org; admission charge*) is located in the historic former Seaboard Air Line station. The building is a fine example of Mediterranean-style architecture, with an arched entryway, stucco walls and a barrel tile roof. The museum preserves the history of railroads in southern Florida and has two impressive model railroad layouts.

Pompano Beach Racetrack (5/10) Harness racers and Quarter Horses use the track to your right.

FORT LAUDERDALE (15/12) One of Florida's main resorts, 'America's Venice' is also well known as a regular port of call for cruise ships. Named after the governor responsible for early Everglades drainage schemes, Fort Lauderdale has eight miles of beaches. An intricate system of waterways makes yachting a common mode of transport. **Ocean World** features sea lions and sharks.

The **visitors bureau** is at 100 E Broward Boulevard (☏ *954 765 4466*). Amtrak's station at 200 SW 21st Terrace opens to the street, and is a busy stop during summer and in the spring break for colleges and universities. You leave past an airport to your left.

HOLLYWOOD (12/20) This eastern Hollywood was founded during the 1920s and grew rapidly until the 1960s. Port Everglades is the second-busiest cruise port in the world. Look for the colourful water tower and a Hollywood Boulevard sign to your left. Tri-Rail commuter trains provide frequent services between Hollywood and Miami International Airport.

You continue past the Opa-Locka flea market and a racetrack at Hialeah. Approaching Miami, look for Miami Beach's hotels away to your left beyond an expanse of junked cars. Freight yards sprawl away complicatedly on the right of the line.

MIAMI America's Casablanca was founded for growing citrus fruits. Only a handful of people lived here when oil billionaire Henry Flagler's Central Florida Railroad arrived in 1896, following a deal struck in a room above a pool hall between Flagler and the visionary Julia Tuttle, who owned the land. Tourism development in the 1920s and the pretty hotels of Miami Beach (10 miles/16km long and 300ft/90m wide) now attract ten million sun lovers and fashion victims every year. More than $1.6 billion has been invested in new hotels on Miami Beach in recent years, including the 789ft (240m) Four Seasons Hotel, the tallest building in Florida.

Greater Miami incorporates Key Biscayne (home of President Nixon's winter White House), upmarket Coral Gables, Hialeah and the elegant Coconut Grove. Half the city's two million population is of Spanish-American descent.

Temperatures can reach 90°F (over 30°C) even in winter, which is the peak season and avoids summer's humidity and showers. Spring and late autumn are the best times to visit.

Miami basics

✆Telephone code 305

≈≈ Station (*Ticket office & waiting room ⊕ 07.00–21.00*) Amtrak's station at 8303 NW 37th Av in Hialeah has bus links to downtown (7 miles/12km south) & Miami Beach. Metropolitan lounge. Lockers, vending machines, newspapers, handcarts, Red Caps, taxi stand. Take bus L for Miami Beach. Amtrak plans to move to the new Miami Central Station, 4 miles west of downtown, which when completed will act as a hub for Amtrak, Tri-Rail & Metrorail.

Connections Tri-Rail trains (✆ *1 800 872 7245*) go to Fort Lauderdale & West Palm Beach.

🚌Local transport Metro-Dade buses run throughout Miami, with free maps & other information from 111 NW First (✆ *891 3131*). Metrorail trains operate every day, with transfers to Metrobus, & its Northside station is close to Amtrak's depot.

🚕 Taxis Metro ✆ 888 8888

🚗 Car rental Avis, 2318 Collins Av; ✆ 538 4441

🚌Greyhound 4111 NW 27th St; ✆ 871 1810

✈ Miami International Airport 8 miles (13km) west by Metrobus #7 & Super Shuttle vans (✆ *871 2000*). Some hotels provide free taxis.

Tours American Sightseeing ✆ 954 463 4805. Boat cruises on the *Island Queen* start from Miamarina, Fifth & Biscayne Bay (✆ *379 5119*).

i Visitors bureau 701 Brickell Av; ✆ 800 933 8448; www.gmcvb.com; ⊕ Mon–Fri. More information from the Chambers of Commerce at Key Biscayne (✆ *361 5207*), Coconut Grove (✆ *444 7270*), Miami Beach (✆ *674 1414*) & the Everglades Visitor Association (✆ *245 9180*).

🏠 Accommodation Miami has an abundance of rooms, from the economical to the ultra-luxurious. Top rates & biggest crowds are in winter, when prices can double. Contact the Miami Beach Hotel Association, 407 Lincoln Rd; ✆ 800 531 3553; www.gmbha.org.

Miami Beach Clay Hotel & International Hostel, 1438 Washington Av, in the historic district; ✆ 534 2988. Take bus #103 from downtown. Members & non-members, **$**.

Downtown hotels include the Hyatt Regency, 400 SE Second Av; ✆ 358 1234, **$$$$**; Holiday Inn Port Of Miami, 340 Biscayne Bd; ✆ 0871 423 4917, **$$$**; Ramada Inn at Dupont Plaza, 300 Biscayne Bd Way; ✆ 358 2541, **$$$**. Courtyard Miami Downtown, 200 SE Second Av; ✆ 374 3000 or ✆ 800 319 4927, **$$$**.

Miami Beach hotels include the Alexander, 5225 Collins Av; ✆ 865 6500, **$$$$$**; Seville Beach, 2901 Collins Av; ✆ 532 2511, **$$$**; Thunderbird, 18401 Collins Av; ✆ 931 7700, **$$$**; Tudor, 1111 Collins Av; ✆ 534 2934, **$$**; Sagamore, 1671 Collins Av; ✆ 535 8088, **$$$$$**; Adrian, 1060 Ocean Dr; ✆ 538 0007, **$$**.

Recommended in Miami

Art Deco District From Sixth to 23rd sts, Miami Beach. Over 800 pastel-coloured buildings with 'eyebrow' balconies & Egyptian architraves make this the world's largest collection of Art Deco architecture. Walking tours start from the Art Deco Welcome Center at 1001 Ocean Drive (✆ *531 3484*).

Wolfsonian Foundation 1001 Washington, in the Art Deco District; ✆ 531 1001; www.wolfsonian.org; ⊕ daily; admission charge. The restored building contains 70,000 cultural items from the 1880s through to the present, including furniture, murals & World War II propaganda.

Seaquarium 4400 Rickenbacker Causeway, on Key Biscayne; ✆ 361 5705; www.miamiseaquarium.com; ⊕ daily; admission charge. The ocean aquarium stars alligators, dolphins, sharks, manatees, stingrays & killer whales.

Vizcaya Museum and Gardens 3251 S Miami Av, in Coconut Grove; ✆ 250 9133; www.vizcayamuseum.org; ⊕ daily; admission charge. An Italianate palace built on the bay as a winter residence by the millionaire James Deering in 1916, with antique Renaissance furnishings brought from Europe. Formal gardens & fountains surround the house.

Historical Museum of Southern Florida 101 W Flagler; ☎375 1492; www.hmsf.org; ☺ daily; admission charge. Located in the Cultural Center, the museum shows Miami's past with hands-on displays & special exhibits. Walking & boat tours are available Sep–Jun.

Metrozoo 12400 SW 152nd; ☎251 0400; www.miamimetrozoo.com; ☺ daily; admission charge. This 327-acre (132ha) zoo features over 2,000 animals, including clouded leopards & Komodo dragons – the largest, most powerful lizards in the world. The zoo has over 70 species of birds, 15,000 Italian honeybees, & more than 1,000 species of trees, palms & other plants, including orchids. Most animals are uncaged on small islands made to resemble their natural habitats. The amphitheatre has wildlife shows throughout the day.

Gold Coast Railroad Museum Near the Metrozoo at 12450 SW 152nd; ☎ 253 0063; www.gcrm.org; ☺ daily; admission charge. Among several Pullman cars displayed is the *Ferdinand Magellan*, used by presidents from Franklin Roosevelt to Ronald Reagan. The steam engines here once belonged to the Florida East Coast Railway. Half-hour train rides at w/ends.

Little Havana Almost a 10th of Cuba's population has settled around Calle Ocho (SW Eighth St) after fleeing Fidel Castro's island, some braving the shark-inhabited Florida Straits on flimsy rafts. Family stores & cantinas are named after Havana streets & this is one of the few places in Miami where people still walk. More information is available from the Little Havana Merchants Association (☎ *428 2758*).

The Cuban Museum of Arts & Culture is at 1300 SW 12th Av (☎ *858 8006*; ☺ *daily; donation*).

Key West Henry Flagler set out to create modern Florida by constructing his East Coast Railway from Jacksonville to the end of the Keys, from where boats would continue to Havana & the Bahamas. He spent $18 million on the railroad, some $12 million on hotels & $10 million on the Key West extension. This continuation – 114 miles/182km long with 17 miles/27km of bridges – was completed in 1912 but a nameless hurricane destroyed the line in 1936.

The right of way now forms the base for a spectacular highway down which Greyhound buses travel from Miami to Ernest Hemingway's old haunts. For visitor information contact the Key West Chamber of Commerce, 510 Greene St, Key West, FL 33040 (☎ *305 294 2587; www.keywestchamber.org*).

18

The *Silver Meteor*
New York–Miami

General route information

The Seaboard Air Line Railroad's original *Silver Meteor*, named in a public contest, began services between New York and St Petersburg in 1939. Today's *Silver Meteor* still travels the eastern part of the United States between New York and Florida, visiting Charleston in South Carolina. Like the *Silver Star* and *Palmetto*, it takes in the nation's capital, the Carolinas and Old Savannah.

Joining the train

NEW YORK For New York City and the route to Washington, see *Chapter 14, The Northeast Corridor* (pages 173–89). For the route from Washington to Rocky Mount, see *Chapter 17, The Silver Star* (pages 202–16).

ROCKY MOUNT (80/80) North Carolina grows the biggest tobacco crop in America and much of it comes here to be traded, along with cotton and other produce.

Wilson (20/60) Tobacco warehouses and curing facilities can be seen on both sides of the track.

Selma (45/35) The *Silver Meteor* continues on the Seaboard Line through tobacco, cotton and soya bean fields.

ESSENTIAL INFORMATION

FREQUENCY Daily. The **southbound** service leaves New York mid afternoon to arrive in Washington by early evening and Charleston very early next day. You reach Jacksonville early in the morning, Orlando around midday and Miami by early evening. Travelling **north**, trains leave Miami early in the morning to reach Orlando by early afternoon and Jacksonville late afternoon. You arrive in Charleston late evening, Washington early next morning and New York by late morning.
DURATION 28+ hours
RESERVATIONS All reserved
EQUIPMENT Amfleet coaches. Movies are shown in coaches, with headphones available for purchase.
SLEEPING Viewliner bedrooms
FOOD Complete meals, snacks, sandwiches, drinks
BAGGAGE Check-in service at most stations.

NEW YORK CITY □

For New York City
and the route to
Rocky Mount, see
The Northeast Corridor
and *Silver Star*

Rocky Mount ○

N
Bradt

Fayetteville ○

Florence ○

Kingstree ○
CHARLESTON ○

Yemassee ○

○
SAVANNAH

For Savannah to
Kissimmee, see
The Silver Star

○ Kissimmee
○ Winter
Haven

For Winter Haven
to Miami, see
The Silver Star

□
MIAMI

Smithfield (60/20) You travel past the birthplace of Ava Gardner then cross the Cape Fear River.

FAYETTEVILLE (80/80) The train crosses Hope Mill Lake at this farming town founded by 18th-century Scottish immigrants. Nearby is Fort Bragg, home of the US Army's 82nd Airborne Division and Delta Force.

Pembroke (25/55) Home of Pembroke State University, the town is located on the banks of the Lumbee River.

Carolinas state line (35/45) You cross from North to South Carolina just before the town of Hamer. You then cross the Little Pee Dee River.

Dillon (45/35) Dillon used to be a haunt of Francis Marion, the 'Swamp Fox' of the Revolutionary War. This is a scheduled stop for the *Palmetto*.

The *Silver Meteor* crosses the Great Pee Dee River 20 minutes later and travels over an area of swampland.

FLORENCE (80/30) General W W Harllee, President of the Wilmington & Manchester Railroad, built his home at the junction of the W&M and the Northeastern and named the town after his daughter. During the Civil War the town was an important railroad repair centre for the Confederacy, transporting troops, artillery and supplies. Florence today is the home of Francis Marion College and the extensive Coast Line yards handle mostly cotton, tobacco and corn. Thruway buses link to Conway and Myrtle Beach.

Amtrak's modern CSX station was built in the same style as the much larger old depot standing next to it, which was bought by the McLoud Regional Medical Center and has been returned to its former magnificence. Look for a steam locomotive parked on your right soon after you leave.

You cross the Lynches River ten minutes from Florence and travel among the farms of the coastal plain. Note the distinctively shaped barns used for storing tobacco.

KINGSTREE (30/45) Amtrak's station was built by the Atlantic Coast Line Railroad in 1909, and is part of the Kingstree Historic District. The building also houses a restaurant. A few minutes later you cross the Black River close to where Robert Mitchum was born. Mitchum's father was a half Blackfoot Indian who died while working as a train brakeman when two cars collided and crushed him.

Santee River (10/35) You cross the river then continue beside **Francis Marion Forest** to your left. Swamps, oak trees, pines and lakes cover an expanse of 250,000 acres (100,000ha). Marion earned his nickname, the 'Swamp Fox', by raiding from these marshlands. He was a master of the surprise attack, never camping in the same place for more than two nights.

Lake Moultrie (20/25) The lake is behind the levee to your left, with Lake Marion further inland. You cross the Cooper River on its way from Lake Moultrie to Charleston, then pass Strawberry Corner shrubs nursery.

CHARLESTON (45/45) Founded in 1670 where the Cooper and Ashley rivers meet on the Atlantic coast, Charleston's position made it one of the most prosperous early American ports and for a time the fourth-largest settlement in the American colonies. Further growth came with the start of America's first train service in 1830, which locals called 'the best friend of Charleston'.

Hundreds of merchants' houses survive and many can be visited during the spring festival. Down on the waterfront you can see spectacular sunsets and watch gulls glide over Battery Park. Charleston's brightly coloured mansions and cobblestone streets have recovered from the hurricane which devastated the city in 1989. For information contact the **Historic Foundation** (*40 E Bay;* ✆ *723 1623; www.historiccharleston.org*).

Charleston basics

✆ **Telephone code** 843
🚉 **Station** (*Ticket office & waiting room* ⏲ *04.05–12.00 & 16.15–23.30; information* ✆ *744 8264*) Amtrak's station is at 4565 Gaynor Av in north Charleston, 7 miles (11km) from downtown (take the Durant Av bus).
Connections No Thruway bus.
🚌 **Local transport** CARTA buses & trolleys (✆ *724 7420; www.ridecarta.com*) operate downtown.
🚕 **Taxis** Yellow ✆ 577 6565. For the Pedicab bicycle cab service, ✆ 577 7088.
🚗 **Car rental** Triangle, 1573 Sam Rittenberg Bd; ✆ 556 1255
🚌 **Greyhound** 3610 Dorchester Rd; ✆ 744 5341
Tours Charleston Tours Inc; ✆ 571 0049. Talk of the Towne; ✆ 888 795 8199. Carriage rides from The Old South Carriage Company (✆ *723 9712*).

ℹ️ **Visitors bureau** 375 Meeting; ✆ 800 774 0006; www.charlestoncvb.com; ⏲ daily, with film shows
🏠 **Accommodation** Contact Historic Charleston Bed & Breakfast, 57 Broad St, Charleston, SC 29401; ✆ 722 6606. Rutledge Victoria Inn, 114 Rutledge Av; ✆ 722 7551, **$$**.

Hotels are expensive downtown but reasonably priced motels can be found across the Ashley River on US 17. Downtown hotels include Best Western King Charles Inn, 237 Meeting; ✆ 723 7451, **$$$$$**; Days Inn, 155 Meeting; ✆ 722 8411 or ✆ 866 723 5361, **$$$$**; Holiday Inn, 125 Calhoun; ✆ 805 7900, **$$$**; Meeting Street Inn, 173 Meeting; ✆ 723 1882 or ✆ 1 800 842 8022, **$$$**; Renaissance, 68 Wentworth; ✆ 534 0300, **$$$$**; Francis Marion, 387 King; ✆ 722 0600, **$$$$**.

Recommended in Charleston

Charleston Museum 360 Meeting; ✆ 722 2996; www.charlestonmuseum.org; ⏲ daily; admission charge. America's 1st museum, begun in 1773, has snuffboxes & silverware among its half a million items. Tickets also give admission to the Joseph Manigault House (an Adam-style mansion) & the 1772 Heyward-Washington House.

St Michael's Church At Broad & Meeting; ✆ 723 0603; www.stmichaelschurch.net. The oldest of Charleston's 181 churches resembles St Martin-in-the-Fields, London. City Hall, the Federal Court, the post office & the County Court House occupy the other '4 corners of law'.
Charles Towne Landing Park 1500 Old Towne Rd, on the site of the first settlement;

18

852 4200; www.charlestowne.org or www. southcarolinaparks.com. The park has trails, a reconstructed village, a sailing ship & an enclosure with wolves & bears.

Fort Sumter 1214 Middle, Sullivan's Island; 883 3123; www.nps.gov/fosu. A short boat ride from the municipal marina. The Civil War began here in 1861 when the garrison surrendered to Confederate general Pierre Beauregard after 2 days of bombardment. Tours of the restored buildings.

Gibbes Museum of Art 135 Meeting; 722 2706; www.gibbesmuseum.org; ☺ Tue–Sun; admission charge. The collection includes American paintings, prints, & drawings from the 18th century to the present, including views of Charleston & portraits of famous South Carolinian citizens. The museum also has miniatures & Japanese prints.

The Best Friend Museum 456 King St, close to the visitor center; 973 7269; ☺ daily; free. The museum has a full-size replica of the *Best Friend of Charleston* – the first (1830) US train to operate in regular passenger service. The engine was constructed from the original plans in 1928 to commemorate the 100th anniversary of the South Carolina Canal & Rail Road Company. Although temporarily on loan to Norfolk Southern for display in their Atlanta GA office building , the steam engine will eventually be permanently placed in a glass-enclosed building on John St, behind the visitor center.

Old Exchange and Provost Dungeon 122 E Bay; 727 2165; www.oldexchange.com; ☺ daily; admission charge. Built in 1771 by the British as the Exchange & Customs House, American Patriots were held prisoner here during the Revolutionary War. You can see part of the Charles Towne sea wall built to defend the colony from pirates in the 17th century.

Drayton Hall 3380 Ashley River Rd; 769 2600; www.draytonhall.org; ☺ daily; admission charge. Completed in 1742, this is the only plantation house remaining on the Ashley River that survived the Revolutionary & Civil wars, & its Georgian Palladian architecture contains much of the original 18th-century craftsmanship. Guided tours & nature walks.

Magnolia Plantation 3550 Ashley River Rd; 800 367 3517; www.magnoliaplantation.com; ☺ daily; admission charge. This pre-Revolutionary War plantation house has fine American antiques & the estate boasts America's oldest gardens, dating from 1680 & featuring azaleas & camellias. Boat rides, wildlife observation tower, art gallery & birdwatching walks.

All aboard!

The *Silver Meteor* pulls out of Charleston among substantial rail yards. You cross the Ashley River before continuing south along the coastal plain.

Jacksonboro (25/20) The town was named after Andrew Jackson. You cross the Edisto River, then the Salkehatchie, Ashepoo and Combahee rivers *en route* to Yemassee.

YEMASSEE (45/45) The town was named after Yemassee Indians. The Charleston & Western Carolina Railroad built the plain-looking station in 1955, and there are plans to restore it to an early 20th-century style. Between 1914 and 1964, when the Marine Corps used the Yemassee depot as a gateway to its basic training at Parris Island, more than 500,000 recruits passed through the station.

Interstate 95 (5/40) The train passes under a highway which runs all the way down the east coast from Maine to Miami.

Savannah River (30/15) Look right for a concrete highway bridge as the train crosses the river into Georgia.

SAVANNAH For Savannah city information and the remainder of the route to Miami, see *Chapter 17, The* Silver Star (pages 202–16).

19

The Northeast Corridor Boston–Newport News

General route information

Three trains a day make the journey from Boston to Washington, following a route formerly taken by the overnight *Twilight Shoreliner*. You follow the Northeast Corridor route to Washington, DC, then travel through Virginia to the state capital. After Richmond, trains turn east towards Newport News on the Atlantic coast, taking in historic Williamsburg and the tidewater region.

Joining the train

BOSTON For Boston city information, the route to Washington and Washington city information, see *Chapter 14, The Northeast Corridor* (pages 187–9). For the Washington to Richmond route, see *Chapter 16, The Crescent,* and *Chapter 17, The Silver Star* (pages 192–201 and 202–16 respectively).

Virginia Science Museum (65/5) Look right for the museum's dome. Housed in the Seaboard Line's former Broad Street Station is a planetarium and space theatre.

RICHMOND (70/50) The beautifully restored Main Street station was built in 1901 by the Seaboard Air Line Railroad (SAL) and the Chesapeake & Ohio Railway (C&O). There are plans to bring Amtrak's *Silver Service* trains to this ornate station with its splendid clock tower.

Trains continue south from Richmond on the Seaboard Coast Line.

James River (2/48) You glimpse the James River to your right before the train crosses a canal and passes through more Chessie yards at Fulton.

ESSENTIAL INFORMATION

FREQUENCY Three trains daily. The **southbound** service leaves Boston early morning, mid morning or late evening to Newport News by early evening, mid morning or midday. Travelling **north**, trains leave Newport News late afternoon or early morning to reach Boston by early morning or late evening.

DURATION 12 hours 15 minutes

RESERVATIONS All reserved

EQUIPMENT Amfleet coaches. Business Class.

FOOD Tray meals, snacks, sandwiches, drinks

BAGGAGE No check-in service

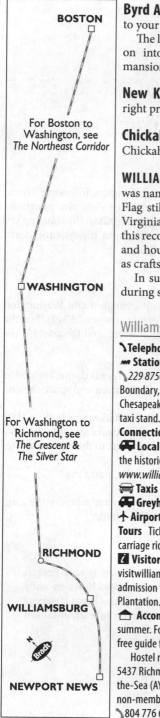

BOSTON

For Boston to
Washington, see
The Northeast Corridor

WASHINGTON

For Washington to
Richmond, see
*The Crescent &
The Silver Star*

RICHMOND

WILLIAMSBURG

NEWPORT NEWS

Byrd Airport (25/40) Aircraft and runways can be seen to your left.

The landscape now becomes flatter as the train continues on into Virginia's tidewater region. Elegant plantation mansions stand next to the river.

New Kent (45/20) The forestry establishment to your right produces thousands of fledgling pine trees.

Chickahominy River (50/15) Seen to your right, the Chickahominy flows towards the James River.

WILLIAMSBURG (65/25) America's largest restored town was named after King William III of Britain, and the Union Flag still flies on the Capitol Building. The town became Virginia's capital in 1699. You can recapture colonial days in this reconstruction of 500 public buildings, taverns, gardens and houses. Costumed townspeople drive carriages, work as craftsmen and add appropriate atmosphere.

In summer it can be hot, humid and crowded, so visit during spring or autumn if possible.

Williamsburg basics

Telephone code 757

Station (*Ticket office & waiting room* ⊕ *07.30–22.00; information* ✆ *229 8750*) Amtrak uses the Williamsburg Transportation Center at 468 N Boundary, located in an elegant restored building formerly owned by the Chesapeake & Ohio Railway (C&O). Lockers, vending machines, handcarts, taxi stand.

Connections No Thruway bus.

Local transport Buses from the visitor center go to most parts of the historic area, best seen by strolling among the buildings (✆ *220 5493; www.williamsburgtransport.com*).

Taxis Yellow Cab ✆ 722 1111

Greyhound Located next to Amtrak's station; ✆ 229 1460

Airport The airport is 16 miles (26km) by bus or taxi from the station.

Tours Tickets are available at the Lumber House (✆ *229 1000*) for carriage rides & walking tours.

Visitors bureau 421 N Boundary; ✆ 229 6511; www. visitwilliamsburg.com or www.history.org; ⊕ Mon–Fri. Passes give admission to all the historic buildings as well as to Carter's Grove Plantation.

Accommodation Rooms are expensive & can be hard to find in summer. For up-to-date information, including guesthouses, pick up a free guide from the visitor center.

Hostel rooms are available at the Pineapple Inn and Housing Center, 5437 Richmond Rd, Williamsburg, VA 23188; ✆ 259 9670. Sangraal-by-the-Sea (AYH) Hostel, 30 miles (48km) away on Route 626. Members & non-members, **$**. Contact 907 Carlton Rd, Route 626, Wake, VA 23176; ✆ 804 776 6500.

Hotel rooms in Williamsburg itself should be booked well in advance. Contact the Williamsburg Foundation, PO Box 1776, Williamsburg, VA 23187-1776; ☎229 1000. Hotels include the Williamsburg Inn, 136 E Francis; ☎229 1000, $$$$$; Crowne Plaza, 6945 Pocahontas Trail; ☎220 2250, $$$; Quality Inn-Colony, 309 Page; ☎229 1855, $$; La Quinta Inn, 814 Capitol Landing Rd; ☎229 0200, $$$; Governor's Inn, 506 N Henry; ☎229 1000, $$; Motel 6, 824 Capitol Landing Rd; ☎259 1948, $$.

Recommended in Williamsburg

College of William and Mary At the end of Duke of Gloucester St is the country's 2nd-oldest college, where Jefferson studied law & the Phi Beta Kappa Society began. Includes the Wren Building (1695) & the President's House (1734).

The Capitol At the other end of Duke of Gloucester St is the place where Patrick Henry denounced King George III's stamp tax. Other buildings include the Raleigh Tavern, the Governor's Palace, the Magazine, Bruton Parish Church & the James Anderson House.

US Army Transportation Museum 300 Washington Bd in Fort Eustis, 20 miles (32km) south of Williamsburg; ☎878 1115; ☉ Tue–Sun; free. Featuring a railroad ambulance car, a hospital kitchen car & an industrial crane, as well as automobiles, motorcycles, aircraft & a marine park.

Busch Gardens 1 Busch Gardens Bd; ☎800 343 7946; www.buschgardens.com; ☉ Mar–Oct daily; admission charge. Voted 'America's most beautiful theme park' for many years in succession, Busch Gardens has also been called

'America's favourite theme park', edging out Disneyland.

Yorktown On Route 31 S at the Colonial Parkway, 10mins from Williamsburg; ☎253 4838 or ☎888 593 4682; www.historyisfun. org; ☉ daily; admission charge. Settled in 1630, Yorktown became a port & trading centre for the tobacco industry, & the Revolutionary War ended here in 1781 with the defeat of Lord Cornwallis. The battlefield is much visited & many colonial buildings survive or have been reconstructed. The **Victory Center** has displays & films.

Historic Jamestowne Reached from Yorktown along the Colonial Parkway; ☎898 3400; www. nps.gov/colo; ☉ daily; admission charge. Part of the historic triangle, along with Yorktown & Williamsburg. English settlers established the New World's first legislature here in 1619, although the old church tower is all that remains standing. Also featured are the Tercentenary Monument, a Confederate fort, replicas of settlers' ships & the foundations of the first state house. Tours by national park rangers.

All aboard!

You depart Williamsburg with the historic district to your right.

Busch Gardens (5/20) Look right also for this Old Country theme park, complete with steam train.

Lee Hall (15/10) Trains no longer stop at the restored station. Soon after passing through Lee Hall you cross a part of the local reservoir.

NEWPORT NEWS Founded in 1619 on a harbour shared with Norfolk, Portsmouth and Hampton roads, where the James, York, Elizabeth and Nansemond rivers flow into Chesapeake Bay (14 miles/22km long and 40ft/12m deep). Newport News boasts the world's largest shipbuilding yard and biggest naval base.

The **Mariners' Museum** (100 Museum Dr; ☎757 596 2222; www.marinersmuseum. org; admission charge) features an outstanding nautical collection and the **War Museum** (9285 Warwick Blvd; ☎ 757 247 8523; www.warmuseum.org; admission charge) has weapons, uniforms and vehicles from the American Revolution to

Vietnam. In Newport News Park you can enjoy boating, fishing and camping. Amtrak's station is at 9304 Warwick Boulevard, from where Thruway buses link to Norfolk and Virginia Beach in Virginia. For information on attractions throughout the peninsula, contact the **visitor center** at 13560 Jefferson Avenue (☏ *757 886 7777 or* ☏ *888 493 7386; www.newport-news.org*).

The *Cardinal*
New York–Chicago

General route information

The *Cardinal*'s 1,147-mile (1,844km) journey takes you through some of America's finest scenery, going from New York City to Washington, DC, then across Virginia to the Blue Ridge Mountains and Shenandoah Valley. You travel west through the Appalachians, the Ohio River Valley and Cincinnati, before crossing the cornfields of central Indiana to Chicago. The *Cardinal* operates over a route formerly used by the *Sportsman* train and the stately *George Washington*, which with its elegant dining cars was the premier passenger service of the Chesapeake & Ohio Railway.

Joining the train

NEW YORK For New York City information, see *Chapter 14, The Northeast Corridor* (pages 179–82). For the route from New York to Charlottesville, see *Chapter 16, The* Crescent (pages 192–201). The *Cardinal* operates between New York and Washington on Amtrak, between Washington and Alexandria on CSX Transportation, between Alexandria and Culpeper on Norfolk Southern, between

ESSENTIAL INFORMATION

FREQUENCY Three trains a week in each direction. The **westbound** service leaves New York early on Sunday, Wednesday and Friday mornings to reach Washington by midday and Charleston mid evening. You arrive in Cincinnati during the night and Indianapolis early the next morning, reaching Chicago mid morning on Monday, Thursday or Saturday. Travelling **east**, trains leave Chicago early evening on Tuesday, Thursday and Saturday to reach Indianapolis around midnight and Cincinnati during the night. You arrive in Charleston early in the morning, Washington early evening and New York late on Wednesday, Friday or Sunday evening.
DURATION 26 hours 30 minutes
RESERVATIONS All reserved
EQUIPMENT Amfleet coaches
SLEEPING Viewliner bedrooms
LOUNGE CAR Movies, hospitality hour. During summer months a CP Huntington Railroad Society guide joins the eastbound train between Charleston and White Sulphur Springs to provide a scenic commentary.
FOOD Complete meals, snacks, sandwiches, drinks
BAGGAGE No check-in service. Bicycle racks available (reservation required).

NEW YORK CITY

N- Bradt

For New York City to
Charlottesville, see
The Crescent

CHARLOTTESVILLE

Staunton

Clifton
Forge
White Sulphur
Springs
Alderson
Hinton
Prince
Thurmond
Montgomery
Charleston

Huntington
Ashland
South
Portsmouth
Maysville
CINCINNATI

Connersville

INDIANAPOLIS

Crawfords-
ville
Lafayette
Rensselaer
Dyer

CHICAGO

Culpeper and Clifton Forge on Buckingham Branch, between Clifton Forge and Dyer on CSX Transportation, and between Dyer and Chicago on Norfolk Southern.

CHARLOTTESVILLE (60/55) Note the colonnaded soccer ground to your right as the *Cardinal* leaves through residential and commercial suburbs, passing over the main street on a trestle. You follow US 250 for some way through western Virginia, travelling among farms, orchards and forests and beginning a steep climb into the Blue Ridge Mountains. It was on this highly demanding route that the Chesapeake & Ohio Railway chose to introduce the first of its powerful American-type steam locomotives in 1911.

The idyllic Shenandoah Valley to your right is the home of bear, bobcat, fox and 200 species of birds. Skyline Drive goes along 100 miles (160km) of mountain ridge, where there are spectacular changes of colour during autumn.

The train passes through Crozet and East Braham then a long tunnel, the first of many on this route, climbing another stiff bank before beginning the descent towards Staunton.

Waynesboro (35/20) After passing this small town beside the river the *Cardinal* continues among cattle and sheep farms with pretty mountains to your right.

Interstate 81 (52/3) Look for a neoclassical building on your right as you pass beneath two highway bridges.

STAUNTON (55/70) Named after English-born Lady Rebecca Staunton, wife of colonial governor Sir William Gooch, Staunton was the birthplace of President Woodrow Wilson. To your right when the train stops on a curve of the tracks beside the large passenger building you can see colourful Chessie System railcars being used as station architecture. Staunton's altitude (1,359ft/414m) is inscribed on the station's canopy. The town's **Frontier Culture Museum** (*1290 Richmond Av;* \ *540 332 7850; www.frontiermuseum.org*) tells the story of the thousands of people who migrated to colonial America, and of the life they created for themselves and their descendants.

You leave among houses perched on hills, with Victorian buildings seen away to your left. As the train climbs, the tops of the tall trees to your left scarcely reach the tracks. Look also for horses, cattle, sheep and eagles.

Elliott Knob (15/55) This dark-purple mountain (4,458ft/1,360m) is visible on the right. Near Clifton Forge the *Cardinal* passes through busy yards of the Chesapeake & Ohio, with freight trains to your left and a picturesque railway building to your right.

CLIFTON FORGE (70/50) This area was wilderness until the railroad arrived and enabled lumber and coal to be exploited. Virginia's **Museum of Transportation** (*303 Norfolk Av, in nearby Roanoke;* ☎ *540 342 5670; www.vmt.org;* ☉ *daily; admission charge*) is housed in a 1917 Norfolk & Western freight depot. The museum features steam, diesel and electric engines, as well as passenger and freight cars, vintage automobiles, trucks and trolleys. The *Cardinal* pulls out of Clifton Forge past a hospital and factories to your right.

Covington (12/38) Below the small town to your right is Highway 64.

The train ascends into the mountains through more of the many tunnels built by the former Chesapeake & Ohio and Virginia Central railroads in this region. The Allegheny Tunnel runs under the crest of the Allegheny Mountains and marks the boundary between Virginia and West Virginia, as well as the eastern continental divide. Look right just before White Sulphur Springs for a golf course and the immaculate grounds of Greenbrier Spa, where US presidents and others have come to bathe in its mineral waters since 1778. The Greenbrier Hotel was once owned by the Chesapeake & Ohio.

WHITE SULPHUR SPRINGS (50/30) Amtrak's unmanned station is at 315 Main. Greenbrier is a 2,600-acre (1052ha) resort with facilities for many sports, including ice skating. The first 'horseless carriage' in these parts arrived in 1900 on a Chesapeake & Ohio freight car.

Somewhere in the surrounding hillside is a secret bunker built in 1958 for Congress to use in the event of a nuclear attack. You can look for this among the wooded mountains and waterfalls on both sides as the train pushes deeper into West Virginia.

ALDERSON (30/30) The restored, orange-painted station dates from 1896 and is typical of the Chesapeake & Ohio designs used between 1890 and 1916. Alderson is a flag stop where trains pause only on request. The building high up to your left is a women's Federal prison where inmates have included jazz singer Billie Holiday and television host Martha Stewart.

Great Bend Tunnel (15/15) The Chesapeake & Ohio Line was mostly built by former Virginia slaves supervised by ex-Confederate army officers. According to folklore, one of the ex-slaves was John Henry, the 'Steel-Drivin' Man', who worked on this tunnel, also known as Big Bend Tunnel, in the early 1870s. When a steam-powered drill was introduced, he challenged it to a contest. With the help of a 'shaker' assistant to turn his drill, and swinging 9lb or 12lb (4kg or 5.5kg) hammers in both hands, he made 15ft to the steam drill's 9ft (4.5m/2.7m). He died of a heart attack soon afterwards but his exploits inspired songs such as 'Take This Hammer' and 'If I Had A Hammer'. A statue of John Henry, stripped to the waist, stands on the mountain above the tunnel.

Greenbrier River (28/2) The river on your right is often reduced to little more than a stream.

For the next 120 miles (192km) you follow the New River as it cuts a tree-lined gorge through America's oldest mountains, the Appalachians. Bluestone Lake and Dam are to your left. The beautiful Sandstone Falls is the largest waterfall in the New River Gorge, dropping about 20ft over a 1,500ft width of river.

HINTON (30/30) Elegant houses stand on the hill. Hinton's busier past is revealed by its large brick station to your right, beside an open space where the rail yards used to be. The **Hinton Railroad Museum** is located in a former department store building at 206 Temple and contains uniforms, tools and other items from the early days of the Chesapeake & Ohio Railway.

Bass Lake (5/25) Look for the ethnic cabins to your right.

PRINCE (30/15) A mountain village with another large depot, from which access to nearby Beckley is by yellow cab. The station dates from 1946, and is a fine example of Art Moderne architecture. The town's founder, William Prince, was involved in the coal business in the 1890s, when coal was transported across the New River in buckets suspended on a wire cable.

THURMOND (15/45) The line curves right into Thurmond, where the *Cardinal* stops only on request. Thurmond was a classic boom town during the early 1900s, when huge amounts of coal were brought in from local mines. It had the largest revenue on the Chesapeake & Ohio Railway and the town's banks were the richest in the state. Fifteen passenger trains a day came through and the depot served as many as 95,000 people a year. With the decline in the coal industry most residents moved away, and Thurmond today is largely untouched by modern development.

The long, narrow slate-roofed wooden depot, built in 1904 by the Chesapeake & Ohio, originally had three waiting rooms: one for men, one for women and one for African-Americans. Painstakingly restored with authentic furniture, fixtures and equipment from the early 20th century, it now also houses a **railroad museum** and a **visitor centre** for the New River Gorge National River.

New River Gorge Bridge (20/25) Spanning 3,030ft (924m), this steel-arch bridge carries Route 19 traffic across the valley. Its arch extends 1,700ft (518m) and at 876ft (267m) is the second-highest bridge in the Americas and the fifth highest in the world.

The *Cardinal* continues through dramatically rugged scenery with waterfalls, mountains and a sheer drop to the boulder-strewn river. This forested national park area is pre-dated in geological history only by Egypt's Nile Valley, and is home to many endangered mammals, birds and amphibians. Look for the stone buildings of Hawk's Nest Lodge and the Gauley Bridge, marking the confluence of the New and Gauley rivers to form the Kanawha River. Much of this picturesque country is visible only by rail or white-water raft. Approaching Montgomery, the tracks diverge from the river and the town mayor's office appears among houses to your left.

MONTGOMERY (45/30) West Virginia's Institute of Technology is on the left. Christopher Janus's poignant novel, *Goodbye, Miss 4th of July*, tells the story of his Greek family's struggles while growing up in Montgomery.

Kanawha River (8/22) The train joins the river to your right and pursues it most of the way to Charleston. Barges can be seen loading coal from a mine on the far side of the river.

You travel through semi-rural scenes, with wooded mountains on the opposite shore and industrial plants below. As you near Charleston, the gold-domed Capitol Building comes into view to your right.

CHARLESTON (30/55) Located on the Kanawha River and surrounded by mountains, Charleston is famous for white-water rafting. Apart from the domed Capitol, the most impressive buildings are the Cultural Center and the Governor's Mansion. Amtrak's stone and brick station is under a highway bridge at 350 McCorkle.

Chemical factories appear on both sides as you cross the river, passing rail yards to your right.

Institute (10/45) Where Union Carbide produces the chemical methyl isocyanate. In 1984, a leak at a similar factory in Bhopal, India, killed 3,800 people.

Approaching Huntington, you pass a large CSX yard on the left then a big shopping mall.

HUNTINGTON (55/20) Founded by Collis P Huntington in 1870 as the western terminus for the Chesapeake & Ohio Railway, which initially stretched from Richmond, Virginia, to the Ohio River. To your right is the historic downtown area of Huntington. **Heritage Village**, located in a former Baltimore & Ohio station, reveals this inland port's railway history and contains the famous Station Restaurant, an authentic locomotive, a renovated Pullman car, and the city's first bank, once robbed by the James gang. Amtrak's small brick depot is to your left at Eighth Avenue and Tenth.

Big Sandy River (15/5) Most of the train comes into view as it crosses the river and takes a long right curve. Look for a concrete highway bridge to your right, linking West Virginia with Kentucky.

ASHLAND (20/55) The historic industrial city to your left is noted for oil and steel. Look right for a major Armco plant. The station at 2001 Greenup Avenue also serves Kenova, West Virginia.

The route between here and Cincinnati takes you along the meandering southern shore of the Ohio River, which forms the Kentucky–Ohio border to your right, so the best views are on this side of the train. When travelling east you should have daylight to observe the river's houses, barges, locks, bridges and power stations. Ohio's bluffs are on the far side.

Greenup Dam (40/15) The lock on this side of the river was built in the 1950s.

SOUTH PORTSMOUTH (55/50) The modest Main Street Station also serves Portsmouth, Ohio, across the river. Note the white Baptist church to your right as the train leaves and passes beneath a suspension bridge. A highway bridge also spans the river, usually busy with freight barges.

Falls City (25/25) The *Cardinal* makes slow progress through this small town before losing touch with the Ohio for a while, travelling among fields and tree-covered hills. The river and industry return near Maysville.

MAYSVILLE (50/85) This atmospheric river city on the edge of bluegrass country was once a centre for the manufacture of wrought ironwork, some of which decorates the buildings of New Orleans. Amtrak's brick and tile station is on W Front.

Augusta (20/65) White houses and an imposing grammar school can be seen to your left but the best viewing remains on the right.

Zimmer Nuclear Power Station (30/55) A cooling tower and chimneys dominate the Ohio shore.

Interstate 275 (50/35) You travel under a highway crossing the river to your right, then cross the Licking River as Cincinnati approaches.

Covington (70/15) At suburban Covington the train dramatically crosses the Ohio River, scene of an extravagant September festival. Other bridges cross the river on both sides and the Riverfront Stadium is to your right, along with the Cincinnati skyline. The suspension bridge on the right was built by John Augustus Roebling, designer of the Brooklyn Bridge in New York. The *Cardinal* skirts the west side of downtown before easing into Union Station.

CINCINNATI (85/100) The 'Queen City of the west' was nicknamed 'Porkopolis' after its pork-packing industry. Another local speciality, Cincinnati chilli, contains not only pork and beans but also a choice of cheese, onions, spaghetti or even hot dog. Many parks, plazas and buildings were created to celebrate Cincinnati's 1988 bicentennial.

Cincinnati basics

Telephone code 513

Station (*Ticket office & waiting room midnight–06.30 Wed–Mon, 23.00–midnight daily; information* 651 3337) Amtrak uses the old Union Terminal at 1301 Vine, a superb example of Art Deco design. Lockers, vending machines, handcarts, shops, cafés, museum, taxi stand.

Connections Thruway buses link with Indianapolis & Chicago.

Local transport Metro bus schedules & information are available from the downtown office at 120 E Fourth (621 4455).

Taxis Yellow 821 8294

Greyhound 1005 Gilbert Av; 352 6012

Tours Ohio River excursions with Celebrations Riverboats at 848 Elm St in Ludlow (859 581 2600)

Greater Cincinnati International Airport 14 miles (22km) southwest across the river in Covington, Kentucky, reached by taxi, limousine & TANK buses (859 331 8265).

Visitors bureau 525 Vine; 621 2142 or 800 543 2613 (for the information line); www.cincyusa.com; Mon–Fri. The Fountain Sq Visitor Center is at 511 Walnut; Thu–Sun.

Accommodation Contact the Clifton House Bed & Breakfast, 500 Terrace Av, Cincinnati, OH 45220; 221 7600; www.thecliftonhouse.com.

Hotels include the Quality Inn Downtown, 800 W Eighth; 241 8660, **$$**; Terrace, 15 W Sixth; 381 4000, **$$$**; Blue Ash Crowne Plaza, 5901 Pfeiffer Rd; 793 4500, **$$$**; Cincinnatian, 601 Vine; 381 3000, **$$$**; Symphony, 210 W 14th; 721 3353, **$$$**; Comfort Inn Northeast, 9011 Fields Ertel Rd; 683 9700, **$$**.

Recommended in Cincinnati

Fountain Square E Fifth & Vine. Features interesting architecture, a historic fountain, gardens, shops & free concerts. Contact Fountain Sq management at 1014 Vine (621 4400; www.myfountainsquare.com; Mon–Fri).

Contemporary Arts Center 44 E Sixth; 345 8400; www.contemporaryartscenter.org; Wed–Mon; admission charge. Includes music events, films & multi-media shows.

Cincinnati History Museum 1301 Western Av; 287 7000; www.cincymuseum.org; daily; admission charge. Walk through the city's streets

as they used to be as costumed interpreters reveal the lives of early Cincinnatians, or take a ride on the sidewheel steamboat.

Museum of Natural History & Science 1301 Western Av; 287 7000; www.cincymuseum.org; daily; admission charge. Explore the Ohio Valley & learn how the natural world works as you travel through a Kentucky limestone cavern. Or visit Cincinnati's Ice Age & experience life 19,000 years ago.

Union Terminal 1301 Western Av; 800 733 2077; www.cincymuseum.org. Now partly a museum, this is one of the most opulent railway stations ever built. It has the highest unsupported masonry dome in the world & the interior of the rotunda (180ft/54m in diameter) features splendid mosaic murals. The ceiling has striking silver, yellow & orange plasterwork. The building, which was renovated & reopened as the Cincinnati Museum Center in 1990, has been named one of the top 50 architecturally significant buildings in America by the American Institute of Architects.

A co-operative project of 7 railroad companies, Union Terminal opened in 1933 to centralise the freight & passenger operations of the Big Four. The Big Four was a railway company formed by the merger of the Cleveland, Columbus, Cincinnati & Indianapolis Railway, the Cincinnati, Indianapolis, St Louis & Chicago Railway, the Indianapolis & St Louis Railway & the Indiana Bloomington & Western Railway. The Big Four was later acquired by the New York Central Railroad (later the New York Central), Pennsylvania, Chesapeake & Ohio, Norfolk & Western, Southern, Louisville & Nashville, & the Baltimore & Ohio railroads.

Taft Museum of Art 316 Pike; ☏241 0343; www.taftmuseum.org; ⊕ Wed–Sun; admission charge, free on Sun. Old master paintings, Chinese porcelains, as well as European & American decorative arts, can be found in the restored interior of the former home of Anna & Charles Taft.

Cincinnati Zoo 3400 Vine; ☏281 4700; www.cincinnatizoo.org; ⊕ daily; admission charge. Opened in 1875, America's 2nd-oldest zoo breeds gorillas & rare white tigers. More than 500 animal & 3,000 plant species make this one of the largest zoo collections in the country.

All aboard!

The *Cardinal* continues north from Cincinnati through scenes of heavy manufacturing.

Hamilton (50/50) Close enough to Cincinnati still to be industrial, Hamilton! is spelled with an exclamation mark in the local telephone directory! The station, built by the Cincinnati, Hamilton & Dayton Railroad is still used by CSX & was a stop for the *Cardinal* until 2005.

Ohio–Indiana state line (80/20) You cross into the Hoosier State in darkness.

CONNERSVILLE (100/80) Founded on the Whitewater River in 1813, Connersville makes everything from auto parts to dishwashers. Automobiles manufactured in 'Little Detroit' have included Auburn, Cord, Duesenberg, Ansted, Empire, Lexington, Jeep and McFarlan (a favourite car for Al Capone).

INDIANAPOLIS (80/65) The birthplace of Kurt Vonnegut and former home town of Steve McQueen is Indiana's capital, located at the geographical centre of the state. The **Indy 500** motor race takes place each Memorial Sunday, drawing the world's largest sports crowd. For tickets and information, ☏636 4556.

Indianapolis basics

☏**Telephone code** 317
⚊ **Station** (*Ticket office & waiting room* ⊕ *midnight–14.15 & 23.00–23.59 Mon–Wed, midnight–06.45 & 23.00–23.59 Thu–Sun ; information* ☏*263 0550*) Amtrak operates from the Union Terminal at 350 S Illinois, next to the Lucas Oil Stadium & the former Indianapolis Union Station.

Connections Thruway buses link with Danville, Champaign-Urbana, Bloomington-Normal, Peoria, Galesburg, Moline, Illinois, & Davenport, Indiana.
🚌 **Local transport** Indy Go buses (☏*635 3344; www.indygo.net*) operate throughout the city.
🚕 **Taxis** Yellow ☏487 7777

🚗 **Car rental**   Avis, 33 N Capitol Av; ☎ 236 1987
🚌 **Greyhound**   Next to Amtrak, at 350 S
Illinois; ☎ 267 3076
✈ **Indianapolis International Airport**
6 miles (10km) southwest of the city, with a
state-of-the-art terminal, the 1st in America
designed & built after 9/11. Indy Go's Green Line
Express bus travels every 20mins between the
airport & downtown.
ℹ️ **Visitors bureau**   30 S Meridian; ☎ 639 4282;
www.indy.org; ⊕ 08.30–17.00 Mon–Fri
🏠 **Accommodation**   The Indy Hostel is at
4903 Winthrop Av; ☎ 727 1696; www.indyhostel.
us, **$$**.

The Crowne Plaza Hotel is housed within
America's first 'Union Station' at 123 W
Louisiana; ☎ 631 2221, **$$$$**. Listed in
the National Register of Historic Places, this
Romanesque Revival-style building has a Grand
Hall with distinctive arches & columns. Its
soaring stained-glass barrel ceiling is matched
by 20ft stained-glass wagon-wheel windows.
The hotel has 26 authentic Pullman train car
sleeping rooms, named & decorated after
famous personalities from the early 1900s.
Other hotels include the Holiday Inn Canterbury,
123 S Illinois; ☎ 634 3000, **$$$**; Stone Soup
Inn, 1304 N Central Av; ☎ 866 639 9550, **$$$**;
Tower Inn, 1633 N Capitol Av; ☎ 925 9831, **$$**;
Day's Inn, 401 E Washington; ☎ 637 6464, **$$**;
Embassy Suites, 110 W Washington; ☎ 236
1800, **$$$$**.

Recommended in Indianapolis

Children's Museum   3000 N Meridian; ☎ 334
3322; www.childrensmuseum.org; ⊕ Tue–Sun,
daily in summer; admission charge. The largest
museum of its kind in the world, containing the
largest water clock in North America. The All
Aboard gallery takes visitors back to the age of
steam with the original 35ft long, 55ton steam
engine designed by Reuben Wells in 1868 to
conquer Indiana's Madison Hill. The museum also
features toy trains, rock climbing, carousel rides
& a petting zoo.
Motor Speedway   4790 W 16th; ☎ 492 8500;
www.brickyard.com; ⊕ daily; free if under 17.
The Speedway is the largest spectator sporting
venue in the world, with more than 250,000
seats. The 2.5-mile (4km) track was built in 1909
& incorporates an entire golf course. Bus tours
except in May.
Indy Hall of Fame   Featuring approx 75
historic cars (inc the Marmon 'Wasp', which
won the inaugural Indianapolis 500 in 1911,
& more than 30 other winning cars), films &
memorabilia.
City Market   222 E Market; ☎ 634 9266; www.
indianapoliscitymarket.com; ⊕ Mon–Sat.
Dating from 1821, this is one of the few original
city markets remaining in the United States.

The restored 19th-century building contains 15
ethnic sections.
Indianapolis Museum of Art   4000 Michigan
Rd; ☎ 923 1331 or ☎ 920 2660 (information line);
www.imamuseum.org; ⊕ Tue–Sun; free. One of
the oldest art museums in the country, located in
a 52-acre (21ha) park with gardens, 5 pavilions,
a theatre & a concert terrace. The collection
includes ancient bronze & masks. Paintings are by
American & European masters, including Gauguin
& post-Impressionist works, with the most
significant collection of works by J M W Turner
outside the UK.
Indiana Historical Society   450 W Ohio; ☎ 232
1882; www.indianahistory.org; ⊕ Tue–Sat; free.
Discover Indiana's past through exhibitions, a
library, publications, educational programmes &
special events.
Indiana Transportation Museum   At Forest
Park, Noblesville, 20 miles (32km) north; ☎ 773
6000; www.itm.org; ⊕ Sat/Sun; admission
charge. Including old vehicles from the Santa
Fe, Burlington & Louisville & Nashville railroads,
as well as locomotives & Henry Flagler's Florida
Coast Line business car. Museum & main line
train rides.

All aboard!

The *Cardinal* departs Indianapolis past the massive RCA Dome, formerly the
Hoosier Dome sports arena, with the downtown area to your right.

Brownsburg (25/40) You pass through a less urban landscape as the train makes for the corn and soya bean fields of central Indiana. You go through several small towns and accompany Interstate 74 to your right. Just before Crawfordsville, the *Cardinal* transfers from former Conrail tracks to those of the Seaboard System (formerly the Monon Railroad). All these tracks are now owned by CSX.

CRAWFORDSVILLE (65/30) Home of Wabash College, one of many educational establishments to be seen on this part of the journey. The country's first official air mail delivery took place in 1859, when John Wise piloted a balloon from Lafayette to Crawfordsville. You cross Cherry Creek then pass beneath Interstate 74.

Linden (10/20) The train crosses tracks belonging to the Norfolk & Western line.

LAFAYETTE (30/50) You accompany a pretty valley with close-up views of this typical mid-American city, where the train used to run directly down Main Street and the old station was simply a storefront. The Big Four depot has been relocated underneath a bridge now used as a pedestrian walkway. Lafayette is the home of Purdue University and was the birthplace of Alvah Roebuck, co-founder of Sears, Roebuck.

Wabash River (10/40) The train crosses the river then travels beneath Interstate 65 on its way to Chicago.

Tippecanoe Battlefield (15/35) On your left is the place where, in 1811, General and future president William Harrison defeated the Shawnee Indian brothers, Tecumseh and Tenskwatawa.

You continue through the small communities of Brookston and Chalmers.

Reynolds (35/15) As you cross the former Toledo, Peoria & Western line you change from Eastern to Central Time, so watches go back an hour (forward when travelling east).

RENSSELAER (50/40) The *Cardinal* crosses the Kankakee River then proceeds through Shelby, Lowell and Creston as it crosses Indiana's plains.

Cedar Lake (30/10) The lake is visible to your left just before you reach a town of the same name.

DYER (40/50) The station is a tiny glass shack with a very short platform, requiring the train to stop several times.

You start to enter an industrial environment which will persist most of the way to Chicago as the *Cardinal* transfers to Norfolk Southern tracks from the CSX route used since Clifton Forge.

Eggers Woods Forest (24/26) Look right for a rare splash of greenery.

Hammond-Whiting (25/25) Hammond-Whiting's modern, yellow-brick station on your right is a stop for Amtrak's *Wolverine* train. Storage tanks belonging to the Standard Oil Company can be seen on both sides as you depart among freight yards. Watch for grain elevators and ships being loaded as you cross the Calumet River on a steel lift bridge.

Roby (35/15) The New Regal Theater to your right was opened by Chicago's first black mayor as a centre for African-American culture. Mayor Washington was subsequently buried in the cemetery to your right. Interstate 90 (the Indiana Toll Road) is to your left.

The route crosses a now-closed Rock Island Railroad track at Englewood then crosses the south branch of the Chicago River. Plans are in hand to turn the old depot and station buildings at Rock Island into a museum in honour of a mighty fine line.

Chicago's Skyway is to your left and the city skyline comes into view on the right, featuring the 110-storey Willis Tower. After crossing the Dan Ryan Expressway, you see the El rail track overhead and Lake Michigan to your right.

Comiskey Park (40/10) The car park on the right is where White Sox baseball used to be played. A new Comiskey Park stadium, completed in 1991, has risen alongside.

Look for Conrail loading facilities to your left, then Amtrak's extensive 21st Street yards on your right. Trains are set up here to travel to every corner of the land. The *Cardinal* lurches into Chicago, reversing slowly into Union Station through a passage beneath the post office building.

CHICAGO For Chicago city information, see *Chapter 5, The* California Zephyr (pages 71–4).

21

The *Adirondack*
New York–Montreal

General route information

The *Adirondack* has been nominated by *National Geographic Traveler* magazine as one of the world's ten best rail trips. It goes from New York to the Gallic charms of Montreal by way of the beautiful Hudson River Valley, the Adirondack Mountains, Lake Champlain, Vermont and the St Lawrence River. This daytime journey is particularly wonderful during autumn.

Adirondack trains operate between New York and Yonkers on Amtrak, between Yonkers and Poughkeepsie on Metro-North Railroad, between Poughkeepsie and Schenectady on CSX Transportation, between Schenectady and Rouses Point on Canadian Pacific, and between Rouses Point and Montreal on Canadian National lines.

Joining the train

NEW YORK For New York City information, see *Chapter 14, The Northeast Corridor* (pages 179–82). Trains from Washington, DC, connect with the *Adirondack*, which leaves Pennsylvania Station on Empire Corridor tracks. The first ten miles were opened in 1991 at a cost of $89 million and this part of the route used to be the New York Central's west side freight line. Constructed by the Hudson River Railroad, passenger services had previously operated until 1872.

You emerge from a tunnel with the Jacob Javits Convention Centre (built on the site of the old 30th Street rail yards) to your left. You then continue through Riverside Tunnel, with Harlem's Cotton Club below to your right as the train exits. The Hudson River and Henry Hudson Parkway are to your left, followed by the North River Water Plant (the world's largest sewage treatment works). You pass beneath the Hudson Parkway, which continues to your right.

George Washington Bridge (8/12) Spanning the river to your left is a suspension bridge which was the longest in the world when completed in 1931. Just before the bridge, look for the 'little red lighthouse' which featured in a well-known children's book and is now preserved.

Fort Tryon Park is to your right beyond the highway before you pass Inwood Hill Park. Among the high-rises on New Jersey's Palisades across the river is the cupola of St Michael Villa, run by the Sisters of St Joseph.

Spuyten Duyvil Bridge (15/5) The *Adirondack* crosses the Harlem River Ship Canal on a 610ft-long (185m) swing bridge, restored to accommodate this line. The Hudson Parkway Bridge is to your right. Metro-North trains join on the right after travelling from Grand Central Station.

IMMIGRATION FORMALITIES US and Canadian citizens must have a passport, Trusted Traveler card or enhanced driver's licence – **an ordinary driver's licence is not sufficient**. Citizens of other countries must have a passport., and in many cases a visa. Passengers aged 15 and under who do not have either a Trusted Traveler card or passport may present a copy of their birth certificate. Passengers aged under 18 and not travelling with both parents require a letter from any parent not present giving permission to cross the border.

For further information and to determine what is required for your particular situation (including permanent residents and others not mentioned above), contact the appropriate US or Canadian government agencies prior to travel. An Amtrak brochure with additional details (*Important Information on Crossing the Border between the United States and Canada*), is available from Amtrak agents.

See also *Chapter 3, Red tape*, page 33, check with your US embassy or contact the Immigration and Naturalisation Service in Washington, DC (see *Chapter 3*, page 34 and *Appendix 2*, page 335). Passengers without proper documentation are prohibited from entering the US or Canada and will be detrained before reaching the US–Canadian border. Neither Amtrak nor VIA Rail Canada accepts any liability if you are denied entry or removed from the train.

FREQUENCY Daily. The **northbound** service leaves New York early in the morning to reach Albany by late morning, Plattsburgh mid afternoon and Montreal by early evening. Travelling **south**, trains leave Montreal mid-morning to reach Plattsburgh just after midday, Albany by late afternoon and New York mid evening.

DURATION Ten hours

RESERVATIONS All reserved

EQUIPMENT Amfleet coaches

LOUNGE CAR National Park Service rangers from the Roosevelt-Vanderbilt National Historic Sites provide a narrative between Croton-Harmon and Hudson, New York, and the Saratoga National Historic Park between Saratoga Springs and Westport weekends except holidays.

FOOD Snacks, sandwiches, drinks. The lounge car serves specialities such as cheesecake baked by nuns of the Canadian New Skete Order.

BAGGAGE No check-in service. Ski racks.

YONKERS (20/20) Where Elisha Otis invented the safety elevator and the **Hudson River Museum** (*511 Warburton Av;* ☎ *914 963 4550; www.hrm.org*) includes an 1876 mansion overlooking the Hudson River and Palisades. Look for other imposing houses among the hills.

Hastings-on-Hudson (6/14) To your left is the home of the promoter Florenz Ziegfeld, whose wife Billie Burke was the good witch in *The Wizard of Oz*.

Irvington (9/11) Named after Washington Irving, creator of *Rip Van Winkle*, and his Sunnyside home can be seen to your right past the station.

Tappan Zee Bridge (10/10) Carrying the NYS Thruway three miles (5km) across the Hudson River ahead to your left. Also to your left is the Phillips Manor, one of many estates in this region which have belonged to the well heeled or famous.

Ossining (15/5) Look for the guard towers of Sing Sing correctional facility, where convicts were sent 'up the river' to do time. The main house is to your left and the annex to your right.

You continue through the most beautiful part of the Hudson River Valley, where maple trees flourish on steep riverbanks in a lush landscape.

CROTON-HARMON (20/35) The 18th-century Van Cortlandt Manor belonged to New York's first lieutenant-governor and was visited by Generals Washington and Lafayette. Across the river are the twin towers of Indian Point atomic power station next to the town of Stony Point.

Peekskill (10/25) Once a frontier trading post, Peekskill was an early American Army headquarters during the Revolutionary War. Across the river is Dunderberg Mountain, at the southern end of the Hudson Highlands. Bear Mountain Bridge carries the Appalachian Trail across the river.

Highland Falls (17/18) The falls cascade 100ft (30m) down cliffs on the far side.

West Point (18/17) The nation's oldest military academy, where cadets have included Ulysses S Grant, Robert E Lee, George Custer, Stonewall Jackson, Dwight Eisenhower and Norman Schwarzkopf. The Gothic chapel features stained-glass windows and the world's largest church organ. Washington positioned troops here during the Revolutionary War.

After West Point the river narrows at the eastern end of Constitution Island. Nearby World's End is the river's deepest place at 202ft (62m). The *Adirondack* travels through Breakneck Tunnel then alongside Sugarloaf Mountain, with Storm King Mountain across the river. Look for blue herons, cormorants and flights of geese.

Bannerman's Castle (24/11) Situated on Pollepel Island in the middle of the river, which narrows to a quarter of its width between Storm King and Breakneck Ridge. The ruined mock-medieval castle was constructed by Scottish immigrant Francis Bannerman during the early 1900s as a private arsenal, complete with moat and drawbridge.

Beacon (26/9) Signal fires on the mountain to your right warned a Revolutionary Army post of approaching British troops. In the 19th century, this was the 'hat-making capital

MONTREAL
□
St Lambert
CANADA
USA
Rouses Point
Plattsburgh
Port Kent
Westport
Port Henry
Ticonderoga
Whitehall
Fort Edward
Saratoga Springs
Schenectady
Albany-Rensselaer
N
Bradt
Hudson
Rhinecliff
Pough-keepsie
Croton-Harmon
Yonkers
□
NEW YORK CITY
For New York City to Washington, see *The Northeast Corridor*
□ WASHINGTON

of the US', with around 50 manufacturers. A bridge links Beacon with the larger city of Newburgh across the river.

Danskammer (28/7) On the far side of the Hudson are the Roseton and Danskammer power plants, then the red buildings of the Royal Kedem winery. As you approach Poughkeepsie look for rock quarries on the near shore.

POUGHKEEPSIE (35/14) Founded by the Dutch in 1683, this manufacturing city was famous for making cough drops and ball bearings. Interesting buildings include Clinton House and Glebe House on the corner of Main and N White. **Vassar College Art Gallery** (*124 Raymond Av;* \ *845 437 5632; www.fllac.vassar. edu*) has Rembrandt prints and Tiffany glass.

Amtrak's splendid station at 41 Main was built in 1918 and has a waiting room modelled on New York's Grand Central Terminal, with a gallery lit during daylight hours by five high-arched windows and three original chandeliers. The 14 chestnut benches are also original and above the wood-panelled walls is a ceiling resembling the one in San Miniato al Monte, an 11th-century church in Florence, Italy.

As the *Adirondack* pulls out of the station, note the cantilever bridge spanning the river. This was the largest rail bridge in the world when completed in 1888, but has been out of use since a 1974 fire. To your right you pass Franklin D Roosevelt's home, where he was born and died, and the enormous mansion of Frederick Vanderbilt. The town of Hyde Park is on the near shore, with Fallkill Creek waterfall to the right.

An old lighthouse with a *trompe l'oeil* window can be seen at the south end of Esopus Meadows in midstream. German-style houses on the other side of the water demonstrate why this valley has been called 'the Rhine of America'. You travel through the neat village of Staatsburg.

RHINECLIFF (14/20) The station at Hutton and Charles was built by the New York Central Railroad in 1914 in Spanish Mission Revival style. This is Amtrak's stop for the attractive towns of Rhinebeck and Kingston. Rhinebeck's historic buildings include America's oldest (1776) hotel, the **Beekman Arms**, which was a favourite with Franklin Roosevelt.

Kingston Rhinecliff Bridge (4/16) The bridge was built in 1957, and on both sides of the track is the marshland of Tivoli Bays, a haven for fish and birds. Across the river, at the mouth of the Esopus River, stands the oldest lighthouse on the Hudson, the Saugerties Light. Look also for the Carmelite Sisters' convent.

Germantown (10/10) First settled by Germans, this is now the centre of a fruit-growing region. Cement plants and barges appear across the river.

Catskill (16/4) Fine houses take advantage of dramatic riverbank locations as you enter a land dominated by the forests and gorges of the Catskills. This recreation area is bigger than Rhode Island and the mountains rise to more than 4,000ft (1,200m).

Roeliff River (15/5) Docks can be seen to your right as the train crosses the river and approaches Hudson. The 1872 Hudson-Athens lighthouse to your left is one of 13 coastguard lights on the river.

HUDSON (20/15) Several television shows, including *The Wonder Years*, have been filmed here. Dutch settlers called this place Claverack Landing because of its luxuriant clover fields and the town was renamed after the explorer Henry Hudson in 1785. Among the former whaling port's gardens and estates is the Persian-style Olana, a 37-room extravaganza designed by landscape artist Frederic Church. Hudson is also home to the **FASNY Museum of Fire Fighting** (*117 Harry Howard Av;* ✆ *877 347 3687; www.fasnyfiremuseum.com*). The railway station at 69 S Front, built in 1874 by the New York Central Railroad, is the oldest on this line.

Castleton-on-Hudson (11/4) The Smith Memorial Bridge appears overhead, followed by a mile-long (1.6km) bridge connecting the New York State Thruway with the Massachusetts Turnpike. As the *Adirondack* nears Albany, look left for the city skyline dominated by the Empire State Plaza. Glenmont power station is seen across the river.

ALBANY-RENSSELAER (15/20) The state capital's port prospered greatly with the arrival in 1825 of the Erie Canal, linking Lake Erie with the Atlantic. The railway came six years later when New York's first steam train, the *DeWitt Clinton*, ran on the Mohawk & Hudson line. Amtrak's busy modern East Street Station is 1½ miles away in adjacent Rensselaer.

Albany's sleek new buildings contrast with the Old State Capitol's Gothic architecture. The Schuyler Mansion is a Georgian house visited by George Washington and Benjamin Franklin. The **New York State Museum** (✆ *518 474 5877; www.nysm.nysed.gov;* ⊕ *daily*) is at the Empire State Plaza. Nearby is the 17th-century **Fort Crailo**, America's oldest fortress, where tradition says a British surgeon wrote *Yankee Doodle Dandy*.

The *Adirondack* crosses the Hudson River after departing Rensselaer past extensive freight yards. The Romantic buildings on your left once belonged to the Delaware & Hudson Railroad and now house State University headquarters. Albany city centre is to your left.

Approaching Schenectady through the environs of General Electric, look right for the gold dome of City Hall. The red-brick Van Curler Hotel to your left is part of a community college.

SCHENECTADY (20/25) 'The city that lights and hauls the world' began in 1661 as a fur trading station, its name being a Mohawk expression for 'through the open pines'. The American Locomotive Company (ALCO) took care of haulage while Thomas Edison's Machine Works created the light. Edison's first job was selling sweets to railroad passengers, money from which he spent on chemistry sets and building a telegraph system out of scrap metal. He was dismissed from his job when he moved his chemistry lab into a baggage car and accidentally set fire to the train.

Apart from the electric light bulb and power stations, Edison developed or invented, amongst other things, the phonograph, motion picture camera, high-speed telegraph, typewriter, electric pen, copier and dictation machines, cement mixer and telephone, eventually holding a record 1,093 patents. The Edison factory eventually became General Electric, still one of the city's main employers.

Amtrak's station at 332 Erie Boulevard was built under the railroad tracks with an elevator and staircase leading to the platform. This was the site of the former Union Station and a replacement building is planned to serve both Amtrak and local transit services. You leave with the 17th-century stockade district to your right. After shaking off Schenectady's factories and power lines you begin to see logging and timber-processing plants among the wooded hills.

SARATOGA SPRINGS (25/20) Before World War I the Vanderbilts and Whitneys came to Saratoga to drink the waters and take curative baths. Mixing only with their own kind, they enjoyed the best hotels, lavish casinos, gardens and America's oldest racetrack. Potato chips (crisps) were allegedly invented by a Native American chef called George Crum when Cornelius Vanderbilt asked for his potatoes to be sliced extra-thin.

No longer an exclusive resort of the rich, Saratoga Springs retains its bathhouses and you can still sample the waters. The 1777 Battle of Saratoga, a turning point in the Revolutionary War, took place 12 miles (19km) to the east and the site is now a military park. Amtrak's station is at West Avenue and Station Lane was built in the 1950s by the Delaware & Hudson Railroad.

After the *Adirondack* passes through a cutting lined with evergreens, look for a junkyard to your left then a field containing pheasants. You cross the river with a highway bridge to your left.

FORT EDWARD (20/22) The original fort was constructed during the French and Indian War (also known as the Seven Years War). A sequence of locks later linked the Hudson River to the Champlain Canal, creating a waterway through to the St Lawrence. Note the wood-framed houses on both sides. Amtrak's East Street Station also serves neighbouring Glens Falls. Lake George, a few miles further north, has cruises, water skiing and winter car races on the ice.

You continue through peaceful country into the heart of the Adirondacks, which were the tallest mountains in the world before the Ice Ages. Home to eagles, bobcat and deer, they became famous in 1869, when the Reverend William H H Murray published *Adventures in the Wilderness*. His book started a fashion for city dwellers to spend their summers in an area recently made accessible by railroads, and rail companies built many big hotels and lodges to accommodate them. Much of this region can still only be seen by train or on foot.

Champlain Canal (10/12) The canal is to your right behind a row of trees, and this is the best side of the train from which to see the scenery ahead.

WHITEHALL (22/25) A lock system connects the canal with Lake Champlain's South Bay. Rutland, served by Amtrak's *Heartland Flyer*, is 20 miles (32km) to the east in Vermont. You leave Whitehall by way of a short tunnel.

Lake Champlain (5/20) Seen to your right as you cross South Bay and enter the six million acres of the **Adirondack Forest Preserve**. These deep, rocky lakes and shallow-running rivers are favoured by hunters and fishermen.

A few minutes later you pass on your right a channel joining South Bay with Lake Champlain. America's sixth-largest lake was named after its discoverer, Samuel de Champlain, and the *Adirondack* follows the clear waters of its shoreline for most of the next 100 miles (160km). In winter, look for ice fishermen fishing from ice houses on the lake. Vermont's tidy farmland is on the far side.

TICONDEROGA (25/25) The name is Iroquois for 'between two waters'. Amtrak's station consists of a small brick box and a telephone on Highway 74, some distance from both town and fort. Ticonderoga's former Delaware & Hudson Railroad station is listed on the National Register of Historic Places but is not served by Amtrak or any other railroad. Visible on bluffs ahead to your right, the fort was built by the French in 1775. This crucial position on the La Chute

River between Lakes Champlain and George was constantly fought over during the Revolution, changing hands several times before the fort was abandoned, destroyed and lately restored.

You leave past the fort to your right and enter a tunnel before continuing among the mountains. Vermont's Green Mountains are across the lake.

PORT HENRY (25/20) Note the magnificent, ornate town hall to the left of the quaint chateau-style station, built in 1888. A Canadian Pacific Alco ore car and a Lake Champlain & Moriah Railroad caboose are on display near the station. Abandoned railroad beds appear forlornly to your right before the train travels on among hay fields, forests and hills. Lake Champlain's rocky shoreline continues to the right.

WESTPORT (20/56) A small fishing town where Thruway buses connect with Lake Placid, site of the 1932 and 1980 Winter Olympics.

The train keeps to a line between Lake Champlain on your right and mountains to your left, crossing high above the lovely Bouquet River. The tranquil lake boasts its own version of the Loch Ness monster called 'Champ', first seen by Samuel de Champlain in 1609.

Willsboro (20/36) Trout and salmon fishing are a major attraction on Lake Champlain and along the dammed Bouquet River. For 25 miles (40km) you travel a route hacked into cliffs 100ft above the lake, with wonderful views as the train negotiates hundreds of curves among birch trees, tunnels and houses.

PORT KENT (42/14) Trains stop here from May to October, when ferries cross the water to downtown Burlington in Vermont. Nearby at Keeseville is Ausable Chasm, a two-mile-long sandstone gorge known as the 'little Grand Canyon of the east'.

Ausable River (45/11) Watch for herons as you cross the tree-lined river, which has its source below the state's tallest mountain, Mount Marcy (5,344ft/1,629m).

Valcour Island (49/7) The *Adirondack* passes several Revolutionary War and French and Indian War battlefields. Benedict Arnold's ships were defeated by the British in 1776 near the island to your right as they competed for control of Lake Champlain.

At this point the train leaves **Adirondack State Park**, the largest state-level protected area in the United States.

Plattsburgh Air Force Base (54/2) Seen immediately to your left as you approach Plattsburgh, with yachts moored on your right.

PLATTSBURGH (56/35) To your left, as the train enters this military and industrial city, you can see a Delaware & Hudson Railroad turntable and the Thomas Macdonough Monument. The monument commemorates a victory in 1814 on Lake Champlain which foiled a British attempt to invade New York State from Canada. Amtrak's green-canopied station waiting room is to your right. Plattsburgh's elaborate French Provincial-style depot was built in 1886 by the Delaware & Hudson Railroad, and resembles a Quebec castle.

The *Adirondack* finally parts company with Lake Champlain before travelling through corn fields and forests towards the Canadian border.

ROUSES POINT (35/45) This is the train's last stop before leaving the United States. The station house is a former US Immigrations Department office near to a now-dilapidated Romanesque brick and stone station built by the Delaware & Hudson Railroad in 1889. The building to your right houses the US Customs checkpoint for those travelling south. In the days of Prohibition, trains crossing from Canada were known as 'bootleggers', since passengers often tried to sneak a few bottles past the border guards in the shanks of their boots. Look for customs stickers adorning checked freight cars to your right.

You cross the US–Canadian border and pass through St Jean, where a cannon on the right guards a military college.

CANTIC (45/30) The Canadian Customs checkpoint for people travelling north, this is not a passenger stop. After inspection the *Adirondack* proceeds over the flat, nondescript landscape of southern Quebec.

ST LAMBERT (30/10) Timber yards and city apartment blocks loom on the right as the train pauses briefly in this residential suburb at a station operated by VIA Rail.

You cross the St Lawrence River on the Victoria Jubilee Bridge, the longest in the world when it opened in 1859. Approaching Montreal through industrial scenes and Canadian National freight yards, the city's high-rise buildings can be seen to your right.

MONTREAL Built on an island where the St Lawrence, Ottawa and Richelieu rivers meet, Montreal hosted the 1967 World's Fair and 1976 Olympic Games. The French settled here in 1642, but explorers had arrived over 100 years earlier. The British took over in 1760, then (for a short time) American revolutionaries.

Montreal today is the world's second-largest French-speaking city, although a third of its three million people have English as their first language. Like the rest of Quebec Province it can be cold in winter, with more snow than Moscow and temperatures well below zero into March, but the city is able to deal with the heaviest snowfall. Tunnels link 2,000 downtown stores. July highs can be in the 80°s Fahrenheit (26–32°C).

Montreal basics

Telephone code 514
Station *(Ticket office ⊕ 07.00–17.00 (Amtrak) & 06.00–21.00 (VIA Rail). Waiting room ⊕ 24hrs; Amtrak reservations & information* 800 872 7245; VIA Rail 800 361 5390) The excellent Gare Centrale (Central Station) at 895 rue de la Gauchetière Ouest is used by Amtrak, commuter trains & Canada's VIA Rail. Restaurants, shops, ATM banking, newspapers, Red Caps, taxi stand.
Connections No Thruway bus.
Local transport STM runs an efficient bus & subway system throughout the city (786 4636; www.stm.info. Le Métro operates 05.30–00.30).
Taxis Champlain 273 2435; Diamond 273 1725

Car rental Budget, Central Station; 866 7675
Greyhound 505 Bd de Maisonneuve; 843 4231. The terminal is also used by Voyageur & Voyageur-Colonial, now owned by Greyhound.
Pierre Elliott Trudeau International/ Dorval Airport 12 miles (19km) from downtown by L'Aerobus (931 9002). Limousines include Montreal Dorval (990 7915).
Tours Gray Line 398 9769; Old Montreal Ghost Trail, available in summer 868 0303; www.fantommontreal.com. Boat trips on the St Lawrence River from Harbor Cruises (842 3871; boat trips ⊕ May–Oct).
Visitors bureau 1255 Peel; 873 2015; www.tourisme-montreal.org; ⊕ daily

🏠 **Accommodation** Contact Chez Taj Bed & Breakfast, 2033 St-Hubert; 📞738 9410 or 📞1 800 738 4338.
 International Youth Hostel, 1030 MacKay; 📞843 3317; www.hostellingmontreal.com. Members & non-members, **$**. Auberge Youth Hostel, 901 rue Sherbrooke E; 📞522 6124; www. aubergemontreal.com, **$**. YWCA, 1355 Rene Levesque Bd; 📞866 9941; www.ydesfemmesmtl. org. Women only, **$$**.

Hotels include Courtyard Marriott, 410 rue Sherbrooke; 📞844 8855, **$$$**; Hotel Kutuma, 3708 St Denis; 📞844 0111, **$$$**; Maritime Plaza, 1155 rue Guy; 📞932 1411, **$$$$**; Château de l'Argoat, 524 rue Sherbrooke; 📞842 2046, **$$$**; Manoir Ambrose, 3422 rue Stanley; 📞288 6922, **$$**; Villa, 57 Sainte-Catherine Est; 📞849 5043, **$$**; Jazz, 1216 rue Saint-Hubert; 📞510 6893, **$$**.

Recommended in Montreal

Mount-Royal Park Reached via Camilien-Houde Parkway or Remembrance Rd; 📞843 8240; www.lemontroyal.qc.ca. Walk, picnic or take time to admire the views in this natural-looking park, dominated by the modest mountain which gave the city its name. The park was planned by Frederick Law Olmsted, designer of New York's Central Park. Winter activities include tubular slides & ice skating.
Museum of Fine Arts 1380 rue Sherbrooke; 📞285 2000; www.mmfa.qc.ca; ☺ Tue–Sun; admission charge. The museum has a gallery devoted to Napoleon as well as European & North American paintings & major international exhibitions.
Museum of Contemporary Art 405 rue Sherbrooke E; 📞847 6226; www.macm.org; ☺ Tue–Sun; admission charge. The collection comprises over 7,000 works of art by more than 1,500 artists, covering contemporary art in Quebec in particular & Canada in general, as well as international artists. The museum is Canada's only cultural complex devoted to both the performing & visual arts.
Canadian Centre for Architecture 1920 Baile; 📞939 7026; www.cca.qc.ca; ☺ Wed–Sun; admission charge; guided tours Sat/Sun. Founded by the architect Phyllis Lambert, this museum & study centre includes the (1874) Shaughnessy House & a splendid sculpture garden is part of the visit of this outstanding place.

St Joseph's Oratory 3800 rue Queen Mary; 📞733 8211; www.saint-joseph.org; ☺ daily; donation. The world's largest church is dedicated to Canada's patron saint. Beneath a green copper dome is the original chapel founded by Brother André, said to have been able to cure the sick.
St George's Anglican Church Pl du Canada, 1101 Stanley; 📞866 7113; www.st-georges. org; ☺ Tue–Sun; free. Built in 1870, this beautiful neo-Gothic church contains wonderful woodwork, including a double hammer-beam roof, & a tapestry from Westminster Abbey.
Exporail/Canadian Railway Museum 110 St Pierre in Saint-Constant, 1 mile (1.6km) south of Montreal; 📞450 632 2410; www.exporail.org; ☺ May–Sep; admission charge. Canada's finest railway museum has over 160 examples of rolling stock, including the country's oldest-surviving steam engines & the Rocket (Montreal's first electric streetcar). Train rides on Sun & holidays.
McCord Museum 690 rue Sherbrooke; 📞398 7100; www.mccord-museum.qc.ca; ☺ daily; admission charge. An introduction to the history of Montreal & its citizens, including toys, photographs & splendid clothes.
Botanical Garden 4101 rue Sherbrooke E; 📞872 1400; www.ville.montreal.qc.ca/jardin; ☺ daily; admission charge. One of the largest in the world, with over 300 outdoor gardens & 10 exhibition houses, including a butterfly house & an insectarium.

22

The *Vermonter*
Washington–St Albans (for Montreal)

General route information

Amtrak's alternative to the *Adirondack* travels from Washington via New York City to St Albans, Vermont. The *Vermonter* follows the Northeast Corridor route before heading north at Amherst. This train replaces the previous night-time *Montrealer*, allowing you to travel through splendid New England scenery by day and see the sun set over the Green Mountains.

Joining the train

The *Vermonter* operates between Washington and New Rochelle on Amtrak, between New Rochelle and New Haven on Metro-North Railroad, between New Haven and Springfield on Amtrak, between Springfield and Amherst on CSX Transportation, and between Amherst and St Albans on New England Central Railroad.

For Washington, DC, and the route from Washington to Springfield, see *Chapters 14 and 15*, *The Northeast Corridor* (pages 173–89 for Washington–New Haven and pages 190–1 for New Haven–Springfield). The *Vermonter* turns north from the Northeast Corridor route after Springfield and travels towards Amherst.

AMHERST (60/45) This is the home of the University of Massachusetts and a college founded in 1821 by Noah Webster (of dictionary fame). The poet Emily

---

ESSENTIAL INFORMATION

FREQUENCY Daily. The **northbound** service leaves Washington early in the morning to arrive in Philadelphia by mid morning and New York before noon. You reach Springfield mid afternoon and St Albans by mid evening. Travelling **south**, the train leaves St Albans early in the morning, arriving in Springfield mid afternoon and New York early evening. You reach Philadelphia by mid evening and Washington late evening.

DURATION 13 hours 45 minutes

RESERVATIONS All reserved

EQUIPMENT Amfleet coaches. Business Class.

FOOD Snacks, sandwiches and drinks

LOUNGE CAR National Park Service rangers from the Springfield Armory National Historic Site provide a narrative from Essex Junction to Springfield, Massachusetts, on Saturdays.

BAGGAGE No check-in service. Bicycle and ski racks are available (reservations required).

Dickinson was born and lived most of her life here, and her house at 280 Main is owned by the college. Another former Amherst poet was Robert Frost. The newspaper editor, Horace Greeley, who invented the slogan 'Go West, young man', was also born here.

Amherst is Amtrak's nearest stop to Northampton, where you can see the Cornet Joseph Parsons House (1658) and Wiggins Tavern (1786). The train leaves and continues north among farms and stately barns, crossing the Connecticut River and the Massachusetts–Vermont border.

BRATTLEBORO (45/30) Named after its original proprietor, William Brattle, the former mill town grew up around Fort Dummer, established by the British in 1724 as Vermont's first permanent settlement. The first train arrived in Brattleboro from Boston in 1849 on the tracks of the Vermont & Massachusetts Railroad. The present Union Station (Brattleboro's first building to be listed on the National Register of Historic Places) opened in 1916. Around 18 trains a day stopped here but passenger service ended in 1966, and the building was transformed into the **Brattleboro Museum & Art Center** at 10 Vernon (\ *802 257 0124; www.brattleboromuseum.org*). Amtrak has a small waiting room in the basement of the building. The **tourist bureau** is at 180 Main (\ *802 254 4565; www. brattleborochamber.org*).

BELLOWS FALLS (30/22) The first bridge across the Connecticut River was established here in 1785, and one of the country's first canals was built around the falls. A fish ladder allows Atlantic salmon to pass on their way upstream to spawn. The **Adams Old Stone Grist Mill Museum** (\ *802 463 4280*) features 19th-century milling equipment, farm tools, machinery and sleighs.

The **Green Mountain Railroad** (*54 Depot;* \ *802 463 3069 or* \ *1 800 707 3530; www.vermontrailway.com*) operates diesel trains with vintage coaches from Union Station to Chester, with other trains going from North Bennington to Manchester or White River to Norwich. Trains use the Green Mountain freight line and tracks which belonged to the former Rutland Railroad. They run from June to September (to Chester) and September to October (to Ludlow).

Between Bellows Falls and White River Junction you fleetingly cross the border into New Hampshire before returning to Vermont.

CLAREMONT (22/10) This is the *Vermonter*'s only stop in New Hampshire. The city was founded in 1762 on the Sugar River, which drops 300ft (90m) and provided water

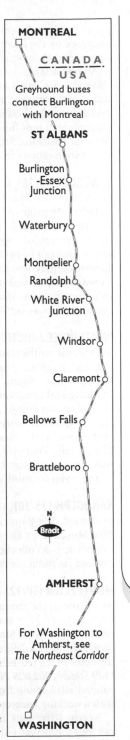

MONTREAL
□

CANADA
USA

Greyhound buses connect Burlington with Montreal

ST ALBANS
○

Burlington
-Essex ○
Junction

Waterbury ○

Montpelier ○
Randolph ○
White River ○
Junction

Windsor ○

Claremont ○

Bellows Falls ○

Brattleboro ○

N
Bradt

AMHERST ○

For Washington to Amherst, see *The Northeast Corridor*

WASHINGTON

The Vermonter Washington–St Albans

power for the old cotton and woollen mills. Historic Mill District walking tours are organised by the Chamber of Commerce, Tremont Square (✆ 603 543 1296; www. claremontnhchamber.org).

Among Claremont's other sights are a 19th-century opera house and New Hampshire's oldest Catholic church, St Mary's. Amtrak's station is at Plains Road and Maple Avenue. Andover's Potter Place Station, built for the Northern Railroad in 1874, is the best 19th-century wooden railroad station surviving in New Hampshire. It now functions as a museum, displaying many items belonging to the Andover Historical Society (www.andoverhistory.org).

The train crosses the Connecticut River again into Vermont.

WINDSOR (10/20) Windsor's pretty Victorian station was originally built in 1871 by the Hartford & New Haven Railroad depot and is listed on the National Register of Historic Places. The former freight house nearby is now an arts centre. The **American Precision Museum** (✆ 802 674 5781; www. americanprecision.org; admission charge) is in a historic building at 196 Main, originally built in 1846 as an armoury. It has the largest collection of historically significant machine tools in the US, as well as products made by them. The **Old Constitution House and Museum** (✆ 802 672 3773; www.historicvermont.org/constitution; admission charge) is located in the tavern where Vermont's first constitution was authored.

WHITE RIVER JUNCTION (20/35) Union Station at Railroad Row was originally built in 1937 to serve the Boston & Maine Railroad, Central Vermont Railway and Rutland Railroad. It serves Lebanon (another mill city) and Hanover (home of Dartmouth College). The elegant station also houses the **New England Transportation Institute and Museum** (✆ 802 291 9838; www.newenglandtransportationmuseum. org; admission charge), and has a splendid Boston & Maine steam locomotive. Nearby **Quechee Gorge State Park** has excellent river fishing and walking trails. Further east is the New Hampshire lakes region, including Lake Winnipesaukee. The 30-mile-long (48km) lake has hundreds of rocky, pine-clad islands and the water is clean enough to drink.

You travel on amid Vermont's hilly forests towards the Green Mountains.

RANDOLPH (35/30) The station at S Main and Salisbury also serves as a local restaurant. The Worcester range of mountains is to your right. The **Porter Music Box Museum** (✆ 802 728 9694; www.portermusicbox.com/Museum; admission charge) has a collection of music boxes as well as a 1926 Steinway Duo-Art Aeolian reproducing piano.

MONTPELIER (30/12) Vermont's capital (population about 8,000) is located on a pass through the mountains along the wooded banks of the Winooski and North Branch rivers. First settled in 1789, it was named after a French city. The 18th-century Greek-style **State House** (✆ 802 828 2228; www.vtstatehouse.org; admission charge) features a delicately beautiful gold dome as well as historic exhibits. Among the items in the red-brick pavilion housing **Vermont's Historical Society Museum** (109 State; ✆ 802 828 2291; www.vermonthistory.org; admission charge) are a hand-painted atlas dating from the Revolutionary War and a railroad station complete with a working telegraph.

Nearby Barre calls itself the granite centre of the world, and at Granitesville you can tour a 100-year-old quarry.

The *Vermonter* continues among green hills, pine trees, rivers and streams, with the graceful orange- and purple-shaded Green Mountains visible ahead as the train climbs.

WATERBURY (12/27) Amtrak's renovated red-brick station was built in 1875 by the Central Vermont Railway and also serves Stowe, a popular tourist destination during the autumn foliage season. Local ski resorts include Sugarbush and Jay Peak.

Bolton Valley (10/17) Another ski area appears to your right as you leave the attractively scattered small town and continue into the 266,000-acre (107,000ha) **Green Mountains National Forest**. Also to your right is the state's highest mountain, Mount Mansfield (4,393ft/1,340m). A toll road from Stowe leads to the summit, from where you can see across Lake Champlain.

BURLINGTON–ESSEX JUNCTION (27/30) Amtrak's station at 29 Railroad Avenue is also the stop for Smugglers Notch ski resort. A white Vermont Federal Bank building features on your left and a graveyard to your right. It was the damming of the Winooski River in the late 18th century which led to the growth of Essex Junction. Six railroad lines converged on this small community by 1853, making it one of the most important rail junctions in the state.

Burlington, seven miles (11km) west, is the smallest US city to be the largest in its state. Located on a hill above the shoreline of Lake Champlain, this is a resort and industrial centre as well as home to the University of Vermont and Trinity College. The city showed its maverick spirit by electing a socialist mayor in 1981, and retaining its old-fashioned downtown area, with its beautiful Italianate, Queen Anne and Colonial Revival-style houses. Burlington has been voted 'best small town for the arts' and *Forbes* magazine selected it as one of the prettiest cities in America.

The Burlington Jazz Festival takes place each June. Except in winter, ferries operate across the lake to Port Kent, New York, served by Amtrak's *Adirondack*. For information throughout the Lake Champlain Valley, contact the **visitors bureau** at 60 Main (✆ *802 863 3489; www.vermont.org*).

Bed & breakfast accommodation can easily be found in this area but you should book early during the foliage season (peaking in mid-October). Contact the Howard Street Guest House, 153 Howard Street, Burlington (✆ *802 864 4668; www. howardstreetguesthouse.com*); Willard Street Inn, 349 S Willard, Burlington (✆ *1 800 577 8712; www.willardstreetinn.com,* **$$$**); Willey's Farm B&B, 5 Red Barn Road, Essex Junction (✆ *802 878 4666,* **$$$**); Willow Pond Farm, 133 Cheese Factory Lane, Shelburne (✆ *802 985 8505,* **$$**).

The **Shelburne Museum** (✆ *802 985 3346; www.shelburnemuseum.org;* ⊕ *May–Oct; admission charge*), seven miles (11km) to the south on Route 7, features the 1890 Shelburne railway depot. The station was originally located in central Shelburne to serve passengers of the Central Vermont and Rutland railroads. Passenger service was discontinued in 1953, and the station was moved to its present site in 1959. Waiting rooms for men and women and the station master's office were restored, and telegraphy systems, railroad memorabilia and maps complete a picture of late 19th- and early 20th-century rail travel. A small annex beside the station exhibits hand tools and equipment used by railroad workers and includes handcarts, picks and shovels, and signal lanterns from railroad lines around the country.

Other highlights at the museum include a Central Vermont steam locomotive, an inspection car from the Woodstock Railroad and the *Grand Isle*, a luxurious rail car built by the Wagner Palace Car Company for the Vermont governor Edward C

Smith. The *Grand Isle* features mahogany panels, an elegant dining room, staterooms and plush furnishings. The museum has a lighthouse, a 220ft Lake Champlain steamboat (the *Ticonderoga*), as well as 37 historic houses and exhibition buildings. The Impressionist paintings include works by Degas and Monet, and you can see one of the country's largest collections of Americana, including carriages, furniture, quilts, dolls and weathervanes. As the *Vermonter* leaves among wooden houses and travels for 30 miles (48km) along part of the Champlain Valley, look for dairy farms, hayfields and logging operations. Warehouses and factories start to intrude on the approach to St Albans.

ST ALBANS The station at 40 Federal, originally built in 1900 as a switch house by the Central Vermont Railway, is the *Vermonter*'s final destination. St Albans is famous for its railroad shops and granite mills. During the Civil War it was raided by a party of Confederates who entered the town from Canada, killed several citizens and robbed the banks of $200,000. They failed in their attempt to burn the place down before fleeing back north of the border. **St Albans Historical Museum** (*Taylor Park;* ✆ *802 527 7933; www.stamuseum.com*) describes the raid and has a collection of railway exhibits including a century-old waiting room and agent's office from a country depot, railroad lanterns, bells, maps and other paraphernalia.

The *Vermonter* terminates in St Albans but it is hoped that a Thruway bus service will be reintroduced to Montreal, 56 miles (90km) further north. For Montreal city information, see *Chapter 21, The* Adirondack (pages 242–3).

23

The *Lake Shore Limited*
Boston/New York–Chicago

General route information

The *Lake Shore Limited* follows the water-level route once travelled by the luxurious *Twentieth Century Limited*. Inspired by the 1932 Broadway musical, the *Twentieth Century Limited* was billed as 'a century ahead of its time' and operated for 65 years from 1902. Boston trains go through central Massachusetts before crossing the Berkshire Hills to Albany, where they are joined by New York trains which have travelled up the Hudson River Valley.

All coaches then accompany the Mohawk River and Erie Canal along a famous Native American highway. The *Lake Shore Limited* touches Lake Erie before hurrying across northern Indiana to Chicago. The *Lake Shore Limited* operates between New York and Yonkers on Amtrak, between Yonkers and Poughkeepsie on Metro-North Railroad (MNRR), between Boston, Poughkeepsie and Cleveland on CSX, and between Cleveland and Chicago on Norfolk Southern (NS).

Joining the train

NEW YORK For New York City information, see *Chapter 14, The Northeast Corridor* (pages 179–82). For the route from New York City to Albany, see *Chapter 21, The Adirondack (pages 235–48)*.

BOSTON For Boston city information, see *Chapter 14, The Northeast Corridor* (pages 174–6).

ESSENTIAL INFORMATION

FREQUENCY Daily. The **westbound** service leaves Boston late morning (or New York mid afternoon) to reach Albany by early evening. You arrive in Cleveland during the night and Chicago by early morning. Travelling **east**, trains leave Chicago mid evening to reach Cleveland early in the morning. You arrive in Albany mid afternoon and Boston by late evening (or New York by early evening).
DURATION 19 hours 30 minutes (New York City); 22 hours 10 minutes (Boston)
RESERVATIONS All reserved
EQUIPMENT Amfleet coaches
SLEEPING Viewliner bedrooms
FOOD Tray meals, snacks, sandwiches, drinks. Complete meals on New York trains.
BAGGAGE Check-in service at most stations

BOSTON
Back Bay Station
Framingham
Worcester
NEW YORK
Springfield
Pittsfield
The Adirondack
Albany-
Rensselaer
Schenectady
Utica
Syracuse
Rochester
Buffalo
Erie
N— Bradt
CLEVELAND
Elyria
Sandusky
Toledo
Bryan
Waterloo
Elkhart
South Bend
CHICAGO

All aboard!

BACK BAY STATION (5/27)
The *Lake Shore Limited* departs Boston's restored South Station to travel along the southern edge of the business district, pausing to pick up passengers at Back Bay Station, opened in 1987 to replace a 1899 former New York, New Haven & Hartford station of the same name. This area was once covered by the Charles River and the railroad tracks had to be built on causeways.

As the train leaves Back Bay you glimpse the city skyline before heading into the wooded landscape of central Massachusetts. Fenway Park, home of baseball's Red Sox, is to your left.

Newton (20/7)
You go through the suburb of Riverside then cross the Charles River.

Wellesley (22/5)
Prestigious Wellesley College, formerly attended by Ali MacGraw, Elizabeth Shue and Hillary Rodham Clinton, is to your right.

FRAMINGHAM (27/30)
A study conducted here in the 1940s was the first to link heart disease with smoking. Framingham's old train station has become a fish restaurant.

The *Lake Shore Limited* continues through the small towns of Ashland, Cordaville, Southville and Westboro.

Lake Quinsigamund (25/5)
The popular watersports area to your right is surrounded by attractive houses.

WORCESTER (30/80)
Past residents have included the humorist Robert Benchley and Isaiah Thomas, publisher of one of America's first newspapers, the *Massachusetts Spy*. Blue and white Holy Cross College can be seen on the hillside to your left. Old Sturbridge village is located 20 miles (32km) southwest.

Worcester's industrial development began in 1828, when the Blackstone Canal linked the town to Providence. A railroad replaced the canal 20 years later. Worcester made America's first carpet loom, first liquid-fuel rocket and first calliope (a fairground music device using steam power to play a set of large whistles).

Amtrak operates out of the grand Union Station at Washington Square in downtown. This impressive 1911 landmark had been quietly decaying for decades before its magnificent twin towers and main hall were renovated at a cost of $32 million and reopened in 2000.

West Warren (45/35)
A miniature golf course features to your left.

Quaboag River (50/30) The *Lake Shore Limited* accompanies the river on the right for several miles.

Chicopee River (60/20) Look right for a waterfall.

SPRINGFIELD (80/75) Birthplace of Dr Seuss and home of the Springfield rifle and Garand semi-automatic, used by US troops during World War II. Springfield began in the 17th century as a trading post on the banks of the Quinnitukqut River (the longest in New England). When the Western Railroad opened a line between here and Worcester in 1839, the city became industrialised.

Springfield is still an important gun-making town and its armoury has one of the world's best military collections. The Basketball Hall of Fame off MA Route 91 (✆ 413 781 6500) honours the game's inventor, James Naismith. The **visitors bureau** is at 1441 Main (✆ 413 787 1548; www.valleyvisitor.com), and Amtrak's station at 66 Lyman. Springfield's large Union Station nearby was built in 1926 by the Boston & Albany Railroad to serve the city's many rail lines, including the Hartford & Springfield, Springfield & New London and Connecticut River railroads. There are plans to turn this long-dormant building into a regional transportation hub.

Connecticut River (5/70) You cross with the stone-arched Memorial Bridge to your left alongside the Eastern States Fairgrounds.

Westfield River (7/68) Look for sawmills and logging operations as the train follows the river through Oronoco, Russell, Huntington, Chester and Middlefield. You travel among some of the state's best scenery, including the Berkshire Mountains and **Chester Blanford State Forest**, where you may see deer, bobcat and wild turkey. Approaching Pittsfield you cross the Appalachian Trail.

PITTSFIELD (75/65) Capital of Berkshire County, surrounded by mountains, forest and lakes, this is where in 1851 Herman Melville wrote *Moby-Dick*. His Arrowhead home is now a museum and the public library includes a room devoted to Melville. The Berkshire **visitors bureau** is at 3 Hoosac Place (✆ 413 743 4500; www.berkshires.org).

Hancock Shaker Village on the slopes of Lebanon Mountain is an open-air museum dedicated to one of the country's oldest religious sects. The **Berkshire Scenic Railway** (✆ 413 637 2210; www.berkshirescenicrailroad.org) offers weekend rides along part of the Housatonic Valley and its museum occupies the restored station at Housatonic and Willow Creek Road in nearby Lenox.

Richmond Pond (10/55) The lake appears to your left. During summer the Boston Symphony Orchestra plays concerts at Tanglewood, the former home of Nathaniel West.

Massachusetts–New York state line (20/45) The train enters the Empire State by way of the Taconic Mountains and State Line Tunnel. Look ahead for views of the Catskill Mountains and Hudson Valley.

Chatham (55/10) A wooden station stands on your right. The 'beefalo' farm on your left cross-breeds cows with buffalo to create a healthier alternative to beef.

The *Lake Shore Limited* rumbles on through such communities as Niverville, Post Road Crossing, Van Hoesen, Brookview and East Greenbush.

ALBANY-RENSSELAER (65/24) For Albany-Rensselaer city information, see *Chapter 21, The Adirondack* (page 239).

SCHENECTADY (24/75) For Schenectady city information, see *Chapter 21, The Adirondack* (page 239).

You cross the Mohawk River on a steel bridge then accompany the river to your left as far as Utica. The Mohawk Trail was the main colonial passage from the east to the Great Lakes. Mohawk Indians fought the Mohicans at Kinquariones, situated on the rocky cliff overhanging the tracks.

Erie Canal (10/65) The train accompanies the canal to your left for much of its route between here and Rochester. Look for the first in a series of locks.

Amsterdam (25/50) Home of Coleco, the company which created Cabbage Patch Dolls. Among the town's buildings are several associated with Sir William Johnson and family, who joined with the Iroquois against the French and their Native American allies during the French and Indian War. Sir William built the mansion to your left for his daughter. Fort Johnson, seen to your right, dates from 1749. Eight missionaries who were killed attempting to convert Native Americans to Christianity are commemorated by a shrine.

You travel on through an attractive valley of woods, hills and dairy farms.

Nelliston (35/40) The stone depot with green shutters to your left is now an Elks Lodge. A marker on the other side of the river indicates the site of a Revolutionary army base at Fort Plain.

Palatine Bridge (40/35) Home of Lifesavers candies and Beech-Nut Products, where the Old Palatine Church (1770) stands next to Caroga Creek on your right.

Fonda (45/30) Montgomery County Courthouse is opposite the station, with the town's fairgrounds to your right.

St Johnsville (48/27) Famous for leather-tanning and dye factories, St Johnsville is the *Lake Shore Limited*'s halfway point along the Mohawk Valley.

Herkimer (60/15) The town featured in Walter Edmond's frontier novel *Drums Along the Mohawk*.

Erie Canal (68/7) You cross the canal above a sequence of locks. Constructed between 1817 and 1825, the waterway spans New York State from Albany on the Hudson to Buffalo on Lake Erie. It was later enlarged and partly relocated to incorporate Lake Oneida. You approach Utica among factories and junk yards.

UTICA (75/45) Located on the Mohawk River and New York State Barge Canal, Utica was called Old Fort Schuyler until it was renamed after a place in northern Africa. Rapid development followed the arrival of the Erie Canal. The beautifully restored Union Station on your left opened in 1914, and extensive rail yards stretch away to your right. The Adirondack Scenic Railroad operates regular excursions from Union Station to Thendara, and eventually Lake Placid ($\backslash$ *800 819 2291; www.adirondackrr.com*).

The train pulls out and continues its journey west. Look right as you near the town of Rome for the sculpture perched above the Paul Revere brass factory.

Rome (15/30) The Stars and Stripes first flew at the Battle of Oriskany in 1777, inspiring Francis Bellamy to compose the Pledge of Allegiance. Fort Stanwix battle site is now part of downtown. The Erie Canal began in Rome on 4 July 1817, and you catch another glimpse of it off to your right as the train leaves for the northern highlands.

SYRACUSE (45/80) Salt City, where for many years the mines produced most of America's favourite seasoning. Extraction methods are demonstrated at the **Salt Museum** (✆ *315 453 6715; admission free*) on the shore of Onondaga Lake. The **Erie Canal Museum** is located in the 1850 weigh lock building at 318 Erie Boulevard (✆ *315 471 0593; www.eriecanalmuseum.org; admission free*).

Look for long Conrail trains being set up on your right as the *Lake Shore Limited* enters the city among factories and warehouses. Amtrak uses the modern William F Walsh Regional Transportation Center near the shore of Lake Onondaga.

LeMoyne College (4/76) Seen high up to your left, the college was named after a French missionary.

Onondaga Lake (8/72) To your right is the place where Father LeMoyne discovered salt reserves.

New York State Fairgrounds (13/67) An annual state fair takes place from late August until early September. The racetrack is to your right.

Erie Canal (32/48) You rediscover the canal on your right soon after Weedsport then cross into a more rural landscape. For the next 40 minutes the train travels among orchards, farmhouses and fields of rich, dark earth.

Clyde (38/42) The town's colonial cemetery is to your left.

East Palmyra (58/22) Look left for a picturesque church standing on the hill. Nearer to Rochester the dairy farms and greenery dwindle, to be replaced by more factories and freight yards.

Sibley Clock Tower (78/2) Named after Hiram Sibley, who was the founder of Western Union.

ROCHESTER (80/55) The city's largest employer is Kodak (established in 1880) and a turreted Eastman Kodak building appears to your right. The Genessee brewery is to your left. Rochester was 'the flour capital of the world' in the early 18th century, when the town grew along the upper falls of the Genessee River. It later became the northern terminal of the Underground Railroad, and has a spectacular lilac festival each May.

The **New York Museum of Transportation** (*6393 E River Rd;* ✆ *585 533 1113; www. nymtmuseum.org;* ⊕ *Sun; admission charge*) in nearby Rush includes a Philadelphia snow-sweeper and a Genessee & Wyoming caboose, along with buses, vintage cars and trolleys. The **Rochester & Genessee Valley Museum** (✆ *585 533 1431; www. rochnrhs.org; admission charge*), in a restored Erie Railroad station south of the city, has locomotives and cars from the New York Central, Baltimore & Ohio and Erie-Lackawanna railroads. As the *Lake Shore Limited* crosses the Genessee River, look for a futuristic Times Square building dominating the downtown area to your left.

Erie Canal (5/50) After you cross the canal for the last time, a massive limestone mine sprawls to your right.

Bergen (20/35) The train passes Bergen on the right as the rolling landscape gives way to flatter countryside approaching the Great Lakes.

Lancaster (47/8) Fences surround Alden Penitentiary to your left and Lancaster's air park is to your right.

BUFFALO (55/90) The city stands next to Lake Erie and is separated from Canada by the Niagara River. After the Civil War many railroads converged here to create important markets and a thriving railroad car industry. Buffalo remains a major rail centre and industrial city.

As the train pauses at Depew Station on Dick Road, note the Art Deco clock tower of the old Buffalo Central Terminal, opened in 1929 by the New York Central Railroad, which used to see 30,000 passengers and 200 trains per day. The Allentown area has Victorian buildings, shops and restaurants. For information, contact the **visitors bureau** at 617 Main (✆ *1 800 283 3256; www.buffalocvb.org*).

Between here and Toledo, the train lives up to its name by skirting the southern shore of Lake Erie, sometimes visible to your right as you travel through a horizontal land of fields and low hedges.

New York–Pennsylvania state line (60/30) You briefly enter the Keystone State, founded by William Penn in 1682.

ERIE (90/90) Pennsylvania's only port on the lake was named after Eriez Indians. During the War of 1812, Admiral Oliver Hazard Perry scored a vital victory over the British and the hull of his flagship *Niagara* is moored at the end of State Street. Dickson's Tavern, his base before the battle, became a station on the Underground Railroad and escaped slaves hid in its walls before continuing to Canada.

The **Lake Shore Railway Museum** (✆ *814 725 1911; ☉ May–Oct Wed–Sun; admission free*) is 15 miles (24km) away at North East. Housed in a New York Central passenger station built for the Lake Shore & Michigan Southern Railway. Its collection includes engines, sleepers, refrigerated freight wagons and a wooden business car.

Pennsylvania–Ohio state line (30/60) Ohio's name comes from an Iroquois word for 'beautiful'. The *Lake Shore Limited* travels through the fishing village of Conneaut before passing the towns of Ashtaboula and Mentor.

CLEVELAND (90/28) Founded in the 18th century by General Moses Cleaveland and misspelled by his men on the official document, Cleveland has been the home of President James Garfield, millionaire John D Rockefeller and Superman, created by Jerry Siegel and Joe Shuster. Ohio's largest industrial city has lately acquired a less sooty image, helped by cultural institutions such as its world-famous symphony orchestra and the **Rock and Roll Hall of Fame**. In 1967, Cleveland elected Carl Stokes as the first black mayor of any major US city.

Cleveland basics

☎ Telephone code 216

🚉 Station (*Ticket office & waiting room* ⏰ *00.00–13.00 & 21.30–23.59; information* ☎ *696 5115*) Amtrak's excellent modern lakefront station is at 200 Cleveland Memorial Shoreway, opposite the Municipal Stadium. Lockers, vending machines, handcarts, taxi stand.

Connections No Thruway buses.

🚌 Local transport RTA buses operate downtown & to outlying areas (☎ *566 5100; www.riderta.com*).

🚕 Taxis Yellow ☎ 623 1550; Americab ☎ 881 1111

🚗 Car rental Hertz, 708 St Clair; ☎ 241 0375

🚌 Greyhound 1465 Chester Av; ☎ 781 2464

✈ Hopkins International Airport 10 miles (16km) southwest by RTA Red Line train & bus #75.

Tours Haunted Cleveland Ghost Tours ☎ 251 0406. Trolley Tours ☎ 771 4484; ⏰ May–Dec. The

Goodtime III cruises Lake Erie & the Cuyahoga & Rocky rivers (☎ *861 5110*).

ℹ Visitors bureau 100 Public Sq; ☎ 875 6680 or ☎ 800 321 1004 (hotel reservations & information hotline); www.positivelycleveland. com; ⏰ Mon–Sat

🏠 Accommodation For rooms in local homes, contact Cleveland Private Lodgings, PO Box 18590, Cleveland, OH 44118; ☎ 321 3213.

Stanford House (AYH) Hostel, 6093 Stanford Rd, Northfield; ☎ 330 467 8711. A historic house 20 miles (32km) south of Cleveland. Beds, **$**.

Hotels include the Renaissance Cleveland, 24 Public Sq; ☎ 696 5600, **$$$$$**; Crowne Plaza, 777 St Clair Av; ☎ 771 7600, **$$$**; Omni International, 2065 E 96th; ☎ 791 1900, **$$$$$**; Holiday Inn Lakeside, 1111 Lakeside Av; ☎ 241 5100, **$$$**; Residence Inn by Marriott, 527 Prospect Av; ☎ 443 9043, **$$$**; Embassy Suite Hotel Cleveland, 1701 E 12th; ☎ 523 8000, **$$$$**.

Recommended in Cleveland

Museum of Art 11150 East Bd; ☎ 421 7350; www.clevelandart.org; ⏰ Tue–Sun; free. An outstanding collection of more than 40,000 works of art, ranging over 5,000 years from ancient Egypt to the present. Includes Picassos, French Impressionists & Rodin's *The Thinker*.

Tower City Center ☎ 771 0033. An ultra-modern extravaganza of shops, offices & mall located in & around the renovated Cleveland Union train terminal. Amtrak's *Lake Shore* train served Union Terminal briefly in 1971 before the *Lake Shore Limited* began in 1975 & Amtrak built its new station on Lake Erie.

Rock and Roll Hall of Fame and Museum 1100 Rock & Roll Bd; ☎ 781 ROCK (7625); www. rockhall.com; ⏰ daily; admission charge. From Muddy Waters & Little Richard to Bruce Springsteen & Neil Young, you can explore the world's largest collection of past, present & future rock music. The Beatles collection includes John Lennon's Sgt Pepper uniform, Paul McCartney's collarless jacket, & handwritten lyric manuscripts.

Cleveland Botanical Garden 11030 E Bd; ☎ 721 1600; www.cbgarden.org; ⏰ Tue–Sun;

admission charge. Exotic indoor biomes & some of the finest public gardens in the Midwest, each with its own personality, including a medieval English garden & the largest herb garden in Ohio.

Museum of Natural History 1 Wade Oval; ☎ 231 4600; www.cmnh.org; ⏰ daily; admission charge. Featuring rare prehistoric exhibits, exotic cultures, rare diamonds & a new planetarium.

Great Lakes Science Center 601 Erieside Av; ☎ 694 2000; www.greatscience.com; ⏰ daily; admission charge. More than 400 interactive exhibits make this one of the largest science museums in the country. Permanent exhibits include Virtual Sports, the Indoor Tornado, giant outdoor mazes & one of the largest video walls east of the Rockies.

Cleveland Metroparks Zoo 3900 Wildlife Way; ☎ 661 6500; www.clemetzoo.com; ⏰ daily; admission charge. 3,000 animals roam 168 wooded acres & 2 indoor acres of tropics. Including the Rainforest, Wolf Wilderness, Birds of the World & Northern Trek, where cool-weather-loving animals like bears, deer, tigers & wolves live.

The Lake Shore Limited   Boston/New York–Chicago

23

All aboard!

The train leaves with the Municipal Stadium on your right and a Goodyear plant to your left. You cross the Cuyahoga River.

Hopkins Airport (10/18) Cleveland's main airport is to your right.

ELYRIA (28/32) Named after Herman Ely, who founded this manufacturing city on the Black River in the 19th century. Oberlin College became the first in the US to enrol African-Americans and women on equal terms with white males.

Amherst (10/22) The New York Central depot has been faithfully maintained and old rail cars stand proudly to the left of the tracks. On your right is a large Pillsbury factory.

Vermillion River (15/17) Look right for a sight of Lake Erie after you cross a river famous for its fishing fleet. You pass through the fishing towns of Vermillion (with its maritime museum) and Huron (where Thomas Edison was born).

Hudson (24/8) You cross the Huron River.

SANDUSKY (32/45) Once another stop on the Underground Railroad, Sandusky's busy port today ships coal and local wine. The city also has a museum devoted to merry-go-rounds. Nearby is the Cedar Point amusement park, America's fifth largest. Amtrak's modest station is on your left at N Depot and Hayes Avenue, and the Lake Erie Islands can be reached by ferry from the waterfront.

The **Mad River & NKP Railroad Museum** (233 York; ✆ 419 483 2222; www. madrivermuseum.org; ⊕ May–Oct daily; admission charge) in Bellevue features a Chicago, Burlington & Quincy dome car (the first in the country) as well as US Army troop sleepers, uniforms, timetables, lanterns, china, locks and historic buildings. Henry Flagler, builder of the Florida East Coast Railroad, once lived on the property where the museum is located.

You go through manufacturing districts then cross Sandusky Bay before veering east towards Toledo. To your right is the top of one of **Cedar Point's** 17 rollercoasters (✆ 419 627 2350; www.cedarpoint.com). The $25 million Millennium Force coaster is one of the tallest and fastest in the world.

Lake Erie (12/33) The lake is visible for the last time away to your right before you cross the Portage River at Port Clinton.

Davis-Bessie Nuclear Plant (20/25) Seen beneath a plume of steam in the right distance before you continue among vineyards, apple orchards and peach trees.

Clay Center (27/18) The town is surrounded by a limestone quarry.

Maumee River (40/5) Scenery becomes ever more industrial as you cross the river, with Toledo's outline to your right. The train curves left among some of the world's largest grain elevators while Conrail trains gather on both sides.

TOLEDO (45/50) Ohio and Michigan argued over this valuable harbour, where the Maumee River meets Lake Erie, until President Jackson settled the issue in Ohio's favour. The Toledo Museum of Art's crystal collection reflects the city's reputation as 'the glass capital of the world' and the Libbey glass factory is to your left. Thruway buses connect with Detroit, Dearborn, Ann Arbor and East Lansing from Amtrak's terminal at 415 Emerald Avenue.

The train pulls out on a 68.5-mile (110km) straight of track known as the air line route, which doesn't have a single curve.

Holland (12/38) Neat farms start to replace industry again.

BRYAN (50/25) A distribution point for agricultural produce, the Fountain City is known for its artesian wells and the Ohio Art Company, maker of Etch-A-Sketch. To your right is WBNO, the first solar-powered radio station in the world.

You cross the St Joseph River and Ohio–Indiana state line.

WATERLOO (25/45) Highest point on the route, situated 995ft (304m) above sea level and 400ft (120m) above the Great Lakes. Waterloo is the train's nearest stop to Fort Wayne.

Elkhart River (25/20) After crossing the river, the train follows a leisurely course through rolling countryside.

ELKHART (45/22) Elkhart has been the world's largest producer of brass musical instruments and mobile homes and is the headquarters of Miles Laboratories, maker of Alka-Seltzer. The Michigan Southern Railroad built repair shops here and this was a division point on the New York Central (later the Penn Central). Amtrak's station is at 131 Tyler Avenue, where shiny New York Central trains wait beside a steam engine across the tracks to your left. Amish and Mennonite Christian communities nearby include Goshen, located five miles (8km) southeast.

The *Lake Shore Limited* leaves among factories and warehouses, approaching South Bend past the old Studebaker car factory to your left, which closed in 1963.

The **National New York Central Railroad Museum** (*721 S Main;* ✆*574 294 3001; www.nycrrmuseum.org; admission free*) in Elkhart shows the creation of the New York Central, Penn Central, Amtrak and Conrail railroads. Adjacent to tracks now controlled by Norfolk Southern and the former main line of the New York Central, the museum lies next to some of the busiest railroad traffic in America. Hands-on exhibits, toy trains and full-size locomotives and rolling stock bring railroad history to life. Three locomotives are in the process of restoration and there is an extensive collection of memorabilia from New York Central stations and rail cars.

SOUTH BEND (22/85) Located on a bend of the St Joseph River where settlers negotiated a treaty with Native Americans under the Council oak tree, which still stands in Highland Cemetery. Look right for the gold dome of Notre Dame University above the trees.

As you travel on you pass from Eastern to Central Time, so watches go back an hour (forward when travelling east).

La Porte (20/65) The town began in 1832 as a trading centre for farmers.

Gary (45/40) Long one of the nation's great steel producers, plants on both sides display a mass of complicated pipelines, pylons and storage tanks. Gary was the birthplace of Karl Malden, Michael Jackson and the astronaut Frank Borman.

23

The train continues sedately through the communities of Pine Junction and Indiana Harbor.

Indiana Harbor Canal (50/35) You cross on a drawbridge. The canal joins the Calumet River to Lake Michigan, seen a short distance away to your right. Look left for more steel mills and a Lever Brothers factory.

Hammond-Whiting (60/25) For Hammond-Whiting and the route to Chicago, see *Chapter 20, The* Cardinal (pages 225–34).

CHICAGO Thruway buses connect with Madison, Wisconsin. For Chicago city information, see *Chapter 5, The* California Zephyr (pages 71–4).

24

The *Capitol Limited*
Washington–Chicago

General route information

The *Capitol Limited* takes you through West Virginia, Harper's Ferry and the beautiful Potomac and Shenandoah valleys. You travel among the Allegheny Mountains, visit a revitalised Pittsburgh and see the cornfields of Ohio and Indiana.

Some of the splendid views experienced on this 780-mile (1,255km) journey are only available by train and for much of the way you follow the original Baltimore & Ohio line along which the very first *Capitol Limited* ran in the 1920s as an all-Pullman sleeping-car train from Pennsylvania Station in New York City to Chicago, via Washington, DC. In 1938, this became America's first diesel-powered streamliner. Today's *Capitol Limited* travels between Chicago and Pittsburgh with Norfolk Southern (NS), and between Pittsburgh and Washington with CSX Transportation.

Joining the train

WASHINGTON For Washington, DC, city information, see *Chapter 14, The Northeast Corridor* (pages 187–9). Thruway buses link with Dulles International Airport and Charlottesville, Virginia.

All aboard!

As the *Capitol Limited* slowly departs Washington, look left for the tiled blue and gold dome of the Shrine of the Immaculate Conception (America's largest Catholic

ESSENTIAL INFORMATION

FREQUENCY Daily. The **westbound** train leaves Washington late in the afternoon, arriving in Cumberland by early evening and Pittsburgh late in the evening. You reach Toledo by early next morning and Chicago by early morning. Travelling **east**, trains leave Chicago early evening to reach Toledo by midnight and Pittsburgh early in the morning. You arrive in Cumberland the next morning and Washington by early afternoon.

DURATION 18 hours

RESERVATIONS All reserved

EQUIPMENT Superliner coaches

SLEEPING Superliner bedrooms

FOOD Complete meals, snacks, sandwiches, drinks

LOUNGE CAR Movies, hospitality hour

BAGGAGE Check-in service at most stations

259

WASHINGTON

Rockville

Harper's
Ferry

Martinsburg

Cumberland

Connellsville

PITTSBURGH

Garfield

Alliance

CLEVELAND

For Cleveland to
Chicago, see
The Lake Shore Limited

CHICAGO

church). You travel north through the suburbs of Takoma
Park and Silver Spring, then turn northwest to begin to
follow Baltimore & Ohio tracks to Pittsburgh. Look left for
the gold spires of a Mormon temple just before you cross
the Beltway, often crammed with commuters' cars.

Forest Glen (12/13) The old building which looks like a
castle was once a speakeasy and house of ill repute, but is
now a post office.

Kensington (19/6) As you cross Rock Creek Park, look
left for the 1891 train station standing beside a row of
antique shops.

Garrett Park (20/5) Named after John B Garrett,
President of the Baltimore & Ohio, this was a summer
retreat for railway executives. Note the attractive Victorian
houses among the trees to your left. Look also for the
small white church of St Mary's, where F Scott Fitzgerald
is buried.

Approaching Rockville you see the town's original red-
brick Baltimore & Ohio station to your left, with beyond it
the Rockville Courthouse. Like many others on this route,
the station was designed by Frances E Baldwin.

ROCKVILLE (25/40) An 18th-century Maryland town
which has become a Washington suburb. METRO and
MARC commuter trains wait on the left beside a spartan
station building.

After Rockville the *Capitol Limited* accompanies the
METRO line for a few minutes to its final stop, Washington
Grove.

Gaithersburg (5/35) The county fairgrounds and
another Baldwin station can be seen to your right before
the train crosses Interstate 270.

After passing through Germantown you begin to shake
off suburbia, travelling instead among the farms and gently
rolling hills of the Atlantic coastal plain. Ahead are the
fertile farms of the Potomac Valley.

Barnesville (10/30) The station to your left is where the
Baltimore & Ohio began a new line in 1866. Look left to see
a steam locomotive stranded in the sidings.

Dickerson (15/25) Sugarloaf Mountain is to your right.
Tall chimneys appear in the distance as the train eases over
to accompany the Potomac along the Maryland–Virginia
border. Between the tracks and the river you can see traces of
a neglected section of the Chesapeake & Ohio Canal. Trees
grow in the cutting and along a towpath which was formerly

used by people hauling barges by mule. The canal dates from the mid 19th century, when it carried huge amounts of freight between Cumberland and Georgetown.

Point of Rocks (23/17) Another Victorian Baldwin depot stands where the line from Washington joins the original Baltimore & Ohio line from Baltimore. You travel 800ft (240m) through Point of Rocks Tunnel, the first of 13 between here and Pittsburgh. The train then loses touch with the river for 15 minutes as it goes through the historic Baltimore & Ohio town of Brunswick.

Appalachian Trail (37/3) The longest (2,050 miles/3,300km) footpath in the world crosses the tracks. Note the canal lock-keeper's white house to your left.

Just before Harper's Ferry you go through a tunnel beneath South Mountain and enter West Virginia's eastern panhandle. Watch for Seaboard trains to your left before you cross the canal then cross the rocky Potomac River on a spectacular long bridge. A second bridge can be seen to your left and beyond it the remains of a third. The Shenandoah River is also to your left.

HARPER'S FERRY (40/20) A trading post was built in 1733 where Virginia, West Virginia and Maryland meet, and the ferry, first operated by Robert Harper in 1749, was in business until a bridge was built across the Potomac River in 1824. The Baltimore & Ohio Railroad built a 900ft covered railroad bridge in 1836.

One of the most important events leading to the Civil War occurred here in 1859 when abolitionist John Brown and his supporters seized the government arsenal. Federal troops led by Robert E Lee came by train to force Brown's surrender – the first time a railroad in North America had been used for military purposes. The arsenal ruins can be seen to your left.

During the war itself, nine bridges were built and destroyed here, and in June 1861, Stonewall Jackson set fire to 42 locomotives and 300 railroad cars. Harper's Ferry has museums, monuments and several buildings that date from before the Civil War. The **visitor centre** is at 171 Shoreline Drive (304 535 6224; www.nps. gov/hafe) and Amtrak's station at Potomac Street, from where MARC commuter trains operate to Washington.

On your right as you leave are the remains of an early hydro-electric plant fed by water from a dam. Wind-powered irrigation pumps appear to your left.

Nearing Martinsburg look right for the two 1860s roundhouses (one partly demolished) standing beside neglected railroad buildings. The stone mansion next to the tracks on your left once belonged to Revolutionary War general Adam Stephen.

MARTINSBURG (20/85) To your left can be seen Martinsburg's restored railroad hotel and a historic Baltimore & Ohio Railroad roundhouse. The 1847 brick station was the only building in town to survive the Civil War and is the oldest working train station in the country. Confederate forces stole 14 Baltimore & Ohio locomotives from Martinsburg during the Civil War and in 1877, the country's biggest-ever rail strike began here.

Hagerstown, 12 miles to the north, was named after a German immigrant, Jonathan Hager, and became known as Hub City when six separate railways converged in the 19th century. Hagerstown still has four lines – Conrail, the Chessie-CSX, the Norfolk-Southern and the Winchester & Western – and rail infrastructure covers 228,000ft^2 (21,000m^2). It has two passenger stations, a roundhouse and the largest turntable in eastern America. The **National Railroad Historic Society** (*300 S Burhans Bd;* 301 739 5598; www.roundhouse.org) has developed a roundhouse museum and intends to make this a working centre for the restoration of steam engines. MARC commuter trains go to Hagerstown from Washington, DC.

The *Capitol Limited* pulls out of Martinsburg and continues past villages, farms, woods and orchards.

Cherry Run (10/75) Fort Frederick, seen across the Potomac to your right, dates from 1756 and was active during the Revolutionary, French and Indian, and Civil wars. You follow the river for over an hour, with fine views apart from the few tunnels.

Hancock (20/65) The small town stands on both sides of the river in three states – West Virginia, Maryland and Pennsylvania. Potomac Park Airport is to your right.

Great Capcon (30/55) You cross the Great Capcon River. Look right on the far side of the Potomac soon afterwards to see the remains of a Chesapeake & Ohio Canal aqueduct.

Orleans Road (35/50) The *Capitol Limited* quits the old Baltimore & Ohio main line at this point and enters the 1,592ft (485m) Graham Tunnel. The tunnel is in Maryland but you emerge back in West Virginia and cross Kessler's Bridge.

Mountains and a tree-lined ravine appear to your right as the Potomac River runs through spectacular, sparsely populated country. Much of this region can only be seen from a raft or by travelling Amtrak. Look for deer among the wooded cliffs which sometimes rise sheer from the river. You cross the Potomac three times before leaving West Virginia.

North Branch (80/5) The Chesapeake & Ohio Canal is visible for the last time before you pass under a highway bridge then under an old railroad bridge. On the approach to Cumberland, coal wagons and trailer trains gather to your left and the *Capitol Limited* leaves the Potomac Valley.

CUMBERLAND (85/130) Otherwise known as Washington Town or the 'Queen City of the Alleghenies'. Early coal, canal and railway barons built mansions here and many attractive houses can be seen on the hillside to your right. Cumberland was the eastern terminus of the Cumberland (National) Road and the western terminus of the Chesapeake & Ohio Canal. The Baltimore & Ohio Railroad arrived in 1842, construction having started in Baltimore in 1828.

The French and Indian War was sparked in 1755, when General Braddock led his forces 220 miles (350km) from Fort Cumberland towards Fort Duquesne. A thousand men died in the battle. George Washington also made expeditions from the fort, of which his log cabin is all that remains. Look left for a miniature fir plantation as the train departs.

The Narrows (5/125) This passage through the Alleghenies provided a route for early traders and the military. The railway came later, followed by America's earliest federal highway (US 40, seen to your left).

Mount Savage (7/123) America's first steel rails were produced at this junction of the Baltimore & Ohio and Pennsylvania railroads.

Maryland–Pennsylvania state line (10/120) You cross the Mason–Dixon Line and enter the most central of the 13 original colonies. Look right for a large red barn.

The *Capitol Limited* climbs laboriously into the mountains, going through Hyndman Station and Falls Cut Tunnel, constructed in 1897.

Wills Creek (40/90) Look right for anglers fishing a stream named after Indian Will, the last of the Shawnees. A flood here in 1984 damaged several small towns and 18 miles (28km) of track.

The train continues to climb a 2% gradient, one of the steepest in these mountains. You go through the small communities of Mance and Manila by way of a series of curves.

Sand Patch Tunnel (47/83) Almost a mile (1.6km) from end to end, the tunnel is the longest and straightest on this route.

Sand Patch (49/81) This pinnacle of the Allegheny Mountains is the route's highest point (2,258ft/685m above sea level). The *Capitol Limited* passes beneath tracks of the former Western Maryland Railroad, now part of CSX Transportation and often busy with freight.

Meyersdale (52/78) Founded in the 18th century, Meyersdale is famous for maple sugar. Look left for Mount Davis (3,213ft/980m) before you continue through the towns of Salisbury Junction and Yoder.

Garrett (60/70) Another town named after the Baltimore & Ohio boss, John Garrett. Helper locomotives were based here in the days of steam.

Atlantic (65/65) The remains of a millstone quarry are visible among the mountains on your right and two abandoned millstones lie in the Casselman River to your left.

As the train continues on a rightwards curve, look left for the boulder called Saddle Rock, shaped like a Western saddle.

Markelton (80/50) Situated on the banks of the Youghiogheny River, Markelton was a resort for Pittsburgh's elite at the beginning of the 20th century.

Confluence (83/47) The Casselman River is joined on the left by the Youghiogheny River and Laurel Hill Creek. A bicycle path runs to Connellsville along a former railroad bed beside the river.

Sugarloaf Mountain (90/40) The mountain's distinctive shape is off to your right as you continue beside the river. Look for canoeists, fishermen, deer and possibly beaver.

Ohiopyle (95/35) Home of Ohiopyle Falls, out of sight to your left. Adjacent Laurel Highlands Park is especially beautiful in autumn and has the state's highest mountain, Mount Davis.

Kaufman's Run (110/20) Frank Lloyd Wright incorporated a small waterfall here inside the house he built and called Fallingwater. It was a weekend retreat for the Kaufman family, owners of a Pittsburgh department store.

Indian Creek (120/10) You cross the creek by an old stone bridge.

CONNELLSVILLE (130/90) Surrounded by coalfields producing the raw material for Connellsville Coke, this was an important railroad town. Service trains paused during World War II so that hundreds of female volunteers could serve food to the troops. Amtrak's station is at Front and Water.

Leaving town, the train passes beneath a railway bridge which crosses the river to your left. You depart the Appalachian Mountains at Layton and descend towards the Allegheny Plateau via the attractive suburbs of Versailles and Smithton.

The *Capitol Limited* encounters heavy industrial scenes as it approaches Pittsburgh. The Duquesne steelworks are to your left, followed by the J Edgar Thompson works built by Andrew Carnegie, the Scottish-born rail and steel tycoon who became a philanthropist.

Braddock (80/10) Named after a British Army general, George Braddock, who died fighting the French in 1755. You pass through another tunnel into Pittsburgh.

PITTSBURGH (90/100) The birthplace of Gene Kelly, Gertrude Stein and Christina Aguilera is America's busiest inland port, where the Allegheny and Monongahela rivers meet to become the Ohio. In the 1750s, this strategic position led to the establishment of a fort named after the British prime minister William Pitt (the Elder). Iron City eventually became so industrial it was known as 'hell with the lid off'. In 1877, 60 people died after soldiers fired on striking railroad workers.

The steel mills have been tamed and the slag heaps eliminated at a cost of $3 billion. Pittsburgh has instead acquired high-tech industry, smart skyscrapers and clean air. Now that the smoke has cleared, even outsiders are impressed by Renaissance City.

Pittsburgh basics

☏Telephone code 412

⇜ Station (*Ticket office & waiting room* ⊕ *24hrs; information* ☏*471 6170*) Amtrak's station is at 1100 Liberty Av. Lockers, vending machines, ATM banking.

Union Station, or Pennsylvania Station, was designed by Daniel Burnham & opened in 1903. This monumental building was constructed from terracotta & brick, with a splendid rotunda & waiting room. It was restored in the mid 1980s, & the office tower converted into apts.

Connections The New Castle Area Transit Authority operates w/day bus services between New Castle, PA & Amtrak's station in Pittsburgh.

⇚ Local transport The Port Authority of Allegheny County operates inclines, light rail, the 'T' subway & bus services throughout the city. For details of routes, a free map & off-peak deals, ☏442 2000.

🚕 Taxis Checker ☏381 5600; Yellow ☏321 8100

🚗 Car rental Enterprise, 120 Sixth St; ☏391 7766

⇚ Greyhound 55 11th & Liberty, near Amtrak's station; ☏392 6504

✈ Pittsburgh International Airport 15 miles (24km) west by Airlines Transportation (☏*321 8147*).

Tours Lenzner; ☏761 7000. River cruises (Apr–Oct) with the Gateway Clipper Fleet at Station Sq Dock (☏*355 7980*). Cable railway inclines take you to an observation deck & restaurants on Mount Washington, from where you can see the Golden Triangle formed by the junction of 3 rivers. The Monongahela Incline (☏*442 2000*) is near Smithfield Bridge & the Duquesne Inclined Plane (☏*381 1665; www.incline.cc*) at Fort Pitt Bridge.

Pittsburgh History & Landmarks Foundation (☏*471 5808 (reservations) or* ☏*877 471 5808 (tour information); www.phlf.org*) offers a wide variety of tours & events, including walking tours of downtown & historic neighbourhoods. Possible tour themes include architectural landmarks of a particular time period or architect; parks, gardens, & sculpture; historic mansions or rowhouses; & notable engineering works.

ℹ Visitors bureau 120 Fifth Av; ☏1 800 359 0758 or ☏281 7711; www.visitpittsburgh.com; ⊕ daily

⌂ Accommodation Hotels include the Omni William Penn, 530 William Penn Way; ☎281 7100, **$$$$**; Marriott Pittsburgh, 112 Washington Pl; ☎471 4000, **$$$$$**; Hilton, 600 Commonwealth Pl; ☎391 4600, **$$$$**; Sheraton, 300 W Station Sq Dr; ☎261 2000, **$$$$$**; Parkway Center-Best Western, 875 Greentree Rd; ☎922 7070, **$$$**; Red Roof Inn, 6404 Stubenville Pike; ☎787 7870, **$$**.

Recommended in Pittsburgh

Andy Warhol Museum 117 Sandusky; ☎237 8300; www.warhol.org; ☉ Tue–Sun; admission charge. Warhol was born in Pittsburgh & this collection (the world's largest devoted to a single artist) includes many films & paintings.

University of Pittsburgh Bigelow Bd, Fifth Av & Forbes Av; ☎624 4141; www.pitt.edu; ☉ daily; admission charge. The Cathedral of Learning Tower (☎624 6000) is a historic landmark & the 2nd-tallest education building in the world, with 27 'nationality rooms' (*www.pitt.edu/~natrooms*) & a 36th-floor observation area.

Point State Park Off Interstate 279, near Fort Pitt Bridge. Featuring the city's oldest building, Fort Pitt Blockhouse, built in 1764 by Colonel Henry Bouquet & now the oldest building still standing west of the Appalachians.

Fort Pitt Museum ☎281 9285; www. heinzhistorycenter.org; ☉ daily; admission charge. The museum shows life inside the fort from the 1750s, including a fur trader's cabin, a casemate storage room for munitions, & a British soldiers' barracks.

Allegheny County Courthouse and Jail 171 Fifth Av & Grant; ☎350 5313; tours by arrangement. This wonderful neo-Romanesque building was designed by Henry Hobson Richardson, with a dominating tower & a 'Bridge of Sighs' where convicts would cross the street from courthouse to prison.

Frick Art and Historical Center 7227 Reynolds, in Point Breeze; ☎371 0600; www. frickart.org; ☉ Tue–Sun; free. Includes the Frick Art Museum (mainly European works), the Car & Carriage Museum (historic automobiles from 1898 to 1940) & the Clayton Historical House featuring Henry Frick's art collection.

Phipps Conservatory One Schenley Park; ☎622 6914; www.phipps.conservatory.org; ☉ daily; admission charge. This huge & splendid Victorian conservatory features tropical plants, cacti, orchids & bonsai.

National Aviary 700 Arch St; ☎323 7235; www. aviary.org; ☉ daily; admission charge. Opened in 1952, the aviary contains more than 500 birds, including many rare & endangered species.

John Heinz Pittsburgh Regional History Center 1212 Smallman; ☎454 6000; www. heinzhistorycenter.org; ☉ daily; admission charge. Housed in the former Chautauqua Lake Ice Company Building, this museum's Great Hall features a 1949 trolley, a Conestoga wagon & the huge Pittsburgh city fire bell that was cast after the Great Fire of 1845. Life-size reconstructions show a log home, an immigrant worker courtyard house & a suburban ranch home.

All aboard!

The train travels on through the night via Ambridge, Beaver Falls and Salem.

GARFIELD (60/40) Named after President James Garfield, who was assassinated in 1881 in the old Washington, DC, station.

ALLIANCE (100/70) An industrial city on the Mahoning River, Alliance makes steel and electrical machinery and is the home of Mount Union College. The unstaffed station on the corner of Main and Webb is Amtrak's nearest stop to Canton, seven miles southwest.

Ravenna (30/40) Founded in 1799, Ravenna has the Northeastern Ohio University College of Medicine.

Hudson (45/25) The town dates from 1826, and was an important stop on the stagecoach route between Pittsburgh and Cleveland.

CLEVELAND (70/110) For Cleveland city information and the rest of the route to Chicago, see *Chapter 23, The* Lake Shore Limited (pages 249–58). The *Capitol Limited* stops at Elyria, Sandusky, Toledo, Waterloo, Elkhart and South Bend.

CHICAGO For Chicago city information, see *Chapter 5, The* California Zephyr (pages 71–4).

The *Pennsylvanian*
New York–Pittsburgh

General route information

After travelling from New York through some of the country's most densely populated areas, the *Pennsylvanian* turns due west at Philadelphia into Pennsylvania Dutch country, home of the Amish people. You follow the Juniata River to the Allegheny Mountains then round spectacular Horseshoe Curve before reaching Pittsburgh.

The prestigious *Broadway Limited*, which first ran in 1912, used this route when it continued to Chicago until the mid 1990s. In 1938, the Pennsylvania Railroad's 'leader of the fleet' was re-equipped as a streamliner that can be seen in action in the 1940 film called *Broadway Limited*.

Joining the train

NEW YORK For New York City, the route to Philadelphia and Philadelphia city information, see *Chapter 14, The Northeast Corridor* (pages 173–89).

PHILADELPHIA (10/26) The *Pennsylvanian* leaves 30th Street Station between apartment buildings on the right and commuter trains to the left.

Overbrook (10/16) Look left for Victorian buildings beyond the wooden station.

Ardmore (12/14) One of several commuter stops occurring between Philadelphia and Paoli. Some stations have elaborately sculpted canopies.

ESSENTIAL INFORMATION

FREQUENCY Daily. The **westbound** service leaves New York late morning to reach Philadelphia around midday and Harrisburg by mid afternoon. You arrive at Pittsburgh mid evening. Travelling **east** (Monday–Saturday), trains leave Pittsburgh early in the morning to arrive in Harrisburg by early afternoon. Philadelphia is reached mid afternoon and New York late afternoon. Travelling east (Sunday), trains leave Pittsburgh early in the afternoon to arrive in Harrisburg by early evening. Philadelphia is reached mid evening and New York late evening.

DURATION Nine hours 20 minutes

RESERVATIONS All reserved

EQUIPMENT Amfleet coaches

FOOD Sandwiches, snacks, drinks

BAGGAGE No check-in service

PAOLI (26/40) Named after Pasquale Paoli, an 18th-century Corsican revolutionary. Just to the north is Valley Forge, site of the base camp where George Washington's fledgling continental army spent a cold and hungry winter (1777/78) during the Revolutionary War. You can visit Washington's headquarters and the memorial chapel. Amtrak's utilitarian depot is located at Lancaster Pike and S Valley Road. There are plans to expand Paoli Station on the site of the former Pennsylvania Railroad–Amtrak–SEPTA train shed and repair facility.

The *Pennsylvanian* continues among residential areas and leafy hills which look especially attractive when dogwoods are in bloom during spring.

Coatesville (10/30) Industry sprawls to your left before the train enters fertile Pennsylvania Dutch country with its many wooden bell-towered churches. Dutch is a misnomer, since this area was largely settled by Germans whose nationality (*Deutsch*) was mispronounced by English colonists.

Many of those now known as Pennsylvania Dutch are members of the Amish Church. Amish people adhere to strict religious beliefs and run their tidy farms much as they have done for 300 years, using mules and ploughs. The 1985 movie *Witness* was set among these white farmhouses, where Amish men dress in black and the women wear plain frocks and traditional bonnets. The Amish have no electricity or television, although mobile phones are allowed and they can drive but not own cars.

LANCASTER (40/18) America's oldest inland city was the nation's capital for a single day on 27 September 1777. Founded in 1718 as Hickory Town before being renamed after a town in England, Lancaster is where the Amish come to market. You can find information on Amish life at the **Pennsylvania Dutch Visitor Center** (*501 Greenfield Rd;* \ *717 299 8901; www.paductchcountry.com*).

Photographs are not allowed but you can visit several families, some of whom make a living selling woven baskets and cookies to 'the English'. Historic Lancaster walking tours depart from 5 W King Street (\ *717 392 1776; www. historiclancasterwalkingtour.com*).

The **Railroad Museum of Pennsylvania** (\ *717 687 8628; www.rrmuseumpa. org;* ⊕ *daily; admission charge*) in nearby Strasburg has one of the world's finest collections of locomotives, passenger cars and freight wagons dating from 1825 up to the present day. The Railroad Weekend in May is one of many special events organised by the museum and the Strasburg Railroad runs daily steam train excursions from April to October. You continue among factories and refineries, with a park to your left. Between here and Harrisburg, the train follows the path of the first telegraph wires. A short distance to the north is Hershey, founded by Milton Hershey in 1903 and dedicated to all things chocolate.

ELIZABETHTOWN (18/20) The town was named after the wife of Captain Barnabas Hughes who purchased the Black Bear Tavern in 1750. The railroad arrived in the 1830s but the town remained mostly agricultural until the early 1900s, when the Klein Chocolate Company opened a factory here and Elizabethtown was a centre for shoe manufacturing.

Three Mile Island (5/15) Two of the power plant's four cooling towers puff plumes of white vapour away to your left. In 1979, this was the scene of America's worst nuclear accident, and the reactor which then suffered partial meltdown has been inoperative ever since.

Harrisburg Airport (8/12) The airport is to your left, with rolling hills beyond the Susquehanna River.

HARRISBURG (20/65) Pennsylvania's capital stands on the east bank of the Susquehanna where the Pennsylvania Canal arrived in 1834. The first trains came two years later and the main Pennsylvania Railroad linked the city with Pittsburgh in 1847.

Harrisburg's Capitol features bronze doors, stained-glass windows and a marble staircase similar to one in the Paris Opera House. Its 272ft (83m) dome resembles St Peter's in Rome. The **State Museum of Pennsylvania** (✆ 717 787 4980; *www.statemuseumpa.org*), situated next to the State Capitol Building at 300 N Street, covers all aspects of Pennsylvania history and has outstanding Civil War exhibits. The **visitors bureau** is at 17 S Second Street (✆ *717 231 7788; www. visithhc.com*).

Bieber Trailways buses connect Amtrak's atmospheric station at Fourth and Chestnut with Scranton and Reading. The current red-brick station, now owned by Amtrak, is the third on this site and is one of the few US stations that still has a train shed above the tracks. It was built by the Pennsylvania Railroad (PRR) in 1887, and rebuilt with its distinctive barn roof in 1905. The **Steamtown National Historic Site** (*150 S Washington Av;* ✆ *570 340 5200; www.nps.gov/stea*) in Scranton reveals early 20th-century railroading in two museums, a theatre and a restored roundhouse. Steam trains travel between Scranton and Moscow, Pennsylvania.

As you depart Harrisburg, look left for the Capitol's green dome beyond the office blocks and car parks.

Susquehanna River (3/62) The *Pennsylvanian* crosses on Rockville Bridge, the longest (3,820ft/1,165m) and widest (52ft/16m) stone-arch bridge in the world.

NEW YORK CITY

N- Bradt

For New York City to Philadelphia, see *The Northeast Corridor*

PHILADELPHIA

Paoli

Lancaster
Elizabethtown
Harrisburg

Lewistown

Huntingdon

Altoona
Johnstown

Latrobe
Greensburg
PITTSBURGH

Duncannon (20/45) For the next 100 miles (160km) you accompany the Juniata River and ascend the Alleghenies. The Susquehanna River fades to your right as farmland gives way to mountains.

LEWISTOWN (65/35) A manufacturing town with a historic station building on the right. The oldest-surviving structure built by the Pennsylvania Railroad, this station was constructed in 1848–49 as a freight handling warehouse. It was renovated and converted into a passenger station in 1868. Lewistown Station closed as a ticket-selling point in 1977, and was purchased by the Pennsylvania Railroad Technical and Historical Society. The building has been restored for use as an archives centre and the society maintains a small waiting room for passengers riding Amtrak trains, making this the oldest continually operated train station in America. Fifty to 60 freight trains a day operate on the former PRR main line, now owned by Norfolk Southern, and branch lines are operated by the Juniata Valley Railroad.

In 1909, a lone gunman held up and robbed a westbound PRR express train a few miles south of the station. He shot the conductor and took $5,000 in gold bullion. Police found most of it the next day and the bandit escaped with only a bag of newly minted pennies. Fifty years later, hunters in the mountains stumbled on a stash of 1909 pennies.

As you move deeper into the Alleghenies, look right for Jack's Mountain and left for Blue Mountain.

HUNTINGDON (35/45) Located next to the Juniata River in an agricultural and fruit-growing region, Huntingdon was the junction of the Huntingdon & Broad Top Mountain Railroad with the PRR, and a port on the main line of the Pennsylvania Canal.

Spruce Creek (15/30) You cross a creek which was fished by former president Jimmy Carter. After negotiating a short tunnel you continue among streams, hills, small towns and rivers. Wooded cliffs appear on both sides.

ALTOONA (45/60) Founded in 1849 by the Pennsylvania Railroad, Altoona was a supply base for railway construction over the mountains. At its peak in the 1920s, the Altoona Works employed 15,000 people and was three miles (5km) long, making it the world's largest rail shop complex. The PRR built 7,873 locomotives here, the last one being in 1946, and the town still provides maintenance facilities. You travel through extensive yards to reach Amtrak's station in the Altoona Transportation Center at 1231 11th Avenue.

The **Railroaders Memorial Museum** (*1300 Ninth Av;* ✆ *814 946 0834; www. railroadcity.com;* ☺ *daily; admission charge*) on your left has many engines, coaches and models associated with the Pennsylvania Railroad. Exhibits include the *Loretto*, a private car that belonged to steel baron Charles M Schwab.

Note the domed cathedral to your right as you go through the middle of Altoona.

Horseshoe Curve (15/45) A 2,355ft (718m) landmark carved out of the Logan Valley hillside in 1854, its central curve measuring 220°, Horseshoe Curve was crucial during the early days of westward expansion since it enabled trains to cope with a demandingly steep gradient. A National Park Service guide is sometimes on board the *Pennsylvanian* to explain the line's history. Look out for an old Pennsylvania Railroad engine to your left next to the modern **visitor centre**.

Gallitzin Summit (25/35) The train travels through a tunnel to the other side of the Alleghenies. Crossing these mountains was a much more laborious affair during the early 19th century, when the Allegheny Portage Railroad, a system of ten inclined planes and a 901ft tunnel carved through solid rock, carried train cars and canal boats 36 miles (38km) between the Juniata and Conemaugh rivers. Charles Dickens, Jenny Lind and Ulysses S Grant were among those who braved the Portage system, which injured passengers on a weekly basis. This unique engineering marvel is explained at the **Allegheny Portage Museum** (✆ *814 886 6150; www.nps. gov/alpo*) with a full-size model and parts of an original stationary steam engine The Allegheny Portage Inclined Plane Railroad operated from 1834 to 1854, when the PRR completed its all-rail line from Philadelphia to Pittsburgh, and played a critical role in opening the interior of the United States to trade and settlement. The railroad's National Historic Site covers 1,249 acres (505ha) and includes a visitor centre, the historic Lemon House, Engine House #6 Exhibit Shelter, the Skew Arch

Bridge, a picnic area and hiking trails. The Staple Bend Tunnel is located four miles east of Johnstown.

JOHNSTOWN (60/45) In 1889, a dam burst on the nearby Conemaugh River after heavy rain. John Hess, an engineer on board the Pennsylvania Railroad's *No 1124*, warned the town of impending disaster by sounding the whistle as his train raced down the valley. He and his fireman jumped to safety just before the train was overtaken by the flood. Many lives were saved because of his warning, but 2,200 people still died in the deluge. Before prohibition, saloons would sometimes have signs reading 'Don't spit, remember the Johnstown flood'.

Further floods in 1936 and 1977 killed 25 and 85 people respectively. Since the steel industry's decline, unlucky Johnstown has also been affected by high levels of unemployment.

You travel for 15 minutes through industrial scenes before forests and mountains return. A sinuously curving river follows below to your right.

LATROBE (45/5) This flag stop is a mostly residential town, used as a training base by the Pittsburgh Steelers football team.

GREENSBURG (5/42) In 1763, Chief Pontiac and the Ottawa Indians were defeated by Henry Bouquet and the British at nearby Bushy Run. Fort Pitt was relieved four days later. Following an economic boom in the 19th century created by coal and Greensburg's importance as a retail and industrial centre, the Pennsylvania Railroad commissioned architect William Cookman to design the new station for the town. This, and rail tracks through Greensburg, were heavily used both for freight and passengers until the late 1940s. The ornate building with its distinctive clock tower is now owned by the Westmoreland Cultural Trust and houses a restaurant and office space.

You continue among green hills with occasional houses and factories, including that of the Westinghouse Brake Company. The train slows down as it begins to approach Pittsburgh, seen ahead to your right.

PITTSBURGH (42/110) For Pittsburgh city information, see *Chapter 24, The Capitol Limited* (pages 264–5).

26

The *Maple Leaf*
New York–Toronto

General route information

The *Maple Leaf* starts in New York and travels more than 500 miles (800km) before reaching Canada's equivalent city, Toronto. The route takes in the Hudson River Valley, the Mohawk Valley, Niagara Falls and Lake Ontario. Travelling north by day gives you maximum viewing opportunities.

ESSENTIAL INFORMATION

IMMIGRATION FORMALITIES US and Canadian citizens must have a passport, Trusted Traveler card or enhanced driver's licence – **an ordinary driver's licence is not sufficient**. Citizens of other countries must have a passport, and in many cases a visa. Passengers aged 15 and under who do not have either a Trusted Traveler card or passport may present a copy of their birth certificate. Passengers aged under 18 and not travelling with both parents require a letter from any parent not present giving permission to cross the border.

For further information and to determine what is required for your particular situation (including permanent residents and others not mentioned above), contact the appropriate US or Canadian government agencies prior to travel. An Amtrak brochure with additional details. *Important Information on Crossing the Border between the United States and Canada,* is available from Amtrak agents.

See also *Chapter 3, Red Tape*, page 33, check with your US embassy or contact the Immigration and Naturalisation Service in Washington, DC (see *Chapter 3*, page 34 and *Appendix 1*, page 331). Passengers without proper documentation are prohibited from entering the US or Canada and will be detrained before reaching the US–Canadian border. Neither Amtrak nor VIA Rail Canada accepts any liability if you are denied entry or removed from the train.

FREQUENCY Daily. The **northbound** service leaves New York City early in the morning to reach Albany by mid morning, Buffalo mid afternoon and Niagara Falls late afternoon. You arrive in Toronto by mid evening. Travelling **south**, trains leave Toronto early in the morning to reach Niagara Falls (Ontario) by midday, Buffalo early afternoon and Albany early evening. You arrive in New York by mid evening.

DURATION 12 hours 30 minutes

RESERVATIONS All reserved

EQUIPMENT Amfleet coaches. Business Class.

FOOD Snacks, sandwiches, drinks

BAGGAGE No check-in service

Joining the train

NEW YORK For New York City and the route as far as Schenectady, see *Chapter 21, The* Adirondack *(pages 235–43)*; for the route from Schenectady to Depew Station, Buffalo, see *Chapter 23, The* Lake Shore Limited *(pages 249–58)*. The *Maple Leaf* operates between New York and Yonkers on Amtrak, between Yonkers and Poughkeepsie on Metro-North Railroad, between Poughkeepsie and Niagara Falls on CSX Transportation, and between Niagara Falls and Toronto on Canadian National.

BUFFALO-DEPEW (55/10) Leaving Depew Station, the *Maple Leaf* picks its way carefully through a mass of tracks. The clock tower of New York Central Station is to your right and a disused evangelical church home on your left. The city skyline appears ahead as you cross Highway 90 before continuing among industrial parks and residential areas. Near Exchange Street Station the eclectic buildings of downtown can be seen to your right.

BUFFALO-EXCHANGE STREET (10/30) Buffalo stands next to Lake Erie, separated from Canada by the Niagara River. After the Civil War many railroads converged, and this remains an important rail centre where freight trains gather on both sides of Amtrak's station. Exchange Street Station opened in 1952 to serve 21 New York Central and Toronto, Hamilton and Buffalo railway trains daily. The New York Central ceased passenger service ten years later and the station was closed until Amtrak reinstated services in 1977.

Look for older, more elegant buildings in the Victorian Allentown District beyond a derelict factory to your right. The **visitors bureau** is at 617 Main (*800 283 3256; www. visitbuffaloniagara.com*).

You leave Buffalo between houses and high-rise apartments, travelling through several tunnels to emerge with Lake Erie on your left. The lake soon begins to narrow as it forms the Niagara River.

Peace Bridge (8/22) The bridge to your left connects the United States with Fort Erie in Canada.

Squaw Island (13/17) The island is linked to the mainland by a drawbridge. You lose touch with the river for a while as the train goes through Tonawanda and crosses the Erie Canal.

Niagara (20/10) The airport on your left lands thousands of honeymooners, as well as visitors to the new casino, from around the world.

As the *Maple Leaf* approaches Niagara Falls, it curves right through ragged-looking yards. Unromantic pylons

NEW YORK CITY

For New York City to Schenectady, see *The Adirondack*

Schenectady

For Schenectady to Buffalo, see *The Lake Shore Limited*

Buffalo

Niagara Falls, New York
U S A
C A N A D A
Niagara Falls, Ontario

St Catharines

Grimsby

Aldershot

TORONTO

Oakville

The Maple Leaf New York–Toronto

26

to your right indicate how much electricity the falls produce. Westinghouse built the world's first hydro-electric plant here in 1896, transmitting power to Buffalo. Nikolai Tesla, inventor of the alternating current, has a statue at the top of the falls.

NIAGARA FALLS, NEW YORK (30/11) Two cataracts pour 600,000 gallons (2.7 million litres) of water a second into the Niagara River below, creating awesome sights and sounds. The American Falls reach 167ft (51m). The Canadian (Horseshoe) Falls are a few feet lower but have a longer, sweeping crest of 2,600ft (790m). The **visitors bureau** is at 10 Rainbow Boulevard (☎ *716 282 8992 or* ☎ *877 325 5787; www.niagara-usa.com*). Previous visitors have crossed the falls on a high wire or gone over the rim in a barrel. Such stunts have now been made illegal but you can enjoy safe thrills on a *Maid of the Mist* cruise or tour caves under the falls (rented rain gear provided). Not so exciting, although less damp, is the observation tower above the falls.

Amtrak's station at 27 Lockport Road was built as a freight depot in 1959 by the Lehigh Valley Railroad. Originally chartered in 1846 to transport anthracite coal from Pennsylvania, the Lehigh Valley Railroad became a major carrier of both freight and passengers between Jersey City, New Jersey, and Buffalo, New York. The current station is some miles from downtown and the falls (take Metro bus #52). You can walk to Canada across the Rainbow Bridge.

US–Canadian border (9/2) The train crosses the Niagara River on a high bridge with the falls away to your left.

NIAGARA FALLS, ONTARIO (11/20) Before you are allowed to leave or continue your journey, the train must pause for a Customs check. A VIA Rail crew replaces Amtrak staff and even the napkins in the lounge car read 'VIA'.

Like its US counterpart, Canada's town of Niagara Falls makes it easy to see the main attraction. Most people prefer the view from this side, where the 520ft (158m) Skylon Tower offers a terrific vantage point and coloured lights create hypnotic effects on the water by night. The **information bureau** is at 5400 Robinson (☎ *905 356 6061 or* ☎ *800 563 2557; www.niagarafallstourism.com*).

Niagara Falls Museum (☎ *416 596 1396; www.niagaramuseum.com*) was established in 1827, making it the oldest in North America. The 700,000 artefacts include dinosaurs and Egyptian mummies.

After leaving Niagara through Canadian National Rail yards, the *Maple Leaf* continues on towards Lake Ontario, travelling among small farms and vineyards.

Welland Canal (15/5) You cross above one of the lock systems which enable ships to be lifted 326ft (almost 100m) between Lakes Erie and Ontario. Just before St Catharines you cross the Old Welland Canal, one of three which pre-dated the present one. The previous canals took much longer for ships to negotiate.

ST CATHARINES (20/15) Garden City is surrounded by orchards, vineyards and wineries. From a viewing platform you can watch the ships of 30 countries pass through the locks. A museum at Lock 3 includes photographs and models explaining the Welland Canal's history. The pavilion-style station was built in 1917 by the Grand Trunk Railway and acquired by VIA Rail in 1986.

More vineyards appear as you travel through pretty, rolling countryside and cross Sixteen Mile Creek.

Jordan (4/11) Lake Ontario is visible for the first time to your right. The train will stay in touch with the lake for most of the next 70 miles (112km) to Toronto.

GRIMSBY (15/30) In the late 18th century, Grimsby had Canada's first town government. Founded by United Empire Loyalist settlers in 1783, it was originally called Township Number 6 or 'The Forty' because of its location at the mouth of Forty Mile Creek.

ALDERSHOT (30/12) Connecting VIA Rail trains link Aldershot with London and Windsor, Ontario. Reservations can be obtained through Amtrak.

The train passes through suburban districts until industry returns on the approach to Oakville. You again cross Sixteen Mile Creek.

OAKVILLE (12/25) Located at the mouth of the creek, Oakville grew as a harbour for exporting oak timber. It now manufactures cars, chemicals and machinery. Watch for the attractive Victorian houses before you leave past a Ford Motor factory and extensive rail yards to your left.

Port Credit (10/15) You cross the Credit River then the Etobicoke and Humber rivers approaching Toronto. The skyline ahead to your right features the giant CN Tower.

Ontario Place (15/10) An amphitheatre and the world's largest movie screen appear to your right in a park built over part of Lake Ontario.

Fort York Park (21/4) The historic British garrison to your right is where Toronto was founded in 1793.

TORONTO Ontario's capital claims to be the most liveable big city in North America. Explored by the French in 1615, it became a trading post and later a British colonial town called York. In 1813, during the so-called War of 1812, York was attacked and burned by an American force commanded by Zebulon Pike, a noted western explorer.

Toronto officially began in 1834, when the town was named after an Algonkian word for 'a place of meetings', but it remained a small town until the railway arrived. Yonge Street, running north from Lake Ontario, is the longest street in the world.

Once scorned as infinitely boring, Canada's largest city has transformed itself into an exciting place of three million people, and among its 70 ethnic groups is the largest Italian community outside Italy. Toronto has acquired a reputation as the Hollywood of the north, with many television series filmed here as well as movies such as *Moonstruck*, *Sea of Love* and *The Fly*.

Freezing temperatures are likely from November to March and midwinter can be very cold, although snow is actually less frequent than in many US cities.

Toronto basics

☏ Telephone code 416
⇼ Station (*Ticket office* ✆ *06.00–13.00.*
Waiting room ✆ *05.30–00.45; reservations &*
information ☏ *1 800 872 7245*) Clean, efficient &
softly lit, the beautiful Beaux Arts Union Station
Building at 65 Front reflects Toronto's character.

Built by the Toronto Terminals Railway (TTR)
& opened by the Prince of Wales in 1927, this
opulent, classically designed structure has 40ft
(12m) stone pillars weighing around 75 tons
each, decorative friezes, arched windows & high
Italian tile ceilings above its 750ft-long hall. Part

of the movie *Silver Streak*, starring Gene Wilder on board a runaway train from Chicago, was filmed here.

Lockers, newspapers, Red Caps, restaurants, shops, ATM banking, taxi stand, subway.

Connections Union Station is also used by subway trains, VIA Rail (☎ *366 8411*) & Ontario Northland Railroad. GO commuter trains operate to Hamilton, Oshawa, Richmond Hill & Georgetown (☎ *869 3200*).

🚍 **Local transport** TTC buses, streetcars & subway trains allow fast travel throughout the city, with day & monthly passes (☎ 393 *4636; www3.ttc.ca*). Toronto has the largest streetcar system in North America.

🚖 **Taxis** Metro ☎ 504 5757; Diamond ☎ 366 6868

🚗 **Car rental** Thrifty, 1108 Bay St; ☎ 515 8800

🚍 **Greyhound** 610 Bay; ☎ 594 1010. The terminal is also used by Gray Line.

✈ **Pearson Airport** 10 miles (16km) west of downtown by TTC bus #58A or the Airport Express (☎ *564 3232*).

Tours Gray Line ☎ 800 594 3310. Olde Town Toronto (☎ *614 0999*) offers sightseeing by trolley & double-decker bus. Toronto Harbour tours (Apr–Nov) leave from 145 Queen's Quay Terminal (☎ *203 6994; www.harbourtourstoronto.ca*).

🛈 **Visitors bureau** 207 Queen's Quay W; ☎ 203 2600; e toronto@torcvb.com; www. seetorontonow.com; ⊕ 08.30–18.00 Mon–Fri

🏠 **Accommodation** Contact Bed & Breakfast Homes of Toronto, PO Box 46093, College Park, 777 Bay St, Toronto, ON M5G 2P6; ☎ 363 6362 or Toronto B&B Inc, Box 269, 253 College St, Toronto, ON M5T 1R5; ☎ 705 738 9449; www. torontobandb.com.

International Youth Hostel, 76 Church; ☎ 971 4440. Members & non-members, **$**. Leslieville Home Hostel, 185 Leslie; ☎ 461 7258. Dormitory beds, **$**, sgls, **$**.

Hotels include the Sutton Place, 955 Bay; ☎ 924 9221, **$$$$**; Admiral, 249 Queen's Quay; ☎ 203 3333, **$$**; Holiday Inn, 370 King; ☎ 599 4000, **$$$$**; Hotel Victoria, 56 Yonge; ☎ 363 1666, **$$$**; Travelodge Downtown, 621 King St W; ☎ 504 7441, **$$**; Clarion Hotel & Suites Selby Downtown, 592 Sherbourne; ☎ 921 3142, **$$**.

Recommended in Toronto

CN Tower 301 Front W; ☎ 868 6937; www. cntower.ca; ⊕ daily; admission charge. In 1995, the CN Tower was classified as one of the 'Seven Wonders of the Modern World' by the American Society of Civil Engineers. The world's tallest tower (1,815ft 5in/553.3m) features outside elevators that rocket you to the Skypod two-thirds of the way up. Even better views can be achieved from the Space Deck, another 33 storeys above & the highest observation platform in the world. Given a clear day you can see as far as Niagara Falls. Try to avoid w/end queues. Next to the Tower is the Rogers Centre, formerly known as SkyDome stadium, with its unique retractable roof & a hotel overlooking the pitch.

Royal Ontario Museum 100 Queen's Park; ☎ 586 8000; www.rom.on.ca; ⊕ daily; admission charge. Free walking tours of the city on Wed & Sun (☎ 586 5797). The collection of 6 million objects includes items from ancient Greece & Egypt, as well as giant totem poles & a dinosaur gallery.

Eaton Centre On Yonge, from Queen to Dundas; ☎ 598 8560; www.torontoeatoncentre. com; ⊕ daily. More than 230 stores & services operate inside this glittering building, with glass elevators & a 16-screen cinema.

New City Hall 100 Queen; ☎ 338 0338. Tours of the building are available by arrangement (☎ *392 7410*). Curved towers enclose a circular council chamber completed in 1965. Next to City Hall is Nathan Phillips Sq, a favourite meeting place for relaxing by the lake (in winter a skating rink).

Art Gallery of Ontario 317 Dundas W; ☎ 979 6648; www.ago.net; ⊕ Tue–Sun; admission charge. The AGO has more than 79,000 works in its collection, including masterpieces by Monet, Cézanne, Van Gogh & Magritte.

First Post Office 260 Adelaide E; ☎ 865 1833; www.townofyork.com; ⊕ daily; free. Dating from the 1830s & still in use. Costumed guides return you to a world of quill pens & sealing wax.

Spadina Historic House & Gardens 285 Spadina Rd; ☎ 392 6910; ⊕ daily; admission charge. Guided tours. This elegant house has one of Toronto's finest restored gardens. Built by businessman James Austin in 1866, Spadina reflects the Toronto art scene of the late 19th & early 20th centuries & their Victorian, Edwardian & Art Nouveau influences.

Toronto Aerospace Museum Downsview Park, 65 Carl Hall Rd; ☎638 6078; www. torontoaerospacemuseum.com; ⊕ Wed–Sun; admission charge. Aircraft important to the history of Toronto are on display, including planes manufactured by Avro Canada, De Havilland & Curtiss.

27

The *Wolverine*
Chicago–Pontiac

General route information

On a fast trip between Chicago and two of America's largest industrial cities, the *Wolverine* train explores a section of middle America. *En route* are lakes, orchards and vineyards, together with manufacturing plants belonging to the likes of Kellogg and Ford. Infrastructure improvements are under way to reduce travel times between Chicago and Detroit by as much as two hours.

Joining the train

CHICAGO For Chicago city information, see *Chapter 5, The* California Zephyr (pages 71–4).

All aboard!

The *Wolverine* train eases out of Union Station through a tunnel under the post office building. Trains are set up in Amtrak's 21st Street yards on your left to travel to every corner of the land, and Conrail loading facilities can be seen to your right.

Comiskey Park (10/15) To your left is a car park where the old White Sox baseball stadium used to be. A new Comiskey Park, renamed US Cellular Field, has risen alongside.

Bronzeville (15/10) The Harold Washington Cultural Center was named after Chicago's first black mayor, who was buried in the cemetery also seen to your left. The Center is on the site of the former Regal Theatre, where African-American

ESSENTIAL INFORMATION

FREQUENCY Three trains daily. The **eastbound** service leaves Chicago early morning, early in the afternoon and early evening, reaching Pontiac mid afternoon, mid evening and early morning. Travelling **west**, trains leave Pontiac early morning, mid morning and late afternoon to reach Chicago late morning, mid afternoon and late evening.
DURATION Six hours 30 minutes
RESERVATIONS All reserved
EQUIPMENT Amfleet coaches. Business Class.
FOOD Snacks, sandwiches, drinks
BAGGAGE No check-in service

icons such as Count Basie and Duke Ellington played. Bronzeville has also been home to great musicians such as Scott Joplin, Louis Armstrong, Jelly Roll Morton, Fats Waller and blues legend Willie Dixon.

Interstate 90 (the Indiana toll road) is on the right. You see the El railway track overhead before you cross the Dan Ryan expressway. Chicago's skyline back to your left features the 110-storey Willis Tower. The train crosses the south branch of the Chicago River and a defunct Rock Island line then crosses the Calumet River on a steel bridge. Look below for grain elevators and ships being loaded.

HAMMOND-WHITING (25/35) The modern yellow-brick station was formerly also a stop for Amtrak's *Capitol Limited* and *Lake Shore Limited* trains.

Several casinos, Lake Michigan and Whiting Park can be seen on your left as the train pulls out. Oil storage tanks proliferate on both sides of the track before you travel east through the towns of Indiana Harbor and Pine Junction.

Indiana Harbor Canal (10/25) The train crosses the canal on a drawbridge. The canal links the Calumet River with Lake Michigan, a short distance away to your left. To your right are a Standard Oil refinery and a Lever Brothers factory.

Gary (15/20) Long one of the nation's great steel producers, with plants on both sides forming a mass of complicated pipelines, pylons and storage tanks. City Hall and the Lake County courthouse are on the right. Gary was the birthplace of Karl Malden, Michael Jackson and astronaut Frank Borman.

MICHIGAN CITY (35/30) The former station house is now a restaurant. Look left for a colourful marina on Lake Michigan, seen just before you cross the Indiana–Michigan state line.

The train moves inland through country famous for producing wine and fruit. You pass from Central to Eastern Time, so watches go forward an hour (back when travelling west).

NILES (30/40) A small railway town which serves local farmers. Note to your left the Romanesque-style Michigan Central Station and clock tower, which has been a location in films such as *Continental Divide*, *Midnight Run* and *Only the Lonely*. Designed by architects Spier and Rohns, this eccentric stone structure was built to impress travellers on their way to Chicago's 1893 World's Columbian Exposition. As well as the 68ft-tall clock tower, the building has stained-glass windows, elaborate wood panels and a steep, pyramid-shaped roof. The clock faces are each 5ft (1.5m) in diameter.

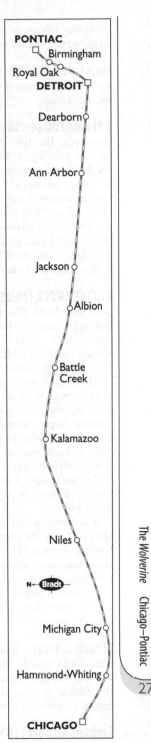

As the *Wolverine* travels on through grape country, look also for cherry trees, strawberries, plums and cider-apple orchards.

Dowagiac (12/28) The beautifully restored station was built by the Michigan Central Railroad in 1903. This is a scheduled stop for one *Wolverine* train daily in each direction.

KALAMAZOO (40/30) The name is a Potawatomi word for 'place where the water boils', and the river has bubbling springs. Pretty 19th-century houses can be seen to your right. The Romanesque-style station, designed by Cyrus Eidlitz for the Michigan Central Railroad, opened in 1887 and originally consisted of three buildings connected by covered walkways. There were separate men's and women's waiting rooms as well as a port cochère (covered carriageway) on the street side of the main building. The city of Kalamazoo bought the depot from Penn Central in the 1970s, and adapted it to serve as a bus/train station. Thruway buses connect with Amtrak's station in Grand Rapids and many other Michigan towns as far north as St Ignace and Sault Ste Marie.

You cross the Kalamazoo River as the *Wolverine* leaves town.

BATTLE CREEK (30/25) The Kellogg brothers invented flaked cereal in the 1890s and made Battle Creek's fortune. 'The cereal capital of the world' is home to the Kellogg Company, Post Cereals and a Ralston Purina plant, all of which can sometimes be smelt as well as seen. A three-day festival in June features 'the world's longest breakfast table'. The **tourist bureau** is at 77 E Michigan Avenue (✆ 800 397 2240; *www.battlecreekvisitors.org*).

Thruway buses connect with East Lansing and Flint from Amtrak's modern station on your left at 104 Capitol Avenue. This station replaced two old stations built by the Michigan Central and Grand Trunk railroads. The Michigan Central depot opened in 1888, and is another Romanesque-style station constructed between Detroit and Chicago in the late 19th century. The massive Grand Trunk Station was built in 1906, and was one of the most elaborate and finely finished depots in the country. Seen on the north side of the track as the *Wolverine* leaves, this was in use as a passenger station until 1971, when Amtrak took over services on the Grand Trunk. Parts of the restored building are open to the public.

Among preserved buildings at the rail town of Coldwater, 40 miles (64km) southeast, are an 1883 depot, freight terminal and railroad granary. The **Little River Railroad**'s 1911 Pacific-type locomotive *No 110* at 29 W Park Avenue makes steam train excursions from Coldwater to Quincy, Michigan (✆ 260 316 0529; *www. littleriverrailroad.com*).

You depart Battle Creek with the Post and Kellogg plants to your right and left. You join the Kalamazoo River to your right and follow its meandering path through a waterlogged terrain.

ALBION (25/22) Albion College campus is to your right. The ornate station house was built in 1882 by the Michigan Central Railroad, which first reached Albion in 1844. It was abandoned in 1971 before being restored to its original condition in the 1980s to serve as a bus and train station. The *Wolverine* pulls out and continues among peaceful farming scenes beside the Kalamazoo River.

Jackson Airport (18/4) Runways appear to your left.

JACKSON (22/35) Look left to see the solid brick-built Michigan Central Station, dating from 1872. A stone tablet in Jackson marks the spot where in 1854 a meeting of Free Soilers, Democrats and Whigs founded the Republican Party. The 500ft (150m) Cascade Falls, America's largest manmade falls, were constructed here in 1932.

The train pulls out among Conrail yards and travels east through the communities of Michigan Center and Leoni.

Grass Lake (10/25) Fire destroyed the station building to your right. You continue through Chelsea then cross the Huron River for the first of many times as it winds between here and Ypsilanti.

ANN ARBOR (35/33) In 1824, two settlers named the town after a grape arbour and their wives, Ann Rumsey and Ann Allen. The Michigan Central Railroad arrived in 1839, linking the town to Detroit. The **visitors bureau** is at 120 W Huron (✆ 734 995 7281; www.annarbor.org).

The University of Michigan, one of the country's oldest and largest, moved here from Detroit in 1841. Located mostly downtown, it has America's biggest college football stadium and witnessed the first anti-Vietnam War teach-in. Note the fine 19th-century Central Michigan building to your right as you leave and cross the Huron River.

Ypsilanti (10/23) Named after a Greek War of Independence hero, Ypsilanti is the home of Eastern Michigan University. **Depot Town** is a historic district preserving old railroad buildings and a large collection of antique cars (✆ 483 4444; www.depottown.org).

Look right just before crossing the Rouge River near Dearborn to see **Henry Ford's Museum** and **Greenfield Village** (✆ 800 835 5237; www.thehenryford.org). A million visitors a year come to look at historic cars, a letter from Clyde Barrow and the chair in which Abraham Lincoln was assassinated in 1865. Among 80 buildings are the Wright brothers' workshop, Edison's laboratory and the courthouse where Lincoln practised law – all brought from their original sites and reconstructed. Also on show are a locomotive built by Ford in 1876 and an 1893 replica of the *DeWitt Clinton*. Steam and diesel trains operate from April to October. Take SMART bus #200 from Detroit.

DEARBORN (33/25) Originally a stop for stagecoaches travelling on the Sauk Trail, the village of Dearborn was established in 1836 and named after patriot Henry Dearborn. Amtrak's plain modern station is at 16121 Michigan Avenue.

Henry Ford built his 56-room **Fair Lane mansion** at 4901 Evergreen Road (✆ 313 593 5590; www.henryfordestate.org; ☻ daily; admission charge) on 1,300 acres (526ha) of farmland next to the Rouge River. He died there by candlelight after floods cut off the power to the house. Ford's private rail car, also named 'Fair Lane', was kept on standby at the Ford Company's siding of the Michigan Central Railroad in Dearborn. Ownership of the estate is being transferred to the University of Michigan-Dearborn and it will close to allow for restoration work before being reopened in phases to celebrate milestones in Ford family history: Henry Ford's 150th birthday in 2013, the estate's 100th anniversary in 2015, and Clara Ford's 150th birthday in 2017.

Soon after Dearborn you see a Ford Company factory to your right and from here to Detroit the *Wolverine* travels through a landscape mostly dedicated to the automobile. Look for Chrysler and General Motors factories as well as many loading docks and rail yards.

DETROIT (25/20) The Midwest's oldest city is the home of crime writer Elmore Leonard and is the birthplace of Joe Louis, Motown music, Alice Cooper, Iggy Pop, Detroit Techno and innumerable cars. Founded by the French in 1701 as Fort Pontchartrain d'Etroit ('of the strait'), Detroit stands between Lakes Erie and Huron. Fought over by French, British and US forces until 1813, it became a staging post on the Underground Railroad for slaves escaping to Canada.

The decline in local industries and the effect of the 1960s race riots have drastically reduced the population, but great efforts have been made to repair the city's image. Julien Temple's documentary, *Requiem for Detroit*, suggests that this is the place to create new ideas about urban futures. Detroit's farming movement is growing and there are ambitious plans for the future, with a fundamental rethinking of what a post-industrial city might become. Among nearby scenic railway routes are the **Southern Michigan** (*320 S Division, Clinton;* ✆ *517 456 7677; www.southernmichiganrailroad. org*), **Walled Lake** (✆ *248 960 9440*) and the **Coopersville & Marne** (*311 Danforth, Coopersville;* ✆ *616 997 7000; www.coopersvilleandmarne.org*).

Detroit basics

✆**Telephone code** 313

⚑ **Station** (*Ticket office* ☻ *06.00–12.00, 13.00–14.30, 16.00–20.00 & 21.00–23.59 daily. Waiting room* ☻ *06.00–01.00; information* ✆*873 3442*). Amtrak's station is at 11 W Baltimore Av. Lockers, newspapers, handcarts, taxi stand. The station was built in 1988 as a replacement for the grand Michigan Central Station, a spectacular 500,000ft^2 (46,000m^2) 1913 building that is under threat of demolition.

Connections No Thruway bus.

🚌**Local transport** The 'people mover' monorail (✆ *224 2160*) stops at many hotels & attractions. DDOT buses (✆ *933 1300*) operate downtown. SMART buses (✆ *866 962 5515*) serve outlying regions.

🚕 **Taxis** Lorraine ✆ 582 6900; Checker ✆ 963 7000

🚗 **Car rental** Thrifty, 29111 Wick Rd; ✆ 734 946 7830

🚌 **Greyhound** 1001 Howard; ✆ 961 8011

✈ **Detroit Metropolitan Airport** 2 miles (3.2km) west by Commuter Transportation bus (✆ *941 3252*).

Tours Kirby ✆ 278 2224. Detroit Tour Connection, 615 Griswold (✆ *283 4332*). Diamond Jack's River Tours, Hart Plaza (✆ *843 9376; www. diamondjack.com*).

ℹ **Visitors bureau** 211 W Fort; ✆ 800 DETROIT (✆ *338 7648*); www.visitdetroit.com; ☻ daily

🏠 **Accommodation** Special rates are available for downtown hotels at w/ends. Hotels include the Courtyard by Marriott at 333 E Jefferson Av; ✆ 222 7700, **$$$$$**; Riverside, 2 Washington Bd; ✆ 965 0200, **$$$**; St Regis, 3071 W Grand Bd; ✆ 873 3000, **$$$$**; Dearborn Inn, 20301 Oakwood Bd; ✆ 271 2700, **$$$**; Westin Book Cadillac, 1114 Washington Bd; ✆ 442 1600, **$$$**; Shorecrest, 1316 E Jefferson Av; ✆ 568 3000, **$$$**; Milner, 1538 Centre; ✆ 963 3950, **$$$$**.

Recommended in Detroit

Detroit RiverWalk This 5½-mile (8.8km) path runs along the river from the Ambassador Bridge to Belle Isle. Free tours from the RiverFront Conservancy (✆ *566 8200; www.detroitriverfront. org*). The east RiverWalk connects an area between Jefferson Av & the river known as **Rivertown**, which prospered in the 19th century as a centre for railroads, shipbuilding & lumber yards. Historic warehouses have been transformed into restaurants, shops & nightclubs.

Detroit Historical Museum At the corner of 5401 Woodward Av & Kirby; ✆ 833 1805; www. detroithistorical.org; ☻ Wed–Sun; admission charge. Displays include the 'Streets of Old Detroit', a fashion library & an old automobile plant body 'drop'.

Detroit Cultural Center 2 miles north of downtown along Woodward Av. 3 buildings make up the core of the Cultural Center – the Italianate Public Library, which has 1 million books & murals showing transport history, the Institute of Arts, & the Horace H Rackham Education Memorial Building. There are also many other museums, galleries, theatres & attractions, as well as Wayne State University & the College for Creative Studies.

Science Center 5020 John R St; ☎ 577 8400; http://sciencedetroit.org; ☺ Tue–Sun; admission charge. Includes spacecraft, a planetarium & the Motorsports Hall of Fame of America.

Detroit Institute of Arts 5200 Woodward; ☎ 833 7900; www.dia.org; ☺ Wed–Sun; admission charge. The 5th-largest fine arts museum in the country houses Renaissance masterpieces in a 1927 Beaux Arts building that resembles an Italian palace. The collection also includes Flemish, Islamic & early American art as well as works by Van Gogh & Brueghel.

Museum of African-American History 315 E Warren; ☎ 494 5800; www.maah-detroit.org; ☺ Tue–Sun; admission charge. The country's largest museum of African-American history & culture includes documents from the Underground Railroad for escaping slaves.

Motown Historical Museum 2648 W Grand Bd; ☎ 875 2264; www.motownmuseum.org; ☺ Tue–Sat; admission charge. Hitsville USA is the original home of Motown Records (derived from Detroit's nickname of 'Motor Town'). Studio A is where Smokey Robinson & Stevie Wonder recorded their hits around the clock in the 1960s.

Fort Wayne 6325 W Jefferson Av, at Livernois; ☎ 224 4356; ☺ Apr–Oct Sat/Sun; admission charge. Built in 1845 as an artillery post to protect the US border, the fort has served as an infantry garrison & induction point for Michigan troops entering every US conflict from the Civil War to Vietnam. During summer, the City's Department of Parks & Recreation hosts historic re-enactments. An Indian burial mound is located at the fort, & ghosts of the Yam-Ko-Desh, the Ottawa name for the mound builders, are said to haunt the site.

Belle Isle Reached via Grand River Bd & the Douglas MacArthur Bridge; ☎ 852 4078. An island 3 miles (5km) from the city centre, granted to French settlers by Detroit's founder, Antoine de la Mothe Cadillac. Larger than Central Park in New York, this beautiful park has a half-mile (0.8km) beach, the **Dossin Great Lakes Museum** & the historic **Anna Scripps Whitcomb Conservatory**.

Fisher Mansion 383 Lenox; ☎ 331 6740; ☺ for tours Mon–Fri; admission charge. This elegant Moorish–Spanish Mission-style mansion belonged to the auto magnate Lawrence P Fisher & its interior has ornate stone & marble, rosewood parquet floors & gold-leaf decorations.

All aboard!

The *Wolverine* continues through Detroit's northern suburbs and industrial districts. Factories specialise in farm implements, electrical equipment and more automobile products.

ROYAL OAK (20/5) This mostly residential suburb is the home of Detroit's Zoological Park. The city's name originated in 1819, when a tree reminded Territorial Governor Lewis Cass of the Royal Oak at Boscobel Wood where England's King Charles II hid after the Battle of Worcester.

BIRMINGHAM (5/12) A small residential town on the banks of the Rouge River in Oakland County.

PONTIAC Located next to the Clinton River on the Saginaw Trail, Pontiac was named in 1818 after an Ottawa Indian chief who fought to hold back British forces and is thought to be buried locally.

Pontiac was one of America's earliest industrial cities and it expanded rapidly after the railroad arrived in the 1880s, making cars, trucks, buses and automotive parts. Motor manufacturing has diminished greatly in recent years. The city is the home of the Silverdome sports arena, where the Detroit Lions play National League football, and many parks and lakes are nearby.

28

Other Amtrak Trains

GENERAL INFORMATION

No reservation or check-in baggage services operate except where stated, and trains run daily unless otherwise indicated.

THE TRAINS

THE *AUTO TRAIN* (LORTON–SANFORD) This is perhaps the world's longest passenger train and is certainly one of Amtrak's finest, much favoured by 'snow birds' escaping the northern winter and by families travelling to Disney World. Being a major money-spinner, the *Auto Train* receives some of the best attendants and best-maintained cars as it operates daily at 70mph (122km/h) over 855 miles (1,376km) of track between Lorton in Virginia and Sanford, Florida. The train is for cars and their passengers only. Amtrak is considering introducing similar services between Chicago and Florida and along the Pacific coast.

The $25 million Lorton terminal at 8006 Lorton Road (just off I-95, Exit 163, 25 miles (40km) south of Washington, DC) was opened early in 2000, with a larger waiting room, snack bar and improved facilities. The 1,500ft (457m) platform enables an entire train to be accepted without having to be split as was previously the case. Sanford station at 600 S Persimmon Avenue (about a half-hour drive north of Orlando in Florida) is fairly basic and dates from when the original, privately run *Auto Train* began in the 1970s. Lorton is for *Auto Trains* only but the Sanford terminal is served by several other trains, including the *Sunset Limited*.

Lorton and Sanford ticket offices and waiting rooms open 08.00–16.00. Cars are accepted by Amtrak staff between 11.30 and 15.00, when the train doors are closed and all passengers must be on board. Trains normally depart at 16.00 but if boarding is complete and the track ahead clear they may leave a little earlier. The only stop during the night is in Florence, South Carolina, where the engine is refuelled and the engineer crew and conductor changed. You arrive at 08.30 the next morning. The train is occasionally delayed by problems on CSX's main route along the eastern seaboard but if this happens to any extent there will be extra meals scheduled and movies shown. If the track has been clear and there have been no delays you may arrive up to an hour early – most likely to happen at weekends.

Boarding times are strictly enforced so it is important to allow for possible heavy traffic, especially on weekends and around Washington. All vehicles must be 65 inches (1.65m) or lower and not have temporary luggage or bike racks. Remember to turn off any car alarms because if one goes off *en route* it could easily drain the battery. There is no check-in baggage except inside vehicles, where you can pack as much as can safely be carried. Personal property left inside your vehicle remains your responsibility. You do not have access to it during the journey so you need to take a small bag of necessities with you when you board.

Northbound fares are lowest between early January and mid-February and from mid-June to mid-December. Southbound fares are lowest between mid-February and late March and from May to December. Special deals are often available, including lodging and tickets to Orlando area attractions as well as your train fare. Amtrak uses Superliner II sleepers and specially designed bi-level lounge cars on this route. The lounge car features improved audio and video systems and booth seating. Complimentary dinner and breakfast in the dining car are included.

Reservations are essential and you should allow at least one hour prior to departure (preferably two hours) for boarding. No pets are allowed and smoking is only permitted in designated areas of the lounge cars, no longer in private compartments. Railfone service is available. For directions and hours of operation there are recorded messages at Lorton (℅ *703 690 3355*) and Sanford (℅ *407 323 4800*). You can also call Amtrak's regular number (℅ *1 800 872 7245*) or the special *Auto Train* toll-free number (℅ *1 877 754 7495*). *Auto Train* fans can join the VIP Club (℅ *1 800 836 6656*) to receive newsletters and updates.

THE *DOWNEASTER* (BOSTON–PORTLAND)

Amtrak's *Downeaster* (*www.thedowneaster.com*) operates five-times daily in both directions, travelling between North Station in Boston, Massachusetts, and Portland, Maine, along part of the former Boston & Maine Railroad. Famous trains such as the *Flying Yankee* used this route from the 1920s until the 1960s, taking passengers on overnight sleepers to New York or Montreal. Amtrak successfully reintroduced services by public demand in 2001, after a gap of 36 years. On its 116-mile journey, the *Downeaster* stops at Woburn, Haverhill, Exeter, Durham, Dover, Wells and Saco, as well as making seasonal stops at Old Orchard Beach (30 April–31 October). There are also plans to extend services further north to Freeport, Brunswick and Lewiston/Auburn. The train is named after the strong winds that used to blow ocean-going ships 'downeast' from Boston, and this route through woods, small towns and farmland is a great way to explore the unspoilt coastline.

All reserved. Business Class available.

THE *CASCADES* (SEATTLE–PORTLAND)

Four European-style trains operate daily in each direction, following the *Coast Starlight* route (see pages 49–70). High-tech Spanish-built Talgo 200 equipment provides wider seats and a bistro dining car. The new trains cut almost half an hour from the previous time on this route. Since the introduction of the *Cascades* service, annual ridership has reached a record high of over half a million passenger trips and this has become Amtrak's most highly rated route for customer satisfaction.

Thruway buses connect Portland's Greyhound depot, opposite the Amtrak station, with Oregon City, Salem, Albany and Eugene-Springfield. Two trains also travel daily between Eugene and Seattle.

All reserved. Checked baggage. Business Class. Bicycle racks. Railfone.

THE *CASCADES* (SEATTLE–VANCOUVER, BC)

Two trains a day follow the *Empire Builder* route (see pages 101–17) to Everett, then continue through north Washington via Stanwood, Mount Vernon and Bellingham before crossing the Canadian border into British Columbia. This train reopened the cross-border Seattle–Vancouver route in 1996 after a gap of 14 years.

All reserved. Complete meals, snacks, sandwiches and drinks, including Red Hook beer and real coffee. Checked baggage. Business Class. Bicycle racks.

THE *CAPITOL CORRIDOR* (SAN JOSE–AUBURN) Sixteen trains travel on weekdays between the Sacramento region and the Bay Area, with eight extended to San Jose and one from Sacramento to Auburn. Eleven weekend trains travel between Sacramento and Oakland, with seven extended to San Jose. Trains follow parts of the *Coast Starlight* and *California Zephyr* routes (see pages 49–79 and 71–89 respectively). Many Thruway buses link with places such as Napa, Santa Rosa and Martinez.

Railfone. Bicycle racks.

THE *ETHAN ALLEN EXPRESS* (NEW YORK–RUTLAND) This train follows the *Adirondack* route (see pages 235–43) from New York City to Fort Edward, then continues to Castleton and Rutland in Vermont. Buses provide connections from Rutland with Brandon, Middlebury, Vergennes and Burlington, as well as with ski resorts such as Killington.

Reservations required north of Albany. Business Class.

THE *KEYSTONE* SERVICE (NEW YORK–HARRISBURG) Thirteen trains a day (seven at weekends) travel in each direction, following the *Pennsylvanian* route (see pages 267–71) as far as Harrisburg. *Keystone* trains are operated by Amtrak in partnership with the Pennsylvania Department of Transportation.

Reservations required north of Philadelphia.

THE *CAROLINIAN* (NEW YORK–CHARLOTTE) This train follows the *Silver Star* route to Raleigh (see pages 202–16) then travels west through wooded hills to Charlotte in North Carolina via Greensboro.

Reservations required, except between New York and Washington. Carolina Business Class service offers complimentary drinks, newspapers, audio and movies between Washington and Charlotte. Check-in baggage. Railfone.

THE *EMPIRE* SERVICE (NEW YORK–ALBANY–NIAGARA FALLS) Six trains a day (four at weekends) travel in each direction, following part of the *Lake Shore Limited* route (see pages 249–58) as far as Albany. Some trains travel on to Niagara Falls, New York.

Business Class. Railfone.

THE *PIEDMONT* (RALEIGH–CHARLOTTE) This train follows part of the *Carolinian* route (see above) and serves fresh barbecued food in a refurbished dining car. Some trains operate between Charlotte and Wilson.

All reserved. Complete meals service. Check-in baggage. Bicycle racks. Railfone.

THE *HIAWATHA* SERVICE (CHICAGO–MILWAUKEE) Seven trains a day (six at weekends) travel in each direction, stopping at Glenview, Sturtevant and Milwaukee Airport. From Milwaukee, Thruway buses link with Fond du Lac, Oshkosh, Wausau and other towns in Wisconsin. You can also catch the train to and from the new Amtrak station at Milwaukee's Mitchell International Airport. Reservations required. Checked baggage service available at Chicago and Milwaukee.

THE *MISSOURI RIVER RUNNER* (ST LOUIS–KANSAS CITY) This route was formerly operated as part of the Missouri Service train network, which included the *Ann*

Rutledge, Kansas City Mule and *St Louis Mule*. Two trains a day travel in each direction via stations that include Jefferson City and Sedalia. Kansas City buses connect to Tulsa and Oklahoma City. As part of the Trails and Rails programme, a National Park Service guide from the Jefferson National Expansion Memorial is on board from St Louis to Kansas City, Missouri.
All reserved. Business Class.

THE *LINCOLN* SERVICE (CHICAGO–ST LOUIS)
Four trains a day follow the *Texas Eagle* route (see pages 154–66) but also stop in Summit and Dwight, Illinois. An interpretive guide from the Jefferson National Expansion Memorial (consisting of the Gateway Arch, the Museum of Westward Expansion and St Louis's Old Courthouse) provides a narrative on board the *Lincoln* service between St Louis and Springfield.
All reserved. Business Class.

THE *BLUE WATER* (CHICAGO–PORT HURON)
An all-reserved train service introduced in 2004, the *Blue Water* runs between Port Huron, Michigan, and Chicago, with intermediate stops at Lapeer, Flint, Durand, East Lansing, Battle Creek, Kalamazoo, Dowagiac and Niles. Named after its home region of Port Huron, this train was reintroduced to replace the Chicago–Toronto *International*. VIA Rail continues to operate a service between Sarnia, London and Toronto but it no longer connects with Amtrak at Port Huron. The *Blue Water* is supported by the Michigan Department of Transportation and provides daily morning departures to Chicago, with return afternoon and evening service for Michigan passengers.
Reservations required.

THE *PERE MARQUETTE* (CHICAGO–GRAND RAPIDS)
The schedule of this all-reserved Chicago–Grand Rapids train mirrors the operating pattern of the *Blue Water*. The *Pere Marquette* is also operated under a contract with MDOT and has a morning departure to Chicago with an evening return to Grand Rapids, stopping at St Joseph-Benton Harbor, Bangor and Holland *en route*. Reservations required.

THE *ILLINOIS ZEPHYR/CARL SANDBURG* (CHICAGO–QUINCY)
This daily service follows the *California Zephyr* route to Galesburg (see pages 71–89), then continues south to Quincy, Illinois, via Macomb.
All reserved. Business Class.

THE *ILLINI/SALUKI* (CHICAGO–CARBONDALE)
Morning and late afternoon departures, following part of the *City of New Orleans* route (see pages 167–72).
All reserved. Business Class. Bicycle racks.

THE *HOOSIER STATE* (CHICAGO–INDIANAPOLIS)
This train operates four days a week along part of the *Cardinal* route (pages 225–34), stopping at Dyer, Rensselaer, Lafayette and Crawfordsville (a flag stop).
All reserved.

THE *HEARTLAND FLYER* (OKLAHOMA CITY–FORT WORTH)
This train travels daily between Oklahoma and Texas, making stops in Norman, Purcell, Pauls Valley, Ardmore and Gainesville. This service is operated by Amtrak on behalf of the states of Oklahoma and Texas. National Park Service guides from the Chickasaw National Recreation Area are on board the *Heartland Flyer* between Oklahoma City and Fort Worth.
All reserved. Bicycle racks.

Other Amtrak Trains THE TRAINS 28

THE *PALMETTO* (NEW YORK–SAVANNAH) A daily service that starts early in the morning and reaches Savannah or New York by mid evening. *Palmetto* trains follow the *Silver Meteor* route, making additional stops in Wilson and Selma-Smithfield (North Carolina) and Dillon (South Carolina). The original *Palmetto Limited*, inaugurated in 1910 by the Atlantic Coast Line Railroad, ran between New York and St Petersburg.

All reserved. Business Class. Checked baggage.

29

US Steam Today

Steam locomotives have always been something special. They seem to possess a soul and to their operators often feel more like living creatures than machines. Early steam engines soon earned people's affection and were given nicknames such as calliope, hog, jack, mill, pig, pot or smoker. Smaller types were called coffee pot, dinky, kettle or peanut-roaster. Their drivers, officially known as engineers, were hog-heads, hog-jockeys, grunts, eagle-eyes or dinkey skinners (if they worked for a logging railroad).

Other words to enter the language were highball (a hand or voice signal to move a train); hostler (someone who services locomotives); shoofly (a temporary bypass track around a damaged track or obstruction); torpedo (an explosive device put on the rail to warn an approaching train of danger ahead); varnish (a passenger train, from the days when coaches were made of wood and varnished); gandy dancer (a track worker named after the Gandy company which made his tools); baby lifter (a brakeman); bakchead, or tallow pot (a fireman); go to beans (go to eat a meal); the brains, or skipper (conductor); brass hat (a railroad executive); car toad (an inspector of freight and passenger cars); crummy (a wooden, two-truck caboose, also called a bean shack when workers lived in them); dead head (a railroad employee travelling on a pass), dinger (a yardmaster); gladhand (metal attachments to which air hoses connect); goat (a yard engine); green eye (a clear signal); kicker (an emergency brake); number dummies (clerks who worked as yard checkers); piglet (a trainee engineer); swing man (a rear brakeman); and yellow eye (a yellow signal).

To 'join the birds' was to jump from a moving engine or car, usually just before it ended up 'in the ditch' (wrecked). Picking up water from between the rails was 'jerking a drink' and a head-on collision was a 'cornfield meet'. Such train language, along with a host of stories, songs and legends, helped railroads become an integral part of American folklore. Even as late as the 1930s and 1940s, being an engineer was a much sought-after occupation and for some it ranked higher than becoming president.

An engineer earned good money, saw new and glamorous places, and was admired by small boys and women everywhere. It could be hard work, though, and getting the most out of a locomotive, often in difficult circumstances, required artistry as much as expertise. The engineer would use the throttle to 'beat on' the engine, making it run sweetly at maximum power. This was a considerable test of both his skill and the locomotive's strength. The fireman regulated the water and fire box to ensure that the engineer had the right amount of steam pressure to drive the engine.

Steam engine numbers peaked at 72,000 just after World War I. Approximately 180,000 steam locomotives were built in the US altogether, culminating in the Union Pacific's 'Big Boys' of the 1940s. These (4-8-8-4) monsters weighed 600 tons, had a capacity of 7,000 horsepower and burned 20 tons of coal an hour. But as technology progressed, lower maintenance costs and safety considerations made the change to diesel increasingly inevitable and no new steam engines were put into service after 1953.

The Norfolk & Western Railroad, centred on Roanoke, was the last steam-powered Class One line. O Winston Link lovingly recorded its demise over a period of six years in the 1950s, making films and sound recordings as well as taking the extraordinary photographs published in *Steam, Steel and Stars*. He even bought his own locomotive, a 1911 Canadian Pacific ten-wheeler. The final Norfolk & Western steam trains ran on 4 April 1960, after which most were scrapped and their metal exported to Japan. The Norfolk & Western merged with the Southern Railway in 1982 to form the massive Norfolk Southern system, with 17,000 miles (27,000km) of track in 20 states.

The age of steam still lives on around the USA though, thanks mainly to the efforts of 40,000 volunteer enthusiasts. It can take up to 30,000 hours of work to restore a single locomotive but more than 200 remain operational out of the 1,875 still in existence in the US and Canada. Most weigh between 100 and 150 tons, but the largest in working order is the Union Pacific *Challenger* (313 US tons/274 tonnes). Some modern reproduction engines have been imported from Europe and China.

Many 'steam chasers' continue to delight in the pungent smell of coal smoke, an echoing whistle and the clickety-clack of the rails. Five million people each year take main-line excursions or dinner trains, visit scenic railways or go to train museums. The leading supplier of books, video tapes and vintage films is **Pentrex** (*PO Box 94911, Pasadena, CA 91109-4911;* ❧ *626 793 3400 or* ❧ *800 950 9333; www. pentrex.com*).

TRAINS, ROUTES AND MUSEUMS

The following are among the most scenic and interesting railways still in regular operation. All are standard gauge except where indicated.

ARCADE & ATTICA (*Mail address: 278 Main, PO Box 246, Arcade, NY 14009-1223;* ❧ *585 492 3100 or* ❧ *585 496 9777; www.arcadeandatticarr.com*) Steam trains travel over a historic route to Curriers from the depot in Arcade, New York, using coaches built around 1915. President Grover Cleveland's honeymoon car, complete with original dishes, is on show at the Arcade Station along with other unique items from railroad history, including lanterns, an antique roll-top desk and two wooden telephones. The authentic ticket office has bars in the window.

Trains leave Arcade past the current station and pass a building which used to be a station of the Tonawanda Valley & Cuba Railroad, predecessor to the Arcade & Attica. You cross a bridge giving great views of Cattaraugus Creek and continue through an attractive wilderness area to Curriers. There the locomotive switches and pulls onto a siding to provide photo opportunities before returning to Arcade, pulling the train in reverse.

Steam trains operate mostly on weekends from Memorial Day (last Monday in May) until September, with foliage specials in October. Special event trains also operate in season and there are diesel-powered trips at other times. The nearest Amtrak stops are Buffalo and Rochester, served by the *Lake Shore Limited*.

AUSTIN & TEXAS CENTRAL RAILROAD (*Mail address: PO Box 1632, Austin, TX 78767;* ❧ *512 477 8468; www.austinsteamtrain.org*) Located at 401 E Whitestone Boulevard in Cedar Park, 20 miles north of Austin, Texas. A vintage Southern

Pacific locomotive and period passenger cars make regular steam excursions into the hill country northwest of Austin, taking a scenic 33-mile route from Cedar Park through the cedar and oak woods of the South San Gabriel River Valley. You cross the river on a spectacular trestle and climb 500ft to the top of the valley before descending a steep grade to the town of Burnet.

The Austin Steam Train Association (ASTA) has trackage rights over this route under an agreement with the city and Capital Metro, which manages the line. The track is also used for weekday freight services and has recently been upgraded. Steam engine *No 786* was built by the American Locomotive Company in 1916, and operated over the Southern Pacific's Texas and Louisiana lines until 1956. After more than 30 years on display in downtown Austin, the 143-ton locomotive was restored to working order in record time to operate out of Cedar Park. Engine *No 786* is undergoing a thorough rebuilding that will return it to service as good as new, and as soon as possible. In the meantime, all of ASTA's regular trains are continuing their schedules uninterrupted, using diesel locomotives. Trains run mostly on weekends from March to December. Amtrak's *Texas Eagle* serves Austin.

BLACK HILLS CENTRAL (*Mail address: PO Box 1880, Hill City, SD 57745;* ☎ *605 574 2222; www.1880train.com*) Trains travel 20 miles (32km) through forests and mountains between Keystone and a former Chicago, Burlington & Quincy station at Hill City near Mount Rushmore, South Dakota. Vintage coaches and a 1919 Baldwin locomotive (star of television's *Gunsmoke* and Disney's *Scandalous John*) run through the beautiful Black Hills of western South Dakota along part of what was once a Burlington Railroad line. You pass the Holy Terror mine, Old Baldy Mountain (5,605ft/1,545m) and Elkhorn Mountain (6,200ft/1,890m), climbing grades of up to 6% past the old tin mine route to Hill City.

Trains operate daily on a two-hour round trip from May to October, with a reduced schedule at other times.

BOONE & SCENIC VALLEY (*Mail address: 225 Tenth St, PO Box 603, Boone, IA 50036;* ☎ *515 432 4249 or* ☎ *1 800 626 0319; www.scenic-valleyrr.com*) A 15-mile (24km) round trip from Boone, Iowa, over the historic Dodge, Des Moines & Southern route, crossing the Des Moines River Valley on two great bridges, including the world's largest and highest double-track rail bridge at 156ft (48m). The railroad was begun in the 1890s to transport coal from Fraser to another railroad at Fraser Junction, now called Wolf, before later extending north to Rockwell, Fort Dodge and Des Moines. Passenger cars operated on an hourly basis and freight business flourished. The Boone Railroad Historical Society purchased a section of the defunct line in 1983 for $50,000, and in 1989 the last commercially built steam locomotive made in China was bought for $350,000 to operate services with restored 1920s passenger cars.

For an additional fare you can travel First Class on the Wolf train, making a 22-mile (36km) round trip to Wolf in an air-conditioned *City of San Francisco* Pullman lounge car with roomettes, an observation platform and free refreshments. The depot was built in 1985 in the style of the one in Rockwell, Iowa, using interior oak woodwork from the depot in Tama. The platform was constructed from bricks brought from several other old platforms. Boone also features **Iowa's Railway Museum**, with free displays and exhibits. Steam trains run on weekends and holidays from May to October, with diesels on weekdays. The nearest Amtrak stop is Osceola, served by the *California Zephyr*.

CALIFORNIA WESTERN (*Mail address: 220 S Sierra Av, Oakdale, CA 95361;* \800 866 1690 or \866 45 SKUNK or 866 457 4864 ; *www.skunktrain.com*) The Skunk line runs 40 miles (64km) between Fort Bragg on the coast and Willits on US Highway 101. A variety of trains and schedules operate from both ends of the line, crossing up to 30 bridges and trestles. From Fort Bragg you can travel with an open observation car along Pudding Creek and the Noyo River, passing through a deep mountain tunnel and seeing splendid redwood trees, wild flowers, grazing cattle and apple orchards. At Northspur you have time to relax before returning to Fort Bragg.

The 90-minute trip from Willits by vintage 1935 M-300 Motorcar begins with a climb into the rolling hills and through a tunnel at the 1,700ft (488m) summit before gently curving down the steep mountain to Wolf Tree then returning to Willits. Steam trains operate Saturdays all year, and Wednesday–Friday during summer. Diesel trains operate daily. Reservations are recommended. Amtrak Thruway buses link Oakland with Willits.

CASS (*Mail address: PO Box 107, Cass, WV 24927;* \ 304 456 4300 or \ 1 800 225 5982; *www.cassrailroad.com*) The Cass Scenic Railroad uses a splendid switchback route built in 1901 as a logging railroad to haul lumber to the mill in Cass. The locomotives are the same ones that were used in Cass and in the forests of British Columbia for more than 50 years. Old logging flat-cars have been refurbished and turned into passenger coaches, transporting you from the restored buildings of Cass into the mountains of West Virginia.

A 90-ton Shay locomotive hauls the train out of Cass past an old water tower from which its tanks are filled. The train then rounds the curve up Leatherbark Creek and chugs laboriously into the mountains, reversing up the steepest grades before reaching open fields. At times the train has to cope with a grade of 11% (11ft/3.6m in altitude for each 100ft/30m of track). A logging camp of the 1940s has been recreated at Whittaker Station, including a rare Lidgerwood tower skidder. You can continue from Whittaker to Bald Knob via a stop further up the mountain to take on more water at a spring. The train then climbs to the summit of Bald Knob, the second-highest point (4,842ft/1,477m) in West Virginia, from where you can see across two states.

Trains travel either eight miles (13km) from Cass to Whittaker (half an hour) or 22 miles (35km) on a round trip lasting 4½ hours to the summit of Bald Knob, operating daily from May to September; weekends in September and October. Amtrak's *Cardinal* stops at nearby White Sulphur Springs.

CONWAY (*Mail address: PO Box 1947, North Conway, NH 03860;* \ 1 800 232 5251; *www.conwayscenic.com*) Diesel and occasional steam trains operate from an imposing 1874 station built by the Portsmouth, Great Falls & Conway Railroad in North Conway, New Hampshire. Nathaniel J Bradlee of Boston designed this beautiful structure, housing separate men's and ladies' waiting rooms, ticket office, baggage room and rest rooms. Two curving mahogany staircases lead to offices in metal-sheathed domed towers and an eight-day clock was installed in the face of the building, opposite the park. The station has changed little since it was built, apart from the incorporation of a gift shop, and has been carefully restored in recent years.

Other buildings include a roundhouse, a free museum, a freight house and an original Boston & Maine crossing tender shanty. There is an outdoor display of restored railcars, operating turntable and roundhouse. The freight house is home to the North Conway Model Railroad Club, open on Tuesday, Thursday and Saturday from July to September.

Some of the 40-plus railroad cars and locomotives are used to take passengers into the White Mountains over part of the Boston & Maine Conway branch line. The Valley train makes a 55-minute round trip from North Conway to Conway (11 miles/17km) or a 1¾-hour round trip from North Conway to Bartlett (21 miles/34km). The Conway route takes you south through farmland, crossing Moat Brook and the Saco and Swift rivers. The Bartlett train travels northwest through fields and woodlands, crossing the East Branch, Saco and Ellis rivers. You can choose Coach Class, the elegant *Chocorua* dining car or the First Class *Gertrude Emma* Parlour observation car. The *Gertrude Emma* was built in 1898 for use on the *Pennsylvania Limited* and has been splendidly restored with wicker and rattan chairs, rich mahogany woodwork and an open observation platform.

The Notch train crosses two spectacular trestles and many streams, steep bluffs and ravines on its way to Crawford Notch (a five-hour round trip) or Fabyan Station (5½ hours). Seating options include Coach Class, the First Class car *Carroll P Reed*, or the dome car *Dorthea Mae*. Live commentary includes history and folklore of the railroad and area as well as other points of interest. The open-air observation coach is available to Coach- and First Class passengers.

Valley trains run at weekends from mid-April to mid-May then daily until mid-October, when a weekend service continues until mid-December. The Notch train operates Tuesday, Wednesday, Thursday and Saturday from June until mid-September, then daily until mid-October for peak foliage season.

CUMBRES & TOLTEC (*Mail address: PO Box 789, Chama, NM 87520;* ☏ *575 756 2151; www.cumbrestoltec.com*) This is the longest and highest narrow-gauge steam railway in America and is one of the world's most scenic routes, taking you through the Rockies by way of tunnels and breathtaking trestles. There are snowdrifts in May, wild flowers in June and brilliant autumn colours in September and October. The 64-mile (102km) Denver & Rio Grande Western track crosses the continental divide at Cumbres Pass (10,015ft/3,055m), then snakes through the Toltec Gorge of the Los Pinos River before making a precipitous descent towards Chama, New Mexico. Power is provided by Baldwin locomotives and trains sometimes have to use one of two preserved rotary snow ploughs to cope with the weather conditions.

The Cumbres & Toltec is one of the last remnants of a rail empire which began in 1871, with the construction of the Denver & Rio Grande Railroad. The original intention was to build a line from Denver to Mexico City via Santa Fe and El Paso. Financed mainly by British investors, this 'happy little railroad' was constructed to a 3ft gauge to cope with the mountainous landscape, although standard gauge was already the norm. By 1876, it had changed its aim from Mexico to the prosperous silver mines of the San Juan Mountains in southwestern Colorado, reaching Silverton via Cumbres Pass and Durango in 1882. After 1955, only one section of narrow-gauge line remained, running from Antonito through Chama to Durango and Silverton, Colorado, and to Farmington in New Mexico.

The states of Colorado and New Mexico purchased the Antonito–Chama section and created the Cumbres & Toltec Scenic Railroad in 1970. The Durango–Silverton line continued to operate and was sold to a private owner in 1981, becoming the Durango & Silverton Narrow Gauge Railroad (see below).

The *Colorado Limited* travels from Antonito to Osier, Colorado, through Toltec Gorge. The *New Mexico Express* leaves Chama, New Mexico, for Osier via Cumbres Pass. You can make through trips either way, returning by road, or make round trips to and from Osier by train.

Trains run daily from late May to mid-October. Dress warmly.

DURANGO & SILVERTON (*Station at 479 Main Av, Durango, CO 81301;* ☎ *970 247 2733 or* ☎ *877 872 4607; www.durangotrain.com*) Durango was founded by the Denver & Rio Grande Railway in 1880 and the 36in-gauge Durango to Silverton line was completed two years later at a cost of $100,000 per mile (see the previous *Cumbres & Toltec* section). The 500 construction workers were mostly Irish and Chinese immigrants, earning an average $2.25 a day for often dangerous work as a ledge was blasted from solid granite above the Animas River. Some of them lived in caves dug out of the hillside near Rockwood in preference to the thin-walled railcars provided. This challenging project ranks alongside that of the Central Pacific Railroad's passage through the Sierra Nevada, and the entire line has been designated a National Historic Civil Engineering Landmark.

The **D & SNGRR Museum** is housed in part of a renovated roundhouse and features full-size locomotives as well as elegant Business Class private cars, railroad paintings, lamps, photographs and books. The original bell from the Union Pacific locomotive *No 119*, present at the Golden Spike ceremony of 1869, is also on display. The **Silverton Freight Yard Museum**, located in the 1882 depot, has more locomotive and freight equipment as well as the 'Casey Jones', a motorised vehicle powered by a 1915 Cadillac engine. Admission to both museums is included in the train ticket price.

Today's Durango & Silverton Railroad has been voted one of the 'top ten most exciting train journeys in the world' by the Society of American Travel Writers. Trains run on a 45-mile (72km) spur of track using coal-fired locomotives built for the D&RGW by the American Locomotive Works (1923) and Baldwin (1925), one of which appeared in the film *Butch Cassidy and the Sundance Kid*. The train has appeared in many other movies, including *Viva Zapata, Around the World in 80 Days* and *How the West Was Won*. Robert Royem's book, *An American Classic: The Durango & Silverton Narrow Gauge Railroad*, contains hundreds of original photographs, including several from the 1880s, as well as a historical overview of the train.

Authentic 1880s coaches make a daily 90-mile (144km) round trip from early May to mid-August among wonderful Rocky Mountain scenery, following the Animas River through the remote wilderness of the San Juan National Forest. The fireman shovels six tons of coal per day on the round trip to Silverton, where there is a two-hour layover. Open-sided gondola cars provide panoramic views. Cascade Canyon winter steam excursions operate daily from 22 November to early May. Reservations are recommended at least a month in advance.

EUREKA SPRINGS & NORTH ARKANSAS (*Mail address: PO Box 310, 299 N Main St, Highway 23 N, Eureka Springs, AR 72632;* ☎ *479 253 9623; www.esnarailway.com*) A four-mile (6.5km) journey through the Ozark Mountains, leaving from the 1913 Eureka Springs depot built from local limestone. The ES&NA collection of vintage rolling stock, including the elegant 1920s *Eurekan* dining car, is one of the Ozarks' largest. Authentic railroad memorabilia recreate a turn-of-the-century era when the railway first brought visitors to Eureka Springs.

Between trains you can check out exhibits such as the restored turntable, a handcar, vintage locomotives and rolling stock that includes an automobile fitted out to run on the rails.

Trains operate daily (except Sunday) from April to October. Sunday trains operate on Memorial Day, 4 July and Labor Day weekends.

FILLMORE & WESTERN (*Mail address: 351 Santa Clara Av, Fillmore, CA 93015; ticket office address: 364 Main St, Fillmore, CA 93015;* ☎ *805 524 2546 or* ☎ *1 800*

773 8724; www.fwry.com) This 31-mile (50km) journey through the unspoilt Santa Clara Valley in southern California uses vintage equipment and the original 1887 station at Tenth Street in Santa Paula is also a museum.

The Fillmore & Western Railway operates many excursions, dinner trains and other speciality trains. It is also engaged in the restoration of historic railroad cars and has recently bought a 1913 Baldwin steam engine originally owned by the Duluth & Northeastern Railroad. The railroad has begun restoring and expanding the track between Fillmore and Piru with a view to running excursions on this route. Steam trains operate mostly on weekends from March to December. Amtrak's nearest stop is Oxnard, served by the *Coast Starlight*.

GEORGETOWN LOOP HISTORIC MINING AND RAILROAD PARK (*Mail address: PO Box 249, Georgetown, CO 80444;* ✎ *1 888 4 LOOP RR (*✎ *1 888 456 6777); www. coloradohistory.org/hist_sites/Georgetown/G_loop.htm*) Journey back in time by visiting the Georgetown Loop Historic Mining and Railroad Park. Located 42 miles west of Denver, the Georgetown Loop is an engineering marvel originally built in 1884 and refurbished in the 1970s that takes visitors through spectacular mountain scenery, twisting and turning over part of the former Colorado & Southern Railway's 36in-gauge line.

The narrow-gauge railroad runs 4.5 miles, connecting Silver Plume and Georgetown, with tracks scaling an elevation of 640ft over mountainous terrain. The 300ft-long Devil's Gate Viaduct formed a spiral where the track actually crossed over itself, making the 'Loop' a popular tourist attraction, but with the end of mining it was dismantled and sold for scrap. Today's route includes a crossing of the new viaduct 96ft (29m) high above Clear Creek. Trains can be boarded in Silver Plume (two miles/3.2km west of Georgetown on I-70) or from the Georgetown depot. Along the route, visitors may stop for guided tours of the historic Lebanon Silver Mine.

Georgetown Loop Historic Mining and Railroad Park is operated in partnership between the Colorado Historical Society (✎ *303 866 3682*) and Railstar Corporation. The park includes an 1884 depot, the Morrison Interpretive Center, an early 1870s silver mine mill, and four reconstructed mine buildings. Trains make 70-minute round trips daily between late May and early October. You can also visit the Lebanon Silver Mine until early September (accessible only by the Georgetown Loop Historic Railroad), which has a guided tour that lasts around 80 minutes. Comfortable walking shoes are recommended and a jacket or sweater is essential. The nearest Amtrak station is Denver, served by the *California Zephyr*.

GRAND CANYON (*Mail address: 233 N Grand Canyon Bd, Williams, AZ 86046;* ✎ *1 800 843 8724 or* ✎ *520 773 1976; www.thetrain.com*) The 1908 depot is at 518 E Bill Williams Avenue, Williams, Arizona, from where trains travel the 65 miles (104km) through ponderosa pine forest, small *arroyos* and high desert plains to the edge of the Grand Canyon. Watch out for the notorious Cataract Creek Gang and the Grand Canyon Railway Marshall. The line was built in 1901 by the Atchison, Topeka & Santa Fe Railway and the canyon's 1910 South Rim Station is one of only three log-built depots still in existence. The original Fray Marcos Hotel (a former Harvey House) in Williams is now occupied by the free **Grand Canyon Railway Museum**, with an authentic steam locomotive and caboose on display outside.

Notable passengers here have included Presidents Theodore Roosevelt, Taft, Franklin D Roosevelt and Eisenhower, as well as Clark Gable, Jimmy Durante and Doris Day. Today's restored 1920s Harriman coaches and vintage engines operate daily, with western entertainment and interpretive guides, and the five classes of service range from Coach to Luxury Parlour Class.

Steam trains run from the last weekend in May to the end of September and vintage 1950s diesel-powered trains in winter, carrying over 170,000 passengers a year. You can choose to stay overnight at the rim and return next day. The train stops in Grand Canyon Village and rooms can be booked at the Maswik Lodge, about a quarter of a mile from the rim and the Bright Angel trailhead. Amtrak's *Southwest Chief* serves Williams Junction, from where there are free shuttle buses to the Fray Marcos Hotel/Grand Canyon Railway depot.

HEBER VALLEY (*Mail address: 450 South 600 W, Heber City, UT 84032;* ☎ 435 654 5601 or ☎ 801 581 9980; www.hebervalleyrr.org) This 32-mile (51km) journey is a 3½-hour round trip from Heber City, Utah, starting from a replica depot constructed in 2001 using techniques from the late 1800s. It looks very similar to the New Meadows, Idaho, depot on the former Idaho & Northern Pacific line (later Union Pacific, now abandoned). The original 1899 Denver & Rio Grande Western depot in Heber City still exists and is used by a stonework/monument dealer. Trains cross farmlands of the Heber Valley, follow the shore of Deer Creek Lake and travel down into a majestic canyon, following the beautiful Provo River to Vivian Park. Look out for the abundant wildlife, including bald eagles, deer and elk.

The Denver & Rio Grande Western was built to serve the pioneers who first settled in this valley. The railroad served the people of this community by hauling freight in and livestock out, and in the 1930s and early 1940s, more sheep were transported by rail from the Heber Valley than from anywhere else in the country. A new highway eventually took away traffic so in 1967 the line was abandoned, becoming a recreational railroad in 1970.

Today, 1920s coaches are pulled by two 1907 Baldwin steam locomotives and three vintage diesel-electrics. Utah's oldest steam railroad has featured in many television shows, such as *Touched by an Angel* and *Promised Land*, and the engine, along with its ten railroad cars, has appeared in more than 30 films over the past 20 years. Special events include Murder Mysteries, Raft the River, the Vivian Park Dinner Train, the Sunset Special Barbecue Train (a steam service with bluegrass musical entertainment), Cinco de Mayo in May, Haunted Canyon in October and Polar Express in November/December. From December to March the 'Tube 'n' Train' offers snow tubing at Soldier Hollow, site of the 2002 Olympic Winter Games biathlon and cross-country skiing events. The steam train service operates daily from May to the end of October, otherwise on weekends year round.

HOCKING VALLEY (*Mail address: PO Box 427, Nelsonville, OH 45764;* ☎ 740 753 9531 (at the depot), ☎ 614 470 1300 or ☎ 1 800 867 7834; www.hvsry.org) Trains make a 14-mile (23km) round trip to Haydenville or a 22-mile (35km) trip to Logan over a Chesapeake & Ohio route. This was part of the original Hocking Valley Railway and is now on the National Register of Historic Places. You leave from Nelsonville, Ohio, where 11 cabooses are on display, including an ex-Hocking Valley caboose. Trains make a stop at the 19th-century settlers' village of Robbins Crossing.

HUCKLEBERRY (*Mail address: 5045 Stanley Rd, Flint, MI 48506;* ☎ 810 736 7100 or ☎ 1 800 648 7275; www.geneseecountyparks.org/huckleberry_railroad.htm) Despite its name, the Huckleberry Railroad is not a toy ride. The name refers to the first *Pere Marquette*-line trains which often travelled so slowly that passengers could hop off to pick huckleberries (wild blueberries) *en route*, then reboard before the caboose reached them. Today's ride is somewhat faster as a historic Baldwin locomotive takes open and closed wooden coaches from the old Denver & Rio Grande Western and Rio Grande Southern for an eight-mile (13km) journey.

The Huckleberry Railroad operates in conjunction with Crossroads Village, a collection of 30 historic buildings that includes a working blacksmith's shop and the Davison depot from the Grand Trunk & Western Railroad. The train travels over a portion of the original *Pere Marquette* roadbed so you ride along the shores of Mott Lake, with great views and a good chance of seeing deer or other wildlife. During special event weekends such as those at Christmas and Halloween, there are decorations along the track.

Trains operate daily from May to early September. Amtrak's *International* train stops in Flint.

KENTUCKY RAILWAY MUSEUM (*Mail address: PO Box 240, 136 S Main, New Haven, KY 40051-0240;* ✆ *502 549 5470 or* ✆ *800 272 0152; www.kyrail.org;* ☺ *daily*) Located in the heartland of Kentucky, the Kentucky Railway Museum is one of the oldest rail museums in the United States. Founded in Louisville in 1954, the KRM now owns 17 miles (28km) of the ex-Louisville & Nashville Lebanon branch, with operating headquarters in New Haven and a passenger boarding area in Boston, Kentucky.

Steam and diesel trains operate on alternate weekends between New Haven and Boston, travelling through the Rolling Fork River Valley on a track built in 1857. A fine collection of Kentucky railway history has been assembled, including the only operating Louisville & Nashville steam locomotive and the largest set of L&N passenger equipment anywhere. A new museum building replicates the original New Haven depot.

Steam train and locomotive cab rides take place from late May to the end of October. Diesel trains operate at weekends until mid-December. Dining trips are available from the Louisville, Harrods Creek & Westport Railroad Foundation on the third Saturday of each month except January.

LITTLE RIVER (*Mail address: 29 W Park Av, Coldwater, MI 49036;* ✆ *260 316 0529; www.littleriverrailroad.com*) From Coldwater, Michigan, trains travel ten miles (16km) to Batavia (80 minutes) or 24 miles (40km) to White Pigeon (2½ hours) over tracks of the Michigan Southern Railroad. The engine used, *No 110*, was built in 1911 at the Baldwin Locomotive Works in Philadelphia. It was made specially for Colonel Townsend's Little River Railroad and is the smallest standard-gauge, Pacific-type steam locomotive ever to be manufactured. Trains operate mostly on Sundays from April to December.

MID CONTINENT (*Mail address: PO Box 358, North Freedom, WI 53951-0358;* ✆ *608 522 4261 or* ✆ *800 930 1385; www.midcontinent.org*) Trains make a seven-mile (11km), 50-minute journey from North Freedom, Wisconsin, along a former branch line of the Chicago & North Western Railroad. This was built in 1903 along the beautiful Baraboo River Valley to an old quartzite quarry. The **Mid Continent Railway Museum** is today dedicated to preserving and interpreting railroad history, especially that of the Upper Midwest during its golden age (1880–1916).

The restored depot was built in 1894 by the Chicago & North Western Railway at Rock Springs, three miles west of North Freedom, and moved to the museum in 1965. Similar designs were used in small communities across the C&NW system in the 1890s, including those at Waunakee and Wonewoc. The interior has two waiting rooms separated by the ticket office, with a freight room on the end, now occupied by the museum gift shop. The exterior has been painted in original C&NW colours. Next to the depot are a dozen steam engines, 33 vintage coaches, 19 cabooses and 33 freight cars, including a wooden tank car for transporting vinegar.

Other structures on site include a Soo Line watchman's tower which formerly stood in Neenah and a tool house for the section crew, moved here from Fond du Lac in 1981. The turntable was removed from an abandoned Milwaukee Road yard and roundhouse in Madison and brought to North Freedom in 1988, but is not yet installed.

Diesel-powered trains operate on weekends from May to early September, with daily operations from Memorial Day through to Labor Day. There are also autumn and winter special excursions.

NEVADA NORTHERN RAILWAY MUSEUM (*Mail address: 1100 Av A, E Ely, NV 89315-0040;* ✆ *775 289 2085 or* ✆ *866 407 8326; www.nnry.com;* ☺ *daily*) The 'best preserved shortline in America' and a National Historic Landmark was one of the last great mining railroads built in the early 20th century, carrying millions of tons of ore from the copper mines at Ely. Completed in 1906 by the Nevada Consolidated Copper Company (later the Kennecott Corporation), the Nevada Northern stretched from Ely to the Southern Pacific Railroad line at Cobre, located about 139 miles (220km) to the north. The rails were later extended west to Lane City and Ruth. This railroad provided regular Pullman services until 1920 and carried passengers until 1938. It ceased regular freight operations in 1983, and that year the line was donated to the White Pine Historical Railroad Foundation to run as a working railroad museum.

Two classic steam locomotives are operated by the railway, pulling an original 1882 Pullman coach, a 1907 baggage/RPO and an open-top flat-car with benches. The 14-mile (22km) round trip takes you around downtown Ely then past the ghost town of Lane City to the historic mining area of Keystone. You travel through one of the few curved tunnels in the world and along the scenic Robinson Canyon. Or you might take the 'Hiline' route above the Steptoe Valley, powered by a vintage Alco diesel engine.

You can visit the roundhouse, machine and blacksmith shops and view the historic rolling stock of steam, diesel and electric locomotives as well as turn-of-the-century passenger and freight cars.

Steam and diesel rides take place on weekends from mid-April and in October, November and December. Daily operations begin in mid-May and go through to September. In February the museum offers special photographers' events. There are guided tours daily from May to October and exhibitions include the general office, depot and dispatcher's office.

NEVADA STATE RAILROAD MUSEUM (*Mail address: 2180 S Carson St, Carson City, NV 89701;* ✆ *775 687 6953; www.nevadaculture.org;* ☺ *daily*) The museum houses over 60 pieces of railroad equipment from Nevada's past, including five steam locomotives and several restored coaches and freight cars. Most of this material is from the Virginia & Truckee Railroad, America's richest and most famous short line.

Museum activities include the operation of historic railroad equipment, lectures, an annual railroad history symposium and other special events. Steam trains operate on some weekends from May to December. Amtrak's *California Zephyr* stops at Reno and Truckee.

NEW HOPE & IVYLAND (*Mail address: 32 W Bridge St, New Hope, PA 18938;* ✆ *215 862 2332; www.newhoperailroad.com*) A vintage Baldwin Consolidation coal-fired steam locomotive takes restored vintage coaches over a nine-mile (15km) round trip in about an hour, leaving New Hope's picturesque 1891 station at 32 W Bridge Street for Lahaska along a branch line of the old Reading Railroad. Steam passenger service between New Hope and Buckingham Valley began in 1966, and the New Hope & Ivyland Railroad ran one of the last regularly scheduled steam-powered mixed freights east of Mississippi. The NHIR became bankrupt in 1971, but the line was successfully operated by McHugh Brothers Heavy Hauling Inc until 1989. From 1980, the volunteer New Hope Steam Railway (NHSR) operated weekend excursions.

The railroad was sold to the present owners, the Bucks County Railroad Preservation and Restoration Corporation, in 1990 and since then the New Hope & Ivyland has been completely restored to its original ambience at a cost of $2 million. The New Hope Station, freight house and boarding platform were refurbished and tracks rebuilt before steam passenger services resumed in 1991. Freight services also continue to expand and prosper.

The Lahaska Station features a pretty picnic grove for the exclusive use of passengers and the freight house at New Hope has a gift shop. Narrated trips take you through attractive Pennsylvania countryside by way of Pauline's Trestle and part of the Underground Railroad route. Passenger steam trains operate daily from April to November, otherwise at weekends. A *Fireworks Express* runs on Independence Day and there are other special trains throughout the year, including fall foliage trains which run the entire length of the railroad and the Evening Star Dinner Train which runs on two Saturdays during the spring, summer and autumn months. Two other steam locomotives are also being restored to operating condition.

The nearest Amtrak stops are New York, Philadelphia, Princeton and Trenton.

NEW YORK, SUSQUEHANNA & WESTERN (*Mail address: PO Box 121, Rochelle Park, NJ 07662;* ✆ *877 TRAIN RIDE or 877 726 7245; www.nyswths.org*) Trains are operated throughout the year by the New York Susquehanna & Western Technical & Historical Society Inc, formed in 1988 to preserve the history of the 'Susquehanna' and its ancestor corporations. All proceeds from the trips are used for restoration of passenger cars, the M-1 motorised coach, steam locomotive *No 142*, and for educational purposes. Trips are powered by historic locomotives, either steam locomotive *Mikado No 142* or e-9 diesels. Passenger equipment consists of coach cars from the 1950s (Long Island RR), deluxe cars from the 1940s (Southern Railway) and a First Class dome car (Santa Fe Railroad).

Trains travel 44 miles (70km) through attractive countryside over a former Lackawanna Railroad line between Syracuse and Tully, New York, and services operate from Thursday to Sunday between April and December.

Amtrak's *Lake Shore Limited* stops in Syracuse.

RAILTOWN (*Mail address: PO Box 1250, Jamestown, CA 95327;* ✆ *209 984 3953 or* ✆ *916 445 6645 (recorded information); www.railtown1897.org;* ☉ *daily*) This California State Historic Park is at Fifth Avenue and Reservoir Road, Jamestown. The Sierra Railway buildings include the only operating steam roundhouse in the west, dating from 1897 and still in original condition. As well as the Sierra's six-stall roundhouse, turntable and main yards, Railtown maintains two operating steam locomotives (with three others located on site) and a wide range of railroad equipment, making this one of the most comprehensive and best-preserved steam railroad sites in the country. Railtown is managed by the **California State Railroad Museum** (CSRM), located in Sacramento.

The Sierra has appeared in more television shows, commercials and movies than any other railway. The first-known filming was in 1919 for a silent serial called *The Red Glove* and the railroad has featured in *High Noon, Little House on the Prairie, Unforgiven* and *Back to the Future III.*

Among the museum's exhibits is a classic Model T purchased in Sonora in 1919, and converted into a railcar for use by the Sierra Railway as a roadmaster's car. Steam trains operate in the 'gold country' of the Sierra Nevada foothills, travelling to the Jamestown Rock siding and back among rolling hills, open pastures and beside a quiet creek. These six-mile (9.6km), 40-minute excursions take place on weekends from April to October and on Memorial Day and Labor Day.

The nearest Amtrak stops are Stockton and Riverbank.

ROARING CAMP & BIG TREES (*Mail address: PO Box G-1, Felton, CA 95018;* ☏ *831 335 4484; www.roaringcamp.com*)

This is America's last steam-powered passenger railroad with a year-round passenger service (weekends only during winter). The Roaring Camp & Big Trees Narrow Gauge Railroad was founded in 1958 by F Norman Clark, who restored two railway lines that operated in the Santa Cruz Mountains from the late 1880s to the early 1920s. The Big Trees rail line dates from 1857, and was used by residents of San Francisco and other East Bay cities on weekends and summers to take them from their communities to the Big Trees (redwood forests) and to Santa Cruz (the beach). It was often referred to as 'the Picnic Line'. Today the Roaring Camp & Big Trees Narrow Gauge Railroad still operates an old-fashioned steam passenger train service providing visitors with a rare opportunity to ride through some of the country's most beautiful and primitive scenery.

Trains leave the 1880 South Pacific Coast depot on Graham Hill Road at Felton, California, for a six-mile (10km) excursion lasting 1¼ hours on a 36in-gauge track between Roaring Camp and the top of Bear Mountain. You travel among the earliest preserved redwoods, then go through Spring Canyon into the Santa Cruz Mountains. On returning to the depot, you can explore an 1880s general store or visit the adjacent **Henry Cowell Redwoods State Park.**

Trains operate daily from April to October, otherwise weekends only. Numerous special events take place throughout the year. The nearest Amtrak stop is San Jose.

SILVER CREEK & STEPHENSON (*Mail address: SCAEC, PO Box 255, Freeport, IL 61032;* ☏ *815 235 2198 or* ☏ *815 232 2306; www.thefreeportshow.com /scs.htm*)

Located at Walnut and Lamm roads, Silver Creek, just south of the Stephenson County Fairgrounds. The Stephenson County Antique Engine Club purchased nearly two miles of rights of way from the bankrupt Chicago, Milwaukee, St Paul & Pacific Railroad in 1983, and volunteers from the club relaid the track. The shed, which houses Heisler, Brookville and Plymouth locomotives and their maintenance facilities, was erected in 1986. The Silver Creek depot, dedicated in 1993, was built from original plans for the Illinois Central depot in Elroy, Illinois. It contains a large collection of railroad memorabilia, including advertising signs and a working telegraph.

Trains leave the replica depot to travel through Illinois farmland, crossing Yellow Creek on a 30ft-high (9m) stone pier bridge, operating on weekends between May and October. Amtrak Thruway buses stop at Rockford, 15 miles (24km) east.

ST LOUIS, IRON MOUNTAIN & SOUTHERN (*Mail address: PO Box 244, Jackson, MO 63755;* ☏ *573 243 1688; www.slimrr.com*)

The route goes from Jackson, Missouri,

along a Missouri Pacific branch line. Journeys last 1½ hours (to Gordonville), two hours (Dutchtown) or five hours (Delta). 'The most daring train robbery on record' took place on the railroad in 1874, when Jesse James and his gang held up the *Little Rock Express* at Gad's Hill. Trains operate on weekends from April to October, and Saturdays in November and March.

TEXAS STATE (*Mail address: PO Box 166, Rusk, TX 75785;* \ *1 800 442 8951 (in Texas only) or* \ *903 683 2561; www.texasstaterr.com*) The railroad is located between Rusk and Palestine on part of the 1896 Texas State Railroad. This line was originally built and run by inmates from the East Texas State Penitentiary to transport iron ore to the prison's furnaces in Rusk. Prisoners were paid 50 cents a day and worked from sunrise to sundown, so the total cost to construct the 32 miles of track was only $573,724. Prison crews made up the train staff (except for the engineer), but when passenger service was extended to Palestine a crew of nine was employed. With the exception of the superintendent and engineer, staff members were paid $1.01 for each day they worked.

The iron furnace was dismantled in 1913, and the penitentiary converted into a state mental hospital. Regular train service was discontinued in 1921, and the line leased to the Texas & New Orleans (Southern Pacific Railroad Company). The Texas Southeastern Railroad leased the line in the early 1960s and continued operations until December 1969, after which it was conveyed to the Texas Parks and Wildlife Department. State inmates were again brought in to rebuild the track by clearing brush, building bridges and replacing ties and rails. The Texas State Railroad State Historical Park opened to the public on 4 July 1976 as part of the nation's bicentennial celebrations.

Two of the railroad's four historic engines simultaneously depart from depots on each end of the shortline, giving passengers a rare chance to see steam locos switch and pass at the midpoint. You board at the historically accurate stations in either Rusk or Palestine for a four-hour, 50-mile (80km) round trip among rolling hardwood creek bottoms and flowering dogwood trees. As well as train excursions, the park offers steam engine shop tours and tours of the 1927 Texas & Pacific *No 610* steam engine, plus train seminars and workshops.

Trains operate from Thursday to Sunday in June and July, on weekends from March to May and August to October, and on the first three Saturdays in November. Amtrak's nearest stop is Longview, served by the *Texas Eagle*.

TWEETSIE (*Mail address: 300 Tweetsie Railroad Lane, Blowing Rock, NC 28605;* \ *828 264 9061 or* \ *1 800 526 5740; www.tweetsie-railroad.com*) The East Tennessee & Western North Carolina Railroad Company was given permission in 1866 for the construction of a railroad from Johnson City, Tennessee, to the iron mines across the state line at Cranberry, North Carolina. The ET&WNC line (sometimes called the 'Eat Taters & Wear No Clothes' Railroad) began operations in 1881 over 50 miles (80km) of track through the Blue Ridge chain of the Appalachian Mountains. The line was extended to Boone, North Carolina, in 1916 to serve passengers and haul lumber.

The railroad was nicknamed the 'Tweetsie' because of the shrill 'tweet, tweet' of its train whistle echoing through the hills. Severe floods damaged sections of the line in 1940, and hastened its closure in 1950. Gene Autry, the movie cowboy, bought engine *No 12*, the last remaining of 13 coal-fired ET&WNC steam engines, intending to use it out west in films. The locomotive was later bought by Grover Robbins Jr for $1 and returned to his home town of Blowing Rock to be restored, along with some of the original ET&WNC railcars.

These are now used on the new Tweetsie Railroad, which had its first run in 1957. Trains follow a scenic three-mile loop through the mountains near Blowing Rock, not far from the original end-of-the-line station in Boone. You can watch cancan girls at the Palace Saloon, chat with cowboys and gunslingers on Main Street, visit the deer park, or ride a chairlift to Miner's Mountain to pan for gold.

Trains operate daily from late May to late August, or on Fridays and weekends from late August to the end of October, plus Labor Day. Amtrak's nearest stop is Gastonia, North Carolina, served by the *Crescent*.

VALLEY (*Mail address: PO Box 452, Essex, CT 06426;* ✆ *203 767 0103; www. essexsteamtrain.com*) The Valley Railroad was created soon after the Civil War, when steamboats ruled the Connecticut River. The line failed to prosper though, since the Connecticut River was sparsely settled and there were insufficient passengers or freight for it to succeed. The railroad was resurrected in 1971 with the running of a passenger train, 100 years to the day after the first one travelled north from Saybrook on the shore of Long Island Sound up the river to Hartford. In 1871, there had been pauses to finish some stretches of track and to saw off pieces of stations that stood too near the tracks. The Essex steam train takes a ten-mile (16km) trip through unspoiled Connecticut countryside between Essex and Chester on a New Haven Railroad branch line, stopping at Deep River. Optional boat trips can be taken on the Connecticut River. Trains operate daily from May to October. The nearest Amtrak stop is Old Saybrook.

VIRGINIA & TRUCKEE (*Mail address: PO Box 339, Carson City, NV 89702-0339;* ✆ *775 885 6833; www.steamtrain.org*) The Virginia & Truckee Railroad was built in 1869 to connect Virginia City with the Carson River Valley. By 1874, the 'Queen of the Short Lines' had been extended to Reno and as many as 50 trains a day carried passengers, supplies and silver ore through Virginia City.

Today you can take half-hour rides along part of the Virginia & Truckee line through the famous Comstock mining area, with the benefit of an informed commentary from the conductor riding in the caboose. Look for exposed silver ore along the track and occasional sightings of wild mustangs in the surrounding Flowery Mountains. The route takes you through Tunnel Number Four, one of six tunnels constructed to allow trains to descend nearly 1,600ft (488m) from Virginia City to the valley floor.

The station is at Washington and F, Virginia City, Nevada. Trains operate daily from May to September, or at weekends in October. Amtrak's nearest stop is Reno, served by the *California Zephyr*.

WESTERN MARYLAND (*Mail address: 13 Canal St, Cumberland, MD 21502;* ✆ *301 759 4400 or* ✆ *1 800 872 4650; www.wmsr.com*) Trains leave Cumberland's 1913 station (which also has the C & O Canal Museum and Visitor Center) and travel west on Western Maryland and Cumberland & Pennsylvania tracks among the Allegheny Mountains, climbing grades of up to 2.8%. On the 32-mile (52km), three-hour round trip you go through the Cumberland Narrows, negotiate the spectacular Helmstetter's Horseshoe Curve and travel through the 914ft-long (278km) Brush Tunnel under Piney Mountain. You also pass the castle at Mount Savage and make a stop at Frostburg's historic restored depot. Make sure you watch the locomotive get turned on the turntable.

Steam trains run from Friday to Sunday between May and mid-September, Thursday to Sunday in October and at weekends. Diesel trains operate on Thursdays from May to August, and on Tuesdays and Wednesdays in October. Steam and diesel trains also operate occasionally for special trains and charters.

Amtrak's *Capitol Limited* stops at Cumberland (about four blocks away).

WHITE MOUNTAIN CENTRAL (*Mail address: PO Box 1, Lincoln, NH 03251;* ☏ *603 745 8913; www.whitemountaincentralrr.com*) A half-hour journey among the attractive White Mountains begins at Clark's Trading Post depot near Lincoln, New Hampshire. Among the other entertainments are an 1890s replica railway station, freight car displays, a haunted house, trained bears, a Victorian-style Main Street and a 1920s garage. The 2.5-mile woodland ride takes you from the trading post up a 2% grade and across the Pemigewasset River through the Howe-Truss covered bridge, the only standing covered bridge still in use. During 1963–65, the bridge was dismantled at its location in East Montpelier, Vermont, before being transported and reassembled here across the river.

The railroad has been in operation for more than 40 years since the Clark brothers began to rescue steam locomotives from the cutting torch to create 'green pastures for Iron Horses'. Salvaged locos now include a 1927 Heisler once owned by the International Shoe Company as well as former Beebe River Railroad and East Branch & Lincoln engines. The restored wood-burning Climax locomotive weighs 42 tons and is one of only three in the world still in working order. The depot opens at weekends from May to mid-October and daily in July and August.

WHITEWATER VALLEY (*Mail address: PO Box 406, Connersville, IN 47331;* ☏ *765 825 2054; www.whitewatervalleyrr.org*) Indiana's longest scenic railway runs between Connersville and the restored town of Metamora, next to the old Whitewater Canal. The Whitewater River formed a natural trade route for Native Americans and early settlers, and a canal was built in the mid 19th century. In 1863, the Indianapolis & Cincinnati Railroad acquired the right to build on the old towpath and its subsidiary, the White Water Valley Railroad, reached Connersville in 1867. It continued on to Hagerstown in 1868, but passenger service ended in 1933 and freight traffic in 1972.

Today's Whitewater Valley Railroad operates along 18 miles (30km) of track purchased in 1983, plus an additional mile in Connersville. It uses historic diesel locomotives and open-window coaches on a regular schedule from Connersville to Metamora. Another service, the Metamora Shuttle, carries passengers further south on a two-mile (3.2km) excursion along the restored canal, past the canal boat dock, a working aqueduct and a restored lock. The railroad's *Baldwin Prairie* locomotive is currently out of action.

Trains operate on weekends and holidays from the first weekend in May to the last weekend in October, as well as at Christmas. Amtrak's *Cardinal* stops in Connersville.

WILMINGTON & WESTERN (*Mail address: PO Box 5787, Wilmington, DE 19808-0787;* ☏ *302 998 1930; www.wwrr.com*) The First State's oldest steam tourist railroad has been in continual operation for more than 120 years. Starting from the impressive new Greenbank Station four miles (6.5km) southwest of Wilmington, trains travel to Mount Cuba over part of a Baltimore & Ohio Landenberg branch line (Sundays, May to December). Or you can travel past Mount Cuba along the Red Clay Creek Valley to Yorklyn or Hockessin (June to October). There are special trains throughout the year, including dinner trains and the *Firework Express*. Amtrak's nearest stop is Wilmington.

29

YOSEMITE MOUNTAIN-SUGAR PINE (*Mail address: 56001 Yosemite Highway 41, Fish Camp, CA 93623;* ☎ *559 683 7273; www.ymsprr.com*) From 1899 to 1931, the Madera Sugar Pine Lumber Company operated many miles of narrow-gauge railroad track. Almost 1½ billion board feet of lumber were harvested and transported to the mill on massive log trains by five wood-burning Shay locomotives.

Located south of Yosemite National Park among California's Sierra Nevada, today's Yosemite Mountain-Sugar Pine Railroad is a restoration of the old 36in-gauge line. A section of the railbed has been reconstructed using the same techniques used originally and two restored Shay steam locomotives were brought from the Westside Lumber Company to provide authentic motive power. *No 15* was built in 1913, and weighs 60 tons (54,000kg). *No 10*, built in 1928, weighs 83 tons (75,000kg) and is the heaviest operating narrow-gauge Shay engine in existence. Railcars which once provided transportation for logging and track repair crews have been refurbished for passenger use on narrated tours. The trains reach 5,000ft (1,800m) before descending through Lewis Creek Canyon and Cold Spring Crossing.

Logger steam trains operate daily from March to October. Antique Model A Ford gas engines power trolley-like 'Jenny' cars over the route every half-hour, except when steam trains are in action. Amtrak's nearest stop is Merced, on the *San Joaquin* route.

YREKA WESTERN (*Mail address: 300 E Miner St, Yreka, CA 96097;* ☎ *530 842 4146 or* ☎ *800 973 5277; www.yrekawesternrr.com*) The *Blue Goose* makes a three-hour, 15-mile (24km) round-trip excursion between Yreka and the historic railroad and cattle town of Montague in California, travelling along the Yreka Railroad which in 1889 linked with the California & Oregon. You travel among lumber mills, cattle ranches and through the Shasta Valley, crossing the Shasta River with magnificent views of Mount Shasta (14,162ft/4,317m) to the south. The 1915 locomotive was built by Baldwin.

You have enough time to visit Montague's 1887 Depot Museum and other historic buildings before boarding the *Blue Goose* for the return trip to Yreka, where you can explore the historic district's attractive Victorian houses and the homes of such luminaries as Bret Harte, Zane Grey and Herbert Hoover.

Trains operate from Wednesday to Sunday between mid-June and early September, and on weekends in May and October. Amtrak's nearest stop is Dunsmuir, served by the *Coast Starlight*.

Part Three

ON CANADIAN RAILS

Location North America, bordering the north Atlantic Ocean to the east, north Pacific Ocean to the west, and the Arctic Ocean to the north
Neighbouring countries USA
Size/area 9,984,670km². The second-largest country in the world (after Russia).
Climate Temperate in the south to sub-arctic and arctic in the north
Status Confederation with parliamentary democracy
Population 34,278,400 (July 2011)
Capital Ottawa
Other main cities Toronto, Montreal, Vancouver, Calgary, Edmonton, Quebec, Winnipeg
Economy Canada has the world's ninth-largest economy and the lowest governmental debt among members of the Group of Eight (G8). Agriculture 2.1%; industry 28.8%; services 69.1% (2011).
GDP Cdn$1.3 trillion (2010)
Languages English 59.3% (official), French 23.2% (official), other 17.5%
Religion Roman Catholic 46%, Protestant 36%, other 18%
Currency Canadian dollar; Cdn$ = 100 cents
Exchange rate €1 = Cdn$1.39, £1 = Cdn$1.62, US$1 = Cdn$1.01 (Nov 2011)
International telephone code +1
Time Canada has six primary time zones. From east to west these are: Newfoundland Time Zone; Atlantic Time Zone; Eastern Time Zone; Central Time Zone; Mountain Time Zone; and Pacific Time Zone.
Electrical voltage 120V/60Hz standard plugs have two parallel flat pins ('American' type) or have two pins with an earth connector. Adapters cost a few dollars.
Weights and measures Metric system (kilometres, litres, etc)
Flag The Maple Leaf has two vertical bands of red, with a white square between them containing an 11-pointed red maple leaf
National anthem 'O Canada'
National flower Maple leaf
National bird/animal Common loon/beaver
National sports Ice hockey, basketball, lacrosse (officially), baseball, American football

RAILWAYS In 2008, Canadian railroads employed about 34,000 people to maintain and operate a total of 48,910 miles of track. This was owned by Canadian National (18,561), Canadian Pacific (13,447), regional and short-line railways (16,059) and others (843). A total of over four million passengers and 361 million tonnes of freight were transported in 2008.

Canadian National (CN) and Canadian Pacific (CP) still dominate, with 85% of activity and revenues and two-thirds of the total rail network, although this is down from 90% in 1990.

VIA Rail operates most inter-city passenger services, with close to 4.2 million passengers in 2007 and almost 95% of total revenues. Other passenger services include the Algoma Central, Ontario Northland and Quebec North Shore & Labrador. Amtrak serves Montreal, Vancouver and Toronto (the last in conjunction with VIA Rail). The Great Canadian Railtour Company has seasonal services between Vancouver, Calgary and Jasper.

30

Canada's Trains Today

Canada may be the only country in the world with a written constitution linking its formation to the building of a railway. British Columbia threatened to join the United States if it wasn't given its rail line, so a parliamentary act in 1867 proclaimed the construction of the Intercolonial Railway 'essential to the consolidation of the Union of British North America'. As a result, 4,000 miles (6,500km) of iron road was laid from the Atlantic to the Pacific. In 1871, British Columbia agreed to join the Confederation and trains have been a crucial part of Canada's history ever since.

A short tramway is thought to have been built in 1720 during the construction of a fort at Louisburg, Nova Scotia, and others later opened elsewhere to transport stone, coal and lumber. Canada's first public railway, the Champlain & St Lawrence, opened in 1836 as a 14-mile (22km) route between Dorchester (now St-Jean), next to the Richelieu River, and La Prairie on the St Lawrence. The success of the Champlain & St Lawrence, and rail companies in the United States, encouraged further development, including the Grand Trunk Railway from Montreal to Toronto.

The Canadian Great Western Railway built the world's first sleeping car in 1857, inspiring the American Pullman design which came two years later. The Great Western originally operated between Windsor and Niagara Falls before extending to Hamilton and Toronto. An accident on the Grand Trunk Railway in Quebec in 1864 took 99 lives, making it Canada's worst-ever railway disaster. The famous circus elephant, Jumbo (over 12ft (3.65m) tall and weighing almost eight tons (8,000kg), was killed on the track at St Thomas in 1885 when he was accidentally struck from behind while being loaded into a GTR freight train.

The great transcontinental Canadian Pacific route opened in 1885, having been blasted through some of the world's hardest rock in temperatures as low as –50°F (–45°C). Among the workers were more than 6,000 Chinese, some of whom had remained in California after building the Union Pacific Railway. Working for a dollar a day (which they considered good money), many died from hard labour, disease and careless use of explosives. Others survived to found the first permanent Chinese community in British Columbia.

Despite financial problems and the exceptionally difficult conditions, the track was completed in only 54 months, almost six years ahead of schedule. The first train ran 3,000 miles (4,800km) from Montreal's Dalhousie Square Station to British Columbia in 1886, travelling 139 hours through a harshly beautiful landscape which was then almost uninhabited. The train arrived on 9 November at its final destination, Port Moody, only one minute late. The 1949 movie *Canadian Pacific* tells the story of the building of the railway rather fancifully but contains many shots of authentic locomotives and rolling stock.

The Canadian Northern line, later to become the Canadian National, reached Vancouver in 1915, going from Montreal via Hawkesbury, Ottawa, Capreol, Fort

Frances, Winnipeg, Dauphin, North Battleford and Edmonton. The Grand Trunk Railway formed the Grand Trunk Pacific to run from Winnipeg to the west, reaching Prince Rupert on the Pacific by way of Yellowhead Pass. These railways and others began to open up the land to immigrants, farmers, mineral prospectors, wealthy travellers and land speculators. They created a crucial sense of nationhood in the world's second-largest country, bringing rapid development to what were otherwise isolated settlements along the way.

The hard-drinking Sir William Cornelius Van Horne, head of the Canadian Pacific, tempted passengers westward by creating a chain of luxurious chateau-style hotels in spectacular settings. The Banff Springs Hotel (half chateau, half Scottish baronial mansion) opened in Banff National Park in 1886, and was succeeded by the Hotel Vancouver, the Empress Hotel in Victoria and Chateau Lake Louise. A railway surveyor, Tom Wilson, had in 1882 been the first white man to see Lake Louise, which is now one of the country's most popular skiing and tourist destinations. Canadian Pacific remains the largest hotel company in Canada.

Canada's rail network was among the biggest in the world by the year 1900, and more than 40,000 miles (64,400km) of track were in place by the end of World War I. The government took over the Canadian Northern company in 1917 and turned it into the Canadian National Railway, subsequently acquiring the Grand Trunk Pacific and other smaller operations. A transcontinental record was set on 4 November 1925 by the Canadian National with a trip from Montreal to Vancouver in 67 hours, when the engine ran non-stop to average 45mph. As in other countries, the 20th century brought increasing competition from airlines, highways and motor cars, but even in the 1950s more than 6,000 locomotives and 200,000 passenger and freight cars were in service.

In 1955, just at the time when air travel was taking over, the prestige *Canadian* train was equipped with glamorous, state-of-the-art stainless-steel coaches. The last Canadian Pacific steam engines ran in 1960. Both CN and CP owned thousands of miles of track and had profitable freight operations, carrying cargoes such as wheat, coal and sulphur, but costs continued to mount for passenger trains. Annual passenger miles fell to around 20 million (one-third of the peak figure) and, like its US counterpart, the Canadian government was compelled to act.

VIA RAIL

Canada's equivalent to Amtrak began in 1977, when it took over most of the country's passenger services. VIA Rail has its own equipment and service personnel but uses tracks belonging to Canadian Pacific and Canadian National. The company now employs over 3,000 people and operates more than 500 trains weekly, using 7,767 miles (12,500km) of track to serve 450 communities. The fleet includes 396 passenger cars and 78 active locomotives. In addition to 159 railway stations, VIA Rail operates four modern maintenance facilities. While VIA Rail owns 138 miles (223km) of track, most of the infrastructure used by its passenger service is owned and managed by the freight railways, including ten different national and short-line operators.

Close to 4.2 million passengers travel on VIA Rail each year and the company joins Amtrak to operate several trains, including the *Adirondack* and *Maple Leaf*, connecting with cities in the United States. VIA Rail's equipment, although sometimes older than Amtrak's, is comfortable and has usually been refurbished to a high standard.

CANADIAN RAILWAYS

Railway

500km
500 miles
0
0

N
Bradt

NEWFOUNDLAND

QUEBEC

Halifax
NOVA SCOTIA
Gaspé
PRINCE EDWARD ISLAND
Moncton
NEW BRUNSWICK
Brockville
Montreal
Jonquière
Hervey
Quebec
Senneterre
Ottawa
Niagara Falls
Toronto
Windsor
Cochrane
Capreol
Sudbury Junction
London
Hearst
Sault Ste Marie
White River

Hudson Bay

ONTARIO

Sioux Lookout

Churchill
Thompson
Lynn Lake
The Pas
MANITOBA
Winnipeg

NORTHWEST TERRITORIES

SASKATCHEWAN

UNITED STATES OF AMERICA

Saskatoon
Edmonton
ALBERTA
Jasper
Kamloops
Prince George
Vancouver
BRITISH COLUMBIA
Courtenay
Victoria
Prince Rupert

YUKON

ALASKA (USA)

Canada's Trains Today   VIA RAIL

30

ARRANGING YOUR TRIP

Information   Information on VIA Rail is available from Amtrak at 400 N Capitol Street, Washington, DC 20001 (℡ *888 842 7245*), or from the following in Canada:

~ Alberta   VIA Rail, 12360-121 St NW, Edmonton, Alberta T5L 5C3

~ Manitoba   VIA Rail Travel Centre, Room 101, 123 Main St, Winnipeg, Manitoba R3C 2P8

~ Quebec   VIA Rail Canada, Rail Travel Bureau, Central Station, Montreal, Quebec H3C 3N3

For telephone information, reservations, special needs and tickets by mail, call the following numbers:

Newfoundland ℡1 800 561 3952
Prince Edward Island ℡1 800 561 3952
Nova Scotia ℡1 800 561 3952
Moncton, New Brunswick ℡506 857 9830
Elsewhere in New Brunswick ℡1 800 561 3952
Montreal, Quebec ℡514 989 2626
Quebec City, Quebec ℡418 692 3940

Elsewhere in Quebec ℡1 800 361 5390
Hamilton, Ontario ℡905 522 7533
London, Ontario ℡519 672 5722
Ottawa, Ontario ℡613 244 8289
Toronto, Ontario ℡416 366 8411
Windsor, Ontario ℡519 256 5511
Elsewhere in Ontario ℡1 800 361 1235
Other provinces ℡1 800 561 8630

People with hearing or speech problems can communicate through teletypewriter (TTY) on ℡416 368 6406 in Toronto and ℡1 800 268 9503 elsewhere.

For Amtrak train information or to make reservations when in Canada, ℡1 800 872 7245.

TICKETS   Information, reservations and tickets can be obtained through the VIA Rail website (*www.viarail.ca*) or from authorised travel agents and VIA sales offices. See *Appendix 3* (pages 335–6) for details of VIA agents abroad. Reservations may be made up to six months ahead and tickets can be ordered by mail and paid for by credit card at no extra cost. If you have not booked ahead, train conductors are able to issue a fare to a passenger not travelling beyond the end of the train run. Cash or credit cards are accepted for payment.

Although VIA Rail does not normally accept responsibility for lost, stolen or destroyed tickets, you can apply for reimbursement by completing a lost ticket indemnity bond obtainable at VIA Rail offices.

Canrailpass   A Canrailpass provides access to the VIA Rail system throughout Canada, giving seven one-way trips in Economy Class within a 21-day period. A trip is defined as a continuous journey between two stations regardless of the duration. In most cases one free stopover is allowed per trip. For example, travelling from Toronto to Vancouver with a stopover at Jasper would count as one trip used. If you wish to make more than one stopover, the trip is broken at the point where the longest stopover takes place. Tickets must be obtained before boarding, and valid photo identification shown if requested by VIA personnel. The number of seats available to Canrailpass holders is limited and bookings must be made at least three days in advance of the travel date.

Tickets booked using a pass may be cancelled at any time prior to the scheduled departure of the train, and the credit for the trip will be returned to the Canrailpass for future use within its validity period. Credits are not granted for tickets cancelled after the scheduled departure of the train. Passes are available both inside and outside

Canada but are not valid for other Canadian railways. Senior citizens (those aged 60 or more), students and anyone aged up to 25 may qualify for senior/youth rates.

VIA offers a choice of two System Canrailpasses. The Supersaver Canrailpass gives the best savings but booking must be made three or more days in advance and availability of seats is limited. The Discounted Canrailpass offers more flexibility and a greater availability of seats, and bookings can be made up to one day prior to departure (subject to availability). The following prices (in Canadian dollars) currently apply, high season being from 1 June to mid-October.

Supersaver Canrailpass	$588 (low season)	$969 (high season)
Discounted Canrailpass	$697 (low season)	$1,114 (high season)
Supersaver Canrailpass (youth/senior)	$545 (low season)	$872 (high season)
Discounted Canrailpass (youth/senior)	$627 (low season)	$1,003 (high season)

Commuter ePass The VIA Rail Commuter ePass is being introduced in some areas of southern Quebec and Ontario. Valid for 20 one-way trips (ten round trips) within a 30-day period between the same two stations, the pass can be purchased and used to book train tickets online. Routes include Ottawa–Montreal (Cdn$543.60) and Toronto–London (Cdn$515.70).

CLASSES OF TRAVEL

Economy Class Economy Class provides adequate space, reclining seats and panoramic views, and is available on all trains. Light meals, snacks and beverages. Most Corridor trains offer free Wi-Fi access and have AC outlets for laptop use. Travel during the off-peak season from mid-October to mid-May and you also have access to the Park car with its panoramic dome and lounges.

Business Class Except for short trips, Business Class is available on Corridor services between Windsor, Toronto, Ottawa, Montreal and Quebec City. This First Class service offers pre-boarding privileges, meals complete with complimentary wine and liqueurs served at your seat, a cellular telephone service, AC power outlets and free Wi-Fi. You also have access to private Panorama lounges with complimentary beverages and newspapers in Toronto, Montreal, Dorval, Quebec City, Kingston, London and Ottawa.

On board, you have a reserved, generously cushioned seat and meals are included in the ticket price. On some trains, Business Class passengers ride in European-designed Renaissance cars.

Sleeper Class Provided to late-night passengers on lengthy routes, Sleeper Class has berth sections and single, double and triple bedrooms which feature bunk beds, electrical outlet, chairs and a private washroom. Each sleeper car (except in the case of Renaissance cars) is equipped with a public shower. Berth seating consists of wide, sofa-style seats which convert at night into berths, with heavy curtains to ensure quiet and privacy. Passengers travelling alone can choose either an upper or lower berth. All necessary pillows and blankets are provided and Sleeper Class passengers have access to a shower room with complimentary soap, shampoo and towel.

Sleeper Touring Class Elite Sleeper Touring Class accommodation is available on the *Canadian* and *Ocean* trains to those who purchase sleeping accommodation. All meals are included and you get exclusive access to the Park car and Skyline

Dome car. The *Canadian* has been restored to its sleek 1950s splendour and its Park car, located at the rear of the train, comprises three separate saloons.

The Dome gives panoramic views from an observation deck, while the uniquely shaped Bullet lounge below features wrap-around windows, armchairs and a relaxed atmosphere. In the Mural lounge you can admire Canadian artworks or play games such as chess and backgammon. With the Sleeper Touring Class service your private room converts into a bedroom at night, with facilities that include a private toilet, washbasin, mirror, razor outlet, small closet, reading lamp and optional table. Single, double and triple bedrooms are available as well as a combined bedroom – actually two double rooms separated by a retractable divider.

Touring Class Available on the *Skeena* during peak period from mid-May to mid-October, Touring Class includes meals served at your seat and exclusive use of the Park car. All meals are included in the ticket price.

LRC Modern LRC (light, rapid, comfortable) equipment is mostly used on VIA's busiest route, the Windsor–Quebec City corridor. Trains travel at speeds of up to 95mph (152km/h).

RESERVATIONS Reservations are required for all First Class seats and sleeping cars, as well as for certain trains between Ontario, Quebec and the Maritime Provinces. Economy Class seats are automatically guaranteed on purchase of your ticket. You can obtain reservations up to six months ahead from most travel agents or use the online booking engine on VIA Rail's website (*www.viarail.ca*) to book your tickets, reserve hotel rooms and rent a car.

DISCOUNTS A discount applies (except during holiday periods) for local travel in eastern Canada. Similar reductions are available in the Quebec–Windsor corridor every day except Friday, Sunday and holidays (five days' notice required). Between Toronto and Vancouver in off-peak periods there is a reduction on Economy and Sleeper Touring classes, and reductions are available on trains to Canada's more remote regions.

Seniors aged over 60 are entitled to a 10% discount on Economy Class fares throughout the VIA system, or up to 50% under certain conditions (advance purchase or restricted periods). Special rates apply for groups of 20 people or more.

CHILDREN Those under two years of age accompanied by an adult (one child per adult) travel free when not occupying a seat. Infants must occupy a seat in Business Class but are entitled to a 25% discount. Children aged two–11 pay half the adult fare in Economy Class and get a 25% discount in Sleeper Class. Those under eight are not allowed to travel unaccompanied. Children aged eight–11 can travel with written permission from a parent or guardian provided certain other conditions are met, such as the signing of a liability waiver form (contact VIA Rail for details).

STUDENTS Full-time students no longer require an ISIC card – an identity card with your photo and date of birth will suffice. Students and travellers aged 12–25 are entitled to year-round discounts in Economy, Sleeper and Sleeper Touring classes. You can also purchase a VIA 6 Pak of tickets at half price, receiving a free telephone card plus discount coupons for accommodation and car hire. VIA 6 Paks can be ordered on VIA's website (*www.viarail.ca*) for delivery by mail or for collection at a station or travel agent of your choice.

CONNECTIONS Published connections with other trains, buses or ferries are not guaranteed and are subject to change without notice. VIA makes every effort to keep to schedules but does not accept responsibility for delays or inconvenience. You should allow at least an hour between trains when planning your itinerary. If a train is running late, its stopping time at stations may be reduced.

PAYMENT Credit cards and travellers' cheques can be used for buying tickets and meals or to upgrade accommodation. Debit cards are accepted at most stations. Personal cheques must be drawn on a Canadian or US bank with your name and address printed on the cheque. Fares and accommodation prices are subject to a 7% goods and services tax.

REFUNDS If your travel plans alter you should notify VIA Rail as soon as possible. Refunds on most tickets, either unused or partially used, can be provided immediately at any VIA sales office or at the travel agency which issued the ticket. If a refund cannot be made straight away a refund application will be taken, and whatever adjustment is due forwarded by mail. Refunds of the Canrailpass and some reduced-fare tickets may be subject to cancellation fees.

For refunds or credit by mail your original tickets and receipt coupon should be sent to VIA Rail Canada Inc, Ticket Refunds, 895 De La Gauchetière West, Montreal, Quebec H3B 4G1.

VIA PREFERENCE This is a frequent-traveller programme which lets you earn points to spend on more rail travel, accommodation on the train, car rental and hotels. You only need to spend Cdn$500 (approximately US$350) to earn a free return trip over a section of the railway. Points can also be earned from certain car-hire companies and hotels when making reservations or checking in. Preference Membership cards can be obtained at most VIA Rail stations or by calling ☏ 888 VIA PREFER (☏ 842 7733).

FACILITIES AND SERVICES
Language VIA Rail provides a bilingual service in English and French.

Baggage Up to 300lb (135kg) of personal baggage may be checked in for each adult fare, the actual amount depending on the route. For Sleeper Touring Class the limits are higher. Each piece of checked baggage should not exceed 50lb (23kg) or measure more than 48in (120cm). Larger items will be counted as two articles and staff may refuse to handle baggage weighing more than 75lb (34kg). Bags should be labelled with your name and address and handed in at least half an hour before departure.

Extra baggage, such as sporting equipment, can be checked subject to a surcharge and you can even bring your canoe if it measures less than 18ft (5.4m). Free boxes are available for transporting bicycles and their use is mandatory where journeys involve a connection. VIA will adjust the price for carrying oversize items to make sure it does not exceed the fare you have paid for travel, except in the case of children's fares.

Carry-on luggage is limited to two items not exceeding 50lb (23kg) each in weight. VIA reserves the right to refuse carry-on baggage measuring more than 26in x 18in x 9in (66cm x 46cm x 23cm). No liability is accepted for loss or damage to carry-on luggage or for articles lost or left on the train, so take out insurance if necessary.

Many stations, including Halifax, Quebec City, Ottawa, Winnipeg, Edmonton and Vancouver, have free luggage carts. Red Caps operate in Montreal and Toronto.

Lost property No liability is accepted for items stolen or left behind in a train, although VIA personnel will make every effort to help you find your belongings.

Boarding The elderly, passengers with young children and those travelling Sleeper Class are encouraged to board trains early at major stations.

Pets With the exception of service animals for visually or hearing-impaired passengers, pets are not allowed in passenger cars. Caged pets such as dogs and cats can be transported in the baggage car on most trains but passengers are responsible for their feeding and exercise. Animals must be claimed immediately on arrival. Cages must be high enough to allow the animal to stand and VIA has the right to refuse cages it deems unsuitable (appropriate cages can be purchased at some stations).

Radios Headphones must always be used when listening to radios, tapes or CDs.

Sleeping Pillows and blankets are not provided for overnight travel in economy accommodation, except on the *Ocean* and *Chaleur* trains. All necessary bedding is supplied in sleeping cars. Roomettes (for one person) and bedrooms (for two people) have a hand basin, mirror, electric razor socket, fold-down table and concealed or separate toilet. Sleeper Touring Class also has showers.

Section accommodation offers two facing couch-style seats which convert at night into an upper and lower berth. Thick curtains provide privacy. A section can be bought separately for one person, either as an upper or lower berth. Toilets are located in each coach.

Smoking All trains offer a completely smoke-free environment, a policy effective everywhere on the network since 1 November 2004, when the last of VIA Rail's western trains became non-smoking. Smoking is still permitted in specifically designated areas at some stations and at certain stops along the way.

Alcohol Alcoholic and other drinks purchased on board must be consumed where served. The law prohibits consumption of personal supplies other than by passengers travelling in enclosed sleeping accommodation.

Special needs Anyone with special needs will be given additional attention on request. Contact VIA in advance and ask for a copy of the brochure on special needs. You should give at least 48 hours' notice for special meals (such as diabetic, kosher or low sodium) and 24 hours for a wheelchair. Special meals are not available in Economy Class.

With the exception of trains running between London and Sarnia in Ontario, all VIA trains are accessible to passengers in wheelchairs, and wheelchairs can be accepted as checked baggage. Passengers unable to care for themselves must travel with an escort, who will be offered free passage in Economy Class (subject to certain restrictions).

Telephone A credit-card mobile-phone service is available in Business Class cars and some LRC coaches. Personal mobile phones should be used with due consideration and set on vibration mode to avoid disturbing other passengers.

Service If you have any comments or suggestions you should write to Customer Relations, VIA Rail Canada Inc, PO Box 8116, Station 'A', Montreal, Quebec H3C 3N3 (e *customer_relations@viarail.ca*).

If you have a complaint or problem which cannot be resolved by discussion with VIA personnel on the spot, you should call ☏ 1 800 681 2561 or write to Customer Relations, enclosing ticket receipts if possible. You can also fill in a comments form on the VIA Rail website (*www.viarail.ca*).

THE ROUTES

Changes to VIA Rail operations and schedules may take place from time to time, so for the latest information, ☏ 888 842 7245. The following passenger services are among those currently operating.

THE *CANADIAN* The government cut the southern transcontinental route through Banff, Calgary and Medicine Hat in 1990, transferring to a more northerly passage via Jasper. At the same time, a Cdn$200 million refurbishment of the *Canadian*'s original 1950s equipment began. Modern comforts such as air conditioning and showers were added to the stainless-steel coaches, and train staff were provided with smart new uniforms.

The *Canadian* now travels three times a week each way between Toronto and Vancouver on the route of the former Canadian National Railway's *Super Continental*, a flagship transcontinental service that replaced the CN's *Continental Limited*. The journey of almost 2,765 miles (4,424km) takes three days and nights and among its 69 stops are several which VIA calls 'dwell time' – brief pauses giving you a chance to stretch your legs on the platform. The train travels through southern Ontario then over the prairies of Saskatchewan, crossing the mountains and gorges of Jasper National Park before reaching British Columbia. In Jasper it connects with the *Skeena* to Prince Rupert.

The *Canadian* leaves Toronto late on Tuesday, Thursday and Saturday evenings to reach Capreol early next morning. You arrive in Winnipeg by early morning on the following day and Saskatoon by late evening. Edmonton is reached early on day three and Jasper by mid afternoon. You arrive in Vancouver on Friday, Sunday or Tuesday morning.

Travelling east, trains leave Vancouver mid evening each Tuesday, Friday and Sunday, arriving in Jasper by mid afternoon on the second day and Edmonton by late evening. You reach Saskatoon early in the morning and Winnipeg mid evening on the third day, then Capreol early on day four, before finally arriving in Toronto on Friday, Monday or Wednesday mornings.

Check-in baggage is available at all major stations. Complete meals service, lounge car, bedrooms and roomettes. Economy Class, with upgrades to Sleeper Touring Class.

← Connections with other VIA routes

Major stations

₩ **Vancouver** *(Ticket office ⊕ 06.00–17.45 Mon, Wed, Thu & Sat, 06.00–20.30 Tue, Fri & Sun; reservations & information ✆ 888 842 7245)* 1150 Station St. Buses connect with the Amtrak network in Seattle, WA. Amtrak's Northwest Corridor trains run between Vancouver & Seattle 4 times a day.

₩ **Winnipeg** *(Ticket office ⊕ 07.30–15.00 Mon, 07.30–23.30 Tue & Thu, 09.30–16.30 Wed, 08.00–16.00 Fri, 07.30–16.00 Sat, 09.00–23.30 Sun; reservations & information ✆ 888 842 7245)* 123 Main St. Lockers, newspapers, handcarts, taxi stand. VIA Rail Headquarters West is at 123 Main St, Winnipeg, MN R3C 1A3.

₩ **Saskatoon** *(Ticket office ⊕ 20.30–midnight Sat, 07.30–14.30 Sun, 17.30–midnight Mon, 07.30–14.30 Tue, 09.30–16.30 Wed, 07.30–14.30 & 20.30–midnight Thu, closed Fri; reservations & information ✆ 888 842 7245)* Unit 38, 1701 Chappell Drive, 4 miles (6.5km) west of downtown. Lockers, vending machines, taxi stand.

₩ **Edmonton** *(Ticket office ⊕ 08.00–23.45 Mon & Wed, 12.00–23.45 Sat, 06.00–13.45 Tue & Sun, 06.00–13.45 Fri, 08.00–15.45 Thu; reservations & information ✆ 888 842 7245)* 12360-121 St NW, Edmonton, AB T5L 5C3. Lockers, newspapers, taxi stand.

₩ **Jasper** *(Ticket office ⊕ 11.30–19.00 Mon, Thu & Sat, 10.00–17.45 Tue/Wed, 09.00–14.45 Sun, 09.00–16.45 Fri; reservations & information ✆ 888 842 7245)* 607 Connaught Dr, Jasper, AB T0E 1E0. Lockers, newspapers, Red Caps, restaurant, shop, taxis. For Jasper National Park contact the information centre (✆ 780 852 6176).

THE *SKEENA* A 725-mile (1,160km) journey among British Columbia's spectacular mountains and snow-filled valleys, starting from Jasper in Alberta and following a route formerly used by Indians, trappers and gold prospectors. You accompany the Fraser River to Prince George then the Skeena River ('river of mists' in the native Gitskan language) to Prince Rupert, only 40 miles (64km) south of Alaska. Prince Rupert is proud claimant to the title of 'halibut capital of the world'.

En route are glaciers, forests, salmon rivers, fishing villages and deserted gold rush towns. An hour from Jasper you can see the highest point in the Canadian Rockies, Mount Robson (12,972ft/3,954m). Look for the abundant wildlife, including moose, deer, bald eagles and an occasional bear.

Before the Grand Trunk Railway arrived in 1914, Prince Rupert was an isolated settlement on Kaien Island. Ferry services now operate north from Prince Rupert to Alaska, or south along the British Columbia and Washington coasts to Seattle. Connections can be made in Prince George with the British Columbia Railway service to Vancouver.

The *Skeena* leaves Jasper soon after midday on Sunday, Wednesday and Friday, reaching Prince George by mid evening. Following an overnight stop in Prince George, trains leave early on Monday, Thursday or Saturday morning to reach Prince Rupert by mid evening.

Travelling east, the *Skeena* departs Prince Rupert early on Sunday, Wednesday and Friday morning to reach Prince George by mid evening. After an overnight stop in Prince George, trains leave early on Monday, Thursday or Saturday morning to reach Jasper by early evening.

Complete meals service and bedrooms. Check-in baggage service only available during the peak period (early June to mid-September). Economy Class, with upgrades to Touring Class during peak period.

VIA uses Prince George's First Avenue and Quebec Station, close to downtown. Lockers, vending machines, handcarts, taxi stand. Prince Rupert Station is at 2000 Park Avenue.

THE CORRIDOR SERVICES VIA's busiest routes are between Quebec City and Windsor as well as to Montreal, Ottawa and Toronto, carrying three million passengers at up to 95mph (150km/h). Montreal and Quebec City are linked by five trains on weekdays, and four on Saturdays and Sundays. Economy Class and Business Class are available. The journey takes just under three hours, and Montreal to Toronto takes less than five hours. There are six departures every weekday from both Toronto and Montreal, with four departures on Saturdays and five on Sundays. Additional services go to Windsor, Sherbrooke (four trains daily in each direction) and Ottawa (five departures every weekday from both Toronto and Ottawa, with three departures on Saturdays and four on Sundays) and Niagara Falls (two trains daily from both Toronto and Niagara Falls, with more added during summer, in addition to Amtrak's *Maple Leaf*). Many trains offer Business Class as well as Economy Class.

Major stations

⋙ Quebec City *(Ticket office* ⊕ *05.00–18.00 Mon–Fri, 07.00–18.00 Sat/ Sun)* The refurbished Gare du Palais is at 450 rue de la Gare du Palais (☏ *888 842 7245).* Quebec's 600-room Hotel Château de Frontenac is another which was built in French style by the Canadian Pacific. The hotel's turrets & bastions still provide the city with its most recognisable landmark.

⋙ Montreal Gare Centrale (Central Station) *(Ticket office* ⊕ *06.00– 19.00 daily. Waiting room* ⊕ *05.30–00.15; reservations & information* ☏ *514 989 2626)* 895 rue de la Gauchetière Ouest, first opened in 1943. It is also used today by Amtrak & commuter trains. The Panorama lounge, for passengers in sleeping-car accommodations on the *Chaleur* & the *Ocean* (☏ *514 871 7759;* ⊕ *05.45–19.00).* Red Caps, restaurants, shops, taxi stand. The **Canadian Railway Museum** *(110 rue St-Pierre, Saint-Constant, Quebec J5A 1G7, located 30mins south of Montreal;* ☏ *450 632 2410 or* ☏ *450 638 1522; www.exporail.org;* ⊕ *late Jun–early Sep daily, otherwise Sat/Sun; admission charge)* houses over 160 historic locomotives & vehicles in enormous train sheds. The collection includes Canada's oldest-surviving steam engine & a steam-operated snow plough (a Canadian invention) as well as the largest steam locomotive built in Canada & the last to be built for a Canadian railway. A replica steam locomotive operates on summer w/ends. For Montreal city information, see also *Chapter 21, The Adirondack* (pages 242–3).

⋙ Toronto *(Ticket office* ⊕ *06.00–22.30 Mon–Fri, 06.00–22.00 Sat, 06.45–23.15 Sun. Waiting room* ⊕ *05.30–00.45. The Panorama lounge* ☏ *416 956 7637;* ⊕ *06.00–19.15 Mon, Wed & Fri, 06.00–22.00 Tue, Thu & Sat, 07.00–19.15 Sun. Arrivals & departures* ☏ *416 366 8411; reservations & information* ☏ *888 842 7245 or* ☏ *1 800 872 7245 for Amtrak)* Clean, efficient & softly lit Union Station is at 65 Front W & York. GO commuter trains operate to Hamilton, Oshawa, Richmond Hill & Georgetown (☏ *416 869 3200).* Lockers, newspapers, Red Caps, restaurants, shops, taxi stand, subway.

For Toronto city information, see *Chapter 26, The Maple Leaf* (pages 275–7).

⇢ Ottawa *(Ticket office* ⊕ *05.00–21.00 Mon–Fri, 06.00–19.00 Sat, 07.30–21.00 Sun; reservations & information* ☏ *888 842 7245)* A modern station at 200 Tremblay, 2 miles (3km) from downtown. Lockers, newspapers, Red Caps, restaurants, shops, taxi stand. The

Canada Museum of Science and Technology *(1867 St Laurent Bd;* ☏ *613 991 3044; www. sciencetech.technomuses.ca;* ⊕ *daily; admission charge)* displays historic steam engines & 1890s rolling stock.

THE *OCEAN* The *Ocean* train first ran on 3 July 1904, making it Canada's longest-running train to have operated over the same line. It takes 18 hours to travel 840 miles (1,352km) along the old Intercolonial Railway (ICR) route between Halifax, Nova Scotia, and Montreal in Quebec. Trains go via New Brunswick and some of the many rural communities of Quebec's south shore, starting out daily (except Tuesday) in both directions.

You leave Halifax just after midday to reach Moncton by late afternoon, Campbellton in New Brunswick by late evening and Montreal early the following morning. A ferry service connects Levis with Quebec City.

Travelling east, the *Ocean* departs Montreal early in the evening to reach Campbellton early next morning, Moncton by midday and Halifax, Nova Scotia, by early evening.

Check-in baggage at main stations. Complete meals service, bedrooms, Park car and Skyline observation car. Economy Class, with upgrades to Sleeper Class or Sleeper Touring Class (available mid-June to mid-October).

Halifax station *(Ticket office & waiting room* ⊕ *09.15–17.30 daily; reservations & information;* ☏ *888 842 7245)* 1161 Hollis. The splendidly restored 1928 station building is adjacent to the Westin Hotel, a former CN property.

Lockers, vending machines, newspapers, Red Caps, restaurant, taxi stand.

THE *CHALEUR* This train operates three days a week, following the *Ocean*'s route between Montreal and Matapédia, then crossing a tributary of the St Lawrence River before continuing along the beautiful Gaspé Peninsula. Don't miss the breathtaking early morning views of the Baie des Chaleurs, after which the train is named. Splendidly restored silver trains leave Montreal early on Wednesday, Friday and Sunday evening to reach Matapédia very early the next morning and Gaspé by midday.

Travelling south, the *Chaleur* leaves Gaspé mid afternoon on Monday, Thursday and Saturday to reach Matapédia late in the evening and Montreal by early next morning.

Park car, Skyline car with observation dome, lounge and café. Check-in baggage. Complete meals service and bedrooms. Economy Class, with upgrades to Sleeper Class.

THE *SAGUENAY* AND THE *ABITIBI* The *Saguenay* travels from downtown Montreal to Lac-St-Jean and Jonquière via the forests and lakes of northern Quebec. The *Abitibi* goes from Montreal to La Tuque then heads northwest through Sanmaur, Parent and Clova to Senneterre, where the station is at 171, 4ième rue ouest. Stations *en route* include Jolette, Shawinigan, Saint-Tite and Chambord. The *Abitibi* and *Saguenay* travel together between Montreal and Hervey Junction, where the *Saguenay* separates and heads north to Jonquière, where the station is at 2439 rue St-Dominique. Both trains leave Montreal on Monday, Wednesday and Friday mornings, arriving 11 hours later in Senneterre or nine hours later in Jonquière. Trains depart for Montreal on Tuesday, Thursday and Sunday. Economy Class only.

THE *HUDSON BAY* Trains travel more than 1,000 miles (1,600km) north from Winnipeg, crossing a bleak desert of ice and snow to sub-arctic Churchill and the polar bear country of Hudson Bay. This is beaver territory, where dams have been known to wash away the track or even wreck a train. The Hudson Bay Railroad opened the line in the 1920s to transport grain for export from Canada's prairies, and the Canadian National's last scheduled steam train (*No 6043*) made its final run between The Pas and Winnipeg in November 1960.

The *Hudson Bay* leaves Winnipeg at midday on Tuesday and Sunday to reach The Pas early next day and Thompson by early afternoon. You arrive in Gillam by late evening and Churchill early on Thursday or Tuesday evening.

Travelling south, trains leave Churchill mid evening on Tuesday and Sunday to reach Gillam early next morning and Thompson by mid afternoon. You arrive in The Pas during the night and Winnipeg late on Thursday or Tuesday afternoon.

Book well in advance, especially during summer. Check-in baggage. Complete meals service, bedrooms and roomettes. Economy Class, with upgrades to Sleeper Class.

Churchill station (*Ticket office & waiting room* ☉ *08.00–08.45 & 19.00–20.30; reservations & information* ☏ *888 842 7245*) This is at 74092 Churchill, on the western edge of town. Left-luggage room.

OTHER VIA RAIL TRAINS On Vancouver Island, the *Malahat* runs daily through beautiful countryside between Victoria and Courtenay through Malahat Pass and the Cowichan Valley. You leave Victoria mid morning or Courtenay mid afternoon for a 140-mile (224km) journey lasting 4½ hours. Snacks, sandwiches and drinks can be bought during station stops at Nanaimo and Courtenay. Economy Class only.

The *Hudson Bay* route connects at The Pas in Manitoba with trains to Pukatawagan. Watch out for polar bear warning signs as you near the edge of the Arctic Circle. Trains leave The Pas late morning and arrive in Pukatawagan mid evening on Monday and Thursday. You can return from Pukatawagan mid morning on Tuesday and Friday to reach The Pas by mid evening. Check-in baggage service available. To book travel on The Pas–Pukatawagan route, contact the Keewatin Railway Company (☏ *204 623 5255*).

VIA Rail's *Lake Superior* trains depart Sudbury on Tuesday, Thursday and Saturday mornings for a 301-mile (480km) journey via Cartier and Franz to White River in Ontario, arriving by early evening. Travelling east, trains leave White River on Wednesday, Friday and Sunday morning to reach Sudbury by mid evening. Economy Class only.

Several VIA trains out of Toronto go to Kingston, Windsor, Stratford and London, Ontario.

ROCKY MOUNTAINEER A leisurely, all-daylight 667-mile (1,112km) journey among the mountains and forests of the Canadian Rockies and on to Jasper or Banff and Calgary, Alberta, makes this one of the most spectacular train trips in the world. The service, originally operated by VIA Rail and heavily subsidised by the government, became *Rocky Mountaineer* in 1990, when the all-daylight journeys were privatised. Under the ownership of *Rocky Mountaineer* the service has become more popular each year since.

Rocky Mountaineer is the largest privately owned passenger rail service in North America, with more than 550 employees. On 12 September 1996, it made the record books by operating the longest passenger train in Canadian history. A total of 37 cars travelled from Vancouver to Kamloops to beat the previous best of 28, set in Regina, Saskatchewan, by the Canadian Pacific's *Dominion* in 1965. The record was later extended to 41 cars in 1999.

The routes *Rocky Mountaineer* uses Canadian Pacific and Canadian National tracks, as well as (briefly) tracks owned by VIA Rail. The entire journey takes place in daylight so that you can absorb the maximum amount of scenery and see animals such as grazing elk, black and grizzly bears, white-tail deer, moose, mountain goats, coyotes, wolves and big-horn sheep. The thick forests of pine and fir are also home to marmots, porcupines and chipmunks. Much of this wildlife has become accustomed to railroad traffic so this is a great opportunity to see more creatures than would otherwise be possible. Bears, for example, have developed a taste for the grain which leaks out of freight cars and ferments beside the track.

William Cornelius Van Horne, first manager of the Canadian Pacific, famously remarked that 'since we cannot export the scenery, we shall have to import the tourists' and this part of Canada has been doing so ever since. *Rocky Mountaineer* leaves Vancouver's Rocky Mountaineer Station and crosses the Fraser River swing bridge before following the Fraser River itself. The passage through the Fraser Canyon was part of the gold rush routes of the late 1880s, when the CN railroad line had to be carved out of the side of the gorge by construction workers using 'dynamite and whiskey'.

At Hell's Gate Canyon, so named because construction work here was so dangerous, a massive rock slide accidentally narrowed the river to 110ft (37m). Look for fish ladders built in the 1940s to allow 40 million sockeye salmon to pass upstream to spawn every year. You continue through a fertile valley of farms and orchards before beginning to climb among snow-capped mountains and glaciers, passing places with names such as Skuzzy Creek, Suicide Rapids and Jaws of Death Gorge. Look for the occasional fields of ginseng, grown under plastic sheets.

After an overnight stop in Kamloops you continue next morning to Jasper by way of the North Thompson River, the Monashee Mountains, Pyramid Falls and Little Hell's Gate. You get an overwhelming view of the highest mountain in the Canadian Rockies, Mount Robson (12,972ft/3,954m), and have the option of continuing on VIA Rail from Jasper, travelling across all of Canada to the Atlantic coast. VIA's *Canadian* train uses the same tracks as *Rocky Mountaineer* from Vancouver to Jasper but travels through the night.

An alternative, and usually preferred, *Rocky Mountaineer* train goes from Kamloops across Glacier National Park to Banff and Calgary. You travel among the ranch lands of the South Thompson River then along the fjord-like shores of the Shuswap Lakes. At Silverdale you pass the spot where in 1904 the American Billy Miner and 'Shorty' Dunn carried out Canada's first train hold-up, getting away with $6,000 of gold dust and $50,000 in US bonds. You also pass the spot where their last train robbery (yielding $15 and a handful of liver pills) took place a year and a half later. The gang were captured shortly afterwards by the RCMP, although Miner later escaped from jail.

At Craigellachie you see a stone cairn indicating where the last spike was driven to complete the Canadian Pacific Railroad on 7 November 1885. *Rocky Mountaineer* travels on through Mount Macdonald by way of the five-mile (8km) Connaught Tunnel, the second-longest in North America. Adjacent Macdonald Tunnel is the longest, at nine miles (14.5km). Both tunnels were built in the early 20th century to protect the tracks from heavy snowfalls and avalanches which had caused over 200 deaths. At Stoney Creek a steel-arch bridge was constructed in 1929 directly above an 1893 bridge which replaced the original wooden structure.

Beyond the Kicking Horse River you go through two unique spiral tunnels located under Cathedral Mountain and Mount Ogden, excavated between 1907 and 1909. These provide a safer and easier route than the original 'Big Hill', an eight-mile stretch which included a 4.5% grade. The upper Spiral Tunnel is 3,255ft (992m) long and turns approximately 250°, emerging 56ft (17m) lower than its entrance. The lower tunnel is 2,922ft (890m) long, turns 230° and comes out 50ft (15m) below. An extra-long freight train may be seen emerging from and entering the tunnel simultaneously.

Rocky Mountaineer leaves Vancouver early in the morning to reach Kamloops by early evening. While in Kamloops, you can enjoy an evening entertainment show such as *Rhythms on the Rails*, a musical dinner show. After an overnight hotel stop you leave Kamloops early next morning for either Jasper or Banff and Calgary.

Travelling west, trains leave Calgary early in the morning (or Jasper mid morning) to reach Kamloops by early evening. After an overnight stop you leave Kamloops early next morning and arrive in Vancouver by late afternoon.

Facilities Each air-conditioned train can carry up to 950 passengers in 22 coaches. Each dome car cost Cdn$1 million, accommodates 72 passengers and was specially built by the Rader Company in Colorado. These were the first completely new coaches to be put into service on a Canadian train for 40 years. Similar ones operate on the Alaska Railroad.

RedLeaf Service gives you a comfortable reclining seat, large picture windows and open-air vestibules. You get complimentary snacks and non-alcoholic drinks as well as an at-your-seat cold meal service. Attendants supply an enthusiastic commentary on the route's history, geography and wildlife. Choose a seat on the left of the train when travelling east, or on the right if going west.

GoldLeaf Service is well worth the extra cost, offering seating in the bi-level Dome car with uninterrupted panoramic views, pre-boarding privileges, an elegant private 36-seat dining room serving Alberta beef, Pacific Ocean fish, regional game and award-winning local wines, rear observation platform and a hotel for the overnight stop in Kamloops.

Timings and booking The season lasts from April to October. You can book one-way or round trips and fares start at about US$789 (Cdn$757). This includes breakfast and lunch on the train, as well as hotel accommodation in Kamloops. Reduced fares are available for children aged two–11.

You should book at least 30 days in advance for best availablity and check in an hour before departure time. For GoldLeaf guests, checked baggage (maximum 66lb/30kg) will be delivered and waiting for you upon arrival at your overnight accommodations in Kamloops. RedLeaf guests are asked to bring a small carry-on bag as their luggage will be delivered to their final destination. To ensure the preservation of the fragile environment of the areas *Rocky Mountaineer* travels through, no smoking is allowed on board. This includes the vestibules between the coaches and restroom facilities.

Rocky Mountaineer trains are run by Rocky Mountaineer, 101-369 Terminal Avenue, Vancouver, British Columbia V6A 4C4 (↖ 00 800 0606 7372 (UK), ↖ 604 606 7245 or ↖ 1 800 665 7245 (Canada/USA); e *reservations@rockymountaineer.*

com; www.rockymountaineer.com). Rocky Mountaineer's station is at 1755 Cottrell Street in Vancouver.

UK ticket agents include First Class Holidays (✆ *0845 644 3545;* e *trains@ 1stclassholidays.com; www.1stclassholidays.com*), Connections Worldwide (✆ *01494 473173;* e *enquiries@connectionsworldwide.co.uk;www.connectionsworldwide.co.uk*), Travel Pack (✆ *0870 121 2020;* e *book.canada@travelpack.co.uk; www.travelpack. co.uk*) and Canadian Affair (✆ *020 7616 9184;* e *mail@canadian-affair.com; www. canadian-affair.com*).

Calgary station The station is at 131 Ninth Avenue SW. Lockers, newspapers, Red Caps, restaurant, taxi stand. For information on the **Alberta 2005 Railway Museum**, contact PO Box 2442, Station M, Calgary, Alberta T2P 3C1 (✆ *281 5989; www.alberta2005rail.com*).

THE *WHISTLER SEA TO SKY CLIMB* (✆ *00 800 0606 7372 (UK) or* ✆ *604 606 8460; www.rockymountaineer.com*) In May 2006, *Rocky Mountaineer* launched two new tourist train routes, connecting into a western Canadian rail network. The *Whistler Sea to Sky Climb* train operates a 3½-hour service between May and September from Thursday to Monday for travellers between the host cities of the 2010 Olympic and Paralympic Winter Games – Vancouver and Whistler, British Columbia. Also launched was the *Rainforest to Goldrush* route, travelling through British Columbia's seldom-seen interior from Whistler to Jasper, Alberta, in the Canadian Rockies.

BRITISH COLUMBIA RAIL LIMITED *Please note that BC Rail ceased operating passenger trains in 2002, but it is hoped that some of its services may return.* British Columbia Rail was formerly known as the Pacific Great Eastern Railway and before that the Howe Sound Pemberton Valley & Northern Railway, founded in 1908.

In July 2004, the Canadian National Railway Company (CN) completed a Cdn$1 billion deal with the British Columbian government and began the gradual integration of BC Rail into its North American system. CN acquired BC Rail Ltd and the BC Rail Partnership (collectively BC Rail), and the right to operate over BC Rail's roadbed under a long-term lease. CN will support the introduction of new train tours over BC Rail between Vancouver, Whistler and northern British Columbia, and has requested proposals from qualified companies to select third parties to operate these trains.

BC Rail formerly operated the *Royal Hudson* steam train between Vancouver and Squamish. King George VI and Queen Elizabeth made a royal tour of Canada in 1939, travelling from Quebec City to Vancouver by a train that was 12 cars long (including two vice-regal cars), painted royal blue and aluminium and pulled by Hudson locomotive *No 2850*. Hudson *No 2851* was used for the pilot train, carrying officials and press, which preceded the royal train by one hour on its 3,224-mile (5,188km) journey. Royal crowns were attached to the running boards of both locomotives. King George was so impressed that he gave permission for all future Hudson engines to carry his coat of arms and be designated '*Royal Hudsons*'.

THE ALGOMA CENTRAL Trains run for 296 miles (475km) between Sault Ste Marie (pronounced 'soo-saint-marie') and Hearst in Ontario. You travel a twisting route opened in 1914 among forests, lakes, waterfalls and ravines, where the mountains resemble the Rockies. There are terrific views of the deep Agawa River Canyon and the train makes a two-hour stop for you to admire more closely the 1,500ft-high (457m) cliffs, pine trees and waterfalls.

The summer service provides northbound trains on Thursday, Saturday and Monday, and southbound trains on Friday, Sunday and Tuesday. The winter service provides northbound trains on Wednesday, Friday and Sunday, and southbound trains on Thursday, Saturday and Monday. During the foliage season (September to October), you should plan a weekday trip if possible and be sure to book early. Dome car service includes breakfast, lunch and a separate bar area with private steward.

The Algoma Central's *Snow Train* operates on weekends from January until March, travelling through a snow-and-ice-encrusted Agawa Canyon. The *Snow Train* makes an overnight stop in the French-Canadian town of Hearst. On certain days throughout the year you can tour the whole length of the railway, including the flat lands of the Clay Belt region with its countless lakes and conifers.

For information or tickets, contact the Algoma Central Railway (*PO Box 130, 129 Bay St, Sault Ste Marie, ON P6A 6Y2;* ☏ *705 946 7300 or* ☏ *800 242 9287; www. agawacanyontourtrain.com*).

THE ONTARIO NORTHLAND In 1932, the Temiskaming & Northern Ontario Railway was built 186 miles (299km) from Cochrane to the Arctic Circle across a demanding physical landscape, opening up the north's mining and forest resources. The railway changed its name to the Ontario Northland Railway (ONR) in 1946, and remains principally a freight line, operating to and from northeastern Ontario and northwestern Quebec. Ontario Northland today provides transportation and telecommunications services to the residents and businesses of northern Ontario. Trains cross farmland, bogs, forests and fields of wild flowers. The year-round *Northlander* passenger train connects northern and southern Ontario, running between Toronto's Union Station and the town of Cochrane via North Bay, Cobalt and Matheson. It provides large, comfortable seats, wide aisles and picture windows. The **Cochrane Railway and Pioneer Museum** (☏ *705 272 4361;* ⊕ *Jun–Sep daily; free*) is housed in several old train coaches opposite Cochrane Station. The *Northlander* leaves Toronto for its 440-mile (705km) journey early in the morning every day except Saturday, reaching North Bay by early afternoon and the gold mining town of Cochrane early in the evening. Travelling south, trains leave Cochrane early in the morning (except Saturday) to reach North Bay by early afternoon and Toronto by early evening. A shuttle service is available to connect to the *Northlander* from Hearst, Iroquois Falls and Timmins. The train is equipped with a dining car, washrooms and plenty of space to read, work or enjoy a hobby while you travel.

The ONR's *Polar Bear Express* is a four-hour, 186-mile (300km) ride down the Arctic watershed, accessible only by rail or plane. You go through a sparsely populated wetland of black spruce forests, lakes, muskeg and scrub, known as 'the bush'. The *Polar Bear Express* proceeds from Cochrane over Ontario's fertile clay belt farmland and Cree Indian territory, crossing the Abitibi and Moose rivers to Moosoonee on the edge of the Arctic Ocean near James Bay. Only 3,000 people live in Moosoonee, which was first settled as a trading post by Revillion Frères of Paris in 1903 in competition with the Hudson Bay Company. Winters can be very cold, freezing the Moose River solid enough to make a road to Moose Factory Island.

Before the Temiskaming & Northern Ontario Railway arrived in Moosoonee in 1932, the journey from Cochrane by canoe or snowshoes took ten days. A green railway car on the right of the station houses a museum of the region's natural and cultural history. A short boat ride will take you from Moosoonee to the historic community of Moose Factory, established as a fur-trading post in 1673, and the oldest English settlement in Ontario. Moose Factory's attractions include a Hudson

30

Bay Company staff house, Centennial Park, St Thomas's Anglican Church, and the Cree Cultural Interpretive Centre where you can meet First Nations people who will share the rich history of the area.

The *Polar Bear Express* operates on weekdays during the summer as a tourist train with full dining-car service and a Dome car offering spectacular views of the lakes, rivers and waterfalls. You can even sit down and sing along to toe-tapping songs with a live entertainer. In the autumn, winter and spring, the train operates as a passenger and freight train that provides a vital link between Cochrane and Moosoonee as there are no roads to the latter. It is about a five-hour trip in each direction and this is one of the last flag-stop trains in Canada. It may halt virtually anywhere, perhaps to pick up a canoeist or camper.

The *Dream Catcher Express* is a train excursion which allows you to enjoy brilliant autumn colours through large viewing windows as well as a Dome car for even more spectacular panoramic views. Six trains operate in late September/early October from North Bay to Temagami, home to a spectacular old-growth pine forest. The region is rich with First Nations history and artefacts and stone drawings dating as far back as 6000BC have been discovered here. The famous naturalist Archibald Belaney, born in England in 1888, worked in Temagami as a fur trapper and married an Ojjibwa woman from whom he learned much about the people. He claimed he was adopted by the tribe and given a name meaning 'Grey Owl'.

For information on all Ontario Northland services, contact 555 Oak Street E, North Bay, ON P1B 8L3 (❨ 705 472 4500; *www.OntarioNorthland.ca*). For information on schedules and fares for the *Northlander* and motor-coach services, contact ❨ 1 800 461 8558. Reservations are required and should be made well in advance for the *Polar Bear Express* and *Dream Catcher Express*. For information and reservations, ❨ 1 800 268 928.

OTHER RAILWAYS AND RAIL MUSEUMS IN CANADA
Royal Canadian Pacific (*201 9th Av SW, Calgary, AB T2P 1K3;* ❨ *403 508 1400 or* ❨ *877 665 3044; www.royalcanadianpacific.com. For extended stays at one of RCP's landmark hotels,* ❨ *1 800 441 1414*) The RCP is mostly a freight-only railroad but several companies operate over its track, including VIA Rail and *Rocky Mountaineer*. Based in Calgary, Alberta, the Royal Canadian Pacific was launched in 2000 and carries a fleet of luxuriously appointed 1920s-era rail cars, built by Canadian Pacific Railway (CP). The eight historic coaches are named after people or events from the history of Canada, and are 80ft (24m) long. They have carpeted floors, mahogany panelling, inlaid marquetry and cut glass, fine china and white linens to conjure up the service of old. The Royal Canadian Pacific (RCP) offers themed tours featuring historic, golfing, fly-fishing and culinary as well as customised private-charter journeys while travelling through the spectacular Rocky Mountains.

As part of their history, these vintage rail cars were used exclusively by CP's executives and on occasion by touring dignitaries. These included US President Franklin D Roosevelt, King George VI and Queen Elizabeth, Princess Elizabeth and the Duke of Edinburgh, and Sir Winston Churchill, who travelled by special train from Montreal to Washington in 1943. These cars were the 'private jets' of their time. In 1999, CP built the Canadian Pacific Pavilion to house its fleet of valuable railway cars. In 2007, the RCP moved its offices into a new building located adjacent to the Pavilion in downtown Calgary. The new headquarters has been built with a theme of a historic steel trestle bridge featuring an open glass concept and housing essential office functions, the sales/booking area and mechanical operations.

The 'Rockies Experience' is a six-day, 650-mile (1,046km) trip from Calgary to Crowsnest Pass and back to Calgary. The fare includes two nights' accommodation at the Palliser Hotel, three nights on board the train, guided tours, meals, baggage handling and admission to off-train tours.

The train heads west from Calgary along the Canadian Pacific Railway main line through the Bow River Valley towards the Rocky Mountains. After a short stop in Banff you continue to Lake Louise and the continental divide, travelling through the famous Spiral Tunnels into Field, British Columbia, where the train stops for passengers to board a motor coach for a tour of Emerald Lake.

You then depart for Golden, British Columbia, where the train leaves the Canadian Pacific Line and goes south along the 'coal route' through beautiful valleys carved by the Columbia River. You also travel through the continent's largest natural wetland, called 'The Rocky Mountain Trench', before making an overnight stop at Invermere. Next morning you travel south to the early 20th-century town of Fort Steele, known as Galbraith Ferry during the 1864 Kootenay gold rush, then to Cranbrook for a visit to the **Canadian Museum of Rail Travel** (see page 326). After reboarding the train at Fort Steele, you travel east to Crowsnest Lake at the top of Crowsnest Pass for a second overnight stop.

The following morning, you leave for Fort McLeod and a guided tour of Head-Smashed-In Buffalo Jump before continuing via the Lethbridge Viaduct – the longest and highest bridge of its kind in the world – then on through rolling ranch country to Okotoks. A motor coach takes you to Homeplace Ranch for a guided horseback tour or scenic walk before the train returns to Calgary.

The Quebec North Shore and Labrador Railroad *(100 Retty, CP1000, Sept-Iles, QC G4R 4L5;* ✆ *418 968 7805)* This line was originally built in the early 1950s to move iron ore from Labrador City to a port at Sept-Iles on the Gulf of St Lawrence, and the line is still used for freight traffic. Construction of the QNSL forms the backdrop for Hammond Innes's 1958 novel *The Land God Gave to Cain*. The author spent some time around Labrador researching for the book when the railway was being built.

QNSL maintained passenger and freight services until 2005, when it sold the Emeril Junction, NL–Schefferville, PQ rail line to Tshiuetin Rail Transportation Inc *(1005 Boul Laure, Suite 305C, Sept-Iles, QC G4R 4S6;* ✆ *418 960 0982; www.tshiuetin. net).* The first ever railway owned by aboriginal people, Tshiuetin means 'North Wind'. Trains depart from Sept-Iles on Monday and Thursday at 08.00 to arrive at Emeril Junction at 15.00. Trains leave Emeril Junction on Tuesday and Friday at 12.00 to arrive in Sept-Iles at 19.00. Passenger trains no longer go to Labrador City so travellers to and from Labrador must take Highway 500 from Emeril Junction, approximately 45 minutes' drive.

White Pass & Yukon Railway *(PO Box 435, 231 Second Av, Skagway, AK 99840, USA;* ✆ *907 983 2217 or* ✆ *800 343 7373; www.wpyr.com)* A daily coach/ train service operates mainly between Whitehorse and Skagway, including a steep narrow-gauge route between Skagway and Fraser. The train hugs precipitous cliffs and crosses flimsy-looking trestle bridges as it follows a route used by many thousands during the 1898 Klondike gold rush, passing waterfalls, glaciers and tunnels carved out of solid granite. You travel in a 1890s-style coach on the train but the part of the journey between White Pass and Whitehorse is operated by motor coach. The whole journey takes 4½ hours and services run from May until mid-September.

Summit Excursions take you from tidewater Skagway to the summit of White Pass, a climb of almost 3,000ft (900m) in only 20 miles (32km). The daily round trip takes three hours.

The *Yukon Adventure* takes you a further 47 miles beyond the summit to Carcross, Yukon (passport required). A two-hour layover at Bennett offers passengers a piping-hot meal and a self-guided walking tour of the historic gold rush town site. At the end of the layover passengers reboard the train and continue on to Carcross. The six-hour round trips from Skagway take place each Sunday, Wednesday and Thursday from late May to August, and the ticket price includes lunch.

On Monday and Friday there are steam train excursions on the route to Fraser Meadows, and the *Chilkoot Trail* hikers' service links Bennett, Fraser and Skagway.

Canadian Museum of Rail Travel (*PO Box 400, 1 Van Horne St, Cranbrook, BC V1C 4H9;* ☏ *250 489 3918; www.crowsnest.bc.ca/cmrt;* ☺ *summer daily, mid-Oct–mid-Apr Tue–Sat; admission charge*) The museum includes a beautifully restored *Trans-Canada Limited* First Class sleeping-car train built in 1929 for the Canadian Pacific Railway. This has 90,000ft² (8,361m²) of inlaid mahogany and walnut panelling as well as large collections of railway china and silverware. Other trains include the 1907 Soo–Spokane *Train Deluxe*. Expansion plans will enable the museum to display five different train sets showing passenger travel between 1887 and 1955, along with heritage railway buildings such as the 1901 Elko Station.

Elgin County Railway Museum (*225 Wellington St, St Thomas, ON N5P 4H4;* ☏ *519 637 6284; www.ecrm5700.org;* ☺ *summer w/ends, by appointment year round; admission charge*) Located in the 1913 Michigan Central Railway shops on Wellington Street, the collection includes a Hudson locomotive formerly used by the Canadian National Railway on its Toronto–Montreal corridor. Other locos are displayed along with an NYC Pullman sleeper, *Cascade Lane*.

St Thomas has been an important railway town since 1856, and was known in its heyday as the 'Railway Capital of Canada'. Around 26 railway lines then passed through, including the Wabash, Pere Marquette, New York Central and London & Port Stanley.

Winnipeg Railway Museum (*PO Box 48, 123 Main St, Winnipeg, MB R3C 1A3;* ☏ *204 942 4632; www.wpgrailwaymuseum.com;* ☺ *daily; admission charge*) Approximately 37,500ft² is filled with railway artefacts and exhibits including the *Countess of Dufferin* (the first steam locomotive in western Canada), a Midland Railway of Manitoba snow dozer, and a combine car (colonist's car) which is now the gift shop.

Waterloo–St Jacobs Railway (*PO Box 40060, Waterloo Sq Postal Station, Waterloo, ON N2J 4V1;* ☏ *519 885 2297; www.steam-train.org*) The railway ceased operation in 2000 due to maintenance costs but in May 2007 the Southern Ontario Locomotive Restoration Society received approval from the city of Waterloo to revive this tourist train. The renamed Waterloo Central Railway now runs passenger services and leases space in the City of Waterloo Visitor and Heritage Information Centre, formerly owned by the Waterloo–St Jacobs Railway. Trains operate three times a day on Tuesday, Thursday and Saturday, beginning in Waterloo at the station at 10 Father David Bauer Drive, with stops at the St Jacobs farmers' market and the village of St Jacobs.

West Coast Railway Heritage Park (*39645 Government Rd, Squamish, BC V8B 0B6;* ☎ *800 722 1233; www.wcra.org;* ⊕ *daily; admission charge*) The park is being developed to show a typical railway facility of the mid 20th century and provides visitors with the opportunity to tour authentic railway equipment in various stages of restoration. The collection consists of 65 pieces of heritage rolling stock plus many railroad-related artefacts, representing the major railways that have served British Columbia – Canadian Pacific, Canadian National, Pacific Great Eastern, BC Electric and Great Northern. The oldest items are the business car *British Columbia* (1890) and a rare Canadian Pacific colonist sleeping car (1905). West Coast Mini Rail line trains circle the park with sights *en route* such as the Garden Railway – a large-scale model railway that operates in woods near Sweet Apple Station. The Skeena River railroad car also features model trains, both HO scale and N scale.

Port Stanley Terminal Rail (*309 Bridge St, Port Stanley, ON N5L 1C5;* ☎ *519 782 3730; www.pstr.on.ca*) Operates over a seven-mile (11km) section of the former London & Port Stanley Railway Line between Port Stanley and St Thomas, which opened in 1856. Over 25 million passengers travelled on the L & PS, many heading for the beach at Port Stanley – 'the Coney Island of the Great Lakes'. Steam trains operated on this route for 59 years, transporting over one million passengers in 1943 alone.

Passenger services were discontinued in 1957 and freight traffic ceased in 1982, but the line was acquired by its present owners the following year and restored by volunteers. Trains again now make over 400 departures each season to cross two bridges and travel the banks of Kettle Creek, where you can see apple orchards and deer as well as plants and trees unique to the north shore of Lake Erie.

Northern Ontario Railroad Museum and Heritage Centre (*26 Bloor St, Capreol, ON P0M 1H0;* ☎ *705 858 5050; www.northernontariorailroadmuseum.ca;* ⊕ *Jun–Aug Tue–Sun, Sep–May by special appointment; admission charge*) This unique museum is a tribute to pioneers who worked along the rails and to settlers who opened the Sudbury region through mining and forestry. The museum is located in the renovated Canadian National Railway Superintendent's house purchased by the town of Capreol in 1997, and explores the local history of the Capreol area through photographs and stories. Displays include an original steam locomotive that helped open up the north, a caboose and a renovated school car. The 'School on Wheels' was one of seven used to teach the isolated children and adults of the northern Ontario wilderness. They began as an experimental joint venture between the Department of Education and the railway in 1926. CN and CP operated school cars on a number of routes throughout northern Ontario, with about six one-week stops at each designated siding. The children would attend school for three–six days and receive further studies to last until the school car returned the following month.

Prince George Railway & Forestry Museum (*850 River Rd, Prince George, BC V2L 5S8 (adjacent to Cottonwood Island Park);* ☎ *250 563 7351; www.pgrfm.bc.ca;* ⊕ *daily; admission charge*) Located on Cottonwood Island, the museum preserves over 70 pieces of rolling stock, nine historical buildings and many smaller artefacts on its eight-acre (3.2 ha) site, displaying the lifestyle of people involved in the railways and industrial development of central British Columbia. The museum's Cottonwood Miniature Railway opened on Canada Day in 2004.

Alberta Railway Museum (*24215-34 St NW, Edmonton, AB T5Y 6B4;* ☎ *780 472 6229; www.albertarailwaymuseum.com;* ⊕ *w/ends from Victoria Day (the Mon* *preceding 25 May) to Labor Day, the 1st long w/end in Sep; admission charge*) Operated by the Alberta Pioneer Railway Association, the museum has more than 60 pieces of equipment, including cars and locomotives formerly owned by Canadian National, Northern Alberta Railways, short lines and industrial railways. The former CN St Albert depot, built in 1909, was moved to the museum grounds in 1980. The station has been completely restored with historic displays and functioning telegraph. Extensive museum archives are located at the Provincial Archives of Alberta, 8555 Roper Road, Edmonton, Alberta.

Train rides operate on holiday long weekends in May, June, July, August and September. Steam engine *No 1392* or diesel *9000* pull a passenger train depending on availability of volunteers. Diesel locomotives are used on Sundays in July and August.

Okanagan Valley Wine Train (*11830 Kingsway Av, Edmonton, AB T5G 0X5;* ☏ *780 452 9999 or* ☏ *866 688 9999; www.okanaganvalleywinetrain.com*) Trains are operated by Funtrain Canada Inc on tracks belonging to the Canadian National Railway and make six-hour excursions through the lush wine and orchard country of British Columbia's Okanagan Valley. The restored vintage coaches are the last-surviving rolling stock of the *Super Continental* that operated across Canada in the 1950s and 1960s.

Trains start out from 600 Recreation Avenue in Kelowna and travel north along the shores of Duck, Wood and Kalamalka lakes, stopping at the historic 1911 station in Vernon before reaching the final destination of Armstrong. Services operate from Wednesday to Sunday between late June and the beginning of September.

New Brunswick Railway Museum (*2487 Main St, Hillsborough, NB E4H 2X7;* ☏ *506 734 3195; www.nbrm.ca*) Home of the Salem & Hillsborough Railroad. Excursion trains formerly ran over an 11-mile (18km) round trip and the equipment is now on static display, in addition to a museum established on the station and shop grounds in Hillsborough. The superb ex-Canadian National steam engine displayed outside the museum was used in constructing portions of the National Transcontinental Railroad and other lines. The locomotive was steamed up in 1998 for the movie *Paradise Siding*.

No passenger trains operate in the Northwest Territories.

Further information The *Trans-Canada Rail Guide* by Melissa Graham (Trailblazer Publications, 1996) gives further detailed information about the trans-Canadian services.

STEAM TRAINS IN CANADA

ALBERNI PACIFIC (*Mail address: Alberni Valley Heritage Network, 5633, Smith Rd, Port Alberni, BC V9Y 8MI;* ☏ *250 723 1376 or* ☏ *250 723 2118; www.alberniheritage. com*) Operates Thursday to Sunday from late June to early September, with holiday excursions at other times of the year. Trains run along the waterfront from downtown Port Alberni to the McLean Hill National Historic Site, which has a 1926 steam sawmill among its 30 preserved buildings. The trip takes about 35 minutes to wind through a forested valley after starting out from the restored 1912 Canadian Pacific station.

The engine is a 1929 Baldwin ex-logging locomotive and the passenger cars are three converted Canadian National transfer cabooses, one of which is open air. The railway is located on Kingsway at Argyle Street near the Harbour Quay in Port Alberni.

ALBERTA PRAIRIE RAILWAY (*Mail address: PO Box 1600, Stettler, AB T0C 2L0;* ☎ *800 282 3994 or* ☎ *403 290 0980 (in Calgary); www.absteamtrain.com*) Between May and mid-October the Alberta Prairie Railway operates steam train rides lasting up to eight hours through central Alberta, complete with staged robberies by the 'Bolton gang'. Different theme trains run throughout the season and an Alberta roast beef dinner is usually included in the fare. A 1920 Baldwin Consolidation locomotive hauls vintage Canadian Northern and Canadian National coaches, including an open-air car and the *Lone Star Saloon*.

Trains travel through Big Valley, the divisional point for the Canadian Northern Railway in the early 1900s when this was a thriving mining centre. Only a few hundred people now live in a community that once numbered 5,000. The restored 1912 station has photographs, blueprints of the gold mine and a complete station master's office.

EAST KOOTENAY (*Mail address: Fort Steele Heritage Town, 9851 Highway 93/95, Fort Steele, BC V0B 1N0;* ☎ *250 417 6000; www.fortsteele.ca*) Trains travel through the grounds of Fort Steele Heritage Park in British Columbia, climbing a double-loop track to give wonderful views from the Kootenay River lookout point. Locomotive *No 1077* featured in several movies, including Jackie Chan's *Shanghai Noon*.

The train runs hourly during summer, and tours of the roundhouse and restored turn-of-the-20th-century steam engines and equipment are available on request.

HULL–CHELSEA–WAKEFIELD (*Mail address: 165 Deveault St, Hull, QC J8Z 1S7;* ☎ *819 778 7246 or* ☎ *800 871 7246; www.steamtrain.ca*) A five-hour journey of 36 miles (57km) from Hull, Quebec, taking you through the forests of the Gatineau Hills, Chelsea and Farm Point. Tour guides describe the line's history and trains make a two-hour stop at the pretty village of Wakefield. The 1907 Swedish locomotive, weighing 93 tons, is revolved on Wakefield's hand-cranked turntable and filled at the water tower.

Trains run daily in July and August; otherwise mostly on Tuesday, Wednesday and at weekends from May to October.

KAMLOOPS HERITAGE RAILWAY (*Mail address: #6–510 Lorne St, Kamloops, BC V2C 1W3;* ☎ *250 374 2141; www.kamrail.com*) The former Canadian National steam locomotive *No 2141* has been fully restored and since 2002, the *Spirit of Kamloops* has carried over 77,000 passengers on 446 runs during July and August. The 182km day trip is between Campbell Creek, 15 minutes east of downtown Kamloops, and Armstrong. Other tours operate throughout the year, including the *Canada Day Fireworks Train*, the *Ghost Train* in October, the *Spirit of Christmas* in December and the *Iron Horse Mystery*.

KETTLE VALLEY STEAM RAILWAY (*Mail address: 18404 Bathville Rd, PO Box 1288, Summerland, BC V0H 1Z0;* ☎ *877 494 8424 or* ☎ *250 494 8422; www.kettlevalleyrail. org (for details of steam excursions on the Kettle Valley Railway between Summerland & the Trout Creek Bridge)*) Enjoy a 90-minute round-trip journey along six miles (10km) of track through the scenic rural beauty of Prairie Valley. The KVSR is powered by a 1912 Consolidation Engine called *No 3716* – rolling stock includes two vintage coaches and three open-air cars. The season is from May to October.

PRAIRIE DOG CENTRAL (*Mail address: The Vintage Locomotive Society Inc, PO Box 33021, RPO Polo Park, Winnipeg, MB R3G 3N4;* ☎ *204 832 5259; www.pdcrailway. com*) The splendid Canadian Pacific engine is the oldest (1882) regularly scheduled operating steam locomotive in North America. This or a vintage diesel takes early 20th-century wooden coaches from Inkster Junction in Winnipeg for a 2½-hour, 35-mile (54km) trip over a Canadian National Railways route to Warren, Manitoba, with a stop at Grosse Isle. Other historic Canadian National locomotives are on display in Winnipeg.

Operates on Sunday from May to September.

SOUTH SIMCOE (*Mail address: PO Box 186, Tottenham, ON L0G 1W0;* ☎ *905 936 5815; www.southsimcoerailway.ca*) Based in Tottenham, Ontario, the railway uses two former Canadian Pacific steam engines dating from 1883 and 1912, as well as a 1948 Southern Railway General Electric 70-ton diesel switcher to haul 1920s vintage cars over part of the former Canadian National Line between Tottenham and Beeton. Departures are from South Simcoe Station at Mill Street West in Tottenham, where there is a gift shop. This old branch line once connected Hamilton with the shipping ports of Barrie and Collingwood.

Operates Sundays and holiday Mondays from May to October, Tuesdays and Wednesdays in July and August, with special events throughout the year.

Steam trains also operate at:

British Columbia Forest Museum 2892 Drinkwater Rd, RR #4, Trans-Canada Highway, Duncan, BC V9L 6C2; ☎ 250 715 1113; www.bcforestmuseum.com
Canadian Railway Museum 110 St Pierre S, Saint-Constant, QC J5A 1G7; ☎ 450 632 2410; www.exporail.org

Fort Edmonton Park PO Box 2359, Edmonton, AB T5J 2R7; ☎ 780 496 8787; www.edmonton. ca; ⊕ May–Sep. A Lima locomotive (*No 2024*) has been saved from the scrap heap & restored to take a passenger train from Midnapore Station.
Heritage Park Historical Village 1900 Heritage Dr SW, Calgary, AB T2V 2X3; ☎ 403 268 8500; www.heritagepark.ca

Appendix 1

331 Appendix 1 USEFUL ADDRESSES A1

USA, GENERAL

American Bed & Breakfast Association
☎250 590 0907; www.americanbedbreakfast.com
American Hotel Association 1201 New York
Av, Suite 600, Washington, DC 20005-3931; ☎202
289 3100; www.ahla.com
Hostelling International USA 8401 Colesville
Rd, Suite 600, Silver Spring, MD 20910; ☎202 783
6161; hiayhserv@hiayh.org; www.hiusa.org
Amtrak Customer Relations Office
60 Massachusetts Av NE, Washington, DC 20002-
4225; ☎215 349 1042
Bed & Breakfast in the USA & Canada Home
Base Holidays, 7 Park Av, London N13 5PG; ☎020
8886 8752; www.homebase-hols.com
BedandBreakfast.com 700 Brazos St, Suite
B-700, Austin, TX 78701; ☎512 322 2710; www.
bedandbreakfast.com
Bed & Breakfast Inns of North America
4516 Lovers Lane, Suite 204, Dallas, TX 75225;
www.inntravels.com
Bed & Breakfast Inns Online PO Box 829,
Madison, TN 37116; ☎615 868 1946; e info@
bbonline.com; www.bbonline.com
BnBFinder 55 Broad St, Suite 3F, New York, NY
10004; ☎212 480 0414; e info@bnbfinder.com;
www.bnbfinder.com
BUNAC 16 Bowling Green Lane, London EC1R
0QH; ☎020 7251 3472; e enquiries@bunac.org.
uk; www.bunac.org
Camp America 37a Queens Gate, London SW7
5HR; ☎020 7581 7373; www.campamerica.co.uk
Great Rail Journeys Saviour Hse, 9 St
Saviourgate, York YO1 8NL; ☎01904 521936;
www.GreatRail.com. Offers escorted tours across
the USA by rail, as well as Eastern Seaboard &
West Coast & Yosemite tours, but cannot arrange
tailor-made or ticket-only requests.

Greyhound International PO Box 660362,
Dallas, TX 75266-0362; ☎1 800 231 2222; www.
greyhound.com
Hostel Handbook for the USA & Canada 730
Saint Nicholas Av, New York, NY 10031; ☎212 926
7030; www.hostelhandbook.com
National Association of Railroad
Passengers 505 Capitol Court NE, Suite 300,
Washington, DC 20002-7706; ☎202 408 8362;
www.narprail.org
National Park Service 1849 C St NW,
Washington, DC 20240; ☎202 208 3818; www.
nps.gov
Pentrex PO Box 94911, Pasadena, CA 91109-
4911; ☎1 800 950 9333; www.pentrex.com
Rail Travel Center 125 Main St, Putney, VT
05346; ☎1 802 254 8844 or ☎1 800 639 3706;
www.railtravelcenter.com
STA Travel 11 Goodge St, Fitzrovia, London,
W1T 2PF; ☎020 7436 7779; www.statravel.co.uk
United Airlines PO Box 66100, Chicago, IL
60666; ☎1 800 864 8331; www.united.com
US Citizenship and Immigration Services
425 I Street NW, Washington, DC 20001; ☎202
514 3636; www.uscis.gov
US Customs Service 1331 Pennsylvania Av NW,
Washington, DC 20004-1710; ☎202 347 7039;
www.customs.ustreas.gov
US embassy 24 Grosvenor Sq, London W1A
1AE; ☎020 7499 9000. For visa information,
☎01891 200290 (premium-rate number).
YMCA of the USA 101 North Wacker Dr,
Chicago, IL 60606; ☎800 872 9622; www.ymca.
net
YWCA USA 2025 M St, NW Suite 550,
Washington, DC 20036; ☎202 467 0801; www.
ywca.org

CANADA, GENERAL

Air Canada PO Box 64239, 5512 Fourth St NW, Calgary, AB T2K 6J0; ☎888 247 2262; www. aircanada.ca

Canada Border Services Agency Ottawa, ON K1A 0L8; ☎1 800 461 9999 or ☎204 983 3500 (outside Canada); http://canada.gc.ca

Canadian Tourism Commission 1400-1055 Dunsmuir St, Box 49230, Vancouver, BC V7X 1L2; www.canada.travel or www.canadatourism.com

Canadian Tourist Office/High Commission Macdonald Hse, 1 Grosvenor Sq, London W1K 4AB; ☎020 7258 6600; www.canada. embassyhomepage.com

CN North America 935 de la Gauchetière St W, Montreal, QC H3B 2M9; ☎1 888 888 5909; www. cn.ca

Hostelling International-Canada 205 Catherine St, Ottawa, ON K2P 1C3; ☎613 237 7884; e info@hihostels.ca; www.hihostels.ca

Hotel Association of Canada 130 Albert St, Suite 1206, Ottawa, ON K1P 5G4; ☎613 237 7149; www.hotelassociation.ca

VIA Rail Canada Inc 3 Pl Ville-Marie, Suite 500, Montreal, QC H3B 2C9; ☎1 888 VIA RAIL (☎888 842 7245); www.viarail.ca

USA STATE TOURISM OFFICES

Alabama 401 Adams Av, Suite 126, PO Box 4927, Montgomery, AL 36103-4927; ☎334 242 4169 or ☎800 ALABAMA or 800 252 2262 ; www. touralabama.org

Alaska 2600 Cordova St, Suite 201, Anchorage, AK 99503; ☎800 327 9372; www.travelalaska. com

Arizona 1110 W Washington, Suite 155, Phoenix, AZ 85007; ☎866 275 5816; www. arizonaguide.com

Arkansas One Capitol Mall, Little Rock, AR 72201; ☎800 NATURAL or 800 628 8725 or ☎501 682 7777; www.arkansas.com

California PO Box 1499, Sacramento, CA 95812; ☎800 862 2543 or ☎916 444 4429; www. visitcalifornia.com

Colorado 1625 Broadway, Suite 1700, Denver, CO 80202; ☎303 892 3885; www.colorado.com

Connecticut One Constitution Plaza, 2nd Fl, Hartford, CT 06103; ☎860 256 2800 or ☎888 288 4748; www.ctbound.org

Delaware 99 Kings Highway, Dover, DE 19901; ☎866 284 7483; www.visitdelaware.com

Florida Suite 300, 661 E Jefferson St, Tallahassee, FL 32301; ☎850 488 5607; www. visitflorida.com

Georgia 75 Fifth St NW, Suite 1200, Atlanta, GA 30308; ☎404 962 4000; www. exploregeorgia.org

Idaho 700 W State St, PO Box 83720, Boise, ID 83720-0093; ☎800 842 5858 or ☎208 334 2470; www.visitidaho.org

Illinois Bureau of Tourism, State of Illinois Ctr, 100 W Randolph, Suite 3-400, Chicago, IL 60601; ☎312 814 4733; www.enjoyillinois.com

Indiana Suite 100, One N Capitol, Indianapolis, IN 46204-2288; ☎888 677 9800; www.in.gov/ visitindiana

Iowa 200 E Grand Av, Des Moines, IA 50309; ☎515 725 3084 or ☎888 472 6035; www. traveliowa.com

Kansas Suite 100, 1000 SW Jackson St, Topeka, KS 66612; ☎785 296 2009 ; www.travelks.com

Kentucky Capital Plaza Tower, 22nd Fl, 500 Mero St, Frankfort, KY 40601; ☎800 225 8747 or ☎502 564 4930; www.kentuckytourism.com

Louisiana 1051 N Third St, Room 313, PO Box 94291, Baton Rouge, LA 70804-9291; ☎225 342 8119; www.louisianatravel.com

Maine 59 State House Station, Augusta, ME 0433-0059; ☎888 624 6345; www.visitmaine.com

Maryland 401 E Pratt St, 14th Fl, Baltimore, MD 21202; ☎866 639 3526; http://visitmaryland.org

Massachusetts State Transportation Bldg, 10 Park Plaza, Suite 4510, Boston, MA 02116; ☎800 227 MASS or ☎617 973 8500; www. massvacation.com

Michigan 300 N Washington Sq, 2nd Fl, Lansing, MI 48913; ☎517 373 0670; www. michigan.org

Minnesota 100 Metro Sq, 121 Seventh Pl E, St Paul, MN 55101; ☎888 868 7476 or ☎651 296 5029; www.exploreminnesota.com

Mississippi PO Box 849, 550 High St, 1100 Walter Sillers Bldg, Jackson, MS 39205; ☎866 SEE MISS or ☎866 733 6477 or ☎601 359 3297; www.visitmississippi.org

Missouri PO Box 1055, Jefferson City, Truman State Office Bldg, MO 65102; ☎573 751 4133 or ☎800 519 2100; www.visitmo.com

Montana 301 S Park, PO Box 200533, Helena, MT 59620-0533; ☎800 VISIT MT (☎800 847 4868) or ☎406 841 2870; www.visitmt.com

Nebraska 301 Centennial Mall S, PO Box 94666, Lincoln, NE 68509-4666; ☎877 NEBRASKA or 877 632 7275 ; www.visitnebraska.gov

Nevada 401 N Carson St, Carson City, NV 89701; ☎800 NEVADA 8 or 800 687 4322 or ☎775 687 4322; www.travelnevada.com

New Hampshire 172 Pembroke Rd, PO Box 1856, Concord, NH 03302-1856; ☎800 FUN IN NH (☎800 386 4664); www.visitnh.gov

New Jersey 225 W State, PO Box 460, Trenton, NJ 08625-0460; ☎800 VISITNJ or 800 847 4865 or ☎609 777 0885; www.visitnj.org

New Mexico PO Box 2002, Lamy Bldg, 491 Old Santa Fe Trail, Santa Fe, NM 87501; ☎800 545 2070 or ☎505 827 7400; www.newmexico.org

New York PO Box 2603, Albany, NY 12220-0603; ☎800 CALL NYS or 800 225 5697 or ☎518 474 4116; www.iloveny.com

North Carolina 301 N Wilmington, Raleigh, NC 27699-4301; ☎800 VISIT NC or 800 847 4862 ; www.visitnc.com

North Dakota Century Center, 1600 E Century Av, Suite 2, Bismarck, ND 58502-2057; ☎800 435 5663; www.ndtourism.com

Ohio PO Box 1001, Columbus, OH 43216-1001; ☎800 BUCKEYE or 800 282 5393 ; www. discoverohio.com

Oklahoma 120 N Robinson Av, 6th Fl, Oklahoma City, OK 73152-2002; ☎800 652 6552 or ☎405 2308 400; www.travelok.com

Oregon 670 Hawthorne SE, Suite 240, Salem, OR 97301; ☎800 547 7842 or ☎503 378 8850; www.traveloregon.com

Pennsylvania Commonwealth Keystone Bldg, 400 N St, Harrisburg, PA 17120-0225; ☎800 847 4872 or ☎717 787 5453; www.visitpa.com

Rhode Island 315 Iron Horse Way, Suite 101, Providence, RI 02908; ☎800 250 7384; www. visitrhodeisland.com

South Carolina 1205 Pendleton St, Columbia, SC 29201; ☎803 734 1700 or ☎888 224 9339; www.discoversouthcarolina.com

South Dakota 711 E Wells Av, Pierre, SD 57501-5070; ☎800 SDAKOTA or 800 732 5682 or ☎605 773 3301; www.travelsd.com

Tennessee 312 Rosa L Parks Av, 25th Fl, Nashville, TN 37243; ☎615 741 2159; www. tnvacation.com

Texas PO Box 141009, Austin, TX 78714-1009; ☎800 888 8TEX or 800 888 8839 or ☎800 452 9292; www.traveltex.com

Utah Council Hall, 30 N State St, Salt Lake City, UT 84114; ☎801 538 1398 or ☎800 200 1160; www.utah.com

Vermont One National Life Dr, 6th Fl, Montpelier, VT 05620-0501; ☎800 VERMONT or 800 828 3239; www.travel-vermont.com

Virginia 901 E Byrd St, Richmond, VA 23219; ☎800 847 4882; www.virginia.org

Washington, DC 901 Seventh St NW, 4th Fl, Washington, DC 2001-3719; ☎202 789 7000 or ☎800 422 8644; www.washington.org

Washington State PO Box 42500, Olympia, WA 98504-2500; ☎800 544 1800; www. experiencewa.com

West Virginia Capitol Complex, Bldg 6, Room 525, Charleston, WV 25305-0311; ☎304 558 2234 or ☎800 982 3386; www.wvtourism.com

Wisconsin 201 W Washington Av, PO Box 8690, Madison, WI 53708-8747; ☎800 432 8747 or ☎608 266 2161; www.travelwisconsin.com

Wyoming 1520 Etchepare Circle, Cheyenne, WY 82007; ☎800 225 5996 or ☎307 777 7777; www. wyomingtourism.org

CANADIAN TOURIST OFFICES

Alberta PO Box 2500, Edmonton, AB T5J 2Z4; ☎800 252 3782; www.travelalberta.com

British Columbia 17, 3318 Oak St, Victoria, BC V8X 1R1; ☎866 810 6645; www.travel.bc.ca

Manitoba 155 Carlton St, 7th Fl, Winnipeg, MB R3C 3H8; ☎800 665 0040; www.travelmanitoba. com

New Brunswick PO Box 12345, Campbellton, NB E3N 3T6; ☎800 561 0123; www. tourismnewbrunswick.ca

Newfoundland and Labrador PO Box 8700, St John's, NL A1B 4J6; ☎800 563 6353 or ☎709 729 2830; www.newfoundlandlabrador.com

Northwest Territories PO Box 610, 5016 52nd St, Yellowknife, NT X1A 2N5; ☎800 661 0788 or ☎867 873 5007; www.spectacularnwt.com

Nova Scotia PO Box 456, 1800 Argyle St, Halifax, NS B3J 2R5; ☎800 565 0000 or ☎902 425 5781; www.novascotia.com

Ontario 10 Dundas St E, Suite 900, Toronto, ON M7A 2A1; ☎800 668 2746; www.ontariotravel. net

Prince Edward Island PO Box 2000, Charlottetown, PE C1A 7N8; ☎902 368 4801; www.gov.pe.ca/visitorsguide

Quebec PO Box 979, Montreal, QC H3C 2W3; ☎800 266 5687; www.bonjourquebec.com

Saskatchewan 189-1621 Albert St, Regina, SK S4P 2S5; ☎877 237 2273 or ☎306 787 9600; www.sasktourism.com

Yukon PO Box 2703, Whitehorse, YT Y1A 2C6; ☎800 661 0494; www.travelyukon.com

Appendix 2

TICKETING AGENTS

AMTRAK INTERNATIONAL SALES AGENTS Amtrak has developed an online booking system that allows for travel agents from anywhere in the world to have access to, and book, Amtrak tickets. The companies that follow have the ability to book Amtrak in these countries but this is not meant to be a comprehensive listing.

Australia Adventure Destinations, 89a Orange St, Bentleigh E, VIC 3165; ☎61 3 9570 4466 or ☎1300 136 330; www.adventuredestinations. com.au. International Rail Australia, Suite 6, Level 1, 69–71 Rosstown Rd, Carnegie, VIC 3163; ☎1300 387 245; www.internationalrail.com.au. Momento Travel, Level 7, Suite 702, 28 Foveaux St, Surry Hills, Sydney, NSW 2010; ☎61 2 9213 0000; www.momentotravel.com.au. Rail Tickets, Level 5, 310 King St, Melbourne, VIC 3000; ☎1300 360 823; www.railtickets.com.au. Rail Plus, Level 4, 10–16 Queen St, Melbourne, VIC 3000; ☎61 3 9642 8644 or ☎1300 555 003; www.railplus.com.au.

Denmark Check Point Travel, Søren Frichs Vej 42M 8230 Åbyhøj; ☎45 86 137 744; www.cpt.dk. Nyhavn Rejser a/s, Nyhavn 31G, 1051 København K; ☎45 33 320 320; www.nyhavn.dk.

France Media Voyages, 55 rue Ney, 69006 Lyon; ☎33 4 72 83 04 95; www.mediavoyages.fr. BMS Voyages, 64 Bd de Sébastopol, 75003 Paris (Rez-de-chaussée face); ☎33 1 42 66 07 07; www. bms-travelshop.com. Comptoir Des Voyages, 2 au 18 rue St Victor, 75005 Paris; ☎33 8 92 23 93 39; www.comptoir.fr. Interface Tourism, 11 bis rue blanche, 75009 Paris; ☎33 1 53 25 11 11; www. interfacetourism.com. JETSET Voyages, 41–45 rue Galilée, 75116 Paris; ☎33 1 53 67 13 00; www. jetset-voyages.fr. Discovery Trains, 29 Bd Henri IV, F-75004 Paris; ☎33 1 42 78 37 26; www. discoverytrains.net. Destination SAS, Château de Pourtalès, 161 rue Mélanie, F-67000 Strasbourg; ☎33 3 88 60 70 70; www.destination-fr.com.

Fab Travel Troyes, 1 bis rue Cardinal Ancher (Pl de la Libération, Préfecture), 10000 Troyes (en Champagne); ☎33 3 25 70 89 19; www.fab-travel.com.

Germany Canada Reise Dienst (CRD International), Stadthausbrucke 1-3, 20355 Hamburg; ☎49 40 300 616 0; f 49 40 300 616 55; www.crd.de. Eberhardt Reisen, Bahnhofstraße 2, 75172 Pforzheim; ☎49 7231 380 243; www. eberhardt-reisen.de.

Italy Gioco Viaggi Srl, Via B Bosco, 57/1a, 16121 Genoa; ☎39 10 553 1169; www.giocoviaggi.com

Mexico Trenes Y Otros Servicios S de RL de CV, Praga #27, Col Juárez, DF 06600; ☎52 55 5207 6620; www.tyoservicios.com

New Zealand International Rail Australia, 171 Darling Rd, E Malvern, VIC 3145; ☎1300 387 245; www.trainticket.com.au. Rail Plus, Level 2, 6 Kingdon St, Newmarket, Auckland, 1149; ☎64 9 377 5415; www.railplus.co.nz.

United Kingdom (Additional sales locations available throughout the UK. Check with your local travel agent.) Cresta World Travel, Cresta Hse, 32 Victoria St, Altrincham, Cheshire WA14 1ET; ☎0845 193 1737; f 0161 929 7951; www. crestaworldtravel.co.uk. Up & Away Holidays, 19 The Mall, Bromley, Kent BR1 1TT; ☎020 8289 5050; www.upandawayholidays.co.uk. Dreamticket, Stoneham Hse, 17 Scarbrook Rd, Croydon, Surrey CR0 1SQ; ☎0845 468 3149; www.dreamticket.com. American Sky, Kings Hse, 1st Fl N, 13/21 Cantelupe Rd, East Grinstead, West Sussex RH19 3BE; ☎0844 332 9390; www.

americansky.co.uk. Haslemere Travel Ltd, 2/4 Petworth Rd, Haslemere, Surrey GU27 2HR; ✆01428 658777; www.haslemeretravel.co.uk. Trainseurope Ltd, 4 Station Approach, March, Cambs PE15 8SJ; ✆0871 700 7722; f 01354 660444; www.trainseurope.co.uk. Emerald Travel, 15/16 New Burlington St, London W1S 3BJ; ✆0844 472 3080; www.emerald.co.uk. Jetline Travel, Colindale Business Centre, 126–128 Colindale Av, London NW9 5HU; ✆0844 493 4600; www.jetlinetravel.com. HIS Europe Ltd, 14 Charles II St, London SW1Y 4QU; ✆020 7484 3337; www.his-euro.co.uk. Aspen Travel, 1 Higher Rd, Urmston, Manchester M41 9AB; ✆0161 748 6864; www.aspentravel.co.uk. Complete North America Limited, Colwick Quays Business Park, Private Rd No 2, Colwick,

Nottingham NG4 2JY; ✆0115 961 0590; f 0845 263 7177; www.completenorthamerica.com. Ffestiniog Travel, 1st Fl, Unit 6, Snowdonia Business Park, Penrhyndeudraeth, Gwynedd LL48 6LD; ✆01766 772957; f 01766 772049; www.ffestiniogtravel.co.uk. Howard Travel, 12/13 Church Walk, Trowbridge, Wilts BA14 8DX; ✆01225 777227; f 01225 777392; www. howardtravel.com. International Rail Ltd, PO Box 153, Alresford, Hants SO24 4AQ; ✆0871 231 0790; f 0871 231 0791; www.internationalrail. com. Trailfinders, 194 Kensington High St, London W8 7RG; ✆020 7938 3939, + many other UK locations – call for information. The Travel Bureau, High St, Wombourne, West Midlands WV5 9DN; ✆0844 815 6212; f 01902 324333; www.thetravelbureau.co.uk.

VIA RAIL INTERNATIONAL SALES AGENTS

Argentina Vanguard Marketing SA, Juncal 840 6˚A, C1062ABF, Buenos Aires; ✆54 11 4322 5100; www.vanguardmarketing.com.ar

Australia Momento Travel, Level 7, Suite 702, 28 Foveaux St, Surry Hills, Sydney, NSW 2010; ✆61 2 9213 0000; f 61 2 9211 0500; www. momentotravel.com.au

Austria Canada Reisen, Buchbergasse 34, 3400 Klosterneuburg; ✆011 43 2243 25594; f 011 43 2243 26198; www.canadareisen.at

Brazil South Marketing International, Franklin Roosevelt Av, 194 GR505 - 20021 120, Rio de Janeiro; ✆55 21 2517 4800; f 55 21 2517 4808; www.southmarketing.com.br

Germany Canada Reise Dienst, CRD International, Stadthausbruecke 1-3, 20355 Hamburg; ✆49 40 3006160; f 49 40 30061655; www.crd.de

Hong Kong Japan Travel Bureau Inc, Room UG3, 3rd Fl, Chinachem Golden Plaza, 77 Mondy Rd, Tsimshatsui East, Kowloon; ✆852 2734 9288; f 852 2722 7300

Japan JTB Tokyo Metropolitan Corp, Travel Designer Shinjuku, Orix Shinjuku Bldg 2F, 4-3-25 Shinjuku, Shinjuku-ku, Tokyo 160-0022; ✆81 3 5366 1780; f 81 3 5366 1595

Korea K S Park Travel Korea, ChungHwa Bldg 4th, Hanam-dong Yongsan-ku, Seoul 140-210; ✆82 2 3785 0127; f 82 2 3785 2076. The Pharos Travelartifex Corp, 4F Bukyung Bldg, 183-1, Chungjin-Dong, Jongno-Gu, Seoul 110-130; ✆82 2 737 3773; f 82 2 737 3883.

Mexico Trenes Y Otros Servicios S de RL e CV, Praga 27 Co Juarez, Mexico 06600 DF; ✆52 55 5207 2258; f 52 55 5207 7154

Netherlands Incento BV, PO Box 1067, 1400 BB Bussum; ✆031 35 69 5 5111; f 031 35 69 5 5155; www.incento.nl

New Zealand Adventure World, 101 Great South Rd, Remuera, PO Box 74008, Auckland; ✆64 9 524 5118; f 64 9 520 6629

United Kingdom First Class Holidays, Trafford Hse, Chester Rd, Old Trafford, Manchester M32 0RS; ✆0844 499 0771 or ✆0161 877 0432; f 0161 877 0423; www.1strail.com

Appendix 3

FURTHER READING

BOOKS It is obviously impossible to produce any sort of comprehensive reading list on countries so vast as the USA and Canada, and all the more so when they also have such a rich and extensive cultural and literary history of their own. The following suggestions, however, may be of help in providing further information on topics likely to interest rail travellers and those new to North America.

USA
Railways

Ambrose, Stephen *Nothing Like it in the World* Simon & Schuster
Bain, David Howard *Empire Express* Viking
Bell, N J and Ward, James Arthur *Southern Railroad Man* Northern Illinois University Press
Best, Gerald M *Iron Horses to Promontory* Golden West Books
Blumberg, Rhoda *Full Steam Ahead: The Race to Build a Transcontinental Railroad* National Geographic
Broggie, Michael *Walt Disney's Railroad Story* Pentrex
Cook, Richard *The Beauty of Railroad Bridges in North America* Golden West Books
Daniels, Rudolph *Trains across the Continent* Indiana University Press
Drury, George H *The Historical Guide to North American Railroads* Kalmbach
Goble, Paul *Death of the Iron Horse* Aladdin
Hidy, Ralph W *Dining by Rail: A History* Harvard Business School
Holbrook, Stewart H *The Story of American Railroads* Crown Publishers
Kennedy, Ian and Treuherz, Julian *The Railway: Art in the Age of Steam* Yale University Press
Kirby, Lynne *Parallel Tracks: The Railroad and Silent Cinema* Duke University Press
Klein, Aaron E *Encyclopedia of North American Railroads* Bison
Link, O Winston *Steam, Steel and Stars: America's Last Steam Railroad* Harry N Abrams
Mayer, Lyn Rhodes *Makin' Tracks* Praeger
Middleton, William D *Landmarks on the Iron Road* Indiana University Press
Perata, David *Those Pullman Blues* Twayne Publishers
Pindell, Terry *Making Tracks: An American Odyssey* Henry Holt
Potter, Janet Greenstein *Great American Railroad Stations* Wiley
Richmond, Al *Rails to the Rim: Milepost Guide to the Grand Canyon Railway* Grand Canyon Railway
Richmond, Al *The Story of the Grand Canyon Railway* Grand Canyon Railway
Roe, Jo Ann *Stevens Pass: The Story of Railroading and Recreation in the North Cascades* The Mountaineers
Ross, David *The Encyclopedia of Trains and Locomotives* Thunder Bay Press
Sandler, Martin *Riding the Rails in the USA* Oxford University Press

Schwantes, Carlos A and Ronda, James P *The West the Railroads Made* University of Washington Press

Schwieterman, Joseph *When the Railroad Leaves Town* Truman State University Press

Shaughnessy, Jim *The Call of Trains* W W Norton

Signor, John R *Donner Pass: Southern Pacific's Sierra Crossing* Golden West Books

Solomon, Brian *Alco Locomotives* Voyageur Press

Solomon, Brian *American Steam Locomotive* Motorbooks International

Solomon, Brian *Baldwin Locomotives* Voyageur Press

Stiles, T J *The First Tycoon: Cornelius Vanderbilt* Knopf

Stover, John *History of the Baltimore and Ohio Railroad* Purdue University Press

Stover, John and Carnes, Mark *The Historical Atlas of the American Railroads* Routledge

Vance Jr, James E *The North American Railroad* Johns Hopkins University Press

Wegman, Mark *American Passenger Trains & Locomotives Illustrated* Voyageur Press

Welsh, Joe *The American Railroad* Motorbooks International

Welsh, Joe and Holland, Kevin J *Union Pacific Railroad* Voyageur Press

Welsh, Joe, Howes, Bill and Holland, Kevin J *The Cars of Pullman* Voyageur Press

White Jr, John H *The American Railroad Passenger Car* Johns Hopkins University Press

Wiatroski, Claude *Railroads across North America* Voyageur Press

Wolmar, Christian *Blood, Iron & Gold* Atlantic Books

York, Thomas *North America's Great Railroads* Brompton Books

Young, Gavin *From Sea to Shining Sea* Hutchinson

General travel

Sakach, Deborah E *The Bed & Breakfast Encyclopedia* American Historic Inns

Soule, Sandra W *America's Favourite Inns, B & Bs, and Small Hotels: USA and Canada* St Martin's Press

Tice, Janet *100 Best Family Resorts in North America* Globe Pequot Press

General – history, the country, the people

Bluestein, G *Poplore: Folk and Pop in American Culture* University of Massachusetts Press

Breidlid, Anders (editor) *American Culture* Routledge

Duchak, Alicia *A–Z of Modern America* Routledge

Evans, Harold *The American Century* Jonathan Cape

Garraty, John A *The American Nation* Longman

Holliday, J S *The World Rushed In: The California Gold Rush Experience* Simon & Schuster

Hughes, Robert *American Visions* Harvill Press

Klein, Joe *Woody Guthrie* Faber & Faber

Mauk, David and Oakland, John *American Civilisation* Routledge

McGlashan, C F *History of the Donner Party* Stanford University Press

O'Callaghan, B *An Illustrated History of the US* Longman

Reid, Brian Holden *The American Civil War* Longman

Scheurer, T E *Born in the USA* University of Mississippi

Skar, R *Movie – Made in America: A Cultural History of American Movies* Random House

Tindall, George B *America* W W Norton

Utley, Robert M *Frontiersmen in Blue* Bison Books

Canada
Railways

Allen, Tom *Rolling Home* Penguin

Berton, Pierre *Steel across the Shield: Canada Moves West* McClelland & Stewart

Berton, Pierre *The Last Spike* Anchor Canada

Berton, Pierre *The National Dream* Anchor Canada
Bohi, Charles *Canadian National's Western Depots* Fitzhenry & Whiteside
Brown, Ron *Ghost Railways of Ontario* Polar Bear Press
Buck, George *From Summit to Sea* Fifth House
Cruikshank, Ken *Close Ties* McGill-Queen's University Press
Doughty, Geoffrey H *Canadian Treasures* TLC Publishing
Eagle, John A *The Canadian Pacific Railway* McGill-Queen's University Press
Fleming, R B *The Railway King of Canada* University of British Columbia Press
Good, Cherry *On the Trail of John Muir* Luath Press
Graham, Melissa *The Trans-Canada Rail Guide* Trailblazer Publications, 1996
Green, Lorne *Chief Engineer* Dundurn
Harris, Chris *BC Rail* Country Light Publishing
Harris, Lorraine *BC's Own Railroad* Hancock House
Klein, Aaron *The Men Who Built the Railroads* Gallery Books
Leggett, Robert Ferguson *Railroads of Canada* Drake
Lovett, Henry Almon *Canada and the Grand Trunk* Ayer
McDonnell, Greg *Canadian Pacific* Boston Mills Press
Murray, Tom *Canadian National Railway* Motorbooks International
O'Reilly, Susan McLeod *On Track* Canadian Museum of Civilisation
Perry, Lorne and MacKay, Donald *Train Country* Douglas & McIntyre
Pindell, Terry *Last Train to Toronto* Henry Holt
Schneider, Ena *Ribbons of Steel* Detselig Enterprises
Secretan, J H *Canada's Great Highway* Ayer
Solomon, Brian *Railroad Stations* Main Street Books
Taber, Thomas Townsend *Guide to Railroad Historical Resources, United States and Canada* Muncy

General – travel, history, the country, the people

Canada Gazetteer Atlas University of Chicago Press
Canada's National Parks Whitecap Books
Carroll, Donald *Canada Traveler's Companion* Globe Pequot Press
Cheng, Pang G and Barlas, Robert *Culture Shock: Canada* Kuperard
Cropp, Richard *Romantic Days and Nights in Vancouver* Globe Pequot Press
Harvey, R G *Carving the Western Path* Heritage House
Kalman, Bobbie *Canada from A to Z* Crabtree
Kranc, Benjamin A *Living and Working in Canada* How To Books
Lechmere, Adam and Catto, Susan *Live and Work in the USA and Canada* Vacation Work
Malcolm, Andrew H *The Canadians* St Martin's Press
McNaught, Kenneth *The Penguin History of Canada* Penguin
Morris, Jan *O Canada!* Robert Hale
Mussio, Russell *The Cariboo* Gordon Soules

WEBSITES The internet is an increasingly popular and useful source of up-to-date travel information which you can use to make reservations, check timetables, purchase tickets and keep in touch with people at home (see *Chapter 3, Media and communications*, page 44). Some of the most useful websites for those intending to travel by train are as follows:

For the USA

Alaska Railroad Operates out of Anchorage. www.akrr.com
Allplaces Statistics, local links & fun stuff. www.allplaces.us
Amtrak A comprehensive, award-winning site. www.amtrak.com

Amtrak California Fare promotions, maps & a quarterly e-zine. www.amtrakcalifornia.com

Amtrak Capitol Corridor For southern California. www.amtrakcapitols.com

Amtrak Cascades For travel between Eugene, Oregon & Vancouver in Canada. www.amtrakcascades.com

Amtrak/Passenger Railroad For travellers, rail fans & railroaders. www.trainweb.org/amtrak

Amtrak Unlimited One of the best Amtrak information sources. www.amtraktrains.com

Coast Starlight Free gifts & historic Parlour cars. www.coaststarlight.com

CPRR Photographic History Museum Stereoviews, engravings, maps & documents illustrating the history of the Central Pacific Railroad. http://cprr.org

Engineering Sights See how engineers turn ideas into reality. www.engineeringsights.org

ETouristUSA Tourism & reservations guide for the United States. www.etouristusa.com

Friends of Amtrak An internet advocacy supporting funding for Amtrak. www.friendsofamtrak.com

Grand Canyon A steam railway built by the Atchison, Topeka & Santa Fe Railway. www.thetrain.com

Grandluxe Rail Journeys Formerly American Orient Express. Travel in luxury over legendary railway routes. www.grandluxerail.com

Green Frog Productions Video, audio & CDs about trains. www.greenfrog.com

ISTC Student travel services, discounts & information. www.istc.org

National Association of Railroad Passengers (NARP) Join & help save the trains. www.narprail.org

National Rail Page Lists all national & international rail websites. www.rrhistorical.com

Onroute Guides to more than 200 places in the USA & Canada. www.onroute.com

Railfan Pictures of trains & other railroad subjects. http://bfcase.railfan.net

The Railfan Network By rail fans for rail fans. www.railfan.net

The Railroad Press Railroad magazine & books with exceptional photography. www.alco628.com

RailServe Guide to 12,000 rail-related websites including train travel, model railroading, railfan resources, & industry sites. www.railserve.com

RailServe Music Page Links to all kinds of railroad songs. www.railserve.com/music

Railwaystation An online community with free stuff for rail fans. www.railwaystation.com

Silver Rails Resort An expanding railroad-themed resort in La Plata, Missouri, with an exhibition of Amtrak history. Ideal for anyone with an enthusiasm for trains or the history of railroading. www.silverrails.com

Texas Eagle Full information for *Texas Eagle* country. www.texaseagle.com

Tour 50 States Profiles, attractions, maps, lodging, dining, local news, weather for the larger cities. www.tour50states.com

Trainweb Masses of information about North American trains. www.trainweb.com

Travelinformation Free travel brochures. www.travelinformation.com

USA by Rail Up-to-date information & tips from other travellers. www.usa-by-rail.com

USA Citylink Detailed city guides as well as official & independent city & state websites. www.usacitylink.com

USA Tourist The latest tourist developments. www.usatourist.com

Visit USA General tips & information. www.visitusa.org

Web Union Station Tourist railroads & train museums. www.webunionstation.net

For Canada

Algoma Central An unofficial website. www.agawacanyontourtrain.com & www.trainweb.org/algoma

Canadian Heritage Museums & galleries throughout the country. www.chin.gc.ca

Discover Canada General information. www.discovercanada.com

Ontario Northland From Toronto to the Arctic Circle. www.ontarionorthland.ca
Rocky Mountaineer Perhaps the most spectacular train route in North America. www.rockymountaineer.com
VIA Rail Download the latest timetables & request brochures. www.viarail.ca
White Pass & Yukon Railway www.wpyr.com

General

Budget Travel For travellers of modest means. www.budgettravel.com
CNN Travel Guide Travel news & booking information. www.cnn.com/TRAVEL
Currency Converter Conversions for 200 different currencies. www.oanda.com/currency/travel-exchange-rates
The Cybercafé Search Engine Lists 2,000 cybercafés in 125 countries. http://cybercaptive.com
Electronic Embassy Page Includes all foreign embassies in the USA. www.embassy.org/embassies
Expedia For transatlantic flights & much else. www.expedia.co.uk
Globetrotters Club For independent travellers. www.globetrotters.co.uk
GoAbroad Alternative travel with information on studying & living abroad. www.goabroad.com
Hostelling International The 'Worldwide Hostels' section lists hostels in 75 countries. www.hihostels.com
Internet Guide to Hostelling One of the largest directories of hostels in the world. www.hostels.com
Journeywoman Online Mainly for women travellers. www.journeywoman.com
Kasbah Travel Information A search engine with 100,000 sites listed. www.kasbah.com
Le Travel Store For travel gear & publications. www.letravelstore.com
Maps Available at www.mapquest.com
Onetravel.com For airfares & accommodation worldwide. www.onetravel.com
Roadnews Everything you need to stay connected while travelling. www.roadnews.com
TrainTraveling.com A comprehensive passenger rail guide & news resource. www.TrainTraveling.com

Bradt Travel Guides

Africa

Access Africa: Safaris for People	
with Limited Mobility	£16.99
Africa Overland	£16.99
Algeria	£15.99
Angola	£17.99
Botswana	£16.99
Burkina Faso	£17.99
Cameroon	£15.99
Cape Verde	£15.99
Congo	£15.99
Eritrea	£15.99
Ethiopia	£16.99
Ghana	£15.99
Kenya Highlights	£15.99
Madagascar	£16.99
Malawi	£15.99
Mali	£14.99
Mauritius, Rodrigues &	
Réunion	£15.99
Mozambique	£15.99
Namibia	£15.99
Niger	£14.99
Nigeria	£17.99
North Africa: Roman Coast	£15.99
Rwanda	£15.99
São Tomé & Príncipe	£14.99
Seychelles	£14.99
Sierra Leone	£16.99
South Africa Highlights	£15.99
Sudan	£15.99
Tanzania, Northern	£14.99
Tanzania	£17.99
Uganda	£16.99
Zambia	£18.99
Zanzibar	£14.99
Zimbabwe	£15.99

The Americas and the Caribbean

Alaska	£15.99
Amazon Highlights	£15.99
Argentina	£16.99
Bahia	£14.99
Cayman Islands	£14.99
Colombia	£17.99
Dominica	£15.99
Grenada, Carriacou &	
Petite Martinique	£14.99
Guyana	£15.99
Nova Scotia	£14.99
Panama	£14.99
Paraguay	£15.99
Turks & Caicos Islands	£14.99
Uruguay	£15.99
USA by Rail	£14.99
Venezuela	£16.99
Yukon	£14.99

British Isles

Britain from the Rails	£14.99
Bus-Pass Britain	£15.99
Eccentric Britain	£15.99
Eccentric Cambrige	£9.99
Eccentric London	£13.99
Eccentric Oxford	£9.99
Sacred Britain	£16.99
Slow: Cotswolds	£14.99
Slow: Devon & Exmoor	£14.99
Slow: Norfolk & Suffolk	£14.99
Slow: North Yorkshire	£14.99
Slow: Sussex & South	
Downs National Park	£14.99

Europe

Abruzzo	£14.99
Albania	£15.99
Azores	£14.99
Baltic Cities	£14.99
Belarus	£15.99
Bosnia & Herzegovina	£14.99
Bratislava	£9.99
Budapest	£9.99
Cork	£6.99
Croatia	£13.99
Cross-Channel France:	
Nord-Pas de Calais	£13.99
Cyprus see North Cyprus	
Dresden	£7.99
Estonia	£14.99
Faroe Islands	£15.99
Georgia	£15.99
Greece: The Peloponnese	£14.99
Helsinki	£7.99
Hungary	£15.99
Iceland	£15.99
Kosovo	£15.99
Lapland	£15.99
Latvia	£13.99
Lille	£9.99
Lithuania	£14.99
Luxembourg	£13.99
Macedonia	£15.99
Malta & Gozo	£12.99
Montenegro	£14.99
North Cyprus	£13.99
Riga	£6.99
Serbia	£15.99
Slovakia	£14.99
Slovenia	£13.99
Spitsbergen	£16.99
Switzerland Without	
a Car	£14.99
Transylvania	£14.99
Ukraine	£15.99
Zagreb	£6.99

Middle East, Asia and Australasia

Armenia	£15.99
Bangladesh	£15.99
Borneo	£17.99
Eastern Turkey	£16.99
Georgia	£15.99
Iran	£15.99
Iraq: Then & Now	£15.99
Israel	£15.99
Kazakhstan	£16.99
Kyrgyzstan	£16.99
Lake Baikal	£15.99
Lebanon	£15.99
Maldives	£15.99
Mongolia	£16.99
North Korea	£14.99
Oman	£15.99
Palestine	£15.99
Shangri-La:	
A Travel Guide to the	
Himalayan Dream	£14.99
Sri Lanka	£15.99
Syria	£15.99
Taiwan	£16.99
Tibet	£13.99
Yemen	£14.99

Wildlife

Antarctica: Guide to the	
Wildlife	£15.99
Arctic: Guide to Coastal	
Wildlife	£15.99
Australian Wildlife	£14.99
Central & Eastern	
European Wildlife	£15.99
Chinese Wildlife	£16.99
East African Wildlife	£19.99
Galápagos Wildlife	£16.99
Madagascar Wildlife	£16.99
New Zealand Wildlife	£14.99
North Atlantic Wildlife	£16.99
Pantanal Wildlife	£16.99
Peruvian Wildlife	£15.99
Southern African Wildlife	£19.99
Sri Lankan Wildlife	£15.99

Pictorials and other guides

100 Alien Invaders	£16.99
100 Animals to See	
Before They Die	£16.99
100 Bizarre Animals	£16.99
Eccentric Australia	£12.99
Northern Lights	£6.99
Tips on Tipping	£6.99
Wildlife and Conservation	
Volunteering: The	
Complete Guide	£13.99

WIN A FREE BRADT GUIDE
READER QUESTIONNAIRE

Send in your completed questionnaire and enter our monthly draw for the chance to win a Bradt guide of your choice.

To take up our special reader offer of 40% off, please visit our website at www.bradtguides.com/freeguide or answer the questions below and return to us with the order form overleaf.

(Forms may be posted or faxed to us.)

Have you used any other Bradt guides? If so, which titles? . . . .
. . . .

What other publishers' travel guides do you use regularly? . . . .
. . . .

Where did you buy this guidebook? . . . .

What was the main purpose of your trip to the USA (or for what other reason did you read our guide)? eg: holiday/business/charity . . . .
. . . .

How long did you travel for? (circle one)

weekend/long weekend   1–2 weeks   3–4 weeks   4 weeks plus

Which countries did you visit in connection with this trip? . . . .
. . . .

Did you travel with a tour operator?' If so, which one? . . . .
. . . .

What other destinations would you like to see covered by a Bradt guide?
. . . .

If you could make one improvement to this guide, what would it be?
. . . .

Age (circle relevant category) 16–25   26–45   46–60   60+

Male/Female (delete as appropriate)

Home country . . . .

Please send us any comments about this guide (or others on our list).
. . . .
. . . .
. . . .

Bradt Travel Guides
IDC House, The Vale, Chalfont St Peter, Bucks SL9 9RZ, UK
☎ +44 (0)1753 893444 f +44 (0)1753 892333
e info@bradtguides.com
www.bradtguides.com

TAKE 40% OFF YOUR NEXT BRADT GUIDE!
Order Form

To take advantage of this special offer visit www.bradtguides.com/freeguide and enter our monthly giveaway, or fill in the order form below, complete the questionnaire overleaf and send it to Bradt Travel Guides by post or fax.

Please send me one copy of the following guide at 40% off the UK retail price

No	Title	Retail price	40% price
1	....	....	....

Please send the following additional guides at full UK retail price

No	Title	Retail price	Total
...	....	....	....
...	....	....	....
...	....	....	....

Sub total ....
Post & packing ....
(Free shipping UK, £1 per book Europe, £3 per book rest of world)
Total ....

Name ....

Address ....

Tel .... Email ....

☐ I enclose a cheque for £ .... made payable to Bradt Travel Guides Ltd

☐ I would like to pay by credit card. Number: ....

　Expiry date: ... / .... 3-digit security code (on reverse of card) .....

　Issue no (debit cards only) .....

☐ Please sign me up to Bradt's monthly enewsletter, Bradtpackers' News.

☐ I would be happy for you to use my name and comments in Bradt marketing material.

Send your order on this form, with the completed questionnaire, to:

Bradt Travel Guides
IDC House, The Vale, Chalfont St Peter, Bucks SL9 9RZ, UK
✆ +44 (0)1753 893444　f +44 (0)1753 892333
e info@bradtguides.com　www.bradtguides.com

NOTES

Index

Page references in **bold** indicate major entries